The Many-Headed Muse

This is the first monograph entirely devoted to the corpus of late clas-sical Greek lyric poetry. Not only have the dithyrambs and citharodic nomes of the New Musicians Timotheus and Philoxenus, the hymns of Aristotle and Ariphron, and the epigraphic paeans of Philodamus of Scarphea and Isyllus of Epidaurus never been studied together, they have also remained hidden behind a series of critical prejudices: political, literary, and aesthetic. Professor LeVen's book provides read-ings of these little-known poems and combines engagement with the style, narrative technique, poetics, and reception of the texts with attention to the socio-cultural forces that shaped them. In examining the protean notions of tradition and innovation, the book contributes to the current re-evaluation of the landscape of Greek poetry and performance in the late classical period, and bridges a gap in our understanding of Greek literary history between the early classical and the Hellenistic periods.

PAULINE A. LEVEN is Assistant Professor of Classics at Yale Univer-sity. She has published articles on Timotheus' language, Athenaeus and the reception of the New Music, Aristotle's *Hymn to Virtue* and fourth-century epigraphy, and is now working on a monograph devoted to Greek and Roman musical myths.

The Many-Headed Muse

Tradition and Innovation in Late Classical Greek
Lyric Poetry

PAULINE A. LEVEN

CAMBRIDGE
UNIVERSITY PRESS

CAMBRIDGE
UNIVERSITY PRESS

University Printing House, Cambridge CB2 8BS, United Kingdom

One Liberty Plaza, 20th Floor, New York, NY 10006, USA

477 Williamstown Road, Port Melbourne, VIC 3207, Australia

4843/24, 2nd Floor, Ansari Road, Daryaganj, Delhi - 110002, India

79 Anson Road, #06-04/06, Singapore 079906

Cambridge University Press is part of the University of Cambridge.

It furthers the University's mission by disseminating knowledge in the pursuit of education, learning and research at the highest international levels of excellence.

www.cambridge.org
Information on this title: www.cambridge.org/9781107018532

© Pauline A. LeVen 2014

First published 2014
First paperback edition 2017

A catalogue record for this publication is available from the British Library

Library of Congress Cataloging in Publication data
LeVen, Pauline Anaïs, 1976– author.
The many-headed muse : tradition and innovation in late classical Greek lyric poetry / Pauline A. LeVen.
  pages   cm
Includes bibliographical references and index.
ISBN 978-1-107-01853-2 (hardback)
1. Greek poetry – History and criticism.   2. Lyric poetry – History and criticism.
I. Title.
PA3110.L48   2014
884´.0109 – dc23   2013022003

ISBN 978-1-107-01853-2 Hardback
ISBN 978-1-108-40166-1 Paperback

Contents

Acknowledgments

This book began as a joint thesis (*thèse de cotutelle*) between the Department of Classics at Princeton University and the Centre d'Etudes Anciennes at the Ecole normale supérieure, Paris, co-directed by Andrew Ford and Monique Trédé; it developed into its current form within the Classics department at Yale University. It is a pleasure and an honor to thank the many individuals who have contributed, on both sides of the Atlantic, to making my work, and myself, into what we are now.

My first thanks go to Monique Trédé, who welcomed me as a *conscrite* at the ENS in 1997 and has been by my side ever since, supporting me in all my endeavors both academic and non-academic. She has taught, guided, and inspired me in more ways than I can acknowledge, and her energy, elegance, and sense of humor are a model that I can only try to emulate.

The dissertation was defended twice, once in Princeton and once in Paris. As a result, I had the unique benefit of receiving perceptive feedback from two fantastic sets of readers. The very diverse realms of expertise but equally large intellectual ambition of my Princeton dissertation committee, Joshua Katz and Josh Ober, made me expand the boundaries of my thinking throughout the dissertation process. A second jury, composed of Claude Calame, Eric Csapo, Paul Demont, and Didier Pralon, gave me detailed responses and thoughtful comments. I could not have dreamt of a more distinguished crew to read my chapters.

I have been lucky to find in the Classics department at Yale a welcoming home in which to develop my ideas further: our librarian, Colin McCaffrey, rescued me countless times on my bibliographical quests, and students and colleagues have been supportive interlocutors, especially Egbert Bakker, Victor Bers, and Emily Greenwood, who were instrumental at all stages as I thought through the arguments of this book, Kirk Freudenburg, Verity Harte, Chris Kraus, and John Matthews, who gave me invaluable advice, and Milette Gaifman and Irene Peirano, whom I count as faithful friends as well as outstanding colleagues.

Many sections of this book were presented as conference papers and talks. I owe particular thanks to Stephen Halliwell, Jason König, and the School of Classics at St Andrews for their hospitality during a terrific and most productive two-week stay there. Audiences at St Andrews and at Berkeley, Cambridge, Cornell, Cremona, Johns Hopkins, Lecce, Paris, Ravenna, Reading, Stanford, the University of Vermont, NYU, Santa Cruz, Yale, and Warsaw have provided me with substantial feedback on various aspects of the argument of the book. Details of chapters were also shaped by inspiring conversations with Andrew Barker, Claude Calame, Marco Fantuzzi, John Franklin, Mark Griffith, Theodora Hadjimichael, Johanna Hanink, Leslie Kurke, Jan Kwapicz, Richard Martin, Natasha Peponi, Andrej and Ivana Petrovic, Lucia Prauscello, and David Sider. Last but not least, many conversations with Felix Budelmann contributed to making me think harder, and I am most indebted to our email exchanges and to his close reading of my manuscript in its final stage.

Several generous scholarships have given me the freedom to pursue research in ideal conditions: the Sibley fellowship from the Phi Beta Kappa Society released me from teaching in the last dissertation year. A year of leave was funded by Yale and allowed me to benefit from a month-long stay at the Fondation Hardt, a setting to "feed the soul" (an expression I owe to Brooke Holmes, whose companionship there was an added boon), and to spend Trinity term at Corpus Christi College, Oxford. My heartfelt thanks go to Ewen Bowie, Jaś Elsner, and Tim Whitmarsh for their hospitality and invigorating conversations, and to Pavlos Avlamis, Gregory Hutchinson, Ian Rutherford, and Oliver Taplin for making my Oxford experience even more stimulating. I also wish to thank Michael Sharp, Elizabeth Hanlon, and Mary O'Hara of Cambridge University Press for their work on my behalf and the press readers for their constructive comments. Deep thanks are due to my research assistant, Caroline Mann, for her industrious work on merciless tasks, to Rona Johnston Gordon, with her perfect ear for the English language, and to Iveta Adams, whose meticulous work helped me eliminate myriads of errors from the text. Their combined care, diligence, and expertise made it possible for the final version of the manuscript to see the light.

Twelve years ago when I set foot as a Fulbright student in Andrew Ford's office, I had no idea that the experience of working with him would prove so transformative: his teaching and tutelage have shaped the way I read, think, and write. Words can barely express my gratitude for his attentive feedback and intellectual generosity, and for his warm encouragement, in our conversations continued over many years, to find my own voice as a scholar.

Neither the dissertation nor the book would have been possible without the support and love of my mother, my families, and my friends – Murielle and Daniel, Michael, Philippe-Etienne, Michelle, Naaman, Stefan, and Ty. Even if, as I hope, they never read these lines, I want to thank them for always being there and keeping things in perspective. This book is dedicated to Thomas, with all my gratitude for his spirit of fun, his loving companionship, his patience and his impatience: on to new adventures now.

Abbreviations

Authors and works are abbreviated following the practice of the *Oxford Classical Dictionary*, and journals according to that of *L'Année Philologique*. Abbreviations of papyri may be found in J. F. Oates *et al.*, *Checklist of Editions of Greek, Latin, Demotic and Coptic Papyri, Ostraca and Tablets*, available online at: http://library.duke.edu/rubenstein/scriptorium/papyrus/texts/clist.html.

Adler   Adler, A. (1928–38) *Suidae lexicon* (5 vols.). Leipzig.

CA   *See* Powell 1925.

CEG   *See* Hansen 1983–9.

CIG   *Corpus inscriptionum Graecarum*.

GVI   Peek, W. (1955) *Griechische Vers-Inschriften*, vol. i. *Grab-Epigramme*. Berlin.

FGE   Page, D. L. (1981) *Further Greek Epigrams: Epigrams before* AD *50 from the Greek Anthology and other sources, not included in "Hellenistic Epigrams" or "The Garland of Philip,"* revised and prepared for publication by R. D. Dawe and J. Diggle. Cambridge.

FGrH   Jacoby, F. (1923–) *Die Fragmente der griechischen Historiker* (4 parts). Leiden, Boston, and Cologne.

FHG   Müller, K. (1841–70) *Fragmenta historicorum Graecorum* (5 vols.). Paris.

Gow   *See* Gow 1965.

HE   Gow, A. S. F. and D. L. Page (1965) *The Greek Anthology: Hellenistic Epigrams* (2 vols.). Cambridge.

IG   (1873–) *Inscriptiones Graecae*. Berlin.

KA   Kassel, R., and C. Austin (1983–) *Poetae comici Graeci*. Berlin and New York.

LIMC   (1981–97) *Lexicon iconographicum mythologiae classicae*. Zurich and Munich.

LSJ   Liddell, H. G., R. Scott, H. Stuart Jones, R. McKenzie, and P. G. W. Glare (1996) *Greek–English Lexicon, with a revised Supplement*, 9th edn. Oxford.

OCD   Hornblower, S., and A. Spawforth (1996) *Oxford Classical Dictionary*, 3rd edn. Oxford.

PMG   Page, D. L. (1962) *Poetae melici Graeci, edidit D. L. Page*. Oxford.

SH	Lloyd-Jones, H., and P. Parsons (1983) *Supplementum Hellenisticum*. Berlin and New York.
SM	Maehler, H. (1987–9) *Pindari carmina cum fragmentis, post Brunonem Snell edidit H. Maehler* (2 vols.: *Pars* I: *Epinicia, Pars* II: *Fragmenta et indices*). Stuttgart and Leipzig.
Σ	scholia.
T	testimonium.
TGrF	Snell, B., R. Kannicht, and S. Radt (1971–86) *Tragicorum Graecorum fragmenta* (5 vols.). Göttingen.
Voigt	Voigt, E. M. (1971) *Sappho et Alcaeus: fragmenta*. Amsterdam.
W²	West, M. L. (1989–92) *Iambi et elegi Graeci ante Alexandrum cantati*, 2nd edn. Oxford.
Wehrli	Wehrli, F. von (1969) *Die Schule des Aristoteles: Texte und Kommentar* (10 vols. and 2 supplements). Basel and Stuttgart.

Note on editions

The texts of the late classical poets are quoted from Campbell's (1993) edition, except for Timotheus of Miletus (*PMG* 791) quoted from Sevieri's (2011) edition, and Philoxenus of Leucas (*PMG* 836) quoted from Olson's (2006–10) edition of Athenaeus' *Deipnosophistae*. Translations are mine unless otherwise noted. Other texts are quoted from the most recent *Oxford Classical Text* edition or from the standard edition as listed in the *OCD*, unless otherwise stated in the Index locorum next to the name of the work.

Introduction: the late classical gap

This book examines the lyric poetry of the late classical period, roughly defined as 430–323 BC. "*Late* classical lyric? Is there any?," a prospective reader might ask. The lyric poetry of the late fifth and fourth centuries has been, for the most part, ignored and left out of standard histories of Greek literature.[1] Or, worse perhaps, it has been obscured by statements such as, "By the middle of the fifth century the creative force vivifying early elegy and lyric had largely spent itself,"[2] "The last twenty years of the fifth century is a period of disintegration and disillusion, in which mannerism and realism live side by side,"[3] or even, "If this turgidity [of the style of one late classical poet] is a fair sample of what was being produced, it is little wonder that poetry went into retirement."[4] Yet as archaeological, epigraphic, and literary evidence suggests, songs were still composed and performed between the time of the death of Pindar, the last great lyric poet of the classical period, and the lyric corpora of Theocritus and Callimachus in the third century BC. About 800 lines of verse have been preserved from the immense corpus of solo and choral songs that were composed and performed between the 430s and the 320s BC, that is, about a hundred fragments, ranging from one mangled word to 240 continuous lines of text, coming from dithyrambs, nomes, paeans, hymns, encomia, and other sung forms accompanied by instrumental music. This evidence is, to be sure, limited – the equivalent of a long book of the *Iliad* – and a frustratingly minuscule part of the whole lyric production of that period. But it is certainly not limited enough to justify the neglect that literary studies showed for this corpus until the past two decades or so. The first goal of this book is thus to present and discuss a varied body of texts that has never been analyzed as a whole.[5]

In fact, it is precisely the diversity of the material available that is daunting. Questions raised, for example, by a hymn inscribed on a stone in a sanctuary

---

[1] It does not appear at all in the histories of Greek literature by Norwood (1925), Murray (1935), Bowra (1967), Campbell (1983), de Romilly (1985), Trédé and Saïd (1997), or Whitmarsh (2004).
[2] Podlecki 1984: 251.   [3] Webster 1939: 197.   [4] Hadas 1950: 64.
[5] It is telling that the texts considered in this book are gathered in not one, but two editions: the "New School of Music" in Campbell 1993, translating and complementing *PMG*, and the epigraphic material, which is edited in *CA*.

in the Peloponnese at the end of the fourth century are different from questions raised by a famous dithyramb performed in Athens at the end of the fifth century. Often these questions are answered by a range of people with different academic specialties, skills, and critical leanings (epigraphy, philology, cultural history, religion, literary criticism, papyrology, history of music, etc.), and they are treated in different volumes. However, the songs – cultic or meant for private celebrations, of lasting fame or barely recalled, judged revolutionary or apparently conservative, Panhellenic and epichoric, preserved in quotations or in epigraphic or papyrus form – are all products of the same era, and they ought to be read together, although there is no need to reconcile one with the other in order to provide, as is all too often attempted, an overall unified narrative. With this diversity in mind, the second goal of this book is to analyze the characteristics of the late classical lyric production in order to locate it within its original socio-cultural context, or rather to treat singing and song production as activities embedded in a larger network of socio-cultural practices. Not only does the archaeological and epigraphic evidence, from lists of victors in poetic competitions and choregic monuments to inscriptions of songs to the gods, suggest that song-and-dance performance was still widespread in the late fifth century and through the fourth century,[6] but references to song composition and performance and to lyric quotations that occur in the work of contemporary prose writers such as Plato, Xenophon, Aristotle and the Attic orators suggest uninterrupted interest and use. This is what Richard Martin notes in connection with dramatic performance, finding a fitting parallel with modern Los Angeles:

This hum of voices – songs in memory, speaking stones – amplified the "buzz" about performance that must have permeated ancient Athens as it does large swathes of modern Los Angeles. An inventory of just the verbal offshoots of dramatic competitions in the fifth through fourth centuries BCE would have to include (apart from the actual dramatic texts), casual compliments, abuse, or anecdotes about poets and actors; oratory and history in which they are mentioned; reminiscences of performances; official didascalic records of the winners; choregic inscriptions; sepulchral inscriptions of those who had once been involved in performance; talk at symposia; and songs, poems, and prose works (such as Plato's *Symposium* and the *Epidêmiai* of Ion of Chios) that are based wholly or in part on performers and their art. And of course the visual inventory, from vases to portrait busts, extended the impact of the stage even further in space and time.[7]

---

[6] Wilson 2000: 265–302.   [7] Martin 2006: 36.

All of these venues for "listening" to after-sounds of drama could be explored for lyric too, but to date such careful and well-merited investigation of lyric has not been undertaken. By analyzing not only the texts but also the discourse about *mousikē* in the late classical period, this book examines the interaction of lyric with contemporary social, cultural, religious, and political contexts and the presentation of lyric as an integral part of late classical civic, religious, and private life, through, for example, symposiastic singing and choral performance.[8]

Finally, the third goal of this project is to study forms of reception of the late classical lyric corpus and to understand why this material has been the object of neglect or condemnation. Three explanations have traditionally been sought for the alleged demise of lyric after the death of Pindar: the Romantic notion that genres have to die, allowing one to succeed the other; the idea that, after the end of the fifth century, talent and public interest turned to genres other than lyric, to philosophical prose and rhetoric in particular;[9] and the argument that, with the end of the early classical period, good taste disappeared when some composers (called by modern critics the "New Musicians") introduced a series of radical tonal, formal, and stylistic transformations in theater music (that is, in the choral parts of drama, in the dithyramb, and in the citharodic nome, all performed in theaters, for musical competitions), which ultimately led to the demise of *mousikē*. As Oliver Taplin explains in the case of late classical vase painting:

I have heard fourth-century Western Greek vase-painting dismissed as "spät und schlecht" (late and lousy). This is clearly a judgment that takes Athenian painting, especially that of the early fifth century, as its ideal of Classical Art. This yearning for noble simplicity can be taken back to the eighteenth-century intellectual Johann Winckelmann; but in the appreciation of vase-painting, it was (Sir) John Beazley, the great connoisseur art historian, who did the most to canonize the Attic ideal.[10]

---

[8] This book is necessarily selective and does not consider aspects of the lyric culture of the late classical period such as quotations of, allusions to, or silences about lyric poetry in Plato, Xenophon, Aristotle, Isocrates, and Attic orators and historiographers. Studies of aspects of this topic include, on the orators, North 1952, Perlman 1964, Ober 1989, Ober and Strauss 1989, Too 1995, and Ford 1999, and, on Plato, especially the *Laws*, Prauscello 2011a, Peponi 2013, and Folch forthcoming.

[9] Mahaffy 1891: I 254: "The student must be reminded that in studying Greek Literature chronologically, he must now turn, before approaching the Attic drama, to the history of prose writing, which was growing silently, and almost secretly, all through the sixth century BC, *though its bloom did not come till after the completion of Greek poetry by Aeschylus and Sophocles*" (my emphasis). On the invention of prose and the contest of authority between the voice of the poet and the voice of the prose writer, see Goldhill 2002, especially pp. 4–6.

[10] Taplin 2007: 16.

The same classicizing vision can be observed in literary criticism. Of Timotheus, author of the *Persians*, the longest surviving piece of lyric of the late fifth century and representative of the so-called revolutionary "New Music," it has been said that "he contradicts in every respect the ideals of Hellenic art and taste. He is a curiosity, a monstrosity" and that he is "the sort of writer who makes 'baroque' an insulting word," and it has been suggested that his "pomposity and bombast, . . . a far cry from the grandeur of Pindar or the grace of Bacchylides, . . . look forward to the worst traits of Hellenistic poetry."[11] This book takes another stance: without wanting to forcibly impute to these lyric poems a genius generally denied them by critics for twenty-five centuries, I question the idea of aesthetic decline at the end of the fifth century and offer literary interpretations that do not judge texts only according to "classical" standards but examine them according to their own aesthetic.

In recognizing the integrity of the late classical corpus, we must not forget its connections to its archaic and early classical predecessors: there are many ways (thematic, linguistic, and rhetorical, inter alia) in which late classical lyric emulates, challenges, and engages with archaic and early classical models. While this type of relationship has been explored in the case of the Hellenistic corpus, much remains to be done in the case of the late classical poets.[12] In particular, careful examination of the aesthetic of the period of lyric history that constitutes the "missing link" between the early classical and Hellenistic periods can reveal much about the roots of Alexandrian art. Some "Hellenistic" features can already be observed in the late classical period, to which the Hellenistic poets might have been indebted more significantly than to the archaic or early classical periods. At the same time, the need to avoid the looming danger of a teleological interpretation in which late classical poetry is read as announcing a later aesthetic and intellectual development should not prevent us from perceiving the late classical period as important in its own right rather than only for what was to come, or what came before.[13]

---

[11] Kenyon 1919: 5, Levi 1985: 382, and Segal 1985: 243 respectively. There are exceptions to these judgments, most notably perhaps Herington (1985: 151–60), who concluded his series of Sather lectures thus, "the outcome of the experiment [of restoring the silent printed letters of Timotheus' *Persians* to a performing context] has been, for me, not necessarily a finer work of art than that which appears in our literary handbooks, but certainly a different and more interesting one" (160).

[12] On the Hellenistic poets' use of the archaic and early classical past, Fantuzzi and Hunter 2004, Morrison 2007a, Acosta-Hughes 2010a, and Prauscello 2011b (for Callimachus' use of the New Music).

[13] For teleological reading, Pickard-Cambridge 1962: 69, Segal 1985: 243. As a reaction, note Acosta-Hughes (2010b), who sees "Hellenistic" hallmarks in archaic poetry.

To achieve its goals, this project as a whole takes the specific form of an investigation of tradition and innovation in late classical lyric. Most studies of the period tend either to emphasize exclusively the supposedly scandalous and disruptive innovations introduced by a group of later fifth- and early fourth-century musicians who are deemed representative of the New Music or to describe the continued tradition of hymn composition; this book examines how in the late classical period, forms of tradition and innovation of all sorts combined, to various degrees, in various places and contexts, and for various purposes. It is possible to examine any musical, visual, or intellectual development in terms of tradition and innovation,[14] but there are two reasons why this approach is particularly useful for the late classical period. First, as Robin Osborne has recently stated in a multi-part project focusing on revolutions, "if change is a historical constant, the nature of change in any particular cultural manifestation is not for that reason uninteresting, nor are all changes equal."[15] Even if changes in music are a constant, the musical changes of the late classical period have particular import because of the controversies they caused and the rhetoric of change with which they are associated. For a second reason too the *problématique* of tradition and innovation is particularly appropriate for the study of late classical lyric: at the end of the fifth century, especially in Athens, changes in many forms took shape, feeding off each other and constituting the background of intellectual culture.[16] Whether they introduced a revolution in lyric poetry and music performance or a series of developments that can be understood as translations or adaptations, the "new musicians" lived in a cultural context in which they would have rubbed shoulders not only with "new architects," "new vase painters," "new scientists," and "new rhetoricians/educators," but also with "new banker-financiers," "new military strategists," "new politicians," and a whole class of nouveaux riches.[17] Only when we take into account the general setting at the end of the

---

[14] On the concept of tradition and innovation as useful for a study of Greek poetry, Pretagostini 1993, Fantuzzi and Hunter 2002 and 2004, and Whitmarsh 2004: 18–31; on classical traditions, J. I. Porter 2006; on innovations in music, D'Angour 2006b and 2007; on novelty in ancient Greek imagination and experience, D'Angour 2011.

[15] Osborne 2007: 2–3.

[16] Akrigg 2007, whose main claim is that "looking at the economic history of Athens can suggest reasons for supposing that a cultural revolution really did take place over this period" (p. 27 for quotation). For the effects of the Peloponnesian War on economy, culture, and society, see Hornblower (1983: 153–80), who defines the fourth century as an age of professionalism in general (156).

[17] On late classical art, see Webster 1956, Schultz 2007, Taplin 2007, and Neer 2012: 318–47. On new scientists, Lloyd 1987: 50–108. On sophists and "new rhetoricians," Taylor 2007. On new military strategists, D'Angour 2011: 175–9. On new politicians, Connor 1971.

fifth century, which was characterized by an intellectual "innovation hype" and socio-economic mobility, from the professionalization of several fields of activity to new constructions of subjectivity, does the full significance of an approach to the lyric corpus from the specific angle of tradition and innovation become evident.

An archaeology of late classical lyric

Late classical poetry is not easily accessed by modern readers. This period of literary history has been ignored, or even hidden from view, primarily because most modern scholars have inherited a series of "selection filters" from ancient authors and critics. Although none of these screens is specific to the period under consideration, five factors, at times overlapping, have helped make the late classical era the missing generation of lyric poetry.

The first filter that has restricted our access to the lyric output of the classical period relates to material. As with most ancient literature, only a fraction of the overall production of late classical lyric has survived, the result of both passive selection – the material accidents that have preserved a particular papyrus or inscribed stone – and active selection, by communities who chose, for example, to inscribe a certain text, and not another, on a stone, by scholars who made editions of particular poets, and not others, or by literary authors who quoted poetic passages and determined what belonged to their canon. Two socio-cultural processes are at stake here: one is linked to technologies of communication, especially writing, as means of preservation, transmission, and diffusion; the other is a cultural and institutional process akin to canon formation and the making of a tradition. The combination of accidents and active choices, the two determining processes, has shaped the corpus as received and accessed today.

A second filter was imposed by ancient authors, including Plato, Aristotle, and Peripatetic scholars as well as pseudo-Plutarch and Athenaeus, their followers in the Imperial period, who wrote *diachronic* accounts of poetic and musical history. Most ancient literary historians describe a watershed in the history of *mousikē* in the mid fifth century and associate the New Music with lyric decline after the golden age of archaic and early classical poetry. They created an opposition between traditional lyric as politically engaged, public, and full of true religious fervor, and New Music as a domestic, formalist *l'art pour l'art* phenomenon, devoid of true inspiration.[18] Modern

---

[18] Pickard-Cambridge 1962: 38–59, Zimmermann 1992: 117–47.

studies have until recently taken these statements at face value, tracing the story offered by Plato, Aristotle, and their followers. This approach is, however, problematic, since ancient political theorists were not so much faithful reporters of musical culture as intellectuals with conservative views who followed their own ideological agenda and wrote their self-interested version of literary and musical history.[19] It is their hostile view of the New Music that we have inherited and their critical categories that for the longest time have been reproduced in diachronic accounts of musical history.

These ancient authors, especially those who wrote several centuries after the fact, have also imposed a third reading screen onto the late classical period that is still strikingly present in modern accounts: they purport to offer a *synchronic* analysis of the New Music and comment on its socio-cultural context and the cultural transformations of the late fifth and fourth centuries. At least until the critical turn marked in the last thirty years or so by performance studies and studies in the material culture of the theater, most modern scholars adopted passages that appear to provide historical context with little critical distance. A careful reading of the source authors often reveals, however, that rather than presenting a faithful and informed synchronic analysis of the period, ancient authors perform a historicist reading of the ancient texts, working with no knowledge beyond what we ourselves possess about the context in which the poems were composed.[20]

A fourth screen is ideological and related to the third. Ancient authors and anecdotists often projected onto the life of the poet elements they read in his poetry. Although the work of Janet Fairweather, Mary Lefkowitz, and, more recently, Barbara Graziosi and Elizabeth Irwin has done much to emphasize the element of fiction in poetic "lives,"[21] scholars of late classical lyric have done remarkably little with their conclusions when considering material related to the New Musicians. Even a canonical book such as Martin West's 1992 *Ancient Greek Music* presents biographies of the poets that tend to veer to a positivist presentation and takes as historical truth ancient anecdotes that describe the excesses of the poets and their lack of poetic discrimination, much as Sir Arthur Pickard-Cambridge did in his *Dithyramb, Tragedy and Comedy* in 1927.[22] It is high time to reconsider these anecdotes and biographical elements to see how they themselves are part of the reception and construction of New Music and its practitioners that we have inherited.

---

[19] Csapo and Wilson 2009a.   [20] LeVen 2010.
[21] Fairweather 1974, Lefkowitz 1981, Graziosi 2002, Irwin 2006.
[22] West 1992: 357–72; Pickard-Cambridge 1927: 53–74 and 1962: 42–58.

Finally, the last screen imposed on reading late classical poetry is that of ancient literary criticism. The comic poets, followed by literary critics and theorists, were especially hostile to the style of the "New Dithyramb," which they describe as vacuous, ridiculously convoluted, and obscure. Many modern studies devoted to analyzing ancient comedy's critical discourse on lyric poems take for granted what the comic poets say.[23] After the explosion of literary critical studies following the publication of the Timotheus papyrus in 1903, hardly any work has been devoted to reading the extant, if fragmentary, texts and analyzing the characteristics and logic of their poetic language or the vividness of their narrative.[24] While Hellenistic poetry, once denigrated, has seen an explosion of sophisticated readings in the last half century, the corpus of late classical, or pre-Hellenistic, lyric poetry still awaits sustained examination by literary critics.

"Late classical lyric"

Two terms in the title of this work are deserving of particular note. "Lyric" can be both too specific and too vague an expression.[25] Etymologically, it suggests an association with the lyre, yet not all "lyric" songs were accompanied by a lyre-type instrument; most, indeed, were accompanied by a wind instrument, the *aulos*. The term "lyric" therefore does not capture all the forms of lyric practice. At the same time, "lyric" has been used to describe not only melic poetry, that is, songs performed to the accompaniment of strings and wind, but also two other forms of poetry, elegy and *iambos*. While performance contexts for elegy and *iambos* are comparable to those for melic poetry, which included the symposium and public festivals, the meter and mode of performance of these compositions were very different: elegy and *iambos* were probably chanted and accompanied by *aulos* music and were composed in stichic meters rather than melic

---

[23] Zimmermann 1988 and 1993.

[24] The only recent detailed studies of the style of Timotheus are Brussich 1970 and Csapo and Wilson 2009a; on the poetics of the New Music in general, with few textual readings, Csapo 2004 and a revised and augmented version in Csapo 2011. Older studies are fascinating for the national ideological prejudices they often betray: Wilamowitz' *editio princeps* of Timotheus' *Persians* in 1903 was followed by articles by Croiset (1903), Mazon (1903), Reinach (1903) (now all conveniently collected in Calvié 2010), Gildersleeve (1903), Kenyon (1903), Danielsson (1903), Ellingham (1921), Ebeling (1925). For works devoted more specifically to the lexis dithyrambica, see Chapter 4, n. 2.

[25] On the definition of lyric, Färber 1936: 7–16, Pfeiffer 1968: 182–8, West 1993: vii–viii, and Calame 1998, who disapproves of the term "lyric" in the narrow sense and prefers "melic," Budelmann 2009b.

cola.[26] Finally, "lyric" understood in the narrower sense of "melic" ought also to encompass the choral odes of drama, which shared many of the characteristics of choral lyric.[27] This book focuses on the narrow sense of "melic" – sung and not chanted words, melic and not stichic meters – and does not include elegy and *iambos*. But neither does it include dramatic melic songs, even though in terms of performance scenario and context these songs had strong affinities with some of the lyric examined in this book. This latter choice was dictated in part by the primary material and the available scholarship: the past fifteen years have seen an explosion of scholarly interest in the dramatic lyric of the late fifth century, especially late Euripides, while much less has been done on the fragmentary corpus of dithyrambs and nomes.[28] The project is thus in dialogue with studies on late fifth-century dramatic lyric but focuses on material that has drawn less attention.

A second term from the title of this work, "late classical," brings us to consider the time frame addressed by this study, which is roughly the period between the beginning of the Peloponnesian War (430s BC) and the end of the reign of Alexander the Great (323 BC). Although, as just indicated, these dates have particular resonance within political history, their selection was determined by cultural considerations.[29] As I explain in Chapter 1, historians of the theater have shown that the 430s saw the beginning of a new era in which the construction of larger theaters began and a real "star-system" was established.[30] This era has been presented as ending when the *chorēgia* (the community-based sponsoring of theater music and popular participation in choral music) is replaced by *agōnothesia* (a system where the tasks of the multiple *chorēgoi* under the democracy are concentrated into a single office), a change most often ascribed to Demetrius of Phalerum.[31] As the uncertainty associated with the exact end of the *chorēgia* shows, those chronological boundaries (430s BC and 323 BC) should not be seen as rigid markers of sudden change or clean-cut watersheds, yet the periodization they denote is the most helpful as we seek

[26] On elegy and iambos, Campbell 1964, E. Bowie 1986, Gentili 1988: 32–6.
[27] Herington 1985.
[28] On fourth-century tragedy, Webster 1956, Xanthakis-Karamanos 1980, Easterling 1993 and 1997, Hall 2007. On late Euripides, Csapo 1999–2000, 2008, 2009, Battezzato 2005, Sansone 2009, Steiner 2011. There are two major exceptions: Hordern (1998, 1999, 2000, 2004) and Power (2010), who deal with the fragmentary corpus.
[29] On the difficulty of periodization, Farell 2001: 85–90, Feeney 2007: 7–11, Hunter 2008: 9–17.
[30] Csapo 2004: 208–14, for the expression see p. 212.
[31] On the issue of passage from *chorēgia* to *agōnothesia*, see Wilson 2000: 270–6, Csapo and Wilson 2009b, who note the "tumultuous and complex process too readily obscured by institutional histories" (68), and Csapo and Wilson 2010.

to understand important changes in theater culture, including the advent of the New Music in the last third of the fifth century and the first quarter of the fourth, and in forms of musical practice.

Chapter layout

Chapter 1 ("A collection of unrecollected authors?") provides a survey of the surviving material and the problems raised by the shape of that corpus. Much more evidence about late classical lyric activity has survived than is often assumed, for its presentation is usually split among genres (dithyrambs and nomes vs. hymns), between media (literary vs. epigraphic evidence), between periods (addenda to the early classical vs. introductions to the Hellenistic period), or, most importantly, among literary criticism, cultural studies, and cultural history. Older studies, often strongly influenced by structuralism, concentrate on stylistic and formal features of the corpus with little regard for the cultural context to which songs belong, while more recent studies focus on the culture of *mousikē* in the classical period, with less attention to the surviving poetic material and its relationship to the poetic tradition. The chapter exposes the evidence in its diversity. It also introduces two important topics that will recur over the course of the book: first, the status, role, and significance of writing in the production, transmission, and dissemination of a sung corpus; and second, the relationship between surviving evidence and our understanding of the evolution of poetic genres over the course of the late classical period.

The next three chapters focus on reception filters, with the aim of exposing the readings that have often been imposed on the surviving corpus and have hindered access to the texts. All these chapters endeavor to explain what later authors might have obscured as they wrote about late classical lyric. Chapter 2 ("New Music and its myths") is devoted to one of the most controversial features of the late classical period: the discourse on the phenomenon that modern critics call the "New Music." The "New Music" or the "New Music revolution" has been associated with the introduction of a series of stylistic, tonal, and formal innovations in theater music, in dithyrambs, nomes, and sung parts of drama. The chapter first outlines three different frameworks used to describe and understand New Music as a phenomenon and its place in literary history. Having examined the phenomenon looking in from the outside, I turn to a description from within, looking out. While any musician or artist might emphasize the novelty of his or her production, no matter how traditional that production is, the New Music poets' rhetoric of self-presentation is well worth our examination. The chapter considers the singular elements of New Music's claim to newness, and the rhetorical means used to propound this new style.[32] One of the significant features of the New Music is that by providing their critics with the vocabulary that shaped their own publicity, the New Musicians staged their own reception in dramatic terms and orchestrated the intense debate about the practice and consumption of *mousikē* at the turn of the fifth century. The chapter focuses on the manipulation of notions of tradition and innovation as powerful rhetorical tools employed by late classical lyric poets in their self-representation, a practice followed also by ancient and modern critics.

The third chapter ("New Music live: poetics of Philoxenia(na)") takes this rhetoric of newness further and examines how the originality of the New Music was represented by later authors in anecdotes about the poets and their lives. Rather than engaging with the historicity of these stories, the chapter considers how anecdotes constitute a stage of reception in themselves and function as an index of the reimagining of the poetics of the lyric composers at different moments in antiquity. The case of the dithyrambist Philoxenus, which constitutes the bulk of the chapter, provides an ideal window, allowing us to see the ways in which stories about the poet's frank speech and liberal dining habits give access to his Odyssean poetics and engagement with comic themes and enable authors to play with important concepts of fourth-century democracy and the place that the poet might occupy within that democracy. In their use of a repertory of themes and motives familiar from the lives of earlier poets, especially stories about Simonides and his relationship with *xenia*, anecdotes about the poet's life, termed here "Philoxeniana," form a cohesive discourse centered on the changed relationship between poet and society and on poetic speech in the city, especially the increasing blurring of public and private spheres.

The fourth chapter ("The language of the New Music") turns to other controversial aspects of the innovations of New Music: its *lexis* (diction) and exuberant style. To this day, the adjective "dithyrambic" can have negative connotations, and ancient comic poets and modern critics have been particularly dismissive of the language typical of late classical dithyramb

---

[32] The bulk of Chapter 2 was completed before the publication of D'Angour's splendid 2011 monograph, *The Greeks and the New: Novelty in Ancient Greek Imagination and Experience.* Many of my considerations on the "newness" of the New Music were anticipated by D'Angour, and wherever possible I refer to his study and indicate points of contact or divergence. To quote D'Angour himself: "In writing about novelty, I naturally hope to say something new; but there are always new things to say and new ways of saying them – and since the passage of time itself brings about the new, the newest thing is what remains to be said" (9).

and nome. With its many compound adjectives, its neologisms, and its long clauses, the diction of the New Music has the features of any elevated language; yet the criticism of the comic poets has framed our reception of this language and has associated New Music diction with vacuity, pomposity, and frigidity. The chapter examines how the innovativeness of the language is not where the comic poets – often mischievously – located it but in its productive reuse of traditional elements of elevated lyric diction. One of the characteristic features of the New Music language is that it defamiliarizes its audience's relationship between things and words. A detailed examination of Timotheus' specific diction shows how the poet's use of compounds, periphrasis, and metaphors and his reliance on a synaesthetic poetics allow him (while reusing his predecessors' vocabulary and images) to engage with the audience's imagination in a way that is characteristically different from the archaic and earlier classical poets. The result is a poetry that allows its audience to apprehend the described objects or phenomena by re-experiencing the poetic past in new ways, and through what can be called, in Michael Silk's terms, "heightened language."[33]

The next three chapters focus more narrowly on the surviving texts and fragments. Chapter 5 ("Narrative and subjectivity") builds on the analysis of language in Chapter 4 and examines the question of *mimēsis* in the New Music. I argue that the major innovation of the narrative lyric of the late classical period resides in a transformation of the relationship between the audience and the world of the narrative. This change is partly located in a switch that Jaś Elsner has described in connection with the visual arts as a shift "from a voice of authority making direct contact with its audience to a performative model whereby the viewer observes an imaginary world that is insulated within its own context and to which he or she must relate by identification or some form of wish-fulfillment fantasy."[34] The chapter examines this evolution in the narrative voice, in the types of character presented, and more generally in the understanding of an audience's subjectivity and relationship with the narrative, first in Timotheus' *Persians* and in the set of themes illustrated in the corpus of surviving fragments, and then in one of the most famous compositions of the late classical period, Philoxenus' *Cyclops*. I suggest that our focus should shift, from looking for novelty in the object (the song and its formal features) to looking for novelty in the response made to the object (the type of interpretive and imaginative work performed by the audience). In all these examples, formal structures of narrative "are most productively analyzed in close relationship to the

---

[33] Silk 2010: 435.   [34] Elsner 2006: 68.

fictional worlds they transmit rather than as items in a catalogue of generic innovations," to use Mark Payne's elegant words in describing Theocritean bucolic.[35] This chapter offers reflections on how poets manipulated the mythical material and stimulated the audience's imagination in ways that were significantly different from earlier narrative poetry and foreshadowed many aspects of Hellenistic and Augustan poetics.

The sixth chapter ("Sympotic mix") pursues this investigation of the relationship between audience and poem by means of a close reading of three poems related to the symposium: Philoxenus' *Dinner Party*, a description of a fancy dinner-cum-symposium, Aristotle's "Hymn to Virtue," a song celebrating Aristotle's father-in-law Hermias and praising virtue, and Ariphron's "Hymn to Health." The last two poems engage with traditional sympotic themes or sympotic forms but were not necessarily performed at, or only at, symposia. While critics have explained the unsettling features of all these songs by connecting them to the "Kreuzung der Gattungen" ("mixing of genres") typically associated with Hellenistic literature or to the invention of a mimetic frame to compensate for the loss of actual performance contexts, I argue that these songs are not generic innovations or experiments but rather illustrate songs' performative fluidity and ability to adapt to new social and cultural environments and to different media, sung and inscribed.

The last chapter ("A canon set in stone?") considers a different type of contextual adaptation and manipulation of the narrative voice in the corpus of epigraphic hymns. Although often deemed "traditional" poetry, the paeans to Asclepius and Dionysus and hymns to Hestia and Apollo actually illustrate changes in the pragmatics of hymns. Crucial to this examination is the idea that epigraphic texts integrate the memory of songs but, because of the ambiguity of the "voice" of the written text, they introduce an additional layer of complexity to the engagement with the audience: I examine the poetic strategies used to negotiate the relationship between the here-and-now of the inscription, memory of orality, and concern for future performances. This less often examined side of the late classical corpus brings to light some intriguing parallels, and contrasts, with the texts preserved in the "literary" tradition and invites us to reconsider processes of canon formation.

---

[35] Payne 2007: 10.

1 | A collection of unrecollected authors?

> Because he found nothing so depressing as the collected works of
> unrecollected authors, although he did not mind an occasional visitor's
> admiring the place's tall bookcases and short cabinets . . .
>
> V. Nabokov, *Ada*[1]

Like the authors in Van Veen's father's tall bookcases, the late classical Greek
lyric poets too are mostly unrecollected, but we have not inherited any
collected volumes of their work. To make up for the gap on our bookshelves,
this chapter presents the surviving corpus of Greek melic poems composed
between the 430s and the 320s BC and sets the scene for the more detailed
studies of texts and contexts that follow in the next chapters. Contrary to
long-standing impression, the variety of material attesting to sung activity
during the late classical period is staggering: names of poets and musicians,
titles of songs, fragments of poetry preserved on stone and papyri and in
quotations, archaeological evidence for musical practice, and the epigraphic
record of choral activity allow us to draw a composite picture of the vibrant
world of Greek songs for men and gods.

Consider, for example, two anecdotes. The first is found in a passage from
the fourth-century music theorist Aristoxenus of Tarentum and comes from
his *Life of Telestes*, reported in Apollonius' *Marvellous Stories*, a work itself
much concerned with musical phenomena:

According to what the music theorist Aristoxenus says in his *Bios* of Telestes, at the
time when [Telestes] was visiting Italy, strange things were happening, among which
one concerned the women: they were the object of such ecstatic fits that sometimes
when they were sitting at the dinner table they would seem to hear somebody calling
them, and would uncontrollably jump to their feet to run outside the city. When
the Locrians and the Rhegians consulted an oracle and asked about the way to get

---

[1] *Ada or Ardor* by Vladimir Nabokov; copyright © 1969, Dmitri Nabokov, used by permission of
the Wylie Agency (UK) Limited. Excerpt from *Ada, or Ardor: A Family Chronicle*, by Vladimir
Nabokov, copyright © 1969, 1970 by the Estate of Vladimir Nabokov; used by permission of
Vintage Books, an imprint of the Knopf Doubleday Publishing Group, a division of Random
House LLC; all rights reserved.

rid of the condition, the god responded that they should sing [twelve] spring paeans for sixty days (εἰπεῖν τὸν θεὸν παιᾶνας ᾄδειν ἐαρινοὺς [δωδεκάτης] ἡμέρας ξ'). This is why there were many paean writers (παιανογράφους) in Italy.

Aristox. fr. 117 Wehrli = Apollonius, *Mir.* 40

This is the only extant fragment of the work that Aristoxenus devoted to Telestes of Selinous, one of the most famous composers associated with the late fifth-century musical and cultural phenomenon that modern scholars call the "New Music," which I discuss in detail in Chapter 2. The story enlarges and adds nuance to the monolithic image of late classical lyric culture often constructed: although it touches only tangentially upon the famous Telestes, it brings to life – if only for a short time – the many anonymous composers who had to keep up with an increased demand for new cult songs. Moreover, rather than focusing on Athens, one of the most important centers for theater music at the turn of the fourth century, the passage describes aspects of musical activity in the West (southern Italy and Sicily), where both Aristoxenus and Telestes are from.[2] Finally, it does not simply focus on the dithyrambs performed at musical competitions for which Telestes was famous, but instead provides glimpses of the world of performance of other types of cult poetry that are often less well attested. The anecdote may very well not be historical, especially as it stages such neat oppositions – what could better bring order back to the Dionysiac fits of female frenzy than the male calming action of the Apollonian songs? But what matters is that Aristoxenus would focus on such a piece of paradoxography, that the theorist's interest in the sociology of *mousikē* complements his theorizing on rhythm and harmonics and his activity as a biographer, and that his approaches to musical practices are diverse. Attention to Telestes' Italian travels incidentally throws light on an important feature of musical life – the "traffic in songs" created by traveling poets, musicians, *choroi*, and songs themselves as they crisscrossed the Mediterranean, eastward and westward between mainland Greece, southern Italy, Sicily, and the coast of Asia minor. The story is a perfect vantage point from which to recognize the intersection of various musical activities throughout the Greek world over the course of the late classical period and to establish a better sense of the variety of practices, in terms of personnel, genre, function, and geography.

The second story, quoted by Athenaeus (6.250b–c), combines some of the issues raised by the first with another question, that of the relationship

---

[2] On music in the West, Morgan 2012.

between the composition of new songs and the performance of the existing repertoire. It stages Dionysius the Elder, the tyrant who ruled Sicily from 406 to 367 BC, and one of his flatterers, Damocles, who is accused of having fomented dissent and injured the general interests of the tyrant while aboard a trireme on an embassy:

> [Damocles] explained that his dispute with his fellow ambassadors arose because after supper the others took up paeans of Phrynichus, Stesichorus, and also Pindar, with some of the sailors accompanying them; but he [Damocles], with those who agreed with him, went through the entire corpus of [paeans] that had been composed by Dionysius himself. And he offered to bring forward undeniable proof of this assertion, saying that his accusers were not even acquainted with the number of his songs, whereas he was ready to sing them all through one after the other. And so, when Dionysius was pacified, Damocles continued, and said, "But you would do me a great favor, O Dionysius, if you were to order any one of those who knows it to teach me the paean that you composed in honor of Asclepius; because I hear that you have taken great pains with that."
>
> Timaeus, *FGrH* 566 F 32

Dionysius is mostly known for his association with another of the famous virtuosi of the late fifth century, Philoxenus of Cythera, and for his infatuation with the musical innovations of the time, as well as for the bad quality of his own tragic compositions.[3] But the anecdote calls our attention to three telling music-related issues. First, while the focus is on the opposition between the old generation (Phrynichus, Stesichorus, and Pindar) and the Nouvelle Vague (represented by Dionysius himself), the story establishes that these kinds of music coexisted, with performances of what we might term "oldies" alongside experimentation with the new. Second, a man who flattered himself for his modernity composed not only songs in the style of theater music that was in vogue in dithyrambic and other musical competitions but also songs for the gods in a non-competitive environment. Finally, the cult song is itself concerned with religious innovation, as it is addressed to Asclepius, recently welcomed in Athens.[4] Like the previous anecdote, the story might not be historical, but it provides us with insight into perceptions of the musical reality of the late fifth century. Even if a heated debate between defenders of the avant-garde and aficionados of "classical" music never took place as described here, the account suggests that the two kinds of repertoire were understood to exist simultaneously,

---

[3] Duncan 2012. On other anecdotes staging Dionysius and Philoxenus, see Chapter 3, pp. 127–34 and 144–8.

[4] On Asclepius in Athens, Garland 1992: 116–35. On songs to Asclepius, Edelstein and Edelstein 1945: 325–36 (*T* 587–607), and Chapter 7 of this book.

and that this coexistence was deemed capable of stirring up passionate disagreement.

Prosopography of late classical *mousikē*

What do we know, then, of late classical poets and musicians? Evidence is of three types: first, literary sources that preserve the names of the poets, quotations of their poetry, and various kinds of information about their life – sometimes invented, sometimes drawn from the poetry itself, sometimes very cryptic – that often provides only limited details about chronology or socio-cultural context; second, the epigraphic record, which preserves the names of composers and musicians (especially *auletai*) and gives a sense of the socio-cultural context in which the songs were performed and chronology, but does not preserve the poetry; finally, a few inscriptions that preserve the song, the name of the poet, and aspects of his biography as officially constructed by the community and the poet himself. The purpose of this section is to draw from these various sources a representative, but probably not exhaustive, picture of the variety of the personnel involved in song composition and instrumental performance in the late classical period.

From larger-than-life figures to shadows of a name

The Telestes of the above anecdote is one of the most famous names associated with the New Music, which dominates accounts of lyric poetry in the late classical period. Although no canon of these New Music poets exists, a few names recur throughout all our ancient testimonies: Melanippides of Melos (*ca.* 475–415 BC), Cinesias of Athens (*ca.* 450–390 BC), Telestes of Selinous (*ca.* 450–390 BC), Timotheus of Miletus (*ca.* 450–360 BC), Philoxenus of Cythera and/or the poet also known as Philoxenus of Leucas (*ca.* 435–380 BC), Polyidus of Selembria (*fl.* 400 BC), as well as the cithara player Phrynis of Mytilene (*ca.* 460–400 BC) and the *aulos* player Pronomus of Thebes (*ca.* 470–390 BC).[5] Most of these composers' names appear on the *Marmor Parium* and on a few inscriptions; they are also recorded in passages of comedy, in musical treatises or works of political philosophy that discuss musical education, and by historiographers.[6] Diodorus of Sicily, for

---

[5] Wilson 2007c on Pronomus' dates.
[6] *Marmor Parium* 65 (Telestes)–76 (Timotheus); for inscriptions, see Table 2, pp. 34–8. On comedy, see Chapter 2, pp. 73–7 and Chapter 4, pp. 152–60.

example, in describing the poetic intelligentsia with whom the tyrant Dionysius of Sicily surrounded himself *ca.* 400 BC, records that

> at that time [that of the tyrant Dionysius], the most distinguished (ἐπισημότατοι)
> composers of dithyrambs were in their prime, Philoxenus of Cythera, Timotheus of
> Miletus, Telestes of Selinus, and Polyidus, who was also an expert in painting and
> music.
>
> Diod. Sic. 14.46.6

All but Cinesias are non-Athenians, and all were famous for composing
solo and choral pieces (nomes and dithyrambs) performed in the Athenian
theater at musical competitions. They are presented as having introduced a
revolution in music in the last third of the fifth century and as occupying
center stage in the musical life of the late fifth and the early fourth centuries;[7]
testimonia often portray them as a group, or as a school, with strong internal
rivalries and collaborations. Because their names occur so often and in
so many contexts, these poets have acquired a greater-than-life existence,
bolstered in particular by anecdotes.[8]

Yet their activity was neither entirely restricted to the theater and to the
genres of dithyramb and nome, nor entirely circumscribed to an Athenian
audience. With its numerous, especially dithyrambic, choruses and theatrical music, Athens was the greatest consumer of musical talent,[9] but the New
Musicians also composed other types of poetry, for other communities and
for private individuals. Besides a *Suda* entry that states that Melanippides
composed, in addition to the dithyrambs for which he was famous, some
"lyric songs" (ᾄσματα λυρικά),[10] Timotheus is credited with the composition of nomes "in hexameters" (δι᾽ ἐπῶν), preludes (προοίμια), adaptations (διασκευάς), encomia (ἐγκώμια), hymns (ὕμνους), and other works
(καὶ ἄλλα τινά), including a paean (*PMG* 800) and perhaps an epigram
(*FGE* 307).[11] Philoxenus composed dithyrambs, but an anecdote presents

---

[7] On which see Chapter 2.
[8] On anecdotes about the New Musicians more generally, see Chapter 3.
[9] Wilson (2000: 245–6), underlining the difference between Athens and the demes, states: "it
   might not be going too far to say that the performance and memorialization of dithyrambs in
   Attike has a 'centripetal' quality. The demes may have offered a training ground for choral and
   poetic performance in the city, but the very performance and scale of the Great Dionysian and
   Thargelian (to which one could add Panathenaïc) *kyklioi khoroi*, with perhaps more than 1600
   Athenian men and boys in their circles each year, may have largely filled Attike's need, and
   exhausted its resources."
[10] *Suda* M 454 (III 350 Adler). There might, however, be no difference between dithyrambs
   and such "lyric songs," since ᾆσμα is the term used in the Hellenistic period to describe
   dithyrambs, on which see Ma 2007: 242.
[11] *Suda* T 620 (IV 556–7 Adler).

him as singing the beginning of a *hymenaion* at a private party (*PMG* 828) and perhaps having composed a funerary epigram (*HE* i.165). The generic classification, as I will consider more fully later in this chapter, might tell of categories used by Alexandrian and later scholars and compilers rather than reflect contemporary practice, but it illustrates the *perceived* variety of their musical output.

Besides the generic diversity, one has to note the geographical mobility of songs and of musicians who composed for very different communities.[12] I have already mentioned the case of Telestes, and Timotheus is presented at the court of the Macedonian king Archelaus, who also hosted Euripides, and Philoxenus is seen at Ephesus, in a Sicilian colony, and at the court of the Sicilian tyrant. Geographical flexibility is especially evident in the case of a processional song (ᾆσμα προσόδιον) by Pronomus of Thebes, described as a specific commission in a note by Pausanias on the tomb of the musician:

> There is also the statue of the Pronomus whose pipe-playing was mesmerizing for the crowd ... and he even composed a song, a processional hymn to Delos (ᾆσμα πεποιημένον προσόδιον ἐς Δῆλον) for the Chalcidians on the Euripus [in Euboia].
> *PMG* 767 = Paus. 9.12.5–6

Nothing else is known of this *prosodion*, but its date of composition or performance is of great significance. Before 411 BC the Euboians were part of the Athenian Empire, and a song to Delos could be understood as a regular choral tribute to the island, following the tradition of performance of Athenian choruses at the Delia earlier in the fifth century.[13] But if the song was performed after 411 BC, and therefore after the Euboians had revolted against Athens, it should be seen as a "first and powerful statement of independence" on the part of the Chalcidians, and of independence too on the part of the poet, who would have been composing for very different communities, for both Athens and her rivals.[14] Such poetic fluidity and geo-political flexibility is also clear in the case of a hymn by Timotheus that was recorded by the Hellenistic poet Alexander of Aetolia in an elegy entitled *The Muses* (*CA* pp. 124–5). Our source for the passage, Macrobius, reports how the *poeta egregius* Alexander described the enthusiasm

---

[12] On Timotheus as traveling musician, Prauscello 2009; on Philoxenus' geographical mobility, see Chapter 3, pp. 134–48 below.

[13] On *theōriai* to Delos, Wilson 2000: 329 n. 201, Rutherford 2004, Kowalzig 2007: 56–128, and especially 85–9 for Pronomus, D'Alessio 2009. On Delos as "offshore Athenian territory," Wilson 2007b: 175–82, for the expression, p. 175.

[14] Kowalzig 2007: 85.

with which the Ephesians ensured that the most talented poets of the day (*qui tunc erant poetae ingeniosissimi*) composed various songs in honor of the goddess Diana (*in deam carmina diversa componerent*) on the occasion of the dedication of the temple. Alexander celebrated in particular Timotheus' poetic skill and underlined his sumptuous, and symbolic, material compensation:

> ἀλλ᾽ ὅγε πευθόμενος πάγχυ Γραικοῖσι μέλεσθαι
>   Τιμόθεον, κιθάρης ἴδμονα καὶ μελέων,
> υἱὸν Θερσάνδρου <κλυ>τὸν ἤνεσεν ἀνέρα σίγλων
>   χρυσείων ἱερὴν δὴ τότε χιλιάδα
> ὑμνῆσαι ταχέων τ᾽ Ὤπιν βλήτειραν ὀϊστῶν,   5
>   ἥ τ᾽ ἐπὶ Κεγχρείῳ τίμιον οἶκον ἔχει,
> et mox
> μηδὲ θεῆς προλίπῃ Λητωΐδος ἀκλέα ἔργα.
>   *PMG* 778a = Macrob. *Sat.* 5.22.4–5

"but [the people of Ephesus] hearing that among the Greeks Timotheus, son of Thersander, was regarded for his skill on the cithara and in songs, asked the famous man to sing, in return for golden shekels, the sacred millennium and Opis [Diana] of the swift arrows, who gloriously inhabits Kenchreios,"

and a few lines later:

"and not leave the deeds of Leto's divine daughter be inglorious."

If the poem in question is the *Artemis* that Cinesias mocked in an anecdote recorded by Plutarch in which Timotheus described Artemis in bacchic terms appropriate for the Ephesian divinity, it attests to the mobility of songs' performances, for the anecdote stages the hymn composed for the Ephesian community, which had sided with Sparta in 412 BC, as later performed in the Athenian theater – a dramatic volte-face in a post-Peloponnesian War context.[15]

Scholarship has, understandably, focused on the showy figures of the New Musicians, and especially on a few characters. But other names, not as frequently or explicitly connected in our sources to the controversies surrounding the New Music, are mentioned in comedy or repeatedly quoted by later authors in ways that suggest that they were important composers in the late classical period: the dithyrambist and rhetorician Licymnius in particular, but also the *melici* Cleomenes, Gnesippus, Lamynthius, Lycophronides,

---

[15] Plut. *Mor.* 170a (*De superst.* 10). Brussich 1990 dates the *Artemis* to 399–390 BC; Hordern 2002: 101–4.

a poet nicknamed or called Stesichorus, and possibly Castorion of Soli, although the surviving fragments invite us to think that he composed (dithyrambs?) under Demetrius of Phalerum at the very end of the period examined here.[16] For each of these poets, a few fragments have survived, and however brief and difficult the reference in Aristophanes or Athenaeus, it provides us with at least the shadow of an image of these poets' activities and a sense of the response their songs elicited. This is not the case, however, for a few lines of poetry by Hermolochus (*PMG* 846), about whom absolutely nothing other than a name associated with a quotation has been preserved. The case of this last poet throws into relief the figure of Cinesias, of whom not a single entire word has survived, but who has become an iconic figure for scandalous late fifth-century dithyrambic music, widely known from comic parodies and anecdotes.[17]

But here the invaluable fifth Loeb volume of Campbell's *Lyric Poetry*, which is devoted to the "new school of poetry," might give us the wrong idea about the material available. The focus on a handful of names of famous or infamous dithyrambic poets provided by the literary sources could lead us to overlook both the artists who were central to the performance of the dithyrambs, the *auletai*, "unsung heroes of the New Music," and also other types of musical performers, especially citharists (players of the cithara) and citharodes (singers who accompanied themselves on the cithara).[18] Both literary and epigraphic records allow us to enlarge the picture of the professionals involved in the large-scale production of choral poetry, especially in the context of the Athenian dithyramb and other musical contests. About seventy names of late fifth- and fourth-century instrumental performers are noted in a variety of literary sources – mainly, again, Athenaeus and Plutarch, but also Lucian, Dionysius of Halicarnassus, and Pausanias – and epigraphic testimonies (see Table 1).

As rich as the literary record is, it is a different type of source that provides by far the largest corpus attesting to the names of lyric composers and/or *didaskaloi* of dithyrambic choruses, whether or not they were the poets:[19] the lists of victors at musical competitions and choregic monuments celebrating dithyrambic victory. Table 2, again representative rather than exhaustive, gives us a sense of the number of reputed dithyrambists active in Greece in the late fifth and fourth centuries BC and of the

---

[16] On Licymnius, see Chapter 4, pp. 163–7. On Cleomenes and Stesichorus, Chapter 5, pp. 222–31. On Gnesippus and Lamynthius, Chapter 6, pp. 267–8.

[17] Cinesias *T* 1–13 in Campbell 1993.   [18] Csapo 2004: 211.

[19] On this aspect, see Wilson 2007b: 160–2.

Table 1. *Literary and epigraphic record for late classical musicians*
*Indicates that more testimonies than listed are available – for which, see Stephanis 1988 and Aspiotes 2006.

Name of musician	Stephanis (1988) entry	Discipline and time period (roman numeral indicates century, arabic specifies quarter century)	Literary and epigraphic sources	Notes and further references
Alcathus of Sicyon	130	Aulete (IV.2)	*SEG* 27 (1977) 16	Aulete for boys' chorus victorious at the Athenian Thargelia 359/8.
Alexippus of Argos	123	Aulete (IV.2)	*IG* II² 3067 *SEG* 27 (1977) 12 and 14	Aulete for boys' chorus victorious at the Athenian Thargelia 363/2 and 361/0.
Andron of Catana	187	Aulete (V–IV)	Ath. 1.22c (= Theophr. fr. 718 Fortenbaugh)	First *aulos* player to sway his body as he played. Cf. West 1992: 106.
Antigenidas of Thebes*	196	Aulete (IV.1–2)	Ath. 4.131d (= Anaxandrides, fr. 42 KA), 14.631f Didymus *in Demosth.* 11.12.60 (= Duris *FGrH* 76 F 36) Plut. *Mor.* 193f, 335a; *Vit. Dem.* 1.6 [Plut.] *De mus.* 1138b *Suda* A 2657 = *PMG* 825	Son of Satyrus of Thebes. Reported to have made important technical innovations on the *auloi*. Wore Milesian shoes and saffron robe for performance of Philoxenus' *Reveller*. Reported to be the *aulos* player at the wedding feast for Iphicrates and the daughter of Cotys, king of the Thracians. Cf. Dinse 1856, West 1992: 367–9, Prauscello 2006b: 48–51, Csapo 2004: 211, 214.
Aratus of Argos	291	Aulete (IV.2)	*IG* II² 3038	Aulete for chorus victor at the Athenian Dionysia 364/3.
Areius	295	Harp player (ψάλτης) (IV.1–2)	Ath. 8.352b (= Callisth. *FGrH* 124 F 5 = Machon, fr.11 Gow)	Time of Stratonicus.

Name	Number	Role	Sources	Notes
Argas	292	Citharode or aulode (iv.1)	Ath. 4.131d (= Anaxandrides, fr. 42 KA); Ath. 14.638c–d (= Phaenias, fr. 10 Wehrli, followed by Alexis, fr. 19 KA, followed by Anaxandrides, fr. 16 KA); Aeschin. *De falsa legatione* 99; Plut. *Vit. Dem.* 4.8; *Suda* Δ 454	Reported to be the singer at the wedding feast for Iphicrates and the daughter of Cotys, king of the Thracians. Said to compose indecent nomes (νόμων μοχθηρῶν, Ath. 14.638c). Nickname of Demosthenes (see Bat(t)alus). See Sutton 1989: 113 (– –)GAS listed as 95 in list of dithyrambographers, with ref. to Arist. *Poet.* 1448a15); West 1992: 372.
Arignotus of Athens	301	Citharode (v.4)	Ar. *Eq.* 1278–9 + Σ, Σ *Vesp.* 1275; Ath. 5.220b	Said to be of great talent and popularity. Brother of Ariphrades.
Ariphrades of Athens	399	Citharode (v/iv)	Ar. *Ecc.* 129 + Σ, *Eq.* 1278–9 + Σ, *Pax* 883, *Vesp.* 1280; Ath. 5.220b; *Suda* A 3940	Brother of Arignotus. Also name of a comic poet (cf. Arist. *Poet.* 1458b); possibly same man? Cf. Degani 1960.
Aristocrates of Thebes	345	Citharode (iv.3–4)	Ath. 12.538e (= Chares, *FGrH* 125 F 4)	Reported to be a citharode at the Susa weddings.
Ariston of Thebes	390	Aulete (iv/iii)	*IG* ii² 713, *IG* ii² 1.2, *IG* vii 1710–12	Honored in Athens for his performance at a contest of Dionysus.
Ariston of Miletus	381	Aulete (iv.2–3)	*IG* xii Suppl. 400	Name of the aulete who excelled in the performance of dithyrambs, recorded on the base of a statue of Dithyrambos, next to a colossal statue of Dionysus and other personifications of literary genres (*LIMC* iii 1 n. 2).
Aristonicus of Olynthus	367	Citharode (iv.2–3)	Arr. *Anab.* 4.16.6–7; Ath. 10.435b (= Theopomp. *FGrH* 115 F 236); Plut. *Mor.* 344e; Polyaenus, *Strat.* 5.44.1	Intimate circle of Alexander.

(cont.)

Table 1 (*cont.*)

Name of musician	Stephanis (1988) entry	Discipline and time period (roman numeral indicates century, arabic specifies quarter century)	Literary and epigraphic sources	Notes and further references
Aristonous (of Corinth?)	369	Citharode and composer (v/iv)	Plut. *Vit. Lys.* 18.5 *FGrH* 239 A67= *IG* xii 5, 444	Time of Lysander according to Plutarch. Six times victorious at Pythian games. Possibly identical with Aristonous of Corinth (author of hymn to Hestia and hymn to Apollo preserved in Delphi – cf. Chapter 7, with additional bibliography).
Aristonymus of Athens	398	Psilocitharist (bare cithara) (iv.3–4)	Ath. 10.452f (= Clearchus, fr. 93 Wehrli); Ath. 12.538f (= Chares, *FGrH* 125 F 4); Ath. 14.637f–8a	Played with riddles (ἔπαιζε γρίφους). Reported to be a citharist at the Susa weddings.
Asopodorus of Phlius	468	Aulete	Ath. 14.631f, 14.639a	See also *SH* 223–4 and Ath. 10.445b (suggests that Asopodorus was a prose-writer, *SH* 222).
Athenodorus of Teos	76	Psilocitharist (iv.3–4)	Ath. 12.538e (= Chares, *FGrH* 125 F4)	Reported to be a citharist at the Susa weddings.
Bacchylides of Opous	514	Aulete (v)	Plato Com. fr. 149 KA = Σ Ar. *Nub.* 331a	
Ba(t)talus of Ephesus*	519	Aulete (iv)	Ath. 4.176d Lucian *Ind.* 23 Plut. *Vit. Dem.* 4 *IG* ii Suppl. 400	Antiphanes wrote a comedy *Batalos*. Nickname for Demosthenes (see Argas, above). Cf. Lambin 1982.
Callistratus of Tegea	1359	Aulete (iv.3)	*SEG* 27 (1977) 19	Aulete for the boys' chorus victorious at the Athenian Thargelia in 349/8.

Name	Number	Type	Sources	Notes
Caphisias (of Thebes?)	1387	Aulete (IV/III)	Ath. 12.538f (= Chares, *FGrH* 125 F 4); Ath. 14.629b Diog. Laert. 7.21 Plut. *Vit. Pyrrh.* 8.7; *Mor.* 184c	Reported to be an aulete at the Susa weddings. Associated with witticisms. Cf. Pickard-Cambridge 1962: 55–6.
Cephisodotus of Acharnae (Athens)	1393	Citharist (IV)	Ath. 4.131c (= Anaxandrides, fr. 42 KA)	Reported to be citharode at the wedding feast for Iphicrates and the daughter of Cotys, king of the Thracians.
Chaeris (of Thebes?)	2593 and 2594	Citharode and/or aulete (V)	Ar. *Ach.* 16, 866 + Σ, *Av.* 858–61, *Pax* 950–5 Pherecrates, fr. 6 KA Cratinus, fr. 126 KA *Suda* x 171	Identity of this character much disputed (cf. Hartwig 2009 for discussion of evidence). Target of comedy. Cf. West 1992: 366 n. 39.
Chares of Thebes	2598	Aulete (IV)	*IG* II² 3106	Aulete for a chorus victorious in Athens in circular chorus and comedy competitions.
Charias of Athens	2604	Aulode (IV.2–3)	*IG* VII 414	Victorious at the Great Amphiaraia at Oropos around mid 4th cent. (366–338).
Charmus of Syracuse	2621	Aulete (V/IV)	Ath. 1.4a–c (= Clearchus, fr. 90 Wehrli); Ath. 8.344c (= Clearchus, fr. 58 Wehrli)	Also a gourmand according to Athenaeus.
Chrysogonus of Thebes	2637	Aulete (V)	Ath. 8.350e (= Callisth. *FGrH* 124 F 5); Ath. 12.535d; Ath. 14.648d (= Aristox. fr. 45 Wehrli) Didymus *in Demosth.* 11.12.61 (= Duris, *FGrH* 76 F 36) Plut. *Vit. Alc.* 32.2 (= Duris, *FGrH* 76 F 70)	Victor at Pythian games in late 5th cent. Author of the Pseudepicharmic text *The Constitution*. Cf. West 1992: 366.
Cleanthes of Sicyon	1416	Aulete (IV)	*SEG* 27 (1977) 13 and 15	Aulete for boys' chorus victorious at Athenian Thargelia 362/1 and for chorus victorious at Athenian Thargelia 360/59.

(cont.)

Table 1 (*cont.*)

Name of musician	Stephanis (1988) entry	Discipline and time period (roman numeral indicates century, arabic specifies quarter century)	Literary and epigraphic sources	Notes and further references
Cleitarchus of Athens	1427	Aulete (iv.2–3)	IG vii 414	Victorious at the Great Amphiaraia at Oropos around mid 4th cent. (366–338).
Cleolas of Thebes	1443	Aulete (iv?)	Ath. 1.22c	"Came after" Andron of Catana – but unknown date. Cf. West 1992: 106, 366 n. 39.
Cleon	1456	Citharode (iv.1–2)	Ath. 8.349d (= Machon, fr. 11 Gow)	Nicknamed "Ox" by Stratonicus.
Cleon of Thebes	1465	Singer / harpist (v.4)	Ath. 1.19b; Plin. *HN* 34.59	Epigram for him in Thebes.
Cleonicus of Athens	1448	Citharode (iv.2–3)	IG vii 414	Victorious at the Great Amphiaraia at Oropos around mid 4th cent. (366–338).
Commes of Thebes	1475	Aulete (v.2)	SEG 27 (1977) 18	Aulete for boys' chorus victorious at Athenian Thargelia 352/1.
Connas (same as below?)	1477	Aulete (v.3–4)	Ar. *Eq.* 534 + Σ; Cratinus, fr. 349 KA; *Suda* K 2027; Hesych. K 3530	Target of comedy (Ameipsias had a *Connos* frr. 7–11 KA). Cf. Winnington-Ingram 1988.
Connos (of Athens?) (same as above?)	1478	Citharist (and citharode?) (v)	Ar. *Vesp.* 675 + Σ; Pl. *Euthyd.* 272c, *Menex.* 235e; *Suda* K 2048	Music teacher of Socrates? Cf. Winnington-Ingram 1988.
Cratinus of Methymna	1494	Psilocitharist (iv.3–4)	Ath. 12.538e (= Chares, *FGrH* 125 F 4)	Reported to be a citharist at the Susa weddings.

Demetria	609	Citharode (iv.3–4)	IG ii² 1557 A 63, SEG 18 (1962) 36	Her name is reported in a list of manumissions.
Dexitheus	596	Citharode (v)	Ar. Ach. 14 + Σ	Very good citharode according to some scholiasts.
Dion of Chios	792	Citharist (v–iv?)	Ath. 14.638a (= Menaechmus, FGrH 131 F 6)	First to play a libation-song in honor of Dionysus on the lyre. Cf. Barker 1982.
Dionysius of Heracleia	723	Aulode (iv.3–4)	Ath. 12.538f (= Chares, FGrH 125 F 4)	Reported to be an aulode at the Susa weddings.
Dionysodorus (of Thebes?)	753	Aulete and composer (iv)	Diog. Laert. 4.22 Plin. HN 37.7	Contemporary and competitor of Hismenias.
Diophantus	783	Aulete (iv.3–4)	Ath. 12.538 (= Chares, FGrH 125 F 4)	Reported to be an aulete at the Susa weddings.
Dorion of Delphi	805	Aulete (iv.3)	Ath. 8.337b–338a (= Machon, fr. 8 Gow); Ath. 10.435b (= Theopomp. FGrH 115 F 236) [Plut.] De mus. 1138a, 1143c Choricius 3.1	Time of Alexander. Attributed some witticisms. Cf. West 1992: 369.
Eudamiscus	937	Aulete (v.2)	IG ii² 3065	Aulete for a boys' chorus victorious at Athenian Thargelia in 365/4.
Euius of Chalcis	952	Aulete (iv.4)	Ath. 12.538f (= Chares, FGrH 125 F 4) Plut. Vit. Eum. 2.2, Mor. 180f Pollux 4.78 IG ii² 3056	Reported to be an aulete at the Susa weddings. Some innovations were attributed to him (invention of νόμοι κύκλιοι). Cf. Wilson 2000: 231–2. Cf. also Table 2.
Heracleitus of Tarentum	1093	Citharode (iv.3–4)	Ath. 12.538e (= Chares, FGrH 125 F 4)	Reported to be a citharode at the Susa weddings.

(cont.)

Table 1 (cont.)

Name of musician	Stephanis (1988) entry	Discipline and time period (roman numeral indicates century, arabic specifies quarter century)	Literary and epigraphic sources	Notes and further references
Hikesius	1264	Aulete (IV.4)	Andoc. 1.12	Witness to mysteries, adduced in trial against Alcibiades, according to Andocides.
(H)ismenias of Thisbe (or Thebes, Steph.)*	1295	Aulete (IV.2–4)	Ael. *VH* 4.16 Diog. Laert. 4.22, 7.125 Lucian, *Ind.* 5 Plut. *Mor.* 174e, 334b, 632c, 1095f, *Vit. Dem.* 1.6, *Vit. Per.* 1.5 Plin. *HN* 37.6	Said to wear many gemstones when performing.
Hyperbolus of Cyzicus	2446	Aulode (IV.3–4)	Ath. 12.538f (= Chares, *FGrH* 125 F 4)	Reported to be an aulode at the Susa weddings.
Lycus of Thebes	1564	Aulete (IV.1–2)	*IG* II² 3046	Aulete for chorus victorious in Athens around mid 4th cent.
Lysander of Thebes	1572	Citharist (IV.2–3)	*IG* VII 414	Victorious (in the children category) at the Great Amphiaraia at Oropos around mid 4th cent. (366–338).
Lysimachides of Epidamnus	1581	Aulete (IV.3)	*IG* II² 3052	Aulete for chorus victorious at the Athenian Dionysia 328/7.
Meles of Athens	1630	Citharode (V.4)	Ar. *Av.* 766 + Σ Aristides 3.231 Pherecrates, fr. 6 KA Pl. *Gorg.* 501e–502a	Father of Cinesias. Said to be a very bad citharode. (Contra: Dunbar 1995, who denies the identification.)
Melissus of Thebes	1633	Aulete (IV)	Plut. *Mor.* 582d	Friend of Epaminondas.

1715	Mnasitheus of Opous	Singer (v/iv)	Arist. *Poet.* 1462a7	Innovated in introducing excessive movement in singing.
1748	Moschus of Acragas	Citharode (v)	Ar. *Ach.* 13 + Σ *Suda* M 1279	Very bad citharode according to scholia.
1830	Nicodromus (of Thebes)	Citharode (iv/iii)	Diog. Laert. 6.89	Contemporary with Crates (*fl.* 326).
1852	Nicomachus	"*mousikos*" (iv)	Plin. *HN* 37.7	Second in the trio Hismenias and Dionysodotus and contemporary with them.
1873	Nicon	Citharode (iv)	Arist. *Rhet.* 1412a34	Contemporary with the actor Theodorus according to Aristotle.
1932	Oeniades of Thebes*	Aulete (v/iv)	*IG* ii² 3064 *SEG* 18 (1962) 66 *SEG* 26 (1976/77) 220 Didymus *in Demosth.* xi.12.62 (= Duris, *FGrH* 76 F 36)	Son of Pronomus. The only "*auletes* [who] had earned himself the honour of being recorded with his patronymic" on a victory-monument (Wilson 2000: 70, 214–15). Cf. West 1992: 366 n. 39. Cf. also Table 2.
1933	Oinopas/Oinonas of Italy	Citharode and parodist (v/iv)	Ath. 1.19f–20a (= Aristox. fr. 135 Wehrli), 14.638b (= Aristox. fr. 136 Wehrli)	Introduced the Cyclops warbling a tune, and Odysseus speaking bad Greek (Κύκλωπα εἰσήγαγε τετερίζοντα). Famous for his imitations of harp-songs. Cf. West 1992: 366 n. 37.
1997	Pantaleon of Sicyon	Aulete (iv.4)	*IG* ii² 3055 = *PMG* 779	Aulete for boys' chorus performing Timotheus' *Elpenor* (victorious in 320/19).
2465	Phaon of Megara (?)	Aulete (iv/iii)	Ath. 8.350f (= Callisth. *FGrH* 124 F 5)	Time of Stratonicus.
2463	Phasimelus	Harpist (iv.3–4)	Ath. 12.539a (= Chares *FGrH* 125 F 4)	Reported to be a harpist at the Susa weddings.

(cont.)

Table 1 (*cont.*)

Name of musician	Stephanis (1988) entry	Discipline and time period (roman numeral indicates century, arabic specifies quarter century)	Literary and epigraphic sources	Notes and further references
Philiscus of Miletus	2505	Aulete (v/iv)	*Suda* Φ 360	Also a rhetor.
Phrynichus	2585	Aulete (iv.3–4)	Ath. 12.538f (= Chares, *FGrH* 125 F 4)	Reported to be an aulete at the Susa weddings.
Potamon of Thebes	2131	Aulete (iv.1–2)	*IG* ii² 8883	Father of Pronomus. Won at Pythian festival. Cf. West 1992: 366 n. 39, Wilson 2007c.
Pronomus of Thebes*	2149	Aulete (v)	Ar. *Eccl.* 98–102 + Σ Ath. 4.184d, 14.631e Paus. 4.27.7, 9.12.5–6 (= *PMG* 767) *Suda* A 385, Π 2527	First to play all scales using one set of *auloi*. Said to have taught the *auloi* to Alcibiades. Cf. West 1992: 366–7, Csapo 2004: 219. Pronomus vase: Beazley *ARV²* 1136, cf. Taplin and Wyles 2010.
Propis of Rhodes	2151	Citharode (iv)	Ath. 8.347f (= Clearchus, fr. 80 Wehrli)	Time of Stratonicus.
S]atyrus of Sicyon	2237	Aulete (iv.3)	*IG* ii² 3068	Aulete for boys' chorus victorious at the Athenian Thargelia in 344/3.
Sogenes of Siphnos	2326	Aulete (iv.1)	*IG* ii² 1951	
Sosistratus of Histiaea	2356	Aulete (iv.2)	*SEG* 27 (1977) 17	Aulete for boys' chorus victorious at the Athenian Thargelia in 355/4.
Stratonicus of Athens*	2310	Citharode (iv.1–2)	Ath. 4.163e, 8.347f–352d (= Machon, fr. 11 Gow = *SH* 737)	Attributed many witticisms. Cf. West 1992: 366–7, Gilula 2000.
Technon	2404	Aulete (v–iv)	Ath. 8.344b (= Clearchus, fr. 58 Wehrli) Alex. fr. 300 KA	Also described as a gourmand by Athenaeus.

Telephanes of Megara (or Samos)*	2408	Aulete (iv)	Ath. 8.351e (= Callisth. FGrH 124 F5 = Machon, fr.11 Gow) Dem. 21.17 Nicarchus, HE iii, 2747–50 Paus. 1.44.6 [Plut.] De mus. 1138a IG ii² 3093 CEG 552 = IG ii² 12778	Probably aulete for boys' chorus victorious at Dionysia at Salamis, early 4th cent. Time of Stratonicus. Pausanias reports seeing his tomb. Cf. Wilson 2000: 161.
Telesias of Thebes	2388	Aulete, composer (iv)	[Plut.] De mus. 1142b–c (= Aristox. fr. 76 Wehrli)	Cf. West 1992: 371.
Tellen (of Thebes?)*	2394	Aulete, poet (v/iv)	Leonidas, HE ix, 2002–3 Plut. Mor. 193f Zenob. 1.45 and 2.15	Proverbially bad aulete.
Theodorus	1151	Hymnist (iv.3–4)	IG ii² 13088	Inscribed song on funeral monument (GVI 1911).
Theodorus	1152	Harpist (iv?)	Ael. NA 7.40	
Theon	1204	Aulete (iv.3)	IG ii² 3042	Aulete for boys' chorus victorious at Athenian Dionysia 335/4.
Thersandrus	1193	Aulete (iv.1)	Polyaenus, Strat. 6.10 Xen. Hell. 4.8, 18–19	
Thyrsus	1237	Aulete (v.4)	Archippus, fr. 27 KA Hesych. Θ 953–4 (= Ar. fr. 411 KA)	Target of comedy.
Timaeus of Elis	2410	Trumpeter (v/iv)	Euseb. Chron. 1.96	Victor at the Olympic games of 396.

(cont.)

Table 1 (*cont.*)

Name of musician	Stephanis (1988) entry	Discipline and time period (roman numeral indicates century, arabic specifies quarter century)	Literary and epigraphic sources	Notes and further references
Timotheus of Thebes*	2417	Aulete (IV)	Ath. 12.538f (= Crates, *FGrH* 125 F 4), Ath. 13.565a Diphilus, fr. 78 KA Duris, *FGrH* 76 F 36 Lucian, *Ind.* 5, *Harmonides* 1 (= *PMG* 777) Dio Chrysost. *Or.* 1.1.1 Themist. *Or.* 26.316c *Suda* O 57, T 620	Reported to be an aulete at the Susa weddings. Teacher of Harmonides (in Lucian). Full beard when he played. Cf. West 1992: 366 n. 39. For another celebrated harpist: see Plutarch *Mor.* 41 d–e.
Zethus	1018	Citharist (IV.1–2)	Ath. 8.351b (= Callisth. *FGrH* 124 F 5 = Machon, fr. 11 Gow)	Time of Stratonicus.

partial nature of the picture to which the literary tradition gives us access.[20]

Table 2 provides the first sobering corrective to the impression given by standard histories of Greek literature, which focus exclusively on names preserved in the literary record. The name Eucles, for example, occurs repeatedly in connection with the boys' dithyramb at the Thargelia, and the poet ought therefore to be considered as one of the fourth century's most successful poets in a specific category of performance.[21]

We must also recognize one last type of sources for this prosopography of late classical *mousikē*. Although most of the evidence for choral songs is related to the dithyrambic production in Athens, we know the names of a few other poets – Philodamus of Scarphea, Aristonous of Corinth, and Isyllus of Epidaurus, whose names were preserved, along with their poetry, on inscriptions in the sanctuaries at Delphi and Epidaurus.[22] The inscriptions offer only tantalizing glimpses of the identity of the poets: nothing further is known of them beyond the status and privileges (*prohedria* ["front-seating"], proxeny, exemptions from taxes) Philodamus and Aristonous acquired in Delphi thanks to their compositions, and the possibly autobiographical event Isyllus recounts, an epiphany of Asclepius that happened when the author, or his son, was a child. We can only speculate whether Isyllus and Philodamus were famous local professional poets who remained unrecorded by the literary tradition or members of the local elite who composed poetry as an educated pastime. Were they perhaps itinerant poets composing for a fee whose talent was snatched up by Delphi or whose *epidēmia* (visit to the sanctuary) was recorded on stone,[23] or victors in a poetic competition whose poems were recorded as a result of their success, on the model described by Andrej Petrovic for epigrammatists?[24] As we consider these inscribed songs and inscribed poets we must remember the reciprocal dynamics that meant that the community honored the poet for his song as much as the poet honored the city with his composition, in a continued network of *charis* that goes back to archaic times.[25]

---

[20] The data are compiled from Stephanis 1988, Sutton 1989, Ieranò 1997, and Aspiotes 2006, with updates or references to more recent discussions, especially Wilson 2000 and 2007a, when available.

[21] Wilson 2000: 304 and 2007b: 162.

[22] All collected in *CA*, pp. 132–40 and 162–73, and Furley and Bremer 2001.

[23] Rutherford 2007: 284–6.   [24] A. Petrovic 2009 and 2013.

[25] For more on these issues, see Chapter 7.

Table 2. *Epigraphic record for dithyrambic victors*
Composers also attested in the literary tradition are given in bold.

Contest	Name of victor (with reference in Sutton 1989/Stephanis 1988)	Date of victory (all dates are BC)	Place of victory	Festival	Source	Notes and further discussion
Dithyramb	Amein[(60 Sutton/ 149 Steph.)	4th cent.	Athens	Dionysia	*IG* ii² 3061	Cf. Wilson 2000: 357 n. 39.
Boys' dithyramb	Antiphilus of Megara (45 Sutton/ 223 Steph.)	354/3	Athens	Thargelia	*SEG* 26 (1976/77) 220	Cf. Wilson 2000: 367 n. 51.
Dithyramb	Archestratus of Athens (31 Sutton/ 437 Steph.)	*ca.* 425–400	Athens	Dionysia	*IG* ii² 3027	Probably to be identified with tragic poet, *TrGF* 1 75. First words also recorded by Plut. *Vit. Arist.* 1.4. Mentioned by Eupolis, fr. 298 KA.
Dithyramb	Aristarchus (25 Sutton/ 308 Steph.)	415/14	Athens	Dionysia	*IG* i³ 960 = *IG* i² 770a	Cf. Wilson 2000: 367 n. 47.
Dithyramb	**Ariphron (96 Sutton, conjecturally identified as dithyrambic victor)**	Early 4th cent. (Wilson: of the 360s?)	Attica	Rural Dionysia	*IG* ii² 3092	Also name of tragic poet (see *TGrF* 1 53). The inscription records other victories, by Polychares and Dicaeogenes, and *chorēgoi* operating in pairs. Difficulties discussed in Wilson 2000: 306–7. See also Table 4.
Dithyramb	Carcidamus of Sotium (58 Sutton/ 1380 Steph.)	320/19	Athens	Dionysia	*IG* ii² 3056	Cf. Wilson 2000: 231.
Dithyramb	Cedeides (26 Sutton/ 1391 Steph.)	Late 5th cent.	Athens	Thargelia	*IG* i² 770	An early 5th-cent. poet of that name (perhaps Ceceides) is mentioned by Aristophanes *Nub.* 985 + Σ.

Genre	Poet	Date	Place	Festival	Reference	Notes
Dithyramb	Charilaus of Locri (56 Sutton/ 2612 Steph.)	328/7	Athens	Dionysia	IG ii² 3052	Cf. Wilson 2000: 368 n. 54.
Dithyramb	**Cinesias of Athens (22 Sutton/ 1406 Steph.)**	Early 4th cent.	Athens	Dionysia	IG ii² 3028	Also *PMG* 774–6. Cf. Wilson 2000: 66, 68, 368 n. 56. See also Table 4.
Dithyramb	Cleidemus of Athens (98 Sutton/ 1419 Steph.)	364/3 (? Sutton)	Athens	Dionysia	IG ii² 3038	
Boys' dithyramb	Corinnus of Opuntia (46 Sutton/ 1482 Steph.)	352/1	Athens	Thargelia	SEG 27 (1977) 18	Perhaps other victory in 327/6; the victor in boys' dithyramb is from Opuntia. Could also be Pheidias (47 Sutton) or Moiriganes I (62 Sutton).
Dithyramb	Dicaeogenes (49 Sutton, conjecturally identified as dithyrambic victor)	Early 4th cent. (Wilson: of the 360s?)	Attica	Rural Dionysia	IG ii² 3092	Also tragic poet, *TrGF* I 52 (see above, Ariphron), mentioned by Arist. *Poet.* 1454b. The inscription records other victories, by Polychares and Ariphron, and *chorēgoi* operating in pairs. Difficulties discussed in Wilson 2000: 306–7.
Dithyramb	Diophon (789 Steph.)	375/4	Athens	Dionysia	IG ii² 3037	
Boys' dithyramb	Epicurus of Sicyon (52 Sutton/ 859 Steph.)	344/3	Athens	Thargelia	IG ii² 3068	
Boys' dithyramb	Eucles (42 Sutton/ 958 Steph.)	365/4	Athens	Thargelia	IG ii² 3065	Cf. Wilson 2000: 304.
		364/3	Athens	Thargelia	IG ii² 3066	
		362/1	Athens	Thargelia	SEG 27 (1977) 13	
		361/0	Athens	Thargelia	SEG 27 (1977) 14	
		360/59	Athens	Thargelia	SEG 27 (1977) 15	
		355/4	Athens	Thargelia	SEG 27 (1977) 17	
		pre-350	Athens	Thargelia	IG ii² 3067	

(cont.)

Table 2 (*cont.*)

Contest	Name of victor (with reference in Sutton 1989/Stephanis 1988)	Date of victory (all dates are BC)	Place of victory	Festival	Source	Notes and further discussion
Dithyramb	Hegemon of Phlius (44 Sutton/ 1051 Steph.)	359/8	Athens	Thargelia	*SEG* 27 (1977) 16	
Boys' dithyramb	**Herm[-]os (54 Sutton/ 894 Steph.)**	Mid 4th cent.	Athens	Thargelia	*IG* II² 3070	See Table 4.
Boys' dithyramb	Lysiades of Athens (51 Sutton/ 1575 Steph.)	352/1 335/4	Athens Athens	Dionysia Dionysia	*IG* II² 3039 *IG* II² 3042	Cf. Wilson 2000: 219–26.
Dithyramb	Meidogenes (61 Sutton/ 1625 Steph.)	4th cent.	Athens	Dionysia	*IG* II² 3057	
Dithyramb Boys' dithyramb	Nauplius (53 Sutton/ 1772 + 2699 Steph.)	344/3 Last quarter of 4th cent.?	Athens Athens	Thargelia Thargelia	*IG* II² 3069 *SEG* 30 (1980) 127	Perhaps also name to be restored in *IG* II² 3060.
Boys' dithyramb	Nicostratus (28 Sutton/ 1862 Steph.)	After 450	Athens	Dionysia	*IG* I³ 961 = *IG* I² 769	Nicostratus was a popular name and other victories could be assigned to the same individual: – *IG* I³ 963 = *IG* I² 768 (before 350) records a victory at Athenian Thargelia by a *didaskalos* Nico[… – *IG* II² 3094 (early 4th cent.) records a victory in Icaria (possibly by a comic poet, or by the same individual). Cf. Wilson 2000: 214.

Type	Name	Date	Place	Festival	Reference	Notes
Dithyramb / Boys' dithyramb	**Oeniades of Thebes** (**38 Sutton/1932 Steph.**)	384/3 / 354/3	Athens / Athens	Thargelia / Thargelia	*IG* ii² 3064 / *SEG* 26 (1976–7) 220	Aulode in 384/3. Son of Pronomus. Also Duris *FGrH* 76 F 36 = *PMG* 840. Cf. Wilson 2000: 70, 214–15, 367 n. 51 See also Table 4.
Boys' dithyramb	Paedeas (48 Sutton/1976 Steph.)	Early 4th cent.	Salamis	Dionysia	*IG* ii² 3093	Cf. Wilson 2000: 244–5.
Boys' dithyramb	Pamphilus (of Hagnus) (57 Sutton/1985 Steph.)	323/2	Athens	Dionysia	*IG* ii² 3054	
Dithyramb	Pantacles (27 Sutton/1992 Steph.)	*ca.* 450–440 / *ca.* 430–420? / End 5th cent.	Athens / Athens	Dionysia / Thargelia	*IG* i³ 958 / *IG* i³ 959 = *IG* i² 771 / *IG* i³ 967	Mentioned by Antiphon in his *De choreut.* 11 and by Aristotle in his *Didascaliae* (fr. 624 Rose). Cf. Wilson 2000: 117, 214.
Boys' dithyramb	Pheidias of Opuntia (47 Sutton/2467 Steph.)	349/8	Athens	Thargelia	*SEG* 27 (1977) 19	
Dithyramb	Philophron (39 Sutton/2554 Steph.)	384/3	Athens	Thargelia	*SEG* 18 (1962) 69	Oeniades was the aulete for victory.
Dithyramb	**Philoxenus of Cythera** (**34 Sutton**)	380/79	Athens		*Marmor Parium* = *FGrH* 239 A 69	Also *PMG* 814–35 (and 836?). See also Table 4.
Dithyramb	Polychares (97 Sutton, conjecturally identified as dithyrambic victor)	Early 4th cent. (Wilson: ot the 360s?)	Attica	Rural Dionysia	*IG* ii² 3092	The inscription records other victories, by Ariphron and Dicaiogenes, and related (Acharnian) *chorēgoi* operating in pairs. Difficulties discussed in Wilson 2000: 306–7.

(cont.)

Table 2 (cont.)

Contest	Name of victor (with reference in Sutton 1989/Stephanis 1988)	Date of victory (all dates are BC)	Place of victory	Festival	Source	Notes and further discussion
Dithyramb	Poly(e)idus of Selymbria (37 Sutton)	399/8 – 380/79	Athens	Dionysia	*Marmor Parium* = *FGrH* 239 A68	Also *PMG* 837. See also Table 4.
Boys' dithyramb	Polyzelus of Thebes (43 Sutton/2097 Steph.)	363/2	Athens	Thargelia	*SEG* 27 (1977) 12	
Dithyramb	Speuseades of Athens (reading uncertain) (55 Sutton)	4th cent.	Attica	Rural Dionysia	*IG* II² 3106	Victory at κυκλίῳ χορῷ καὶ κωμῳδιοῖς. Cf. Wilson 2000: 244, 306.
Dithyramb	Stesichorus II of Himera (41 Sutton)	370/68 (369/8 Sutton)	Athens	Dionysia	*Marmor Parium* = *FGrH* 239 A73	Also *PMG* 814. See also Table 4.
Dithyramb	Telesias (35 Sutton/2389 Steph.)	Early 4th cent.	Athens	Dionysia	*IG* II² 3029	Cf. Wilson 2000: 367 n. 51, 368 n. 56.
Dithyramb	Telestes of Selinus (36 Sutton)	402/1	Athens	Dionysia	*Marmor Parium* = *FGrH* 239 A65	Also *PMG* 805–12. See also Table 4.
Boys' dithyramb	Timotheus of Miletus (33 Sutton)	320/19	Athens	Dionysia	*IG* II² 3055	Reperformance of the *Elpenor*. Also *PMG* 777–804. Cf. Wilson 2000: 227. See also Table 4.

The surviving texts

Late classical songs have survived in three forms: inscriptions, literary quotations, and papyri. Altogether, this evidence amounts to about one hundred fragments and eight hundred attributed lines. The bulk of the data is related to very public forms of lyric: not only the theater music composed for the musical competitions of the Dionysia, Thargelia, and Panathenaea, but also the many other hymns composed for these and other festivals.[26] Much less material is available about scolia, encomia, and epithalamia, which were less civic and less religious kinds of lyric, either because they were no longer being composed (a possibility to which I will return) or because of the way these types of song were preserved.[27] The dearth of material evidence for genres that were not memorialized or recorded in public places or through civic gestures is accentuated by the fact that while the Alexandrians made editions of the archaic corpus that contained a variety of songs for gods and songs for men, including epinicians, *thrēnoi*, and *partheneia*, there seems to have been no Alexandrian edition of fourth-century melic poets.

Papyri

The longest surviving passage of late classical lyric comes from a papyrus that has preserved the last 240 lines, probably the last third, of a citharo-dic nome (the *Persians*) composed by Timotheus of Miletus (*PMG* 791 = *P. Berol.* 9875).[28] Although a few lines from the piece were already known from quotations, it is difficult to overstate the importance of this papyrus: it is by far the longest, and nearly the sole, surviving fragment of a genre, the citharodic nome, that was immensely popular through antiquity;[29] it is one of the oldest papyri to have surfaced; and it is the only surviving example of a late classical text preserved in papyrus form.[30]

Other papyri have preserved works quoting late classical lyric but no text transmitted directly. The Hibeh papyri (dated 280–240 BC) contain six quotations (*PMG* 925) on the topic of Odysseus' meeting with his mother in the underworld, which have been connected to Timotheus' *Elpenor*. A fragment of a prose work (*PMG* 929, Rainer papyrus dated around 200 BC) quotes dithyrambic fragments in which the names of famous New Music composers (Melanippides, Philoxenus, and possibly Telestes) occur.[31]

---

[26] For an overview of the diversity and complexity of these festivals, see Slater 2007.
[27] For sympotic lyric, see Chapter 6.
[28] *Editio princeps*: Wilamowitz-Moellendorf 1903. Other editions are *PMG*, Janssen 1984, Campbell 1993, Hordern 2002, and Sevieri 2011 (based on Hordern's text).
[29] On the genre, Power 2010 is now fundamental.
[30] On the papyrus, see further in this chapter, pp. 55–7.   [31] Oellacher 1932.

Finally, papyrus fragments, including one of Aristoxenus' *Rhythmics* (*PMG* 926), quote passages that display some of the features characteristically associated with the dithyrambic style.[32] It is tempting to take these snippets of evidence, fragile as they are, as sources for more dithyrambs, but to date a poem or assign it a genre on the basis of its style often runs the risk of circular reasoning, since style is one of the features most easily parodied.[33] Yet even if these fragments do not add to our collection of late classical texts, they contribute to the documentation of musical controversies and technical discussions of late classical *mousikē* in its various aspects, rhythmic, harmonic, and linguistic.[34] And other fragments could also throw light on cultural and scholarly practices associated with lyric poetry. *PMG* 927 and 928, for example, are fragments of papyrus that list compound adjectives, one of the marked features of the elevated diction of the dithyramb.[35] *PMG* 927 is a list of three items, of which the last two are triple compound nouns: vv. 49 χρυσὸς αἰγλήεις ("gleaming gold"), 55 βοτρυοκαρποτόκος ("bringing forth the fruit of the grape"), 56 ἀστερομαρμαροφεγγής ("star-flashing light"). Although not linguistically related, the adjectives are thematically linked in their use of light imagery and the presence of Dionysiac elements. Some of these remarks could be extended to *PMG* 928, another list of compounds – although organized differently (alphabetically) – which picks up, as we will see in the next chapter, some keywords of the New Music, including the verbal base καμψι-. What function might such lists have had? And what is the relationship between the fragments? Can we extend hypotheses about one to the other? One might speculate that they were school exercises or commentators' exercises that illustrated the principles of compound formation in dithyrambic texts, some of which were Homeric borrowings. Such evidence may tell us of the intellectual and institutional activity that continued to be associated with the dithyrambic corpus outside the context of performance, either ritual or theatrical, although its scanty nature limits us to speculation only.

Epigraphy

The second type of epigraphic evidence for surviving texts of late classical songs is epigraphic. Table 3 sums up the surviving texts.

---

[32] *P. Oxy.* 2687 (= *P. Oxy.* 9+): see Pearson 1990, 36–44, 77–86.

[33] On the danger, already Bowra 1933.

[34] Wallace 1995b; Barker 2009 on the schools of harmonics; J. I. Porter 2010: 235–9 on the quarrel between Aristoxenus and Alcidamas, and pp. 335–9 on Alcidamas.

[35] The sources are *P. Hamb.* 128 (*ca.* 250 BC), Theoph. *On Diction* = *PMG* 927; and *P. Hib.* II 172 (*ca.* 270–230 BC) = *PMG* 928 + *SH* 991. On *PMG* 927, Maehler 2004: 26–7 notes that four of the compounds only appear in Bacchylides.

Table 3. *Hymns surviving in epigraphic form*
(Square brackets indicate hymns for which a fourth-century date has been proposed but is not secure.)

Genre of song	Author – number of preserved lines in parentheses	Date of song composition	Place where the stone was found	Occasion of song performance	References and other comments
Paean	Anonymous (27)	380–360 BC	Erythrea + 3 other places (later versions found in Ptolemais, Athens, Dion)	Cult of Asclepius	CA 136–8 + 140 There are 4 inscriptions, with slight variations.
Hymn/paean (no *Paian epiphthēgma*)	Ariphron of Sicyon (10)	Early 4th cent.?	Asclepeion in Athens and Epidaurus	Cult of Hygieia. Also described as sung at dinner to finish *Deipnosophistae*	Furley and Bremer 2001: II 175–80. See also Tables 2 and 4.
Paean to Dionysus (*iē Paian epiphthēgma*)	Philodamus of Scarphea (156)	340–339 BC	Delphi	Celebration of reconstruction of the temple of Apollo (at Theoxenia)	CA 165–71.
Paean (*iē Paian epiphthēgma*)	Aristonous of Corinth (48)	333 BC	Delphi	Cult of Apollo (at Theoxenia?)	CA 162–4.
Hymn to Hestia	Aristonous of Corinth (17)	333 BC	Delphi	Cult of Hestia	CA 164–5.
Paean (*iē Paian epiphthēgma*)	Isyllus of Epidaurus (85)	Last quarter of 4th cent. BC	Epidaurus	Cult of Asclepius (paean sung in procession)	CA 132–6.

(*cont.*)

Table 3 (*cont.*)

Genre of song	Author – number of preserved lines in parentheses	Date of song composition	Place where the stone was found	Occasion of song performance	References and other comments
[Paean (*iē Paian epiphthēgma*)]	[Macedoni(c)us (32)]	[?]	[Asclepeion in Athens]	[Cult of Asclepius]	[CA 138–9. Stone dates from Roman period, song may be from Isyllus' time (CA).]
[Hymn to Zeus Kouros (prosodion?)]	[Anonymous (66)]	[4th–3rd cent.]	[Palaikastro (Crete)]	[Cult of Zeus Kouros]	[CA 160–2.]
[Hymn to the Idean Dactyls]	[Anonymous (35)]	[4th–3rd cent.?]	[Crete]	[Cult of Idean Dactyls]	[CA 171–3.]
[Hymn to Pan]	[Anonymous (19)]	[4th cent.?]	[Epidaurus]	[Cult of Pan]	[Furley and Bremer 2001: II 192–8.]
[Hymn to the Mother of the gods]	[Anonymous (26)]	[4th–3rd cent.?]	[Epidaurus]	[Cult of the Mother of the gods]	[Furley and Bremer 2001: II 167–75. 2 half choruses?]
[Hymn to all the gods]	[Anonymous (15)]	[??]	[Epidaurus]	[Cult of all the gods (starts late 4th cent.)]	[Furley and Bremer 2001: II 202–5.]

This table is inclusive and necessarily approximate. The dating of the songs brings up two different, but connected, problems: does it correspond to the date of the composition of the song or to the moment when a community decided to inscribe a hymn that could have been composed many centuries before? The table includes poems that might still have been performed in the fourth century BC but were composed much earlier, as seems to be the case with the hymn to the Idean Dactyls, and with some of the Epidaurian hymns, for example, for which dating ranges from the fifth century BC to the third century AD. Some stones record poems that might have been composed in the fourth century BC but were still performed in the first centuries of the Christian era, as is the case with the reinscription of the Erythraean paeans.[36] Only three texts can be dated, thanks to prose dedications that indicate the archonship under which the inscription was made, and it is on these texts that the discussion in Chapter 7 will focus.

Literary quotations

Literary evidence for the poetic production of the late classical period is our final category of source. About one hundred passages amounting to 228 lines are cited for a variety of reasons and by a variety of authors, and they range from the fourth century BC to the fifth century AD. Our main literary sources are Athenaeus, Plutarch, and Stobaeus, who respectively provide us with twenty-one fragments amounting to 175 lines (or 77.5 percent of the total lines), eight fragments with eleven lines (or 4.8 percent of the total lines) and four fragments with ten lines (or 4.4 percent of the total lines). These three authors alone account for nearly 87 percent of the surviving quotations. Table 4 lists the original sources that quote the late classical poets and the total number of extant lines of these poets.

Additionally, a few passages evocative of the dithyrambic style are quoted in technical treatises on poetry. Dionysius of Halicarnassus (*PMG* 1027), for example, commenting on rhythms, quotes a series of lines whose vocabulary and theme are evocative of Timotheus' *Persians*.[37] Aelian, in the context of a description of dolphins' love of song and pipe music, quotes a hymn of

---

[36] On the dating of the Hymn to the Idean Dactyls, Powell and Barber 1921: 49–50; on the dating of the Hymn to Zeus Kouros, Powell and Barber 1921: 50–3; West 1965; Alonge 2005. On the Hymn to the Mother of the gods, see Powell 1933: 204–8, West 1970: 212–15, Wagman 1995: 109–46.

[37] Dion. Hal. *Comp.* 17 = *PMG* 1027. For example, οἱ δ' ἐπείγοντο πλωταῖς ἀπήναισι χαλκεμβόλοις ("and they led on their bronze-beaked nautical chariots") has been attributed to Timotheus' *Persians* by Usener, Wilamowitz, Diehl, and Edmonds, and deemed "not out of place in the iambo-trochaics of the *Persae*" by Hordern (2002: 131).

Table 4. *Literary record of late classical lyric poets and fragments*

Literary sources	Literary tradition (biographical information, anecdotes about author, elaborate context of quotation). Sources that preserve anecdotes or other details are listed in chronological order.	No tradition (no biographical information in source, only mention of name). Sources are listed in chronological order.
Surviving fragments or titles (the number in parentheses after the name of the poet is the number of preserved lines of poetry; it does not include paraphrases). Reference to main edition of fragments and entry in Stephanis (1988) and/or Sutton (1989) and Aspiotes (2006) follow in square brackets. Sources that preserve fragments or titles are noted in bold.	SOPHOCLES [*PMG* 737] [Luc.] *Demosth. Encom.* 27; Philostratus, *Vit. Apoll.* 3.17; **Philostratus, *Imag.* 13.4**; *Suda* Σ 815 EURIPIDES (7) [*PMG* 755–6] **Plut. *Vit. Alcib.* 11; *Vit. Demosth.* 1.1** MELANIPPIDES (20) [*PMG* 757–66; 18 Sutton] Xen. *Mem.* 1.4.3; Arist. *Rhet.* 1409b; Praxiphanes, fr. 18 Wehrli (= Marcellin. *Vit. Thuc.* 29); Meleager (*HE* i, 3932); **Phld. *De piet.* (p. 23 Gomperz); Plut. *Mor.* 758c, 1095c**; [Plut.] *De mus.* 1136c (= Aristox. fr. 80 Wehrli), 1141c–d (= Pherecrates, fr. 155 KA); **Clem. Al. *Strom.* 5.14.112; Ath. 2.35a, 10.429c, 14.616e–f, 14.651f; Stob. 1.49.50 (quoting Porphyry)**; *Suda* M 454–5, Φ 393; **Σ bT Hom. *Il.* 13.350; Σ bT Hom. *Il.* 18.570c** PRONOMUS [*PMG* 767; 2149 Stephanis] Ar. *Eccl.* 102; Paus. 5.27.7, **9.12.4–6, 9.27.7**; Ath. 4.184d, 14.631e; *FGE* anon. xxiii LICYMNIUS (8) [*PMG* 768–73; 29 Sutton] Pl. *Phdr.* 267b–c (+ Σ); Arist. *Rh.* 1405b, 1413b, 1414b; **Phld. *De piet.* (p. 13 Gomperz with Henrichs 1984); Dion. Hal. *Demosth.* 26, *Lys.* 3, *Thuc.* 24; Parth. *Amat. narr.* 22; Ath. 13.564c–d, 13.603d; Sext. Emp. *Math.* 11.49; Stob. 1.49.50 (quoting Porphyry)**	ARIPHRON (10) [*PMG* 813; *96 Sutton] **Plut. *Mor.* 450b, 479b; Lucian *Pro lapsu* 6; Max. Tyr. 7.1; Ath. 15.702a–b; Sext. Emp. *Math.* 11.49** LYCOPHRONIDES (8) [*PMG* 843–4] **Ath. 13.564a–b** (= Clearchus, fr. 22 Wehrli), **15.670d–f** (= Clearchus, fr. 24 Wehrli) CASTORION (7) [*PMG* 845, *SH* 310; 99 Sutton] **Ath. 10.454f–455b** (= Clearchus, fr. 88 Wehrli = *SH* 310), **12.542** (= *SH* 312 = Dem. Phal. fr. 34 Wehrli, from Duris, *FGrH* 76 F 10) HERM[OLOCHUS] (5) [*PMG* 846; 54 Sutton] **Stob. 4.34.66; Photius, *Bibl.* 167** (p. 115a Bekker), quoting list of poets used by Stobaeus

(cont.)

<u>CINESIAS (1 word)</u> [*PMG* 774–6; 22 Sutton]

Ar. *Av.* 1372–1409 + Σ, *Nub.* 332 + Σ, *Ran.* 152–61 + Σ, 366 + Σ, 1437–42 + Σ; Lys. 21.20; Pl. Com. fr. 200 KA (= Gal. *in Hipp. aphor.* 18a); Pl. *Gorg.* 501e–502a; **Phld. *De piet.* (p. 52 Gomperz); Erotian (ῥαβοειδέστατον)**; Plut. *Mor.* 22a, 170a, 348b; [Plut.] *De mus.* 1141e–f (= Pherecrates, fr. 155 KA); Ael. *VH* 10.6; **Ath. 12.551c–552b** (= **Lysias fr. 195**), **551d**; *Suda* K 1639, T 693

<u>TIMOTHEUS (31)</u> [*PMG* 777–804; 33 Sutton]

Pherecrates, fr. 155 KA (= [Plut.] *De mus.* 1141f); **Antiphanes, fr. 6 KA (= Ath. 10.455f), fr. 110 KA (= Ath. 10.433c)**; Anaxandrides, fr. 6 KA; Arist. *Met.* 993b; ***Poet.* 1448a, 1454a, *Rh.* 1415a; Machon, fr. 9 Gow (= Ath. 8.341d); Chrysippus, *On negatives* 10**; Satyrus (*P. Oxy.* 1176 fr. 39 col. xxii); Polyb. 4.20.8–9; **Hegesander, fr. *FHG* IV.416 (= Ath. 8.338a)**; Artemon, fr. 11 *FHG* IV.342 (= Ath. 14.636e–f); Diod. Sic. 14.46.6; Cic. *De leg.* 2.39; Dion. Hal. *Comp.* 17, 19; Dio Chrys. *Or.* 32.61, 33.57; Plut. *Mor.* 22a, **32d, 170a**, 187b, 238c, **327e, 334b, 539c, 659a**, 795d, *Vit. Agis* 10, ***Vit. Agesil.* 14.2, *Vit. Demetr.* 42, *Vit. Philopoem.* 11**; [Plut.] *De mus.* 1132d, 1135c–d, 1138b, 1141c, 1142c; Paus. 3.12.10, **8.50.3**; Nicomachus, *Harm. Excerpta ex Nicomacho* 4; **Lucian, *Harmonides* 1**; [Censorinus] *Gramm. Latin.* VI.610; Heph. *Poem.* 3.3; Clem. Al. *Strom.* 1.16.78; **Ath. 3.122cd, 8.352a, 11.465c; Diog. Laert. 7.28; Stob. 1.49.61 (quoting Porph.)**; Themist. 26.316c; **Macrob. *Sat.* 1.17.20, 5.22.4–5**; Boethius *Mus.* 1.1.182; Steph. Byz. (Μίλητος); Phot. *Bibl.* 320a 33; *Suda* T 620; Σ A Hom *Il.* 9.219b; ***Etym. Magn.* ὀρίγανον**

<u>TELESTES (25)</u> [*PMG* 805–12; 36 Sutton]

Aristox. fr. 117 Wehrli (= Apollon. *Hist. Mir.* 40); **Phld. *De piet.* (p. 18 and p. 23 Gomperz)**; Dion. Hal. *Comp.* 19; Plin. *HN* 35.36.109; Plut. *Vit. Alex.* 8.3 (from Onesicritus, *FGrH* 134 F 38); **Ath. 11.501f–502a (= Theopompus Com. fr. 4 KA), 14.616f–617b, 14.626a, 14.637a**; *Suda* T 265

Table 4 (cont.)

Literary sources	Literary tradition (biographical information, anecdotes about author, elaborate context of quotation). Sources that preserve anecdotes or other details are listed in chronological order.	No tradition (no biographical information in source, only mention of name). Sources are listed in chronological order.

PHILOXENUS OF CYTHERA (13) [*PMG* 814–35; 34 Sutton]

Pherecrates, fr. 155 KA (= [Plut.] *De mus.* 1142a; **Ar.** *Nub.* 335 (+ Σ), **Plut. 290–301 (+ Σ)**, **fr. 745 KA** (= **Hsch. μεσαύχενες**); **Antiphanes, fr. 205** (= Ath. 10.446ab), fr. 207 KA (= Ath. 14.643d–e); Arist. *Poet.* 1448a, **Pol. 1342b**; Ephorus *FGrH* 70 F 2, F8 (= Ath. 8.352c); Sopater, fr. 23 KA (= Ath. 8.341e); **Clearchus, fr. 57 Wehrli** (= Ath. **1.5f–6b**); **Duris,** *FGrH* 76 F 58 (= **Σ Theocr. 6f**); **Phaenias, fr. 13 Wehrli** (= Ath. **1.6e–7a**); Machon, fr. 9 Gow (= Ath. 8. 341a–d); **Hermesianax, fr. 7 CA** (= **Ath. 13.598e**); **Theophr.** *De ventis* 38 (Wimmer); Polyb. 4.20.8–9; **Antig. Car.** *Mir.* **127**; Phld. *Mus.* 1.23 (ix 67 fr. 5, p. 9 Kemke); **Didymus in Demosth. 11.12.61** (= **Duris** *FGrH* 76 F 36); Diod. Sic. 15.6; Dion. Hal. *Comp.* 19; **Plin. *NH* 37.31**; Plut. *Vit. Alex.* 8.2 (= Onesicritus, *FGrH* 134 F 38), **Mor. 14d**, 334c, 471e, **622c, 762f, 831f**; [Plut.] *De mus.* 1135d, 1141c, 1142a–c; Lucian, *Ind.* 15, *Cal.* 14; Ael. *VH* 12.44; **Zenob. 5.45**; **Σ Theoc. (6f)**, **Σ Theoc. 11.1–3b**; Ath. **2.35d, 13.564e, 15.692d**; Diog. Laert. 4.36; **Synes. *Epist.* 121**; Stob. *Anth.* 2.31.86, 3.13.31, *Flor. Mon.* 260; Hsch. Δούλωνς; ***Anth. Pal.* 9.319** (= **Philoxenus,** *HE* i 3036); *Suda* A 2862, Δ 1178 = EI 291, **E 336, Θ 475**, Φ 393–5, 397

PHILOXENUS OF LEUCAS (if different from above Philoxenus) (73) [*PMG* 836; *94 Sutton]

Pl. com. fr. 189 KA (= Ath. 1.5b–c); Arist. fr. 83 Rose; **Plut. *Mor.* 668c**; Ath. 1.6d, **4.146f–147e, 4.156e, 9.409e, 9.410b, 11.476e, 11.487a–b, 14.642f–643e, 15.685d**; *Suda* O 1091, Φ 395, 398

POLYIDUS [*PMG* 837; 37 Sutton]

Arist. *Poet.* 1455a, 1455b; Diod. Sic. 14.46; [Plut.] *De mus.* 1138b; Ath. 8.352b; ***Etym. Magn.* 164.20** (= **Tzetzes on Lycophron *Alex.* 879**)

CLEOMENES [*PMG* 838; 21 Sutton]

Epicrates, fr. 4 KA (= Ath. 13.605e); Chionides, fr. 4 KA (= Ath. 9.638d); **Ath. 9.402a**, 14.620d; Σ Ar. *Nub.* 333a

LAMYNTHIUS [*PMG* 839]

Epicrates, fr. 4 KA (= Ath. 13.605e); **Clearchus, fr. 34 Wehrli** (= **Ath. 13.596f**); Phot. *Lex.* Λαμύνθιος

OENIADES [PMG 840; 38 Sutton]
Didymus in Demosth. 11.12.62 (= Duris, FGrH 76 F 36)

STESICHORUS II [PMG 841; 41 Sutton]
Aristox. fr. 89 Wehrli (=Ath. 14.619d); Didymus, in Demosth. 11.12.62 (= Duris FGrH 76 F 36); Strabo 8.3.20

ARISTOTLE (21) [PMG 842]
Didymus in Demosth. 10.6.21–36 (= Duris FGrH 76 F 36); Ath. 14.696a–f (= Hermippus fr. 48 Wehrli); Suda A 3929

HIERONYMUS [20 Sutton; 922 Aspiotes]
Ar. Ach. 387 + Σ; Σ Ar. Ach. 835; Σ Ar. Nub. 347; Suda A 676, K 1768

PHRYNIS [23 Sutton; 2583 Stephanis]
Ar. Nub. 969–71 + Σ; Pherecrates, fr. 155 KA (= [Plut.] De mus. 1141f); Arist. Metaph. 993b; Phaenias, fr. 10 Wehrli; Plut. Mor. 84a, 220c, 549c, Vit. Agis 10; [Plut.] De mus. 4.66; Photius, Bibl. (p. 320b Bekker, quoting Procl. Chrest.); Suda Φ 761

CREXUS [32 Sutton; 1131 Aspiotes]
Philodemus De mus. 4.10.2 (p. 74 Kemke); [Plut.] De mus. 1135c, 1140b

DICAIOGENES [41 Sutton; 548 Aspiotes]
Arist. Poet. 1454b; Harpocr. Δικαιογένης; Σ Ar. Eccles. 1; Suda Δ 1064

ANAXANDRIDES [50 Sutton; 118 Aspiotes]
Chamaeleon, fr. 43 Wehrli (= Ath. 9.373f)

DIONYSIUS I
Diod. Sic. 15.6; Lucian, Ind. 15

GNESIPPUS [556 Stephanis]
Eupolis, fr. 148 KA (= Ath. 14.638e); Chionides, fr. 4 KA (= Ath. 14.638d); Cratinus, fr. 17 KA (= Ath. 14.638d–f), 104 KA (= Ath. 14.638e), 276 KA (= Ath. 14.638f); Teleclides, fr. 36 KA (= Ath. 14.639a); Σ Ar. Nub. 332a

LEOTROPHIDES [*91 Sutton; 1189 Aspiotes]
Ar. Av. 1406 + Σ; Hermippus, fr. 36 KA (= Ath. 12.551a); Suda Λ 278

TELLEN OF THEBES [2394 Stephanis]
Leonidas of Tarentum (HE ix 2002–3); Zenob. 1.45 and 2.15; Lib. Ep. 633; [Plut.] Παροιμίαι 1.27

No preserved fragments

LYSIMACHUS Lycurg. fr. 5.8 (= Harpocr. Λυσίμαχος); Suda Λ 862

PHILOTAS Machon fr. 11 Gow (= Ath. 8.352b)

DIONYSIUS [Plut.] Vitae Decem Oratorum 839d

thanksgiving to Poseidon that he attributes to Arion (*PMG* 900), which, as Campbell and others have noted, is in the dithyrambic manner of *ca.* 400 BC.[38] But, again, precisely because the "dithyrambic manner of *ca.* 400 BC," to use Campbell's phrase, was imitated, parodied, and characterized by critics as early as Aristophanes, we must be wary of imitations or forgeries that proved all too easy to generate.

A filtered corpus: choice and chance

As an examination of the record of names and texts makes evident, two processes account for the shape of the surviving corpus of early classical lyric. The first process can be termed passive filtering. No late classical song has survived solely as an oral and musical phenomenon: songs have survived both because they were written down at some point and for some reason, and because the stone or papyrus or text that contained them has been preserved by a combination of choice and chance. A second, simultaneous, process, which can be called active filtering, lies behind the selection of passages to preserve or quote or the mentioning of the names of a handful of late classical poets; this process is characterized by active decision making, by authors or communities with specific agendas. These two processes of canonization are of a different nature, and sometimes, but not always, overlap: passive filtering has to do with the technique of communication of writing, the socio-anthropological phenomenon of literacy, and choices made by the Alexandrians, scholars operating within an academic institution; active filtering reflects cultural and ideological biases and impetuses.

Active filtering: biased memory

Active filtering is particularly evident in the case of literary sources. The quotations of late classical lyric that have survived are a direct reflection of the authors' or quoters' interests, and we can never forget how their preoccupations, biases, and methods have shaped our image of the late classical poetic production. In particular, given that 80 percent of the late classical fragments quoted come from Athenaeus, it is overwhelmingly Athenaeus' thematic interests that are illustrated in the selection. It should be no surprise, then, that in the narrative setting of the *Deipnosophistae* ("Sophists at dinner") many late classical fragments focus on sympotic matters: wine, food, and musical entertainment. This selection undoubtedly introduces

---

[38] Campbell 1993: 361. Also Bowra 1963, West 1982, Mantziou 1989, and Csapo 2003.

some distortion but is a reality we must accept: if we had the *Iliad* or *Odyssey* only in a selection by Athenaeus, the epics might seem to be more concerned with feasting and playing the *phorminx* than with fighting the Trojans or sailing back to Ithaca. But by the same token, this antiquarian interest in convivial practices of older times is also the reason why we have much of the archaic lyric poetry that has survived, as well as Philoxenus' *Deipnon*, the longest fragment of New Music after Timotheus' *Persians* and preserved only by Athenaeus, and many passages devoted to poetic statements about music. Moreover, as a result of Athenaeus' completist approach, that is, his tendency to have his *sophistai* characters, most of them grammarians, present an erudite dossier containing many mutually reinforcing sources of information, we have many elements of discourse *on* the poets – anecdotes or later judgments, for example – in addition to the fragments themselves.[39]

Besides taking into account Athenaeus' deipnosophistic thematic filter, it is also crucial that we reflect on his method. Long thought interesting only on account of the encyclopedic mind of its author and for the encyclope-dically minded reader,[40] Athenaeus' imposing *Deipnosophistae* has recently been the object of re-evaluation, and a much more nuanced view of the author's interests and approach has surfaced.[41] In the case of musical mat-ters in particular, Andrew Barker has analyzed the author's interest in music and has shown that the musical quotations preserved in Athenaeus were selected "whether deliberately or subconsciously, through a distinctly curi-ous process of filtration, which has systematically sieved out everything that had ever been of interest to genuine students and connoisseurs of music."[42] Part of the explanation for this selectivity may lie in the sources that were available to Athenaeus: the fact, for example, that only metamusical pas-sages from Telestes have survived might suggest that Athenaeus was using a compilation from the New Musician, perhaps that realized by Aristoxenus, who had a *Life of Telestes*, rather than the texts of the poet himself. But part of the explanation may also lie in the conservative ideology reflected in the discourse of the deipnosophists, elite Greek men under the Roman

---

[39] Although Athenaeus quotes Antiphanes' parodies of Philoxenus' style at several points (fr. 180 KA *ap.* Ath. 4.169e–f and fr. 55 KA *ap.* Ath. 10.449b–d), he also quotes a passage of Antiphanes that provides a positive evaluation of the dithyrambist's art – if we are to take the passage at face value: Antiphanes, fr. 207 KA *ap.* Ath. 14.643d–e, on which Fongoni 2005.

[40] E. Bowie (2000: 124): "Put a piece of poetry in front of [Athenaeus] that 'Longinus' might pick out for sublimity, or Plutarch for a profound moral lesson, and [Athenaeus] will home in unhesitatingly on the unusual word or form."

[41] For a re-evaluation of Athenaeus, Romeri 1997, Braund and Wilkins 2000, Canfora 2001, Jacob 2001 and 2004, König and Whitmarsh 2007, Lenfant 2007, Louyest 2009: 11–18, LeVen 2010.

[42] Barker 2000: 437. On Book 14, see also Restani 1988.

Empire who did not so much practice music like professional musicians as talk about music in an educated way. More generally, scholars have emphasized that Athenaeus' book engages with preoccupations of imperial culture and that his choice of quotations, including those of conservative political philosophers, is indicative of an idealizing view of classical culture, and the view of musical culture that accompanies it.[43] In this regard, the era of the New Music, and the late classical period in general, is an ideal time period for an imperial reader: one can choose either to identify with this epigonic moment, in a nostalgic view of the classical past, or to distance oneself from it, and see it as a step past the classical.[44]

One way of correcting the Athenaean thematic and ideological distortion is to listen to other voices and to give weight to remarks attesting to other thematic choices. Different authors come with different biases: the pedagogical purpose of Stobaeus' collection and the moralizing approach of Plutarch (who represent respectively 4.6 percent and 5 percent of the total number of lines quoted) guide their selection of poetry, and the late classical lyric they quote illustrates a different set of interests. Given Stobaeus' didactic goal in compiling passages from Greek literature for his son, it is not surprising to find fragments of classical lyric that deal with moral subjects or ethical outlooks, material which is not very different from archaic poetry and underlines the continuity of some traditions, such as moral disquisitions on man and life, regardless of performance mode. This is the case with a passage of Hermolochus:

> ἀτέκμαρτος ὁ πᾶς βίος οὐδὲν ἔχων πιστὸν πλανᾶται
> συντυχίαις· ἐλπὶς δὲ φρένας παραθαρσύνει· τὸ δὲ μέλλον ἀκριβῶς
> οἶδεν οὐδεὶς θνατὸς ὅπᾳ φέρεται·
> θεὸς δὲ πάντας †ἐν κινδύνοις θνατοὺς† κυβερνᾷ·
> ἀντιπνεῖ δὲ πολλάκις εὐτυχίᾳ δεινά τις αὔρα.   5
>
> Hermolochus, *PMG* 846

> Baffling is one's whole life, without anything certain and led astray by incidents. Hope emboldens one's heart; but no mortal knows the future clearly and where it is leading to: a god steers all †mortals among dangers†. Often an awful wind blows against good fortune.

Nothing in the diction or themes of this material distinguishes it from the work of archaic authors or from philosophy. Indeed the quotation appears among prose extracts. As for Plutarch, he quotes late classical lyric at key

---

[43] E. Bowie 1970; in general Braund and Wilkins 2000, König and Whitmarsh 2007, and König 2009. On the quotations of philosophers with a conservative cultural agenda, Trapp 2000.
[44] On the classical past(s), J. I. Porter 2006, with D'Angour 2006b on music.

points in his works and consistently seems to consider them as known to his intended audience of *pepaideumenoi*. *How to Read the Poets*, for instance, opens with a quotation of Philoxenus;[45] the *Erotikos* quotes Melanippides, and right after quoting Sappho, a protagonist asks where a line of Philoxenus comes from, as if it were as natural to know Philoxenus as it was to know Sappho.[46] This expected familiarity is also true of isolated remarks in a variety of earlier authors: an aristocrat in Xenophon's *Memorabilia*, for example, sees no difficulty in making the New Musician Melanippides equal to Homer, Sophocles, Polycleitus, and Zeuxis in their respective arts and genres.[47] Aristotle, who is rarely enthusiastic about contemporary lyric poetry, underlines the major contribution of Timotheus and quotes or refers to him no fewer than six times.[48] The Hellenistic poet Hermesianax pairs Philoxenus with Philotas, after Sophocles and Euripides, in his historical catalogue of canonical poetic lovers.[49] We find the same process in some pages of Philodemus, where the names of Timotheus and Philoxenus are quoted by Philodemus, or those he refutes alongside those of Homer and Pindar.[50] These examples suggest that as early as Xenophon's time and down to the first centuries of the Common Era, the New Musicians were assimilated into a form of lyric canon, as a form of "classics," even if they were not part of the Alexandrian canon. We can read how well regarded they are also in the testimony of the middle comedy poet Antiphanes (fr. 207 KA), who compares Philoxenus, the "old master" who surpasses all poets (πάντων τῶν ποιητῶν διάφορος) and is "a god among men" (θεὸς ἐν ἀνθρώποισιν), to poets of his own day, mere poetasters composing "wretched songs with wretched words, weaving in other people's melodies" (μέλεα μελέοις ὀνόμασι . . . ἐμπλέκοντες ἀλλότρια μέλη).[51]

Other testimonies make this early canonization of some lyric figures even clearer. At the end of the second century BC, Polybius describes how children in Arcadia learn to sing the songs of Philoxenus and Timotheus as part of their patriotic repertoire:

These practices are known and familiar to all: first that in Arcadia and hardly anywhere else, children are trained from babyhood to sing according to customs hymns and paeans (κατὰ νόμους τοὺς ὕμνους καὶ παιᾶνας), with which they each

---

[45] Plut. *Mor.* 14e (*De audiendis poetis* 1) = *PMG* 836 (f).

[46] Plut. *Mor.* 758c (*Amatorius* 15).   [47] Xen. *Mem.* 1.4.3.

[48] Arist. *Metaph.* 993b15: "If there were no Timotheus, we would not have much melody (μελοποιίαν); but if there were no Phrynis, there would be no Timotheus."

[49] *CA*, pp. 98–105 (fr. 7.69–74).

[50] Wilamowitz (1872: 21 n. 28) recognized Philodemus' predilection for late classical lyric.

[51] On the tone of the passage, Fongoni 2005. See also above p. 49 and n. 39.

sing of their local heroes and gods according to tradition (κατὰ τὰ πάτρια). Then they learn the songs (νόμους) of Philoxenus and Timotheus and demonstrate great love of honor in dancing every year accompanied by the Dionysian *aulos* players in the theaters – boys taking part in the boys' competition, young men in the so-called men's competition.

Polyb. 4.20.8–9

Perhaps Polybius is projecting an idealistic vision of his native Arcadia that corresponds with the image of an ideal conservative musical culture or perhaps he is projecting anti-Athenian values onto Arcadia and using *mousikē* as a cultural symbol; whichever is the case, the nomes (νόμους) of Timotheus and Philoxenus are presented as part of the musical Arcadian tradition (νόμους).[52] What is more, they can even achieve canonical, or classic, status by being part of the educational institution. Two second-century BC inscriptions honoring Menecles, a Teian citharode sent to Crete to obtain the status of inviolability (*asylia*) for his city, confirm the impression of an Athenian New Music that has become classical:

Menecles often performed on the cithara the songs of Timotheus and Polyidus and our old [Cretan?] poets (τά τε Τιμοθέω καὶ Πολυίδω καὶ τῶν ἁμῶν ἀρχαίων ποιητᾶν) beautifully and as befits a gentleman (ὡς προσῆκεν ἀνδρὶ πεπαιδευμένῳ).

CIG 3053

There is no opposition between the innovative songs of the former (the dithyrambists operating in Athens) and the traditional songs of the latter (the Cretan poets), and the clause "as befits a gentleman" even seems to apply to the songs of Timotheus and Polyidus, in an ideological orientation that is radically different from the Athenian discourse on the decadence of the New Music.[53]

In the end, these testimonies suggest that our classicizing view of the archaic and early classical past stands in the way of our appreciating late classical compositions for their own sake;[54] we must keep in mind other canons or other ways of thinking of the relationship between the innovations of the late classical period and our view of "the tradition," which most often does not include this type of belated poetry. An anecdote preserved by Aristoxenus ultimately gives us a good idea of how artificial it is to separate early and late classical moments of musical history, and shows that the late classical musicians already had an iconic, if not canonical, status in the fourth

---

[52] Stehle 1997: 66, Wilson 2000: 300–1, Kowalzig 2007: 4–5, and Prauscello 2009: 188–94.

[53] On the inscription, Rutherford 2007: 285–6, Prauscello 2009: 192–3, Patterson 2010: 111–12, and Barker 2011: 171–4, 176.

[54] For a re-evaluation of the notion of tragic canon, see Easterling 1993 and 1997.

century. The story (fr. 76 Wehrli *ap.* [Plut.] *De mus.* 1142b–c) presents the musician Telesias of Thebes as having first trained thoroughly in his youth in the most beautiful kind of music (ἐν τῇ καλλίστῃ μουσικῇ), in the old style of Pindar, Dionysius of Thebes, Lamprus, and Pratinas; tricked, or seduced (ἐξαπατηθῆναι), by the complex and modern style of Timotheus and Philoxenus (τὰ ποικιλώτατα καὶ πλείστην ἐν αὐτοῖς ἔχοντα καινοτομίαν), he utterly failed, however, to compose as they did because of the excellent training he had received in his childhood. Several tropes associated with the innovations of the late classical period can be found here, but most importantly, the musician Telesias is presented as having been able to try out, with different degrees of success, both styles, which existed alongside each other. As the opening anecdote, by Diodorus of Sicily, demonstrated, what is often constructed as different stages, the old followed by the new, ought rather to be seen as two contemporary musical options that could be performed by the same person, as the three cases preserved in very different testimonies about musical practice suggest – Telesias' experiment, Polybius' Arcadian children, and Menecles' career.

Passive filtering: a "record" of songs

The passive filter involves a different process of selection, but one no less rich and complex than that of the active filter. Beyond the element of chance that is common to the history of all ancient artifacts that have survived down to our time, the surviving corpus of *songs* raises specific issues about the technology of transmission and communication and about changing cultural practices in the late classical period.[55] To put it in crude terms, the classical period seems to sit uneasily as a period of transition between the song culture of the archaic period and the book culture of Hellenistic times. Eric Havelock's work on the mechanisms of social change in the classical period has suggested that the rise of literacy caused the decline of song culture.[56] Havelock saw the fact that "the Muse learned to write" in Hellenistic times as a consequence of the fact that her audiences had learned to read and that communication practices overall had changed over the course of the fifth and fourth centuries BC. Yet this characterization leads to an awkward divide between orality and literacy, and although

---

[55] As Kowalzig (2007: 6) explains about choral cultic lyric of the archaic and early classical periods: "[the texts of] traditional oral hymns . . . were only picked up by tradition when they presented peculiar features, such as the crow song mentioned by Athenaios [*PMG* 848 = Ath. 8.360b–d]."

[56] Havelock 1982 and 1986.

Havelock's thesis has been influential, several objections need to be kept in mind.

First, Kevin Robb, building on Havelock's work, has asked whether "the degree of literacy acquired replaced in the *fifth* century the traditional, oral methods for transmitting the Hellenic paideia to a new generation." At the term of his analysis, Robb underlines that "an increasing popular literacy in the fifth-century Athenian democracy seems clearly to have been oriented to civil, legal, and diplomatic matters, with some mercantile development, *not to producing a revolution in the methods of traditional education.* We must resist the automatic assumption of an alliance between literacy and paideia based on a model familiar to us, however natural" (my emphasis).[57] That a significant portion of the population might have developed an ability to read did not necessarily translate into a sudden change in traditional education practices. The rates and uses of literacy should not be overstated, nor should the evidence available for Athens be applied to Greece as a whole without careful consideration. Moreover, orality and literacy are not two distinct and successive eras of technology: since the archaic period, they had overlapped and mingled in complex ways, as studies by William Harris, Rosalind Thomas, and the various contributors to the *Mnemosyne* supplements devoted to orality and literacy have shown.[58]

Second, in the case of the late classical corpus, it has not been acknowledged enough that the written word and the practice of writing songs down, either on papyrus or in stone, had very different meanings and purposes. Writing as a way of *recording* a text greatly predates the late classical period: as Herington has shown, there might have been written "texts" of songs as early as their first performance.[59] Besides having ritual, symbolic, or even magical value, as in the case of songs preserved on stone *inside* a sanctuary,[60] written texts could be used for teaching in schools, and perhaps for composition purposes, as well as for preservation in aristocratic family archives.[61] All these uses are quite independent of a purpose aimed at public transmission and dissemination.

Moreover, although writing can be understood as a way of *transmitting* and *disseminating* texts, that process differs between papyri and stones and involves a different type of relationship with reading, and performing,

---

[57] Robb 1994: 189.
[58] Harris 1989, Thomas 1989 and 1992, Yunis 2003, Mackie 2004.
[59] Herington 1985: 45–7; Ford 2003.
[60] On the case of Pindar's *Olympian* 7, inscribed in gold letters inside the temple of Athena Lindia on Rhodes, see Chapter 7.
[61] Herington 1985: 201–6, Harris 1989, Thomas 1989 and 1992, Hubbard 2004, Currie 2005, and Morrison 2007b about Pindar.

communities. Stones preserve texts but do not travel; they make the text available to whoever is able and/or willing to read it on site and often ground their own rhetoric in that reality of an open, anonymous, readership.[62] By contrast, books can travel. Leaving aside the details of the book market, the issue of the transmission of late classical texts deserves special attention.[63]

Other than the Timotheus papyrus, no papyrus preserving a late classical song has surfaced to date. But we know from a few isolated references that at the end of the classical period some texts of famous dithyrambs were transmitted in written form. Plutarch (*Vit. Alex.* 8.3) reports that Onesicritus, a contemporary of Alexander, mentions in his *History* the circulation of βίβλοι (papyrus rolls) of dithyrambic texts at the time of Alexander:[64]

And when he [Alexander] ran out of other books (ἄλλων βιβλίων) in the up-country, he ordered Harpalus to send him some, and Harpalus sent him the papyrus rolls (βίβλους) of Philistus and many of the tragedies of Euripides, Sophocles, and Aeschylus, and the dithyrambs of Telestes and Philoxenus.

Onesicritus, *FGrH* 134 F 38

Our epigraphic and literary sources attest that texts circulated while the songs were still performed. An inscription records the victory of a boys' chorus in a reperformance of Timotheus' dithyramb *Elpenor* in 320/19 BC;[65] a dialogue of Lucian refers to the aulete Timotheus' performance of Timotheus' *Madness of Ajax* in the late fourth century; and Plutarch describes a reperformance of Timotheus' *Persians* in Nemea in 205 BC for Philopoemen.[66] But in the case of Onesicritus, the existence of a "book" (or text) is tightly linked to issues of cultural capital. This situation, where a Macedonian, in Upper Asia, asks for what is in effect the "canon" of Athenian tragedians (Aeschylus, Sophocles, Euripides) and of dithyrambists (Telestes and Philoxenus) active in Athens to be sent to him in book-form, bears striking parallels with that of the Timotheus papyrus, found in Egypt, to which I now turn.

The Timotheus papyrus was discovered in 1902 by Ludwig Borchardt and his German archaeological team in a Greek necropolis in Abusir, Egypt, along with a few objects that included a sponge and coins. The imagery of the coins invites us to think that the papyrus had been deposited (or lost? or

---

[62] Svenbro 1976, Bing 2002 and 2009, Day 2010.

[63] On the book market, Kenyon 1951 and Turner 1952: 21.

[64] On βίβλοι as texts, and not musical scores, Prauscello 2006b: 43 n. 129; contra: Bélis 1988: 30, 38 n. 7 and 1999: 158–9, 274 n. 3. On musical notation, see further below, pp. 57–8.

[65] *PMG* 779 = *IG* ii² 3055.

[66] Lucian, *Harmonides* 1; *PMG* 788 = Plut. *Vit. Phil.* 11.

discarded?) in the tomb "in the time of Alexander the Great at the latest, and possibly somewhat earlier," since they do not depict Alexander "as might have been expected from perhaps the middle of his reign and certainly later."[67] Like true or fictional, minimal or explicit, explanatory notes by an author who is quoting literary fragments, the archaeological evidence surrounding the papyrus provides clues to the relationships between the text and the cultural context in which it was circulated and between the papyrus and the dead man in whose tomb it was found. The presence of a sponge among the grave goods might suggest that the deceased was a scribe but nothing else allows us to confirm this attractive hypothesis, which is, indeed, dismissed by Hordern, one of the most recent commentators on the poem. The presence of the text in Egypt gives weight, however, to the evidence provided by Onesicritus that texts of nomes were circulating in the late fourth century in Hellenized communities, even, or especially, at some distance from Athens, the center of theater culture, and relatively long after their original production.

Moreover, the aesthetic quality of the Timotheus papyrus might say something about the function that the text, as object, played. The writing is extremely clear, inspired by epigraphic *stoichedon* writing, in which each letter occupies the same amount of space.[68] That the papyrus looks similar to the other earliest surviving specimen (the Derveni papyrus) suggests that this kind of script was in use in the late fourth century, yet the coronis that separates the end of the narrative from the *sphragis* again highlights the special care invested in the production of the manuscript as a beautiful object.[69] It is a very stylized bird, perhaps an ibis, which Gildersleeve, tongue in cheek, assimilated to the poetics of the poem in his spirited review of Wilamowitz' *editio princeps*.[70] The design plays with the iconic

---

[67] On the papyrus, Wilamowitz-Moellendorff 1903, Schubart 1911, Turner 1952, Hordern 2002: 62–73, with quotation on p. 63.

[68] On the aesthetics of *stoichedon* writing, J. I. Porter 2010: 464–70.

[69] Turner 1952: 5–6: "It is a pleasing notion that this roll was the precious possession of a wandering singer, perhaps an Ionian, who could attract an audience even for modern Greek music in a foreign land . . . I do not doubt that this is the oldest book known to us, but I challenge the assumption often made that it can be regarded as a typical example." On the coronis, see Fischer-Bossert 2005.

[70] Gildersleeve 1903: 231: "Ibis-like, Timotheos has swallowed and digested all the departments of Greek poetry, epic, lyric, dramatic," with the unfortunate follow-up, "But, honestly, I do not think that they have been improved by the process." The bird also announces something that will become more frequent in Hellenistic poetry: the attention to the status of the text, including its paratextual marks (title, sphragis, coronis), as object. For Hellenistic epigrams staging the *coronis*, see Bing 2008: 33–5.

status of the bird and with the homonymy between coronis as typographical mark and the mythical Coronis, a maiden who was turned into a crow for sleeping with a mortal after being impregnated by a god in her "longing for things far away," according to Pindar (*Pyth.* 3). But the bicultural nature of the coronis – an Egyptian bird paired with a classical Greek myth – brings to the fore the ideological and symbolic function of the material object itself and of its content: the *Persians*, as text and object, allows Greece and Egypt to be aligned, as it celebrates a Greek victory over the Persians and has a particularly strong symbolic and emotional value for a Greek living in Egypt, itself dominated by Persia in the late fourth century.[71]

Nothing suggests that there were other texts on the papyrus of Timotheus. Nor does anything suggest that the Alexandrians made editions of the *dithyrambopoioi* in their great attempt to categorize the available body of songs.[72] As noted above, the absence of editions of the *dithyrambopoioi* might be understood in the light of performance practices: dithyrambs and nomes were still composed and performed at the end of the fourth and in the third century, texts of "singles" circulated, and early examples of the New Music, now classics, were still performed, in a continued tradition. The Alexandrians probably did not feel a need to preserve texts that were still being produced by a continued performance culture.

As for the musical notation of late classical songs, direct information about textual transmission is relatively scarce.[73] Some papyri with musical notation of late fifth- and fourth-century compositions have survived, but the genre of the songs they record is often difficult to establish.[74] Pöhlmann and West have suggested, for example, that some papyrus fragments not-ing fourth-century musical texts (P. Ashm. Inv. 89B/29–32, dated third–second century BC), "might [be expected to] be citharodes' repertoire, either excerpts from tragedies or citharodic nomes or dithyrambs."[75] But as tan-talizing as this instance of late classical musical notation possibly used for performance is, we cannot examine it without considering what musical

---

[71] On that aspect, Van Minnen 1997.
[72] On the Alexandrians' attitude toward lyric, Wilamowitz-Moellendorff 1900, especially pp. 1–24, 63–71; Pfeiffer 1968: 181–9. On the formation of the canon, Hadjimichael 2010.
[73] Pöhlmann and West 2001: 40–60; frr. 7–18.
[74] For example, *P. Berol.* 6870, first published by Schubart, who "left the musical notation for others to analyse." Bélis (1998) argues it is the score of a dithyramb, Timotheus' *Ajax*; Pöhlmann and West (2001: 58), with reference to West 1992: 361–4, argue on the basis of the nature of the modulations for the notation of a tragedy of the late classical or early Hellenistic period.
[75] Pöhlmann and West 2001: 38.

notation *meant* and without taking into account the kind of textual, cultural, and institutional practice to which it belonged.

Questions similar to those raised by the transmission of words can also be asked of musical notation. *Why* is the music inscribed, and what for? Is it as a means of transmission or dissemination? Does the transcribed music record an anomaly rather than a norm? As Andrew Barker states very clearly, "when a written notation, melodic or rhythmic, was added to a text in Greek antiquity, it was never designed as the vehicle of the music's publication to a wide readership, as it is in the modern world. It served precisely as an aide-mémoire for performers."[76] The various uses of musical notation have been thoroughly examined by Lucia Prauscello in a seminal study on music between practice and textual transmission that investigates "possible paths, in terms of traditional channels, followed by texts originally conceived for performance."[77] Taking issue with antithetical premises in modern scholarship – one (Fleming and Kopff 1992) "arguing for an early symbiosis, in terms of textual transmission, between *Lesetexte* and *Bühnenexemplare*," the other (Pöhlmann 1960) splitting the two traditions, the merely textual and the scenic, into two distinct media – Prauscello shows how "the high degree of uniformity posited by both approaches runs the risk of oversimplifying the processes of textual transmission by forcing into a straightforward frame a reality that seems to have been, fortunately or not, far more unsettled and 'contaminated.'"[78] The surviving evidence, which includes the direct evidence of papyri and epigraphy and the indirect evidence of anecdotes, iconography, and descriptions of cultural practices, leads her to a skeptical conclusion, that restricted circles of professional musicians "could well have occasionally resorted to musical scores by that time [the fifth century] but this is quite different from positing a whole strand of musical transmission closely associated with the textual one."[79] Prauscello's detailed analysis of the Alexandrian scholars' use of two texts with musical notation additionally suggests that ancient "scores" contain evidence of variants "most likely to be ascribed to actual performance" and that "the renewed Hellenistic context could in fact entail a whole range of modes of performance different from those codified by classical theatrical practice."[80]

In this context, a tangentially related question is that of the textual transmission of choral lyric parts in fourth-century drama. The presence of merely the word XOPOY (chorus part), instead of a choral ode, in

---

[76] Barker 1995: 59–60.   [77] Prauscello 2006b: 9.   [78] Prauscello 2006b: 10.
[79] Prauscello 2006b: 48.   [80] Prauscello 2006b: 182–3.

manuscripts of Aristophanes' *Plutus* and probably of Agathon's tragedies
has led scholars to hypothesize about a change in musical practices, especially the introduction of *embolima*, choral odes with no relationship to
the plot that were supposedly recycled from play to play.[81] Yet there is no
evidence of professional choruses who would be used for the choral parts
of drama until the Hellenistic period, and there is no reason to assume that
dramatists stopped composing their own choral odes for performance by
citizen choruses.[82] Aristophanes, in particular, gives us grounds to think
that Agathon composed hymnic odes.[83] Rather, the change introduced by
the mention of XOPOY reinforces the picture suggested by the evidence of
dithyrambic manuscripts and musical notation, that is, of a multiplicity of
oral and written channels of transmission of both music and words, and of
the multiplicity of recording and transmission practices.

Late classical lyric in context

Questions about performance practices and the fluid identity of songs are
tied to a larger issue, that of genre. So far I have tended to consider the corpus
of early classical lyric as a whole, but focusing on song types forces one
to wrestle with synchronic and diachronic elements and to reflect on what
makes songs resemble each other through time even as formal, performative,
and other changes take shape. As Ian Rutherford describes in the first pages
of his fundamental book on paeans:

In most places there was a demand (at least in the classical period) for an ever increasing repertory of new material. On the other hand, innovation took place within
a fixed canon of genres, some sacred (e.g. the διθύραμβος, προσόδιον, ὑπόρχημα,
ὕμνος, δαφνηφορικόν, ὠσχοφορικόν), other comparatively secular (the ἐπινίκιον,
ἐγκώμιον, θρῆνος, παρθένειον). The generic "canon" is thus essentially a conservative factor, though it is itself not immune to change (and we seem to see some
changes from the end of the fifth century BC).[84]

The very notion of "genre" actually encapsulates the challenges of thinking
about such tradition and innovation, in terms of forms, practices, and
contexts, and deserves special attention.[85]

---

[81] Lévêque 1955, Xanthakis-Karamanos 1980: 9–11.
[82] Wilson 2000: 128–9 on the socio-cultural background of choruses.
[83] Rothwell 1992 against the demise of the comic chorus in the fourth century.
[84] Rutherford 2001a: 3–4.
[85] Gentili 1988: 61: "The diachronic setting for the phenomenon of lyric is the middle ground
between tradition and innovation."

Song types: literary critical and formal approach

Defining ancient lyric genres, or song types, is a notoriously difficult problem.[86] One of the reasons for it being difficult is that, in ancient sources, the notion of genre, and the activity of defining a song's type, meant different things to different people at different times. In an important 1955 article, A. E. Harvey tackled the question of the classification of lyric poetry, and his prudent and "depressingly negative" conclusions can be used as helpful guidelines here.[87] Harvey made clear that the principles which the Alexandrian scholars adopted to distinguish between different song types (εἴδη) of the archaic and early classical lyric poets – hymn, dithyramb, paean, epinician, *thrēnoi*, encomia, etc. – derived from practical considerations. This type of distinctions "tells us, not of the difference between certain types of poetry which were important when the poetry was written, but only of those differences which were regarded as distinctive when it came to be edited."[88] Even the vocabulary that the poets themselves used to describe their song types (ὕμνος or κῶμος, for example) is, in the end, not very helpful, as the terms were vague and their usage changed over time.[89]

In light of the challenges presented by ancient definitions or reflections on genres, scholars have offered a variety of other methods to distinguish song types from each other. A first method starts with the surviving body of ancient lyric and characterizes a genre according to a series of formal features that can be observed in the texts. Stylistic, syntactic, or metrical features that distinguish one category of song from another enabled critics to define "paean" or "dithyramb" by contrast with other song forms.[90] This approach however is hampered by the limited size of the surviving corpus, which risks generating a distorted sense of the essential nature of these songs: the surviving Pindaric dithyrambs or paeans, for example, might be taken

---

[86] The literature on lyric genres is extensive, and I refer here only to representative and recent studies: Harvey 1955, Rossi 1971, Fantuzzi 1980, Davies 1988, Calame 1974 and 1998, Depew and Obbink 2000, Rutherford 2001a, Cingano 2003, Ford 2006, Swift 2010.

[87] Harvey 1955: 175.   [88] Harvey 1955: 157.

[89] Rossi 1971 on the famous distinction between "non-written rules to be followed" in the archaic period, and "written rules that can be ignored" in the Hellenistic period. Also Rutherford 2001a: 4–6 on the change from the notion of genre as descriptive category in the early fifth century to a taxonomic tool in the late classical period.

[90] Fairbanks 1900 on paean; Pickard-Cambridge 1962: 1–59 on dithyramb; Rossi 1971: 71 discussing various genres; Seaford 1977–8 on post-450 dithyramb; Hamilton 1990 on Pindaric dithyramb.

as representative of tradition when they ought probably to be considered exceptional or innovations in themselves.[91]

Critics have also identified narrative as one of the essential elements that allow the generic identity of a song to be ascertained. The link between dithyramb and Dionysiac themes, for example, appears in our earliest piece of evidence, Archilochus, fr. 120 W[2].[92] One could say the same about the paean, whose narrative content is often linked with Apollo, as early as Homer (*Il.* 1.473). Yet, not all dithyrambs have a Dionysiac narrative content and not all paeans have an Apollonian theme, nor are pieces with Dionysiac or Apollonian contents necessarily dithyrambs or paeans, as Bacchylides' dithyramb 16 and Philodamus' fourth-century BC "Paean to Dionysus" show.[93]

Scenarios of performance: text-based cultural history

To deal with these difficulties, a different approach to categorization has been sought in the last thirty years. As Ian Rutherford explains, "what songs have to have in common in order to be perceived as adhering to the same genre seems usually to be a shared function, or shared performance scenario."[94] Song types, as their names often suggest, are linked to specific performance scenarios and social and ritual contexts. Paeans, for example, are songs addressing a divinity called Paeon/Paian that are sung by a community of performers accompanied by instrumental music and dance steps.[95] Andrew Ford has proposed we go further and use the term "paian" for any choral song in which the circumstances call for the "paian" cry (victory, celebration, imploration, apotropaic prayer, etc.), regardless of the actual presence of the cry, which could be added *extra metrum*, or of the connection with Apollo.[96]

---

[91] Seaford 1977–8: 92, and highlighting the same idea but in a very different way, Kowalzig 2007: 7, who sees the great archaic choral poets as composing "on specific occasions to mark a special festival, to make a point about a particular performance or otherwise to label an event as important and different."

[92] The fragments of dithyrambs quoted by metricians or music critics suggest a more obvious Dionysiac connection: *PMG* 926 (from Aristoxenus or an Aristoxenian) contains quotations of fifth- or fourth-century compositions that refer to bacchic choruses, spring flowers, dancing maidens, and Dionysus. The same is true of *PMG* 929b, on which see Powell 1933: 178–9, and Hamilton 1990.

[93] Rutherford 2001a: 21–3 and Fearn 2007: 163–225 fully discuss methodology and problems of defining, respectively, paean and dithyramb in formal terms.

[94] Rutherford 2001a: 4.   [95] Rutherford 2001a: 18–58.   [96] Ford 2006.

The case is more difficult for the dithyramb. Even when we look at performance scenario or context, it is not easy to find a common denominator that accounts for the diversity, endurance, and constant reshaping of the dithyramb through time and space.[97] The earliest evidence suggests it was a processional song, but later sources describe it as choral, sung and danced in a circle by fifty choristers.[98] The same diversity characterizes its contexts of performance. The prime setting for the performance of dithyrambs at Athens was the musical contests of the City Dionysia in honor of Dionysus, but the worship of Dionysus was not the only occasion for dithyrambic performance. Dithyrambs were also performed at Athens' most important city festival for Apollo, the Thargelia.[99] Bypassing these issues to some extent and arguing as in the case of the paean genre for a more performative model, Andrew Ford has suggested that the only element that defines a dithyramb is that it is a song that addresses a divinity as *dithyrambos* and uses the cletic adjective.[100]

If song types are to be defined by their performance context, the evolution of that context presents a challenge. In response to that challenge, up until some thirty years ago scholars relied almost entirely on literary sources and wrote a cultural history of music that was mostly text based. One fundamental source for many theories of the evolution of lyric genres and scenarios is Plato's description of the development of the musical panorama in the classical period:

Our music used to be divided according to genres (εἴδη) and forms (σχήματα), so one genre was that of the prayer to the gods, which they called hymns. And there was another genre of song, opposite to that one – one would specifically call them dirges – and another paeans, and another, the creation of Dionysus I think, called dithyramb (Διονύσου γένεσις οἶμαι, διθύραμβος λεγόμενος). And they called another "nomes" as a different type of song, qualifying them as "citharodic." Such were the categories and other ones too, and it was not possible to go from one song to another when using them . . . When things were thus organized, the citizen mass was content to be governed, and they did not have the audacity to judge thanks to their hubbub. But after this, with the passage of time, appeared some composers who, although creative by nature, started unmusical law-breaking; they

---

[97] Fearn 2007; Wilson and Kowalzig forthcoming presents a variety of approaches to defining the dithyramb genre.

[98] Archil. fr. 120 W^2. On how the dithyramb got its circular shape, D'Angour 1997. On dithyramb and *kyklios khoros*, Fearn 2007: 163–256.

[99] On the problem of the existence of dithyrambs for Apollo, Pickard-Cambridge 1962: 3–4 and 26–8, Parker 1996: 95, Wilson 2000: 33 and 2007b: 164–75. Conversely, there seem to have been no performances of paeans or citharodic *nomoi* in honor of Apollo in Athens.

[100] Ford 2011b.

didn't know what was just and acceptable in music. In a bacchic frenzy, and held by pleasure beyond what is right, they mixed dirges with hymns, and paeans with dithyrambs, and imitating *aulos*-songs with their *kithara*-songs, brought everything together with everything else, thus involuntarily, because of their stupidity, giving false witness against music, alleging that music has no standard of correctness, but that it is judged most correctly according to the pleasure of the listener, whether he is a good man or a wretch. By creating such compositions and by choosing corresponding words, they have instigated among the populace lawlessness toward music, and the effrontery to suppose they were capable of judging it. As a result the audiences, once silent, made their voice heard, as if they perceived what is good in music and what is not, and a musical aristocracy has given place to a degenerate theatocracy.

Plato, Leg. 700a–701a (trans. inspired by Barker 1984)

This passage accounts for two of the most widespread ideas in modern criticism about the lyric culture of the late classical period: first, that songs that used to have a religious and social function and celebrated the gods became divorced from their ritual significance and were turned into mere entertainment art forms; and second, that, because of that loss of cultic roots and a civic base, genres became mixed and new hybrid forms were invented. It is these two positions at the root of the *interpretatio Platonica* that one finds either combined or explored separately in most of the histories of lyric genres (be it that of the dithyramb or of the paean), and of lyric culture in general.

In one of the most influential books written on the dithyramb, for example, Pickard-Cambridge explains the changes that occurred in the later part of the fifth century thus: "no lyric poetry of any importance was composed apart from the dithyrambs, *nomes*, and paeans required for performance at festivals; *from the festivals themselves the religious interest was probably fast disappearing*, and it is natural that in these also the desire for novelty and freedom should find expression" (my emphasis).[101] This statement assumes the Platonic scenario in which musicians catered to the frivolous masses by giving them the music they liked, the New Music, leaving out any indication of the ritual or religious function of the songs.

In the same spirit, Bernhard Zimmermann's 1992 *Dithyrambos* accounts for the evolution of the dithyramb as a consequence of changes in social and political conditions. Zimmermann posits a first evolution, during the time of Arion or Lasus of Hermione, from a simple Dionysiac cult song (*Kultlied*) to a cultic poem (*kultische Dichtung*). A second evolution would

---

[101] Pickard-Cambridge 1962: 38–9.

have then taken place, as the dithyramb developed from cult poetry (archaic *ritual* dithyramb) into a civic manifestation (classical *civic* dithyramb, acted by the community as it performed its citizenship). The last modification would have occurred in the late fifth century, with the New Music and the transformation of the civic dithyramb into a mere art-for-art's-sake display of mannerism, its lack of cultic or political associations a sign of the decadence of the democracy: "So sind die Phänomene Gattungsmischung, Manierismus und Archaismus letztendlich Ausdruck derselben grundlegenden Änderung der Kommunikationsverhältnisse: des Zusammenbruchs des demokratischen Konsenses, der die Grundlage der Gattungen der Polis darstellte" ("In that way, the phenomena of mixing of genres, mannerism and archaism are, at the end of the day, an expression of the fundamental changes in behaviors of communication: an expression of the collapse of the democratic consensus that represents the basis of the genres of the Polis").[102] In Zimmermann's scenario, artistic features become divorced from ritual and civic function, and genres – for he extends his argument from the dithyramb to all genres – turn into formal categories isolated from socio-religious contexts.[103]

The background assumed in histories of the paean is little different. In his examination of this genre, Lutz Käppel describes a change at the end of the fifth century, when the features of the genre became "automatized." Käppel highlights the characteristics of a fourth-century paeanic specimen (its attention to using the right names and adjectives, its *epiphthēgma*, structure, and the overall sobriety of the narrative part) to conclude that the formal elements of the songs are dictated by a standardized pattern and suggest little literary creation.[104] Against this theory, Stephan Schröder has argued that the anonymous paeans inscribed in different versions were not an early example of the increased importance of formal elements in the

---

[102] Zimmermann 1992: 134–6, 135 for the quotation.

[103] On the deceptive and erroneous character of this dichotomy, see Fearn's (2007: 183–4) forceful judgment, on the dithyramb: "There is something very wrong in both these assessments [Pickard-Cambridge 1962 and Zimmermann 1992]. Behind both of them lurks the assumption that if any art form is seen to have lost a primary and original religious function (in this case, praise of Dionysos), the motivation for this must be explained by a shift from religion towards popular demand, politics, or entertainment. For Greece of the fifth century, any such notion needs to be dispatched forthwith since it is also suggestive of a false dichotomy between serious religion and popular, and hence more frivolous, artistic phenomena. Rather, it should be clear that music, like all cultural productions, is part of a discourse which can overlap with, intersect with, or compete against, the discourse of religion. Neither could ever have had any independent existence."

[104] Käppel 1992: 200–6.

definition of the genre but, rather, an instance of less elaborated cult poetry, which constituted the majority of compositions from which the major early classical poets distinguished themselves. Käppel's and Schröder's opposing views converge, however, on one idea: they both create a dichotomy between "literary" paean and merely "cult" paean, just as other theoreticians of genre have created a dichotomy between "literary" dithyramb and "cult" dithyramb. Yet one should note that while scholars of the dithyramb see no difficulty in separating literary and cultic function and present the dithyramb as a mere literary *l'art pour l'art* shell in the late fifth century, scholars of the paean offer the reverse scenario and present the paean as a mere cultic shell. In even the most sophisticated accounts of genre evolution, the specter of Plato's scenario still hovers in the background. For instance, in a detailed description of the evolution of the socio-cultural conditions of performance of the paean, Ian Rutherford states: "Along with the change in social conditions and canonization of earlier models *goes a change in artistic taste: the traditional genres of song and dance will have been regarded as old-fashioned and parochial in an age which demanded novelty and complexity*" (my emphasis).[105] Once again, the evolution of the paean genre is set against a novelty-crazed crowd corrupted by theater music.

So far I have discussed the most public and ritual genres, but a similar understanding of social, civic, and ritual decline also explains the demise of other, and more private, melic forms, especially those associated with the symposium. Numerous studies have focused on the connection between the archaic and early classical symposium as a place of socio-political interaction and as a context of performance for several poetic genres (elegy, iambs, and various lyric forms such as scolia, epinician, and encomium).[106] One of the main changes that historians of literature present in connection with socio-political development in the classical period is the progressive evolution of the symposium, from place of performance of political poetry to place of mere literary entertainment, a movement that is deemed to run in parallel and in step with the perceived loss of civic or religious function in other genres: "Auch wenn Xenophons und Platons *Symposia* wohl kaum als repräsentativ für das Symposion angesehen werden dürfen, so ist die Entstehung dieser neuen literarischen Gattung doch paradigmatisch für die im 4. Jh. *weitgehend abgeschlossene Verwandlung des Symposion vom*

---

[105] Rutherford 2001a: 127.
[106] Rösler 1983, E. Bowie 1986, Gentili 1988, Kurke 1991 (introduction), Stehle 1997, Ford 2002: Chapters 2–3, and Irwin 2005.

politischen, sozialen und kulturellen Zentrum des gesellschaftlichen Lebens zu einem fiktiven literarischen Ort" (my emphasis) ("Even though the *Symposia* of Xenophon and Plato should hardly be seen as representative of the symposium, the emergence of this new literary genre is paradigmatic of the transformation, largely completed in the fourth century, of the symposium away from the political, social, and cultural center of societal life and into a fictitious literary place").[107] Most of the surveys of different genres and most overviews of the settings of performance suggest that, in the late fifth century, "literary" (*sic*) or poetic innovation became separated from engagement with ritual or civic participation and dominated by either daring mannerist innovations or retreat into stale tradition. In all these cases, literary historians see a fracture between, on the one hand, social, political, and ritual significance and, on the other, musical reality, be it in public settings such as festivals, or in private ones such as symposia. In this understanding, the late classical period has been seen as a period already looking forward to the Hellenistic era, where songs start to be attached to fictive contexts, and compensate for the loss of actual venue of performance by describing fictive performance contexts in the text.[108]

The Plato passage quoted above also forms the basis of a second and related idea, that of the mixing of genres. With the socio-ritual context lost, critics argue, formal features of different song types could intermingle. Fantuzzi and Hunter, for example, use the concept famously identified by Kroll as "Kreuzung der Gattungen" as "one of the distinctive characteristics of the refined poetry which flourished in the Alexandria of Callimachus in the first half of the third century BC."[109] As they note, however, "generic 'contamination' was not the exclusive prerogative of the learned poetry of third-century Alexandria," and they quote the passage from the *Laws* to document changes that had already occurred in the fourth century.[110] Yet the idea of contamination implies a view of genres that is much too rigid and, at the same time, unstable. Rather than giving criteria for what makes

---

[107] For changes in fora and modes of communication, Wallace 1994 and 1995a, and Seidensticker 1995: 189. For a presentation of the evolution of the symposium in the fourth century BC, Wilamowitz-Moellendorff 1900: 14–15, and for the symposium in the Hellenistic period, Gützwiller 1998: 119–22. Against the alleged decline of symposium practices, Cameron 1995: 72–6.

[108] On fictive performance contexts for Callimachus' hymns, Depew 1993, for example.

[109] Fantuzzi and Hunter 2004: 17, Kroll 1924. See Barchiesi 2001 for an illuminating discussion of Kroll's expression, which "must be understood as a specific ideal of the 1920s, as specific as transatlantic ships, the rise of Argentina, and Russian aristocrats driving taxicabs... A modern equivalent of the idea, similarly related to contemporary obsessions, would be *generic engineering* (a pun I owe to Michael Haslam)" (145).

[110] Fantuzzi and Hunter 2004: 18.

a genre a genre, the "mixing" fuses apples and oranges: in Plato, it combines narrative content ("birth of Dionysus") and function ("*thrēnos*"), while Kroll assimilates metrical features and content, thus sliding over the very problematic, and elusive, notion of genre itself.

Material-based cultural history

Over the past thirty years, the relationship between, on the one hand, changes in society, religion, culture, economics, and politics, and, on the other, changes in music has been explored in a series of studies that take a third approach, that of a material-based cultural history of *mousikē* which explores the intersection of socio-political history, musical discourse, and cultural practices. In the introduction to his 2007 edited volume, Peter Wilson justifies this new understanding of how the history of the theater should be written:

The approach collectively exemplified in this volume advocates recognition of the specificity and complexity of the material conditions of dramatic production as they varied over time and place; and the recognition of the importance of close contact with the raw data relating to the organization and operation of theatre and festivals. Attention to such information need not represent a retreat to naïve empiricism. Analysed with the appropriate care and sophistication, the documentary evidence can become a more eloquent testimony to the ideological and historical complexity of its societies. Interpretation arrives at an apprehension of such complexity through a "bottom-up" approach, from the evidence for material conditions, rather than via the "top-down" method of some of the more abstract forms of structuralism and post-structuralism.[111]

This materialist bottom-up method of investigating musical culture has had impressive results, including Wilson's seminal *Khoregia*.[112] Starting from material culture, rather than from accounts about culture, it allows the correction of traditional claims both about the decline of lyric culture and about the demise of *mousikē* in conjunction with the decline of democracy. Where other histories of the genre have focused on the surviving literary evidence, this recent work has underlined the vividness of theater culture and the importance of *mousikē* and its institutions. Rather than describing a loss of religious spirit and communal values linked to a supposed decline of democracy, Wilson argues for the continuity of a very strong theater culture in the late classical period, not only in Athens but in the Greek world in general. Others have emphasized the continued importance of festivals and

---

[111] Wilson 2007a: 2–3.   [112] Wilson 2000.

theater as civic institutions,[113] but Wilson is perhaps the most explicit in his assertions: "The best part of a century of lavish festival expenditure was to pass before, in the last third of the 4th century, both the ongoing rhetorical and ideological 'debate' and actual practice show significant shifts." And even more clearly:

What th[e] testimony [of Lykurgos' activity at the head of Athenian finances and public policy] certainly shows is that the *khoros* as a social and poetic form continued to be an important tool of social and cultural formation in late fourth-century Athens. This is one argument to add to others against the familiar story of choral decline as concerns drama in the fourth century. The persistent flourishing of non-dramatic choral performance does not of course prove the necessary persistence of the *khoros* in drama. But it is something to set against the argument, largely from silence, for the early death of the dramatic *khoros*.[114]

Set against such a backdrop, the contextualized interpretation of literary testimonies and fragments along the lines of Pickard-Cambridge or Zimmermann becomes much harder, and our understanding of the evolution of theater genres needs to be re-evaluated.

Similarly, in looking for historical changes in the performance of theater lyric, Eric Csapo, who starts from the epigraphic and archaeological record, has shown that a new era began in the 430s BC, as larger theaters began to be built. Theatrical production was no longer "sponsor-directed," but resembled instead something more akin to the "mass entertainment industry."[115] In connection with these material changes, the socio-cultural status of actors, musicians, and singers was also transformed. The demand for such performers grew, and the nature of the performance changed, along with the nature of the theatrical experience.[116] Musical practice was professionalized, following the model of other areas of knowledge, especially higher education, rhetoric, ethics, politics, and medicine, which became the province of sophists, politicians, rhetoricians, philosophers, and doctors. For music, this development marked the beginning of the star system, which developed fully in the fourth century with famous virtuoso performers in specific genres.[117]

Additionally, as a corrective to Pickard-Cambridge's and Zimmermann's descriptions of the loss of the religious nature of the dithyramb, Csapo has

---

[113] Junker 2010.   [114] Wilson 2000: 265 and 267.

[115] The first expression is Bremer's (1991: 59); the second Csapo's (2004: 402).

[116] Csapo and Wilson 2009a, Csapo 2010.

[117] Neoptolemus and Theodorus for tragic roles, for example – the latter specialized in female roles – and Satyrus for comedy; see Easterling and Hall 2002, Hall 2006, and Csapo 2010.

argued elsewhere for a "come-back to Dionysus" in the New Music, espe-cially in the choral odes of late Euripides and in the dithyramb.[118] According to Csapo, references to Dionysus and to divinities associated with him (espe-cially Eastern deities such as the Great Mother), adjectives suggesting circle performance, and references to possession and to the Dionysiac in general all suggest a conscious reliance on the cultic element and tell of the great importance of the link between performance and cult. Csapo's thesis has not gone unchallenged, but when taken along with the re-evaluation of the theater culture of the late classical period, it creates a framework that is entirely different from that assumed in all examinations of the intellectual and social context of late classical music to date. Far from seeing the decline of theater lyric, Csapo and Wilson have argued for the expansion of its geographic, economic, and institutional scale of production, and see the theater continuing as an important civic institution.[119] This book aims to provide the re-evaluation of the evolution of song genres made necessary by this new understanding of theater lyric.

The many-headed Muse

This chapter has laid out the material available for a study of the late classical melic corpus. As cultural historians seek to rectify the distorted image of late classical *mousikē* inherited from historicist approaches, which were based on the reading of texts, they draw mainly from material history. As a result, their interpretation of the lyric poems themselves is not always contextualized in the lyric tradition and tends to be less sensitive to dynamics of allusion, emulation, and intertextuality than literary studies, especially those that focus on Hellenistic poetry. The chapters that follow here seek to keep to a middle road, relying largely on ancient texts as their source, read within a diachronic (literary) history of *mousikē*, but taking material history mainly as the synchronic context within which to read the poems. Yet although my principal interest is for the surviving corpus, I do not wish to pursue the analysis of already fragmentary remains of fourth-century poetic objects in a cultural vacuum, along the lines introduced by New Critics. This study of the surviving fragments of melic poetry occupies what I see as an unexplored space, a gap left between, on one hand, a cultural sociology of late classical *mousikē* that focuses on the institution rather than its artistic products and,

[118] Csapo 1999–2000; contra: Scullion 2002, with a response in Csapo 2003.
[119] Junker 2010.

on the other hand, a purely formal criticism of the surviving lyric corpus that lacks reference to actual performance context. The many-headed Muse serves as an illustration of the multiplicity of approaches to a varied corpus that this book offers: close readings, narratological analysis, and a focus on the rhetoric and pragmatics of texts.

2 | New Music and its myths

> M. Chopin increasingly affects the crudest modulations. Cunning must
> be the connoisseur indeed, who, while listening to his music, can form
> the slightest idea when wrong notes are played.
>
> Henry Fothergill Chorley, reviewing a Chopin recital in
> London in 1843

> Those who do not believe that genius is evident in superabundance of
> noise, looked in vain for a new musical message in Mr. Prokofiev's work.
> Nor in the Classical Symphony, which the composer conducted, was
> there any cessation from the orgy of discordant sounds. As an exposition
> of the unhappy state of chaos from which Russia suffers, Mr. Prokofiev's
> music is interesting but one hopes fervently that the future may hold
> better things both for Russia and listeners to Russian music.
>
> *Musical America*, December 1918

Every era has its new music, and late classical Athens was no exception.
Although neither the term "New Music" nor "musical revolution" was
used in antiquity, modern scholars employ both expressions in referring
to a moment of musical history mostly associated with the late fifth-
century musicians Melanippides, Phrynis, Cinesias, Telestes, Timotheus,
and Philoxenus, and with the tragedians Agathon and Euripides.[1] Ancient
sources depict these poets as having introduced a series of tonal, instrumental, and formal innovations in dithyrambs and nomes, as well as in the
solo and choral lyric parts of drama, changes apparently so dramatic that
they caused the "demise of *mousikē*" or even, more dramatically, the end of
an era.[2] But there is a surprising continuity across the vocabulary used by

---

[1] On the term "New Music," Csapo 2011: 66: "written as a proper noun, [it] is useful but
misleading." D'Angour 2006a: 267: "[the terms 'revolution' and 'New Music'] are
unapologetically applied by modern scholars to inventions in the late fifth century." What
modern scholars refer to as "New Music" was called by the ancients "theater music" (σκηνική or
θεατρική: see Arist. *Pol.* 8.1342a17–21, Aristox. fr. 70 Wehrli, [Plut.] *De mus.* 1140d–e, 1142c).
Because the term is so entrenched in modern vocabulary, I will continue using it as shorthand
for the spectacular choral and solo *mousikē* performed in a competitive setting in theaters in the
late fifth century and after.

[2] Σ Ar. *Nub.* 333d specifically ascribes the "demise of *mousikē*" (διαφθορὰν μουσικῆς) to the
dithyrambs.

these ancient critics – comic poets, musical and political theorists, and later authors writing musical histories – to describe the New Music of the late fifth century BC, and the vocabulary used by music critics of the nineteenth and early twentieth centuries to describe the music of their contemporaries, as illustrated by the two opening quotations, selected from the *Lexicon of Musical Invective*.³ The music of Philoxenus and the music of Chopin may not have much in common, yet their critics have employed much the same terminology in reacting to their "affecting the crudest modulations" – or what the comic poet Pherecrates calls "bends" (καμπαί).⁴ The music of both Timotheus and Prokofiev, no matter how harmonically different, is qualified by a "superabundance of noise" – as is suggested by Pherecrates' three references to "twelve notes" (χορδαὶ δώδεκα). And Prokofiev's music is deemed "an orgy of discordant sounds," the musical expression of an "unhappy state of chaos," terms reminiscent of the "most shameful" (αἴσχιστα), even "perverse" (ἐκτραπέλους), melodic runs of Timotheus.⁵ As is most evident in this last example, the parallels between ancient and modern responses to musical innovation go beyond the use of a similar critical lexicon and range of metaphors: both the comic poet and the critic writing for *Musical America* rely on an equivalence of music and morals, especially sexual morals, to describe the offence committed by the musicians and to represent the threat they embody for "the future of Russia" or that of Athens. The "newness" of the music is thus as much in the ears of the critics as in the music itself.

In light of this observation, the present chapter focuses on the myths of the "New Music revolution." By "myths" I mean two things: first, because the New Music is accessed more often through the comments of critics than through a reading of its texts, it is very much a critics' construct. As with a myth, its "history *is* the story of [its] reception."⁶ Not that there were no changes whatsoever in musical practice in the late fifth century: as stated in the previous chapter, historians of the theater have shown that momentous transformations took place in the scale of the production, performance, and consumption of *mousikē*.⁷ But my focus is less on the aural reality of the New Music than on its discourse and rhetoric: we must bear in mind that literary sources are not, as has all too often been thought,

---

³ Slonimsky 1953: 5–6.   ⁴ Pherecrates, fr. 155 KA.
⁵ Pherecrates, fr. 155 KA, lines 20 and 23 respectively.
⁶ Csapo and Wilson 2009a: 277 about Timotheus, but the comment can be extended to the whole phenomenon.
⁷ As noted in the previous chapter, Csapo 2004, revised in Csapo 2011, is fundamental to understanding the material conditions of the New Music and the changes introduced after 440 BC; D'Angour 2006a, 2007, and 2011: 184–206 for aspects of the aural reality of the experience of New Music.

straightforward documents about this musical phenomenon, but rather chart the reactions, creations, and reinventions of later critics. Second, the New Musicians themselves were the first to contribute to this myth, by their self-invention and their self-presentation, which included, but was not limited to, a reinterpretation of the concept of novelty. Other musical myths, including narratives about the origins of the instruments accompanying the songs, are an integral part of this self-definition, and one of the ways the New Musicians related to the poetic past was by engaging with the same kind of narrative material as their predecessors had used to shape and reshape the melic tradition to which they belonged. Before examining the rhetoric of self-presentation of the New Musicians, however, it is necessary to consider how the New Music has been presented, and created, by critics both ancient and modern, and how these selection screens have themselves determined our appreciation of the phenomenon of the New Music.

Labeling the New Music

Staging the New Music

The most familiar image of the New Music comes from Old Comedy, the earliest source for the reception of lyric: Aristophanes' parodies of Cinesias in the *Birds*, of Euripides and Agathon in the *Thesmophoriazousae*, and of Philoxenus' *Cyclops* in the *Plutus* describe and imitate the changes the New Musicians introduced. The novel features of the New Music presented in these parodies can be summarized under four headings: the use of *anabolai* (often translated "preludes," that is, response-less passages that replaced the triadic structure characteristic of choral songs in the dithyramb and odes of drama);[8] a mix of a greater variety of meters;[9] the use of melism (the dragging of one syllable onto different notes);[10] and a florid, exuberant

---

[8] Aristotle (*Rh.* 1409b26–30) reports that the fourth-century citharode Democritus of Chios described "a long *anabolē* [as] the greatest evil to its composer" (μακρὰ ἀναβολὴ τῷ ποιήσαντι κακίστη), referring to the songs of Melanippides. Aristotle (*Poet.* 1456a29–32) also refers to tragic *embolima*, choral odes that are "thrown in" and have little to do with the rest of the dramatic plot. On *anabolē* and the dithyramb, Comotti 1989; on the epic prehistory of the term *anabolē* used to describe the New Musicians' astrophic songs, Power 2010: 185–7.

[9] [Arist.] *Pr.* 19.15 (918b), on the necessity of having professionals, rather than amateur citizen choruses, perform polymetric and astrophic pieces. Heph. *Poem.* 3.3 describes Timotheus' citharodic nomes as composed "loosely" (ἀπολελυμένα) and "without meter" ⌈ἄνευ μέτρου⌉. On the polymetry of the New Musicians, Hordern 2002: 55–60.

[10] On melism, Pöhlmann 1960: 29–48, especially 34–6, Borthwick 1994: 31–2, Csapo 2004: 223–5, also Irigoin 2006, who discusses Dionysius of Halicarnassus' reading of the Euripides musical papyrus.

diction characterized in particular by compound words and neologisms.[11] These New Music labels are the singular features that allow a poet to make the "new Muse" a recognizable laughing stock for a comic audience.

The parody of Cinesias in the *Birds* (412 BC) distils nearly all these features. Appealing to Peisetairus to be admitted into the newly founded Cloudcuckooville, the poet boasts of "snowy preludes" (νιφοβόλους ἀναβολάς) on which, he specifies, the dithyrambists' art relies (1385–7). His song imitates the mix of rhythmic patterns typical of the New Music: when asked by the city founders what he wants, Cinesias starts with the regular iambic trimeter form of spoken dialogue (ὄρνις γενέσθαι βούλομαι, "I want to become a bird" 1380) but ends the line with a pherecratean typical of sung passages (λιγύφθογγος ἀηδών, "a mellifluous nightingale"), a metrical switch immediately underlined by Peisetairus (παῦσαι μελῳδῶν, "stop singing!" 1381) – in case the audience did not catch it. Similarly, in the *Frogs*, Euripides' odes and monodies are parodied as long astrophic arias, featuring instances of melism (εἰειειειλίσσετε, "twiiiiiirl" 1314, εἰειειειλίσσουσα, "twiiiiiirling" 1349) and a complicated metrical pattern that partly reflects the metrical variety of Euripides' compositions, but also illustrates Aristophanes' parodic exaggeration, which incidentally allows the comic poet to display his own New Music skills.[12]

Up until thirty years ago, this Identikit picture of the New Music, made up of a series of stylistic or musical traits reproduced in comedy, was the main means used (mostly by French, German, and Italian scholars) to describe the lyric innovations of the late classical period. Besides looking at the parodies of Aristophanes and at the formal characteristics of the late choral odes of Euripides, critics also focused on fragments in which New Musicians defined their own musical practice and on "metamusical" passages in drama. In this approach, 415 BC marks a turning point, as the date of Euripides' *Trojan Women*, in which Euripides uses the term "new songs" (καινῶν ὕμνων, 512), presumably to self-referentially acknowledge his innovations and his recourse to "dithyrambic odes."[13] His use of the term does not, however, tell

---

[11] On the diction of the New Musicians, see Chapter 4.

[12] On Aristophanes' own lyric art, Silk 1980 and 2000: 170. For lyric in the *Birds*, especially the hoopoe's monody: Pretagostini 1988, Zimmermann 1993, Dunbar 1995: 209–27, Trédé 2000, Barker 2004, Pöhlmann 2011a: 40–4; in the *Clouds*: Dover 1968: 137–42, Silk 1980, Sommerstein 1982: 176–8; in the *Frogs*, Pöhlmann 2011a: 51–61.

[13] One of the most influential studies treating the connection between New Music and tragedy remains Kranz' 1933 *Stasimon*, which devotes thirty-four pages to New Music (post 415 BC Euripidean tragedy), with a focus on the "dithyrambic stasima." This material is revisited in Panagl 1971, Webster 1967 and 1970, Pintacuda 1978. More recently, on the New Music of the *Trojan Women*, Battezzato 2005 and Sansone 2009.

us much about the tonal, instrumental, and musical characteristics of the
New Music, so critics have, again, turned to comedy, where they read these
changes in particular in a passage in Pherecrates' comedy *Cheiron* (fr. 155
KA), which describes the innovations introduced by the New Musicians.[14]

Pherecrates' passage stages Mousike (Mrs. Song-and-Dance), who
explains to Dike (Lady Justice) the outrage she has suffered at the hands
of musicians and their "modern" instruments. Each of their innovations is
metaphorically translated in sexual terms, and the New Music is again item-
ized, dissected into a series of traits. The passage starts with Melanippides
and Cinesias, and crescendoes with Phrynis and Timotheus, and possibly
Philoxenus:

> ἐμοὶ γὰρ ἦρξε τῶν κακῶν Μελανιππίδης,
> ἐν τοῖσι πρῶτος ὃς λαβὼν ἀνῆκέ με
> χαλαρωτέραν τ’ ἐποίησε χορδαῖς δώδεκα.   5
> ἀλλ’ οὖν ὅμως οὗτος μὲν ἦν ἀποχρῶν ἀνήρ
> ἔμοιγε . . . πρὸς τὰ νῦν κακά.
> Κινησίας δέ <μ’> ὁ κατάρατος Ἀττικός,
> ἐξαρμονίους καμπὰς ποιῶν ἐν ταῖς στροφαῖς,
> ἀπολώλεχ’ οὕτως, ὥστε τῆς ποιήσεως   10
> τῶν διθυράμβων, καθάπερ ἐν ταῖς ἀσπίσιν,
> ἀριστέρ’ αὐτοῦ φαίνεται τὰ δεξιά.
> ἀλλ’ οὖν ἀνεκτὸς οὗτος ἦν ὅμως ἐμοί.
>
> Pherecrates, fr. 155 KA (3–13)

It is Melanippides who started my troubles. He first took hold of me
and loosened me and made me slacker with his twelve strings. But that
fellow was still all right with me, compared to my present troubles. Then
Cinesias, that damn one from Attica, introduced some exharmonic twists
in my strophes, destroying me in such a way that, in the making of his
dithyrambs, the right seems to be the left, as a reflection on a shield. But
that fellow was still okay with me . . .

One of the most important melodic changes is the proliferation of καμπαί ("turns, bends"), a term used as a form of *terminus technicus* to refer
to harmonic modulations specifically within strophes.[15] These were made
possible by the structural alteration of both *aulos* and cithara, which allowed

---

[14] On the passage: Düring 1945, Borthwick 1968, Restani 1983; Zimmermann 1993, Dobrov and
  Urios-Aparisi 1995, Henderson 2000, Trédé 2000, Franklin forthcoming.

[15] The term is used two more times in the passage, lines 15 (κάμπτων με καὶ στρέφων, "bending
  and turning me") and 28 (καμπῶν, which puns on καμπή ["bend, modulation"] and κάμπη
  ["caterpillar"]). See also Ar. *Nub.* 333 ᾀσματοκάμπτας ("song-bender"), Ar. *Nub.* 969 κάμψειέν
  τινα καμπήν ("introduced a bend/modulation"), and Ar. *Nub.* 970 τὰς κατὰ Φρῦνιν ταύτας τὰς

a greater melodic range:[16] the twelve strings (χορδαὶ δώδεκα) that Pherecrates describes in reference to Melanippides, Phrynis, and Timotheus (lines
5, 16, 25) and the *strobilos* that Phrynis shoved in (14) allowed the use of
more notes and different *harmoniai*.[17] The introduction of *anabolai*, which
replaced the tighter triadic choral structure, is underlined by the reference
to the "more relaxed" form (χαλαρωτέραν, 5) that Melanippides gave to
mousikē, and to the destruction of the strophes introduced by Cinesias in
the making of his dithyrambs, "where the right seems to be the left, as a
reflection on a shield" (καθάπερ ἐν ταῖς ἀσπίσιν, ἀριστέρ᾽ αὐτοῦ φαίνεται
τὰ δεξιά, 11–12).

As Dobrov and Urios-Aparisi have neatly summarized, "Pherecrates'
conspiracy of metaphor, vagueness, repetition and comic topoi [and one
could add exaggeration and deformation] continues to engage students of
Greek music," and what the poet is describing, distorting, or even inventing
is not always evident.[18] What is clear, however, is that the passage uses a
limited number of "technical" terms (turns, many strings, looser structure),
and that it plays with the priamel form to present a comically distorted
version of musical history entirely focused on strings music. The repetition
of some expressions in particular (χορδαὶ δώδεκα and variations on ἀλλ᾽ οὖν
ἀνεκτὸς οὗτος ἦν ὅμως ἐμοί) is in tension with the crescendo of the priamel
intended to build toward the innovations of Timotheus: there is no clear

---

δυσκολοκάμπτους ("those difficult bends in the manner of Phrynis"). On modulations, Hagel
2000: 81–7 and Franklin forthcoming.

[16] Pherecrates' passage focuses on *cithara* players, not *aulos* players, but Pausanias (9.12.5–6)
refers to Pronomos' invention of a rotating collar for the *auloi*, which allowed a greater variety
of notes. On the multiplicity of pitches and modulations allowed by the technical innovations,
Hagel 2010: 377–90.

[17] The exact number of strings used by the New Musicians is debated. Both Timotheus and Ion of
Chios (fr. 32.1 W²) refer to a lyre with eleven, rather than twelve, strings. (On Ion's passage,
Levin 1961, Comotti 1972, Power 2007). The twelve strings Pherecrates refers to could be
generic and mean "many" (Düring 1945: 182, Maas 1992: 78, Zimmermann 1993: 41). But in
the three instances in which it occurs in Pherecrates, the expression χορδαὶ δώδεκα seems to be
used as a form of metrical and rhythmical stopgap, used to "fake" the language of musical
experts rather than to describe any musical reality. Moreover, it is difficult to make much
musical sense of the "twelve *harmoniai* on five strings" (ἐν πέντε χορδαῖς δώδεχ᾽ ἁρμονίας ἔχων,
16) in the case of Phrynis unless one accepts the theory of a pentatonic tuning of a few-stringed
lyre, which would allow for the possibility of creating a variety of notes by stopping or
strumming the strings – and thus creating "a dozen" *harmoniai* – on a simple instrument.
The hypothesis for a tuning of this form was refuted by Winnington-Ingram 1956. The
existence of the *strobilos*, maybe a pinecone-shaped device used to modulate between
harmoniai, is not well attested: Düring 1945: 186–94, Barker 1984: 94–5 and 237 n. 201,
Anderson 1994: 131. For a recent argument that takes into account archaeological evidence,
Pöhlmann 2011b: 126–31.

[18] Dobrov and Urios-Aparisi 1995: 157. Also Franklin forthcoming.

indication of musical evolution, but rather repetition and a great degree of self-absorption.

Othering the New Music

Another major element of Pherecrates' rhetoric relies on the confusion of musical, moral, and sexual categories.[19] The abuse of the body of a person-ified Mousike is not simply a metaphorical representation of the changes introduced by New Musicians (especially, in the case of this fragment, focused in the field of *kitharōidia*): it tells also of a moral evaluation of the art and its practitioners. The title of the play to which the quotation belongs, *Cheiron*, even suggests that the presence of Lady Mousike herself was motivated by the play's engagement with a specific genre of discourse, the "precepts of Cheiron," which was concerned with the education of young men and the transmission of wisdom through *mousikē*.[20] In the fragment, Mousike uses an aristocratic frame of reference to judge the New Musicians: to introduce her monologue, she relies on archaizing vocabulary: λέξω μὲν οὐκ ἄκουσα· σοί τε γὰρ κλυεῖν | ἐμοί τε λέξαι θυμὸς ἡδονὴν ἔχει ("I will hap-pily tell you: for it gladdens your heart to listen, and mine to tell"), using archaic κλυεῖν, rather than ἀκούειν. She also describes Timotheus' offense with reference to a context where she was "walking by herself" (μοι βαδι-ζούσῃ μόνῃ, 24), thus evoking the image of monodic song, accompanied by the amateur lyre, which any elite male would pride himself on being able to perform.[21] Moreover, when she tells Justice about the sexual abuse she has experienced, sex is not a matter of private preferences, but of norms: in the three quasi-formulaic lines in which she presents Melanippides, Cinesias, and Phrynis, Mousike underlines that the assault was, after all, tolerable.[22]

---

[19] On this common trope in musical discourse, Zimmermann 1993 and Dobrov and Urios-Aparisi 1995.

[20] Kurke 1990; on Pherecrates: "the collocation of μουσική and Chiron tends to confirm the inference that the Χείρωνος Ὑποθῆκαι was a text associated with the education of young men" (93). Other fragments of Pherecrates' *Cheiron* present reminiscences of the sympotic practices of the past (frr. 157–8 KA) and considerations on youth and old age (fr. 156 KA). Cratinus' comic *Cheirons* also contains a reference to the "precepts" (fr. 253 KA, a self-presentation of the chorus) and complaints about the decadence of music (frr. 247, 248, 254 KA), on which Bakola 2009: 54–5.

[21] See for example Ar. *Nub.* 1353–76, where Strepsiades asks his son Pheidippides to pick up the lyre and sing the "Shearing of the ram" or the Harmodius song. On this Aristophanic passage, see further Chapter 6, pp. 264–6.

[22] On that aspect, Power 2001: 198–200 and LeVen 2011: 249–50. One could perhaps also read the comic topos (*Lysistrata*-like) of the sex-craved female in what would be Mousike's not completely sincere complaints – in the formulaic repetition of "he wasn't that bad after all"

The vocabulary she uses to describe the offense has socio-political reson-
ances in the context of late fifth-century Athens: the "bends" and modulations that the New Musicians introduced are not quite in keeping with the
"straight" moral and ethical standards associated with the good citizen.[23]
Most explicitly, in the case of Timotheus, she uses the vocabulary of the
kaloskagathos: what Timotheus did to her was αἴχιστα ("most shameful")
and ἐκτραπέλους ("perverse"), the latter an adjective used, for example, by
Theognis in a couplet encapsulating aristocratic ideology.[24]

In this regard, the New Music is a creature not too different from the New
(Asianic) Rhetoric that Dionysius of Halicarnassus introduces in the opening paragraph of the preface of his *On the Ancient Orators*. The Old Attic
Rhetoric is described with an image strikingly similar to Pherecrates': she,
the freeborn, chaste, lawful wife, has been trampled in the mud (προπηλακι-
ζομένη), subjected to dreadful abuses (δεινὰς ὕβρεις ὑπομένουσα), and
threatened with disappearance (μικροῦ δεήσασα εἰς τέλος ἠφανίσθαι). By
contrast, the New Rhetoric, a harlot (ἑταίρα) who has just come from
Mysia, Phrygia, or Caria, is described as shameless, histrionic (θεατρικῇ),
and without an ounce of philosophy or education (οὔτε φιλοσοφίας οὔτε
ἄλλου παιδεύματος οὐδενὸς μετειληφυῖα ἐλευθερίου).[25] Dionysius uses similarly gendered and politically charged discourse to equate the abuse of the
sexual personified body of the art with the decadence of its practitioners.
One could say of the New Music what critics have noted about the Asianic
rhetoric: that as a new, lascivious, foreign, and low-class female, she is the
polar opposite of the construct of the idealized, autochthonous, upright,
and aristocratic Muse of the past, to which the conservative critics assimilate.
So whether the juxtaposition is with Old Music or Old Rhetoric, representation of the "New Muse" is equally influenced by the socio-political biases
of the sources, and fits into a discourse on the decadence of the culture of
the idealized past they associate themselves with.

This type of analysis has been provided by a more recent and mostly
Anglo-Saxon trend within scholarship on the New Music. In addition to

---

there is space to imagine that Mousike secretly did not dislike what was happening to her as
much as she tells Justice (on Mousike as hetaera, Henderson 2000).

[23] See Thgn. 535–6 W[2] for example: οὔποτε δουλείη κεφαλὴ <u>ἰθεῖα</u> πέφυκεν, | ἀλλ' αἰεὶ <u>σκολιὴ</u>
καὐχένα λοξὸν ἔχει ("never is a slavish head by nature <u>straight</u>, but always <u>crooked</u>, and it keeps
its neck askew"). See also Solon, fr. 4.36 W[2]: εὐθύνει δὲ δίκας <u>σκολιάς</u> ("[good order]
straightens crooked judgments"), on which Chapter 7, p. 320 n. 76.

[24] For the term, Thgn. 289–90 W[2]: νῦν δὲ τὰ τῶν ἀγαθῶν κακὰ γίνεται ἐσθλὰ κακοῖσιν | ἀνδρῶν·
γαίονται δ' <u>ἐκτραπέλοισι</u> νόμοις ("now the evils of good men are the noble deeds of bad men;
and those rejoice in <u>perverse</u> customs").

[25] Dion. Hal. *De antiquis oratoribus* 1.

continued reliance on the comic poets, critics have used a second series of descriptions of the New Music: reflections on music by fourth-century philosophers and theorists – Plato, Aristotle, and Aristoxenus. Like the comic poets, these authors judge the New Music in moral terms and make it the cause of the demise of *mousikē*, but they also extend the decadence to society, to both performers and *consumers* of this decadent art. The passage of Plato's *Laws* (700a–701a) quoted in the previous chapter describes how the new (vulgar, democratic, professional) musicians, by contrast with the musicians of old times (elite, aristocratic amateurs), sinned against the laws of music, were ruled by pleasure rather than good taste, and inspired the audience to be a noisy theatocracy. In the *Politics*, Aristotle expresses a similar idea in referring to a revolution (μεταβάλλειν) that occurred in the *audience* of musical pieces performed for competition – the kind of music affected by the New Music revolution – and explains that in music performed for competitions,

the practitioner does not strive for his own excellence, but works for the pleasure of the audience, and it is a vulgar (φορτικῆς) pleasure. Wherefore we judge it to be the practice not of free-born men (οὐ τῶν ἐλευθέρων τὴν ἐργασίαν) but somewhat menial (θητικωτέραν). And performers do become vulgar (βαναύσους), for the goal that they aim at is lowly (πονηρός). Thus it is the baseness of the spectator that usually alters the music (ὁ γὰρ θεατὴς φορτικὸς ὢν μεταβάλλειν εἴωθε τὴν μουσικήν), so that it gives a specific type of personality to the performers that practice it, and to their body because of the movements involved.

Arist. Pol. 8.1341b

Rather than discuss musical, melodic, or instrumental features, Aristotle bases his depiction of the New Music on ethical and socio-political considerations. A similar discourse on the professionalization of music, said to have brought with it vulgarity, baseness, and lack of moral standing in both performers and audiences, is evident when Aristoxenus complains that "theaters have been barbarized, and vulgar *mousikē* has brought with it great ruin" (τὰ θέατρα ἐκβεβαρβάρωται καὶ εἰς μεγάλην διαφθορὰν προελήλυθεν ἡ πάνδημος αὕτη μουσική).[26] Finally, this nostalgic presentation is epitomized in the pseudo-Plutarchian *De musica*, a treatise whose importance "lies in its lack of originality."[27] This work is principally a collage of quotations and passages of earlier authors on musical history, practice, and theory, especially the Peripatetics Aristoxenus and Heraclitus of Pontus,

---

[26] Fr. 124 Wehrli. The terms used by Aristoxenus, διαφθορὰ μουσικῆς, are the exact same as those used in Σ Ar. *Nub.* 333d to describe the demise introduced by dithyrambs.

[27] Barker 1984: 205.

and it reproduces their elite conservative ideology while following a loose narrative framework. The dialogue refers several times to the composers associated with the New Music and settles on three terms that encapsulate the changes introduced by the revolution in *aulos* and cithara music: καινοτομία ("thirst for innovation"), πολυχορδία ("use of many strings"), and ποικιλία ("elaboration").

The *De musica* opens with a presentation of "what inventions time has brought to the advancement of the history [of music]" (τί εὗρεν πρὸς αὔξησιν ταύτης ὁ χρόνος, 1131e). The long list runs through innovations in musical practice (cithara-, *auloi*-, and panpipes-playing), in rhythms, musical genres, melodic structure, and instrument technology. After introducing mythical, quasi-mythical, and historical figures, from Amphion and Orpheus to the sixth-century Sacadas and Lasus, it abruptly concludes with a short mention of the late fifth-century composers:

> Crexus, Timotheus, and Philoxenus and other poets of the same period who were particularly vulgar and interested in novelty (φορτικώτεροι καὶ φιλόκαινοι) pursued the style nowadays called "popular" and "profiteering" (τὸ φιλάνθρωπον καὶ θεματικόν). The result was that music limited to a few strings and simple and dignified in character (τὴν ὀλιγοχορδίαν καὶ τὴν ἁπλότητα καὶ σεμνότητα τῆς μουσικῆς) went quite out of fashion (ἀρχαικὴν εἶναι συμβέβηκεν).
>
> [Plut.] *De mus.* 1135c–d

The first speaker's evaluation of the music of Timotheus and his contemporaries is, once again, moral and political.[28] The anti-democratic vocabulary of the passage is even reminiscent of that of Aristotle in his discussion of music in *Politics* 8, quoted above: the adjective φορτικώτεροι ("more vulgar") is used twice (1340b and 1341b) by Aristotle to describe the tastes of the mob, and θεματικόν and φιλάνθρωπον ("popular" and "profiteering") are reminiscent of Aristotle's description of the professional musicians as θητικωτέρα ("somewhat menial"). The New Musicians' love of innovation is portrayed as differing in nature rather than degree from the ancients', for ancient innovations were still ruled by "good" taste (οὐκ ἀφεστῶσαι τοῦ καλοῦ, 1135c).[29] This distinction is also expressed, and in an even more radical way, by the second speaker of the dialogue, Sotesichorus:

---

[28] For the meaning of θεματικόν: Poll. 3.153 explains that the sacred contests fell into two categories, the *stephanitai* (where the prize was a crown) and the *thematikoi* (where the prize was money). For a different interpretation, Lasserre (1954 ad loc.) and Barker (1984: 218 n. 90), who deems the account "almost devoid of content."

[29] Although καινός is used of Terpander, Polymnestus, Thaletas, Sacadas, Alcman, and Stesichorus, all are associated with classicism and with a sense of measure. Thaletas and Sacadas, for example, are described as "not straying from the canon of beauty" (οὐκ ἐκβαίνοντες μέντοι τοῦ καλοῦ τύπου, *De mus.* 1135c).

One could say: "So my friend, you mean that the archaic poets made no invention or innovation (οὐδὲν . . . προσεξεύρηται καὶ κεκαινοτόμηται)?" To which I too say that there were inventions (προσεξεύρηται), but they were done in accordance with what is noble and befitting (μετὰ τοῦ σεμνοῦ καὶ πρέποντος).

[Plut.] De mus. 1140f

The two other characteristics of the New Music described in the treatise are its reliance on many strings (*polychordia*) and elaboration (*poikilia*):

The lyric poet Melanippides who flourished later did not remain within the kind of music that had preceded him, nor did Philoxenus or Timotheus. For Timotheus scattered about and increased the number of notes on the lyre (διέρριψεν εἰς πλείονας φθόγγους), which had been seven-noted (ἑπταφθόγγου) as far back as Terpander of Antissa. *Aulos*-playing also introduced a change in music, from simplicity to greater complexity (αὐλητικὴ ἀπὸ ἁπλουστέρας εἰς ποικιλωτέραν μεταβέβηκε μουσικήν).

[Plut.] De mus. 1141c–d

The passage highlights the same features as those presented by Pherecrates and reproduces the Platonic and Aristotelian fantasy of a simple and digni-fied archaic music that the New Music revolutionized. As Csapo and Wilson have noted, "most or all the central terms relating to the technical develop-ments in music seem to have been the site of ideological struggle: plurality, changeability, innovation, openness, liberation, inclusiveness and mixing," and they continue, "it was a very easy step to make those 'multiple notes' (*polychordia*) an icon of democracy's pluralistic excess, a babble of noise and voices (*polyphthongia*) like the masses in Assembly."[30]

While some of the most recent and most stimulating accounts of the New Music have sprung from this type of socio-political interpretation, one needs to keep in mind a few more interpretative options. For the New Music was not *only* an invention of conservative critics who exploited the political associations of the terms used by the musicians themselves, and it was not *the only* musical revolution. Greece underwent. No matter how politicized and charged the terms used by the musicians were, they also described tonal and instrumental changes. Passages from the *De musica* itself, testimonies of historiographers and historians of music, and fragments of earlier lyric poets suggest that the New Music revolution of the late fifth century has to be understood against the background of earlier Argive and Athenian revolu-tions, in the early sixth and late sixth/early fifth centuries respectively.[31] First, Polymnestus, Sacadas of Argos, and Lasus of Hermione were representative

---

[30] Csapo and Wilson 2009a: 291–2, with further reference to Csapo 2004, now developed in Csapo 2011, especially p. 88 n. 123 on the critical vocabulary of multiplicity.

[31] On the earlier musical revolutions, Cassio 1971, Barker 1984: 47–61, Wallace 2003, Prauscello 2012, Franklin forthcoming.

of the Argive efflorescence that Herodotus situates during the reign of Poly-crates (*ca.* 540–522 BC), "[when] the Argives were held to be first among the Hellenes in music."[32] The *De musica* (1141c) ascribes to Lasus the introduction of many-notedness in *aulos*-playing (πλείοσί τε φθόγγοις καὶ διερριμμένοις χρησάμενος), based on the wide range of the instrument (τῇ τῶν αὐλῶν πολυφωνίᾳ). It also ascribes (1142f) to Sacadas compositions in alternate modes, the first in the Dorian, the second in the Phrygian, and the last in the Lydian, illustrating an early case of modulation, which Philoxenus took further in his dithyramb *Mysians*.[33] Later Pythocles, Agathocles, and Lamprocles, all Athenians, were involved in experimentations with *harmoniai* as well (1136c), and there is substantial evidence that even Pindar and Simonides, often considered representatives of the old style, participated in an Athenian *aulos* revolution that followed the Argive efflorescence but predated the New Music of the late fifth century.[34] Two *Lives* of Pindar in particular make the poet a student of the innovators Lasus and Pythocles; one of Pindar's prooemia celebrated the innovative aulete Sacadas of Argos, and one of his dithyrambs (fr. 70b SM) seemed to emulate Lasus' experimentation with asigmatism.[35] It is certainly easy to imagine that the author of the *De musica* retrojected some of the features of the New Music onto more archaic *mousikē* and reimagined the past in the light of the present. But scholars of ancient music have shown specific differences in the nature of the changes introduced by these revolutions. In particular, in a detailed investigation of the nature of the "turns" and modulations introduced by the New Musicians in the late fifth century, John Franklin highlights an important aspect of the first musical revolutions Comparing the uses of the terms *kampē* and *strophē* across choral lyric metaphors, Attic tragedy terms, and later rhetorical terminology, Franklin shows that the modulations introduced by the early *aulos* composers were modulations *at strophic boundaries*, while those of the New Musicians were modulations that *did not correspond to strophic boundaries*. He concludes that

there were two strata of meaning and practice for the term *kampê* in its application to modulation, corresponding to the earlier and later phases of the "*aulos* revolution"

---

[32] Hdt. 3.131. Also [Plut.] *De mus.* 1134a–b.

[33] On the modulations, Hagel 2010: 388–90, Fongoni 2011. The musician Pythagoras of Zakynthos also invented a cithara with three sides that allowed him to modulate between three modes (Artemon, *ap.* Ath. 14.637c–e), on which D'Angour 2006a and 2011: 182–3.

[34] For Pindar as representative of the old style, Dion. Hal. *Comp.* 22.10–12, which quotes a dithyramb of Pindar (fr. 75 SM) as representative of the αὐστηρὰ ἁρμονία; [Plut.] *De mus.* 1142b. On Pindar as representative of the early fifth-century revolution, Wallace 2003: 77–81, Prauscello 2012, who thoroughly examines the paradox, and Franklin forthcoming.

[35] For the prooemion, Paus. 9.30.2; on Pindar's asigmatic dithyramb, D'Angour 1997.

(Lasus, Simonides, Pindar *et alii* versus the New Music respectively). They support the thesis that the innovation attributed to Clonas and Sacadas in the historiographical tradition was not some one-off experiment, but became common and acceptable usage in choral poetry by the end of the Archaic period, and continued to be elaborated thereafter.[36]

The work of Hagel, Wallace, Franklin, and Prauscello, who examine the features of the late fifth-century revolution in the light of the features of earlier revolutions, goes a long way to correcting the bias introduced by a certain type of criticism that depicts the late fifth-century New Music as *the* New Music revolution, when in fact it was only the latest, and best documented, in a series of revolutions.

Economic and cultural context

The constantly changing nature of *mousikē* needs, however, to be read also in the light of a third, and final, type of ancient testimony, a source that describes the social, cultural, and economic background of the New Music, especially the economic and cultural changes introduced by the "professional music" of the *aulos*. A passage from the *De musica* and a series of late classical lyric quotations from Athenaeus' *Deipnosophistae* suggest that one of the most spectacular changes associated with the New Music was the growing importance of the *auloi* and their place in musical performance.[37] At the opening of the penultimate book of the *Deipnosophistae*, a guest launches into a discussion of entertainment with a quotation of Melanippides, whom he presents as disparaging *aulos*-playing (διασύροντα τὴν αὐλητικήν) in his *Marsyas* in the following words:

> ἁ μὲν Ἀθάνα
> τὤργαν' ἔρριψέν θ' ἱερᾶς ἀπὸ χειρὸς
> εἶπέ τ'· ἔρρετ' αἴσχεα, σώματι λύμα·
> ὔμμε δ' ἐγὼ κακότατι δίδωμι.

> 4 Wilamowitz: ἐμὲ δ' ἐγὼ codd., ἐμὲ δ' ἐγὼ <οὐ> ci. Maas

> Melanippides, *PMG* 758 *ap.* Ath. 14.616e

Athena cast the instruments away from her holy hand and said: "away with you, shameful things, outrage to my body! I relegate you to misery!"[38]

---

[36] Franklin forthcoming.

[37] For the radical material, economic, and aesthetic changes introduced by the *aulos* and the growing class of auletes, Csapo 2004, revised in Csapo 2011.

[38] The text of this fragment is uncertain, but Campbell's reading is more convincing than Maas' (ἐμὲ δ' ἐγὼ οὐ), which would imply that Athena dwells on her own attitude to the *auloi*: "I do

In a manner typical of the progression of the *Deipnosophistae*, a second guest counters by saying that Telestes, doubting this myth, "took up arms against Melanippides" (ἀντικορυσσόμενος) and defended the art of *aulos*-playing in his *Argo*:[39]

(a) †ὃν†σοφὸν σοφὰν λαβοῦσαν οὐκ ἐπέλπομαι νόῳ
δρυμοῖς ὀρείοις ὄργανον
δίαν Ἀθάναν δυσόφθαλμον αἶσχος ἐκφοβη-
      θεῖσαν αὖθις χερῶν ἐκβαλεῖν
νυμφαγενεῖ χειροκτύπῳ φηρὶ Μαρσύᾳ κλέος·
τί γάρ νιν εὐηράτοιο κάλλεος ὀξὺς ἔρως ἔτειρεν,   5
ᾇ παρθενίαν ἄγαμον καὶ ἄπαιδ᾽ ἀπένειμε Κλωθώ;

ὡς οὐκ ἂν εὐλαβηθείης τὴν αἰσχρότητα τοῦ εἴδους διὰ τὴν παρθενίαν, ἑξῆς
τέ φησι·

(b) ἀλλὰ μάταν ἀχόρευτος ἅδε ματαιολόγων
φάμα προσέπταθ᾽ Ἑλλάδα μουσοπόλων
σοφᾶς ἐπίφθονον βροτοῖς τέχνας ὄνειδος.

μετὰ ταῦτα δὲ ἐγκωμιάζων τὴν αὐλητικὴν λέγει·

(c) ἂν συνεριθοτάταν Βρομίῳ παρέδωκε σεμνᾶς
δαίμονος ἀερθὲν πνεῦμ᾽ αἰολοπτέρυγον
σὺν ἀγλαᾶν ὠκύτατι χειρῶν.

      Telestes, *PMG* 805 *ap.* Ath. 14.616f–617a

(a) I cannot conceive of the clever lady, divine Athena, taking the clever instrument in the mountain thickets, and, fearing shamefulness unpleasant to see, immediately throwing it away from her hands to be the *kleos* of the hand-clapping nymph-born beast Marsyas! No, why would a keen love for lovely beauty distress her, to whom Clotho allotted marriageless and childless virginity?

[So he says,] because she, being a virgin, does not care about the ugliness of her features, and he goes on:

(b) But this is a tale unsuitable for the chorus that has idly flown to Greece, told by idle servants of the Muses, an invidious insult to the clever art among mortals.

Then in praise of the art of *aulos*-playing, he says:

not give myself to debasement." Campbell's text makes Athena's pronouncement a performative statement: by stating that she throws away the *aulos*, she consigns them to misery in the poetic tradition too.
[39] On the text, Livrea 1975, Comotti 1980.

(c) which the uplifted quick-fluttering breath of the august goddess, along with the swiftness of her splendid hands, gave to Bromius as a most helpful attendant.

The passage is immediately followed by a historical contextualization that describes a change in the relationship with auletes and chorus, illustrated by a passage of Pratinas:

When mercenary auletes and choreutes (αὐλητῶν καὶ χορευτῶν μισθοφόρων) started invading the dancing-places [in the theaters], Pratinas of Phlias says that some got angry[40] at the fact that the auletes no longer accompanied the chorus, as in the good old days, but that instead the chorus accompanied the auletes (ἐπὶ τῷ τοὺς αὐλητὰς μὴ συναυλεῖν τοῖς χοροῖς, καθάπερ ἦν πάτριον, ἀλλὰ τοὺς χοροὺς συνᾴδειν τοῖς αὐληταῖς). So the opinion he holds of those behaving in such manner, Pratinas makes clear in the following *Hyporchema* [*PMG* 708].

Ath. 14.617b–f

This passage is quoted after two fragments of the New Musicians Melanippides and Telestes, and the thematic continuity has led critics to make Pratinas contemporary with the late fifth-century musical revolution. But both the date of the Pratinas passage and the tone of the criticism are hard to assess. In their discussions, modern critics have had to juggle two sets of data, the date and the tone: if Pratinas is to be dated early (late sixth or early fifth century), as most other ancient sources suggest, the chorus could be reacting against an earlier musical revolution.[41] If Pratinas is to be dated to the later fifth century, as a contemporary of the New Musicians, the chorus could be either resisting the changes in musical culture, perhaps genuinely, or advertising them with mock indignation by mouthing the opinion of conservative critics.[42] Regardless of the actual date of Pratinas, the general picture a reader gets from Athenaeus' account of the three passages is that at some point in the fifth century BC, the playing of the *auloi* became a

---

[40] My translation follows Olson's Loeb text, which prints ἀγανακτεῖν τινας. Gulick 1941, Campbell 1991, and Canfora 2001 (after Wilamowitz) print ἀγανακτήσας.

[41] The details of the debate over Pratinas' chronology are discussed and documented by Prauscello 2012: 73 n. 89 and Franklin forthcoming. For an early date (fifth century or earlier), Seaford 1977–8, West 1992: 343, Ieranò 1997: 218–26, Napolitano 2000, Barker 2002: 56, Cipolla 2003, Power 2010: 397–8, Prauscello 2012: 73–4. For a late fifth-century date, Pickard-Cambridge 1962: 17–20, Lloyd-Jones 1966, Zimmermann 1986 and 1989: 29–30, Hamilton 1990, Wallace 2003: 85 (who distinguishes between the "Pratinas" author of the hyporcheme and an earlier Pratinas), Csapo 2004: 214; Franklin forthcoming. I favor the earlier dating, exactly for the two reasons that Prauscello cogently presents.

[42] On the tone: Csapo 2004 argues that the chorus of this late fifth-century piece is a pastiche of conservative critics. D'Alessio (2007: 118 and n. 53) suggests that *PMG* 708 might be a late fifth-century pseudepigraphic piece ascribed to the sixth-century Pratinas.

major topic of cultural debate and prompted three poets, two of whom are securely associated with the New Music, to take sides, either condemning or defending *aulos* music in their songs.[43] Athenaeus, moreover, locates the cause of this "revolution" in the changed economic situation of *aulos* players and choreutes, who ceased being representatives of the civic body and became mercenaries.

A second passage, from the *De musica* (1141c–d), presents a strikingly similar situation, including the change in the source of the auletes' pay, but explicitly makes it a later fifth-century phenomenon:

> In the old days, up to the time of Melanippides, the composer of dithyrambs, the auletes used to receive a salary from the poets (τοὺς αὐλητὰς παρὰ τῶν ποιητῶν λαμβάνειν τοὺς μισθούς), which shows that poetry was the main actor and the auletes were subordinate to their instructors (πρωταγωνιστούσης δηλονότι τῆς ποιήσεως, τῶν δ' αὐλητῶν ὑπηρετούντων τοῖς διδασκάλοις). But later even this changed, as the comic poet Pherecrates shows by staging *mousikē* in the guise of a woman whose body has been completely mistreated [in the following passage (fr. 155 KA)].
>
> [Plut.] *De mus.* 1141c–d

The ideological bias of this fragment is the same as in the fragment of Athenaeus. They both describe similar scenarios, and both authors locate the cause of the revolution in economic change. But the parallel might be suspect, in particular since the verb used in the *De musica* to describe the traditional relationship between musical accompaniment and song, ὑπηρετούντων, is formed on the distinctive image of "service" contained in ὑπηρέτας (*PMG* 708.7), used in the poem of Pratinas quoted in the *Deipnosophistae*. One likely hypothesis is that the source on which both pseudo-Plutarch and Athenaeus rely was glossing the Pratinas poem in a historicist reading typical of ancient musical scholarship. If Pratinas belongs to the early fifth century, the source in question would be interpreting the passage of the hyporcheme (which says nothing about the actual social or economic conditions of *aulos*-playing) in the light of the second, late fifth-century, musical revolution.

Strategies of self-representation

The ancient portraits of the new Muse and the modern approaches that I have reviewed draw on different types of literary testimony to describe the

---

[43] Given these verbal echoes, we should not exclude the possibility that Melanippides and Telestes are playing with a third (lost) text, to whose imagery or phraseology they both allude.

New Music. Starting from these sources, scholars have emphasized either change in the formal features of songs, tonal, rhythmic, and instrumental innovation, altered attitudes toward instruments and what they mean, or transformations in the social and economic base of musical practice. In most of these accounts, New Music is the Other; it represents the decadence of democracy, or radicalizes, for the worse, anything that earlier revolutions started. But behind the multiplicity of approaches and overlapping images of the New Music lies something important: the rhetoric of the New Musicians themselves. Many of the key terms that the critics use and the images they present are based on the *persona* the New Musicians presented in their own compositions. So after the "outside in" approach I have presented above, I turn now to an "inside out" approach, to show how the image that the New Musicians presented of themselves and their art in their compositions contributed to shaping their critics' vocabulary. The New Musicians relied on a series of polysemic ideas (including that of novelty and of *poikilia*), terms, and myths, that allowed them to create a complex self-image and to manipulate in different ways the tradition to which they belong.

Kainotomia: *the rhetoric of the old*

The new Muse is as old as Homer. Telemachus, a prototype of the literary critic, is the first to use the new Muse topos and state the appeal of novelty in songs:

> τὴν γὰρ ἀοιδὴν μᾶλλον ἐπικλείουσ᾽ ἄνθρωποι,
> ἥ τις ἀκουόντεσσιν νεωτάτη ἀμφιπέληται.
> Hom. *Od.* 1.351–2[44]

> For men praise most that song which comes the newest to their ears.

Most lyric poets made the same claim about novelty, all the while using diction, motives, and themes that link them to the poetic past. This is the case, for example, with Pindar, who in one of his epinicians refers to his new composition with an adjective that echoes a Homeric formula:

> λάμβανέ οἱ στέφανον, φέρε δ᾽ εὔμαλλον μίτραν,
> καὶ <u>πτερόεντα νέον</u> σύμπεμψον ὕμνον.
> Pind. *Isthm.* 5.62–3

---

[44] Plato (*Rep.* 424b) quotes a slightly different version of the second line, ἥτις <u>ἀειδόντεσσι</u> νεωτάτη ἀμφιπέληται (which comes newest to the <u>singers</u>), which focuses on the production, rather than on the reception, of novelty. On this passage, D'Angour 2011: 184–90.

> Take a crown for him, bring a headdress of fine wool, and send along my
> winged new song.

The adjective πτερόεντα ("winged") is unmistakably Homeric (cf. the formula ἔπεα πτερόεντα, "winged words"), but the reality it describes, a νέον
ὕμνον ("new song"), is different from Homer's both in nature and in time:
not spoken words (ἔπεα) but a melic composition; not the utterances of
heroes of the past but words freshly produced for the latest pancratic victor at the Isthmian games. Another Pindaric ode underlines the temporal
dimension in νέος ("new, fresh"):

> ἔγειρ' ἐπέων σφιν οἶμον λιγύν,
> αἴνει δὲ <u>παλαιὸν</u> μὲν οἶνον, ἄνθεα δ' <u>ὕμνων</u>
> <u>νεωτέρων</u>.
>
> <div align="right">Pind. <i>Ol.</i> 9.47–9</div>

> Rouse for them the clear-sounding path of song – praise wine that is <u>aged</u>,
> but the flower of the <u>freshest songs</u>.

As D'Angour has made clear, one of several ways in which the Greeks
conceived of novelty was in the opposition between νέος and παλαιός (what
has been around for a long time). νέος designates the youngest, latest, freshest
in a series and inherently contains "an organic or generational metaphor,
one of growth and development over time."[45] Yet the novelty that Pindar
advertises does not seem to be the same as that associated with the New
Musicians. For one thing, the adjective often used by critics to refer to the
New Musician's novelty is καινός, not νέος. The contrast in nature that exists
at the end of the fifth century between the two adjectives is illustrated in a
passage from Euripides' satyr-play *Cyclops*:

> {Σι.} <u>τὰ καινά</u> γ' ἐκ τῶν ἠθάδων, ὦ δέσποτα,   250
> ἡδίον' ἐστίν. οὐ γὰρ οὖν <u>νεωστί</u> γε
> ἄλλοι πρὸς ἄντρα σοὺσαφίκοντο ξένοι.
>
> <div align="right">Eur. <i>Cyc.</i> 250–2</div>

> Silenos: <u>Novelties</u> [i.e. things new in kind] that change from your regular
> diet, Master, that's what's most pleasant; for it's not <u>fresh news</u> [i.e. at the
> newest point in time] that strangers have come to your cave.

Silenus underlines the difference between νέος, the latest chronologically,
and καινός, what is novel, newly invented, different in quality, or perceived

---

[45] D'Angour 2011: 187.

as such – the flesh of strangers by contrast with the cheese-and-vegetables diet of the Cyclops.[46]

The most explicit contrast between the two adjectives, and explicit positioning of the notion of "novelty," appears in a passage of Timotheus that is taken to be part of the *sphragis* of one of his compositions:

> οὐκ ἀείδω τὰ παλαιά,
> καινὰ γὰρ ἁμὰ κρείσσω·
> νέος ὁ Ζεὺς βασιλεύει,
> τὸ πάλαι δ' ἦν Κρόνος ἄρχων·
> ἀπίτω Μοῦσα παλαιά.   5
>
>   Timoth. *PMG* 796

I don't sing the ancient songs, because the novel ones I compose are better. It is the young Zeus who is king, but in ancient times Cronos was the ruler. Let the Muse of old go away!

The fragment relies on two distinctions, between older and more recent, and between old-fashioned and new age. Since τὰ παλαιά is the concept common to both, the *persona loquens* of Timotheus' poem is playing on the blurring of the two concepts of newness and novelty, in time and in kind, and makes overly explicit that he is pursuing the novel. Yet there are some traditional features even in his ambitious revolutionary statement: by using the metaphor of divine genealogy and a tone reminiscent of gnomic or didactic poetry, the poet draws on a well-established theogonic model.[47] At the same time, the adduced succession model hints at the revolutionary potential of his songs: the transfer of power from Cronos to Zeus was not exactly peaceful, and the choice of subversive metaphor provides the critics with a political vocabulary they could, and eagerly did, use against the musicians.

One would be hard-pressed, however, to find this kind of revolutionary manifesto throughout the corpus of New Music: this overly explicit defense of novelty is an isolated phenomenon in the self-presentation of poets. The

---

[46] The lexical opposition does not seem to exist before the late fifth century, and the term καινός is not used in Homer or Pindar: when Telemachus describes the "new" (νέος) song that pleases men's ears in the passage previously quoted, he is describing a different theme, a symbolically novel topic that marks the young hero's own new beginning. For a detailed analysis of the semantics of novelty, D'Angour 2011: 19–27. On the emergence of καινός, D'Angour 2011: 71–84.

[47] The parallel with Pratinas, who also describes the situation of music in cosmo-political terms, might be significant: Pratinas, *PMG* 708.6 τὰν ἀοιδὰν κατέστασε Πιερὶς βασίλειαν ("the Pierian one has established song as queen").

tone of other self-reflexive passages is much more restrained than the fragment just examined, and the strategy of self-presentation more complex, as illustrated in particular by the most famous passage of New Music, the *sphragis* of Timotheus' *Persians*. Three features of the rhetoric of this passage, all of which also appear in other late classical metamusical statements, are particularly important: the reliance on older poetic and rhetorical tropes to legitimize newness; a self-presentation that mixes literary criticism and literary history to describe an invention of tradition; and the careful construction of innovation as a constant progress that amounts to a tradition of innovations.

Legitimizing newness

The *sphragis* of Timotheus' *Persians* is the part of this poem that has received the most attention.[48] It opens with a traditional apostrophe to Apollo:

> ἀλλ' ὦ χρυσεοκίθαριν ἀέ-
>   ξων Μοῦσαν νεοτευχῆ,
> ἐμοῖς ἔλθ' ἐπίκουρος ὕμ-
>   νοις ἰήϊε Παιάν.   205
>   Timoth. *PMG* 791.202–5

But you who protect the <u>newly fashioned Muse</u> with the golden cithara, come as an ally to help me defend my songs, Iē Lord Paean.

In contrast to the passage quoted above (*PMG* 796), these lines are not a violent manifesto for a radical new music. The cautious tone of the ending of the *Persians* responds to the careful hexametric opening of the poem. According to the *De musica*,

[Timotheus] sang the beginning of his nomes in hexameters (πρώτους νόμους ἐν ἔπεσι) while mixing dithyrambic diction (διθυραμβικὴν λέξιν), to avoid making it obvious that he was immediately breaking the laws of ancient *mousikē* (παρανομῶν εἰς τὴν ἀρχαίαν μουσικήν).

[Plut.] *De mus.* 1132e

An anecdote recounted by Plutarch in his *Life of Philopoemen* and by Pausanias (8.50.3) actually preserves one of the first hexameters of the song:

> <u>κλεινὸν</u> ἐλευθερίας τεύχων <u>μέγαν</u> Ἑλλάδι <u>κόσμον</u>.
>   Timoth. *PMG* 788

making the <u>great and glorious ornament</u> of Freedom for Greece.

---

[48] Kranz 1962, Nieddù 1993, Ercoles 2010, Power 2010: 516–49. On the relationship between this passage and the rest of the narrative, see Chapter 5.

It is not simply the meter of the line but also its *ethos* that recall earlier poetry on the Persian Wars, including an encomium of Simonides celebrating the men who died at Thermopylae:

> μαρτυρεῖ δὲ καὶ Λεωνίδας,
> Σπάρτας βασιλεύς, ἀρετᾶς μέγαν λελοιπὼς
> κόσμον ἀέναόν τε κλέος.
>
> Simonides, *PMG* 531.7–9

> Witness Leonidas, the king of Sparta, who has left behind the great ornament of his manly virtue and his imperishable glory.

Just as the opening lines of the song rely on the memory of a public encomium that could have been performed at a remembrance ceremony at a shrine in Sparta, the concluding *sphragis* sounds like a traditional hymnic appeal to the Muses or to their leader, Apollo.[49] Yet behind what looks like a rhetorical gesture giving an artificial old frame to a new kind of song, there is much more.

The first reference to novelty is introduced in the apostrophe to Apollo (ὦ χρυσεοκίθαριν ἀέξων Μοῦσαν νεοτευχῆ, *PMG* 791.202–3), depicted with his celebrated attribute, the cithara, the very instrument that the performer of the *Persians* would be playing.[50] The use of the compound νεοτευχής ("newly fashioned") to qualify the Muse that Apollo protects is representative of the poem's rhetorical strategy as it combines what looks like a metatextual claim for originality with a Homeric hapax. The adjective was used in the *Iliad* (5.193–4) to describe the "eleven beautiful chariots, newly fashioned and constructed for the first time" (ἔνδεκα δίφροι καλοὶ πρωτοπαγεῖς νεοτευχέες) found in Lykaon's mansion. As Hordern (2002 ad loc.) notes, the compound suggests that "Timotheus regards . . . music as a craft." But just as in the only other post-Homeric instance in which the compound adjective is used – in Theocritus, *Idyll* 1. 28, of a "newly fashioned double-handed drinking-cup, still redolent of the chisel" (κισσύβιον . . . ἀμφῶες, νεοτευχές, ἔτι γλυφάνοιο ποτόσδον) – the use of the adjective here is also a programmatic statement about the song's poetics.[51] While the transfer of an epithet qualifying a war item (a chariot) in Homer to a domestic piece of tableware in Theocritus signals a shift from epic to bucolic poetry, the shift accomplished by the passage from the *Persians* is of a different nature. The adjective can be perceived as transferred from an actual chariot to a metaphorical chariot – the chariot of song – in a very self-conscious and

---

[49] On the conditions of performance of Simonides' poem, Bowra 1961: 342–9, Podlecki 1968, West 1975: 308–9.

[50] Power 2010: 11–27, on the visual and symbolic power of the instrument itself.

[51] Hunter 1999 ad loc. On craft as a metaphor for poetry, Steiner 1986, 52–65; Ford 2002: 113–30.

self-reflexive move.[52] In qualifying his poetic process with a compound adjective used in Homer of a real artifact, Timotheus simultaneously practices Homeric scholarship, for he gives new life to what appears to be an archaic hapax, and acknowledges his poetic debt, by attaching the heroic topic of the *Persians* (the battle of Salamis) to an epic predecessor.

This generic cue is particularly charged, as a contemporary of Timotheus, Choerilus of Samos, uses a similar image and compound.[53] In the opening apology of his new epic narrative on the Persian Wars, Choerilus laments:

> ἆ μάκαρ, ὅστις ἔην κεῖνον χρόνον ἴδρις ἀοιδῆς,
> Μουσάων θεράπων, ὅτ' ἀκήρατος ἦν ἔτι λειμών·
> νῦν δ' ὅτε πάντα δέδασται, ἔχουσι δὲ πείρατα τέχναι,
> ὕστατοι ὥστε δρόμου καταλειπόμεθ', οὐδ' πῃ ἔστι
> πάντῃ παπταίνοντα νεοζυγὲς ἅρμα πελάσσαι.
>
> Choerilus, *SH* 317

> O blessed he, who was skilled at song, a servant of the Muses, at that time when the meadow was still undefiled; but now that everything is divided, there are boundaries to the arts, to the point that <u>we are left behind last in the race</u>, and it is not possible for me, although I peer everywhere, to steer <u>a newly yoked chariot</u>.

As D'Angour notes, "[Choerilus'] complaint reads as an original trope in its own right. Rather than simply registering it as a cry of despair, it is a self-conscious bid to be original by means of deliberately *reversing* familiar epic claims made by poets such as Homer, Hesiod and Parmenides."[54] D'Angour goes on to compare the poet's claim with two ancient Egyptian texts from the end of the third millennium BC that touch on the limits of art and on the anxiety over repetition. The comparison is already important in the context of a reflection on the psychology of the creative act, but the parallel with Timotheus is even more significant and polemically charged. While Timotheus relies on a traditional rhetorical posture, that of the poet in need of help from a divine agent, to create a new image of Apollo as a god who fosters innovation, Choerilus adduces the so far unparalleled motive of the impossibility of innovation. The image – the newly yoked chariot – that Choerilus uses to describe his impossible innovation

---

[52] For the metaphor, compare Pind. *Ol.* 9.81 ἐν Μοισᾶν δίφρῳ ("in the Muses' chariot"). Also *Ol.* 6.22–8 ζεῦξον ἤδη μοι σθένος ἡμιόνων ("yoke for me the strength of the mules"); *Pyth.* 10.64–6 τόδ' ἔζευξεν ἅρμα Πιερίδων τετράορον ("he yoked this four-hourse chariot of the Pierian Muses"). On these images, Simpson 1969 and Steiner 1986: 41, 79, and 85.

[53] On the relative chronology and relationship of the two poets, McFarlane 2009: 219 n. 1, picking up on themes in McFarlane 2002: 214–73. On the passage, D'Angour 2011: 57–61.

[54] D'Angour 2011: 58. Emphasis in text.

is similar to that of Timotheus, but developed in a different poetic way and combined with a different motive. Choerilus' metaphor evokes not so much the chariot used in war as that used in athletics, especially in the race of *Iliad* 23, where the contestants need to turn the boundary (the τέρματα, Hom. *Il.* 23.358) before getting to the finish line. The two poets' choice of compound adjectives belonging to the same semantic field throws light not only on the creative interactions between genres, motives, and poets, but also on the innovation hype and radicalization of concerns about novelty in the last quarter of the fifth century. As the agonistic and learned game played by Timotheus and Choerilus illustrates, innovation is no longer a topos, a logistic and psychological reality with which poets have to wrestle in the creative process, but an abstract object of investigation in itself, a realm of competition, and an integral part of the "innovationist turn" that D'Angour has described.[55]

Inventing the tradition

One specific form of engagement with novelty as a theme in Timotheus' poem is illustrated in the next lines of his apology:

> ὁ γάρ μ' εὐγενέτας μακραί-
>   ων Σπάρτας μέγας ἀγεμών
> βρύων ἄνθεσιν ἥβας
> δονεῖ λαὸς ἐπιφλέγων
> ἐλᾷ τ' αἴθοπι μώμῳ,   210
> ὅτι <u>παλαιοτέραν</u> <u>νέοις</u>
> <u>ὕμνοις</u> Μοῦσαν ἀτιμῶ·
> ἐγὼ δ' οὔτε <u>νέον</u> τιν' οὔ-
>   τε <u>γεραὸν</u> οὔτ' ἰσήβαν
> εἴργω τῶνδ' ἑκὰ<ς> ὕμνων·   215
> τοὺς δὲ <u>μουσοπαλαιολύ-</u>
>   <u>μας</u>, τούτους δ' ἀπερύκω,
> λωβητῆρας ἀοιδᾶν,
> κηρύκων λιγυμακροφώ-
>   νων τείνοντας ἰυγάς.   220
>   Timoth. *PMG* 791.206–20

For the well-born and long-lived Spartan people, a great leader, swarming with the flower of youth, drives me about in its blazing hostility, and harasses me with burning reproach, saying that with <u>new songs</u> I dishonor

---

[55] D'Angour 2011: 216–24.

> the Old Muse. Yet for my part I don't keep anybody, either <u>young</u> or <u>old</u>
> or a <u>peer</u>, away from these songs. It is <u>the old corruptors of the Muse</u> that
> I reject, debauchers of songs straining the howls of far-shouting heralds.

The poet describes his detractors' criticism and establishes his "inclusive" poetics. Scholars have speculated on the identity of Timotheus' Spartan critics, but the attack Timotheus describes certainly does not need to be historical: although many anecdotes emphasize Timotheus' difficult relationship with Spartan power, we should bear in mind that these anecdotes themselves are likely to have been derived from a reading of this part of the poem.[56] More importantly, the attack allows Timotheus to define his own poetics and delineate his critical reception of other poets and his relationship with his own audience, including the one listening to the current song. In defending his "new songs" (νέοις ὕμνοις, 211–12) Timotheus not only relies on the same generic, unmarked vocabulary that Pindar used to refer to his own compositions, but also draws on one of the best-attested and most fundamental oppositions and strategies of Greek poetry: that between praise and blame. Timotheus starts by exposing the attacks leveled against him (206–12) and, in particular, the blame he suffers (αἴθοπι μώμῳ) and contrasts them with his own attitude to poetry (ἐγὼ δ'. . . , 213–15); then he states his own poetic stance and proceeds to praise of his citharodic predecessors. In characterizing the Spartan critics' attack, Timotheus employs, in a way that Hordern (2002 ad loc.) interprets as satirical, words that Spartan poets used to define their own noble origins (εὐγενέτας), ancestry (μακραίων), and the vigor of Sparta's people (βρύων ἄνθεσιν ἥβας). But in this form of praise, whether real or feigned, he also weaves into his description of Spartan detractors who harass him (δονεῖ, ἐλᾷ) with the hostility of fire (ἐπιφλέγων, αἴθοπι) terms that are reminiscent of the military vocabulary used in the rest of the narrative of the *Persians* (especially φλέγω, in περίβολα πυρὶ φλεγόμεν', 27). Adopting Spartan praise language and a Spartan set of values here is a rhetorical strategy used by Timotheus to accentuate the unfairness of the critical reception of his poem: while he is ready to embrace Spartan imagery when describing his critics, his detractors only receive the new poetry according to their own values and their love of the past. But by the same token, the use of the very terms that the Spartans are proud of (in particular Σπάρτας μέγας ἀγεμών, "Sparta's great leader," 207) might sound Persian overtones (especially of "Great King") in an Athenian ear and further distance the audience. This strategy allows the poet and his multiple audiences to have it both ways.

---

[56] Prauscello 2009; on anecdotes and their interpretative strategies, see Chapter 3.

This displacement of potential criticism onto Sparta is also a means whereby Timotheus can ward off critics in Athens, where it is likely the premiere took place.[57] If his Athenian critics condemn his "new songs," they will be adopting the same attitude as their current political opponents in the Peloponnesian War and sharing the cultural backwardness and stiff traditionalism associated with Sparta in the Athenian imagination. In the next lines (213–20), Timotheus refines his response to potential detractors by defining not only his own poetics, but also his ideal audience. Dithyrambic diction here verges on comic invective, as the poet rejects the μουσοπαλαιολύμας ("old corruptors of the Muse," 216–17). The characterization is carefully constructed. On the one hand, the temporal reference in μουσοπαλαιολύμας builds on his opponents' accusation that he is dishonoring the <u>older</u> Muse with his new songs (212–13) and on Timotheus' defense of his "democratic," inclusive poetics. Such argument may have prompted the first conservative critics, Aristophanes and others, to interpret the New Music in political terms. But as Timotheus illustrates, the reference to chronology (young versus old) is not useful: the reference to an audience that includes young (νέον), old (γεραόν), and contemporary (ἰσήβαν) suggests a timeless view of poetic reception. It might also allow the poet to suggest that his audience has an intimate understanding of what *mousikē* is about, as the terms echo the categories of choral performers (youth and men) at musical competitions. On the other hand, the term μουσοπαλαιολύμας also inverts, and interiorizes, the critical paradigm used by his accusers: the expression is ambiguous and can be taken to mean "corruptors of the old Muse" or "old corruptors of the Muse." If the former, Timotheus would be internalizing the vocabulary of the comic critics, in the vein of Pherecrates, depicting the New Musicians as debauchers of the respectable old Muse.[58] If the latter, Timotheus would be contrasting himself with bad musicians, corruptors of the art vilified as old-fashioned by contrast with his own forward-looking attitude. Although the force of the compound resides in its ambiguity, it is tempting to translate the

---

[57] The issue of the date and place of the premiere of the *Persians* has been much debated. Wilamowitz (1903: 61–4) offered Miletus or Mycale as a place of performance. The most widely accepted date and place for the first performance (against which I see no tenable objection) is an Athenian festival, probably the Panathenae, around 410 BC: Bassett 1931, Janssen 1984: 13–22, Hansen 1984, Herington 1985: 151–2, van Minnen 1997, Hordern 2002: 15–17, Phillips 2003: 212–13, Rosenbloom 2006: 148–54, Power 2010: 522–4, 538–42. On the dating of the *Persians* by stylistic comparison with Euripides' *Iphigenia in Tauris*, Firinu 2009.

[58] This kind of rhetoric is illustrated in *PMG* 802.3, where Timotheus celebrates his victory over Phrynis by labeling his opponent τὸν ἰωνοκάμπταν ("the Ionian bender") with the same type of critical vocabulary that was used against him (on "bends" as describing an important aspect of the New Music, see earlier in this chapter, pp. 72 and 75–6).

compound in this latter way, as it continues the reference to an ageless Mousike appreciated by an ageless audience, rather than introducing a new comic trope.[59] Those described as μουσοπαλαιολύμας are finally further qualified as destroyers of songs, λωβητῆρας ἀοιδᾶν (218). Here the contrast between the two words is striking: that λωβητῆρας is a very strong marker of abuse and outrage throws into even starker relief the dignity of the ἀοιδή, the oldest term used for the epic song that encapsulates the prestige of the bardic past.[60] This evaluative description is defined much more specifically in the lines that follow.

But, with telling parallels to Aristophanes' *Frogs*, Timotheus' attack on his critics is not so much a trope as it is a precise definition of bad poetry, in terms of both composition and performance. Here invective gives way to literary criticism as all aspects of the art of song are described – production, performance, and reception. In particular, the poet moves from blame to description, using more technical vocabulary, of the quality of the voice of the composers he rejects. Both the verbal action of "straining" (τείνοντας) and the noun "shrieking" (ἰυγάς, 219–20) indicate what the persona of Timotheus sees as musical monstrosities:[61] the ἰυγαί (220) of the bad poets belong to the realm of joyful or painful sounds and emotions but not to that of songs (ἀοιδή), while the only quality praised in the voice of those called "far-shouting heralds with a shrill voice" (κηρύκων λιγυμακροφώνων) is its range, which is more appropriate to the realm of communication than to that of inspired poetry.[62]

These few lines combining self-defense and critical attack rely on a precise musical vocabulary that could reproduce the "critics' chatter" heard in the literary milieu at Athens, both in Aristophanes' descriptions of the poetic scene and in the sophists' discussions of language.[63] That vocabulary allows Timotheus to characterize his ideal audience by contrast with an ignorant crowd – a subtle maneuver in a musical competition. His poetry is meant for anybody, that is, for anybody who has an ear for good music. More than

---

[59] Contra: Power 2010: 534–7.

[60] The expression echoes Dionysus' verdict on young tragedians, whom he calls λωβηταὶ τέχνης (Ar. *Ran.* 92–5).

[61] The verb τείνω is used in Aesch. *Pers.* 574, *Eum.* 201; Eur. *Med.* 201, *Hec.* 1177. Whether one connects it with tragic (female) lament or with τόνος and ἐντείνω, it has a technical dimension. On the verb, Rocconi 2003: 13–22.

[62] Κηρύκων λιγυμακροφώνων builds on an expression from the epic register (κηρύκεσσι λιγυφθόγγοισι, "shrill-voiced heralds," used in Hom. *Il.* 2.50, 2.442, 9.10, 23.39, *Od.* 2.6); but it could also refer to another form of musical competition, that between heralds announcing victory, a contest far less prestigious than *kitharōidia*, on which see Poll. 4.91, Dem. 19.338, and *PMG* 863, 865.

[63] Ford 2002: 279.

a strict social or political identification, the poet creates a form of aesthetic identification for his audience and provides the terms that allow them to discuss what makes good poetry, and that allow the judges to make up their mind.

This tactic is reminiscent of the poetico-critical strategy of the *Frogs*. As Andrew Ford states in his study of the origins of criticism, "by 405, Aristophanes could address his audience as 'veterans' in the wars of criticism, and *Frogs* is only one among a number of comedies that attest to an interest on the part of the Athenian public in the most innovative and startling new approaches to poetry."[64] One cannot deny that these references to a knowledgeable, discerning, interested audience, which includes the judges awarding the contest prize, can be part of the *captatio benevolentiae* of the poet and can participate in the overall rhetoric destined to convince the judges of the poet's worthiness. As Martin Revermann has noted, comic commentaries on dramatic audiences' competence are not straightforward evidence. But, as he observes, "perhaps the most interesting aspect surrounding the rhetoric of audience praise and vilification is its very existence: audience competence is a matter of concern to playwrights, a part of the theatrical experience which is subject to reflection, exploration and challenge."[65] In the same way, Timotheus' "defense," genuine or not, taps into a contemporary development: the new technical discourse of music and language.[66] The poet appeals to his audience's critical sense, which has been honed by their many poetic experiences both as audience members and as performers in one of the many boys' and men's choruses, but he provides them too with a specific critical vocabulary that they might also have heard on the comic scene.

A tradition of innovation

The end of the song moves from this mix of polemical posturing and reliance on technical vocabulary to a description of the tradition to which Timotheus belongs:[67]

πρῶτος ποικιλόμουσον Ὀρ-
    φεὺς <χέλ>υν ἐτέκνωσεν

---

[64] Ford 2002: 188, with reference to Dover (1993: 25–8) for a survey of other comedies, now lost, on "literary topics."
[65] Revermann 2006: 103.
[66] On the development of literary critical expertise among comic audiences, Ford 2002: 188–9.
[67] The passage is reminiscent of the catalogue of poets (Orpheus, Museus, Hesiod, and Homer) that Aeschylus goes through in Ar. *Ran.* 1030–6 to illustrate the boons they brought to mankind.

υἱὸς Καλλιόπα<ς κόρας
Διὸς> Πιερίαθεν·
Τέρπανδρος δ' ἐπὶ τῷ δέκα   225
ζεῦξε Μοῦσαν ἐν ᾠδαῖς·
Λέσβος δ' Αἰολία ν<ιν> Ἀν-
            τίσσᾳ γείνατο κλεινόν·
νῦν δὲ Τιμόθεος μέτροις
ῥυθμοῖς τ' ἑνδεκακρουμάτοις   230
κίθαριν ἐξανατέλλει,
θησαυρὸν πολύυμνον οἴ-
            ξας Μουσᾶν θαλαμευτόν·
Μίλητος δὲ πόλις νιν ἁ
            θρέψασ' ἁ δωδεκατειχέος   235
λαοῦ πρωτέος ἐξ Ἀχαιῶν.
ἀλλ' ἑκαταβόλε Πύθι' ἁγνάν
ἔλθοις τάνδε πόλιν σὺν ὄλβῳ,
πέμπων ἀπήμονι λαῷ
            τῷδ' εἰρήναν θάλλουσαν εὐνομίᾳ.   240
            Timoth. *PMG* 791.221–40

Orpheus, son of Calliope daughter of Zeus and native of Pieria, was the
first to beget the tortoiseshell lyre of dapp<u>led music.</u>[68] Then Terpander
yoked the Muse to ten songs. Aeolian Lesbos gave birth to this man to give
fame to Antissa. And now Timotheus with meters and rhythms of eleven
strokes makes the cithara spring up, opening the treasure rich in songs
hidden in the thalamus of the Muses. It is the city of Miletus that brought
him up, twelve-walled, the first of the Achaean people. Now far-shooting
Pythian, come to this holy city with prosperity, and send to this people, to
be protected from plagues, the peace that flourishes in good order.

Timotheus starts his "history of the lyric tradition" with the mythological hero Orpheus. This son of a Muse is credited with the creation of
the tortoiseshell lyre, the prototype for the ancient and venerable art of
kitharōidia. The epithet that qualifies the instrument transfers the dappled
aspect of the tortoise shell to the variegated nature of the music such that
Orpheus as innovator is qualified with the same terms as the New Musicians.
The concise description of Orpheus' contribution to *kitharōidia* contrasts

---

[68] The text of lines 221–8 is uncertain. For a detailed apparatus criticus, see Ercoles 2010. Editors
differ on the following points: the case of ποικιλόμουσος (221, either nominative or accusative)
and the supplement in 223–4. I follow Sevieri's edition, which differs from Page 1962 and
Campbell 1993 in emending ποικιλόμουσος to an accusative, thus modifying the chelus-lyre
rather than Orpheus, and in providing the supplement κόρας Διός in 223–4. For an ingenious
supplement, see Ercoles 2010, who suggests Οἰάγρου τε.

with the boyish version of the divine origins of the instrument as exuber-
antly told in the Homeric *Hymn to Hermes*: Hermes killed the tortoise, but
Orpheus begot (ἐτέκνωσεν) the elaborate music, the real rebirth of the art
that improved on the simpler version invented by the baby god.

The catalogue then moves on to Terpander, skipping over other early and
equally iconic citharodic figures, including Amphion and Arion, and more
recent famous predecessors, who include the Lesbian citharode Phrynis of
Mytilene. Timotheus' praise is selective: although Terpander is variously
credited with the invention of seven nomes or with the addition of strings
to the four-string lyre, Timotheus leaves the exact nature of his contribution
vague. Whether we take the δέκα ("ten") to refer to the number of songs
he composed, strings/notes he played, or meters he used, it does not match
any of the other attestations of his innovations.[69] This might be a case of
Timotheus *inventing* a Terpandrian innovation, and also a tradition into
which that innovation can be fitted. Moreover, although there is a tradition
of Terpander at Sparta, Timotheus only mentions the musician's Lesbian
(Antissan) connection. Yet even a mention of the name of Terpander is likely
to have brought up in an audience's mind the other associated tradition,
that of Terpander's Spartan victory at the first Carneia.[70] Placing himself in
the lineage of Terpander is a subtle but effective way for Timotheus, literally
or fictionally hounded by Spartan critics, to connect himself to the tradition
of Eastern citharodes victorious in Sparta.

The descriptions of Orpheus and Terpander function in the same way
in the priamel: an allusive or riddling reference to musical innovation is
followed by a reference to the musicians' geographical origins. Timotheus'
self-presentation caps the list: to refer to his own musical contribution
(μέτροις ῥυθμοῖς τ' ἐνδεκακρουμάτοις κίθαριν ἐξανατέλλει, θησαυρὸν πολύυμνον οἴξας Μουσᾶν θαλαμευτόν, 229–33), he relies – as also noted earlier, in
the case of his use of a Homeric compound – on a traditional technical and
metaphorical register for poetic activity. First, what he seeks to "bring to
new life" (ἐξανατέλλει) is the κίθαρις. To our knowledge, the noun κίθαρις
had been exclusively Homeric, and in Homer it refers both to an instrument
(a four-stringed round-based box lyre, also called *phorminx*) and to the art

---

[69] On Terpander's innovations, *Suda* T 354 (IV 527 Adler). Terpander's invention of the
cithardic nome: [Plut.] *De mus.* 1132d–e, Poll. 4.66. On his addition of strings to the cithara,
[Plut.] *De mus.* 1141c, with only seven (and not ten) strings. Hordern (2002: 243–4) presents
possible interpretations of this reference to the (untraditional) number ten. On the number of
strings, see also above, n. 17.

[70] On Terpander and Sparta, Clem. Al. *Strom.* 1.16.78.5, [Plut.] *De mus.* 1134b; Hellanicus of
Lesbos *ap.* Ath. 14.635e (= *FGrH* 4 F 85a) for his Carnean victory.

of playing that instrument.[71] The important point is that Timotheus' image of the awakening of the instrument is built on the poetic past of the word.[72] This reliance on traditional diction is even more clearly illustrated in the next lines: in 232–3, the metonymy of the "treasure rich in songs hidden in the thalamus of the Muses" (θησαυρὸν πολύυμνον . . . Μουσᾶν θαλαμευτόν) relies on a striking image – song as treasure house – with an illustrious past, for it had been used by Pindar in the opening of his sixth *Pythian*.[73] Timotheus' debt to the lyric past and contribution to poetry is thus activated in his reworking of both expressions: the poet adds to the metaphorical treasure house, that is, the poetic tradition itself, by appropriating and transforming the metaphor, while introducing a linguistic coinage, the neologism θαλαμευτόν. In the same way, Timotheus appropriates the image of the Homeric *kitharis*, concentrates the epic past of the instrument (or practice) in one noun, and qualifies this noun with an ambiguous linguistic coinage (μέτροις ῥυθμοῖς τ᾽ ἐνδεκακρουμάτοις, "with meters and rhythms of eleven strokes").[74] This wording has been taken to refer to the addition of strings to the seven-string cithara or to the ten-string Terpandrian cithara. But the number, just like the noun *kitharis*, might be used more for its evocative power than for its organological precision: the series of numbers applied to items of a different nature (the ten songs/notes associated with Terpander, the eleven strokes of Timotheus, and the twelve walls of Miletus) gives a sense of ineluctable development, as does the geographic progression from the Muses of Pieria (224) to Lesbos (227) to Miletus (234) and back to Pythian Delphi (237), in a sort of grand tour of important citharodic capitals, with no explicit mention of Sparta.[75] This is the final argument of Timotheus' rhetoric of legitimization: he is not doing something radically new but continuing a tradition of innovations that started with Orpheus.

Geopolitical considerations are an integral part of this careful mythicopoetic recreation. The citharode's birthplace, Miletus, is described with a

---

[71] Barker 1984: 96. On the Homeric *kitharis*, see Maas and Snyder 1989: 5–6 and 30–1, West 1992: 50–6. That instrument starts being "less common than the square-based type" after 600 BC (West 1992: 55). The only testimony that underlines a structural difference between *kitharis* and cithara as instruments is Aristoxenus (fr. 102 Wehrli), which post-dates our text.

[72] It might also pick up on the technical ἀναβάλλομαι ("strike up a prelude") of epic bards and rhapsodes and on a verb derived from it, ἀνακρούομαι ("begin"). The expression ἐνδεκακρουμάτοις κίθαριν ἐξανατέλλει could be a periphrastic gloss on ἀνακρούομαι.

[73] Pind. *Pyth.* 6.7–8: ἑτοῖμος ὕμνων θησαυρὸς ἐν πολυχρύσῳ | Ἀπολλωνίᾳ . . . νάπᾳ ("a treasure house of hymns at hand in the Apollinian vale rich in gold").

[74] For a tentative interpretation of the compound "eleven-struck," see LeVen 2011.

[75] For the numerical progression, already Barker 1984.

striking formula, πρωτέος ἐξ Ἀχαιῶν ("first of the Achaeans"), an expression that, as Nagy notes, in the *Iliad* is applied to no Achaeans other than Diomedes, Agamemnon, Ajax, and Achilles.[76] Here, however, the Iliadic formula is inverted and reappropriated for an Ionian city. It is not the first inversion, or reappropriation, eastward that the poet devises. I have mentioned earlier the use of the adjective νεοτευχής to qualify Lycaon's chariots. Timotheus' use of the adjective describing a Trojan, not Achaean, object to qualify the god protecting his poetry takes on new significance in light of this formula. So too does the selective presentation of mythical citharodes: the Theban Amphion or the adoptive Corinthian Arion also belong not simply to the citharodic tradition, but more specifically to the tradition of "Asiatic" Lesbian *kitharōidia*.[77] This is all the more striking in view of the final invocation of Pythian Apollo and the appeal to εὐνομία ("good order") in "this holy city" (238). The noun puns on good singing in the nome (*nomos*) genre and good administration (*nomos*) of the city, in Solonian vocabulary (εὐνομίη, fr. 4.32 W²) but, as an echo of the title of a poem of Tyrtaeus (frr. 1–4 W²), it also has Spartan connotations. This use of a key word of Spartan ideology completes the rhetorical posture adopted earlier in the *sphragis*, showing the narrator putting his own words into practice, even as he adopts the vocabulary of his detractors. The abstract noun finally creates a ring composition, from the Athenian ἐλευθερία ("freedom") of the opening line to the peace and εὐνομία ("good order") of the city in the closing lines. In this context, the deictic (238) is tantalizing, as it does not give us information about the actual performance setting, but makes the song adaptable to as many places as the traveling musician will take it to. I have focused on the effect of the rhetoric of the song for its likely premiere in Athens, but this imaginary tour could be activated to the citharode's benefit wherever he performed it, including on the Ionic coast, where an audience could relive, and reconnect with, the grand mythological tradition of Eastern cithara-playing continued by Timotheus and subsequent performers.

Poikilia: *the new colors of sound*

Newness may be the most enduring and most suspect topos that poets use to advertise their composition, but it is not the only term that the

---

[76] Nagy 1979: 32.

[77] This tradition of Lesbian citharodes is reported by Hellanicus of Lesbos in his *Carnean Victors*, on which Franklin 2012.

New Musicians employ in their traditionalizing rhetoric to describe their poetry. *Poikilia* (variegatedness, complexity) is a second critical term provided for their critics by the New Musicians in the self-fashioning of their reception.[78]

Poetic *poikilia* starts with birds and snakes. In archaic lyric, the term often describes the natural world: animals (snakes, birds, horses), vegetation (flowers), or natural phenomena (wind) that display an intriguingly intricate, changing, and variegated quality in color or movement are called ποικίλος or αἰόλος.[79] This intricacy is what links the expression to its other main – and metaphorical – use, in connection with objects that illustrate the technical abilities of mortals displayed in handiwork, artifacts, and cunning inventions.[80] *Poikilia* links the two aspects – on the one hand, the aesthetic and sensorial, especially visual but also aural, and on the other hand, the intellectual – by referring to the cunning skills (the *mētis*) of the designer or user.[81] Pindar and Bacchylides use the term to refer to musical, instrumental, or intellectual artifacts (including thoughts or lies) that deserve attention, in addition to the many objects and natural elements with a mottled appearance.[82] One fragment in particular illustrates especially well the metaphorical use of *poikilia* as a term of early poetic criticism. In the passage of Pratinas criticizing the new place of the *auloi* in musical practice, *poikilia* is used as a term of both praise and blame: the tune the chorus sings is described as "a swan of variegated plumage" (οἷά τε κύκνον ἄγοντα ποικιλόπτερον μέλος, 5); by contrast, the tone of the *aulos* is compared to the breath of a spotted toad (τὸν φρυνεοῦ ποικίλαν πνοὰν ἔχοντα, 10). In both instances, the expression draws attention to the aesthetic qualities of the musical items described and suggests that the musician's skills compete with those of natural vocalists (birds and frogs). But in addition to defining a specific quality or pattern in itself, *poikilia* turns our attention to the visual intricacy of the object it qualifies.

[78] On the *poikilia* of New Music, Zimmermann 1992: 123–4, Barker 1995, Wallace 2009, LeVen 2013b, with further bibiliography.

[79] Of a dragon or snake, *PMG* 1.66, Pind. *Pyth.* 8.46, 10.46, 4.249; of a toad, Pratinas *PMG* 708.10; of a bird, Alc. fr. 345.2 Voigt; of a horse, Pind. *Pyth.* 2.8; of the wind, Pind. *Isthm.* 3/4.36, Sim. *PMG* 508.6.

[80] Of Aphrodite's throne, Sapph. fr. 1.1 Voigt; of sandals, Sapph. fr. 39.2 Voigt, Anac. *PMG* 358.3; of a headband, Sapph. fr. 98(a)11 Voigt, Pind. *Ol.* 8.15; of clothes, Ibyc. *PMG* 316.1; of a bow, Bacchyl. 10.43.

[81] On *poikilos/poikilia* as reflective of *mētis*, Détienne and Vernant 1974: 32–57.

[82] Of lies similar to truth: Pind. *Ol.* 1.29; of counsels: Pind. *Nem.* 5.28; of the mind: Alc. fr. 69.7 Voigt; of a charm: Pind. *Pyth.* 4.214; of a song: Pind. *Ol.* 6.87, *Nem.* 5.42; Pratinas, *PMG* 708.5; of the music of the cithara: Pind. *Ol.* 3.8, 4.2, *Nem.* 4.14.

Similarly, *poikilia* is used by critics of the New Music to define one of its fundamental features: its aural complexity. The New Musicians themselves use the metaphorical realm of nature and the notion of *poikilia* to describe their art. Telestes describes the art of *aulos*-playing as αἰολοπτέρυγον ("quick-fluttering," *PMG* 805c.2) and αἰολομόρφοις ("of quick-moving forms," *PMG* 806.3), and in the *sphragis* of the *Persians*, as we saw above, Timotheus qualifies his predecessor Orpheus' lyre as ποικιλέμουσον ("of dappled music," *PMG* 791.221). In describing their music as intricate, the New Musicians thus tap into a traditional image. Yet this semantic continuity can be interpreted in two ways. On the one hand, the appropriation of *poikilia* as a term of criticism can be seen as participation in archaizing poetics along the same lines as the traditional reliance on the motive of newness. By using the idea of variegation to describe music with which they associate themselves, Telestes and Timotheus are merely doing what archaic poets did, or rather, they are appropriating the prestige of the past to describe – and thus legitimize – their innovations. But one could also read the New Musicians' use of the traditional notion of *poikilia* as engaging with the musical claims of Pindar, not as a representative of tradition, but as a representative of revolution.[83] If Pindar belonged to an earlier *aulos* revolution, and if the term *poikilia* refered to his own tonal modulations, then the New Musicians' reference to *poikilia* should be interpreted as a legitimizing reference that links not to old musical practice but to the inventions of previous generations: just as Timotheus justifies his innovations by contextualizing them in a history of citharodic transformations, Telestes relates the *poikilia* of his *aulos*-playing to earlier instances of creative auletic variegation.

This tactic can also be detected in the New Musicians' recourse to specific references to various *harmoniai*, rather than to the general term *poikilia*, when they talk of their modulations.[84] A few passages (*PMG* 802, 806, also 810, and possibly *PMG* 791.227) use ethnic markers (Phrygian, Dorian, Lydian, even Ionian and Aeolian) evocative of different modes. These scanty references make straightforward associations between metamusical adjective and melody or type of rhythm impossible (for example, correlating a reference to something Phrygian to performance in the Phrygian mode), yet two remarks can be ventured.[85]

[83] On Pindar as belonging to an earlier musical revolution, see above, pp. 81–3.

[84] West 1992: 364–6 on Philoxenus' *Mysians*. Dion. Hal. *Comp.* 19.2 describes the innovation in tunings (τρόποι) introduced by the contemporaries of Philoxenus, Timotheus, and Telestes. Also Fongoni 2011.

[85] As Prauscello 2006b: 28–33 explains, the question has been examined for Pindar, and the debate goes back to Apollonius *eidographos*. Critics have since been divided between believers

First, two fragments of Telestes that share the same scenario make explicit references to Dorian, Phrygian, and Lydian musical realities and need to be examined together.[86] The first is *PMG* 806 *ap.* Ath. 14.617b:

ἢ Φρύγα καλλιπνόων αὐλῶν ἱερῶν βασιλῆα,
Λυδὸν ὃς ἅρμοσε πρῶτος
Δωρίδος ἀντίπαλον Μούσας νόμ ον αἰολομόρφοις
πνεύματος εὔπτερον αὔραν ἀμφιπλέκων καλάμοις.

3 Dobree (νόμον), Wilamowitz (αἰολομόρφοις): νομοαίολον ὄρφναι cod. αἰόλον ὀμφᾷ Schweighäuser

or the Phrygian King of the holy fair-breathing *auloi*, who was the first to fit together the Lydian tune, opponent of the Dorian Muse, weaving around it on his reeds of quick-moving forms the well-fledged breeze of his breath.

The second is *PMG* 810 and comes later in the *Deipnosophistae* (14.625f–626a):

πρῶτοι παρὰ κρατῆρας Ἑλλάνων ἐν αὐλοῖς
συνοπαδοὶ Πέλοπος Ματρὸς ὀρείας
Φρύγιον ἄεισαν νόμον·
τοὶ δ' ὀξυφώνοις πηκτίδων ψαλμοῖς κρέκον
Λύδιον ὕμνον.

The first to sing to the accompaniment of the *auloi*, beside the mixing bowls of the Greeks, the Phrygian tune of the Mountain Mother were the companions of Pelops. And they played the Lydian hymn to the high-pitched plucking of the *pektis*.

The movement is similar in both passages: as Athenaeus explains in his introduction to the fragment, "Phrygian and Lydian *harmoniai* originated with the barbarians and came to be known to the Greeks from the Phrygians and the Lydians who settled in the Peloponnese." This strategy of legitimization is particularly important for Telestes, a native of Sicily, who might be defending his own contribution to *mousikē* by pointing to the mythological precedent of foreign influence in *aulos*-playing and, even more pointedly, by going back to the mythological model of the first *aulos* revolution. The agonistic aspect of this archaeology of music also provides the confrontational

in a correspondence between rhythmic and melodic pattern (starting with Boeckh 1811–21) and skeptics (Anderson 1994).
[86] On these fragments, Comotti 1993.

topos activated in Timotheus' *sphragis*.[87] But one also ought to remark that the choice of the harmonies to which Telestes refers in both passages is archaizing: as Athenaeus again underlines (Ath. 14.635c), Phrygian, Dorian, and Lydian were the only kinds of early melodies employed by Anacreon.[88] While earlier innovators, especially Lasus (*PMG* 702) and Pratinas (*PMG* 712a–b) and later Pindar (fr. 191 SM), debate about the use of other harmonies (Iastian, Locrian, and Aeolian), Telestes can be seen as adopting a conservative attitude by referring only to ancient harmonies associated with Anacreon. Moreover, Telestes does not refer to the actual mixing of modes (or modulation) but uses the suggestive image of the mixing bowl, next to which different peoples might mix, in a proto-sympotic context: the sociology of music, as much as its theoretical and ethical dimension, is at stake in this self-definition.

Second, the next passage that Athenaeus quotes (635e–f) gives an additional twist to Telestes' narrative: the Pindaric lines describe an instrument, the *barbitos*,

> τόν ῥα Τέρπανδρός ποθ' ὁ <u>Λέσβιος</u> εὗρεν
> πρῶτος, ἐν δείπνοισι <u>Λυδῶν</u>
> ψαλμὸν ἀντίφθογγον ὑψηλᾶς ἀκούων πακτίδος.
>
> Pind. fr. 125 SM

> which long ago the <u>Lesbian</u> Terpander was the first to invent, when he heard at the dinner parties of the <u>Lydians</u> the plucking that responds to the high-pitched *pektis*.

While Telestes' passage is remarkably similar to Pindar's in depicting a westward movement and sympotic setting, it focuses on the archaeology of wind-playing, not on an archaic string instrument specific to the symposium. This rhetorical move from strings to winds needs to be understood in the larger context of the discourse on *aulos*-playing manipulated by the New Musicians, to which I now turn.

Instruments of invention: aulos *and cithara*

As I have suggested above, an important set of passages by the New Musicians focuses on the myth of Athena and the *auloi* and seems to refer to a cultural debate about the instrument's ideology and the practice of playing it. The

---

[87] See, for example, the parallel with Pind. fr. 140b.1–3 SM, with the restoration proposed by Schröder and Ferrari, "rival of the Ionian Muse" (Ἰων[ίδος ἀντίπαλον Μοίσας).

[88] See also [Plut.] *De mus.* 1134a for the same early harmonies "in the time of Polymnestus and Sacadas."

myth of Athena and Marsyas was certainly well known in Athens in the mid fifth century. It even occupied a significant religious space on the Acropolis, in the form of a bronze group sculpture made by Myron and depicting "Athena striking the satyr Marsyas for picking up the *auloi* when the goddess wanted to get rid of them for good."[89] This apparent ambivalence in classical Athens about the instrument was also reported in a number of anecdotes, most famously stories about Alcibiades refusing to play the instrument, and on vase painting that depicted *auloi*-playing satyrs.[90] Most of the stories, however, are much later representations of the early classical period, and as McKinnon states, "there is little trace of antagonism towards the aulos or of opposition between it and the kithara up to the time of Plato and Aristotle."[91] As McKinnon also makes clear, the same conservative screening of the sources that demonizes the New Music also condemns the *aulos*-playing with which it was specifically associated. Yet the Myron group, the lines of Melanippides, and Telestes' "response" to Melanippides *do* stage an opposition, real or imagined, that needs serious consideration and invites us to analyze the rhetoric of the two poets, in particular their use of the *aulos* myth and the fashioning of their reception.

In the case of Melanippides, one first has to take stock of the provocative stance of the lines and of the publicity potential offered to the dithyrambist or even to the dithyrambic chorus, if the *Marsyas* is indeed a dithyramb, in the description of the rejection of the instrument that provides the song's accompaniment.[92] Whoever is speaking the lines and presenting the myth is ventriloquizing an elite attitude and presenting the elite discourse later often repeated by Plato that aligns musical, ethical, aesthetic, and civic elements. Athena is depicted as rejecting the instrument that deforms her features with a vocabulary that collapses moral and aesthetic categories.[93] As for Telestes, whether he is responding to Melanippides or engaging with the same type of story, he adopts a traditional rhetorical trope illustrated

[89]   Paus. 1.24.1; Plin. *HN* 34.57–8. On the relationship between the group and Melanippides' victory, Boardman 1956. On representations on vase painting, Froning 1971: 29–44, Bundrick 2005: 34–42, 131–9.

[90]   Plut. *Vit. Alc.* 2.5–7. The evidence is thoroughly presented by Wilson (1999), who explores what he calls the "extremely ambivalent position" (p. 58) of the *aulos* in Athenian life. Wilson (2003b: 184) also argues that the *aulos* was demonized by the elite as early as the fifth century, and "an attachment to stringed instruments as a basis for the 'free man's' formation persisted well into the democratic period."

[91]   McKinnon 1984: 209.

[92]   The genre is not made explicit, but Melanippides is mostly presented as a composer of dithyrambs, see *Suda* M 454 (III 350 Adler).

[93]   These elements have been thoroughly explored in Wilson 1999, 2003b, 2004, 2010, and Martin 2003.

by Pindar's *Olympian* 1 and fr. 70b SM and Stesichorus' *Palinode*: myth revision and criticism of alternate versions. Telestes' rejection of the myth is also based on a motive typically found in Pindar's epinicians, that of the critics' envy (ἐπίφθονον ὄνειδος, "envious reproach," *PMG* 805b.3), and it is qualified with a traditional adjective: that myth is ἀχόρευτος, unfit for a chorus, with all the elite connotations associated with the term.[94] One can see here a witty, even sophistic, reply that makes Telestes, or rather the *persona loquens* of the lines, recuperate the same type of ideology as Melanippides, in presenting himself as an even greater defender of good *mousikē* and its myths.

But from this traditional agonistic stance, Telestes also defines bad critics (ματαιολόγων μουσοπόλων, "servants of the Muses with idle speech," *PMG* 805b.1–2) and thus influences his own audience with a rhetoric similar to Timotheus'. Two details are striking. First, Telestes' use of yet another compound of Μοῦσα (Muse) combines a mythical, traditional reference and a more precise definition and recalls Timotheus' use of the term in νεοτευχῆ Μοῦσαν ("newly fashioned Muse," *PMG* 791.203), παλαιοτέραν Μοῦσαν ("older Muse," *PMG* 791.211–12), μουσοπαλαιολύμας ("old corruptors of the Muse," *PMG* 791.216), ποικιλόμουσον ("of dappled music," *PMG* 791.221), and Μοῦσα παλαιά ("Muse of old," *PMG* 796.5). All these forms suggest that "muse" is becoming a common noun, subject to a variety of redefinitions, rather than a mythological entity.[95] The noun still echoes some of the authority of the daughters of Mnemosyne invoked by the archaic and early classical poet, whom Choerilus describes as Μουσάων θεράπων, "servant of the Muses," but the nine divine sisters have been replaced by as many muses as poets. It might well be this new critical approach to the muse-ful poetic discourse that Aristophanes parodies in the *Frogs*, in staging Euripides' Muse. One ought to consider Aristophanes' Euripidean Muse not as a personification of the tragedian's poetics, but as the personification of the *critical discourse* of the time and of the multiplication of definitions of Muses.[96] The Muses are not epiphanic, Heliconian creatures, the source of inspiration and divine agents one invokes to secure poetic authority. They have turned so pedestrian that they are rarely found as stand-alone nouns any more and need to be defined by an adjective, preferably a compound adjective.

---

[94] Pind. *Ol.* 1.47, 6.74, 8.55, *Pyth.* 1.85, 2.90, 7.19, 11.29, 11.54, *Nem.* 4.39, 8.21, *Isthm.* 1.44, 5.24, 7.39.

[95] The only traditional use of the noun is Μουσᾶν θαλαμευτόν, "thalamus of the Muses," *PMG* 791.233. See also μουσεῖα ("concert hall of the Muses") in Euripides' *Helen* (174, echoed in 1108) and σπανίαν Μοῦσαν ("narrow Muse") in *Ion* fr. 32.4 W².

[96] On that aspect, Hall 2000 and 2006: 170–83.

The second distinctive feature of Telestes' fragment is that the poet, just like Timotheus in his *sphragis*, defines his position in a larger Panhellenic context. The mention of the idle tale about Athena that "flew to Greece" (προσέπταθ' Ἑλλάδα, *PMG* 805b.2) places the myth in a fluid network of musicians and musical narratives and allows the narrator to present himself as the insider, the true defender of tradition against outside rival influences. The narrator's position can certainly be read as ironic, since Telestes, like most of the New Musicians, was not an Athenian, and Athens, "the Greece of Greece" (Ἑλλάδος Ἑλλάς) in an epitaph (*FGE* 307) attributed to Timotheus or Thucydides, had always been receptive to other musical influences.

Overall, this defense of *aulētikē* contains the praise and blame motif also found in Timotheus' defense of his citharodic art: both vividly describe a position against which they define themselves and present their own argument, thereby shaping their own image and influencing their reception by their audience. But rewriting the *aulos* myth is also a means for Telestes to retell, and reappropriate, other musical and instrumental aetiologies. The retelling relies on a traditional element of discourse on the body in relation to *aulos*-playing: how, asks the narrator of Telestes' piece, could the virgin Athena care about her disfigured features, since cosmetic issues lie beyond the realm of virgins' concerns? Yet far from denying Athena any sexuality by stating the goddess' presumed lack of interest in good looks, the narrator suggests it merely by naming what the goddess does not have (she is ἄγαμον καὶ ἄπαιδ᾽, "marriageless and childless") and teases the audience by accumulating erotic images: the mountain thickets (a favorite place for sexual predators of nymphs and other vulnerable females), the "nymph-born beast" (νυμφαγενεῖ φηρί, that is, the satyr Marsyas), the "distressing love for lovely beauty" (εὐηράτοιο κάλλεος ὀξὺς ἔρως), and the very multiplication of love in the phrase describing it. Moreover, highlighting the goddess' desire, it also activates the sexual connotations of the *aulos*. As iconography attests, the "clever instrument" (σοφὸν ... ὄργανον) belongs to the same phallic realm as the satyr.[97] While the instrument is traditionally domesticated in the world of the symposium, in Telestes' fragment, for a few lines probably sung to the accompaniment of the *auloi*, the instrument is given back its wild, phallic, subversive characteristics, before being solemnly – and not entirely without humor – handed over to Dionysus himself, the god of the dithyramb, as he presides over the festival at which the poem would have been performed.

It is clear that Telestes offers much more than a defense of *aulos*-playing in this passage of the *Argo*. Besides appropriating diction and rhetorical

---

[97] Lissarague 1990, Wilson 1999: 82–3.

posture to legitimize his place in the lyric tradition, the poet also offers an alternate version of the invention of the *aulos*, in a composition whose title itself, *Argo*, has a programmatic charge and engages with the theme of technological innovation. The invention of the *auloi* as recounted by Telestes is reminiscent of two other organogonic myths: a different version of the creation of the instrument as narrated by Pindar in *Pythian* 12 (perhaps itself a rejection of other myths about the invention of the *auloi*), and the invention of the *chelus* (tortoiseshell lyre) in the Homeric *Hymn to Hermes*. These two models give authority to Telestes' own narrative and legitimize his poetic status as much as the status of the instrument. Both myths are worth examining in detail.

Pindar's *Pythian* 12, the only victory ode composed for a musician (Midas, victor at the 490 BC *aulētikē* competition), is one of the competing versions of the origins of the *aulos* and makes Athena the inventor of the instrument and the art:[98]

> . . . ἐπεὶ ἐκ τούτων φίλον ἄνδρα πόνων
> ἐρρύσατο παρθένος αὐλῶν τεῦχε πάμφωνον μέλος,
> ὄφρα τὸν Εὐρυάλας ἐκ καρπαλιμᾶν γενύων   20
> χριμφθέντα σὺν ἔντεσι μιμήσαιτ' ἐρικλάγκταν γόον.
> εὗρεν θεός· ἀλλά νιν εὑροῖσ' ἀνδράσι θνατοῖς ἔχειν,
> ὠνύμασεν κεφαλᾶν πολλᾶν νόμον,
> εὐκλεᾶ λαοσσόων μναστῆρ' ἀγώνων,
> λεπτοῦ διανισόμενον χαλκοῦ θαμὰ καὶ δονάκων,   25
> τοὶ παρὰ καλλίχορον ναίοισι πόλιν Χαρίτων
> Καφισίδος ἐν τεμένει, πιστοὶ χορευτᾶν μάρτυρες.
>   Pind. *Pyth.* 12.18–27

> . . . once she had delivered her dear hero [Perseus] from those toils, the maiden fashioned the all-voiced song of the *auloi*, to imitate by means of an instrument the far-resounding scream that assailed her ears from the fast-moving jaws of Euryale. The goddess was the inventor. But she invented it for mortal men to have, she called it the "many-headed nome"

---

[98] Wilson 1999: 61 n. 9: "precisely the same 'contradiction' [between different versions of the myth] exists, significantly, for Dionysos himself, the god who came from the east, but is a native-born son of Thebes. Linguists and archaeologists concur with the widespread tradition that makes the *aulos* an outsider in Greece, but as the modern history of the worship of Dionysos shows, we must pay as much attention to the semi-autonomous dynamic and logic of myth as to the facts uncovered by archaeology and historical linguistics." In other compositions, Pindar could be engaging with other *auloi*-creation myths, in referring to the figure of Olympus (fr. 157 SM), favorite and disciple of Marsyas, known as the creator of the *tibia obliqua* (Plin. *HN* 7.204) and the creator of the many-headed nome ([Plut.] *De mus.* 1133e).

destined to be a famous reminder in popular musical contests, a tune that quickly passes through the delicate bronze and the reeds growing close to the city of the Graces, city of beautiful choruses, in the precinct of Cephisus' daughter, trustworthy witnesses of dancers.

In Pindar, Athena's body is conspicuous by its absence: nothing is said about the looks of the maiden who invented the *aulos*, but the *parthenos* (19) is recalled by the evocation of Medusa and her sisters, described by their terrifying maidenly heads (παρθενίοις ἀπλάτοις κεφαλαῖς, 9), their beautiful cheeks (εὐπαράου κρᾶτα, 16), and the fastness of their jaws (ἐκ καρπαλιμᾶν γενύων, 20).[99] There are too many cheeks in the span of four lines to *not* think of the aulete's own features while playing the *aulos*. But the constructed silence about Athena's own face also shows the goddess' impossible position between her beautiful *parthenos* side (the Medusa side) and her more technical, functional, banausic side (the Euryale side).

The *Pythian* passage is thus strongly indebted to the elite discourse on the integrity of the body, and it is this ideology that Telestes, tongue in cheek, highlights by rejecting it. But instead of rejecting the banausic, technical aspects of music-playing, Telestes endorses them fully while tapping into another tradition, which connects the *aulos* with the East and Dionysus. The *aulos* is bestowed, as a privilege, by Athena on Dionysus (Βρομίῳ παρέδωκε, *PMG* 805c.1), which allows Telestes to legitimize the instrumental practice of the New Musicians: by "rejecting" the traditional myth of Athena's condemnation of the *auloi*, he recalls that myth, in diction and in scenario, and legitimizes the practice of virtuoso playing. At the same time, he combines the myth of the invention of the *aulos* with another story, that of the introduction of the instrument from Phrygia by Dionysus. If the composition was a dithyramb, this reference to Dionysus would only re-emphasize the ritual connection of the genre, in an archaizing return to the Dionysiac roots of the genre that recent criticism has made a hallmark of the New Music.[100]

The combination of the two myths (that of the invention of the instrument and that of the distribution of power between gods) is itself modeled on the pattern of another musical aetiology: the invention of the lyre in the Homeric *Hymn to Hermes*. The most explicit connection between the

---

[99] On Pind. *Pyth.* 12, Gerber 1986, Leclercq-Neveu 1989, Strauss Clay 1992, Frontisi-Ducroux 1994, Segal 1994, Gentili and Luisi 1995, Papadopoulou and Pirenne Delforge 2001: 41–7.

[100] In particular Csapo 1999–2000 ("the later Euripides and the New Musicians self-consciously put their music in cultic and Dionysiac dress," p. 417) and Csapo 2003. See also chapter 1, pp. 68–9.

two myths is in the repetition of σοφὰ τέχνα, which appears twice in the Homeric hymn:

> ὅς τις ἂν αὐτήν
> <u>τέχνη καὶ σοφίη</u> δεδαημένος ἐξερεείνη
> φθεγγομένη παντοῖα νόῳ χαρίεντα διδάσκει
>
> *Hymn. Hom. Herm.* 482–4

> and whoever cunningly enquires with <u>art and skill</u> to play it, him she teaches, uttering all sorts of delightful things for the spirit

and

> αὐτὸς δ' αὖθ' <u>ἑτέρης σοφίης</u> ἐκμάσσατο <u>τέχνην</u>·
> <u>συρίγγων</u> ἐνοπὴν ποιήσατο τηλόθ' ἀκουστήν.
>
> *Hymn. Hom. Herm.* 511–12

> but he in turn found <u>another artful skill</u>: he created for himself the sound of the <u>syrinx</u> that resounds afar.

This verbal echo linking ancestral lyre-playing and modern *aulos*-playing is important, and so is the traditional association of music and *sophia*. But most significant perhaps are the structural and ideological parallels: an instrument (the lyre/the *aulos*) is handed over by its inventor god (Hermes/Athena) to become the *timē* of another god (Apollo/Dionysus). The inventor is not the player, and was never meant to be, but the instrument keeps the original characteristics of its inventor (*sophia* of Athena and *mētis* of Hermes) while integrating the cultural values of the god to whom it is given.[101] The parallels between the two myths do not stop here: just as the lyre of Hermes/Apollo was associated with a series of transgressions and inversions, so too are the *auloi* of Athena/Dionysus: the lyre is a mix of animal (tortoiseshell, cattle horns, strings) and vegetal (the reeds that make the bridge) and its invention story mixes death and violence with light-hearted play and joyful celebration. In the same way, the *auloi* mix vegetal (the reeds that make the mouthpiece and the wood of the body) and metal elements (the bands that join the mouthpiece and bulb to the wooden pipe) and weave death and violence with future joyful celebration.[102] Reliance on the parallel with the divine string instrument reinforces Telestes' rhetoric of legitimization in the passage, as the supposedly decried *aulos* can take on all the positive (divine, Apollonian) characteristics of the cithara, while

---

[101] On that aspect, see Leclercq-Neveu 1989, Brown 1947.

[102] On a similar mix of life and death in a musical invention, Soph. *Ichneutai* 292–3;
       Cleoboulina's riddle on the *aulos* in Plut. *Mor.* 150e–f (*Septem Sapientium convivium* 5).

competing with its prestige. This passage also throws light, retrospectively, on Timotheus' own presentation, which might be using the motif of the attack on the *aulos* and transferring it to his own art in feigned self-defense, in an intra-New Music *agōn*. Besides the opposition between the old and new guards, one has to take into consideration the internal rivalries, real or imagined, often featured in anecdotes, which allowed both citharodes and dithyrambists to boast about their own art with ever more complex and sophisticated rhetoric.[103]

New Music: a label

What the "New Music" was about cannot be captured fully by either understandings of "newness" or any set of "musical" features, such as complexity or the use of many strings, *anabolai* or polymetry. The poets' position in the history of *mousikē* is best defined by their own rhetoric of self-presentation and by the self-consciousness of their engagement with the past in the context of an agonistic present. Undoubtedly because fragments of New Music have come down to us in the compilations of ancient authors interested in metamusical statements, the New Music texts show a great degree of self-consciousness and reflexivity and great sophistication in constructing their position in the lyric tradition and in using traditional lyric tropes and images. These strategies are not uniform, and poets use traditional rhetorical posturing (praise and blame, rejection of myth, construction of an elaborate poetic persona, and so on) to present new themes, or variously present themselves as part of a tradition of innovators, or invent traditions. Most importantly perhaps, they define the terms of their own reception by providing audience and critics with a series of technical, or pseudo-technical, terms with which to think through innovation itself. The New Music is not *just* a rhetorical creation, devoid of any tonal, metrical, instrumental, or musical reality: from musical papyri and musicological treatises to material evidence for a changing scale of musical production, non-literary sources independently underline important changes. But an important part of the success of these innovative songs lay in the way the New Musicians created the language of their own reception, to the beat and tune of an ever-new music.

---

[103] On rivalries between Phrynis and Timotheus, for example, Plut. *Mor.* 539c (*De laude ipsius* 1); between Timotheus and Cinesias, Plut. *Mor.* 170a (*De superst.* 10); between Timotheus and Dorion, Hegesander, *Hypomnemata* (*FHG* IV 416 fr. 14); on Stratonicus' witticisms against contemporary musicians, Machon frr. 8–11 Gow. For aspects of anecdotes, see next chapter.

> When some brick makers were singing some of his songs out of tune,
> Philoxenus came upon them and trampled their bricks under foot,
> saying, "As you spoil my work, so I will spoil yours."
>
> Diogenes Laertius, *Life of Arcesilaus* 4.6.11

As the last chapter suggested, the New Music is commonly associated with the death of *mousikē*, but it itself had a long, anecdotal, life. The quotation from Diogenes Laertius above is one of many narrative snippets staging a New Musician in a social setting. Rather than focusing narrowly on the musicological controversies associated with the New Music, such accounts provide insight into the poets' dealings with fellow citizens – in the theater, at the market place, or in bed, for example – their position in society, and their relationship with city, tyrants, and kings. No study has paid much attention to this eclectic corpus drawn from historiographers, philosophers, and biographers that throws light on a different aspect of the traditions and innovations associated with the New Music and the lasting popularity of the phenomenon in critics' imagination.

On encountering such narratives, one can treat them as historical truth and combine them into a mostly coherent "biography," while cautiously dismissing suspicious elements.[1] Or one can treat them as mostly fictional, as has Mary Lefkowitz in her influential *Lives of the Greek Poets*: most anecdotes, she argues, can be read as inventions born from a reading of the poet's production.[2] Although Lefkowitz's book does not contain a chapter on the New Musicians, if it were written, it would emphasize, for example, how the anecdotes staging Timotheus being criticized by the Spartans for his overstringed lyre are based on his lines about "meters and rhythms of eleven strokes" and defense against Spartan attacks (*PMG* 791.229–36), or how anecdotes staging Philoxenus' love of food are a reading of the gastronomically themed *Dinner Party* (*PMG* 836). Even if one treats biographical anecdotes as fiction because they are a form of early reception of

---

[1] The historicist approach is illustrated for example in the mini-biographies of the poets in overviews of the New Music by Pickard-Cambridge (1962: 58–71), Pintacuda (1978: 157–64), and West (1992: 356–72).

[2] Lefkowitz 1981; see also Fairweather 1974.

the poet's production and a creative engagement with the poetic corpus, they also inform us about the meaning and significance of a poet for specific audiences and about his or her lasting popularity.[3] Whether Philoxenus ever trampled bricks, as the epigraph to this chapter recounts, is less important than the fact that brick makers are depicted as singing one of Philoxenus' hits while on the job and that Philoxenus sets a parallel between his song and the product of another craft.

The pages that follow focus mostly, although not exclusively, on one figure, Philoxenus, for whom the most abundant data survive. I do not try to determine whether events of his life as glimpsed from anecdotes are historical or not, but rather analyze why such stories were given their specific form and consider the poetic figure and his place in the poetic tradition as they emerge from the intersection of several types of narrative. Anecdotes crystallized around what were felt to be problematic aspects of the musician's persona – his dithyrambs' poetics and his relationship with either *polis* or tyrant.[4] It is these problems and discourses, rather than the actual "life" of Philoxenus, that I am interested in. Ultimately, these stories open into the cultural narrative of a fascinating figure and his time, and into another facet of perceptions of the evolution of musical and socio-cultural history.

Biographic strategies

Apart from Aristoxenus' *Bios* of Telestes, we know of no other *Life* of a New Musician. Yet the narrative strategies used by ancient authors in documenting aspects of the existence of the New Musicians deserve attention, for they serve as background for detailed readings of anecdotes connected to Philoxenus. What Glenn Most says of the tradition of Sappho's *Bios*, or rather *Bioi*, can be adapted for biographical snippets about the New Musicians: in attempting to come to terms with a complex set of data about a poet's life, "authors have tended to apply one or the other of three basic strategies: duplication, narrativization, and condensation."[5]

Duplication, the first process, can be used to account for biographical details that are mutually contradictory, by assigning them to more than one

---

[3] Graziosi (2002) on Homer; Irwin (2006) on Solon.

[4] Building on Foucault's fundamental essay "Qu'est-ce qu'un auteur?," Claude Calame has suggested that we think about poets in terms of the *fonction auteur* ("author function"), "which characterizes the mode of existence, circulation, and functioning of some discourses within a society" (Calame 2004b: 12, quoting Foucault 1969: 798 – my translation). The figure we associate with a name, with "Solon" for example, is the product of a complex construct based on institutional, judicial, and poetic parameters.

[5] Most 1995: 17.

person. In the case of Sappho, Most explains, authors have distinguished between two consistent and plausible individuals, both called Sappho, to make sense of the wealth of data about the artistic and romantic existence of "Sappho": there was Sappho the poetess, and another woman of the same name, a prostitute.[6] Some anecdotes are connected with the poetess, but the stories that do not fit in well are attributed to the life of the other Sappho. The same process has been used in the case of the New Musicians as a means of accounting for discrepancies in data or fuzziness in chronology. The *Suda* for example lists two Melanippides;[7] Aristotle distinguished between two Cinesias;[8] the *spuria* of Stesichorus I are attributed to a second Stesichorus of the fourth century BC; and there were at least two late classical melic poets called Philoxenus.[9] One possibility in this last case is that several contemporary poets could have shared the same name, especially if they were relatives who all participated in the family trade, but the case of the duplication of Philoxenus remains worth examining in detail.

Tradition distinguishes between, on the one hand, a Philoxenus of Cythera, a notorious gourmand and author of dithyrambs that included the famous *Cyclops* or *Galatea*, and, on the other hand, a homonymous poet from Leucas, the alleged author of a poem on food, of undetermined genre, the *Deipnon* (*PMG* 836). In four of the five passages where Athenaeus quotes this *Deipnon* (*Dinner Party*), he uses the phrase ἐν τῷ ἐπιγραφομένῳ Δείπνῳ ("in the work entitled the *Dinner Party*") and attributes the piece to Philoxenus of Cythera (frr. d and e), or simply to Φιλόξενος δ' ὁ διθυραμβοποιός ("Philoxenus, the composer of dithyrambs") (frr. a and c);[10] in the fifth instance, however, he introduces some doubt as regards the identity of the *Dinner Party*'s author by attributing it thus:

Philoxenus of Cythera in the work entitled *Dinner Party* – if he is indeed the one the comic poet Plato refers to in his *Phaon* (εἴπερ τούτου καὶ ὁ κωμῳδιοποιὸς Πλάτων ἐν τῷ Φάωνι ἐμνήσθη), and not Philoxenus of Leucas – describes the following dinner preparation [thus: *PMG* 836 fr. b].

Ath. 4.146f

Modern editors and critics, including Bergk, Smyth, Diehl, Wilamowitz, Page, and Campbell, take Athenaeus' hesitation seriously and attribute the *Deipnon* to Philoxenus of Leucas.[11] But given the scanty evidence about

6 Nymphodorus of Syracuse *FGrH* 572 F 6.
7 *Suda* M 454–5 (III 350). On the doubtful existence of two Melanippides, Garrod 1920: 132.
8 Σ to Ar. *Av.* 1379.
9 See *PMG* 814–35 (Philoxenus of Cythera) and *PMG* 836 (Philoxenus of Leucas).
10 Ath. 11.476e, 11.487a–b, 14.642f–643d (ἐν τῷ Δείπνῳ), 15.685d.
11 For skeptical positions on the existence of two separate Philoxeni: Gulick (1927–41: I), who, in the index of proper names, lists Philoxenus of Leucas as "identical with P. of Cythera?

Philoxenus of Leucas, this one parenthetical mention is barely enough to justify their persistent refusal to attribute the *Deipnon* to the dithyrambic poet or to see the piece as a dithyramb. These two problems, that of genre and that of authorship, are distinct but can be treated as two aspects of the same issue: this attribution to another Philoxenus seems to be a symptom of the discomfort that the *Deipnon* as a poem causes.[12] Since the content of the poem (the narrative of a lavish dinner) does not match generic expectations attached to what is traditionally understood as a dithyramb (a choral song performed at city festivals, on heroic or divine themes often related to the worship of Dionysus and offering a framework within which to praise *Dithyrambos*), the need was felt, I propose, to distinguish between a dithyrambic poet and another poet. The duplication of Philoxenus is thus a solution by ancient and modern interpreters that is intended to explain the variety of the Philoxenian production, or at least the oddity of the *Deipnon* within that production.

But the evidence related to the said Philoxenus of Leucas invites a further suggestion that would justify Philoxenus of Cythera's duplication as Philoxenus "of Leucas." The only mention of a poet of that name comes from a passage of the comic poet Plato's *Phaon* quoted by Athenaeus:

τοῦ Φιλοξένου δὲ τοῦ Λευκαδίου Δείπνου Πλάτων ὁ κωμῳδιοποιὸς μέμνηται·

{Α.} ἐγὼ δ' ἐνθάδ' ἐν τῇ ἐρημίᾳ
τουτὶ διελθεῖν βούλομαι τὸ βιβλίον
πρὸς ἐμαυτόν. {Β.} ἐστὶ δ', ἀντιβολῶ σε, τοῦτο τί;
{Α.} Φιλοξένου καινή τις ὀψαρτυσία.
{Β.} ἐπίδειξον αὐτὴν ἥτις ἔστ'. {Α.} ἄκουε δή.
"ἄρξομαι ἐκ βολβοῖο, τελευτήσω δ' ἐπὶ θύννον."
{Β.} ἐπὶ θύννον; οὐκοῦν †τῆς τελευτ† πολὺ
κράτιστον ἐνταυθὶ τετάχθαι τάξεως.
{Α.} "βολβοὺς μὲν σποδιᾷ δαμάσας καταχύσματι δεύσας
ὡς πλείστους διάτρωγε· τὸ γὰρ δέμας ἀνέρος ὀρθοῖ.
καὶ τάδε μὲν δὴ ταῦτα· θαλάσσης δ' ἐς τέκν' ἄνειμι."

Ath. 1.5b–f

Parodist"; Dalby (1996: 113–16), Olson and Sens (2000: xxxix–xliii), who underline (xlii) that the "Philoxenian" passage closely resembles Archestratus' poem; Wilkins (2000), who sums up the problem (347): "it is not easy to see how the Philoxeni are to be disentangled from each other given their similar areas of interest, their use of an identical poetic form, their contemporaneity and the similar place they share in the discourse of luxury." Olson (2006–10) in his note to Ath. 1.5b: "Philoxenus of Leucas and Philoxenus of Cythera are hopelessly confused in ancient sources."

[12] For a reading of the *Dinner Party*, see Chapter 6.

The comic poet Plato [fr. 189 KA] mentions the *Dinner Party* of Philoxenus of Leucas: "A.: Here in this deserted spot, I want to go through this book by myself. B.: What is it, tell me please? A.: A *Nouvelle Cuisine* by Philoxenus. B.: Show me what it's like! A.: All right, listen. 'I will start from the purse-tassel bulb and will end with the tuna.' B.: With the tuna? So it's much better to be positioned here at the back then! A.: 'The purse-tassels, tame them with ash, drench them with a sauce, and eat as many as you can. For it erects one's manhood. That's it for that; I move on to the children of the sea.'"

On the one hand, the quoted passage differs from Philoxenus' *Deipnon* not only in its meter (dactylic hexameters, while the *Deipnon* is in dactylo-epitrites) and narrative technique (a series of injunctions rather than an *ekphrasis*), but also in that it focuses on cooking and on the aphrodisiac effect of food items, rather than on the dinner as a social event. On the other hand, the way the passage is introduced, as a καινή τις ὀψαρτυσία (a *Nouvelle Cuisine*), echoes one of the buzzwords of the New Music (*kainotomia*) with which Philoxenus of Cythera is associated. In the light of the complex discourse on food and poetry as τέχνη ("art") in the late classical period, it is difficult not to see a connection between the two themes.[13] The *Nouvelle Cuisine* that the character reads is a systematic adaptation, for aphrodisiac needs, of the food items described in the *Dinner Party*. I propose that the passage is not a direct quotation of a parodist, Philoxenus of Leucas, but rather a *Platonic* parody (in dactylic hexameters) of Philoxenus of Cythera, whom Plato calls "Philoxenus of Leucas."[14] I cannot prove this theory, but the alternative geographical origin, Leucas, that Athenaeus attributes to Philoxenus is significant, even too overdetermined to be ignored. Both the title of Plato's comedy, *Phaon*, and most of the fragments of that work that survive (frr. 188–98 KA) introduce a special connection with Sappho's life:[15] Phaon was allegedly the lyric poetess' lover, for whom she jumped from the Leucadian rock, and most of the fragments are concerned to some

---

[13] Nesselrath 1990: 280–330, Wilkins 2000: 396–408, Dobrov 2002. For an example of such assimilation of musical and culinary discourse, see Damoxenus, *Foster Brothers* (fr. 2 KA *ap.* Ath. 3.102f–103a), where the cook acts like a composer and uses the vocabulary of the *harmonikoi* to describe his cooking.

[14] On that aspect, Olson and Sens 2000: xl–xliii. This claim is stronger than that of Gulick, who, in his annotation of the passage, suggests that Philoxenus of Leucas is a parodist. I propose that Plato *himself* writes a parody of Philoxenus of Cythera and calls him "Philoxenus of Leucas."

[15] On the Old Comedy poets' interest in Sappho, Campbell 1982, *T* 25 and 26 with n. 1: "Other comedies which may have dealt with Sappho were *Phaon* by Plato Comicus and Antiphanes . . . and the *Leucadian* by Menander, Diphilus, Alexis, Antiphanes and Amphis."

degree with the apothecary of love (love formulae, drugs and aphrodisiacs, etc.). The associations of Leucas with events of Sappho's "life" could justify the connection between Philoxenus of Cythera, the author of a poem related to food, and Leucas, a metonymy for destructive *eros*. In Anacreon, for example, we find:

ἀρθεὶς δηὖτ' ἀπὸ Λευκάδος
πέτρης ἐς πολιὸν κῦμα κολυμβῶ μεθύων ἔρωτι.

Anac. PMG 376

Once again I stand up and dive from the Leucadian rock into the grey wave, drunk with love.

The term "of Leucas" would be a joke on Philoxenian poetics: given the erotic nature of the parodic passage, it seems natural that the dithyrambic poet of Cythera (Aphrodite's island), who wrote about the Cyclops in love, would be a citizen of Leucas, just as Sappho is Leucadian because of her love poetry and tumultuous romantic biography.[16] I do not have any proof that Plato actually called Philoxenus of Cythera Philoxenus "of Leucas," but neither is there any proof, other than this fragment of Athenaeus, that there ever existed a "Philoxenus of Leucas."

Now, to return to the different processes employed to construct the lives of the poets: Most highlights narrativization as the second means used to account for the rich data about the life of Sappho. Its earliest use is *Heroides* 15, attributed to Ovid. In this fictitious letter, the author creates a rich image of Sappho by accepting as many of the traditional details of the poetess' life as possible and by temporalizing these various elements.[17] Since so little has survived of, and about, the New Musicians, it is extremely difficult to trace such narrativization of their lives, but we might see something like a "narrativization instinct" in the *Suda* entries and other notes devoted to the New Musicians. By making, for example, Melanippides the grandson of an earlier Melanippides and the master of the slave Philoxenus, the *Suda* connects different musicians in a larger narrative framework and ties up the poetic loose ends.[18] Making Phrynis a pupil of Aristocleitus, himself descended from Terpander, a scholiast legitimizes the position of Phrynis in a quasi-mythical Lesbian citharodic lineage.[19] To these familial narratives, one could add a larger narrative about the evolution of *mousikē* as marked by a series of innovations. The New Musicians, just

---

[16] The same kind of process is deployed by Aristophanes, for example, when using "Socrates the Melian" to refer to Socrates (of Athens), Aristophanes mixes together two characters, Socrates and Diagoras the Melian, who shared a reputation for impiety.

[17] Most 1995: 20.   [18] *Suda* M 454–5 (III 350 Adler) and Φ 393 (IV 728–9 Adler).

[19] Σ Ar. *Nub.* 969.

like Sappho, are each associated with one innovation: Sappho invented the plectrum;[20] Melanippides introduced *anabolai*;[21] Phrynis added strings to the lyre, from seven to nine, and introduced harmonic modulations;[22] Timotheus also added strings; Pronomus invented the multimodal *auloi*;[23] Crexus is credited with the introduction of polyphony and recitation.[24] Just as the narrativization of the life of Sappho is a way of making sense of contradictory events, so too is attaching each composer to a specific innovation a way of giving some direction in the meta-narrative of *mousikē*.

The third process presented by Most consists of *condensing* into a single person the many contradictions furnished by the tradition. Most successfully used by the Romantics in the case of Sappho, it is also illustrated by an anecdote told by Satyrus in his life of Euripides:

When Timotheus was held in little esteem [?] in Greece because of his musical innovations (διὰ τὴν ἐν τῇ μουσικῇ καινοτομίαν), and when he was so discouraged that he nearly attempted to put an end to his life, only Euripides laughed at the audiences instead: realizing how great Timotheus was in his genre, he cheered him up with words as encouraging as possible, and even wrote for him the proem of his *Persians*, with which he won and stopped being despised . . .

Satyr. Vit. Eur. 17–18 = P. Oxy. 1176 fr. 39 col. 22

In a proto-romantic way, Satyrus condenses the ambiguity in the reception of Timotheus' production: to reconcile the criticism laid on Timotheus' poetry, whether actual or extrapolated from the *sphragis* of the *Persians*, with the later success of the *Persians*, Satyrus creates a story that stages Timotheus as a lonely genius, ready to take his own life out of despair and commitment to his art, and Euripides as a loyal friend with the insight of a rare art critic. The scenario combines tragic suicide attempt, disinterested male friendship, and the triumph of art,[25] in a way that makes Timotheus' existence, in Schlegel's words, "a constant oscillation, like the stormy wave – just now it seemed to touch the eternal stars, and already it has fallen into the terrifying abyss of the sea."[26]

Character, body, and type

Yet some features of the narrative of the New Musicians' lives do not fall into the categories just described. A first type of comments on the New Musicians belongs to another type of discourse, heir to the comic, and

---

[20] *Suda* Σ 107 (IV 322–3 Adler).   [21] Arist. *Rh.* 1409b26–30 for *anabolai*.
[22] [Plut.] *De mus.* 1133b–c.   [23] Paus. 9.12.5, Ath. 14.631e.
[24] [Plut.] *De mus.* 1135c–d, 1141a.
[25] Kris and Kurz 1979: 1–12, on the idea of the heroization of the artist.
[26] Schlegel, *Studien*, 43, quoted by Most (1995: 22).

iambic, tradition, which projects onto the body of the poet, or onto the body of a personified Mousike, aspects of the poet's work.[27] In a way that announces the Hellenistic poets' association of literary and portrait styles, Aristophanes exploits this trope in the *Thesmophoriazousae* (149–52), by equating Agathon's effeminate and languid body with his topic and style.[28] The same is true of the *Birds*, where Cinesias' limping gait (ποδὰ . . . κυλλὸν ἀνὰ κύκλον κυκλεῖς, "you circle your bandy-legged foot in circle") is described in a circumlocutory way representative of the poet's diction. The circular motion of the poet, moreover, stands in for the circularity of his compositions (*kyklioi choroi*). Additionally, other sources comment on Cinesias' thinness: his lack of physical substance is connected with the lack of substance of his dithyramb.[29]

By contrast, a second type of stories is not specifically related to one person. These stories can be used interchangeably of one musician or another: stories about Phrynis appear in other passages as anecdotes about Timotheus, and the name of Terpander, or even that of Empedocles or Plato, can be substituted for that of Timotheus.[30] In his examination of the ethical origins of the biography genre, Arnaldo Momigliano has accounted for this feature: "lives" are more "types of life" than actual accounts of individual existences.[31] This Peripatetic interest in types, rather than particulars, explains why some stories illustrate ethical points or characters, rather than personal features. The following story for example speaks to the ideology of excess of the New Music rather than illuminating the biography of Timotheus:

When Timotheus was competing at the Carneia, one of the ephors took a knife and asked the poet from what end of his instrument he wanted the strings in excess of the traditional seven cut out.

Plut. *Mor.* 238c–d (*Inst. Lac.* 17)

---

[27] Muses on the comic stage: Mousike herself appears in Pherecrates, *Cheiron*, fr. 155 KA; Aeschylus' Muse (Ar. *Ran.* 939–44) and Euripides' Muse (Ar. *Ran.* 1304–64) are described in physical terms. On personifications of musical ideas, Hall 2000 and 2006: 170–83.

[28] On Aristophanes, Muecke 1982. On Hellenistic epigrams on portraits of poets, Prioux 2007: 7–74.

[29] Ar. *Av.* 1373–1409. Dunbar links the emaciated birds in the parody of Cinesias with the thinness of the poet, called φιλύρινος "limewood" Cinesias. See also Ar. frr. 156.10–11 KA; Plato Com. fr. 200 KA; Galen, *On the Aphorisms of Hippocrates* 18.1; Ath. 12.551d–552b, quoting Strattis' *Cinesias* 17 KA. More generally on character, body type, and performance: Cameron 1991, Worman 2002: 14–19, with reference to Bakhtin 1984, Foucault 1985, Butler 1990, Bourdieu 1991.

[30] For Timotheus, Phrynis, and Terpander, see below. The opening anecdote told by Diogenes Laertius about Philoxenus is also reminiscent of the story of Homer's dealing with the potters (pseudo-Herodotus, *Life of Homer* 32).

[31] Gemoll 1924 on how anecdotes, taken as slices of life, illustrate virtues and vices. Momigliano 1993: 69–70, on individuals as types; also Bell 1978 on Simonides.

The reference to Timotheus appears in a passage concerned with Spartan musical conservatism, which explains that "if anyone tried to sin against traditional music, [the Spartans] would not allow it" (εἰ δέ τις παραβαίνοι τι τῆς ἀρχαίας μουσικῆς, οὐκ ἐπέτρεπον), and also adduces the example of Terpander. In another version of the story, told this time about Timotheus' contemporary Phrynis, the ephor's name (Ecprepes or Mr. *Comme Il Faut*) fittingly underlines the issues at stake: what is important is the appropriate number of strings, and what counts most are the middle strings.[32] But the same story can have a contrary conclusion: Athenaeus, for example, refers to an anecdote told by Artemon of Cassandreia in his *On the Dionysiac Guild* according to which Timotheus, in response to the accusation of *polychordia*, pointed to a little statue of Apollo playing a similarly many-stringed *magadis* and was acquitted.[33] Both narratives can be read at different levels: as discourses on lyric practice and its evolution and as discourse on moral norms and the place of the outsider in society, a status determined in this case by the failure to respect acceptable metrics. In the end, what really happened to Timotheus at Sparta matters much less than the intersection of ethical and musical discourse illustrated by this type of episode.

The poet's voice and the poet's throat

That these narrative forms – discourse on the poet's body and reading of an ethical type – sometimes overlap is illustrated by a short anecdote, a four-line *chreia* from the mid third-century BC comic poet Machon quoted by Athenaeus in his catalogue of famous *opsophagoi* in Book 8, which is devoted to discussions of fish, musicians, and fish-obsessed musicians. Machon's *Chreiae*, only preserved through quotations in the *Deipnosophistae*, is a collection of passages presenting the witty sayings of hetaerae, parasites, and musicians or poets. A majority of the anecdotes are connected with the lower functions of the body – especially those concerning sex and food – but the overall purpose of the collection remains a matter of debate.[34] Even the main point, and significance, of each anecdote is often difficult to grasp.

---

[32] Plut. *Mor.* 220c (*Apoph. Lac.* 8), about the ephor Ecprepes cutting two supernumerary strings on Phrynis' nine-string lyre. The story is repeated in *Mor.* 84a (*De prof. virt.* 13) and in *Vit. Agis* 10.4, about both Timotheus and Phrynis. In both versions, the lines following the anecdote make explicit its symbolism and connect music and politics. In *De prof. virt.* a comparison is drawn between the instrument and the state: progress toward virtue consists in a mean between excess in either direction (μετρίον). In the *Life of Agis*, the magistrates of the times of Phrynis and Timotheus "were watching out to prevent the pompous and excessive in music (τὸ ἐν μουσικῇ σοβαρὸν καὶ περιττόν) from getting to the point where the lack of measure and the out-of-tuneness (ἀμετρία καὶ πλημμέλεια) in lives and manners would make the city discordant and out of tune (ἀσύμφωνον καὶ ἀνάρμοστον)."

[33] *FHG* IV 342 fr. 11 *ap.* Ath. 14.636e–f.   [34] Gow 1965: 23–4, Kurke 2002.

The anecdote I cite below lends itself, I suggest, to three kinds of reading: an ethical reading, a literary critical reading, and a political reading:

Φιλόξενός ποθ', ὡς λέγουσ', ὁ Κυθήριος
ηὔξατο τριῶν σχεῖν τὸν λάρυγγα πήχεων,
ὅπως καταπίνω, φησίν, ὅτι πλεῖστον χρόνον
καὶ πάνθ' ἅμα μοι τὰ βρώμαθ' ἡδονὴν ποιῇ.

Machon, fr. 10 Gow

> Philoxenus of Cythera, as the story goes, once prayed his throat were four foot long, "so that I could take," he said, "as much time as possible to drink, and all the food could cause me pleasure at once."

On one level, the anecdote focuses on the body and the satisfaction of its desires. In a remark mostly made of superlative terms, the poet expresses the fantasy of a body that would allow him maximum gastronomic pleasure, liquid and solid. The story is quoted in different versions and attributed to different characters in Athenaeus and in the Aristotelian corpus.[35] In Athenaeus, the quip appears in a series of variations on disorderly eating, while in the Aristotelian corpus it is quoted in passages variously discussing excess and profligacy (ἀκολασία), self-control (σωφροσύνη), and continence (ἐγκράτεια). In these passages, the story as suggested above has less to do with Philoxenus as an individual and more to do with Philoxenus as a type.

Yet, even if one recognizes that the passage is typical of the ancient biographic anecdote genre, there is something distinctive about having a lyric poet, condemned elsewhere for his excessive innovations, ask for an enormous throat. The choice of that particular organ, instead of the more practical mouth, tongue, or belly, as the site of gastronomic pleasure is particularly apt for discourse on music and norms: even if in discussing the optimal use of the body Philoxenus says nothing about the musical possibilities of a formidable throat specifically, the emphasis on the laryngeal features of Philoxenus underlines his proximity to natural lyricists – the birds.[36] Moreover, what Philoxenus fantasizes about is based on an aesthetics of *mélange*. The poet does not make any distinction between food and drink; he not only wants to enjoy everything at the same time (ἅμα), but also uses a plural noun (πάντα τὰ βρώματα) to describe the food he consumes, which

---

[35] Ath. 1.6b–d; Arist. *Eth. Eud.* 1231a, *Eth. Nic.* 1118a; [Arist.] *Pr.* 28.7 (950a 4–5).

[36] In the epitome of Athenaeus (1.6b–d), where other versions are related in connection with Philoxenus the son of Eryxis or Melanthius, the throat is explicitly described as that of a crane or a long-necked bird. I have not found any convincing argument to explain how πῆχυς, which can be used of the arms of the lyre (LSJ s.v. III), could have a musical meaning in this passage.

obliterates the individual qualities of the fare. This particular preference can be interpreted as a commentary on Philoxenus' musical aesthetics, a gastronomic illustration of the poet's mixing of modes attested in other sources.[37] The four lines also condense a discourse on performance and pleasure, which is in keeping with conservative criticism of the populist appeal of the New Musicians, eager to please the crowds. In the *chreia* though, Philoxenus' remark blends the role of the audience and that of the poet: the poet presents himself at the same time as potential performer (offering a marvelous sight) and as audience (experiencing the pleasure created [ποιεῖν] by the food). One can extend to the image of Philoxenus in the four lines of Machon the correlation between body and poetry that Deborah Steiner reads in descriptions of eating practices in archaic and early classical poetry: "composers in a variety of poetic genres were working within a social and linguistic paradigm that constructed intimate links between decorous dining and decorous speaking, and that saw breaches in the registers of eating and speech as joined and expressive of one another: what goes into the mouth and what comes out turn out to be very closely related."[38] Here too, what travels down the poet's throat and what comes out are tightly connected: the fantasy of a monstrous throat allowing endless mélange to enhance pleasure echoes commentaries on New Music and its practice as presented by conservative critics.

But Philoxenus' wish can also be interpreted in a more political way. If one takes into consideration the setting in which *chreiae* were performed or shared, the witticism gains a new dimension. When set against the background of aristocratic sympotic ideology, Philoxenus the dissolute man (ἀκόλαστος) challenges the values associated with the elite symposiast. By being the opposite of the "middling" man, Philoxenus turns on their head a traditional feature of lyric poetry – praise of pleasure in orderly consumption of wine and music in good company – and the acceptable metrics of the society he belongs to.[39] The personal hedonistic ideal he describes (physical monstrosity, or animality, to satisfy bodily desires) could not be in greater opposition to that of the *kaloskagathos*: his wish for a monstrous throat inverts the values of self-control and temperance associated with the *kaloskagathos*, who prides himself on his personal discipline and physical integrity. What Philoxenus prays for is actually an anti-symposium: the

---

[37] Dion. Hal. *Comp.* 19 for modulation between *harmoniai* within the same piece, on which Fongoni 2011.

[38] Steiner 2002: 297.

[39] Morris 1986. Also Kurke 1999: 145, who comments, "the figure of the grotesque body serves as the representational weapon of popular tradition against aristocratic mores and ideology."

solitary self-indulgent and undiscerning consumption of food and wine in a deformed body.

Opsophagia and philoxenia

The biographic and critical strategies I have presented above are useful for explaining many of the features of the stories connected with the New Musicians, but a number of anecdotes about Philoxenus deserve special consideration. All are connected with the issue of the poet's name, and they stage a recurring threefold element: the poet's relationship with food, *xenia*, and speech or poetry.

Philoxenus apparently had several names throughout his life: according to the *Suda*, he was called Myrmex, or Mr. Ant, a name that reflects the characteristics of New Music's tortuous melodies called μυρμηκιαί ("ant paths").[40] Hesychius also reports that Philoxenus was called Doulon, Mr. Slave, because he had been a slave, first of Agesylus, then of the poet Melanippides.[41] But the entry under which the *Suda* gives these details, Philoxenus (Mr. Hospitable, or lover of *xenia*), is itself loaded with connotations and encapsulates a problem: that of the status of the poet in a social network. Starting with the Demodocus of the *Odyssey*, the archaic and early classical poet-singer is linked to the community to which he belongs through *xenia* (hospitality, guest-friendship, or ritual friendship); as Carson notes, "poets ... participated in the gift economy of their communities as *xenoi* of the people who enjoyed their poetry."[42] Philoxenus' name itself collapses literary criticism and socio-political categories and captures the complexities of the poet's societal status: most of the anecdotes told about Philoxenus also revolve around this very issue, as if enactments of his loaded name.

"Like an overcooked hare"

Philoxenus, however, is not the first poet lover of *xenia*. After the archaic period, the tension surrounding the mercenary Muse and the monetary value of poetry in society is described by Pindar and, to a lesser extent, Bacchylides in their compositions,[43] but the most elaborate anecdotal

---

[40] *Suda* Φ 393 (IV 728–9 Adler). Μυρμηκιαί is used of Timotheus' and Agathon's melodies, Pherecrates, fr. 155 KA, 23; Ar. *Thesm.* 100.

[41] Hsch. Δ 2261.   [42] Carson 1999: 14. On *xenia* in the *Odyssey*, Finley 1954: 103–9.

[43] On models of prestige and the professionalization of the Muse, Nagy 1989. On *xenia* in Pindar as a way of conceptualizing the relationship of poet and victor, Kurke 1991: 135–59.

tradition staging the problems of a poet's complicated relationship with *xenia* and love of money is attached to Simonides.[44]

In her study of Simonides, evocatively entitled *Economy of the Unlost*, Ann Carson has analyzed some of the stories related to Simonides' stinginess in the light of Marxist views of money and commodities' value. The anecdote that Chamaeleon tells of Simonides and the hare is a good starting point:

About hares, Chamaeleon says in his *On Simonides* that Simonides was having dinner with Hiero, and that he did not get a hare, when everyone else had one on their table. When Hiero later gave him his portion, Simonides improvised: "wide it was, but not wide enough to reach to here" (οὐδὲ γὰρ <οὐδ'> εὐρύς περ ἐὼν ἐξίκετο δεῦρο). In fact, Simonides was, according to Chamaeleon, a real cheapskate (κίμβιξ) and a sordid profit-lover (αἰσχροκερδής). In Syracuse for example, when Hiero used to send him lavish daily provisions, he would sell most of what had been sent to him and keep for himself only a small portion. When asked the reason, he said, "so that Hiero's munificence (μεγαλοπρέπεια) and my sense of moderation (κοσμιότης) be clear to all."

Chamaeleon, fr. 33 Wehrli

In the first part of the story, Simonides improvises a witty parody on a line of Homer, οὐδὲ γὰρ οὐδ' εὐρύς περ ἐὼν ἐδυνήσατο πάσας ("and wide was [the beach at Troy], but not wide enough to contain all the ships," *Il.* 14.33), to address the unfairness of the hare distribution. As Carson explains,

Likening skimpy hare to the beach at Troy is a witticism aimed at easing an awkward social moment. But it may also cast a wry side glance at an earlier age and other values. Homer's community would surely have guaranteed him not only a complete dinner but a full livelihood, "so that he might eat and so that he might be folded close," as Odysseus once said [*Od.* 8.477–8 and above].[45]

One can also add that in the first part of the story poetry, especially with a reference to the epic past and a non-straightforward (nearly oracular) way of speaking, is the way for the poet to establish his authority and wisdom.[46] This practice requires his addressee's knowledge and understanding of the same set of references. The juxtaposition of this first story with the second one, told by Chamaeleon, makes the ambiguity Simonides feels with regard

---

[44] Bell 1978, Carson 1999.   [45] Carson 1999: 21.
[46] On the traditional connection between poet and wisdom, Svenbro 1976: 85–8. Also Gentili 1988: 161–3, especially 162: "In breaking away from the traditional mold of the inspired poet and the model of the poet as master of truth, Simonides inaugurates a process of secularization that replaces a special, privileged type of knowledge with what is essentially a lay person's knowledge, more accessible and political."

to his different economic relationships even clearer: "Once again Simonides is pointing to a tension between two economic systems. Food is transformed into money in the story, as use value is transformed into exchange value when a society adopts coinage . . . Simonides' wording is deliberate. *Megaloprepeia* ("munificence") and *kosmiotēs* ("sense of order") are terms drawn directly from the aristocratic vocabulary of gift exchange."[47] These anecdotes underline the two-sided nature, like that of a coin, of the poet's relationship with a patron in the fifth century BC. Simonides' situation embodies the problem surrounding the production of song in the city, in a new age of commerce and growing professionalization. Two models of thinking about the value of poetry and remuneration of the poet are in competition: on the one hand, the archaic *xenia* and gifts model, which embeds the poet in an aristocratic economy and treats poetry as a form of *charis* ("favor, beautiful gift"), and, on the other hand, the money model, which deems poetry a commodity.[48] In Carson's economical words, "money has imploded the meaning of *xenos*. For alongside 'guest' and 'host,' the Greek word *xenos* denotes 'stranger,' 'outsider,' 'alien.' At one time it made sense to blend these meanings in a single word because the reality was unitary. Stranded between 'guest' and 'alien,' Simonides sits watching this rich and ancient reality fall apart like an overcooked hare."[49]

This early classical Simonidean background is necessary to understand two other anecdotes, one of which stages Philoxenus, the other Timotheus. The Timothean story is preserved in Plutarch:

When Archelaus seemed too sticky fingered when it came to gift giving (γλισχροτέρῳ περὶ τὰς δωρεάς), Timotheus often used to hint at the matter with the following line: "you commend earth-born silver" (σὺ δὲ τὸν γηγενέταν ἄργυρον αἰνεῖς). To which Archelaus answered, not without wit (οὐκ ἀμούσως), "and you demand it" (σὺ δέ γ᾿ αἰτεῖς).

Plut. Mor. 334b (De Alex. fort. 1)

The Macedonian king is here reminiscent of Hiero: both rulers appear to have abandoned the aristocratic archaic practice of keeping a poet in a network of commensality and gifts (δωρεάς), and both poets use their poetic wit to point out that the poet could use the tyrant's generosity. But unlike Simonides, who has his eyes on a rabbit, a non-monetary gift, Timotheus hints at something that cannot be eaten – silver.[50] In his witty request, the

---

[47] Carson 1999: 25.   [48] On *charis*, Kurke 1991: 103–7.   [49] Carson 1999: 22.

[50] The connotations of the metal are important: it is not the gold of gods and aristocrats (on which Kurke 1999: 45–60), nor the base bronze of "token coinage" (on which Kurke 1999: 304–9). Kurke 1999: 12: "if Kroll [1998] is right, we might see the development of silver money

poet still relies on motives of a non-money model: he makes silver sound noble, Titan-like (γηγενέταν), a pre-coinage entity, and refers to a poetic function – praise (αἰνεῖς). With a pun, however, Archelaus returns the quip and puts the sentence back in its actual context, that of the poet asking (αἰτεῖς) for cash. The Simonidean and Timothean anecdotes encapsulate the same problem: the breakdown of a system in which the poet can rely on a patron, and the poet's use of his poetic persona and wit to remind the patron of his socio-economic responsibility. In the Simonides passage, the exchange still takes place against the background of a gift economy, looking back to a model as archaic as Homer, while in the Timotheus anecdote the poet uses archaizing rhetoric to take aim at new concerns: money and metal, especially the Athenian metal of choice, with its middling connotation – silver.[51]

Philoxenus' fishy tyrant: Dionysius and Galatea

A second anecdote, staging Philoxenus and another tyrant, Dionysius of Sicily, takes the embeddedness of poetry in social and economic networks to another level. The passage is from the Peripatetic author Phaenias and probably comes from his *On the Tyrants in Sicily*.[52] It is more complex than the Simonidean anecdote, as it explicitly mixes this issue of socio-economic and symbolic status with questions of poetics and reception:

Philoxenus the poet of Cythera, a lover of delicacies (περιπαθὴς ὢν τοῖς ὄψοις), was once having dinner with Dionysius when he saw that a large red mullet had been served to the tyrant and a small one to himself; Philoxenus took the small fish and put it to his ear. When Dionysius asked what he was doing that for, Philoxenus replied that he was writing a *Galatea* (γράφων τὴν Γαλάτειαν) and wanted some information about Nereus from the red mullet, but the fish had replied that she was too young when she was caught and so could not follow; the fish that had been served to Dionysius on the other hand was older and had a clear understanding of all he wanted to know. Dionysius laughed and passed to Philoxenus the fish that was set in front of him.

---

before coinage as the first general-purpose money, that crosscut and thereby began to break down the rigid hierarchy of ranked spheres of exchanges through which the elite maintained authority. Finally, the minting of coin would represent the state's assertion of its ultimate authority to constitute and regulate value in all the spheres in which general-purpose money operated simultaneously – economic, social, political and religious."

[51] Kurke 1999: 305.

[52] Phaenias also probably composed *On the Slaying of Tyrants for Motives of Revenge* (frr. 14–16 Wehrli), on which see Wehrli's commentary (pp. 30–3), and Podlecki 1969.

Dionysius also used to like getting drunk with Philoxenus. But when the poet was caught making advances to Dionysius' mistress Galatea, he was thrown to the quarries, where, working on his *Cyclops* (ποιῶν τὸν Κύκλωπα), he made what had happened to him into a story (συνέθηκε τὸν μῦθον εἰς τὸ περὶ αὐτὸν γενόμενον πάθος), casting Dionysius in the role of the Cyclops, the flute girl in that of Galateia, and himself as Odysseus.

Phaenias, fr. 13 Wehrli

The anecdote is twofold. The first part presents the poet at dinner with the Sicilian tyrant, with a scenario that echoes the setting of the Simonidean story; the second covers post-dinner entertainment, which would correspond to the Greek sympotic part of the evening. The two parts are strongly connected thematically and deal with the relationship between appetite, poetry, and socio-economic relationships.[53] Again our story lends itself to more than one type of reading: here, one that throws light specifically on the early reception of the poet's production and one that reflects the perception of the new social relationship of a poet with a tyrant.

The anecdote starts with the same issue of food distribution as in the Chamaeleon episode, but this is a different kind of food. While hare was featured at Hiero's table, Dionysius serves fish. Hare eating, and recreational hare hunting, are connected with the aristocratic world.[54] Whatever the reality of the hare market in fifth-century Sicily, Hiero's hare was more likely a product of aristocratic gift exchange than a purchase. As iconography suggests, gifts of hare in particular "claimed a central place in the ideology of aristocratic masculinity in Athens" and especially in pederasty.[55] Fish occupies a very different position in Athenian ideology, where it is the *opson par excellence* and has associations widely different from those of both the farinaceous element of a man's diet (the *sitos*) and meat, which was mostly enjoyed by citizens at civic festival meals and whose apportionment was religiously regulated.[56] This anecdote, which stages seduction, is a reminder that in ancient Greece, and especially Athens, fish, and red mullet in particular, was "treated as quite irresistible, lusted after with a desire that comes close to a sexual one."[57] But fish is also a product from the market, sold

---

[53] On Dionysius' relationship with the arts, Loicq-Berger 1966. Cicero called him *doctus a puero et artibus ingenuis eruditus* (*Tusc.* 5.63).

[54] On hunting hares, Xen. *Cyn.* 5–6; on the ideal hunter, Xen. *Cyn.* 2.1–3.

[55] Barringer 2001: 72.

[56] Athens dealt with the problem by distributing pieces of meat on the basis of lot casting (Détienne and Vernant 1979: 23–4). On sacrifice and civic community, see also Schmitt-Pantel 1992: 49–52, Davidson 1997: 15–18.

[57] Davidson 1997. Red mullet was, among fish, one of the finest and most appreciated; see also Gow 1965: 67. Davidson (1997: 8) underlines the continuity between Athens and Sicily in

and bought, acquired with currency. The sexual objects associated with the two kinds of food are thus diametrically opposed: where an aristocratic boy might be persuaded with a gift of a hare, a courtesan can be acquired with the money that might buy fish.

The two anecdotes engage with the same fundamental issue, the negotiation of the relationship between poet and patron through food, but each poet handles the situation with a different kind of rhetoric. Simonides' use of the Homeric line is a way for the poet to give a witty conclusion to an unfortunate episode and pay back, as it were, the tyrant for the food handout. Philoxenus, by contrast, uses an animal fable, an *ainos*, to make the tyrant smile and substitute big for small fish: he uses the riddling language of the symposiast to get the mullet. His expression is not straightforward, but he talks as among equals who share the same language and expects his fellow drinkers to understand sentences imbued with *sophia*, the kind of rhetoric described by Theognis:

> ταῦτά μοι <u>ἠνίχθω</u> κεκρυμμένα τοῖς ἀγαθοῖσι·
> γινώσκοι δ' ἄν τις καὶ κακόν, ἄν <u>σοφὸς</u> ἦ.
>
> Thgn. 681–2 W²

<u>let these things be riddles</u> hidden by me for gentlemen:
    one would recognize even evil, if he is <u>wise</u>.[58]

It is also possible here to read Philoxenus in the tradition of the wise man who visits the tyrant and delivers wisdom, as other testimonies about Philoxenus explicitly suggest.[59]

But there is more to the anecdote. For one thing, we are not told how Dionysius acquired the big fish. If he did not grab it himself, then, just as in the case of the tyrant Polycrates, the mechanisms of tyranny have fed off themselves, enabling the tyrant, as always, to get the big fish, or power.[60] To

---

matters of fish appreciation: "The strength of this Athenian appetite is demonstrated most graphically by passages in which fish are involved in a literary or metaphorical seduction." Even more explicitly: "Fish seduces and conquers. It functions like the forces of persuasion, or the allure of a hetaera, or the magical power of charms" (10); "Fish you were free to fall in love with, grabbing the best bits for yourself. Here in this very small section of the Athenian economy in the fifth and fourth centuries BCE we have what looks like a fully-fledged system of consumer objects" (16).

[58] Following Nagy (1990: 149), I adopt the manuscript reading, κακόν, rather than the emendation printed by West (κακός).

[59] On the tradition, Gray 1986. For parallels between Simonides and Philoxenus, see Ephorus (*FGrH* 70 F 2 *ap.* Ath. 8.352c), who underlines that both poets were aiming for εὐτραπέλια ("wit"). For Philoxenus as a provider of wisdom: Plut. *Mor.* 831f (*De vitando aere alieno* 8), Stob. 2. 31, *Flor. Mon.* 260, 261.

[60] On food and power, Davidson 1997: 292: "In the light of Greek insistence on the equality of the sacrificial community, then, an equality re-enacted in practice at every blood-sacrifice, the

mess with these mechanisms is to court a bitter end, as the conclusion of
the story illustrates. Moreover, Philoxenus, like any good trickster, ends up
ahead, in his case with the best, or at least bigger, share of the fish. Philoxenus
seems at least as interested in the fish as in wisdom and good stories, an observation that takes on additional significance given the erotic connotations
of the whole scene. Philoxenus presents himself as working on a *Galatea* –
a song that takes its name from a Nereid and sets up a thematic expectation: like most of her mythical sisters and their land counterparts, the
nymphs, Galatea is a love object. He starts his little skit by taking the mullet
(τρῖγλα, feminine in Greek) in his hands. Not only does the verb, ἀναλαμ-
βάνω ("grab"), indicate violence, including the violence of unwilling sex (the
very verb that Mousike uses to refer to the musicians' assault in Pherecrates'
passage, fr. 155 KA, 4), but the εἰς τὰς χεῖρας also involves more physical
contact with the fish than a Greek used to proper table manners would
want.[61] Even the fish's fictional talk is full of sexual innuendoes, as if she
were playing with the poet's desire by using the vocabulary of the hunt (with
ἁλοίη, "to be caught"), usually associated with the quest for the beloved, and
by referring to her tender age (νεωτέρα). Phaenias' language indicates that
Philoxenus might desire his fish more than he wants to show: his passion
for the mullet might be even greater than his desire for making a point to
the hungry tyrant. In this light, Philoxenus appears as a character with an
appetite more tyrannical than a tyrant's, rather than as a wise man delivering
a lesson to a greedy ruler. What are we to make of this disturbing feature?

The second part of the anecdote might provide an answer. After getting
drunk with Dionysius (συνεμέθυε), the poet tries to seduce the tyrant's
mistress, Galatea. As a punishment for his overbearing behaviour, Dionysius
has Philoxenus thrown into the quarries, a particularly charged place after
the Sicilian expedition attempted by the Athenians.[62] Philoxenus, who had
previously adopted the riddling language of the aristocrat, has behaved as a
bad symposiast, showing *hybris* and lack of *sophrosyne* in his incapability to
contain his appetite for drink and sex. Philoxenus is here the fourth-century
BC version of Alcibiades, a fellow symposiast who displays *paranomia*, "[a]
disregard for norms . . . considered dangerous in any society and . . . typical
of tyrants."[63] Anxiety about tyrannical behavior that accompanies or is

---

descriptions of politicians eating greedily has automatic overtones of a power-grab." "The idea
of a fish 'worthy of your rule' is a perfectly plausible notion in Greek terms" (289).

[61] On "sea animals" as a double entendre for sexual parts, Henderson 1991: 142. For other
parallels between fish, hetaerae, and political discourse, see Ar. *Vesp.* 493–502.

[62] Thuc. 7.87.

[63] Davidson 1997: 299. About Alcibiades, Davidson continues with words that could describe
Philoxenus: "This *paronomia* . . . is not mere delinquency, some general disregard for all laws or

made manifest by excessive drinking is expressed in wisdom poetry, for example in the *Theognidea*:

οἶνόν τοι πίνειν πουλὺν κακόν· ἢν δέ τις αὐτόν
πίνῃ ἐπισταμένως, οὐ κακὸς ἀλλ᾽ ἀγαθός.
Thgn. 211–12 W²

Drinking lots of wine is bad; but if one drinks it reasonably, he is not a bad man, but a gentleman.

That anxiety is closely connected to injunctions about moderation and middleness associated with civic behaviour:

μηδὲν ἄγαν ἀσχαλλε ταρασσομένων πολιητέων,
Κύρνε, μέσην δ᾽ ἔρχευ τὴν ὁδὸν ὥσπερ ἐγώ.
Thgn. 219–20 W²

Don't get excessively distressed, Kurnos, when your fellow citizens are causing trouble, but walk down the middle of the road, as I do.

The second part of the Philoxenus story thus turns the first part on its head: the poet is the real tyrannical man, a slave to his belly and a threat to his fellow symposiasts, and Dionysius, the illuminated ruler who accepts the lesson of the wise man in the first part of the story, turns out to be the proper symposiarch, the one who regulates excess (εὐθυντῆρα κακῆς ὕβριος ἡμετέρης, Thgn. 40 W²), prevents the rise of a potential tyrant, and brings an unruly gathering of fellow drinkers back to order (*kosmos*) and good measure (*metron*).

In retrospect, the first part of this anecdote was only preparing for the second: the alleged subject of Philoxenus' first dithyramb (Galatea) announces the second, real, dithyramb, which the poet will end up composing, inspired by the eponymous mistress. Moreover, by a not-so-subtle conflation of images, the poet's seizing of the fish paves the way for the seizing of the homonymous girl, and the poet's uncontrollable appetite for the tyrant's dinner proves to have been a hint of his desire for the tyrant's partner. The two parts are closely linked, thematically and structurally: Philoxenus starts by seeing (εἶδεν), then silently performs (seizing the fish, ἀναλαβών), and finally makes the connection with his poetry, when he answers Dionysius. The next part of the anecdote involves the same elements (gaze, action,

authority, it is a disregard for the limits of appetite, for the laws and protocols that control desire, particularly in Alcibiades' case, the rules that govern sex and drinking." On the good symposiast, who governs good deeds and knows rightful thoughts (τὰ δίκαια φρονεῖν), see also Ion of Chios, fr. 26.13–16 W².

and poetry) but in reverse order: this time, it is Philoxenus who is seen (ἐφωράθη), in the act of seducing the tyrant's mistress, and he is the object of a violent action (ἐνεβλήθη, seized and thrown to the quarries). The subject of his miseries (τὸ περὶ αὐτὸν γενόμενον πάθος) he transforms into a poem.

The second part of the anecdote has often been read as a fiction explaining features of Philoxenus' *Cyclops* or *Galatea*.[64] Elements in the poet's life, including the innovations introduced in the Homeric Polyphemus story, are invented to explain characteristics of the poetry in a form of early reception, and the dithyramb is seen as an allegorized narrative of an event in the poet's life. The Philoxenian Cyclops' character, for example, would be a projection of Dionysius' character, Galatea's of the tyrant's mistress', and Odysseus' of Philoxenus'. The parallels are particularly fitting: both Sicilians have poor eyesight,[65] have to deal with breaches of the rules of hospitality, and have to come up with a political expedient when a Greek does not act as a proper *xenos* but enters their home and has a go at their cheese, fish, or mistress. And both overreact equally violently against guests who go too far. As for Galatea, in the light of the first part of the anecdote, she can be seen as illustrating the new status of commodities in a market economy, be they fish, poems, or courtesans: money can buy any of these items. Finally and most importantly, Philoxenus as staged by Phaenias is a new Odysseus, a man driven by his belly and a master riddler.

But the connections between Phaenias' anecdote and the *Odyssey* episode are so rich that they also suggest more than a scenario invented to explain features of Philoxenus' *Cyclops*. The Phaenias story is a meditation on the name of Philoxenus himself and on the poet's connection with *Odyssey* 9. Consider the following lines. Upon reaching the island of the Cyclops, Odysseus goes exploring

> αὐτὰρ ἐγὼ σὺν νηΐ τ' ἐμῇ καὶ ἐμοῖσ' ἑτάροισιν
> ἐλθὼν τῶνδ' ἀνδρῶν πειρήσομαι, οἵ τινές εἰσιν,
> ἤ ῥ' οἵ γ' ὑβρισταί τε καὶ ἄγριοι οὐδὲ δίκαιοι,   175
> ἦε <u>φιλόξεινοι</u>, καί σφιν νόος ἐστὶ θεουδής.
>   Hom. *Od.* 9.173–6

> I will go on my ship with my comrades to test these men, find out what kind of people they are, whether they are violent and savage, or just and <u>stranger-loving</u>, with a god-fearing mind.

The last line is formulaic but takes on new meaning in the context of the Cyclops story.[66] Both Odysseus' ethnographic curiosity and his interest

---

[64] Hordern 1999, 2004; Power forthcoming.
[65] <'Ο> Διονύσιος οὐκ ὠξυδόρκει. John Tzetzes, Σ in Ar. *Pl.* 290.
[66] For example, Hom. *Od.* 6.121, 8.576, 13.202.

in material goods bring him to test the Cyclops. In his account of their discovery of the Cyclops' cave and assault on the Cyclops' cheeses, Odysseus explains that his comrades begged him to leave,

> ἀλλ' ἐγὼ οὐ πιθόμην, ἦ τ' ἂν πολὺ κέρδιον ἦεν,
> ὄφρ' αὐτόν τε ἴδοιμι, καὶ εἴ μοι ξείνια δοίη.
>
> Hom. *Od.* 9.228–9

but I did not obey – it would have been so much better – because I wanted to see if he would give me gifts of ritual friendship (*xenia*).

The first words of the Cyclops (Ὦ ξεῖνοι, τίνες ἐστέ; "O *xenoi*, who are you?," 9.252) give a very different meaning to Odysseus' words: by *xenos*, Polyphemus does not mean "ritual guest-friend" but "stranger," by which he means, in this case, "trespasser." Odysseus concludes his introductory speech by using no fewer than five forms of *xenos* (in the sense of guest-friend) in the last five lines:

> ἡμεῖς δ' αὖτε κιχανόμενοι τὰ σὰ γοῦνα
> ἱκόμεθ', εἴ τι πόροις ξεινήϊον ἠὲ καὶ ἄλλως
> δοίης δωτίνην, ἥ τε ξείνων θέμις ἐστίν.
> ἀλλ' αἰδεῖο, φέριστε, θεούς· ἱκέται δέ τοί εἰμεν.
> Ζεὺς δ' ἐπιτιμήτωρ ἱκετάων τε ξείνων τε,   270
> ξείνιος, ὃς ξείνοισιν ἅμ' αἰδοίοισιν ὀπηδεῖ.
>
> Hom. *Od.* 9.266–71

But we've ended up here and are reaching for your knees, to see if you can give us some provisions for guests or otherwise provide us with presents, which it is just to give to guests. Have reverence for the gods, my good fellow: we are your suppliants, and Zeus of Strangers is avenger of suppliants and guest-friends and attends reverent guest-friends.

Three meanings of *xenos*, guest, host, and stranger, and two different versions of hospitality are thus activated in the Homeric episode. Rather than explaining specific features of Philoxenus' dithyramb, the Phaenias anecdote seems to work as a form of reading that problematizes the name of the poet who wrote about the Cyclops against the background of the Odyssean episode and its engagement with *philo-xenia*. There is something even more intriguing in seeing Philoxenus, the wandering poet born on an island, as an Odysseus figure: both characters share rhetorical skills and a *mētis* that Philoxenus has shown in the previous part of the story, with his ability to change the situation to his benefit. This last and explicit example of Philoxenus as an Odyssean figure is only one in a series of stories in which Philoxenus' Odyssean features can be read. If we look back at the first part of the episode, for example, the witty way in which Philoxenus gets his fish from the tyrant is reminiscent of a passage of *Odyssey* 14 in which Odysseus gets a coat from his host, the swineherd Eumaeus, in a sympotic-like setting. Having already been lavishly entertained by Eumaeus, Odysseus, in his beggar disguise, tells a clever but far from straightforward tale. The story explains how Odysseus, who on a cold night at Troy had forgotten to take his coat when going on an embuscade, tricked a comrade into giving him his own coat. The account bolsters his heroic persona just as Philoxenus' story bolsters his poetic persona and also sends a clear message to Eumaeus: the swineherd gets the point, promises that his guest will get a coat the next day, and even identifies the speech form:

> ὦ γέρον, α<u>ἶνος</u> μέν τοι ἀμύμων, ὃν κατέλεξας
> οὐδέ τί πω παρὰ μοῖραν ἔπος νηκερδὲς ἔειπες.
> Hom. *Od.* 14.508–9

Old fellow, this is for sure a blameless <u>tale</u> that you have told, and you haven't spoken an unprofitable word out of place!

Before I turn to additional Philoxenian stories that are evocative of an Odyssean persona, let me sum up the different, and not mutually exclusive, readings to which the episode lends itself. On the one hand, the second part of the story can be read as a fiction explaining features of Philoxenus' dithyramb, including the innovation introduced in the Polyphemus story, with the figure of Galatea as love object. On the other hand, the whole anecdote can be interpreted as a complex form of engagement with the problem of the poet's relationship with *xenia*. At the tyrant's court, Philoxenus, like Odysseus, appears as a stranger relying on a host's hospitality. Like Odysseus, Philoxenus is a trickster, who not only gets the big fish (or coat) for himself thanks to his rhetorical play and indirect speech, but is also a guest who tests the limits of hospitality. That these concerns surround the figure of Philoxenus and are more than an ad hoc explanation for his poetry is illustrated by other episodes.

Philoxenus, Odysseus, and the politics of *xenia*

A fragment from Clearchus quoted in the epitome of the *Deipnosophistae* (1.5f–6b) stages the same elements as the previous stories: food, poetry, and socio-economic webs of relationship:[67]

---

[67] The passage might have come from the philosopher's *On Lives*, a work that presents moralizing anecdotes about political, artistic, and poetic figures, frr. 37–62 Wehrli. Clearchus must have

Philoxenus used to go round among the houses in his own city and others as well, freshly bathed, with an escort of slaves carrying oil, wine, fish paste, vinegar, and other seasonings (ἡδύσματα). He would then enter strangers' houses and season whatever was cooking for the rest of the company, throwing in what was lacking. Then he would stoop and greedily feast on the food. He once landed at Ephesus, and finding the fish market (ὀψόπωλιν) empty inquired about the reason. When he learned that everything had been sold out for a wedding, he bathed and showed up uninvited (ἄκλητος) at the bridegroom's house. And after the dinner he sang the wedding song beginning "marriage, most radiant deity" (Γάμε θεῶν λαμπρότατε) and enraptured (ἐψυχαγώγησεν) everybody (for he was a dithyrambic poet). The groom then said, "Philoxenus, will you dine in this way tomorrow also?" (Φιλόξενε, εἶπε, καὶ αὔριον ὧδε δειπνήσεις·) "Yes," said Philoxenus, "if there is no fish for sale" (ἂν ὄψον, ἔφη, μὴ πωλῇ τις).

Clearchus, fr. 57 Wehrli

The anecdote is, again, twofold: the first part shows the peculiar dining habits of Philoxenus, the second is the story of a particular dinner that retrospectively sheds light on Philoxenus' character as presented in the first part. The very location of the anecdote, Ephesus, creates a specific backdrop for a story about a musician. Ephesus, the hometown of the iambic poet Hipponax, was in the late fifth and fourth centuries BC a city "oligarchic in temper,"[68] which took sides with Sparta after it revolted in 412 BC. This Spartan connection – and Sparta's reputation for austere barley porridge and musical conservatism – is particularly important in a story that stages a musician who defines himself by his *opsophagia*.

In the first sentences, Clearchus presents Philoxenus as a strange hybrid. On the one hand, Philoxenus acts as a guest-friend (*xenos*), about to be entertained after having a bath (προλουόμενος). But he is the one who provides *opson* (the condiments, the most delicate part of the meal) for the dinner, and by generously seasoning his guests' food, he acts like a host (*xenos*). In a word, Philo-*xenos* lives up to his name. What he does to other people's food (τὰ ἑψόμενα τοῖς ἄλλοις <u>ἀρτύειν</u> <u>ἐμβάλλοντα</u> ὧν ἦν χρεία, "he would <u>season</u> whatever was cooking for the rest of the company, <u>throwing in</u> what was lacking") is a gastronomic illustration of his poetry: the verb ἀρτύω is used "of things that require skills or cunning" and suggests an obvious parallel between the use of cookery and the use of poetry, and the participle ἐμβάλλοντα ("throwing in") recalls the *embolima* (the odes

---

had a good knowledge of, or at least interest in, fourth-century poetry and linguistic and poetic phenomena (frr. 83–95b Wehrli), since he is one of our only sources for several fourth-century figures: Lycophronides (frr. 22 and 24 Wehrli), Castorion (fr. 88 Wehrli), and Eriphanis (fr. 32 Wehrli).

[68] *OCD* s.v. Ephesus.

"thrown in") of the New Musicians.[69] So Philoxenus' image as a skillful *saucier* is a commentary on the activity of the poet, as one who brings delight to people's life by providing ἄλλα ἡδύσματα ("other seasonings").[70]

But Philoxenus is also the *xenos*, the foreigner – neither really a guest (since he is not invited) nor a host (since he goes to other people's houses). It is again difficult not to read an echo of the Homeric Odysseus, especially in the light of the story discussed above. Like Odysseus, Philoxenus barges into a stranger's place and helps himself to his food. Like Odysseus, who brings wine as *opson* (and quite ironically, the flesh of the companions that Polyphemus will feast on as well), Philoxenus brings the *opson* to his perhaps unwilling hosts. But in another way too, Philoxenus is like Odysseus. The adjective ἄκλητος, used in the next part of the story, makes Philoxenus a very special kind of guest. Along with ἀσύμβολος, in Greek comedy this standard epithet cues the reader into a link with a parasite.[71] The attitude of Philoxenus the *opson*-bringer confirms that he is indeed a parasite: he is depicted as an intemperate glutton, bending over to feast. No matter what reading we choose,[72] the sentence illustrates Philoxenus' lack of control or, rather, it underlines how he plays the parasite and acts greedily, just as would be expected of an *aklētos*. Burkhard Fehr emphasizes this performance aspect:

Firstly, during the banquet the *akletos* displays his ugliness, weakness, voracity, or whatever by chance and unintentionally, thus making the invited guests laugh as they feel their superiority. Secondly, the physical and moral inferiority of the *akletos* is revealed consciously and on purpose: the *akletos*, as it were, performs himself. Thus he confirms the image the invited guests have of people of his sort; enjoying this, they become inclined to give the *akletos* what he asks for and are less likely to use violence.[73]

---

[69] On *embolima*, Arist. *Poet.* 1456a29–32.

[70] The parallel between cooking and rhetoric is a topos. See for example Pl. *Grg.* 462e–463e; also Arist. *Poet.* 1449b25 on the poetic language of tragedy (ἡδυσμέμῳ λόγων, "seasoning of speeches").

[71] On the rich social history of the *aklētoi*, Fehr 1990: 185: "Other people, who contribute to the entertainment of the symposiasts as well, arrive without being called (*aklētoi*). They do not possess property and – for whatever reasons – do not earn their livelihood by some useful *techne*. Driven by their hungry stomachs they appear wherever they hope to gain a meal. These *aklētoi* had a not unimportant role in the Archaic cultural and social history of the *symposion*... The very first *aklētos* is Odysseus."

[72] Olson's Loeb edition of the *Deipnosophistae* gives κᾆθ' οὕτως <εἰς ἑαυτὸν> κύψαντα εὐωχεῖσθαι. Müller's reading of the manuscripts gives ἀνακάμψαντα, "gulp down," while the *Suda* (Φ 395, IV 728–9 Adler) has εἰς ἑαυτὸν κύψαντα, "bend over." Like the English translation, the verb has sexual connotations (root of κύβδα, one of the positions referred to in ancient sex manuals). On the reading of this passage, Bartol 2004 and Roskam 2006.

[73] Fehr 1990: 186.

This performance could not be further from the image of the *xenos*: in place of a network of mutual indebtedness between equals tied by a web of *symbola*, the Cytheran poet at Ephesus is the *asymbolos* and performs his foreignness. Odysseus too, uninvited, performs his "beggarness" when going back to Ithaca, both at Eumaeus' house, where his discourse and persona are focused on the "wretched belly," and when he meets with Iros.[74]

The relationship between Philoxenus' generosity and his greed acquires new significance in the next part of the story. When there is nothing for sale at the deli, Philoxenus invites himself to a wedding and literally sings for his supper, enrapturing everybody in the process (πάντας ἐψυχαγώγησεν).[75] The verb is used to refer to the power of language, both poetry and rhetoric, and conveys that *mousikē* has magical, beguiling power. It echoes descriptions of the Homeric bards Phemius and Demodocus, who charm their audience by means of a delightful song (θελκτήριον, *Od.* 1.337), but whose activity, just like Philoxenus', is also closely connected to food.[76] In the last lines, however, Philoxenus breaks away from the model he has just adopted: in his response to the groom, he switches from the vocabulary of symbolic value used by his host ("will you dine in this way," ὧδε δειπνήσεις, as a guest-poet, in the old fashion way of *xenia*) to that of the market economy ("if there is no fish for sale," ἂν ὄψον μὴ πωλῇ τις). Unlike Phemius, who is "a locus for both the *gastēr* and *thelgein* themes,"[77] Philoxenus does not assimilate himself to a court poet, but treats his delightful song as a form of occasional currency, to be used when food cannot be obtained by money. This conclusion brings us back to the first part of the previous story, where Philoxenus made a statement about the new type of relationship into which the poet enters, a type that contrasts with the aristocratic *xenia* model. But this interpretation does not exhaust the possible readings of this anecdote and one can also read the anecdote another way, in the light of two other stories.

Philoxenus and the wisdom of the octopus

Another *chreia* of Machon, also quoted in Book 8 of the *Deipnosophistae* (341b–d), revolves again around the issue of Philoxenus' appetite but places

---

[74] Pucci 1987: 181–7.   [75] On the verb, and its magic connotations, see de Romilly 1975: 3–11.

[76] On song and *thelgein*, Pucci 1987: 191–213. At 193: "*Thelgein* points to the psychological effects of poetry and defines them as 'pleasurable enchantment' and 'ruinous fascination.' The use of *thelgein* (to designate aesthetic effects) is exclusively Odyssean and gives a special twist to the other epic terms – such as *kharis, terpsis*, 'joy,' 'pleasure' – that traditionally describe the pleasurable effects of poetry, for *thelgein* describes a supplementary structure whereby the 'pleasure' produced by poetry contains simultaneously the 'loss of oneself.'"

[77] Pucci 1987: 196.

the poet in a different social context. This time, nothing is said about Philoxenus' dining companions:

ὑπερβολῇ λέγουσι τὸν Φιλόξενον
τῶν διθυράμβων τὸν ποιητὴν γεγονέναι
ὀψοφάγον. εἶτα πουλύποδα πηχῶν δυεῖν
ἐν ταῖς Συρακούσαις ποτ' αὐτὸν ἀγοράσαι
καὶ σκευάσαντα καταφαγεῖν ὅλον σχεδόν
πλὴν τῆς κεφαλῆς, ἁλόντα δ' ὑπὸ δυσπεψίας
κακῶς ἔχειν σφόδρ'· εἶτα δ' ἰατροῦ τινος
πρὸς αὐτὸν εἰσελθόντος ὃς φαύλως πάνυ
ὁρῶν φερόμενον αὐτὸν εἶπεν, Εἴ τί σοι
ἀνοικονόμητόν ἐστι διατίθου ταχύ,
Φιλόξεν', ἀποθανῇ γὰρ ὥρας ἑβδόμης.
κἀκεῖνος εἶπε, Τέλος ἔχει τὰ πάντα μοι,
ἰατρέ, φησί, καὶ δεδιῴκηται πάλαι.
τοὺς διθυράμβους σὺν θεοῖς καταλιμπάνω
ἠνδρωμένους καὶ πάντας ἐστεφανωμένους,
οὓς ἀνατίθημι ταῖς ἐμαυτοῦ συντρόφοις
Μούσαις. Ἀφροδίτην καὶ Διόνυσον ἐπιτρόπους –
ταῦθ' αἱ διαθῆκαι διασαφοῦσιν, ἀλλ' ἐπεὶ
ὁ Τιμοθέου Χάρων σχολάζειν οὐκ ἐᾷ,
οὐκ τῆς Νιόβης, χωρεῖν δὲ πορθμὸν ἀναβοᾷ,
καλεῖ δὲ μοῖρα νύχιος ἧς κλύειν χρεών,
ἵν' ἔχων ἀποτρέχω πάντα τἀμαυτοῦ κάτω
τοῦ πουλύποδός μοι τὸ κατάλοιπον ἀπόδοτε.

Machon, fr. 9 Gow

Philoxenus the dithyrambic poet was, they say, excessively fond of fish. One day in Syracuse he bought an octopus three feet wide, prepared it, and ate it almost entirely except for the head. As he got very sick to the stomach and was doing very badly, a doctor came to visit him. Seeing the poet's terrible condition, he said, "If you have any business that needs to be taken care of, Philoxenus, attend to it at once, because you won't live to the seventh hour." Philoxenus replied, "Everything is settled (τέλος), doctor, and has been in order for a long time. By the gods' grace I leave my dithyrambs behind grown up and all crowned with garlands, and I dedicate them to my foster sisters (συντρόφοις), the Muses. For guardians (ἐπιτρόπους), they will have Aphrodite and Dionysus – my will makes all of this clear. But since Timotheus' Charon, the one in his *Niobe*, does not allow lingering but shouts that the ferryboat is leaving, and gloomy Fate who must be obeyed is calling me – so that I can run below with all my stuff, fetch me the rest of that octopus!"

The passage opens with ὑπερβολῇ ("excessively"), a term that keys the reader into one of the main themes of the *chreia:* excess.[78] On the one hand, this anecdote brings us back to the now familiar figure of Philoxenus as *ako-lastos*, going always further in his gourmand quest. But while building on this motive, the story also goes to some length to create an elaborate *poetic* persona for Philoxenus, even before his death. Philoxenus describes his post-mortem arrangements (δεδιῴκηται, "everything is in order"), a response to the injunction of the doctor to "take care of business" (διατίθου), which the poet understood as "make a will" (διαθήκη). The description that follows corresponds to what could actually be written on his tombstone. It is a purely metaphorical will. First, the dithyrambist calls himself a σύντροφος of the Muses, not a recipient of their gift or even a familiar connection but a foster brother. His last gesture is to entrust his dithyrambs to the Muses. Described in the vocabulary of poetic dedication (ἀνατίθημι), his is a self-perpetuating gesture: he dedicates to the Muses the very product of their inspiration, which also contributes to isolating him from the society of men.[79] The guardians who will be taking care of his poetic offspring are gods, Aphrodite and Dionysus, who are associated respectively with the Charites and with the dithyramb. Finally, Philoxenus presents the end of his life as if it were dictated by the injunction of a poetic character, the Charon of Timotheus' *Niobe*. In this last speech, he has already left the society of men to inscribe himself in the poetic world and has created the postmortem persona that is the Philoxenus figure.[80]

But this reading is complicated by the poet's association of his poetry with the city, by underlining the successful *paideia* his "children" received and their status as respectable citizens (ἠνδρωμένους) crowned with the wreath (ἐστεφανωμένους) of the agonic victor. In this poetic death, one can even read echoes, I suggest, of Socrates' death. Philoxenus' last words as presented by Machon seem to parody Socrates': τοῦ πουλύποδός μοι τὸ κατάλοιπον ἀπόδοτε ("fetch me the remains of the octopus") here echoes the ὦ Κρίτων, ἔφη, τῷ Ἀσκληπιῷ ὀφείλομεν ἀλεκτρυόνα· ἀλλὰ ἀπόδοτε καὶ μὴ ἀμελήσητε ("'O Crito,' he said, 'we owe a cock to Asclepius: go fetch it, and don't forget'") of the last lines of Plato's *Phaedo* (118a8), except that the cock

---

[78]　The adverb appears also in two other anecdotes of Machon, frr. 12 and 13 Gow, and in all three cases signals excess in appetite, for sex or food.

[79]　See Gow's note on line 79: "So in *A.P.* 7.26 (Antipater Sid.) Anacreon is φιλακρήτου σύντροφος Ἁρμονίης ['foster brother of Harmony fond of sheer wine']."

[80]　One can compare this with the anecdote staging Diogenes' death, also by eating a raw octopus: Diog. Laert. 6.76, Ath. 8.341e; or with Zeno's death (for the quotation from the *Niobe*): Diog. Laert. 7.28.

owed to Asclepius is substituted by the head of the octopus. Moreover, while Socrates' execution is determined by the arrival of the boat from Crete, Philoxenus presents his death as determined by the mythical departure of Charon's boat, as evoked in Timotheus' *Niobe*. But the *Niobe* is not any kind of song; it is a *nomos* ("nome"), the homonym of the figures (the *nomoi*, "laws") who convince Socrates that he should die (Pl. *Cri.* 50a–51b). While Socrates uses the fictional speech of an abstraction to connect to the city, Philoxenus has already entered the poetic pantheon and can connect with the Niobe, or the *Niobe*, of Timotheus.[81]

Yet, in the last lines of the anecdote, Philoxenus inverts the paradigm of Socratic death that he seemed to have just created. Unlike Socrates, who covers his face in a sign of his denial of the existence of the body after death,[82] Philoxenus presents death as a physical event in which the body participates (ἀποτρέχω κάτω, "run below") and where belongings (ἔχων . . . πάντα τἀμαυτοῦ, "with all my stuff") still matter. Most importantly, Philoxenus asks for the remains of the octopus. Why does Philoxenus on his deathbed eat even the head of the mollusc? Was he still hungry, or was he making a statement? What does that gesture represent? How should we explain the parallels with, and the divergences from, the philosopher's death?

One level of understanding implies poetic and generic considerations. This anecdote belongs to Machon's *Chreiae*, a type of exercise that, in the rhetorical tradition, mostly stages wise men and reports their pithy sayings or meaningful acts.[83] Philoxenus' Socratic moment would be in keeping with the tradition of philosophical *chreiae*, the parody of philosophical maxims. But as Leslie Kurke has emphasized in an article entitled "Gender, politics, and subversion in the *Chreiai* of Machon," "when we ask why Machon should choose to parody this philosophical genre by recasting it as the doings and sayings of Athenian low-lifes, we run up against the problem that there are no extended examples of 'straight' philosophical *Chreiai* extant."[84] The anecdote staging Philoxenus as a hero of *chreia* might

---

[81] For a reading of the anecdote that focuses on issues of intertextuality, LeVen 2013b.

[82] Pl. *Phd.* 118a.

[83] Gow 1965: 12–13: "To the rhetors of the imperial age the word χρεῖαι had a technical and specific meaning, and Hermogenes, Theon, and Aphthonius all devote a section of their προγυμνάσματα to the subject . . . *The literary genre however had existed since at least the fourth century* BC" (my emphasis). For use of *chreia* in Progymnasmata, see Hock and O'Neil 1986, especially pp. 3–60. On Machon's contribution to the literary genre, Kurke 2002; at p. 21: "read all together, the individual anedotes of the *Chreiai* are short and punchy . . . funny (when we can figure out the joke), and frequently highly obscene . . . But most of all, Machon's *Chreiae* seem oddly subversive or askew in relation to the values and hierarchies we expect to find."

[84] Kurke 2002: 24.

be a case in which the intertext with philosophical models is the clearest. Machon draws attention to the image of the poet as wise man, while at the same time debunking philosophical death and casting Philoxenus as an anti-Socrates. It is not for the afterlife of the soul but for the afterlife of his poems in the world of men that Philoxenus has prepared himself – and up to that moment, he will continue enjoying the life of the body and the remains of the cephalopod. Rather than illustrating a dichotomy between body and soul, the last moment of the dithyrambist illustrates a divorce between the dyspeptic body of the mortal poet and the eternal nature of his poetic corpus.

It is worth pointing out one additional element of the anecdote. Philoxenus' last moments take place in Syracuse. Although not stated explicitly, it is understood that Philoxenus is in Syracuse as a poet working in the entourage of the tyrant Dionysius. And here might be the point of the story: while at Syracuse working for a tyrant, Philoxenus frames his life in relationship to Athens and Athenian values, including his death in relation to Socrates', but turns those values upside down. For Machon, the figure of Philoxenus works as a paradoxical marriage between a poet composing in a civic genre, celebrated, for example, by public monuments, and an individual speaking for the triumph of pleasure and consumption and adaptation to the rules of a tyranny. This idea of Philoxenus speaking for Athenian values while using the Sicilian tyrant's ethos to his advantage is reminiscent of the anecdote that staged Philoxenus with Dionysius' fish and mistress. There too, Philoxenus was defending *isonomia* – or at least equal shares of fish – while grabbing the tyrant's portion for himself.

If, going back to Philoxenus and the octopus, that story throws light on what use Machon might have made of Philoxenus, what can it tell us specifically about the poet? A second type of reading brings another telling aspect of the anecdote into focus. Just like the hare in the Simonides story or the red mullet at Dionysius' table, the octopus that caused Philoxenus' death is meaning-laden, for it can be read as a commentary on the dithyrambist's poetics and politics. An octopus is not just any creature. As a dish, it is a delicacy known for its aphrodisiac capacities – which again reinforces the connection with the love of pleasure that Philoxenus exhibits in matters of food.[85] But Athenaeus also has a long disquisition on the live octopus in his discussion of fish in Book 7 of the *Deipnosophistae* (7.316a–318f) that throws light on the symbolism of the mollusc. The polyp distinguishes itself not only by its eight arms, but also by its intelligence, its versatility, and

---

[85] Ath. 7.316 c = Diocles, fr. 222 van der Eijk.

its skill at adaptation, as attested in a passage quoted by Clearchus.[86] The physical ability of the polyp to use its arms to attach to something is evoked in a simile in the *Odyssey*. Shipwrecked Odysseus has finally reached the island of the Phaeacians, but the shore is difficult to access and the hero is described as clinging to a rock,

> ὡς δ' ὅτε πουλύποδος θαλάμης ἐξελκομένοιο
> πρὸς κοτυληδονόφιν πυκιναὶ λάϊγγες ἔχονται,
> ὣς τοῦ πρὸς πέτρῃσι θρασειάων ἀπὸ χειρῶν
> ῥινοὶ ἀπέδρυφθεν· τὸν δὲ μέγα κῦμα κάλυψεν.   435
>
> Hom. *Od.* 5.432–5

as when an octopus is dragged out of its lair, and strips of pebbles are stuck in its tentacles, so from his strong hands clinging to the rock, strips of skin were ripped. And a great wave covered him.

Roles are inverted in this simile. It would seem natural for the pebbles to be compared to the rock, and Odysseus to the octopus. But the image specifically focuses on Odysseus' hands, whose skin is ripped away as pebbles are ripped away from a rock when an octopus holds on to it with its suckers while it is dragged out. In the comparison, Odysseus has blended with the rock covered with pebbles, just as an octopus takes on the appearance of the rock to which it clings, as Theophrastus attests.[87] The comparison between Odysseus and the octopus is not explicitly stated in the simile but is, as it were, enacted, and illustrates Odysseus' octopedalian qualities in practice.

Indeed the comparison of Odysseus with the octopus goes further than the hero's ability to cling to rocks, and the connection between octopus, Odysseus, and Philoxenus is worth examining further. In a classic discussion of the octopus, Marcel Detienne and Jean-Pierre Vernant explain that, like the fox, the octopus defines a certain type of human behavior.[88] They cite Theognis, who instructs:

> θυμέ, φίλους κατὰ πάντας ἐπίστρεφε ποικίλον ἦθος,
>   ὀργὴν συμμίσγων ἥντιν' ἕκαστος ἔχει·
> πουλύπου ὀργὴν ἴσχε πολυπλόκου, ὃς ποτὶ πέτρῃ,   215
>   τῇ προσομιλήσῃ, τοῖος ἰδεῖν ἐφάνη.
> νῦν μὲν τῇδ ἐφέπου, τοτὲ δ' ἀλλοῖος χρόα γίνου.
> κρέσσων τοι σοφίη γίνεται ἀτροπίης.
>
> Thgn. 213–18 W²

---

[86] Clearchus, *On Proverbs*, fr. 75 Wehrli: πουλύποδός μοι, τέκνον, ἔχων νόον, Ἀμφίλοχ' ἥρως | τοῖσιν ἐφαρμόζου τῶν κεν <κατὰ> δῆμον ἵκηαι ("with the mind of an octopus, my son, heroic Amphilochus, assimilate yourself to those whose country you come to").

[87] Ath. 7.317e–f = Theophr. 365b Fortenbaugh.   [88] Detienne and Vernant 1974: 47.

My heart, adapt your versatile character to different friends, blending your disposition with that of each. Maintain the disposition of the crafty octopus, who assimilates its aspect to the rock to which it clings. Follow one model one day, and the next, adopt another color: *sophia* prevails over inflexibility.

Pindar's account of Amphiaraus' advice to his son departing from Thebes is very similar:[89]

ὦ τέκνον, ποντίου θηρὸς πετραίου
χρωτὶ μάλιστα νόον
προσφέρων πάσαις πολίεσσιν ὁμίλει·
τῷ παρεόντι δ' ἐπαινήσαις ἑκών
ἄλλοτ' ἀλλοῖα φρόνει.

Pind. fr. 43 SM

My son, let your mind behave like the skin of the rocky beast of the sea, and consort with men of all nations. Praise willingly the one who is present, but change your mind according to the circumstances.

The advice seems to be Odysseus' own motto and defines the hero's ever-changing (πολύτροπος) qualities. But how does it qualify Philoxenus? Again we face the question of why Philoxenus eats the rest of the octopus. I suggest that the form of the poet's death, an overdose of octopus, is a fitting embodiment of his socio-political stance: the position of the dithyrambist in society, as described by many anecdotes, is characterized by his capacity to adapt to new environments. This better explains, for example, the last story and the poet's use of his octopedalian wisdom when negotiating *opsophagia*, poetic skill, and social setting. While the image of the octopus in Pindar and Theognis is a reflection on the poet's need to be flexible vis-à-vis a patron, Philoxenus uses it as an invitation to adapt his social conduct to best suit the circumstances and navigate between different settings. Against this background, Philoxenus takes further the motive of the mercenary Muse, which I discussed in the first anecdote: while Simonides and Pindar see the beginning of professionalization and grit their teeth at

---

[89] On which Gentili 1988: 132: "The nobleman's ability – his *sophía* – lies precisely in his capacity to adjust himself to the situation at hand and not to lose his inbred, intuitive sense for what is opportune to say or not say in the presence of a given audience. Without such vigilant attention to the social context in which he is moving, the nobleman falls into an obtuse inflexibility – a true condition of *atropía*, dulled perceptions, and inability to extricate himself adroitly in difficult situations."

the change, Philoxenus is staged as flexible in his understanding of the correlation between music and food. For Philoxenus, the relationship between poetry, food, and money (or market) depends on place and circumstance, and although the market model is his default position, he, like an octopus, will blend with other environments – even if that means turning into an overbearing tyrant when in Syracuse.

Philoxenus and the politics of literary criticism

The last anecdote to receive our attention in this chapter is related by Diodorus of Sicily and stages the poet's dealings with the Sicilian tyrant Dionysius. It shares some of the already discussed features of other anecdotes, including the poet's relationship with poetry and Sicilian power. It too revolves around the poet's mouth, but in this instance the focus on what comes out of that mouth (frank speech) and the point seen in Machon's *chreia* (the readiness of the poet to adapt to the circumstances at hand) are reinforced.[90]

The story belongs to an aside in Diodorus' narrative and presents the literary activities of the tyrant Dionysius in time of peace:

> In Sicily, once Dionysius the tyrant of Syracuse had abandoned the war against the Carthaginians, he had plenty of peace and leisure. Hence he started writing poems with great zeal and he invited over the famous poets of the time, granted them great honor (προτιμῶν αὐτούς), and spent time in their company, having them as instructors and editors of his poems (τῶν ποιημάτων ἐπιστάτας καὶ διορθωτὰς εἶχεν). Flying high with the words with which these men were repaying his benefactions (διὰ τὰς εὐεργεσίας τοῖς πρὸς χάριν λόγοις), Dionysius boasted a lot more about the poems than about his success in the war.
>
> Diod. Sic. 15.6.1

This introductory paragraph already sheds light on the ambiguous character of the tyrant. Two aspects are emphasized: on the one hand, Dionysius' love of letters and poetic zeal (μετὰ πολλῆς σπουδῆς) and his features as an enlightened ruler; on the other, the tyrannical aspect of his relationship with poetry. For the tyrant, poetry is only another way of managing his power in times of peace, and the famous poets of the time play along with the game of the tyrant, feeding his hubristic appetite for recognition (μετεωριζόμενος).

---

[90] On *parrhēsia*, Sluiter and Rosen 2004, Saxonhouse 2006. Two fourth-century figures presented in Machon's *Chreiae* deserve further examination in connection with the issue of *parrhēsia*: Philoxenus and Stratonicus. On Stratonicus (put to death for his *parrhēsia*: Ath. 8.352d), see Gilula 2000; on Philoxenus, Prioux 2009.

The honors (προτιμῶν) Dionysius gives to poets are the money he pays them for his poetic education, and benefactions (εὐεργεσίας) in return motivate their appreciation of his poetry (τοῖς πρὸς χάριν λόγοις). The poems are to peace what military successes are to war; the parallel is reinforced by the use of κατωρθωμένοις ("set up right, brought to success"), the participle of a verb also found in nominal form in διορθωτάς ("his correctors").

Philoxenus' attitude contrasts with that of his contemporaries. His refusal to praise the tyrant's poetry is described in the next sentences:

[a] Among the company of poets surrounding him, there was Philoxenus the composer of dithyrambs, who had a great reputation for the elaborateness of his own poems (κατὰ τὴν κατασκευὴν τοῦ ἰδίου ποιήματος). During the symposium, after the tyrant's poems were read (they were truly wretched), he was asked for his judgment of the poems. When Philoxenus replied in a very frank way (παρρησιωδέστερον), the tyrant was offended by his words, and reproaching the poet for slandering him out of jealousy, ordered his attendants to immediately bring Philoxenus to the quarries. [b] The next day, after the tyrant's friends petitioned him to give his absolution to Philoxenus, Dionysius invited the same group to the symposium. As the drinking advanced, when once again Dionysius was bragging about his own compositions, he recited some lines that seemed to him to be well composed and then asked: "What do you think of these poems?" The poet said nothing else but, calling Dionysius' attendants, ordered them to bring him [Philoxenus] to the quarries. So this time, because of the wittiness of his reply, the tyrant smiled and could take the frankness, since humor blunted the reproach (διὰ τὴν εὐτραπελίαν τῶν λόγων μειδιόσας ὁ Διονύσιος ἤνεγκε τὴν παρρησίαν, τοῦ γέλωτος τὴν μέμψιν ἀμβλύνοντος). [c] Soon after though, when Philoxenus' acquaintances and those of Dionysius asked him to stop using untimely frankness (ἄκαιρον παρρησίαν), the poet made a paradoxical offer. In his answer he would, he said, at the same time respect the truth *and* show respect to Dionysius. And he did not lie: for after the tyrant read some lines that depicted miserable events and Philoxenus was asked what he thought of the poem, he answered "pitiful!" (οἰκτρά), thus keeping both promises thanks to the ambiguity of the term (διὰ τῆς ἀμφιβολίας ἀμφότερα τηρήσας). For Dionysius took "pitiful" to mean miserable and deserving pity, the very effects achieved by good poets, and hence understood that the poet was approving of them. The rest of the company however, grasping the real intent, understood the adjective as describing the wretched nature of the endeavor.

Diod. Sic. 15.6.2–5

In the part that I have labeled [a], we are confronted with a typical case of inappropriate *parrhēsia*. The poet, asked to give his opinion, tells the unadulterated and unflattering truth. By doing so, he shows that poetry is not a matter of negotiation; talent cannot be bought, and wretched poetry must be rejected. With the (unnamed) *en vogue* poets of his times described in the passage above, the principle of tyrannical reciprocity worked fine: by admiring Dionysius' poems, the *melici* merely offered a kind of praise different from that of the early classical lyricists. Whether he pays for a song that praises his horse or his latest martial victory, as did Sicilian tyrants employing Simonides, Pindar, or Bacchylides, or for praise of his poetry, the tyrant compensates the poet for his service (διὰ τὰς εὐεργεσίας). For the tyrant, this kind of exchange is fair, but in the eyes of an Athenian, this is flattery and demagogy. Philoxenus simply refuses to admire bad poetry and speaks his mind, illustrating the *parrhēsia* of the democratic citizen who takes risks when speaking openly.[91]

This poetic integrity, which ignores the octopus wisdom, is at odds with the principles of tyranny, and Dionysius' response is not surprising. The unspoken rule of tyranny is that to say the tyrant's poems are wretched is to say the tyrant is wretched. The tyrant's poetry is only a synecdoche for his power. Outside a democratic context, there is neither law nor appeal to protect Philoxenus, who has to follow the rules set by Dionysius. Only the personal plea of the poet's friends (οἱ φίλοι) can gain him the monarch's forgiveness (τῶν φίλων παρακαλούντων συγγνώμην δοῦναι τῷ Φιλοξένῳ).

In [b], Philoxenus, forgiven, is once again called upon to give his advice. This time, instead of straightforwardly opposing the ruler, he phrases his criticism wittily. He has anticipated the tyrant's reaction to criticism, and by making the tyrant deduce the poet's critical judgment, rather than hear a harsh statement, and draw conclusions for himself, Philoxenus avoids raising Dionysius' ire. The process involved here is known in rhetoric manuals as λόγος ἐσχηματισμένος, "figured speech"[92] – a form of communication that consists of disguising frank advice-giving to a ruler and making that

---

[91] Saxonhouse (2006: 88) describes the two most important aspects of *parrhēsia* thus: "1) the daring and courageous quality of the practice; those who spoke openly in Athens may have been at risk of legal action if they spoke on behalf of proposals contrary to the established laws and if they questioned the fundamental principles of their system of government; and 2) the unveiling aspects of the practice that entailed the exposure of one's true thoughts, the resistance to hiding what is true because of deference to a hierarchical social and political world or a concern with how one appears before the gaze of others, that is, shame."

[92] [Demetr.] (*Eloc.* 287–95), Quintilian (*Inst.* 9.2.65–99), and pseudo-Dionysius of Halicarnassus (*Ars rhetorica*, Chapters 8–9) comment on this rhetorical strategy. Chiron 2001: 224–36 defines "figured speech" as "a figure that pushes boundaries: it consists in not completely saying what one is saying, in making it possible to be understood, sometimes subtly, but without helping in an obvious way. One could gloss it every time it is used with two phrases: 'figure it out if you can' and, in an innocent self-realization, in case the interlocutor is suspicious: 'Me? I didn't say anything!'" (p. 226 – my translation). Figured speech is not a democratic practice, and one could contrast two attitudes in addressing a political superior as early as the *Iliad*: that of Chalcas, who uses figured speech in *Il.* 1.74–83, and that of Thersites, the democratic figure *par excellence*, who uses *parrhēsia* in *Il.* 2.225–42.

advice more amenable to the recipient by including him in the process of sense-making. This is precisely what happens with Dionysius: instead of being a criticism addressed to Dionysius, Philoxenus' comment both shows the poet's unwillingness to insult the tyrant directly by openly criticizing him and relies on the tyrant's understanding and appreciation of wit. His remark is not criticism addressed as among equals in a democratic setting, but wit with which the tyrant will play along, in a hierarchic relationship that once again recognizes his superiority and flatters his pride. The text even identifies the rhetorical process at stake: both the form (τὴν εὐτραπελίαν τῶν λόγων, "the wit of his speech") and the principle (τοῦ γέλωτος τὴν μέμψιν ἀμβλύνοντος, "humor blunting the reproach") are pointed out by Diodorus himself.[93]

At the same time, however, such un-straightforward speech can be set in parallel with the rhetoric that works at the symposium, requiring equality between speaker and recipient and supposing the sharing of certain communication codes.[94] That this might be the game that Philoxenus is playing with the tyrant is confirmed by the last part of the story: in [c], the tyrant and the poet's acquaintances address the question of Philoxenus' untimely frankness (ἄκαιρον παρρησίαν). The issue at stake is once again that of power management: even Philoxenus' wit is untimely since what the tyrant ultimately wants is unequivocal praise and affirmation of his superiority. The apparently paradoxical solution Philoxenus proposes (pleasing the tyrant and being frank) is founded on another strategy: it is not a question of rhetoric anymore, but of hermeneutics. Once again, Philoxenus' mastery over language and wit is illustrated here, as he proposes a term ambiguous enough to accept several interpretations (ἀμφιβολίας). The recipient's will and the *homophronēsis* ("sameness of mind") of the audience will motivate the right interpretation: with "pitiful," his ambiguous answer to the question of what he thought of the poem, Philoxenus resorts to a *sophos* statement, whose interpretation depends on whether or not knowledge is shared with his interlocutor. The underlying principle, as explained by Diodorus, is that

[93] Arist. *Eth. Eud.* 1234a defines wittiness (εὐτραπελία) as a middle state (μεσότης), the witty person being midway between the intractable boor and the buffoon (ὁ εὐτράπελος μέσος τοῦ ἀγροίκου καὶ δυστραπέλου καὶ τοῦ βωμολόχου). Wittiness is also called an "educated insolence" (πεπαιδευμένη ὕβρις), Arist. *Rh.* 1389b11–12.

[94] On this aspect, Nagy 1990: 148–50, quoting Thgn. 681–2. In his description of the *ainos*, Nagy underlines the three features of ideal listeners: they must be *sophoi, agathoi, philoi*, the latter being "those who are 'near and dear' and who are thereby interconnected to the poet and to each other, so that the message that is encoded in the poetry may be transmitted to them and through them: communication through community" (148). This is exactly the relationship staged in Philoxenus' response, the message being encoded in the poet's direct speech to Dionysius.

those who share the poet's mind understand the true intent of the words (οἱ δ' ἄλλοι <u>τὴν ἀληθινὴν διάνοιαν</u> ἐκδεξάμενοι).

In the course of the story, Philoxenus covers the ground from democratic *parrhēsia* [a], to figured speech addressed to a tyrant [b], to sympotic *sophos* discourse [c]. The anecdote summarizes the main characteristic of tyranny, and Philoxenus shows his independence from tyranny's mechanisms: he is not offering *charis* to Dionysius (τοῖς πρὸς χάριν λόγοις) but neither is he acting like a democratic critic, as an equal to the tyrant – from the start the tyrant wants to be admired but does not want to see the mechanisms of admiration or criticism. In parts [b] and [c] Philoxenus uses his wit to illuminate practical aspects of the relationship between speech and power: without *actually* exercising free speech and straightforward, in his case literary, criticism, he shows in [b] that he is ready to face the consequence of his *parrhēsia*, by accepting that he will be taken off to the quarries, but navigates around that threat by positing himself as an equal of Dionysius, for they share the same kind of discourse. There is even an added layer of meaningfulness in his invitation to bring him to the quarries: the Athenian prisoners of war were kept at the quarries after the defeat of the Sicilian expedition in 415 BC and therefore, by asking to be brought there, Philoxenus assimilates even more closely with the Athens whose value (*parrhēsia*) he had spoken for in the previous part. Part [c] illustrates another model of the relationship between speech and power: form is not the issue anymore, but reception. The social networks that the recipient belongs to determine meaning. Using an ambiguous word ("pitiful"), the poet exercises a form of *parrhēsia* for a certain audience (those who are in the know) while addressing an acceptable discourse to the tyrant. Ultimately, the anecdote reinforces the image of Philoxenus as a master of discourse who can act successively as critic, wise man, and court poet and is unwilling to compromise on any position.

Philoxeniana – or the octopus in the quarries

The stories I have discussed, what I call "Philoxeniana," are culled from different authors belonging to different time periods, but surprisingly they converge on several points. Whether or not these traits represent the historical poet is impossible to tell in most instances, but in my view this is not, in any case, the most interesting question to consider. The figure of Philoxenus allows glimpses into the representation of the relationship between poet and society in its various social, economic, and aesthetic contexts, a relationship that has evolved considerably in comparison to its archaic model. As is to be expected given the genre of ancient biographical stories, Philoxenus shares anecdotal features with other figures, especially Simonides. Staging both Simonides and Philoxenus allows authors to address the poet's socio-economic status and his changed relationship with his patron in an age of growing professionalization. But despite the similarity of tropes, it is impossible to ignore the difference between the socio-political context of production of Simonides and that of Philoxenus, especially in the latter's engagement with specifically Athenian political and cultural institutions, in particular democracy, frank speech, and theater. But a core of Philoxenian features also emerges from these different readings. We are left with the image of an octopus in the quarries. The octopus literally connects Philoxenus to the (Athenian) classical discourse on delicate food, passion, and excess, while it metaphorically ties the poet to Odysseus, especially the Odysseus of the Cyclops episode. The theme of *philoxenia*, inherited from the anecdotal tradition about Simonides, finds a very different resonance when it is used as a means of talking about the author of a famous *Cyclops*. That theme allows authors staging Philoxenus not only to re-examine a question central to one of the poet's most celebrated compositions, but also to pun on the issues raised by the very name of the poet, thus treating Philoxenus not as a person but as a distinct moment in a poetic tradition.

4 | The language of the New Music

> On voit dans toutes les littératures apparaître, plus ou moins tard, une langue mandarine, parfois très éloignée de la langue usuelle; mais, en général cette langue littéraire est déduite de l'autre, dont elle tire les mots, les figures, les tours les plus propices aux effets que recherche l'artiste en belles-lettres. Il arrive aussi que les écrivains se fassent un langage singulier.
>
> P. Valéry, *Je disais quelquefois à Stéphane Mallarmé…*

One of the most important features of the New Music not discussed so far is its language. Critics both ancient and modern have not looked kindly on the *lexis* of nomes and dithyrambs of the late classical period. From the proverbial expression "you make less sense than dithyrambs" (διθυράμβων νοῦν ἔχεις ἐλάττονα) to Pickard-Cambridge's famous qualification of the text of Timotheus' *Persians* as "vapid and silly libretto," many descriptions of the New Music style have either underlined the contrast between the wildness of the language and the dullness of the thought or emphasized the overwhelming importance of the music and spectacle, and minimized the role of the lyrics, deemed variously too vacuous or too enigmatic.[1] But consider the following passage:

> σμαραγδοχαίτας δὲ πόν-
> τος ἄλοκα ναΐοις ἐφοι-
> νίσσετο σταλά[γμασιν,
> κρ]αυγᾷ βοᾷ δὲ [συ]μμι[γ]ὴς κατεῖχεν·
> ὁμοῦ δ[ὲ] νάϊος στρατός   35
> βάρβαρος ἄμμι[γ' αὖτις
> ἀντεφέρετ' ἐ[π' ἰχ]θυ[ο]-
> στεφέσι μαρμαροπ[τύχ]οις
> κόλποισιν [Ἀμφιτρί]τας.
> Timoth. *PMG* 791.31–9

---

[1] *Suda* Δ 1031 (ɪɪ 92 Adler). Pickard-Cambridge 1962: 51. Croiset and Croiset 1904: 405: "These virtuosos needed *a poetry richer in words than in ideas*, lavish of pretty tones and images…"; Dover 1997: 47: "The language [of the *Persians*] is elaborate, exuberant, highly coloured; Timotheus has a genuine gift of imagination and a sense of dramatic realism, but also *a lack of taste which leads him close to absurdity*… His poetic style had no lasting influence; his music did" (my emphasis).

The emerald-haired sea was reddened in its furrows by the naval drops, and shouts mixed with cries filled the air. The barbarian navy was carried back in confusion upon the fish-wreathed bosom of Amphitrite with its marmoreal folds.

This is the first description of the sea a reader encounters in the surviving text of Timotheus' *Persians* and a representative example of the diction of the New Music. Critics have derided the stylistic features of such descriptions:[2] "far-fetched adjectives are piled up in the attempt to impress. There is a marked tendency to puzzle the reader with bold periphrases . . . "; "extravagant compounds, concatenations of adjectives, nouns, or participial phrases . . . stringing of subclauses, usually paratactically, often asyndetically"; "flashing metaphors and heavy magnificence of the strong style as an affected decoration." We might not be surprised to see included in this list "far-fetched metaphor, enigmatic paraphrase, newly coined words, new uses of current words, ambiguous phrases", surely an apposite description of Timotheus' work. But this quotation in fact qualifies the art of Aeschylus, compelling evidence that a catalogue of distinctive features alone is insufficient as a means of distinguishing the language of New Music.[3] Moreover, one needs to observe that, despite the lexical exuberance, the syntax of the Timothean passage is simple and the narrative easy enough to follow: the narrator describes a naval battle and the movement of the barbarian fleet. Furthermore, part of the passage's effect resides in the violent juxtaposition of colors and in the poignant antithesis of the personification of the sea, bejeweled with emerald and wreath, and the crudeness of the battle with its blood and shrieks.

   With the major exception of Eric Csapo's now classic 2004 study of the politics of New Music, critics have tended to skirt the poetics of such passages and have not paid much attention to the way stylistic features work together to "make a verbal message a work of art" – to use Jacobson's definition of poetics. Csapo has changed the way one interprets the stylistic aspects of the New Music by accounting for a series of characteristic phonetic, syntactic, and semantic features as a direct result of the "material cause of the new style," the music of the *auloi*.[4] In particular, the "agglutinative syntax" of the

---

[2] On the *lexis dithirambica*, Schönewolf 1938: 24–6, Zimmermann 1992: 118–21, Ieranò 1997: *T* 165–88b, Csapo 2004: 226–9. More specifically on the language and style of Timotheus, Wilamowitz-Moellendorff 1903: 38–55, Croiset 1903: 337–43, Reinach 1903: 76–80, Brussich 1970, Hordern 2002: 36–55, Csapo and Wilson 2009a.

[3] Respectively Lesky 1966: 416, about Timotheus; Csapo 2004: 225, about the New Music; Webster 1939: 197, about Timotheus and Antimachus; Stanford 1942: 132, about Aeschylus.

[4] Csapo 2004: 217.

New Music can be explained by the "potentiality of the pipes for indefinitely sustained tones and phrases."[5] Yet neither this material approach nor a more traditional philological approach that focuses on lexical or dialect choice (as offered by Brussich and Hordern) alone is sufficient for interpreting the language of Timotheus' *Persians*, the images of Philoxenus' *Dinner Party*, or the effect achieved by Timotheus' *Cyclops*.[6] A fresh tack is therefore needed, one that can account for the poetic logic of the *lexis* of late classical dithyrambs and nomes and for the style of each poet. This chapter adopts such an approach: it considers the language of late classical dithyrambs and nomes together, under the larger umbrella of "language of the New Music," without differentiating between the two genres that shared the same (theatrical) performance venue, and shows that it is not so much certain stylistic features per se that make New Music a distinct poetic language, but rather the way these features work together to create an experience that relies heavily on defamiliarization. Ultimately, the specific logic and aesthetics of this interaction of the various characteristics of the New Music define a unique relationship between the audience and the poetic world created – an aspect that I will examine in greater depth in the next chapter.

Behind the comic screen

The idea that the New Music style can be encapsulated in a list of stylistic features goes back to its first literary critics, contemporary with the New Music: the comic poets and, first of all, Aristophanes.[7] Aristophanes is an invaluable source of representations of the lyric poets' rhetoric, persona, and style,[8] yet he is also largely responsible for the neglect and derision of the language of the New Music. Aristophanes certainly provides caricatures of the lyric poets' style, but we must also note that he imposes a distorting lens onto our perception of late classical lyric language, often failing to reproduce, and even *keeping us away from*, important features of these compositions.

---

[5] Csapo 2004: 226.

[6] On the imagery of the New Music, Csapo 1999–2000, 2003, 2008, 2009, Steiner 2011.

[7] For a representative of such a method, Zimmermann 1992: 118: "the main source for stylistic and formal criticism of the New Dithyramb are the comedies of Aristophanes." Willi 2003: 6: "the example [of Euripides] shows that some characteristic features of tragic language are reconstructable on the basis of their comic reflection. *There is no reason why a similar procedure should not lead to trustworthy results with other linguistic varieties, where the 'original' is lost*" (my emphasis).

[8] For parodies of the New Music style in Aristophanes and other comic poets, Ieranò 1997: *T* 195a–201 and pp. 297–303 for discussion.

The comic force of the parodies comes from the careful imitation of the *lexis* of the New Music poets, but the parody is emptied of the specific logic and energy that make the original successful as a work of art and narrative and is reframed through the particular lens of the comic poet *qua* literary critic.

Elevated diction and poetic flop

The character of Aristophanes' critical engagement with the New Music can be observed in the parody of Cinesias in the *Birds*, a scene whose humor relies on a play on physical and metaphorical "poetic elevation." One of many uninvited visitors coming to the recently founded Cloudcuckooville, Cinesias presents himself to Peisetairus to ask for wings. His arrival works as a counterpart to the earlier visit of the old-fashioned encomiastic poet (lines 904–57). Chapter 2 has referred to the first part of the scene, where Cinesias defines his contribution to *mousikē* (his new, frigid, wing-flitting preludes), but it is the second part that I want to focus on here. Despite Peisetairus' resistance, Cinesias announces he will go through the dithyrambic "airs" (1392) and starts singing:

> εἴδωλα πετηνῶν
> αἰθεροδρόμων
> οἰωνῶν ταναοδείρων
>
> . . .
>
> ἁλίδρομον ἀλάμενος   1395
> ἅμ' ἀνέμων πνοαῖσι βαίην
>
> . . .
>
> τοτὲ μὲν νοτίαν στείχων πρὸς ὁδόν,
> τοτὲ δ' αὖ βορέᾳ σῶμα πελάζων
> ἀλίμενον αἰθέρος αὔλακα τέμνων.   1400
>   Ar. *Av.* 1393a–4, 1395–6, 1398–1400

> I will go through the whole air for you: "Phantoms of winged coursers of the aether, of long-necked birds . . . leaping in a course over the sea, may I go on the breath of the winds . . . now going over the moist road, now approaching with the Boreus, cleaving an inhospitable furrow of aether."

The opening apostrophe reproduces two of the most characteristics elements of dithyrambic diction: its love of compound adjectives (αἰθεροδρόμων, 1393b; ταναοδείρων, 1394; ἁλίδρομον, 1395b) and of periphrasis. The exuberant and enigmatic nature of the diction characteristically associated with the New Music is illustrated in the apostrophe: "phantoms of winged coursers of the aether, of long-necked birds" is both unsettling and, if not pleonastic, at least redundant: what exactly are "phantoms of birds"? Are they to be taken literally, as emaciated volatiles reflecting the notoriously thin body of Cinesias himself, or metaphorically, as describing, for example, clouds?[9] And are not the birds "long-necked" because they are flying, as suggested by both πετηνῶν and αἰθεροδρόμων? The dithyrambic diction is further evoked by the abundance of uncoordinated adjectives (in lines 1392–4, for example), the lexical repetitions (in particular, αἰθεροδρόμων and ἁλίδρομον), and a marked taste for assonance and aurally mimetic effects, especially in the last line, ἁλίδρομον ἀλάμενος | ἅμ' ἀνέμων πνοαῖσι βαίην (1395b–1396), which combines quasi anaphora (*hali, hala, hamanemōn*) and repetition of liquids and nasals (*l, m, n*), evocative of a wing flutter. But after the initial surprise caused by this florid language has passed, one has to acknowledge that Cinesias' diction is, actually, not earth-shatteringly new. Most of the compounds are neither especially obscure nor original: τανανδείρων, in particular, is used by the "old" encomiastic poet earlier in the play (254). The language that Cinesias uses is merely elevated diction, the same type of language that Aristophanes himself uses in his choral odes.[10] It is not so much the language itself, but rather the intense reaction of Peisetairus, and probably the stage business surrounding Cinesias' "performance," that create in part the effect and comic reception of Cinesias' *lexis*.

Aristophanes' parody does not limit itself to dithyrambic diction though, and a second feature of the neo-dithyrambic style is closely tied to the New Music's *lexis*: the poets' rhetoric and choice of metaphors. Chapter 2 has examined the reuse of traditional images as an aspect of the rhetoric of legitimization of the New Musicians. This practice can account for the line Cinesias speaks upon entering the stage: ἀναπέτομαι δὴ πρὸς Ὄλυμπον πτερύγεσσι κούφαις ("I surge toward Olympus on light wings") is a direct borrowing from Anacreon (*PMG* 378). But while Anacreon's couplet continues by referring to the truant winged-god Eros who "does not want to be young with [him] anymore" (διὰ τὸν Ἔρωτ'· οὐ γὰρ ἐμοὶ < – ˘ > θέλει συνηβᾶν), Aristophanes' Cinesias continues the metaphor in earnest: πέτομαι δ' ὁδὸν ἄλλοτ' ἐπ' ἄλλαν μελέων ("I fly sometimes this road of song, sometimes another," 1374). Aristophanes' parody seems to extend the poet's rhetoric by developing in earnest the image of the inspired "winged" poet with a

---

[9] On the thin body of Cinesias and the relationship with his poetry, see Chapter 3, n. 29. For the metaphor, compare Ar. *Nub.* 337, where clouds are γαμψούς τ' οἰωνοὺς ἀερονηχεῖς ("birds with a crooked beak floating in the air"), on which see below, p. 166.

[10] On Aristophanes as lyric poet, see p. 74, Chapter 2, n. 12. On features consistently associated with elevated diction, Griffith 1977: 149–57.

second, traditional, metaphor, that of the path of song.[11] But it also introduces a deformation: the flight metaphor is developed literally and drawn out to the point that it loses its tenor (inspiration, or escape from the everyday in general) and that the vehicle (flight) becomes the whole object of stylistic attention. The parody emphasizes the loss of connection between the original image of the "flight" of the inspired poet and Cinesias' all too literal obsession with wings, suggesting that by overdeveloping an old image in a new way, the dithyrambist makes that image lose its evocative power.[12]

These two aspects of the parody reveal two different, but complementary, comic mechanisms: the literalization (and materialization) of language and the thematization of some stylistic features. By literalization of language I mean that the metaphorical "elevation" of the style of the New Dithyramb is described or represented as the real elevation of the poet. Cinesias introduces his song by stating "I want to go through the whole air" (ἅπαντα γὰρ δίειμί . . . τὸν ἀέρα, *Av.* 1392), a polysemic expression that Dunbar explains as meaning both that the poet will go through the air culling preludes (continuing the image of the flying dithyrambist) and that he will go through the air that constitutes his preludes. In the same way, in the *Peace* Trygaeus tells how he saw "two or three souls of composers of dithyrambs (διθυραμβοδιδασκάλων) up in the sky" upon his return from Olympus (*Pax* 829). A variant on this type of representation of language through physical elevation occurs in the famous weighing scene in the *Frogs* (*Ran.* 1364–1413): Euripides, as a representative of the New Music and its style, never pulls his metaphorical weight in the poetic contest with Aeschylus, be it with his images, his themes, or his rhythms. His language levitates while Aeschylus' makes the scales tip. Again the visual power of the metaphor is developed until it becomes a comic element. A further type of comic deformation in Aristophanes' parody of Cinesias' diction resides in the thematization of stylistic features themselves. Features such as levity, airiness, and elevation are made the *topic* of Cinesias' song: in a song that displays features of the elevated style, Cinesias sings of birds that fly high and of other aerial phenomena (wind, breeze, aether).

The combination of the two comic mechanisms appears most clearly in another caricature of dithyrambists, found in opening scenes of the *Clouds*.

---

[11] In addition to Homer's "winged words" (ἔπεα πτερόεντα), for the flight of the poet: Thgn. 237–54; Pind. *Pyth.* 8.34, *Nem.* 3.80, 5.21, 7.22; Bacchyl. 5.16–33. For the path of song: Hom. *Od.* 8.73–4; Pind. *Ol.* 1.110, *Pyth.* 4.247–8, 9.45, 11.39, *Nem.* 6.54. On the metaphor, Giannisi 1997 and 2006.

[12] Silk 2000: 140–6, on metaphor "sustained enough to become a miniature norm in its own right, which is then disrupted by the unpredictable intrusion of the tenor terminology" (141); Hunter 2009: 4–5.

After the Clouds have made their entry, in the elevated diction typical of hymnic invocations, Socrates describes them as a new type of Muse:

> ... μεγάλαι θεαὶ ἀνδράσιν ἀργοῖς,
> αἵπερ γνώμην καὶ διάλεξιν καὶ νοῦν ἡμῖν παρέχουσιν
> καὶ τερατείαν καὶ περίλεξιν καὶ κροῦσιν καὶ κατάληψιν.
>
> Ar. *Nub.* 316–18

> ... great goddesses for idle men, who provide us with thinking and expression and logic and imagination and circumlocution and deception and comprehension.

He further identifies these idle men as "experts" (σοφιστάς, 331): prophets, professors of medical theory, idlers, and "song-benders of circular choruses" (ᾀσματοκάμπτας, 333). All are "men-with-their-heads-in-the-sky" (ἄνδρας μετεωροφένακας, 333), who do nothing, feed off the clouds, and poeticize about them (οὐδὲν δρῶντας βόσκουσ' ἀργούς, ὅτι ταύτας μουσοποοῦσιν, 334), an image that recalls Cinesias' description of the dithyrambic art as depending on the clouds (κρέμαται μὲν οὖν ἐντεῦθεν ἡμῶν ἡ τέχνη, *Av.* 1386). Socrates' reference to the lyricists gives Strepsiades the opportunity to "quote" some dithyrambic expressions (335–8), all of which again display the features of elevated diction described above.[13] But the expressions also function as ways of materializing the language and thematizing the comic poet's aesthetic judgment. All the expressions describe either terrifying monsters (for example, πλοκάμους θ' ἑκατογκεφάλα Τυφῶ, "hundred-headed Typho with his locks") or misty, hazy, disembodied, and floating entities: ὑγρᾶν Νεφελᾶν στρεπταίγλαν δάϊον ὁρμάν ("the destroying onset of the moist Clouds edged with twisted brilliance" – a thunderstorm?), πρημαινούσας τε θυέλλας ("hard-blowing squalls"), ἀερίας διερᾶς γαμψούς τ' οἰωνοὺς ἀερονηχεῖς ("misty and aerial crooked birds floating in the air" – clouds?), ὄμβρους θ' ὑδάτων δροσερᾶν νεφελᾶν ("storms of water of the moist clouds"). Just as was the case with the representation of the dithyrambic subject matters that live high in the sky, the lack of substance of the clouds, mists, and gales functions as a visual parallel for the lack of substance of the dithyrambs themselves, and is turned into the topic of the dithyrambists' expressions.[14]

---

[13] The last expression appears, according to a scholiast to the *Clouds* passage, in a poem by Philoxenus (*PMG* 830), although the respective chronology of Aristophanes' *Clouds* and Philoxenus is problematic (on which, see Dover 1993 ad loc.).

[14] One has to observe, however, that many of the fragments of the dithyrambists are actually devoted to air-, aether-, or wind-related topics: see *PMG* 803, 835, 962, 963, and 1006.

In both the *Birds* and the *Clouds*, the mix of images, themes, and, one can assume, props and staging creates a dizzying mirror effect: the metaphors of the poets are literalized and given a comic, physical presence, while the features of their style are thematized. The "wings" of Cinesias are probably the most symbolic detail of this process: the poet sings of metaphorical wings (*Av.* 1375) before asking for literal ones (1383) and describes the nature of his preludes in winged terms (ἀέρια, πτεροδόνητα, 1389–90) as an introduction to a song with a volatile theme.

Elevation and heightening

But this relationship between metaphor and things is only one side of the comic strategy of dithyrambic representation. At the heart of Aristophanes' system of judgment, as the hinge for his misrepresentation, is the relationship between words and things. It is not specifically the elevation of the New Music language that Aristophanes ridicules. In the parodos of the *Clouds*, the poet himself uses the same type of elevated diction as "Cinesias," and in the *Frogs* Aeschylus' language is characterized by similar linguistic features – compounds, impressive adjectives, and words that are "as big as oxen, with crests and brows, terrible and hideous to behold, unknown to the spectators" (ῥήματ᾽… βόεια… | ὀφρῦς ἔχοντα καὶ λόφους, δείν᾽ ἄττα μορμορωπά, | ἄγνωτα τοῖς θεωμένοις, *Ran.* 924–6) – not so far from the "hundred-headed Typho with his locks" described in the dithyrambists' phrase. This abundance of neck-breaking words (ῥήμαθ᾽ ἱππόκρημνα, 929) makes it difficult to grasp their meaning, and the general lack of clarity contributes to creating loftiness and bombast (ὄγκος).[15] But here Aristophanes' parodies distinguish between two types of elevated diction created by the same linguistic means. Aeschylus' elevated language is associated with bovine, equine, and martial imagery that represents the tragedian's weighty concerns, lofty themes, and impressive rhythms. Imposing as the warriors in full armor staged by Aeschylus' tragedies are, this elevation is still grounded, planted on its feet (including its metrical feet) like an ox. By contrast, the New Musicians' style is associated with feather-light, winged, and aerial images.[16] It resists gravity, pulls upwards, and is always on the verge of diluting and evaporating into nothingness; without lead in its shoes,

---

[15] On Aeschylus' style, Stanford 1942, Fowler 1967, Rosenmeyer 1982, Citti 1994, Silk 2010: 437–8. On the passage of the *Frogs*, O'Sullivan 1992: 8–9, 109–29, Hunter 2009: 6–52. Compounds are also associated with weight and ὄγκος (on which, Earp 1944: 56–72, especially 57–8, on the style of Sophocles).

[16] Both Cinesias himself and Socrates describe the dithyrambs as ἀέρια (*Av.* 1389, *Nub.* 337).

which Cinesias needs to resist wind gusts, the poetry of the New Musicians threatens to fly away. While Aristophanes' parody introduces distortion, it is certainly not a blunt tool: not all compounds are ridiculous and elevation is not always synonymous with levity.

In the same way, "obscurity" is not to be disparaged in itself. Cinesias defined his brilliant preludes (τῶν διθυράμβων τὰ λαμπρά) as obscure and dark-gleaming (σκοτεινὰ καὶ κυαναυγέα) (*Av.* 1388–9), but there are different types of obscurity. The *Frogs* contrast Aeschylus' obscurity (his being ἀσαφής, "unclear," *Ran.* 1122) with Euripides' clarity (σαφῶς, 1434): the obscurity of Aeschylus comes from his σοφία, that is the "richness and variety of thoughts and the intensity of the poet's passion."[17] This obscurity is different from the misty obscurity of the sophists and the New Musicians, an obscurity that comes from the cloud of words in front of simple things, as Cinesias again illustrates, by piling up four (antithetical) adjectives to describe his song (*Av.* 1389–90). The difference in the representation of those two types of obscurity can be nicely summed up by a quaint formulation: the obscurity of Aeschylus is "that of condensation – a pregnant obscurity, as contrasted with the redundant obscurity of some modern poets."[18]

This comparison of different types of obscurity brings us to a consideration of the adequation, or lack thereof, of words and things themselves. In Aristophanes' parodies, elevation of the diction and periphrastic way of describing things cannot make up for the vacuity or triviality of the thing itself. This is also the aspect that the *Thesmophoriazousae* parodies in the case of sophistic language: in the opening lines of the play, Euripides describes everyday things and phenomena (eyes, ear, hearing, and seeing) in riddling language influenced by philosophical theories: the Sky fashioned the eye as "an imitation of the solar disk" (ὀφθαλμὸν ἀντίμιμον ἡλίου τροχῷ, *Thesm.* 17) and perforated "a funnel for hearing" as the ear (ἀκοῆς δὲ χοάνην ὦτα, 18).[19] The periphrases puzzle the kinsman, unfamiliar with clever speech (δεξιῶς λέγειν, 9) and intellectual exchange (σοφαὶ συνουσίαι, 21).

---

[17] Stanford 1942: 129. On Aeschylean obscurity, Stanford 1942: 126–37. On Aristophanes' discussion of the poets' *sophia*, Dover 1993: 10–37.

[18] The expression, and the reference to the "modern poets," is not from a late fifth-century BC conservative critic, but from a late-Victorian historian of Greek literature, Mahaffy (1891: I 275). Stanford (1942) adds an interesting note after quoting this very passage of Mahaffy: "After the lapse of half a century this needs only one qualification. The poets of the 1930s and 1940s are nearer Aeschylus in their obscurities and ambiguities than were the 'modern' poets of Mahaffy's day, though among them Browning and Hardy show Aeschylus's direct influence" (128). This qualification makes "vacuous obscurity" a quality of modern poetry in general, regardless of its time.

[19] The language recasts Hesiodic theogony in more scientific-sounding words, but Colin and Olson (2004 ad loc.) also mention the possibility of Anaxagoran or Democritan influence.

For the kinsman, the expression verges on the paradoxical and only shows the vacuity of periphrastic language, which is as needlessly convoluted as the expression "being lame in both legs" (χωλὸς εἶναι τὼ σκέλει, 24). But ultimately, what Aristophanes' parody of different high styles illustrates is a distinction between two literary qualities: elevation and heightening. These categories, which I borrow from Michael Silk's terminology, account for much of Aristophanes' work and for much of the distortion he introduces in the representation of style. Elevation, in general, is characteristic of various poetic languages and styles. In Aristotle's words, poetry should be οὐ ταπεινή ("not low").[20] It is "solemn and distanced from everyday language" (σεμνὴ καὶ ἐξαλλάττουσα τὸ ἰδιωτικόν, *Poet.* 1458a21–2). Elevation can be obtained by linguistic and stylistic "exotic" tools (ξενικοῖς), including the use of γλῶττα (an obsolete or foreign word that needs explanation), μεταφορά (metaphor), ἐπέκτασις (lengthened form), and, in general, "everything that diverges from standard use" (πᾶν τὸ παρὰ τὸ κύριον).[21] But according to Silk, and this is a crucial distinction, although all lyric language is elevated – that is, it differs significantly from everyday speech – not all elevated language is heightened, and heightened language is not necessarily found in high style:

Heightened language is what Ezra Pound . . . called "language charged with meaning to the utmost possible degree." Such extra "meaning" is created by what T. S. Eliot . . . calls "words perpetually juxtaposed in new and sudden combinations," that is, by unexpected mobilization of the connotations of words or of their sound or rhythmic properties in the cause of the sensuous enactment of meaning or the suggestion of new meaning.[22]

In parodying the *lexis* of Euripides and the New Musicians by contrasting it with that of Aeschylus, Aristophanes presents Aeschylus' language as combining elevated diction with maximum heightening, while Cinesias' dithyrambic style is, on the Aristophanic account, elevated diction with minimal or no heightening. In this reading, the repetition of some nominal elements in the compounds, for example, grounds the mind and reduces the imagination's possibilities. While Aristophanes' Aeschylus matches the impressive nature of his topic with the bombast of a varied diction, loftiness of thought, stately rhythms, and evocative sounds, his dithyrambic poet falls short of "perpetually juxtapos[ing] in new and sudden combinations"

---

[20] Arist. *Rh.* 1404b4–5, *Poet.* 1458a18.
[21] In the language of the *Frogs*, this would be a ῥῆμα γενναῖον, what Dover (1993: 10) glosses as "the real expression, the bold image, the provocative idea neatly expressed in one striking line."
[22] Silk 2010: 436, who explains how the heightened language of Aristophanes is not elevated.

words, sounds, and images but recombines them in repetitive and conventional patterns. One can find an illustration of this lackluster product in the monotonous reconfiguration of the same elements in new compounds in the *Birds*: rather than bringing together unexpected elements in the two elements joined together, adjectives like ἀεροδονήτους, πτεροδόνητα, αἰθεροδρόμων, and ἁλίδρομον rely on a limited number of operative elements (the idea of whirling, fast movement, and airiness) completed by another element that adds only a little information (either location, direction, or means). Instead of helping the imagination take flight by adding "variety, stature, and simultaneously conciseness,"[23] the string of compounds reproduced by Aristophanes achieves the opposite effect: it stifles the imagination by making it go back to a limited number of ideas used repeatedly in various compositions, grounding the thought in the same referent and mostly producing redundancy.

The overall poetic lameness of Cinesias' dithyrambs is embodied in the poet's limping gait, which keeps him close to the ground and signifies his poetic flop. Such parodies and critical screens frame our appreciation of the new dithyramb as elevated language with no heightening and encompass the stylistic faults associated with the New Music in general. Because Aristophanes' voice is so loud, it all too often prevents us from listening to the specific forms of heightening the language takes.[24]

Redeeming the text: dithyrambic heightening

When audiences went to the theater to hear a dithyramb or a nome, they must have expected to hear a specific kind of language; they must also have been used to their distinctive, although unsettling, communication strategies, which were reused in comedy, and have had interpretive tools at the ready. The dynamic relationship between, on the one hand, the elevated diction and, on the other, other poetic features responsible for "heightening" and determining the singular style of the New Music is addressed in the following pages.

---

[23] These features (ποικιλίαν τινὰ . . . καὶ μέγεθος, καὶ ἅμα καὶ συντομίαν τινά) are what [Demetr.] *Eloc.* 92 describes as specific to the use of compounds, associated with the grand style.

[24] Another important frame contributing to the misrepresentation of the dithyrambic diction is that of Middle Comedy. On Middle Comedy's parodies of dithyrambic language, see Hunter 1983: 18–9 and commentary on Eubulus, fr. 75, Nesselrath 1990: 241–80, Conti Bizzarro 1993–4.

Compounds and periphrasis: defamiliarizing the familiar

As already noted, one of the most striking, and most often parodied, features of the New Music is its use of compounds. Yet compounding is exclusive neither to the genres of dithyramb and nomes, nor to the late classical period. No matter how narrowly or broadly understood, compounding is a feature of the Greek language, used abundantly in all song types, from Homer, Aeschylus, and a whole range of hymns to the Hellenistic and Imperial poets, as well as by a variety of prose writers, including the sophists and prose authors contemporary with the New Musicians.[25] Not all compounds are equally puzzling, interesting, or productive though. Some words, although morphologically compounds, might have barely been perceived as still composed of two morphemes, as in ἐμβόλοις (*PMG* 791.1) or πανήγυϱις (*PMG* 791.171). Others were not puzzling, because the morphological, syntactic, or semantic relationship between the two (or more) members of the compound seemed straightforward in light of their obvious syntax and/or their poetic familiarity, as in "grey-eyed" Athena or "far-shooting" Apollo (although this familiarity might sometimes make us forget that their cultic or ritual associations remained unclear).

So can we highlight a specific use of compounds by the New Music poets? Several times in the *Rhetoric* and the *Poetics* Aristotle notes that compounds (and especially double compounds) are particularly *appropriate* to the dithyramb.[26] The way his remarks are presented suggests that they are more than an observation on the frequent occurrence of compounds in dithyramb, old and new: there is something in the *nature* of compounds that makes them particularly suited to the genre. As Aristotle underlines in both the *Poetics* and the *Rhetoric*, because of their sheer size, compounds have great expressive potential and allow multiplying aural, even mimetic, effects. Dithyrambic poets particularly appreciate compounds because they are noisy (ψοφώδεις, *Rh.* 1406b2), but their excessive use in prose, Aristotle

[25] Compounds bring up linguistic, stylistic, and literary critical problems. On the relationship between morphology and syntax in compounds, Benvéniste 1967: 15–16. For an original overview of compounds in Greek, Meyer 1923: 153–72 for the dithyramb; on compounds in Indo-European poetics: Clackson 2002. On compounds in Pindar, Bräuning 1881; in Aeschylus, Citti 1994: 6–19; in Sophocles, Earp 1944: 56–72; in Euripides, Breitenbach 1934: 3–131; in New Dithyramb, Schönewolf 1938: 24–6 and Hordern 2002: 41, 47–50; in late epic poetry, Giangrande 1973.

[26] Three different passages use the same kind of vocabulary to underline fittingness of compounds: *Poet.* 1459a8–10 τὰ μὲν διπλᾶ μάλιστα ἁρμόττει ("the double compounds are most fitting"); *Rh.* 1408b11–12 τὰ δὲ ὀνόματα τὰ διπλᾶ καὶ τὰ ἐπίθετα πλείω καὶ τὰ ξένα μάλιστα ἁρμόττει λέγοντι παθητικῶς ("double compounds, an abundance of epithets, and exotic words are most fitting for an emotional speaker"); *Rh.* 1406b1–5 χρησιμωτάτη ἡ διπλῆ λέξις τοῖς διθυραμβοποιοῖς ("compounds are much used by composers of dithyrambs").

continues, makes a text overly poetic or, literally, "made-up" (ποιητικά, *Rh.* 1406a5) and emotional, two aspects that many later testimonies about the "dithyrambic style" emphasize and that the modern definition of the adjective still conveys. This use of double compounds as "expressive intensification" might well be reproducing what is at stake in the sonorous dithyramb cry itself:[27] Pratinas, for example, describes Dionysus' celebration with a reference to the "much-clashed Dionysian altar" (Διονυσιάδα πολυπάταγα θυμέλαν, *PMG* 708.2), and Dionysus' epithet Bromius reproduces the god's fondness for noise. The duality of the double compound belongs in particular to the very nature of Dionysus, a god of mysteries and "twice born" according to some etymologies of his epithet (*di-thyrambos*).[28]

But as Aristotle states in the *Rhetoric* (1406a35–6), double compounds are more generally used when things do not have a name, as in τὸ χρονο-τριβεῖν ("pastime"), for example. Compounds have an inherent neologic potential and allow the combining of familiar morphemes in unfamiliar ways to refer to a new thing or concept. They are also, or rather *especially*, used to refer in an unfamiliar way to something that has a familiar name. The effects of the compound are underlined by [Demetrius] (*On Style* 91), who, speaking of compounds in general, says that they should not be like those of dithyrambs (οὐ τὰ διθυραμβικῶς συγκείμενα) but like those formed by usage (ἐοικότα τοῖς ὑπὸ τῆς συνηθείας συγκειμένοις), thereby suggesting that the dithyrambic compounds are not like those of everyday language. This dis-habituating effect is a precursor of the vocabulary used by Russian Formalists to refer to "defamiliarization." Dithyrambic compounds offer a way to describe the world in an unfamiliar way that gives listeners fresh access to things – an insight that so far has not received the attention it deserves. By challenging the audience to engage in the process of recognition and identification, dithyrambic compounds too participate in the Dionysian play with mask and identity; they both hide their referent and reveal something new of its nature.

New Musicians and sophists on the truth of language

Defamiliarization also underlies the process of referring to things in a periphrastic way.[29] The process is described explicitly not by Aristotle, but

---

[27] For the expression, and on double compounds' appropriation of the cultic association with Dionysus, Ford 2011b. Earlier, Pickard-Cambridge 1962: 50.

[28] Ieranò 1997: *T* 2–23, especially 4a and b, 12, 14–16, 19–21.

[29] On periphrasis as defamiliarization, Bers 1984: 192–4.

by [Demetrius] (*On Style* 92), in the lines following his discussion of compounds; it is known from scholars of Old English as kenning.[30] As I have
noted in the previous section, defamiliarization is also characteristic of
sophistic expressions, or rather it is a feature of the caricature of sophistic
expressions one gets from Aristophanes in the *Clouds*: rather than giving
immediate access that brings the audience closer to the object or concept
described, the sophists, as depicted by Aristophanes and Plato, introduce
distance, thanks to periphrasis and neologisms. As the parodos of the *Clouds*
(316–18) suggests, diction cannot be separated from reflection: the powers
of expression (διάλεξις, itself a linguistic coinage for diction, and περίλεξις)
that the Clouds grant are linked to logic, reflection, and imagination, and
to performance skills that demonstrate these powers (κροῦσις, "deception,"
and κατάληψις, "comprehension").[31] While the passage conveys the kind
of attack regularly directed at the New Musicians, it also points out that
keenness for verbal innovation is linked to the sophists' attempt to defamiliarize the audience's relationship to things through words, an idea stated
with particular clarity later in the *Clouds* when Worse Argument, who aims
to win over Strepsiades and have him study under his tutelage, promises
to shoot at him new words and reasonings (ῥηματίοισιν καινοῖς αὐτὸν καὶ
διανοίαις κατατοξεύσω, *Nub.* 943–4).[32] These new words are not just smart
ways of talking about the world as we know it, but a new way of thinking
about our relationship with it, especially through language.

This connection between the language of the New Music and contemporary prose runs deeper than the use of compounds and periphrases. The
language of the New Music relies on processes that are associated in particular with Gorgianic prose style,[33] and sources identify a specific connection
between the sophists and the New Musicians, several of whom, including
Licymnius, are reported to have been students of Gorgias. In particular,

---

[30] On kennings, Waern 1951, who compares the "mannerism" of Ion of Chios and Timotheus.
Her treatment of the language is, however, rather hasty, as the following statement illustrates:
Timotheus' kennings "seem to have been used, to a high degree as *l'art pour l'art*... They make
a rather cold impression because they are quite unpathetic. The complete absence of the
affective kenning also suggests the lack of pathos" (97–8).

[31] Borthwick (1959) suggests that it is significant that the last two terms, κροῦσις and κατάληψις,
have a musical meaning (Σ Ar. *Nub.* 317): the sophists are often described as causing the same
(ensnaring?) effects as musicians; see de Romilly 1975: 4–14.

[32] The sophists' interest in new words (ὀνόματα καινά) is mocked in Aristophanes' *Banqueters*
(fr. 205 KA), on which Cassio 1977: 32–6.

[33] Homoioteleuton, for example, is illustrated in Timotheus, *PMG* 778: θυιάδα φοιβάδα μαινάδα
λυσσάδα ("frantic, prophetic, menadic, full of panic").

Aristotle describes Licymnius' (dithyrambic) style as appropriate for reading (ἀναγνωστικός) rather than fit for competition (ἀγωνιστικός):

Most popular are the authors who can be read (οἱ ἀναγνωστικοί), like Chaeremon – he is precise as a speech writer (ἀκριβὴς γὰρ ὥσπερ λογογράφος) – and Licymnius among the dithyrambic poets.

Arist. Rh. 1413b12–14.

As a matter of fact, besides composing dithyrambs, Licymnius wrote on language and rhetoric, and Aristotle criticizes him for having introduced some dithyrambic expressions into his technical prose.[34] More specifically, Licymnius seems to have attributed great importance to the physical qualities, and beauty, of *lexis*. As Aristotle also explains in the passage where he condemns Licymnius' style, "metaphors should also be derived from things that are beautiful, the beauty of a word consisting, as Licymnius says, in its sound or sense, and its ugliness in the same" (*Rh.* 1405b6–8). This euphonic view of language might be at the root of the perceived vacuity of dithyrambic language, which would seem to put more emphasis on sound than sense. Dionysius of Halicarnassus, for example, highlights that some of Plato's passages (from *Menex.* 236e) are concerned as much with pleasing oral effects as with meaning, in a way close to the style of contemporary poets: commenting on a sentence in the *Menexenus*, Dionysius observes how Plato dresses up (καλλωπίζει) his language with affected and exaggerated figures of speech in a manner reminiscent of Agathon or Licymnius:

For he says "we need a speech such that it praises adequately the dead, but gently encourages the living." He balances adverb with adverb, and verb with verb, "adequately" balancing "gently" and "praises," "encourages," and these are equally balanced. And these are not the words of a Licymnius or an Agathon, saying "hybris or Cypris for a salary or toil for the fatherlands" (ὕβριν ἢ <κύ>πριν μισθῷ ποθὲν ἢ μόχθον πατρίδων), but the brilliant Plato expressing himself.

Dion. Hal. Dem. 26 = Licymnius, PMG 773

He further refers to how Gorgias and his pupils Licymnius and Polus wrote compositions that were vulgar (φορτικήν) and inflated (ὑπέρογκον) and (quoting Plato's *Phaedrus*, 238d) "not far from dithyrambs" (οὐ πόρρω διθυράμβων τίνων).[35] In another passage, *Thucydides* 26, Thucydides' use of ostentatious figures of speech (θεατρικῶν σχημάτων, "histrionic figures,"

---

[34] Arist. *Rh.* 1414b15–18: "But one must only adopt a name to express a distinct species or a real difference; otherwise, it becomes empty and silly (κενὸν καὶ ληρῶδες), like the terms introduced by Licymnius in his *Art*, where he speaks of 'wafting' (ἐπούρωσιν), 'wandering from the subject' (ἀποπλάνησιν), and 'ramifications' (ὄζους)."

[35] Dion. Hal. *Lys.* 3.

which Dionysus defines as τὰς παρισώσεις καὶ παρομοιώσεις καὶ παρονο-
μασίας καὶ ἀντιθέσεις, "balancing of clauses, assonances, play on sounds, and
oppositions"), is described as similar to that of Gorgias, Polus, Licymnius,
and their followers.[36]

Besides the connection between sense and sound, the adequation of sig-
nifier and signified is itself illustrated in another series of passages, the most
striking of which comes from Plato's *Cratylus*. Socrates gives as the origin of
the familiar σελαναία the compound σελαενονεοάεια ("beams-always-old-
and-new"). When he hears that etymology, Hermogenes exclaims, "That
word does look dithyrambic!" (διθυραμβῶδές γε τοῦτο τοὔνομα).[37] The
remark is paradigmatic of what is associated with "dithyrambic language" –
long words with puzzling meaning. Yet there is a more deep-seated truth in
Hermogenes' remark. In the same way as Socrates in the *Cratylus* plays with
fantastic etymology, finding truth in word collocations and following the
logic of words and puns, some passages of the New Music poets display an
interest in suggestive and expressive (as opposed to scientific) etymologies.
Just like Socrates' inventions, these etymologies are works not of scholarship but of the imagination, and they create connections between words and
things based on the logic and sound of language rather than (anachronistic)
linguistic rules.[38] They emphasize what truth a word might have, in itself,
about the thing to which it refers. Thus Melanippides derives the name of
the Acheron from ἄχεα ("pains"), thereby suggesting a strong connection
between sound and meaning:

> καλεῖται δ᾽ <εἵνεκ᾽> ἐν κόλποισι γαίας
> ἄχε᾽ εἶσι προχέων Ἀχέρων.
>   Melanippides, *PMG* 759

> It is called Acheron because of the pains that it goes pouring in the bosom
> of the earth.

In addition to the jingling effect of ἄχε᾽ ... προχέων Ἀχέρων, the alliteration
in the stops [g], [k], [kh] imitates the pangs and beating effect that the
words describe. Licymnius illustrates the same mimetic process in two
further instances: while proposing the same etymology as Melanippides for

---

[36] On Dionysius' ambiguous relationship with poetic language, de Jonge 2008.
[37] Pl. *Cra.* 409b11–c3.
[38] "Serious" etymologies in the *Cratylus* are relatively few (a little over twenty) compared to the
language games that Plato plays in the rest of the 120 etymological explanations. On ancient
poetic etymologies and an oral culture's interest in paronomasia, wordplays, and alliterations,
Pfeiffer 1968: 4–5, 61–4, Tsitsibakou-Vasalos 2007, especially pp. 5–6 and pp. 13–33.

Acheron, by accumulating occlusive sounds, the poet evokes the feeling of pain he describes:

(a) μυρίαις π̱α̱γ̱αῖς δ̱ακρύων ἀ̱χ̱έ̱ω̱ν τε β̱ρ̱ύει,
καὶ πάλιν

(b) Ἀ̱χ̱έ̱ρ̱ω̱ν ἄ̱χ̱ε̱α̱ π̱ο̱ρ̱θ̱μεύει β̱ρ̱ο̱τοῖσιν.

> Licymnius, *PMG* 770

(a) with thousands of sources it rushes with tears and <u>pains</u>
and again
(b) <u>Acheron</u> carries <u>pains</u> for mortals.

The two passages provide an etymology for Acheron as connected with ἄχος ("pain") – or, more specifically, with a form of its plural, ἄχεα – but also suggest different types of poetic work in the process of etymologizing. These two passages even suggest the existence of an agonistic relationship between poets, who always "up" each other, and possibly illustrate a form of competition in scholarship: while Melanippides doubly justifies the sound χε (as part of ἄχε᾽ and προχέων) and presents straightforwardly the etymology of the noun, Licymnius integrates the etymology in the narration, in something that looks like, but is not, a *figura etymologica*.[39] Any poet or prose writer, of course, exploits the aural and musical potential of language, but what connects neo-dithyrambists and sophists is their apparent interest in finding *truth* in language, which leads them to pursue the logic of language and its expressive possibilities, and playing with (and discussing) the "material" elements of language. This concern is particularly well illustrated in two passages of Telestes related to *aulos*-music (*PMG* 805 and 806), which describe the breezy sound of the pipes in lines that use the materiality of language to evoke musical features. The poet creates texture through lexical repetitions of important words ("clever" in σοφὸν σοφάν, *PMG* 805a.1), polyptoton ("love" and "lovely" in εὐηράτοιο ἔρως, *PMG* 805a.5, μάταν . . . ματαιολόγων, *PMG* 805b.1; καλλιπνόων . . . πνεύματος, *PMG* 806.1–4), as well as paronomasia (εὐηράτοιο . . . ἔτειρεν, *PMG* 805a.5; ἄγαμον καὶ ἄπαιδ᾽ ἀπένειμε, *PMG* 805a.6; πνεύματος εὔπτερον αὔραν ἀμφιπλέκων, *PMG* 806.4). This form of *poikilia* (variegation) relies on the physical characteristics of speech and syntax, with the syllables and vowels (the *stoicheia* of language) forming the elements that create the music of language, a process again familiar to the sophists, and to Gorgias in particular.[40] Far from being unique to Telestes or to any New Musician, these aural processes imitate features that are being described – giving

---

[39] On the process of narrativized etymology, Nagy 1979: 69–93, Peradotto 1990: 94–170, Calame 1995: 174–85, Tsitsibakou-Vasalos 2007: 57–9.

[40] Ford 2002: 165–7, J. I. Porter 2010: 205–60, 276–307.

virtuosity to a passage that describes virtuosity, and lightness to a passage that describes the breeziness of music – but what is more specific to them is the self-consciousness of the poet-theoretician of language, who describes a musical process while activating it through language.

Metaphors and the logic of images

The challenges of disentangling different features of dithyrambic diction have already come into focus. Compounds are often neologisms and work semantically as periphrasis, exploiting the aural quality of words and refreshing our access to the thing described. Such features make for an indirect form of communication. But this description and also most list-based descriptions of the features of the New Music style leave out the single most important feature at the heart of this process: metaphor.[41] An understanding of the specific functioning of the New Musicians' metaphors, and of the logic of language on which it relies, can help to define better the specificity of neo-dithyrambic language beyond its linguistic features.

Since it is impossible to distinguish between lexical and other poetic features, let me start with some observations on the metaphorical relationship at work in a compound found in a fragment of Telestes that I have already quoted in Chapter 2 and referred to above:

μετὰ ταῦτα δὲ ἐγκωμιάζων τὴν αὐλητικὴν λέγει·

(c) ἂν συνεριθοτάταν Βρομίῳ παρέδωκε, σεμνᾶς
δαίμονος ἀερθὲν πνεῦμ᾿ αἰολοπτέρυγον
σὺν ἀγλαᾶν ὠκύτατι χειρῶν.
Telestes, PMG 805c

Then he praises the art of *aulos*-playing and says:

(c) [the art of *aulos*-playing] which the uplifted quick-fluttering breath of the august goddess, along with the swiftness of her splendid hands, gave to Bromius as a most helpful attendant.

In Telestes' praise of the art of *aulos*-playing, the goddess' breath is imagined as something volatile, pictured as winged, and the wings themselves are described by their quick-fluttering movement.[42] The metaphor (the breath as a bird) is thus developed with an adjective (αἰολοπτέρυγον, "quick-fluttering") appropriate to the vehicle (the bird) rather than the tenor – unless the quickness of movement (αἰολο-) applies, in a metamusical way,

---

[41] On metaphors, Nowottny 1962, Lakoff and Johnson 1980, Fauconnier and Turner 2002, Boys-Stones 2003. On the singular appeal of metaphor as "the figure of figures, a figure for figurality," Culler 1981: 188–209; p. 189 for the expression.

[42] Already ποικιλόπτερον μέλος ("a song of variegated plumage") in Pratinas, *PMG* 708.5.

to the divine music-playing and the ποικιλία ("variegation") associated with it. In the compound, a metaphorical relationship is thus established between the adjective and the noun, based on an analogy: Athena's uplifted breath is *like* a bird. But the compound, and the metaphor on which it relies, plays a particular role: among the functions that Winifred Nowottny defines, the metaphor does not really make clearer, as through a diagram, nor does it make more immediate, as if through the senses. Instead it has the "power to bring . . . associations and suggestions with it. The figurative words bring with them a diffused aura of their literal use; I say 'aura' deliberately, to emphasize that it is rather indeterminate."[43] As Nowottny makes clear, an audience's word-associations and associations with their experience of life of course varies. But there is also another way in which the poet can develop metaphors and follow the "aura" of words, based this time on an audience's poetic memory.

This aspect of the New Music has not been explored so far, and can be observed in the process needed to make sense of the term συνεριθοτάταν in our passage, the adjective used to describe the art of *aulos*-playing. Συνέριθος, "female helper" (a word of unknown origin),[44] is how Athena presents herself in the *Odyssey* when she wakes up Nausicaa to invite her to do laundry since her girlhood is coming to an end:

> καί τοι ἐγὼ <u>συνέριθος</u> ἅμ' ἕψομαι, ὄφρα τάχιστα
> ἐντύνεαι, ἐπεὶ οὔ τοι ἔτι δὴν <u>παρθένος</u> ἔσσεαι.
> Hom. *Od.* 6.32–3

I will come with you as a <u>fellow worker</u>, so that you may quickly make your preparations, since you won't be a *parthenos* for long any more.

It is significant that in its compound form συνέριθος is a hapax in Homer, used for Athena who offers handiwork help to Nausicaa. In the lines that come immediately before our passage, Athena is described as appearing to Nausicaa "like a breath of wind" (ἀνέμου ὡς πνοιή, *Od.* 6.20) and "hovering over her head" (στῆ δ' ἄρ' ὑπὲρ κεφαλῆς, 6.21). Can we read in the "uplifted breath" (ἀερθὲν πνεῦμ') a synecdoche for the goddess that works as a miniature piece of scholarly exegesis of the Homeric simile which appears in a passage where maidenhood is at stake? And in describing Athena's handing over the breath of the *aulos* as most helpful assistant to Dionysus could Telestes be relying on the "pneumatic" description of Athena as helper in the Homeric line? This interpretation of the Homeric hapax might

---

[43] Nowottny 1962: 64.
[44] The *Suda* (E 2901, II 403 Adler) connects the epithet Ergane with ἐργασίας, "work," and scholia on the passage with ἔρια, "wool."

be facilitated by the reference to the cult of Athena Ergane, supervisor of spinning and weaving, two activities requiring the "swiftness of splendid hands" (ἀγλαᾶν ὠκύτατι χειρῶν) described with reference to the playing of the *aulos*.[45] This interpretation of συνέριθος suggests that neo-dithyrambic florid and disorienting diction is more than long words with no meaning used merely as sound effects or as a source of flashy images for mindless listeners. One productive way to think about such adjectives is to interpret them as glosses on rare Homeric words and as forms of scholarly engagement with the poetic past in a self-consciously belated way that we usually associate with Hellenistic scholarship.

Other adjectives in Telestian fragments and, one can assume, in many others, also rely on the interpretation process illustrated above: in developing the "aura" associated with the vehicle (to use Nowottny's term), the (compound) adjective develops an idea and image that are rather independent of the noun it qualifies. This process can be taken so far that it transforms the expression into a form of riddle,[46] as is the case with the following fragment referring to music:

> ἄλλος δ' ἄλλαν κλαγγὰν ἱείς
> κερατόφωνον ἐρέθιζε μάγαδιν
> πενταρράβδῳ χορδᾶν ἀρθμῷ
> χέρα καμψιδίαυλον ἀναστρωφῶν τάχος.
> 　　　　　　　　　　　　Telestes, *PMG* 808

> Each lets out a different clamor, and rivals the horn-voiced *magadis*, swiftly running his hand up and down around the turning post, on the five-staffed joining of strings.

All the scholarship on this passage focuses on the technical difficulties entailed by the description, especially on the nature of the instrument (the *magadis* – if it is an instrument) and its technique of playing, and on deciphering the musical reality that the adjectives might describe.[47] But very little has been written on the way this reality is described and on the effect the compounds achieve. To start with, each line in the Telestian fragment works as a small syntactic unit that also corresponds to a unit of meaning and does not spill over into the next line. This is in fact true of most other Telestian fragments in the surviving corpus: the very simple syntax and the absence of enjambment makes it possible to isolate each line

---

[45] On Athena Ergane, Bruit Zeidman and Schmitt Pantel 1992: 189–91, Mikalson 2005: 118–19, 165–6.

[46] I have examined two such examples of learned riddling in a compound adjective in LeVen 2011 and LeVen 2012. The discussion below is an edited version of LeVen 2012: 51–5.

[47] On the *magadis*, Comotti 1983, Barker 1984: 298, 1988, 1998; Hordern 2000.

as an independent unit of sense, an "intonation unit."[48] Second, each noun is modified by an adjectival compound (κερατόφωνον, πενταρράβδῳ, and καμψιδίαυλον) that introduces an image. Rather than creating a sense of flow in the passage, each adjective holds a metaphorical relationship with the noun and encapsulates a miniature image quite independently from the rest. The *magadis* has a voice of horn, the joining of strings has five lines, and the hand completes a *diaulos* race. The levels of explicitness and vividness vary: the last compound, καμψιδίαυλον, for example, works through the analogy between a hand running up and down the strings and a runner completing a turn in a *diaulos* race, around a turning post (καμπτήρ). Just like αἰολοπτέρυγον, it puts the emphasis on technical features of *magadis*-playing, which is reminiscent of the emphasis on "bends" to qualify the New Music, as described in Chapter 2.

But the first compound adjective opens a new way to think about the metaphorical relationship, especially the nature of the analogy, established in the compound. The *magadis*, most often taken to be a twenty-string lyre, is described as having a "voice of horn." Campbell remarks "resonant like the military instrument," but how can a string instrument sound like a trumpet?[49] Gulick and Olson suggest that it was struck by a (horn) plectrum, but this interpretation barely fits with other descriptions of the *magadis* as a plucked, rather than struck, instrument. I think that the compound develops another association, of the same type as that observed in the compound αἰολοπτέρυγον. The interpretation hinges on one word in particular, the participle ἀναστρωφῶν. In the famous Homeric passage where this participle, a hapax, is used, it describes Odysseus' handling the bow after his return to Ithaca:

> ὁ δ' ἤδη τόξον ἐνώμα
> πάντη <u>ἀναστρωφῶν</u>, πειρώμενος ἔνθα καὶ ἔνθα,
> μὴ <u>κέρα</u> ἶπες ἔδοιεν ἀποιχομένοιο ἄνακτος.   395
> Hom. *Od.* 21.393–5

He was already handling the bow, <u>turning it on every side</u>, making trial of it here and there, lest the woodworms ate the <u>horn</u> in the absence of the master.

Two Homeric words appear in the Telestian fragment (ἀναστρωφῶν, and the κέρα-compound), and the image of the anxious owner going over the

---

[48] On intonation units, Chafe 1994, Bakker 1997a: 48–53, 68–71.

[49] Unless the *magadis* is a form of *aulos*, which is suggested by a few passages of Athenaeus that collect earlier sources: Ath. 4.182d–183a and 14.634c–637a, which concludes with our passage of Telestes.

bow and touching it all over (ἔνθα καὶ ἔνθα) in the Homeric passage is evocative of the busy hands of a strings player moving back and forth all over the instrument. Even more important is the comparison between bow and *phorminx* in the next lines of the *Odyssey*: Odysseus tightens the bow the way a professional *aoidos* would tighten the strings of a *phorminx*:

> ἀτὰρ πολύμητις Ὀδυσσεύς,
> αὐτίκ᾽ ἐπεὶ μέγα τόξον ἐβάστασε καὶ ἴδε πάντη,　　　　　405
> ὡς ὅτ᾽ ἀνὴρ φόρμιγγος ἐπιστάμενος καὶ ἀοιδῆς
> ῥηϊδίως ἐτάνυσσε νέῳ περὶ κόλλοπι χορδήν,
> ἅψας ἀμφοτέρωθεν ἐϋστρεφὲς ἔντερον οἰός,
> ὣς ἄρ᾽ ἄτερ σπουδῆς τάνυσεν μέγα τόξον Ὀδυσσεύς.
> Hom. *Od.* 21.404–9

But wily Odysseus at once was holding the great bow and looking it all over, as when a man expert in the *phorminx* and song easily stretches anew a string around a peg, fastening from both ends the well-twisted sheep-gut string, in the same way Odysseus effortlessly stretched the great bow.

The image in the compound κερατόφωνον is thus developed from the familiar comparison between bow and string instrument, κλαγγά and χορδᾶν applying both to a bow (as to Apollo's bow in *Il.* 1.49, for example) and a *phorminx*. In this instance, again Telestes might be playing with a Homeric hapax and giving it new life or simply relying on the understanding of a common image (bow = *phorminx*) when qualifying the *magadis* as horn-voiced – that is, it lets out, when plucked, the same resounding sound as that made by a horn bow when it is strung. Similar strategies might be called for in the interpretation of the other compounds, some of which have been already suggested.[50] This consideration of the compounds is, I contend, an important step toward re-evaluating the diction and the nature of the audience's engagement with meaning in New Music texts. As I have suggested elsewhere, and as the next chapter further explains, this kind of approach to the language of the New Music is not antithetical to thinking about New Music in, and as, performance. It *adds* meaning to what Csapo has called the overall "experience" of late classical theatrical music: besides the aural experience of the performance and the overall overstimulation of senses and imagination through music and spectacle, the type of analysis I have proposed, which highlights the self-conscious and agonistic

---

[50] In particular, Barker (1998) on the five-rodded joining of strings, which he interprets as a riddle for the hand. I would only add to his convincing argument the parallel with πεντόζοιο ("with five branches") in Hesiod's *Works and Days* (742), which suggests a familiar pattern in seeing the hand as an object particularly fit for riddling descriptions.

engagement of the dithyrambic poet with Homeric language and a form of early Homeric scholarship, emphasizes the role of the audience's experience (in the sense of familiarity) as listeners of poetry in their processing of the songs.[51]

Adjectives between pleonasm, actualization, and synaesthesia

In the passages quoted above, it is difficult not to observe the repeated use of epithets qualifying each noun, sometimes with no coordination. But one has to notice, once again, that the use of adjectives in dense texture (coordinated *or* in asyndeton) is not specific to the neo-dithyrambists.[52] In particular, any cletic address packs in a lot of adjectives as part of the ritual invocation of a god and in realizing his or her epiphany.[53] While some adjectives are not specific to a single god (σεμνός, for example, or πολυώνυμος), others underline local cultic titles. In this latter case, ritual adjectives work as *Zaubermittel* and have performative power.[54] The literature on the subject is very rich but, again, can we identify something specific to the neo-dithyrambists, in this instance in their use of epithets, besides a tendency to add verbal padding lacking any substance?

A fragmentary address to Health by Licymnius provides some insight:[55]

> λιπαρόμματε μᾶτερ ὑψίστα θρόνων
> σεμνῶν Ἀπόλλωνος βασίλεια ποθεινά
> πραΰγελως Ὑγίεια . . .
> > Licymnius, *PMG* 769

> gleaming-eyed mother, highest queen of the holy throne of Apollo, longed-for, gentle-laugh Health . . .

In a manner typical of cletic invocations, the address consists exclusively of nouns and adjectives (of its ten words, six are adjectives, of which two are compounds). Some divine qualities of Health are reminiscent of those in the invocation of Hera in the opening of the Homeric *Hymn to Hera*:

---

[51] On dithyrambic language in performance, LeVen (2012) emphasizes the importance of the similarity of festival context and musical contest for the performance of rhapsodic and dithyrambic poetry.

[52] On the defamiliarizing use of epithets, Arist. *Rh.* 1406a14–15 ἐξαλλάττει γὰρ τὸ εἰωθὸς καὶ ξενικὴν ποιεῖ τὴν λέξιν ("it removes familiarity from diction and gives it an 'exotic' air").

[53] On the use of epithets in hymn and prayer, Meyer 1923: 48–67, Guthrie 1930, Harvey 1957, Furley and Bremer 2001: 152–63. For epithets of the gods, Dee 2001.

[54] Meyer 1923: 48.

[55] *PMG* 769 is possibly not a dithyramb but what Sextus Empiricus calls a prelude: προειπών (or an address?) in dactylic meters. On Licymnius and New Music, J. I. Porter 2010: 314–15.

"Ηρην ἀείδω χρυσόθρονον ἣν τέκε Ῥείη,
ἀθανάτην βασίλειαν ὑπείροχον εἶδος ἔχουσαν
Ζηνὸς ἐριγδούποιο κασιγνήτην ἄλοχόν τε . . .
Hymn. Hom. Hera 1–3

Hera I sing, golden-throned, whom Rhea bore, immortal queen, of
supreme beauty, sister and wife of loud-sounding Zeus . . .

Three features – the mention of the throne, the connection with another
Olympian, and reference to beauty – are common to both invocations, but
other adjectives placed at key points in the lines in the Licymnian invocation
(the opening word and the final adjective accompanying Health's name)
emphasize physical qualities associated with Health's personification –
not so much her anthropomorphization, but her manifestation in those
whom she visits, who become "figures of health." Two of these adjectives
are compounds, and neologisms. With respect to the first adjective, the
shininess expressed with λιπαρο- points out, since Homer, high status and
qualifies heroes as well as cities.[56] Compounds in λιπαρο- appear in many
lyric or epic texts, including Bacchylides' λιπαρόζωνος and Pindar's λιπαροπλόκαμος and λιπαράμπυξ.[57] In these examples, the quality of shininess
applies to the head of the compound: the girdle, the diadem, or the lock of
hair, and the brilliance is a marker of divine status, that of the daughters
of the Asopus river in Bacchylides or of Mnemosyne and Delos in Pindar.
In Licymnius' address, however, the material meaning of the adjective (unc-
tuous, liquid) is reactivated and qualifies the radiance of Health's eyes, and
of the eyes of whomever she grants her favor to, as Aristotle attests in
Physiognomy 808a – a passage where compounds abound. In the same
way, the second compound, πραΰγελως, a Licymnian coinage, can be compared to Pindar's πραΰμητιν ("of gentle mind," Pind. *Ol.* 6.42) and Erinna's
πραΰλόγος ("of gentle speech," *SH* 401.46): again, the adjective emphasizes
a physical, sensual quality (the gentle tone of the laugh) rather than a status
and applies proleptically to the recipient of health.

This example shows the poetic work accomplished by epithets (and compounds) in Licymnius' fragment: while contributing to the invocation and
characterization of deities as in any traditional hymn or prayer, the dithyrambist adds layers of significance by playing on the traditional epithets of a

---

[56] In Pindar, of Marathon (*Ol.* 13.110), Thebes (*Pyth.* 2.3), and Athens (*Nem.* 4.18, *Isthm.* 2.20,
fr. 76.1 SM).

[57] Λιπαρόζωνος: Bacchyl. 9.49–50; λιπαροπλόκαμος: Pind. fr. 33c.1 SM, also in Hom. *Il.* 19.126;
λιπαράμπυξ: Pind. *Nem.* 7.15, also parodied in Ar. *Ach.* 671, as an epithet of fish sauce.
Reminiscent of λιπαροκρήδεμνος, "with bright headband," Hom. *Il.* 18.382, *Hymn. Hom.
Cer.* 459.

non-traditional divinity and by blurring the boundaries between, on the one hand, physical qualities that describe her in anthropomorphic terms and, on the other, features that describe her in technical and quasi-scientific terms in her epiphany. A slightly different use of epithets is found in Philoxenus' *Deipnon* (*PMG* 836).[58] Fragment b is structured around a list of dishes:

> πάρφερον ἐν κανέοις
>   μάζας χιονόχροας ἄλλοι·
> <τοῖς> δ᾽ ἐπὶ πρῶτα παρῆλθ᾽
>   οὐ κάκκαβος, ὦ φιλότας,
>   ἀλλ᾽ †ἀλλοπλατεῖς† τὸ μέγιστον
> †πάντ᾽ ἔπαθεν λιπαροντες
>   εγχελεα τινες ἄριστον
> γόγγροι τοιωνητεμων†
>   πλῆρες θεοτερπές· ἐπ᾽ αὐτῷ
> δ᾽ ἄλλο παρῆλθε τόσον,
>   βατὶς δ᾽ ἐνέην ἰσόκυκλος·
> μικρὰ δὲ κακκάβι᾽ ἧς
>   ἔχοντα τὸ μὲν γαλεοῦ
>   τι, ναρκίον ἄλλο < . . . >
> < . . . > παρῆς ἕτερον
>   πίων ἀπὸ τευθιάδων
>   καὶ σηπιοπουλυποδείων
> < . . . > ἁπαλοπλοκάμων.
>
> Philoxenus, *PMG* 836 fr. b, 6–13

Others brought <u>snow-skinned</u> barley cakes in baskets: after these then first came not a cooking pot, my dear, but [corrupt] the biggest †everything he experienced, <u>shining</u> eels and congers, as lunch, cutting in some way†, full and capable of delighting the gods. After this then came another, just as big, which contained a perfectly round skate; and there were small pots, one with a piece of dogfish, another with a ray . . . Another was there, rich, made of squid and cuttlefish-octopus . . . <u>with their soft locks.</u>

As opposed to the lists of comedy, where the mere accumulation, juxtaposition, and random order of the items in the list create a comic effect, the list Philoxenus offers makes each new dish the object of careful attention. It starts with the baskets of bread, qualified by an adjective that almost personifies them (μάζας χιονόχροας, "snow-skinned barley cakes," 6). This descriptive adjective combines both the visual (the white of the snow) and the tactile (the surface of the skin or that of the snow), allowing the poet

---

[58] On Philoxenus' *Dinner Party*, see Chapter 3, pp. 115–18 and further Chapter 6, pp. 245–64.

to mix the different senses and thus create a sort of synaesthetic poetics: what describes the color of the bread (white) also describes its skin-like texture (soft under a thin crust). The same technique is used to describe the cuttlefish-octopus "with their soft locks" (σηπιοπουλυποδείων < . . . > ἁπαλοπλοκάμων, 12–13): what describes the visual aspect of the "chameleon of the sea" (the arms, seen as soft locks of hair, with many-colored reflection) also describes its texture (ἁπαλός).[59]

With all these adjectives, Philoxenus asks the audience for a response that is different from that expected from, for example, the use of Homeric adjectives. The picture created with their use is more layered, as their meaning shifts: the ἁπαλός quality of the "locks" of the cuttlefish-octopus (13), for example, recalls the ἁπαλός quality of the boy (παιδίσκος) who brings the dishes earlier in the passage (2). But the picture created with the adjective ἁπαλοπλόκαμος requires a medial term that connects the reality described (the soft arms of the mollusc) and the adjective used to describe it. The term is an elaboration on the traditional adjectives εὐπλόκαμος ("of the lovely tresses") or καλλιπλόκαμος ("with beautiful tresses") found in epic and lyric poetry, and adds a tactile detail to the metaphor while conjuring up the image of the female characters described by these adjectives.[60] Just like the participle †λιπαροντες† ("gleaming"?, 8) that describes the eels, the adjectives that Philoxenus applies to food usually qualify people, and in particular women, and the poetic memory associated with the word enriches the image: χιονόχροας mixes for the audience reminiscences of the Homeric formulae τέρενα χρόα or χρόα λειριόεντα, both used of a female or soft warrior and suggesting the whiteness of youth.[61] This use of adjectives chosen not only for what they describe but also for the literary memory they trigger would make Philoxenus an Alexandrian *avant la lettre*: the pleasure at hearing the lines thus comes as much from the recognition, or the distant evocation, of a certain idiom working as a poetic model as from the final image suggested. In Philoxenus' list, there is a constant oscillation between familiar-sounding terms and periphrases that create a form of "titillation de l'énigme," without being frustratingly obscure.[62] These learned games and the verbal inventiveness create a new type of connection between things, language, and audience, and between everyday and poetic language. More than the stylistic features themselves, it is the way the

---

[59] Contrast the plainer πολύπου πολυπλόκου ("many-locked octopus," Thgn. 215 W²).

[60] For example, Hom. *Il.* 18.407, *Od.* 12.449; Pind. *Ol.* 3.1, fr. 33c1 SM; Archil. fr. 8.1 W².

[61] See, for example, for τέρενα χρόα ("soft skin"): Hom. *Il.* 4.237, 13.553, 14.406; Hes. *Theog.* 5, *Op.* 552; χρόα λειριόεντα ("lily-like skin"), Hom. *Il.* 13.839.

[62] For the suggestive expression, Guilleux 2009: 225.

traditional markers of elevated diction work together that is striking: periphrasis, compounds, epithets, and neologisms can create ambiguity in interpretation, or rather defamiliarize everyday things, and are best understood as concentrating poetic features that can be observed in earlier poetry while also responding to sophistic experiments with language and relying on the pleasure created by the engagement of all the senses, and the mind, in the process of interpretation. As I will discuss further in the next chapter, these features are specific to the style and aesthetics of the New Music rather than to the genre of the dithyramb.

Heightened and elevated style

The stylistic features described above can be observed in a short passage from Timotheus' *Cyclops*:[63]

> ἔγχευε δ' ἐν μὲν δέπας κίσσινον μελαίνας
> σταγόνος ἀμβρότας ἀφρῷ βρυάζον,
> εἴκοσιν δὲ μέτρ' ἐνέχευ', ἀνέμισγε
> δ' αἷμα Βακχίου νεορρύτοισιν
> δακρύοισι Νυμφᾶν.   5
>
> Timoth. *PMG* 780

He [Maron? Polyphemus? Odysseus?] <u>poured into it one ivy-wood cup</u> brimming with the foam of the <u>black</u> ambrosian drops, and <u>then he poured in twenty measures</u>, and mixed the blood of Bacchus with the newly poured tears of the nymphs.

The description combines descriptive terms (the ivy-wood cup) with metaphorical language (blood of Bacchus). It suggests many layers of experience, not only sensual but also intertextual, as the passage relies heavily on the diction of *Odyssey* 9, where it draws from two distinct passages in particular,

> τὸν δ' ὅτε πίνοιεν μελιηδέα οἶνον ἐρυθρόν,
> <u>ἓν δέπας ἐμπλήσας ὕδατος ἀνὰ εἴκοσι μέτρα</u>
> <u>χεῦ'</u>, ὀδμὴ δ' ἡδεῖα ἀπὸ κρητῆρος ὀδώδει,
> θεσπεσίη...
>
> Hom. *Od.* 9.208–11

---

[63] The passage is probably paraphrased in Antiphanes, fr. 55 KA. On Timotheus' *Cyclops*, Hordern 2002: 106–16, 2004.

> And whenever they [Maron and his wife] drank the honey-sweet red wine, <u>he would fill one cup and pour on top twenty measures of water</u>, and a sweet smell would come from the crater, divine . . .

and

> καὶ τότ' ἐγὼ Κύκλωπα προσηύδων ἄγχι παραστάς,
> <u>κισσύβιον</u> μετὰ χερσὶν ἔχων <u>μέλανος</u> οἴνοιο . . .
>
> Hom. Od. 9.346–7

> and then, I stood in front of the Cyclops and said to him, as I held in my hands the <u>ivy-cup</u> of <u>dark</u> wine . . .

Timotheus' description heightens the sensual elements of the Homeric passage by condensing many more nuances, adding color (black), texture (froth), and movement (drips and trickles) to the Homeric scene. Perhaps more important even is that the passage collapses two distinct moments of the *Odyssey*: the description of Maron mixing the splendid wine in the crater for his wife in a very secret ceremony (only he, his wife, and a faithful servant know about the special wine), and the description of Odysseus giving the rustic ivy-wood cup to Polyphemus in the reverse guest-friendship scene of Book 9. The subject of the verb is unspecified and, in the absence of context, it is unclear whether Timotheus describes Maron, the Cyclops, or Odysseus as mixing the liquids. If the subject is Polyphemus, Timotheus is offering a picture of the Cyclops close to that of the aesthete of Euripides' satyr-drama: the elaborate language would be evoking the savage's delight at such an unusual sight. But if the subject is Maron, the description of Odysseus' host using the Cyclopic cup has chilling connotations: the cup full of wine is described with words (μέλας and σταγών) commonly used to describe blood, and announces the periphrasis "blood of Bacchus" for wine. This final periphrasis itself condenses the poetic texture by recalling the Dionysiac element of the first two lines, the ivy-cup and the image of it teeming with wine (βρυάζον). The images imbue the text with more narrative allusions: the blood of Dionysus prefigures the blood of the wounded Cyclops, and the fresh-flowing tears of the nymphs, the giant's own tears.[64] There is a horrifying discrepancy between the elaborate images and the narrative situation, as if in Timotheus' highly packed diction, the drama of the blinding of the Cyclops was already actualized in the language describing Maron's wine. Read the other way around, the description of Odysseus, or

---

[64] The image of mixing Bacchus and the nymphs (for wine and water) also appears in Euenus, fr. 2.3 W²: <u>Βάκχος</u> χαίρει κιρνάμενος δὲ τρισὶν <u>Νύμφαισι</u> τέταρτος ("Bacchus rejoices when making a fourth with three <u>nymphs</u>").

the Cyclops, mixing liquids referred to as male (Bacchus) and female (the nymphs) would activate some of the very intimate elements of the scene of private wine consumption by Maron and his wife. Part of this blurring of images and the vertiginous effect of the passage's diction come from the very nature of the reality described: if there is one substance, and one god, which makes one see double and allows one to mix images to create a new kind of reality, it is Dionysus and his beverage. Here the distance, and the blurring, created by the language and the mix of images – a distance originally associated with the inherent doubleness and alienation of the Dionysiac – only contribute to the effect of the description. The heightening of the language could not be clearer: the lines are bursting with intertextual echoes, and the learned transformation of the Odyssean episode provides a diction that is both familiar and dazzling because of its concentration of details. This assessment is far from accusations of vacuity or meaninglessness: close examination of the *lexis* and images of the fragment reveals not emptiness but an elaborate and *poikilos* style that reconfigures elements of Homeric diction to create an aesthetic experience based on the tension between known and new elements of diction.

Timotheus' *langue mandarine* and *langage singulier*

One could object that all the readings suggested in the previous pages try to fit a case-by-case explanation to isolated fragments, or even expressions, and force an aesthetic strategy onto independent passages. In this section, rather than isolating images or metaphors, I would like to examine how all these features function as a system in Timotheus' text of the *Persians*. I propose to start again with an examination of compounds, in order to see how this linguistic feature, which cannot be isolated from metaphors, periphrases, metonyms, sound patterns, etc., allows us access to Timotheus' *langage singulier*. This language, I argue, is characterized by its elasticity, and by its ability to concentrate or extend poetic expressions, mostly Homeric, in ways that engage senses, intellect, and memory of the poetic past in a new manner, in order to defamiliarize the relationship between language and things and to heighten the overall aesthetic experience.

From formula to compound

Timothean compounds used to describe the sea are a particularly striking example of the creative interaction of linguistic tradition and innovation. The sea is qualified by many different formulae in Homer, perhaps as a reflection of its ever-changing nature:[65] formulae describe its appearance, especially its color ("wine-dark" in ἐπὶ οἴνοπα πόντον, "violet" in ἰοειδέα πόντον, "dark" in ἐπ' ἠεροειδέα πόντον, "grey" in ἁλὸς πολιοῖο), its surface ("billowy" in ἐπὶ πόντον κυμαίνοντα, "stormy" in πολυκλύστῳ ἐνὶ πόντῳ), or its content ("teeming with fish" in πόντον ἐπ' ἰχθυόεντα) and its expanse ("limitless sea" in ἐπ' ἀπείρονα πόντον, "vast sea" in εὐρέα πόντον), as well as what it evokes: a "moist road" (ὑγρὰ κέλευθα) or an unfertile expanse (in the formulae ἐπ' ἀτρύγετον πόντον and ἁλὸς ἀτρυγέτοιο). In the *Persians*, many descriptions of the sea are constituted by an accumulation of, and elaborate variations on, Homeric compounds and formulae, as illustrated in the description of the sea with which this chapter opened. There, the description reconfigures a set of Homeric phrases and images. The first striking image, that of the reddening of the furrows of the emerald-haired sea (σμαραγδοχαίτας δὲ πόντος ἄλοκα . . . ἐφοινίσσετο, *PMG* 791.31–3), combines two Homeric ideas:[66] first, the qualification of a marine divinity by the color or aspect of his or her hair (as is the case, for example, for Poseidon, called κυανοχαίτης, "dark-haired," or for Thetis, qualified by καλλιπλόκαμος or εὔκομος, "of the lovely locks" or "with beautiful hair");[67] and second, the metaphor of the sea as a piece of land along which one can dig a furrow.[68] This last image, condensed in the accusative of respect ἄλοκα, functions as a variation on and inversion of the formula ἐπ' ἀτρύγετον πόντον,[69] and the σμαραγδοχαίτας qualifying the sea evokes not so much a color as a mineral quality, again reminiscent of the infertility of the Homeric ἀτρύγετον. These elaborate reworkings of Homeric expressions are all the easier because the syntax is very simple: there are very few subordinate clauses and the independent clauses are linked with a very narrow range of particles. Because the grammar develops linearly (with no complex clauses embedded), most of the focus can be on the development of nouns and adjectives and the images they create.[70]

---

[65] On poetic treatments of the sea, see the classic study of Lesky 1947, especially pp. 149–214. On epithets for the sea, Gray 1947, especially pp. 109–11; Dee 2002. On three-word expressions for the sea, Bers 1974: 12–14, and 34, on enallages for the sea and bodies of water.

[66] On the reddening of the sea at Salamis, see also Hdt. 8.77.1 αἵματι δ' Ἄρης πόντος φοινίξει ("and Ares will redden the sea with blood").

[67] Hom. *Il.* 13.563, 14.390, 15.174, 15.201, 20.144, 20.224, *Od.* 3.6, 9.528, 9.536; Pind. fr. 52f SM; Bacchyl. 5.33, 9.53, 11.83.

[68] The image appears in Hom. *Od.* 3.174–5 and 13.88. Also in *PMG* 939.16–17 ἄλοκα Νηρείας πλακὸς | τέμνοντες ("cutting a furrow in Nereus' plain") and Ar. *Av.* 1400, in the parody of Cinesias: αὔλακα τέμνων ("cutting a furrow [in the sky]").

[69] Hom. *Il.* 1.312, *Od.* 3.71, 4.842, 9.252, 15.474.

[70] The most often used particles are δέ, ἀλλά, γάρ, καί, τε δέ, and μέν. There are very few or no instances of δή, ἄρα, ἀτάρ, τοι, ἤτοι, γε (see Hordern 2002: 53–5 for parallels with the other neo-dithyrambists).

In the next two lines (ἐπ' ἰχθυοστεφέσι μαρμαροπτύχοις κόλποισιν Ἀμφιτρίτας, "upon the fish-wreathed bosom of Amphitrite with its marmoreal folds," 37–8), a different kind of expression personifies the sea, but compounds function in a similar way, as developments of Homeric formulae. As Hordern notes, Amphitrite (if the supplement is correct) is not an unknown metonymy for the sea. Although not used in the *Iliad*, the noun appears four times in the *Odyssey*, always in descriptions of a rough sea.[71] This turbulence associated with Amphitrite is concentrated here in the description of the shining folds of her bosom (μαρμαροπτύχοις κόλποισιν). The image of the sea's bosom is itself Homeric,[72] as is the marmoreal gleaming of the waves,[73] and the compound "fish-wreathed" (ἰχθυοστέφεσι) develops the formula πόντον ἰχθυόεντα, used in both the *Iliad* and the *Odyssey*, to complete the personification.[74] The inversion of the elements, the shining white (usually of the top of the wave) qualifying the folds of the sea, and the fish (usually at the bottom) qualifying its top, contributes to a description of not only the roughness of the water but also the topsy-turviness of the whole situation. Are we again to see a (pre-Hellenistic) sophisticated scholarly game, one in which in this case the poet concentrates in the same passage two expressions referring to the sea used only once in Homer? This interpretation is very tempting indeed, especially since a process that glosses rare Homeric words and collapses them into a compound also occurs, as I have argued above, in two passages of Telestes. Competition in Homeric rewriting would thus be an additional element in the agonistic relationship between composers of different song types who performed in the same musical contexts.

At the same time, as we have seen in the case of Philoxenus, compounds are one of the main elements of a synaesthetic poetics, and contribute to creating a complex, because many-layered, picture and a rich description that combines elements of color, contrast, movement, and sometimes sound.[75] They help generate a thicker poetic texture, for, by using the same elements in different combinations, they allow the creation of long sequences of interconnected images. Thus, the purple of the blood of the dying Persians contrasts with the darkness of the sea and the whiteness of its waves, while the emerald color and mineral-like quality of the sea (σμαραγδοχαίτας πόντος, 31) are echoed by two other compounds that repeat the same phonic

---

[71] Hom. *Od.* 3.91, 5.122, 12.60, 12.97.

[72] Hom. *Il.* 18.140 θαλάσσης εὐρέα κόλπον ("the large bosom of the sea"), and closer to our passage: *Od.* 5.52–3 ὅς τε κατὰ δεινοὺς κόλπους ἁλὸς ἀτρυγέτοιο | ἰχθῦς ἀγρώσσων πυκινὰ πτερὰ δεύεται ἅλμη ("like a seagull who searches for fish in the frightening gulfs of the infertile sea and drenches its wings in the briny sea").

[73] Hom. *Il.* 14.273 (ἅλα μαρμαρέην, "the shining sea").   [74] Hom. *Il.* 9.4, *Od.* 3.177.

[75] Csapo 2004: 226–7.

pattern (α-α-ο sequence in five-syllable compounds: μαρμαροπτύχοις, 38, and later <u>μαρμαρο</u>φεγγεῖς, 92).

Grammar of metaphors: personification and synecdoche

While compounds are an important locus in Timotheus' poetry for the concentration and development of Homeric expressions (both formulae and hapax), they can barely be isolated from other stylistic features. Another process that creates the elasticity I have identified in Timotheus' language is the sustained use of personification and synecdoche throughout the song: all through the poem the boats are personified, and parts of the boats are synecdoches of the body. The oars are the "hands of fir" (χεῖρας ἐλατίνας, *PMG* 791.5–6) or the "mountain feet of the boat" (ὀρείους πόδας ναός, 90–1), and the puzzling "gleaming children of the mouth" (στόματος δ᾽ ἐξήλλοντο μαρμαροφεγγεῖς παῖδες, 92–3) have been interpreted as the rams at the prow (the "mouth") of the ships;[76] boats have limbs (γυῖα, 14), sides (πλευράς, 15), and an (iron) head (cf. σιδαρῷ κράνει, 20). This way of condensing meaning into expressions is illustrated by the "naval drops" (ναΐοις σταλάγμασιν, 33). Hordern (2002 ad loc.) comments: "the adjective is infelicitous, since the blood should strictly belong to the sailors." The point is precisely that a listener takes the shortcut and makes the connection, for there is a simple but powerful logic to the accumulation of periphrases and a grammar of images with which an audience needs to become familiar: the sea is a body that the barbarians fight against.[77] This is more than a clever game of riddling: this fractured view of the battle scene corresponds to the breakdown of the fighting order and the overall confusion, and the accumulation of words for limbs and parts reproduces the accumulation of live and dead bodies in the narrow straits of Salamis. These metonymies, synecdoches, and personifications further narrow down the narrative perspective to human dimensions, in close-ups that have dramatic effects.

    Moreover, these sustained networks of association work together and build off each other. The boundaries between maritime and land elements are blurred: again, the sea is a field where a furrow is traced (ἄλοκα, 32), a navigable plain (πέδιος, 40; πεδία πλόϊμα, 78),[78] but the first time dry land is described, it is still very much a maritime landscape (ἀκταῖς ἐνάλοις,

---

[76] Janssen 1984: 74. Contra: Reinach 1903: 71, Edmonds 1922–7: III 317 n. 3, Campbell 1993: 101 n. 14, and Hordern 2002: 178.

[77] For example, πλαγὰ ῥηξίκωπος ("oar-blasting blow," 8–9); νῦν δέ σ᾽ ἀναταράξει ἐμὸς ἄναξ ἐμὸς πεύκαισιν ὀριγόνοισιν ("my lord, yes my lord, is about to stir you up with his mountain-born pines," 75–7).

[78] Compare Aesch. *TGrF* III fr. 150 δελφινοφόρον <u>πόντου πεδίον</u> ("the dolphin-bearing <u>plain of the sea</u>").

"with marine promontories," 98). The analogy continues when the land is described with one of the terms that depicted the sea earlier: while the sea was ἰχθυοστεφέσι μαρμαροπτύχοις ("fish-wreathed, with marmoreal <u>folds</u>," 38), Mysia is described as having δενδροέθειραι πτυχαί ("tree-crowned <u>folds</u>," 105). Compounds that rely on recurring elements and create some sort of repetition and pattern in an otherwise disorienting text facilitate this process: the ships, for example, are first "sea-going loud-ringing pines" (πολυκρότους <u>πλωσίμους</u> πεύκας, 12), then the continuity between land and sea is underlined by the metaphors of the "mountain-born pines" stirring up the navigable plain of the sea (πεύκαισιν ὀριγόνοισιν . . . πεδία πλόϊμα, 78), with ὀριγόνοισι replacing πλωσίμους, an echo of which is still heard in πλόϊμα. There is a poetic logic to the new images created by Timotheus: both the compounds and the many adjectives underline the connection between terrestrial and maritime elements, and the violent confrontation between boats, sailors, and water. What might seem at first glance a gratuitous propensity for indirect language is actually a way to condense at the linguistic level the very nature of the battle of Salamis, a sea battle fought in a small space. This indirect way of speaking, as we have seen in the case of the sophists, enables defamiliarization through language, allowing an audience to feel, in an eerily physical way, the unsettling character of the battle of Salamis, even several generations after its being fought.

Intertexts, logic of language, and langage singulier

In Timotheus' descriptions of the sea we also encounter another aspect of this deployment of compounds: the intertextual use of some passages, in which "old" words are given renewed life in a changed context (an aspect of which I have described in Chapter 2 and to which I will return in the next chapter). In a further passage of the *Persians* narrative, a Persian "man from the plain" is drowning. Beating the sea with fists and feet, gnashing his teeth, he curses her:[79]

> ἤδη θρασεῖα καὶ πάρος
> λάβρον <u>αὐχέν'</u> ἔσχες ἐν
>   πέδᾳ <u>καταζευχθεῖσα</u> λινοδέτῳ τεόν.
>   Timoth. *PMG* 791.72–4

Already before, for all your arrogance, you had your turbulent <u>neck yoked</u> in <u>flax-bound</u> shackles . . .

---

[79] On swimming, drowning, and Greek identity, Hall 1994.

Both the image of the neck of the sea (later recalled in "sailing of the long neck of the sea," μακραυχενόπλους, 89–90) and its yoking in flax-bound shackles appear in the parodos of Aeschylus' *Persians*:[80]

> λινοδέσμῳ σχεδίᾳ πορθμὸν ἀμείψας
> Ἀθαμαντίδος Ἕλλας,   70
> πολύγομφον ὄδισμα
> ζυγὸν ἀμφιβαλὼν <u>αὐχένι πόντου</u>.
> > Aesch. *Persians* 69–72

> crossing on a <u>flax-bound</u> raft the strait of Helle, Athamas' daughter, throwing around <u>the neck of the sea a yoke</u>, a <u>many-bolted</u> road.

These lines, spoken by a Persian, perhaps make clearer than any other passage how poetic language always recreates itself while relying on its previous uses as poets emulate their predecessors or engage with the tradition in suggestive new patterns. It is the adjectives that interest me in particular. While the Homeric raft (σχεδίη) Odysseus used for his eventful *nostos* was "bound with many ropes" (πολύδεσμος, Hom. *Od.* 5.33), the ships Hesiod describes in the account of his short and unheroic poetic crossing to Euboea were "bolted with many nails" (πολύγομφοι, Hes. *Op.* 660). This πολύγομφος is, in turn, the very compound Aeschylus uses to describe the bridge of ships made by Xerxes to cross the Hellespont, a "road bolted with many nails" (πολύγομφον ὄδισμα, Aesch. *Pers.* 71), which is also described metaphorically as a "flax-bound raft" (λινοδέσμῳ σχεδίᾳ). The three texts play with the same set of words arranged in different collocations to describe sea voyages whose significance resides partly in their relationship with mythical (epic, heroic, or didactic) predecessors. It is thus no surprise that in his *Persians*, Timotheus uses the Aeschylean compound λινόδεσμος "flax-bound," to describe the shackles put on the neck of the sea, while the helplessness of the drowning Persian gnashing his teeth (γόμφοισι ἐμπρίων, *PMG* 791.69) is described with an adjective reminiscent of one used by Aeschylus (πολύγομφον, *Pers.* 71). In this last expression, Timotheus plays with the homonymy between γόμφοι ("bolts") and γομφίοι ("molars")[81] to echo even more of the Aeschylean text, appropriating the language used of Xerxes' historical conquest for the description of a single drowning Persian.

This kind of intertextual reading inevitably brings up questions about audience response. What type of audience would have recognized the

---

[80] Analysed by Croiset (1903: 330–5), who gives parallels with Eur. *Or.* and suggests some more intertexts with Choerilus' *Persika*.

[81] Γομφίοι = γόμφοι, cf. LSJ s.v. 1.3, quoting Hesychius.

Aeschylean echo of the *Persians* over the sound of music and the excitement of the narrative? How could the precise words of Aeschylus' *Persians*, performed about sixty or seventy years earlier than Timotheus' song, be known to the generation of Athenians listening to the late fifth-century nome? How does this elaborate literary critical analysis relate to the material approach to the poetics of the New Music? And what is lost when these erudite games of interaction with poetic predecessors never reach the consciousness of an audience? One goal of such a reading is to bring to the consciousness of modern readers the fact that texts of the New Music have never received the same type of detailed analysis as any other lyric text susceptible to raising the same type of methodological objection. Moreover, as I have briefly suggested earlier in this chapter and elsewhere, a literary critical reading of this sort is not incompatible with attention to performance setting and to the dynamics of performance itself:[82] the vocabulary of Homeric epics, in particular, would have been heard in the very same musical context as dithyrambs and nomes, and, on the cognitive level, the simplicity of the syntax of the New Music texts allows an audience to concentrate on its images much better than on an ode of Pindar, for example, where the structure, syntax, and images challenge the listener on several fronts at the same time. Perhaps what is of greatest importance in this analysis is that it encourages us to take stock of the self-consciousness of the New Music texts. The self-referential tags that I have analyzed in Chapter 2 have received such attention but, by contrast, these subtle, learned, sometimes subversive games played with poetic predecessors need to be highlighted, enabling the rehabilitation of the New Music poets within the tradition.[83]

But some of the most compelling images in the *Persians* rely on a different process of combination of "traditional" and "innovative" language. The force of these passages comes from extending the logic of everyday language or reactivating the latent potential of words, rather than from the new use of a rare form or the creation of a sustained network of metaphorical associations. A few kennings show how Timotheus develops images from everyday language itself and follows the logic of that language. One example can be drawn from the description of the drowning man of the plain, which comes before the curse quoted above:

> ὅ]τε δὲ τᾷ λείποιεν αὖραι,
> τᾷ δ' ἐπεισέπιπτον, ἄφ-

---

[82] LeVen 2012 and n. 51 in this chapter.
[83] On the New Musicians as pre-Hellenistic poets, Acosta-Hughes 2010b.

ρει δ' ἀβακχίωτος ὄμβρος,
εἰς δὲ τρόφιμον ἄγγος
ἐχεῖτ'.   65

      Timoth. *PMG* 791.60–4

and whenever the winds were letting off on one side, they would attack
on another, and unbacchic rain would foam and pour into his alimentary
vessel.

The image of "unbacchic rain" that foams (ἄφρει, 61–2) as a description
of seawater and the use of the "alimentary vessel" (τρόφιμον ἄγγος, 63)
for the stomach have seemed preposterous to many. But the first phrase,
ἀβακχίωτος ὄμβρος, plays on two expressions: the Homeric οἴνοπα πόντον
("dark-wine sea") and the phrase οἶνος ἄκρητος ("unmixed wine"). The
Timothean kenning activates the Homeric image contained in an unexpressed formula: the sea *is* associated with wine, although in a negative
form, ἀβακχίωτος. But it is also an "ironic inversion" of οἶνος ἄκρητος:
in the text, it is the water, not the wine, that is unmixed.[84] Timotheus is
playing with the phraseology and ideology of the symposium and on the
frequent parallels between symposium and sailing, wine and sea.[85] With
the periphrasis, "we would have a unique and rare reversal of sympotic
discourse."[86] There is no sustained network of reference; the expression is
a spin-off and mix of different kinds of language that play on the liquid
associations of seawater, water, and wine.

    The second kenning, τρόφιμον ἄγγος ("alimentary vessel," 63), continues
the metaphor of unbacchic water: LSJ glosses ἄγγος (vessel) as part of the
body, but it is primarily used of containers, for wine, water, or milk,[87] and
thus complements the metaphor of liquid. The unsettling effect comes from
the juxtaposition of the rain with the domestic vessel, but it is the adjective
ἀβακχίωτος that might, again, motivate and justify the choice of ἄγγος, for
the metaphorical recipient of "unbacchic water" might be qualified with
the same word as the recipient of wine or water. Despite the oddness of the

---

[84] Janssen 1984: 52.   [85] Slater 1976.

[86] Gargiulo 1996: 78. Gargiulo does not cite parallels for the image, but there are similarities with
Dionysius Chalcus, who consistently uses maritime images for sympotic activities: εἰρεσίη
γλώσσης ("oarage of the tongue" = poetry); Μουσῶν ἐρέται ("oarsmen of the Muses" =
poets); εἰρεσία Διονύσου ("oarage of Dionysus" = banquet); συμποσίου ναῦται ("mariners of
the carouse" = symposiasts); κυλίκων ἐρέται ("oarsmen of the cups" = poets). Also Telestes,
PMG 811, who calls a goblet (φιάλη) a boat (ἄκατος). There is a further connection between
the foam of the sea (Hom. *Il.* 18.403, for example) and that of the wine (Timoth. *PMG* 780.2,
Antiphanes, fr. 55 KA).

[87] Of wine: Hom. *Od.* 2.289, 16.13–14, Hes. *Op.* 613 (in reference to a vat); of milk: Hom.
Il. 2.471, 16.643, *Od.* 9.222, 9.248.

expressions, it is not unlikely that an audience member would also think of the Homeric οἴνοπα πόντον when hearing ἀβάκχιωτος ὄμβρος: even if hard to pin down, there is something familiar in the image, but in contrast to the understanding of periphrases in Hellenistic poets, no high level of poetic competence is necessary. The images proceed by simply elaborating or reversing the logic of everyday language and by using the polysemy of words and their figurative potential.

In the same way, in the Celaenaean's prayer in broken Greek, there are, in quick succession, two highly evocative expressions that both derive from the idea that speech is something physical. That idea is activated in the Homeric formulaic question "What has escaped the barrier of your teeth (ἕρκος ὀδόντων)?," but also in lyric metaphors where words, sung or spoken, can be woven, stitched, or plaited together. The same idea lurks in Timotheus' passage:

> ὁ δ' ἀμφὶ γόνασι περιπλεκείς   145
> ἐλίσσετ', Ἑλλάδ' ἐμπλέκων
> Ἀσιάδι φωνᾷ διάτορον
> σφραγῖδα θραύων στόματος,
> Ἰάονα γλῶσσαν ἐξιχνεύων·
> "ἐγώ μοί σοι κῶς καὶ τί πρᾶγμα;"   150
>   Timoth. *PMG* 791.145–50

> He, embracing his knees, was supplicating [the Greek], and weaving Greek with Asian language, piercing and shattering the seal of his mouth to track the Ionian tongue: "I for me with you how and what thing?"

Preverbs (ἐξ, ἐν, περί) play an important role in the passage. The panicked words coming out of the shattered seal of the Persian's mouth are first represented as an animal that has broken the gate of its cage and needs to be chased (ἐξιχνεύων, 149). The metaphor is particularly appropriate as an illumination of the difficulty of tracking words in a foreign language and works as the reverse of the traditional poetic weaving of words (ἐμπλέκων, 146). The participle is used here as a visual echo of what the Caeleanian does (embrace the knees of the Greek, περιπλεκείς, 145). Moreover, the image of the shattered seal (σφραγῖδα) expands on the unexpressed Homeric formula that gives the lips as a liminal space and speech as something physical. The seal image emphasizes the notion of authenticity: the mouth is really the physical marker that, once crossed, reveals the foreignness of the Phrygian. The shattered seal of the mouth thus works as a sign of values and perception: Greek sounds piercing (διάτορον) to a Phrygian, just as Phrygian sounds muddled, "barbarian," to a Greek. This is another instance in which a more general thematic concern of the song, in this case the cultural encounter between Persians and Greeks in battle, is reflected and developed in a tiny detail that is given human proportions and contains an elaborate miniature of the whole narrative.

Conclusion: heightening and truth of language in New Music

Our appreciation of the language of New Music is most often influenced by the comic poets' and ancient literary critics' remarks on the style of the dithyramb. "Dithyrambic" has become a label for obscure, ornate, labored, bombastic, or vacuous language, features that are all slightly different from each other but that all correspond to elevated diction with no heightening. Such judgment obscures an important fact about the way the language of New Music operates: lexical, rhetorical, and stylistic features work together to create a charged and unsettling language, close in many respects to the experiments of the sophists. While some critics have emphasized the connection between this type of language and the cultic (Dionysiac) roots of the dithyramb, another path provides us with a different vantage point. The novelty of the language of the New Musicians resides less in some linguistic tools characteristic of elevated diction (compounds, strings of adjectives, etc.) than in the way these features are used to explore the relationship between language and things. Several examples have shown how sound games, which are often interpreted as a quest for mimetic effects that attests to the emptiness of a "decorative" language that focuses more on sound than on sense, can be seen as strategies for exploring the expressive truth of language itself. As readings of the text of Timotheus have shown, the poet often develops the logic of language and leaves the audience's imagination and ear for language to perform the work that sense alone will not perform, especially in the play with homonyms. But at the same time, and this is the aspect that perhaps deserves the greatest emphasis, all the New Music passages I have discussed display a very high level of self-consciousness and awareness of the poetic tradition (including of both Homeric and tragic diction). One should keep in mind, in this regard, the competitive nature of the language games played by the poets, and their agonistic relationship: as we have seen in the case of Licymnius and Melanippides, there was competition in creating etymologies and establishing as evocative as possible a relationship between sound and sense. Another form of competition is found in the exploration of Homeric *hapax legomena* and their redevelopment in a new narrative context (as we have seen in several cases in both Telestes and Timotheus) as a form of early scholarship. But no matter how Hellenistic this process seems to be, the interpretive context of the language of New Music is different from that of Alexandrian times: New Music is a type of poetry (as Timotheus claims in the *sphragis* of the *Persians*) that excludes nobody. There is neither a recondite image whose interpretation depends on knowledge of an obscure reference, nor any convoluted formulation whose pay-off relies on the recognition of a source passage. When we focus in particular on the breathtaking language of Timotheus' *Persians*, what is most striking is the feeling of elasticity in a text that constantly reconfigures Homeric formulaic language: formulae are either compacted in new compounds, extended in periphrasis, or combined in a form of synaesthetic poetics that highlights more sensual nuances than any single Homeric adjective. The play on the logic of language and the reuse of familiar Homeric expressions creates a sense of familiarity, but because the processes change all the time, they are also essentially unsettling. Most important in the *Persians* is that the poetic tropes (metaphors, synecdoches, metonymies, personifications) that contribute to the richness, and unsettlingness, of the language reflect the narrative perspective: close-ups on individual details, for example, or attention to pathetic events. In this regard, a comment of Philodemus neatly encapsulates the relationship between diction and narrative work. Commenting on the relationship between the language of Pindar and that of Philoxenus, Philodemus notes:

If one should compare the dithyrambic styles (δειθυραμβικοὺς τρόπους) of Pindar and Philoxenus, there would be a great difference in the characters shown (ἐπιφαιν-ομένων ἠθῶν), but the style would be the same (τὸν αὐτὸν . . . τρόπον).

Philodem. *Mus.* 1.23 (ix 67 fr. 5, pp. 9–10 Kemke)

The comparison that Philodemus draws is difficult to interpret, not least because of the lack of surviving evidence. But it offers a way to think about different, yet related, areas of inquiry. Having focused on aspects of the style (τρόπον) and diction, I now turn to the "characters shown" (ἐπιφαινομένων ἠθῶν) and to the world created by the songs.

5 | Narrative and subjectivity: *mimēsis* and theater music

"A champion fish!" he cried, taking off his mask. "I was following the little ones! He swallowed one, and then I . . ." And he described the scene, stammering with emotion. It was impossible to catch a bigger, more beautiful fish; Zeffirino would have liked the signorina finally to share his contentment.

I. Calvino, *Difficult Loves*[1]

Building on the previous chapters, this chapter explores the relationship between audience, language, and narrative world in late classical compositions. Central to this discussion is the concept of *mimēsis*: New Music, ancient and modern critics tell us, was more mimetic than any other music before. But several features are often conflated under this broad claim. With its fluctuating constellation of meanings, *mimēsis* can describe a *mode* of representation, the *process* by which reality is represented, and the *status* of the world created by a work of art.[2] Most recent discussions have focused on the performance aspect of *mimēsis* and, following on from the comments of Plato, Aristotle, and other conservative critics, have examined the growing tendency of New Music artists to reproduce through their evocative physical performance some of the features described in the narrative. Aristotle, for example, complains of the excessive gyrations of contemporary tragic actors,[3] who

πολλὴν κίνησιν κινοῦνται, <u>οἷον οἱ φαῦλοι αὐληταὶ</u> κυλιόμενοι ἂν δίσκον δέῃ <u>μιμεῖσθαι</u>, καὶ ἕλκοντες τὸν κορυφαῖον ἂν Σκύλλαν αὐλῶσιν.

Arist. *Poet.* 1461b30–1

---

[1] Excerpt "Big Fish, Little Fish" from *Difficult Loves* by Italo Calvino, translated by William Weaver. Copyright 1949 by Giulio Einaudi editore, Torino. Copyright © 1958 by Giulio Einaudi editore, s.p.a. Torino, English translation copyright © 1983, 1984 by Houghton Mifflin Harcourt Publishing Company; reprinted by permission; all rights reserved. Published by Secker & Warburg; reprinted by permission of the Random House Group Limited.

[2] On *mimēsis*, fundamental are Auerbach 1953 and Halliwell 2002. For *mimēsis* as performance, Bakker 2005: 56–70. On the status of a work of art as *mimēsis*, Laird 1993: 153: "The world of a story is the *mimēsis* (or 'poetic imitation') of space, time, values, characters, events, etc. generated by the narrative of a text, and at the same time circumscribed by it."

[3] Arist. *Pol.* 8.1341b15–18.

engage in much gesticulation, <u>like inferior auletes</u> who spin round if they
have to <u>represent</u> a discus or drag the chorus leader about if they are
playing the *Scylla*.

Even some New Musicians themselves, adopting the stance of reactionary
critics, point out their contemporaries' tendency to overdo the gymnastic
aspect of theatrical performance. The aulete Dorion, for example, mocked
Timotheus' performance of the nome *Nauplius*, saying that he "had seen
a bigger tempest in a boiling pot (ἐν κακκάθᾳ ζεούσᾳ μείζονα ἑωρακέναι
χειμῶνα)," and an anecdote of Machon presents the citharode Stratonicus
as attending a performance of Timotheus' *Birth Pangs of Semele* and won-
dering "what kind of screaming she would have done if she were giving
birth to a contractor, not a god."[4] This histrionic tendency was apparently
adopted by citharodes as well as auletes, and the image of a musician "performing himself" and contorting his body to follow the narrative or the
melodic modulations plays an integral part in an elite critical discourse that
equates physical and ethical behavior or the somatic and political integrity
of the adult male citizen and sees indecorous physical abandonment by the
performer as a threat to the morals of a righteous audience.

But *mimēsis* in performance could also extend beyond the gymnastics
of representation to other aspects of the performance, including a form of
onomatopoeic *mimēsis*.[5] Plato notes, for example, that

> there is another type, the baser he is, the more he will narrate anything, and he thinks
> nothing unworthy of himself. He will endeavor to imitate (μιμεῖσθαι) everything with
> zeal especially when he has a large audience, even what we were just describing –
> thunder and the noise of wind and hail and axles and pulleys and the sounds of the
> trumpet, the *auloi* and the panpipe and all other instruments, and even the cries of
> dogs, sheep, and birds. And so all his narrative will be through imitation of voices
> and gestures (διὰ μιμήσεως φωναῖς τε καὶ σχήμασιν) and will have little narration
> (σμικρόν τι διηγήσεως).
>
> Pl. *Resp.* 397a

Here the kind of imitation that Plato finds fault with is musical, verbal,
and aural, rather than visual and dynamic.[6] As the previous chapter noted,

---

[4] Respectively *PMG* 785 (= Hegesander [*FHG* iv 416 fr. 14] *ap*. Ath. 8.338a) and *PMG* 792 (= fr.
11 Gow) *ap*. Ath. 8.352a. Also, about Pronomus' movement, Paus. 9.12.6.

[5] Pickard-Cambridge 1962: 51: "[the dithyramb was] perverted by the passion for *mimēsis* in the
sense of mere reproduction of sounds (often non-musical sounds) and other effects." See also
Zimmermann 1992: 127–8 and Csapo 2004: 212–16.

[6] On the Plato passage, Stanford 1973.

New Music composers were often presented as relying on the expressive potential of words rather than on their discursive power. An anecdote reported by Plutarch (*De audiendis poetis* 22a), for example, describes Cinesias as being outraged on hearing a line of Timotheus' *Artemis* (*PMG* 778b) composed entirely of homoioteleuta: θυιάδα φοιβάδα μαινάδα λυσσάδα (frantic, prophetic, menadic, full of panic). Cinesias may be echoing here the kind of accusations made against *his own* dithyrambic language, but be that as it may, his anger, whether true or staged, is directed at the citharode's overuse of the incantational power of the rime, seen as engaging the appetitive part of the soul of the audience rather than their intellect. This accusation is different from that which targeted the bewitching spectacle of the musician's body in performance and its effect on the senses: here, the New Musicians are indicted for using an emotive language that tends to rob *logos* of its discursive force and instead emphasizes impressions and feelings.[7]

As Plato's discussion further suggests, the New Music is also associated with yet another type of *mimēsis*. Critics have described the "dramatization" of dithyrambs and nomes. On their reading, the genre described by Plato in the *Republic* (394c) as "purely" narrative (diegetic) began to adopt more *mimēsis*, including direct speech that could be impersonated by the performers. Starting with Bacchylides, lyric narrative parts are said to have been sung and impersonated by a half-chorus, rather than being narrated by the whole chorus.[8] One pseudo-Aristotelian *Problem* (19.15 [918b]) even goes so far as to suggest that the dithyramb became monodic, and scholars have proposed that dithyrambs included musical-dramatic solos by vocal virtuosos and even instrumentalists.[9] Again such evolution can easily be explained by the ubiquitous *interpretatio Platonica* (described in Chapter 1): genres "contaminated" each other, with the established dramatic forms

---

[7] Csapo 2004, 222–5, 235, with references to Pl. *Resp.* 424e–444e, 543a–592b, *Leg.* 669a–670a, 689a–e, and *Plt.* 291a–b. Csapo 2011: 117–20 for the political risks connected with the musical reliance on the appetitive part of the soul.

[8] For example, the two half-choruses in Bacchyl. 18, on which Burnett (1985: 114–28) in a chapter tellingly entitled "The tragic Muse." The evidence for mimetic musical display in Bacchylides and the New Dithyramb is examined by Fearn (2007: 192–3), who remains overall cautious in his assumptions.

[9] Boardmann (1956) argues from the evidence of visual arts that Melanippides' *Marsyas* included a showdown between the aulete leading the dithyramb and a cithara player. West 1992: 363–4: "it seems that [Philoxenus' *Cyclops*] was not related by the chorus as part of a chorus, but performed by a solo singer." Power (forthcoming) suggests that Philoxenus' *Cyclops* relied on the exchange between the voice of a solo singer and that of the chorus.

influencing the narrative manner of the musical genres, while the musical genres added histrionics to the performance of drama.[10]

While recent work has put much emphasis on the performer, the spectacle he offered, and the greater role played by the senses in the experience of New Music, I consider here a different aspect of the "mimetic revolution" introduced by the New Music. My focus is not on the relationship between performer and audience or between performer and world created, but rather on the relationship between audience and world created. The mimetic shift that took place at this level is of tremendous importance as it constitutes a move away from the archaic lyric model and gives center stage to the subjectivity of the audience, not the persona of the poet. Rather than connecting to the world created by the narrative mainly through the visual spectacle of the artist, as has been recently argued, late classical audiences, I suggest, were called to connect with the world of the song through the narrative work of the poem. Musical and visual *mimēsis* (that is, reproduction by musical and visual means of aspects described by the narrative) complemented or enhanced the imaginary experience created by the text but ultimately depended on the narrative *mimēsis*. This new relationship between audience and narrative world manifested itself in the characteristically different way the narrator addressed his audience and depicted a fictional world and in the psycho-poetic experience offered to listeners.

Far from being a retreat to a mostly textual approach to lyric and a step back from the "performance turn" that has contributed to a much more sophisticated understanding of the musical culture and soundscape of the ancient world, my approach seeks to ground remarks about *mimēsis* (as physical impersonation) in a close analysis of the song as *mimēsis* (as representation of a world, in terms of its language, themes, and narrative technique): the performative element relies on a change in the *narrative* aspect of the song and cannot be understood without close scrutiny of the way the poet stimulates the audience's imagination in his narrative. Such an examination can help us understand crucial aspects of the development of theater lyric (nome and dithyramb) with respect to other features of the musical revolution (including the type of music, performance style, and language), and even with respect to other artistic forms of expression (tragedy, comedy, and the visual arts) over the course of the classical period. Adopting this audience-centered approach to the text allows us to perceive a crucial switch located in the relationship between the voice of the narrator

---

[10] See Chapter 1, pp. 61–7.

and the subjectivity of the audience, a change that provides a framework within which features I have described in previous chapters can be placed. In this context, the significance of Jaś Elsner's reflections on the Greek Revolution in the visual arts cannot be overestimated:

Many of the other major innovations of Athenian culture in the fifth century BC can be defined broadly by the shift from a voice of authority making direct contact with its audience to a performative model whereby the viewer observes an imaginary world that is insulated within its own context and to which he or she must relate by identification or some form of wish-fulfillment fantasy. While the changes in tragedy took place in the early fifth century, at about the same time as those in the visual arts, the fundamental analogous changes in comedy and philosophy came in the fourth century.[11]

Elsner says nothing of lyric, but this gap, or silence, begs to be explored. This is what I propose to do by examining first the role of the narrator in the longest surviving narrative fragment, Timotheus' *Persians*, before turning to more elusive fragmentary material. I will conclude with another important composition, Philoxenus' dithyramb *Cyclops*, and examine how late classical dithyramb and nome might create a world "insulated within its own context" which can be accessed by "identification or some form of wish-fulfillment fantasy."

Making the Salaminian world present: narrative and fiction in Timotheus' *Persians*

In Plato's description of the different modes of poetic representation in the *Republic* (394c), the citharodic nome is not named explicitly, but it falls into the category of "mixed narrative." Timotheus' *Persians*, which comprises a narrative (*diēgesis*) of the naval battle of Salamis and four direct speeches spoken in the voice of characters (*mimēsis*), illustrates this hybrid narrative nature. Thematically, the text belongs to a poetic tradition of describing the Persian Wars and the events leading to them. Phrynichus had composed tragedies, *The Sack of Miletus*, probably around 493–491 BC, and the *Phoenician Women* in 476 BC, which recounted the defeat of Xerxes at Salamis.[12] Simonides had poems on the sea battles of Artemisium and

---

[11] Elsner 2006: 89.
[12] The dates of Phrynichus' plays are unknown, but for *The Sack of Miletus* Rosenbloom has suggested that the period 493–491 BC is most likely; see Rosenbloom 2006: 20–2. On the *Phoenician Women*, Hall 1996: 7, 12, 14.

Salamis (*PMG* 532–6), and an elegy on the battle of Platea, probably composed around 470 BC.[13] Aeschylus composed the tetralogy that included
the *Persians*, winner at the City Dionysia in 472 BC; comic poets staged
different *Persians*, and a contemporary of Timotheus, Choerilus of Samos,
an epic *Persika* in the last years of the fifth century BC (*SH* 316–23).[14] Each
of these compositions made the world of Salamis present to an audience in a
different way, depending on the chronological distance from the events, the
context for the performance of the poem, its mode of artistic representation
(dramatic, narrative, or mixed), its language, and its performance.

Modes of the Persian Wars

We know little of Phrynichus' tragedy *The Sack of Miletus* other than
Herodotus' comment that the Athenians fined Phrynichus 1,000 drachmas
because the poet had composed a tragedy that struck too close to home. By
staging the pain that the Ionians, Milesians, colonists, and allies had experienced, Phrynichus had reminded the Athenians of their own woes (οἰκήϊα
κακά, Hdt. 6.21.2) and "forc[ed] the audience to relive the pain of Miletus'
fall."[15] Simonides' poem on Salamis has also not been preserved, but his
Plataea elegy gives a good idea of its probable contrast with a dramatic mode
of representation. The longest surviving fragment of the elegy starts with a
hymn to Achilles and features a direct address by the narrator to the Muse,
asking her to come as an ally:

ἀλλὰ σὺ μὲ]ν νῦν χαῖρε, θεᾶς ἐρικυ[δέος υἱέ
  κούρης εἰν]αλίου Νηρέος· αὐτὰρ ἐγώ[20
κικλήισκω] σ' ἐπίκουρον ἐμοί, π[ολυώνυμ]ε Μοῦσα,
  εἴ περ γ' ἀν]θρώπων εὐχομένω[ν μέλεαι·
ἔντυνο]ν καὶ τόνδ[ε μελ]ίφρονα κ[όσμον ἀο]ιδῆς
  ἡμετ]έρης, ἵνα τις [μνή]σεται ὕ[στερον αὖ
ἀνδρῶ]ν, οἳ Σπάρτ[ῃ τε καὶ Ἑλλάδι δούλιον ἦμ]αρ   25
  ἔσχον] ἀμυνόμ[ενοι μή τιν' ἰδεῖν φανερ]ῶ[ς
οὐδ' ἀρε]τῆς ἐλάθ[οντο, φάτις δ' ἔχε]ν οὐρανομ[ήκ]ης
  καὶ κλέος ἀ]νθρώπων [ἔσσετ]αι ἀθάνατο<ν>.
                       Simonides, fr. 11 W² 19–28

---

[13] Frr. 1–22 W² and the "New Simonides": Boedeker and Sider 2001.
[14] Comic *Persians*: Epicharmus' *Persians* (frr. 110–11 KA), Chionides' *Persians or Assyrians* (T1
      KA), Pherecrates' *Persians* (frr. 132–41 KA) and *Lydians* by Magnes. On Choerilus and the
      tradition, McFarlane 2009.
[15] Rosenbloom 2006: 21.

Hail to you, <u>famous</u> son of the marine daughter of Nereus. For my part, I call you as an <u>ally</u>, Muse of many names, if you care about the prayers of men. Fit out the sweet adornment of our song, so that posterity will in turn remember those men who held the line and warded off the fate of seeing the day of slavery from Sparta and Greece; they did not lack heart, their fame rose to heaven and their *kleos* will <u>never die</u> on earth.

The adjective ἐπίκουρον ("ally," 21) is military and ties the poet's self-referential statement to the theme of the elegy.[16] Rather than giving a detailed account of the historical expedition, the narrator only alludes to the events in a metonymic fashion, using epic motives and diction; rather than relating the recent past, Simonides presents to the audience's imagination the glorious mythical paradigm of the Trojan War. The only action described is the march (ἵκοντ', 35; ἵκον, 40) led by Pausanias, who is himself described in heroic terms as "noble son of godlike Cleombrotus" (υἱὸς θείοιο Κλεομβρότου ἄριστος, 33), with a periphrasis that recalls the description of Achilles as "famous son of the marine daughter of Nereus" a few lines earlier (19–20). The idea that the victors of Plataea will have immortal fame (κλέος ἀθάνατον, 28) creates particular continuity between the heroic Achillean narrative and this celebratory civic motive. Retelling the exact nature of the events that just occurred is less important than commemorating the glory of the Plataean heroes, the new Achaeans of the Trojan War, in the moment of the performance of the elegy, and preserving their name for posterity.[17] The circumstances in which the elegy was performed, whether we imagine a public festival or a symposium, must have created a particularly powerful link between audience and narrative.[18] Some of the men hearing the performance would likely have fought in the battle, and if the occasion of its performance was a festival – as I believe it would have been – the performance itself would have been echoed by the surrounding landscape of memory: city ruins, inscriptions, epitaphs, and monuments for the dead would have enabled the elegy to be received in stereo.

The mode of representation of Salamis is entirely different in Aeschylus' *Persians*. Most of the dramatic action on stage is not related to the events of the war: instead of bringing Salamis to the Athenian theater, Aeschylus stages only the royal Persian family, who did not participate in the battle, and a

---

[16] For different interpretations of the use of ἐπίκουρον, Boedeker and Sider 2001: 45–6, 107–13.

[17] Compare with Bakker 2005: 60, speaking of rhapsodic poetry: "the storytelling event . . . is of central cultural importance *because it is the occasion when the community allows a meaningful past to shape its present*" (my emphasis).

[18] On the circumstances of performance, E. Bowie 1986, Schacter 1998, Aloni 2001, Rutherford 2001b: 40–1, Kowerski 2005, Lulli 2011: 50–8, and Nobili 2011 for most recent bibliography.

messenger who gives them, and the tragic audience more broadly, an account of the historical events.[19] The first strategy employed by the messenger to make his audience "believe" in Salamis and explain his narrative position is the rhetoric of presence: he will describe it as he saw it, because he was there, he was an eyewitness, and this is not a second-hand account (καὶ μὴν παρών γε κοὐ λόγους ἄλλων κλύων, 266–7).[20] The messenger proves his reliability by describing his, and only his, perception of the scene:

> καὶ <u>νὺξ</u> ἐχώρει, κοὐ μάλ' Ἑλλήνων στρατός
> κρυφαῖον ἔκπλουν οὐδαμῇ καθίστατο·   385
> ἐπεί γε μέντοι <u>λευκόπωλος ἡμέρα</u>
> πᾶσαν κατέσχε γαῖαν εὐφεγγὴς ἰδεῖν,
> πρῶτον μὲν <u>ἠχῇ κέλαδος</u> Ἑλλήνων πάρα
> <u>μολπηδὸν</u> ηὐφήμησεν, ὄρθιον δ' ἅμα
> ἀντηλάλαξε νησιώτιδος πέτρας   390
> <u>ἠχώ</u>· <u>φόβος</u> δὲ πᾶσι βαρβάροις παρῆν
> γνώμης ἀποσφαλεῖσιν.
>
> Aesch. *Pers.* 384–92

<u>Night</u> was giving way and the Greek army was not making a furtive exit anywhere. When <u>the shine of the day with her white horses</u> was embracing the whole of earth, first an ominous <u>cry like a song rang out</u> from the Greeks and straightaway an <u>echo</u> from the island's rocks was heard in response. <u>Fear</u> befell all barbarians, mistaken in their expectations.

What makes the scene vivid, and believable, for the audience is that the messenger describes his own perceptions from his truncated point of view: he *saw* the receding night (384) and the brightness of day (386), he *heard* the cry (389) and the echo (391), he *felt* the terror (391), but he does not tell the audience either who utters the cry or why, for he himself does not know. In the vocabulary of ancient critics, Aeschylus' messenger achieves vividness (*enargeia*) by relating his own perceptions in order to call upon the emotions (*pathē*) of the audience – by telling of the fear that resulted from seeing the scene, he creates fear. To conclude his narrative, the messenger again relies on his own emotional state of mind and his (calculated) inability to recount the whole scene in a way reminiscent of a Homeric *recusatio*:

> <u>κακῶν δὲ πλῆθος</u>, οὐδ' ἂν εἰ δέκ' ἤματα
> στοιχηγοροίην, οὐκ ἂν ἐκπλήσαιμί σοι.   430
>
> Aesch. *Pers.* 429–30

---

[19] On the narratology of Aeschylus' *Persians*, Hopman 2009.
[20] Although this might be at the same time the very sign that it is not believable. On the concept of belief, and the double-edged character of "I have seen it," Feeney 1993: 239.

This plethora of ills I wouldn't be able to describe fully, even if I had ten days to go through it line by line.

This psycho-poetic process has been well explained in the past, starting with Plutarch's comments on Thucydides' historical narrative art:

> καὶ τῶν ἱστορικῶν κράτιστος ὁ <u>τὴν διήγησιν ὥσπερ γραφὴν</u> πάθεσι καὶ προσώποις <u>εἰδωλοποιήσας</u>. ὁ γοῦν Θουκυδίδης ἀεὶ τῷ λόγῳ πρὸς ταύτην ἁμιλλᾶται τὴν <u>ἐνάργειαν</u>, <u>οἷον θεατὴν ποιῆσαι τὸν ἀκροατὴν</u> καὶ τὰ γινό-μενα περὶ τοὺς ὁρῶντας <u>ἐκπληκτικὰ</u> καὶ ταρακτικὰ πάθη τοῖς ἀναγινώσκ-ουσιν <u>ἐνεργάσασθαι</u> λιχνευόμενος.
>
> Plut. *Mor.* 347a (*De glor. Ath.* 3)

And of the historians the most powerful is the one who depicts a <u>narrative as if a painting</u>, thanks to the <u>depiction</u> of emotions and characters. Thucydides in any case is always eager to achieve this *enargeia* [vividness] in his narrative, <u>aspiring to turn his audience into a spectator</u> and to <u>make vivid</u> for his readers the <u>striking</u> events and emotions that struck those who witnessed them.

This verbal painting (τὴν διήγησιν ὥσπερ γραφήν), which works through the creation of a likeness (εἰδωλοποιήσας) of emotions and characters, is intended to create on a reader or an audience effects similar to those it describes in the narrative.[21]

But there is a second, and related, way by which the Aeschylean messenger creates *enargeia*: this internalized narration, which relies on vision, has the effect of mentally transporting the audience through both time and place. To use the vocabulary of narratologists, the text can "transport" a spectator by operating a "shift of deictic center," from the here-and-now of the performance to the there-and-then of the events. This mental displacement of the audience is linked to the pragmatics of communication: it relies on the very grammar of speech and on the use of verb tenses. When the messenger starts narrating the actual battle, he opens with aorists (underlined in the quotation below), but once the deictic shift is realized, he turns to the imperfect (in bold):

> εὐθὺς δὲ ναῦς ἐν νηῒ χαλκήρη στόλον
> <u>ἔπαισεν</u>· **ἦρξε** δ' ἐμβολῆς Ἑλληνική
> ναῦς, <u>κἀποθραύει</u> πάντα Φοινίσσης νεὼς   410

---

[21] Walker 1993: 360: "What gives a narrative *enargeia* is its representation of *pathē*, especially . . . *pathē* that are attendant on visual perception . . . The *enargeia* of a text is contingent upon the reader's experience of *pathē* like those suffered by the spectators of the original event."

κόρυμβ'· ἐπ' ἄλλην δ' ἄλλος ηὔθυνεν δόρυ.
τὰ πρῶτα μέν νυν ρεῦμα Περσικοῦ στρατοῦ
ἀντεῖχεν· ὡς δὲ πλῆθος ἐν στενῷ νεῶν
ἤθροιστ', ἀρωγὴ δ' οὔτις ἀλλήλοις **παρῆν**,
αὐτοὶ δ' ὑπ' αὐτῶν ἐμβόλαις χαλκοστόμοις   415
παίοντ', **ἔθραυον** πάντα κωπήρη στόλον . . .
                          Aesch. *Pers.* 408–16

> A ship immediately struck its bronze prow against another ship. A Greek
> vessel started the ramming and shattered the entire stern of a Phoenician
> ship, each captain steering his vessel straight against the other. First, the
> flux of the Persian fleet puts up a resistance, but as the crowd of vessels
> had gathered in the straits, there was no aid for one another, and they
> struck the others with bronze-mouthed rams, they shattered all the fleet
> furnished with oars . . .

As Egbert Bakker has shown, to do justice to the narrator's strategy, neither
the grammatical explanation offered by traditional grammars that emphasize the intrinsically durative aspect of the imperfect, nor the insights provided by narratology, which posits a relationship between tense and point
of view, are sufficient.[22] Bakker suggests that instead we consider tense in
terms of closeness or distance of consciousness: "In this way, we can define
tense without recourse to the notions of knowledge and reference: in terms
of perception and observation, present tense is the expression of *immediacy*,
perception in the here-and-now; past tense, on the other hand, is a matter
of *displacement*."[23] He uses the concept of *pretended immediacy* to describe
Thucydides' use of verb tenses in the description of the Athenians' reception
of the fleet's defeat in the battle of Syracuse. In his analysis, the imperfect
may "displace an observation to the past." By contrast, "the aorist does not
by itself effect a displacement from the present to the past. Rather, it relates
an event vis-à-vis a given consciousness that is situated either in the present
or in the future, or . . . in the past."[24] This distinction helps us understand
the use of tenses in the Aeschylean passage presented above and the switch
between the aorist and the imperfect. After the messenger has related the
actions that started the battle, presenting them by reference to his "now"
(his relating the battle to Queen Atossa and the royal family), he locates

[22] On the intrinsically durative aspect of the imperfect, Goodwin 1889: 11–13, 16–18, Smyth
1956: 427, Comrie 1976: 16–40, Rijksbaron 1988. On the relationship between tense and point
of view, Bakker 1997a: 67–8, 1997b: 11–16.

[23] Bakker 1997b: 16–18 (p. 18 for the quotation). On the aorist: "in fact, the aorist is not a tense
at all, in view of the fact that it is not limited to a single temporal relation between an event and
a speaker's situation: it may be present, past, or future" (21).

[24] Bakker 1997b: 19 and 21.

the events in the past and transports his listeners – the royal family and, by extension, the Athenian audience – into the chain of events, giving them through the imperfects the illusion that they are observing events on the spot.[25] Rhetorical and grammatical processes complement each other in creating for the audience the presence of Salamis. The narrator first gains the audience's trust by presenting himself as an eyewitness; now willing to follow him, the audience can displace itself into the past and, for the duration of the speech, witness the events at the mental site of Salamis. For the duration of the speech, spectators of the play are called to watch not the actions of the character on stage but another site that has appeared in their mind's eye, an imagined Salamis.

Timotheus' ekphrastic Salaminian mode

Detailed analysis of Aeschylus' messenger narrative provides an important foundation for understanding Timotheus' own mode of representation of Salamis and the relationship that his *Persians* creates between its audience and the world of the Persian Wars. The performance framing of Timotheus' nome, and of nomes in general, is different from that of both elegy and drama. Drama is based on the tacit convention that the audience knows that what they get is not what they see: they agree, for example, that Nicostratus, the famous actor, is before their eyes, yet they are not watching Nicostratus but Nicostratus *as* messenger, or *as* Darius' ghost. By contrast, in the case of a citharodic performance, the performer, arrayed in a magnificent robe and singing and accompanying himself on the cithara, never "plays" anything other than the citharode. Yes, this role itself had magical and mystical connotations, and part of the glamour of the citharode came from the spectacle of his robes and impressive and ornate instrument.[26] There is, however, no implicit convention, or even tacit agreement, that what an audience sees when a citharode steps onto the podium is not a citharode (just as a rhapsode is never taken for anything other than a rhapsode). To use the vocabulary of performance studies, *kitharōidia* remains fundamentally non-matrixed: no imaginary circumstances are provided to the audience.[27]

---

[25] Bakker 1997b: 26. Also p. 28: "Rather than locating the action in time, the imperfect has the effect of displacing us into the past. The observer, and hence the narrative perspective, is not the historian in his present, but a remote consciousness to which he has access – really or fictionally – by way of remembering, empathy, or hearsay."

[26] On "citharodic glamour and the economics of visual display," Power 2010: 11–31 (especially 24–5), 136–48.

[27] For matrixed and non-matrixed events, Kirby 1972.

By contrast with the Aeschylean character, who inscribes himself in the retelling of the events and gains the trust of his audience by presenting himself as an eyewitness, the position of Timotheus' narrator is unknown. At the point at which the text becomes readable in the part of the papyrus of the *Persians* that has survived, we do not know how the narrator has introduced the narrative, who he is, where his knowledge is from, or whether he was present at the events he narrates. There is no rhetorical framing, and narrative alternates with direct speeches. The situation of Timotheus' song seems at first the reverse of that of Aeschylus' drama: the nome's narrator introduces direct speeches that represent different voices, whereas Aeschylus had a long narrative of Salamis spoken in the voice of one character. But in the course of the Aeschylean tragedy, the messenger himself has become a narrator and has displaced the attention from real spectacle on stage to fictional spectacle in speech.

And here lies the greatest "dramatic" resemblance between the ways Timotheus' and Aeschylus' narrators depict the world of Salamis: throughout the 200 lines of narrative of Timotheus' *Persians* (I exclude here the *sphragis* to which I will return later), the imperfect is, with two exceptions, the only tense used in the indicative in main clauses. The use of the imperfect allows the same displacement effect, and displaced immediacy, as in the Aeschylean passage. Take, for example, the beginning of the *ekphrasis* of the naval battle as it has survived in the papyrus:

> ἀλλ' εἰ μὲν [ἐ]νθένδ[' ἀπρόσο]ι-
> στος ἐπ[ιφ]έροιτο πλαγά
> ῥηξ[ίκωπ]ος, πάντες [ἅμ'] ἀνέ-
> πι[πτον] ἐκεῖσε να[ῦ]ται·   10
> εἰ δ' ἀντίτοιχος ἀκτ[ὰ
> πρ]οσ[ά]ξειεν [πο]λυκρότο[υς
> πλω]σίμους πεύκας, πάλιν ἐφέροντο·
> αἱ δ'[ἀκρ]αινῆ γυῖα [δ]ιαφέρουσα[ι
> πλ]ευρὰς λιν[ο]ζώστους ἔφαι-   15
> νον, τὰς μ[ὲν μολυβδίνο]ις
> σκηπ[τοῖς] ἐπεμβάλλ[ο]ντες ἀνε-
> [χ]αίτιζον, αἱ δὲ πρα[νεῖς
> ἔδυνον καθ' ἅλμ]ας ἀπηγλαϊ-
> σμένα[ι] σιδα[ρ]ῷ κράνει.   20
>   Timoth. *PMG* 791.7–20

If from one side an [unendurable] oar-blasting blow was dealt, the sailors would all tumble in that direction. But if a promontory on the other side shattered the sea-going loud-ringing pines, they were thrown backward

again. And when some ships [powerlessly] flashing their limbs were showing their flax-bound sides, others were capsized by the attack of the [lead]
thunderbolts, while other boats were sinking, prow first, down to the deep,
stripped of their adornment by the iron helmet.

James Hordern explains: "This use of the imperfect is no doubt intended
to *add to the generic nature of the scenes* described in the *Persae*, but also
adds to the vividness of the details... This should be contrasted with the
narrative passages in e.g. Aeschylus, where the aorist is standard for single
events... though the present tense *may be used for vivid descriptions*."[28]
Hordern puts his finger on something important – the vibrancy of detail
and the generic nature of the scene – but he does not connect the two, nor
does he explain how the use of the imperfect is different from the use of
the aorist in creating vividness. The model used by Bakker allows the effect
of the imperfect here and in the following lines to be explained: through
displaced immediacy, Timotheus' narrative, which traditional narratological
approaches would call "externally focalized," works like a camera, following
general movement, actions, and gestures without guessing at or presenting internal thoughts. The text immerses its audience in a scene, without
mediation by an omniscient narrator or internalization, thus creating for
that audience the impression that it is directly observing something. The
something might be a specific moment, but that moment described in the
imperfect is taken as a narrative synecdoche of the entire narrative: it is
a fragment that gives access to the whole. It is in this context, when the
narration has created this displacement, that it can zoom in, and out, on
different events. We encounter this process in action in the first description
of a character, when the text zooms in from the naval army (νάϊος στρατὸς
βάρβαρος, 35–6) to a single man:

> ὅ]τε δὲ τᾷ λείποιεν αὖραι,
> τᾷ δ᾽ ἐπεισέπιπτον, ἄφ-
>   ρει δ᾽ ἀβακχίωτος ὄμβρος,
> εἰς δὲ τρόφιμον ἄγγος
> ἐχεῖτ᾽· ἐπεὶ δ᾽ ἀμβόλιμος ἅλ-
>   μα στόματος ὑπερέθυιεν,   65
> ὀξυπαραυδήτῳ   65α
> φωνᾷ παρακόπῳ
>   τε δόξᾳ φρενῶν
> κατακορὴς ἀπείλει
> γόμφους ἐμπρίων

---

[28] Hordern 2002: 52 (my emphasis).

δινούμενος λυμεῶ-   70
νι σώματος θαλάσ<σ>α.
Timoth. *PMG* 791.60–71

and whenever the winds were letting off on one side, they would attack
on another, and unbacchic rain would foam and pour into his alimentary
vessel. But when the surging brine was raging over his mouth, with shrieking voice and frenzied mind, glutted, he threatens the sea, jaws gnashing,
whirling in the sea, destroyer of his body.

This Persian landowner, whose "territory it takes one day to cross" (40–
2), has become a ship, on his first sea travel (ἔπλει, 45). Buffeted by the
wind in the same way as the sailors were blown around on the ships, he
is drowning.[29] As he takes in and spews out seawater in a reified torrent
of insults (βλοσυρὰν | δ᾿ ἐξέβαλλ᾿ ἄχναν ἐπανε|ρευγόμενος στόματι βρύχιον
ἅλμαν, "disgorging shaggy froth, he was spitting out from his mouth the
deep salty sea," 83–5), he reproduces the tragic inversion of sea and land
that I described in the analysis of language in the previous chapter.[30] With
this vignette, as in the general scene of battle, the audience is brought to the
scene and left to observe for itself the intensity of the emotions (*pathē*).

This zooming technique is extended to the whole narrative. Traversing
horizontally, the narrator's camera moves from a description of movements
at sea (1–96), to what is happening on the shores (97–139), to events on land
(140–88), and finally to Xerxes' retreat inland (189–95). But there is even
more movement, as the focus dramatically oscillates between the insults of
a single sputtering barbarian (72–81) and a panoramic view of the whole
army, the sea, and the flow of the battle (86–95), or switches from the teeth,
"the shining children of the mouth," of a single sailor (92–3) to a grand
cosmic vista that encompasses two sublime and chilling images, the sea
"starry with bodies" (κατάστερος πόντος, 94) and the "shores heavy [with
corpses]" (ἐβρίθοντο δ᾿ ἀϊόνες, 97).

Ekphrasis *and jump cuts*

Although this sustained *ekphrasis* of a battle is created by the use of the
imperfect, I want to focus on two significant exceptions to the use of this
tense, both of which appear in the last part of the narrative. The first occurs in
the depiction of the Persians' collective moment of realization that they have
lost the battle at sea. The narrator describes (in the imperfect, underlined

---

[29] On the tragic irony of the islander who cannot swim, Hall 1994.   [30] See above, pp. 178–82.

in the text below) their gestures of lament, the hands dropping javelins, the nails tearing at faces. Nothing is said about feelings; what is shown is only the manifestations of grief:

> Περσίδα στολὴν περὶ στέρ-
> νοις <u>ἔρεικον</u> εὐϋφῆ,
> σύντονος δ' <u>ἁρμόζετ</u>' Ἀσιάς
> οἰμωγὰ πολυστόνῳ <γόῳ>.   170
> <u>κτύπει</u> δὲ πᾶσα Βασιλέως πανήγυρις
> φόβῳ τὸ μέλλον εἰσορώμενοι πάθος·
> ὁ δὲ παλινπόρευτον ὡς
> **ἐσεῖδε** Βασιλεὺς εἰς φυγήν
> ὁρμῶντα παμμιγῆ στρατόν,   175
> γονυπετὴς <u>ᾄκιζε</u> σῶμα,
> <u>φάτο</u> δὲ κυμαίνων τύχαις . . .
> > Timoth. *PMG* 791.167–77

> They rip the well-woven Persian robes about their chest, and the high-pitched Asian wailing is tuned to the many-tongued lament, and all the entourage of the King clamors, looking in fear at their future fate: and the King, when he saw his army in confusion flying in retreat, falls on his knees and abuses his body, and says, rolling in the wave of misfortune . . .

Since the narrator has moved the deictic center to the past, there is virtually no difference between the use of the imperfect or a present to describe the ripping, wailing, and clamoring of the Persians as a direct perception (and as a matter of fact Page prints a present, κτυπεῖ, at 171). This description of a perception leads to the description of the King's entourage as specta-tors of their own pathos (εἰσορώμενοι πάθος). The moment when we, as audience, see the spectators, who themselves see, is followed immediately by the King's own spectation, in the aorist (ὡς ἐσεῖδε Βασιλεύς). Perhaps here, retrospectively, we are given the key to the perspective on the scene throughout the whole narrative – it has been focalized through the Great King's emotionless eyes, watching the sea battle as reported by Aeschylus and Herodotus.[31]

But the direct perception of the Persian subjects' voices also leads to perception of the King's own lament, in direct style, which concludes with an injunction to burn his tent and riches (193–5). His last performative utterance (μηδέ τις ἡμετέρου γένοιτ' | ὄνησις αὐτοῖσι πλούτου, "let them not

---

[31] Aesch. *Pers.* 466–7: "he had a seat with a clear view of the whole navy (ἕδραν παντὸς εὐαγῆ στρατοῦ), on a lofty hill near the sea"; Hdt. 8.90.4: Xerxes was "seated at the foot of the hill opposite Salamis" (καθήμενος ὑπὸ τῷ ὄρει τῷ ἀντίον Σαλαμῖνος).

profit from our riches," 194–5) brings an abrupt jump cut in the narrative. The next lines transport the listener in place and time:

> οἱ δὲ τροπαῖα στησάμενοι Διός
> ἁγνότατον τέμενος, Παιᾶν᾽
> **ἐκελάδησαν** ἰήϊον
> ἄνακτα, σύμμετροι δ᾽ **ἐπε-**
> **κτύπεον** ποδῶν   200
> ὑψικρότοις χορείαις.
>   Timoth. *PMG* 791.196–201

> They [the Greeks] set up trophies as most sacred sanctuary of Zeus, <u>sang</u> the Lord invoked with *iē Paian*, and in rhythm they <u>started to stamp</u> a high-resounding choral dance.

After the last royal imperative, nothing more is said about the battle. With the symbolic burning of the royal tent, the narrative has consumed the imaginary setting. It now turns to the Greek victory, materialized with the nearly formulaic trophies, paean, and dance, and introduces the first aorist used in an independent clause since the beginning of our narrative. This switch is of great significance: it marks the shift from the voice of the narrator as displaced consciousness, making the audience observe a scene directly, to the voice of the narrator as master of the narrative.[32] Rather than generating a mental spectacle and putting it in front of an audience, as was the case with the imperfect that created the impression of "perceived immediacy," the narrator now states facts. Using the aorist is a performative gesture that allows him to remove the spectators from the created mental place to which he had led them, the glorious past of Salamis, and to bring them back to the reality of the situation, in which a citharode performs for an audience. Bolstered by Bakker's insights again, we can see this short passage in the aorist transform the narrator from a viewer who allows others to view into a knower who addresses his audience with the voice of authority. At exactly this point in the narrative the Timothean narrator transforms from an Aeschylean messenger into the narrator of the Simonides elegy: there is no description of the beauty of the trophies, the tonal quality of the song, or the effect of the paeanic performance; instead, the Greek victory is described metonymically, thanks to the civic signs of the community, and

---

[32] Hordern (2002 ad loc.) notes: "The imperfect is standard in narrative, although we find a few cases of the aorist in temporal clauses (P. 163, 174) and also at the conclusion (198 ἐκελάδησαν), *where it has the effect of marking the end of the narrative*" (my emphasis), but this assessment does not do justice to the complexity of the psycho-poetic process.

not by means of individual details as was the case in the description of the battle.

This narrative switch introduces a second jump cut: after the evocation of the victory paean, the narrator uses a different type of speech act, and addresses Apollo directly before introducing his *sphragis*. Before turning to that aspect, however, I turn to the parts of the narrative that I have not yet examined: the direct speeches, in which the narrator adopts, as a form of *mimēsis*, the voice of other characters.

Inhabiting the Salaminian world

Scholars have commented on the presence of direct speeches in Timotheus and New Music in general,[33] but none has offered an analysis that is sensitive to the singularity of the relationship between narration and direct speech and to the mode of the relationship between narrator and audience. Let us go back to the first speech embedded in the *ekphrasis* of the battle, that of the drowning Persian lord who utters threats at the sea:

> "ἤδη θρασεῖα καὶ πάρος
> λάβρον αὐχέν' ἔσχες ἐν
>   πέδα καταζευχθεῖσα λινοδέτῳ τεόν·
> νῦν δέ σ' ἀναταράξει   75
> ἐμὸς ἄναξ ἐμός
> πεύκαισιν ὀριγόνοισιν, ἐγ-
>   κλήσει δὲ πεδία πλόϊμα νομάσι ναύταις,
> οἰστρομανὲς παλαιομί-
>   σημ' ἄπιστόν τ' ἀγκάλι-   80
>   σμα κλυσιδρομάδος αὔρας."
>   Timoth. *PMG* 791.72–81

"Already before, for all your arrogance, you had your turbulent neck yoked in flax-bound shackles; but now my lord, yes my lord, is about to stir you up with his mountain-born pines and enclose your navigable plain with his roaming sailors, you mad-raging, hated thing of old, untrustworthy darling of the racing, drenching winds."

The opening words used by the Persian, ἤδη . . . καὶ πάρος ("already before"), might seem initially to be a reference to the historical past (πάρος) and to Xerxes' first attempt to bridge the Hellespont, destroyed by the arrogance

---

[33] On direct speech in New Music, Bassett 1931: 161, Kranz 1933: 259, Brussich 1970: 76–7, Herington 1985: 154, 156–7, Zimmermann 1989: 30, J. R. Porter 1994: 203, Csapo 2004: 215–16.

of the sea.[34] But the adverbs also cue their audience into another allusion: they refer to the *poetic* past of the sea and underline the closeness to words already used before to describe the yoking of the sea, as I discussed in the previous chapter.[35] Part of Timotheus' vocabulary and images is borrowed from the parodos of Aeschylus' *Persians*:

> λινοδέσμῳ σχεδίᾳ πορθμὸν ἀμείψας
> Ἀθαμαντίδος Ἕλλας,   70
> πολύγομφον ὅδισμα
> ζυγὸν ἀμφιβαλὼν αὐχένι πόντου.
> > Aesch. *Pers.* 69–72

Crossing on a <u>flax-bound</u> bridge the strait of Helle, Athamas' daughter, throwing <u>around the neck of the sea a yoke</u>, a many-bolted road.

With the temporal adverbs, the Timothean narrator hints at this double take on the past. Ἤδη καὶ πάρος blurs the distinction between historical events at Salamis and the fictional past of the sea, and between the body of water that Aeschylus was describing (the Hellespont) and that which the drowning nameless Persian addresses (the water at Salamis).[36] The image of the shackling of the sea is itself reminiscent of another passage in Aeschylus' *Persians*: the ghost of Darius had referred to his son's arrogance (θράσει, 744) in binding the sea with the following words:

> καὶ πόρον μετερρύθμιζε, καὶ <u>πέδαις</u> σφυρηλάτοις
> <u>περιβαλὼν</u> πολλὴν <u>κέλευθον</u> ἤνυσεν πολλῷ στρατῷ.
> > Aesch. *Pers.* 747–8

And he altered the form of the straits and <u>threw over it</u> iron-wrought <u>shackles</u> to make a great <u>road</u> for a great army.

The adjective θρασύς ("arrogant") encapsulates the reversal of perspective: in Timotheus, it refers no longer to the folly of King Xerxes, blamed by his wise father Darius, but instead to the folly of the sea, blamed by a hybristic subject of Xerxes. This echo reinforces the impression that Timotheus' Persian lives in the world of a properly Aeschylean Xerxes and shares the blindness of his master.

These Aeschylean intertexts have not escaped the attention of critics,[37] but they have been interpreted as either random poetic reminiscences or

---

[34] Hdt. 7.34–7.   [35] See Chapter 4, pp. 182–7.   [36] Rosenbloom 2006: 151–3.

[37] For example, Croiset 1903: 330–5 ("Timothée avait la tête pleine de fragments, de vers, d'expressions, d'images … qu'il acceptait parfois sans beaucoup de critique," 335), Janssen (1984: 118), arguing contra Wilamowitz (1903: 54), Rosenbloom 2006: 151–4, Hunter 2001: 243–6.

weak imitation, or in the light of the rhetoric of legitimization that Timotheus displays in the *sphragis*. While the words are clear echoes of Aeschylus' tragedy, the dramatic situation evinces no such parallels: it would be hard to find any features of the old Persian King of Aeschylus in Timotheus' spitting and drowning Persian. This difference in narrative content should not be overlooked. As Mark Payne observes, "manifest differences in content with regard to archaic and classical poetry may not be indications of the author's agonistic relationship to his predecessors, *but extensions and developments of the repertory of fictional worlds available to him.*"[38] Timotheus uses Aeschylean expressions, and especially expressions from the *Persians*, to establish his narrative authority and flag his place in a poetic tradition of celebration of the Persian Wars, but he also employs such expressions as a way to connect with the "story world" of Salamis.[39] These expressions are meant to convey persuasion, not simply because they refer to "known items, places, features of the actual past," but because, as Andrew Laird explains, there is "community with, or reference to, other stories, making the world of the story in question more complex and substantial."[40] These expressions are ways, for an (ideal) audience,

to construct for [it]self, and to construct quite actively, a *world* in which the story takes place. All of us, whenever we read a book or see a play or film, have to do this passively, if a narrative is going to work on us. But it is not generally a process we notice ... This degree of credibility is also achieved, and increased, by the very inclusion of details which themselves happen to *find their origin in other literary fictions* ... Not just details from what is perceived as the actual past, but *also the cross-referencing to other stories that the ideal reader knows, boost the credibility of this story.*[41]

A narrative about Salamis is not just *any* story: this story already has a history, and the historical reality of Salamis, whatever it was, cannot be the same after stories told about Salamis – in the messenger speech of Aeschylus, in Simonidean elegies, perhaps even after Choerilus' *Persika*. As Laird explains further:

In general for a story to work well it must appear as plausible and true-to-life to its audience as it can. We can see two features by which *The Magician's Nephew* [the example with which Laird opened his essay] lays claim to credibility, discernible

---

[38] Payne 2007: 9 (my emphasis). Also: "What is needed now is an equally detailed account of the kinds of world-making that are the outcome of this activity – how formal innovations are related to fictionality and the mimetic function" (ibid.).

[39] On the notion of story worlds, Laird 1993.

[40] Laird 1993: 152.   [41] Laird 1993: 151–2 (my emphasis).

in the passage quoted and applied throughout. These features exist, with vary-
ing degrees of intensity and conspicuousness, in *all* stories, whether we call them
"fictional" or "factual". They are: (i) community with the world of the (expected)
reader's experience, beyond the obvious minimum of using his or her language:
e.g. reference to known items, places, features of the actual present or past. (ii)
Community with, or reference to, other stories, making the world of the story in
question more complex and substantial.[42]

Reliance on vocabulary from Aeschylus' *Persians* is one means for Timotheus
to give credibility to the imaginary site of Salamis to which he has displaced
his audience: part of the realism of the distressed Persian's speech comes
from the incorporation in the Greek of Aeschylus' *Persians* of an iconic
moment that led to the Persian Wars (Xerxes' yoking of the Hellespont).
The two processes – use of elevated diction and images of tragedy *and* use
of direct speech – are not two distinct features but rather depend on each
other, together reinforcing the psycho-poetic experience of a listener.

　　After this flashback to Xerxes, the Persian turns to his future (νῦν δέ σ'
ἀναταράξει ἐμὸς ἄναξ..., "now my master will stir you...," 75–6). The
adverb νῦν here takes a tragically ironic dimension. There is a gap between
the future as the character imagines it and the historical past as the audience knows it: since the audience knows that the Persians lost the war,
they also know that the Persian's master *will not* stir up the sea with his
mountain-born pines. But for a moment, that audience might feel the
enraged pathos of the islander, relate to his miseries, and even believe, or
at least hope, that his master will punish the sea. For the duration of the
Persian's speech, the audience is brought into the fantasy world of the character and led to think about alternate futures. Aeschylean echoes linger
for one more line after the end of the direct speech: the "deep salty sea"
(βρύχιον ἅλμαν, Timoth. *PMG* 791.96) that the Persian belches out is one
last Aeschylean drop from the *Persians* (ἔπαισαν ἅλμην βρύχιον, "they struck
the deep salty sea," Aesch. *Pers.* 397). The rare adjective is brought back to
life, but rather than being used to describe the assault of the Greek fleet,
its oars beating the sea in unison, it is a synonym for the "shaggy froth"
(βλοσυρὰν ἄχναν, Timoth. *PMG* 791.83–4) pouring into the Persian's belly.
Once again, the echoes are neither a specific reference to the text of Aeschylus' *Persians* nor an affected archaism used to legitimize daring musical
features but instead give texture to the world into which the audience has
been displaced and which they look upon through the eyes of one participant. Just as the adjective θρασύς recast the Aeschylean regal perspective

---

[42] Laird 1993: 152.

and refocalized it through a nameless individual's speech, the "deep salty sea" transforms the Persian fleet's communal, nearly choral, experience of the sea to make it the last image in the description of a single struggling Persian.

Interpreting the Persian's intertextual speech in story-world terms gives a greater role to the audience and allows the focus to be shifted from the relationship between poets and their use of the poetic tradition to the relationship between poet, audience, and world created. Two processes that I have described successively here – the use of the imperfect to operate the mental transport and give the audience the impression of displaced consciousness, and the intertextual link with the world of Aeschylus' *Persians* through the direct speech – in practice work simultaneously. Their conjunction defines in part the specificity of the mode of narrative of the citharodic nome. Many narrative genres, from epic to Bacchylidean dithyramb, rely on the mental transport of the audience to create their effect: one has only to think of the description of the shield of Achilles couched entirely in the imperfect to realize that the specificity of the narrative technique of the *Persians* relies on something more. Its characters (fictional and anonymous, apart from the Great King) inhabit the narrative world created by the poet. These figures, starting with the drowning landowner just examined, are modeled on other poetic figures or speak in the words of other poetic texts but are transformed in the process, becoming characters an audience can project into. The process that I have described above on the example of the inversion of perspective in the intertextual Aeschylean θρασύς, βρύχιον ἅλμαν, and the description of the yoking of the sea extends to the whole of Timotheus' *Persians*: each character from Timotheus' gallery of foreigners, I would argue, comes from a story world but is transformed into someone whom the audience can not only observe directly but also project into, in the form of wish-fulfillment fantasy that Elsner has described in relation to the visual arts.[43] These speaking characters are not entirely realistic – their speech is mediated by other poetic words and therefore they do not speak as the audience itself would speak in their situation – but neither are they entirely fantastic or mythical, precisely because the presence of the intertext gives more weight, and credence, to the words they speak.

---

[43] For another clear statement about the change of relationship, see Elsner 2006: 91: "In moving from being directly addressed by the divine or by a voice of inspired authority (religious or civic) to becoming the observer of a series of social interrelations like our own, but heightened through artistic representation to the levels of sculptural, tragic or philosophical heroics (or reduced to comic bathos), the subject and the collective subjectivity are fundamentally transformed."

The second speech in the *Persians* is a choral lament (θρηνώδει ὀδυρμῷ, 103) in which a group of Mysians call to their native land ([γᾶν] πατρίαν ἐπανεκα[λ]έοντ᾽, 104):

> "ἰὼ Μύσιαι					105
> δενδροέθειραι πτυχαί,
> [ῥύ]σασθέ μ᾽ ἐνθένδε· νῦν ἀήταις
> φερόμεθ᾽, οὐ γὰρ ἔτι ποτ᾽ ἀμόν
> [σῶ]μα δέξεται [πόλ]ις."
>> Timoth. *PMG* 791.105–9

O Mysian folds crowned with trees, protect me here: we are now being carried by blasts of winds, no city will ever again receive my body.

The very ethnicity of the group may have been chosen because of the connotations of "Mysian lament," and the opening lines could even be an echo of Aeschylus' *Mysians*.[44] But another intertextual echo is more significant: Euripides' *Medea*. The lines the Mysian group utters reconfigure two lines spoken by Medea in the monologue in which she states her plight as a foreign and exiled female:

> "τίς με δέξεται πόλις;
> τίς γῆν ἄσυλον καὶ δόμους ἐχεγγύους
> ξένος παρασχὼν ῥύσεται τοὐμὸν δέμας;"
>> Eur. *Med.* 386–8

What city will welcome me? What host will offer the protection of his land and the refuge of his house to save my life?

The Colchian heroine in despair and the Mysians, who are castaways on a foreign shore with no hope of going back to their land, definitely have something in common. The situation of the latter seems even more desperate as the mourners turn the Euripidean question "What city will receive me?" into a negative ("no city will ever again receive my body") and the sinister overtones of σῶμα replace Medea's δέμας.[45] The parallel is even clearer in their next exclamation:

> εἴ[θε μ]ὴ στέγην ἔδειμε
> [δ]ῆτ[α] τελεόπορον ἐμός					115

---

[44] Aesch. *Mysians* (*TGrF* iii fr. 143) opens with ἰὼ Κάικε Μύσιαί τ᾽ ἐπιρροαί ("Oh, Mount Caicus and streams of Mysia"). The lament form itself is associated with Mysia: Aesch. *Pers.* 1054: καὶ στέρν᾽ ἄρασσε κἀπιβόα τὸ Μύσιον, "beat your breast and shout the Mysian lament."

[45] The words would have even more chilling overtones if performed after the naval battle at Arginousae in 406 bc, where the bodies of the Athenians were not recovered.

[δ]εσπότης· οὐ γὰρ ἂ[ν Τμ]ῶλον οὐδ᾽
ἄστυ Λύδιον [λι]πὼν Σάρδεων
ἦλθον ["Ε]λλαν᾽ ἀπέρξων Ἄρ[η·
νῦν] δὲ πᾷ τις δυσέκφευκ[τ]ον εὕ-
ρῃ γλυκεῖαν μόρου καταφυγήν;   120

Timoth. PMG 791.114–20

Would that my master had never built a deck that made the crossing! For I would not have left Tmolus or the Lydian city of Sardis to come to ward off the Greek Ares. But now, where to find a sweet refuge from fate?

The impossible wish recalls the opening lines of Euripides' *Medea*:

εἴθ᾽ ὤφελ᾽ Ἀργοῦς μὴ διαπτάσθαι σκάφος   1
Κόλχων ἐς αἶαν κυανέας Συμπληγάδας,
μηδ᾽ ἐν νάπαισι Πηλίου πεσεῖν ποτε
τμηθεῖσα πεύκη . . .

Eur. Med. 1–4

Would that the hull of the Argo had never passed the Clashing Rocks and flown to the land of Colchis, and that the pine had never been felled in the glens of the Pelion . . .

Both statements rely on a contrafactual sequence and hold a sea-going vessel (the Argo and the anonymous στέγην) responsible for their woes.[46] They each relive a voyage through evocative foreign places: Tmolus, Lydia, and Sardis for the Persian; Colchis and the Clashing Rocks for Medea. The speech of the Mysians channels the voice of Medea, their chorus speaking the solo voice of the mythical character. Their words are all the more believable because they borrow from a fictional world with which an audience could, or would, be familiar.[47] But Medea is a mythical witch who can take off in the chariot of the sun, and no matter with which character of the *Medea* the audience most sympathize, they cannot entirely identify themselves with her; by contrast, the group of lamenting Mysians are realistic, or believable, characters with whom the audience can connect. Once again, I am locating the force of the intertextual echoes not only in the relationship between the

---

[46] The reference to the cutting of the pines forms a sharp contrast with the opening appeal to the glens of Mysia, still untouched (106). Already in Hom. *Il.* 5.63, the boats Paris had built are ἀρχεκάκους ("starters of ills").

[47] I cannot tackle here the question of the status of Aeschylean tragic reperformances in the late fifth century BC, and of the actual possibility of an audience member remembering the exact lines of a play composed two generations before. But this question, which one can raise about any allusive reading strategy, does not invalidate the fact that there are strong intertextual echoes in the text of Timotheus' *Persians*, which need to be interpreted.

poet and his predecessors (a feature that I will explore further in the follow-ing pages) but also in the relationship between the narrator and the audi-ence, and ultimately in the relationship between the audience and the world created, a world inhabited by fictional creatures removed from the realm of the heroic and mythical.

After the impossible wish (would that the boat that conveyed us had never been built), the Mysians explore the only possible way out of their predicament:

> Ἰλιοπόρος κακῶν λυσαί-
>   α μόνα γένοιτ᾽ ἄν, εἰ
>   δυνατὰ πρὸς μελαμπεταλοχί-
>   τωνα Ματρὸς οὐρείας
> δεσπόσυνα γόνατα πεσεῖν   125
> εὐωλένους τε χεῖρας ἀμφιβάλλων
> λισ<σοίμαν· σῶ>σον χρυσοπλόκαμε
> θεὰ Μᾶτερ ἱκνοῦμαι
> ἐμὸν ἐμὸν αἰῶνα δυσέκφευκτον, ἐπεί
>   μ᾽ αὐτίκα λαιμοτόμῳ τις ἀποίσεται ἐνθάδε   130
>   μήστορι σιδάρῳ
> ἢ κατακυμοτακεῖς ναυσιφθόροι αὖραι
> νυκτιπαγεῖ βορέᾳ δια<ρ>-
>   ραίσονται· περὶ γὰρ κλύδων
> ἄγριος ἀνέρρηξεν ἅπαν   135
>   γυίων εἶδος ὑφαντόν·
> ἔνθα κείσομαι οἰκτρός, ὀρ-
>   νίθων ἔθνεσιν ὠμοβρῶσι θοίνα.
>   Timoth. *PMG* 791.121–38

A crossing to Ilion would be the only release from ills, if I could fall to the queenly knees of the Mountain Mother with the black-leaved gar-ment, and casting my fine arms around them utter the prayer: "Golden-tressed divine Mother, I beseech you for this existence of mine, mine, hard to escape from, since someone will carry me off soon from there, with a throat-cutting iron assistant, or the ship-destroying winds, melt-ing the waves, will dash me to pieces with a night-freezing Boreus. Indeed a savage billow has ripped all of the woven warmth from my limbs. And here I shall lie, wretched, a feast for the tribes of flesh-eating birds."

The striking feature of this prayer to the Mountain Mother is that it is not actually performed by the Mysians but only *imagined* in another conditional system. The description of the ritual gesture (embracing the knees of the divinity they supplicate) replaces the event itself. Yet the words they use in the prayer to describe their miserable fate (περὶ γὰρ κλύδων ἄγριος ἀνέρρηξεν ἅπαν γυίων εἶδος ὑφαντόν, "a savage billow has ripped all of the woven warmth from my limbs," 134–6) replicate the reality the narrator described earlier, including the Mysians freezing, naked (γυμνοπαγεῖς, 99), on the shore. Similarly, the risk that they might be killed or carried off at sword point (λαιμοτόμῳ τις ἀποίσεται ἐνθάδε μήστορι σιδάρῳ, 130–1) will be realized in precisely these terms in the description of the Celaenaean being carried off (σιδαρόκωπος Ἕλλαν, ἄγεν κόμης ἐπισπάσας, "an iron-bladed Greek, dragging him by the hair, carries him off," 144–5). The two voices, that of the narrator and that of the character, feed off each other, and the solo voice of the singer performing the nome brings to life a choral voice that recasts the solo words of Medea – or, rather, the solo voice of the singer impersonates the choral voice of the group of Mysians, who have acquired the individuality, and realism, of a tragic character.

The text continues to play with modes of representation of reality, from the wished-for prayer in which the Mysians confess their fears to a description a few lines later that actualizes these fears. Once brought into the world of the Mysians, the audience can observe their mental life, and explore with them a series of non-real possibilities, impossible wishes, prayers, and worst fears. This process, finally, brings them in the last line (ὀρνίθων ἔθνεσιν ὠμοβρῶσι θοινά, "a feast for the tribes of flesh-eating birds," 138) strikingly close to another story world, that of the opening lines of the *Iliad*, in a perfect ring-composition that includes the initial ambiguous word, Ἰλιοπόρος ("the crossing to Ilion," 121).

The next speech, by a Celaenaean man supplicating in Greek, introduces a shift of register, but the technique remains the same:

ἐγώ μοί σοι κῶς καὶ τί πρᾶγμα;   150
αὖτις οὐδάμ' ἔλθω·
καὶ νῦν ἐμὸς δεσπότης
δεῦρό μ' ἐνθάδ' ἥξει·
τὰ λοιπὰ δ' οὐκέτι, πάτερ,
οὐκέτι μαχέσ' αὖτις ἐνθ<ά>δ' ἔρχω   155
ἀλλὰ κάθω·
ἐγώ σοι μὴ δεῦρ', ἐγώ
κεῖσε παρὰ Σάρδι, παρὰ Σοῦσ',
    Ἀγβάτανα ναίων·
Ἄρτιμις ἐμὸς μέγας θεός   160
    παρ' Ἔφεσον φυλάξει.
          Timoth. *PMG* 791.150–61

Me for me to you, how, and what thing? Never again I come back. Now my
master has brung me here to this place; but from now on no more, father,
no more I come again here for fight. I sit still. I no come here to you . . . I
for you there I go to Sardis, to Susa, living in Agbatana. My Artemis the
great goddess will protect me at Ephesus.

Here again Timotheus looks to the poetic world of the East and relies on
his audience's belief in this fictional world to bring his own character to life,
but this time the narrator draws on comedy. Tragic barbarians do not speak
any differently from Greeks on the late fifth-century stage; to compensate,
they self-consciously emphasize their foreignness.[48] But Timotheus had at
his disposal a full cabinet of comic barbarians: the Persian ambassador in
Aristophanes' *Acharnians*, the Scythian archer in his *Thesmophoriazousae*,
the Triballian god in the *Birds*, to list only figures from extant comedies (and
assuming the *Persians* was composed later).[49] All these characters speak a
Greek full of "barbarisms," which in addition to giving the impression of
incomprehensible chatter might also imitate Asiatic dialects, including their
semantic and phonological features, and pick up on Persian vocabulary. We
find such a case in the *Acharnians*:

{ΨΕΥΔΑΡΤΑΒΑΣ} ἰαρταμαν ἐξαρξας ἀπισονα σατρα.   100
{ΠΡΕΣΒΥΣ} Ξυνήκαθ' ὃ λέγει;
{ΔΙ.}   Μὰ τὸν Ἀπόλλω 'γὼ μὲν οὔ.
{ΠΡ.} Πέμψειν βασιλέα φησὶν ὑμῖν χρυσίον.
Λέγε δὴ σὺ μεῖζον καὶ σαφῶς τὸ χρυσίον.
{ΨΕ.} Οὐ λῆψι χρυσό, χαυνόπρωκτ' Ἰαοναῦ.

Ar. *Ach.* 100–104

Pseudartabas: Iartaman exarxas apisona satra.
Ambassador: Did you understand what he is saying?
Dicaeopolis: By Apollo, no, I didn't.
Am.: He says the King is going to send you gold.
[To Pseudartabas:] Speak louder, and clearly, about the gold.
Ps.: You not vill get goldo, you gaping-ass Iaonian.

After the striking assonance of his first line – ten [a]-sounds in thirteen
syllables – the Aristophanic ambassador uses the term "Ionian," an echo of
the Old Persian name for the Greeks (Yauna) and the very expression that

---

[48] Bacon 1961: 115–40; "gorgeously cacophonous passages like those of Aeschylus do not occur in
Euripides" (143 n. 29).

[49] On barbarians in comedy, and features and effects of their language, Long 1984, Hall 1989:
76–8, 117–21, Halliwell 1990, Colvin 1999: 287–95, Willi 2002: 142–9, Hall 2006: 225–54. For
details of Timotheus' character's barbarisms, Hordern 2002: 207–14.

Timotheus uses before introducing the Persian's speech (Ἰάονα γλῶσσαν ἐξιχνεύων, "hunting for the Ionian tongue," 149). Timotheus' Phrygian also reproduces elements of barbaric phonology, including Ἀγβάτανα (for the Greek Ecbatana) and Ἄρτιμις (for Artemis). Nowhere is the use of poetic texture or reliance on a story world clearer than here, for around 480 BC the exotic locations that the Persian invokes (Sardis, Susa, Ekbatana, Ephesus) were filled with Greek mercenaries and could not have been places to which the Persian character would really have wanted to go. This is proof, if more be needed, that the poet relies more on the power of names associated with the distant past than on historical references. In his speech, the Persian once again inverts what we see in the Aristophanic scenario: the man from Celaenae is not a representative of a whole people, but an individual appealing to the Greek with whom an audience could identify.

Even in this short and foreign-sounding speech, the structure is the same as in the other monologues: it starts with a reference to the present (ἔγω μοί σοι κῶς καὶ τί πρᾶγμα; "Me for me to you, how, and what thing?," 150), then turns to the future, with a promise that we know the Celaenaean man will not be given the opportunity to make good (αὖτις οὐδάμ' ἔλθω, "never again I come back," 151), and then back to his present (καὶ <u>νῦν</u> ἐμὸς δεσπότης | δεῦρό μ' ἐνθάδ' ἥξει, "<u>now</u> my master has brung me here to this place," 152–3), that is, to the past to which the audience has been transported. There is one more fascinating instance of what I would call "story-world of enslaved Phrygian": that of Euripides' *Orestes* (1368–1502), which stages a terrified singing Asiatic. The parallel between the two characters is tantalizing, but one can only speculate whether Euripides furthered the possibilities of what a barbarian *can* do, including in a monody, or Timotheus undid the *Orestes* and exploited the comic potential latent in Euripides.[50]

The last speech is that of the Great King. Battered just as the Persian was literally battered by the sea, the King is "borne on the wave of destiny" (κυμαίνων τύχαισιν, 177) with a metaphor that continues the nautical register of the narrative:

> "ἰὼ κατασκαφαὶ δόμων
> σείριαί τε νᾶες Ἑλλανίδες, αἵ
>   κατὰ μὲν ἥλικ' ὠλέσαθ' ἥ-   180
> βαν νέων πολύανδρον·
> νᾶες δ' οὐκ ὀπισσοπόρευ-

---

[50] On the Persian slave's monody, J. R. Porter 1994: 173–213, especially 199–207 for the *Orestes'* "clear debt to the Timothean nome" (199). Also Bassett 1931, who argues for the priority of the *Persians*. Contra: Ebeling 1925, Janssen 1984: 13–22.

τόν <νιν> ἄξουσιν, πυρός
δ' αἰθαλόεν μένος ἀγρίῳ
σώματι φλέξει, στονόεντα δ' ἄλγη   185
ἔσται Περσίδι χώρᾳ·
<ἰ>ὼ βαρεῖα συμφορά,
ἅ μ' ἐς Ἑλλάδ' ἤγαγες·
ἀλλ' ἴτε, μηκέτι μέλλετε,
ζεύγνυτε μὲν τετρά<ορ>ον ἵππων   190
     ὄχημ', οἱ δ' ἀνάριθμον ὄλ-
     βον φορεῖτ' ἐπ' ἀπήνας·
πίμπρατε δὲ σκηνάς,
μηδέ τις ἡμετέρου γένοιτ'
     ὄνησις αὐτοῖσι πλούτου".   195
               Timoth. *PMG* 791.178–95

O utter destruction of my palace! Oh you scorching Greek ships that destroyed the youth of my ships, my numerous contemporaries. No vessel will carry them on the backward journey, the blazing force of the fire will consume them with its fierce body, and it will be groaning pains for the Persian land. O heavy misfortune, you who brought me to Greece! But enough – don't delay any longer, yoke my four-horsed chariot, and carry onto my wagons my innumerable riches: burn the tent and let them not profit from our riches.

The King's speech, like the Mysians', opens with a lamenting apostrophe and what seems like an exact quotation of Aeschylus' *Choephoroi*:

ἰὼ πάνοιζυς ἑστία,
ἰὼ κατασκαφαὶ δόμων.   50
ἀνήλιοι βροτοστυγεῖς
δνόφοι καλύπτουσι δόμους
δεσποτᾶν θανάτοισι.
               Aesch. *Cho.* 49–53

O all unhappy hearth, O utter destruction of my palace! Sunless shadows hateful to mortals shroud the hall after the masters' death.

As the parallel with the other quotations suggests, I am not privileging a direct intertextual relationship with the *Choephoroi*, in which reliance on that play as "source" or "model" text overloads the speech of the Great King with meaning. In speaking like the Aeschylean chorus lamenting the destruction of the greatest house of Argos, the Persian King, I contend, acquires the fictional stature of a tragic chorus. Once again, we see the type of inversion I have highlighted in the previous speeches: by talking like their poetic predecessors the characters are granted fictional weight. But while the Mysians were speaking the voice of a single character, this time the Persian King speaks the voice of a community: rather than being one of the mythical characters of the house of Atreus from the *Oresteia*, the King has the fictional presence of a chorus, and speaks for his subjects. Both Oresteian chorus and Persian King use the metonymy of the house for the destruction of their power and kingdom, regardless of the fact that, as he goes on to explain, the King lost not his palace, but his fleet. Once again what matters is that the speech of the character that the citharode brings to life acquires some of its credibility and, paradoxically, its naturalism by recasting a tragic choral voice. Xerxes, who in Aeschylus' *Persians* has the quasi-mythical dimension of an epic hero, acquires in the Timothean narrative the citizen voice of the chorus of the *Oresteia*. The King's speech, like that of the other characters, then turns to the future (νᾶες δ᾽ οὐκ ὀπισσοπόρευτον <νιν> ἄξουσιν, "no vessel will carry them on the backward journey," 182–3) and in stating that his ships will not make the voyage back cancels out the string of compound adjectives suggesting flight that had been used in the description introducing the lines (παλίμπορον φυγὴν, "retreating flight," 162–3; παλινπόρευτον φυγήν, "fleeing in retreat," 173–4). Here again we can observe the back-and-forth between speech of a character and voice of the narrator that can also be found in each of the mimetic speeches explored above.

To sum up: the meaning of the speech in these four passages is not dependent on a "source text" and a source scenario; allusion is not the key. Rather, the intertextual echoes in all four passages give weight to fictional characters. By connecting the drowning Persian or the Great King to other dramatic figures and by giving their voices recognizable fictional and poetic texture, the Timothean narrator boosts his own credibility and reinforces the imaginary experience of his audience. Each character is isolated in a specific story world, but the audience's belief in that character comes from a stored memory of other stories. Most importantly, each intertext instantiates a moment when a fictional or mythical character staged in a source-text narrative becomes an individual whom the audience can observe, continuing the fiction through wish-fulfillment fantasy. The illusion is never broken off; there is a voyeur's pleasure in observing a self-contained and, I would add, vicariously close, world. This strategy provides the simplest and strongest explanation for the absence of any mention of Athens or any other proper name in the narrative: a reference to Athens would return the audience to the here-and-now of the performance, to wherever the song was actually performed, while the evocation of Susa, Egbatana, or Mysia contributes to the mental transport of an Athenian, Spartan, or Milesian audience to remote locations, loaded with poetic memories. The same is true of personal names: anonymity allows projection and is an important mechanism for following the fiction.[51] The characters themselves deepen this exercise in projection, for each relates to his past, present, and future in a different way. That the characters' expressions of despair are in part the words of other story worlds contributes to their fictional weight, or naturalism.

This reading provides us with an important way to talk about dramatization. The dramatic nature of Timotheus' *Persians* does not stem primarily from the citharode's embodiment of the topic in a gymnastically evocative performance – how long could the effect of such a spectacle last without an audience getting seasick? – or only from the work's inclusion of many direct speeches, or because the author borrows voices, tone, or even lines from tragedy and comedy in the mixing of genres that has been seen as typical of the late classical and Hellenistic periods. Rather, the citharodic performance can be seen as dramatic in that listeners of the song, transformed into musical voyeurs, are called to believe for the duration of the song in the mimetic existence of the speakers and to explore their mental world by means of a form of mental projection which recalls that required of spectators of tragedy. While my focus has been on narrative technique and on the mimetic story worlds of the speeches, I do not ignore mimetic effects as mentioned above: some words could have been matched by mimetic sounds – the high-pitched Asian wailing (169–70), for example, or the resounding paeanic stamping of the performer's feet (200–1) – and the King's injunction to burn his tent and riches (193–5) would have found a striking visual echo in the spectacle of the citharode himself, splendidly arrayed in a rich στολή ("garb") and playing a valuable instrument. The reactionary critics complain loudly about the New Music's *mimēsis*, but one must not forget that dithyrambs and nomes were not framed as drama or pantomime: the force of any momentary dramatic assimilation of performer and fictional character, by means that include gestures and sounds, is fundamentally dependent on the audience's willingness to commit to a mental displacement. And this mental displacement is itself predicated on narrative *mimēsis* and on the construction of an imaginary world, with its own space, time, and characters, through narration.

---

[51] Payne 2007: 14–15: "Anonymity is a marker of fiction where it is found in earlier literature [Finkelberg 1998: 130], and the presence of unnamed characters in the bucolic poems seems to be programmatic: while fictional beings elsewhere people the interstices of mythical narratives – the shield of Achilles in the *Iliad*, whose invented cities are filled with anonymous inhabitants, or the messengers and minor characters of tragedy – here they alone occupy the stage."

Narratorial voice

We turn now to the *sphragis* (cited in Chapter 2, pp. 90–8). I have already noted that the trophy setting in the very last lines of the narrative functions as a metonymy for the end of the war and that the shift to the aorist signals a change in the position of the narrator as he asserts his control over the story rather than allowing the audience to perceive the scene for themselves. The reference to the paean sung by the Greeks also serves as another kind of pivot, bringing the second, and final, jump cut, from the narrative to the direct address to Apollo. There is a tight performative bond between the description of the Greeks singing *iē Paian*, and the narrator's cletic address and his own Paian invocation.[52] In asking the god of the golden cithara to come as an ally (ἐπίκουρος) to his songs, Timotheus specifically borrows the words of the Simonidean narrator in the Plataea elegy (fr. 11 W², line 21), calling on the Muse as an ally (ἐπίκουρον) to his own narrative. It is possible to see this use of the word as one way in which the New Musician legitimizes his own project within the elaborate strategy of authorization that I have described above,[53] but I would rather interpret this echo, or more specifically this reliance on military vocabulary and invocation of a divine protector, as a means of creating the narrator's changed persona. In this context, the repetition of words describing the battle in the poet's own defense take on added significance: the way Timotheus describes the Spartan leaders hounding him (μέγας ἀγεμὼν βρύων ἄνθεσιν ἥβας, "a great leader, swarming with the flower of youth," 207–8) recalls Xerxes' blaming the Greek ships for the destruction of his peers (αἴ κατὰ μὲν ἥλικ' ὠλέσαθ' ἥβαν νεῶν πολύανδρον, "[the ships] that destroyed the youth of my ships, my numerous contemporaries," 179–81). And the violence of the poet's critics (δονεῖ λαὸς ἐπιφλέγων ἐλᾷ τ' αἴθοπι μώμῳ, "the people drives me about in its blazing hostility and harasses me with burning reproach," 209–10) is a metaphorical echo of the fiery destruction of the Persian navy (πυρὸς δ' αἰθαλόεν μένος ἀγρίῳ σώματι φλέξει, "the blazing force of the fire will consume them with its fierce body," 183–4). By activating the military vocabulary used in the description of the battle of Salamis in the description of his own fight, Timotheus adds a very distinct civic note. Moreover, he borrows from the authority of the poet of the Persian Wars not simply to legitimize his own project, but also to establish the same type of relationship with the audience that the Simonidean narrator had with his: his too is to be a voice of authority, and through that voice the community will experience

---

[52] For a generic link between paean and nome, Rutherford 1995.
[53] See Chapter 2, pp. 97–101.

its civic cohesiveness as the mythical past is brought into the present. It is in such a capacity that Timotheus, probably in the last years of the Peloponnesian War, addresses his audience in the closing lines of the poem, having offered them the imaginary spectacle of Salamis, one of the most powerful icons of Athenian patriotic discourse.[54] Timotheus' use of the vocabulary of battle in the *sphragis* continues the trope started by the reference to Simonides – the narrator takes it upon himself to defend the city's civic ideal. Borrowing from the elegiac register of Simonides, just as Simonides borrowed from Homer, Timotheus aligns himself not only thematically but also ideologically and functionally with the early classical poet and adopts the narratorial persona projected into the elegy, that of a poet recalling the recent past in a ritual and civic moment of celebration for his community.

Calling on Apollo citharode as an ally (ἐπίκουρος) for his paean hints at the double genealogy in which Timotheus inscribes himself: on the one hand, the musical tradition of the citharodes Orpheus and Terpander, calling on their patron Apollo as mythical cithara player; on the other, the civic and religious tradition of Simonides, who evoked the world of the Persian Wars to address his community directly. This twofold relationship gives double-edged meaning to the poet's claim that he "does not keep anybody away from his new songs": all are invited both to join in witnessing the fantasy of Salamis and to gather for this utopian celebration of the glorious past with its divinely and civically inspired narrative that is like Simonides', in which the narrator projects a voice of authority for the gathered community.

Narrative worlds

The detailed analysis of the relationship between the audience and the narrative world that is possible for Timotheus' *Persians* is impossible for the rest of the corpus, since the fragments are for the most part too short to give a sense of a narrative. An overview of the variety of the narrative material (*what* stories songs told) provides, however, a useful complement to an analysis of the narrative technique (*how* songs told stories). This overview enables us to recognize a new type of theme that matches the new type of relationship that composers sought to establish between audience and

---

[54] Power 2010: 542, "a highly effective utopian entertainment, nostalgic and escapist, but also inspiring and hopeful," with further reference to Phillips 2003: 212–13, on the morale-boosting effect of the *Persians* in this context of geopolitical anxiety.

world of the song. Investigation of the themes treated by late classical poets in their dithyrambs and nomes confirms the impression that poets offered audiences not only a certain type of imaginary world to explore but also, by positing a different type of audience's subjectivity, new ways to explore these worlds.

Titles

A quick survey of the surviving titles of theater lyric already makes this clear. Titles of dithyrambs and nomes – it is often impossible to establish the genre of a composition – fall into three categories. The first category encompasses divine and theogonic material (when sources provide indications of the genre of the piece, these are marked):

> Melanippides, *Persephone* (*PMG* 759)
> Telestes, *Asclepius* (*PMG* 806–7)
> Telestes, *Birth of Zeus* (*PMG* 809)
> Timotheus, *Birth Pangs of Semele* (*PMG* 792) – dithyramb
> Timotheus, *Artemis* (*PMG* 778a and b) – citharodic hymn, sung in
>   Ephesus and Athens
> (Probably) Cinesias, *Asclepius* (*PMG* 774)

The second category contains mythical and heroic material:

> Cleomenes, *Meleager* (*PMG* 838) – dithyramb
> Melanippides, *Danaids* (*PMG* 757)
> Melanippides, *Marsyas* (*PMG* 758)
> Oeniades, *Cyclops* (*PMG* 840) – dithyramb
> Philoxenus, *Cyclops* or *Galatea* (*PMG* 815–823) – dithyramb
> Philoxenus, *Genealogy of the Aeacides* (*PMG* 814) – "lyric song"
> Stesichorus II, *Cyclops* (*PMG* 840) – dithyramb
> Telestes, *Argo* (*PMG* 805)
> Telestes, *Hymenaeus* (*PMG* 808) – dithyramb
> Timotheus, *Elpenor* (*PMG* 779)
> Timotheus, *Cyclops* (*PMG* 780) – nome
> Timotheus, *Laertes* (*PMG* 785)
> Timotheus, *Scylla* (*PMG* 796) – dithyramb
> Timotheus, *Madness of Ajax* (*PMG* 777) – dithyramb
> Timotheus, *Nauplius* (*PMG* 785) – nome
> Timotheus, *Niobe* (*PMG* 786) – nome
> Timotheus, *Sons of Phineus* (*PMG* 795)

And the third category contains a number of non-divine, non-mythological, historical, or fictional titles:[55]

> Licymnius, *Dithyrambs* (*PMG* 768)
> Philoxenus, *Dinner Party* (*PMG* 836)
> Philoxenus, *Syrus/Syrian* (*PMG* 827)
> Philoxenus, *Mysians* (*PMG* 826) – dithyramb
> Timotheus, *Persians* (*PMG* 791) – nome
> (Perhaps) Philoxenus, *Komastes* (?) (*PMG* 825) – dithyramb

Keeping in mind the crudity of the poetic panorama that is generated by a mere overview of surviving titles and the distortion necessarily introduced by the thematic and ideological biases of the sources preserving those titles, as noted in Chapter 1, one can venture two observations. First, most of the heroic titles tend to fill in Homeric gaps or explore short episodes of the Homeric, and especially Odyssean, narrative, rather than the main Trojan, and especially Iliadic, themes treated in Attic tragedy (with the exception perhaps of Timotheus' *Ajax*). This is the case with Timotheus' titles, *Cyclops*, *Elpenor*, *Scylla*, and *Laertes*. These four pieces covered aspects of the *Odyssey* narrated in the *apologoi* and could together have composed an *Odyssey* cycle.[56] Similarly, the *Meleager* of Cleomenes treats a topic, the Calydonian hunt, that was treated only in an embedded narrative in the *Iliad* (the speech of Phoenix to Achilles, *Il.* 9.529–86). The surviving fragments also tend to focus on neglected, or minor, heroes rather than on the major Theban or Trojan war characters staged in the Athenian theatre – a feature that will be developed more systematically in the Hellenistic period.[57] Furthermore, there is some overlap between, on the one hand, comic and tragic titles and, on the other, titles of theatrical lyric: the *Persians* obviously meets this assessment, as does Melanippides' *Danaids*, which overlaps with a play that belonged to the Aeschylean trilogy which included the *Suppliants*. The most significant overlap, however, is between titles of dithyrambs and nomes and titles of satyr drama. Euripides composed a satyr-play entitled *Cyclops*, a topic that was treated in at least four late classical dithyrambs and nomes, by Timotheus (*PMG* 780–3), Philoxenus (*PMG* 815–24), Oeniades, and Stesichorus II (*PMG* 840); Achaeus had a *Linos satyrikon* (*TGrF* II F 6),

---

[55] Aristotle (*Poet.* 1451b20–1) makes a point of stating that Agathon composed a tragedy based on a fiction, *Antheus*.

[56] Gerhard (1938), first editor of the Heidelberg fragments, attributed *PMG* 925 to Timotheus' *Elpenor*, but Page (1942: 389) doubts the attribution to Timotheus, mostly on stylistic grounds. On the Odyssean cycle, Hordern 2002: 12–13.

[57] On "epic in a minor key" in the Hellenistic period, Fantuzzi and Hunter 2004: 191–245.

which was the topic of a dithyramb of Melanippides,[58] and three titles or themes treated in dithyrambs, *Argo* (*PMG* 805), *Atlas* (*PMG* 837), and *Persephone* (*PMG* 759), were possibly also titles of satyr-plays.[59]

The thematic continuity between dithyramb and satyr-play is reinforced by the marked musical, or metamusical, interest shown by both genres.[60] Other titles are inherently musical, for example *Marsyas*, *Linus*, and *Hymenaeus* (the latter two of whom have musical connections already mentioned by Pindar, fr. 128c SM, 7–9), and the intriguing *Dithyrambs* of Licymnius.[61] The hero Hymenaeus actually appeared in Licymnius' *Dithyrambs*, where he was said to be the lover of Argynnus. Although it is not clear whether Hymenaeus was the main subject of the whole composition or only mentioned incidentally, a note by Philodemus informs us about Licymnius' treatment of one aspect of his myth:[62]

> φησὶν δὲ καὶ [Κλε]ιὼ τὴν Μοῦσα[ν ἀνδρὸ]ς ἐρασθῆναι [Λι]κύ[μ]νιος, οἱ δὲ καὶ [τὸ]ν Ὑ[μ]ένα[ιο]ν υἱὸν α]ὐτῆς [εἶν]αι νο[μίζουσι]ν.
>
> Licymnius, *PMG* 768A = Philodem. *De piet.*: *P. Herc.* 243.vi.12–18

> According to Licymnius, the Muse Clio as well fell in love with a man, and some think that Hymenaeus was her son.

Beyond the musical connotations of the hero, these last two titles and testimonies open onto another thematic aspect present throughout the surviving fragments: the New Musicians' interest in narrative "romance."

Romance, pastoral, and exoticism

As Mark Griffith summarizes, "romance" and "romantic" have two distinct but overlapping spheres of meaning:

(i) works of fiction that include themes of travel, adventure, exotic location, and often erotic encounters, too, culminating in a happy ending... (ii) erotic

---

[58] *Linos* is also the title of a comedy by Alexis (140 KA).

[59] *TGrF* II *Argo*: F 1e, *Atlas*: F 1f, *Persephone*: F 8h. Also Griffith 2008: 74 n. 50.

[60] Some titles in particular suggest a topic that could be embodied by a dithyrambic chorus of fifty men or boys: the fifty daughters of Danaus in Melanippides' *Danaids*, for example, and perhaps, although there is no way to prove it, the fifty daughters of Nereus in Philoxenus' *Cyclops*, on the model of Bacchyl. 15, which staged the fifty sons of Antenor: on which Fearn 2007: 240–1, 313–15.

[61] *PMG* 768 = Ath. 13.603d. The plural in the title *Dithyrambs* may suggest that the piece, which is by a poet-theoretician, was meant to illustrate Licymnius' language theory, but it might only be the common noun in the plural. Amphis also had a comedy named *Dithyrambus* (frr. 14–15 KA).

[62] On which, Henrichs 1984.

engagement, courtship, sexual passion and falling in love . . . as distinct from "low" and crudely anatomical or violent depictions of sexual conquest and activity on the one hand, and non-erotic representations of marriage and other intimate relations on the other.[63]

Aspects of these themes are treated throughout the Greek poetic corpus, from the Homeric episode of Odysseus in Scheria to Euripidean "romantic" tragedies as well as satyr-plays, especially Sophoclean, as a form of "middlebrow drama,"[64] and they will be further developed in New Comedy, Theocritean idylls, and in the novel. But an interest in romance is probably the most distinctive thematic trait one can observe in the collection of late classical lyric fragments: despite the diversity of the sources from which they are derived, a majority of titles, testimonia, and fragments attest to the late classical poets' interest in both meanings of the term "romance," and to the frequent overlap of these meanings.

The most famous case that combines the two meanings of romance is probably Philoxenus' dithyramb *Cyclops* or *Galatea* (*PMG* 815–24), which adds a romantic twist to the fantastic episode of *Odyssey* 9 by portraying Polyphemus as the unsuccessful lover of the nymph Galatea. A similar slant is given to a story of the dithyrambist Licymnius of Chios, from whom Parthenius draws the narrative of Nanis and Croesus, a tale of seduction and promises, persuasion and deception, in an Eastern setting (*PMG* 772).[65] About other titles, we can only speculate. For example, the title of Lamynthius' song *Lyde* (*PMG* 839), quoted in Clearchus' *Erotica* (fr. 34 Wehrli *ap.* Ath. 13.597a), also suggests a tale of romantic love with an "exotic" (βαρ-βάρου) component. The late fifth-century poet Antimachus had composed a bombastic elegiac *Lyde*, and Lamynthius' poem may have been a model to emulate, in a lighter tone, an "*Antilyde*," although not necessarily in dithyrambic or nomic form.[66] We are also told by Athenaeus that Cleomenes, a poet known as a composer of erotic songs, based a dithyramb on the Meleager story. The story of the Calydonian hunt recounted in the *Iliad* is the central myth of a Bacchylidean victory-ode (*Ode* 5) that stages Heracles facing the weeping shade of Meleager in the underworld. But the version that Ovid preserves (*Met.* 8.260–444) reports a much more dramatic and romantic version of the hunt that includes a love-at-first-sight encounter between Meleager and Atalanta, the only woman among the heroes who came to help kill the Calydonian boar. Ovid recounts how she was the first to wound

---

[63] Griffith 2005: 51 n. 1.   [64] Griffith 2005 and 2008.

[65] The story is preserved in Parthenius, on which Lightfoot 1999: 504–7.

[66] On Antimachus' *Lyde*, Matthews 1996: 26–39. On the difference of meters employed to treat different "levels" of poetry in the Hellenistic poets, Fantuzzi and Hunter 2004: 34 n. 138, 69.

the boar, and the one to whom Meleager gave the hide; how rivalry followed between the heroes whose manhood had been slighted; and how Meleager killed his uncles.[67] We do not know anything about the narrative content or tone of Cleomenes' dithyramb, but the hunt and the love story would have had an appropriately romantic and dramatic (rather than heroic) potential.

As vague or fragmentary as they are, these titles and plot indications suggest that the works to which they were attached opened the possibility for an audience to become voyeurs of a fictional spectacle isolated in its own world, to which they could relate by projection. This is even truer when the plot took place in an exotic location. A general interest in oriental characters is attested in other late fifth-century genres, tragedy, comedy, and epic: Euripides' late plays in particular are often set in exotic settings (*Helen* and *Iphigenia in Tauris*) or stage oriental characters (the Phrygian slave in the *Orestes*) or choruses (including the Phoenician women).[68] Aristophanes stages a Persian envoy, a Scythian archer, and hymns foreign gods (Sabazius and Cybele in the *Birds*); Pherecrates had a comedy entitled *Persians* (frr. 132–41 KA), and Antiphanes the *Scythians* (fr. 197 KA), the *Lydian* (fr. 144 KA), and *Oenomaus* or *Pelops* (fr. 170 KA), in which he "presents a Persian description of the differences between Greek and Persian eating which is similar to those found in *Acharnians*."[69] Choerilus composed an epic *Persika* (*SH* 316–23), and tragic fragments also illustrate an interest in oriental themes.[70] New Music compositions with titles suggesting an exotic (Eastern) setting included Melanippides' *Danaids*, Timotheus' *Persians*, a dithyramb of Philoxenus entitled *Mysians*, and another possibly entitled *Syrus*.

The thematic interest in exotic lands or people was not new, but there is something specific about the way late classical songs mobilize this exotic world. In David Rosenbloom's economical phrasing, "if tragedy depicts the other as the self, comedy depicts the self as the other."[71] As far as we can tell from surviving dithyramb and nome fragments, melic narratives, tragedy-like, also paint the other as the self. But in the process, the features of the world that the self inhabits take on a richness of their own. I have already described Timotheus' specific mode of engagement with the East: the direct speeches favor a Persian point of view, but in place of the speech

---

[67] Also Apollod. *Bibl.* 1.64–75; Hyginus 171–4.   [68] Saïd 1984.

[69] Wilkins 2000: 276; also Rosenbloom 2006: 154–6, on Persians in comedy, and Willi 2002.

[70] *TGrF* II *Cresus*? F 5a, *Gyges*, F 664, *Mysoi*? F 327c, *Persai* F 8f. F 685 fr. 3 has a reference to the "race of Persians."

[71] Rosenbloom 2006: 154.

of an omniscient narrator who emphasizes the strangeness of the Persians, the narrative offers an *ekphrasis* that allows an audience to mentally displace itself, to observe and explore. Instead of creating an othering discourse that helps polarize the relationship between listener and narrative world, the poem depicts the detailed features of a world that calls in the audience. Displacement and exploration are privileged by means of a combination of detailed description and unsettling diction that allows access to a world that is both familiar and can be experienced anew, as I discussed in an earlier chapter.[72] We get the impression of a similar strategy in the fragments, as attested, for example, by a few lines of Melanippides. The passage describes the Egyptian Danaids' unusual mode of life:[73]

> οὐ γὰρ ἀνθρώπων φόρευν μομφὰν ὄνειδος
> οὐδὲ τὰν ὀργὰν γυναικείαν ἔχον,
> ἀλλ' ἐν ἁρμάτεσσι διφρούχοις ἐγυμνάζοντ' ἀν' εὐήλι' ἄλσεα πολλάκις
> θήραις φρένα τερπόμεναι,
> <αἱ δ'> ἱερόδακρυν λίβανον εὐώδεις τε φοίνικας κασίαν τε ματεῦσαι   5
> τέρενα Σύρια σπέρματα.

> Melanippides, *PMG* 757

> For they did not bear opprobrium, the reproach of the world, nor did they have a womanly temper, but they exercised on chariots in the groves bathed in sun, often taking delight in hunting, seeking the sacred-tear incense and fragrant dates, and the tender Syrian seeds of cinnamon.

These lines show a particular sensitivity for adjectives that give a feeling for texture, sensuality, or details that require the participation of the listener's senses: sight, in the description of the groves with the sun piercing through the branches (εὐήλι' ἄλσεα) and the sacred tears of incense (ἱερόδακρυν λίβανον), smell for the fragrant dates (εὐώδεις φοίνικας), and touch for the tender cinammon (κασίαν τέρενα) – or a mix of these senses. The Danaids also allow the inversion of the male and female spheres to be experienced vicariously:[74] although their space is outside, not inside, in the sun and not even in the city but in the woods, and although they hunt and exercise like men, they do not give cause for reproach as would women acting as men in "our" world. The narrative creates an atmosphere of fantastic voluptuousness and abundance, an exotic *locus amoenus*, which auditors are allowed to mentally experience through their senses for the duration of the description. Rather than confronting us directly with mythical women

---

[72] See Chapter 4, pp. 161–2.   [73] Hall 1989: 202.
[74] On the gender blurring in the passage, Moreaux 1994–5; also Lloyd-Jones 1968.

acting as men on stage – Clytemnestra-, Antigone-, or Medea-like – and polarizing the relationship between audience and staged characters, the power of the short *Danaids* narrative passage stems from its effect on the senses. Its sensual vividness draws us into the Danaids' world, allowing us to observe and mentally experience it, vicariously, voyeur-like.

This is for the first meaning of "romance." But "romance" in the second sense, with its sexual overtones, is also illustrated by a variety of fragments. A passage of Licymnius describes the love story of Sleep and Endymion:

> Ὕπνος δὲ χαίρων
> ὀμμάτων αὐγαῖς, ἀναπεπταμένοις
> ὄσσοις ἐκοίμιζεν κόρον.
> Licymnius, *PMG* 771

> And Sleep, rejoicing in the rays of his eyes, would make the young man sleep with eyes wide open.

The three lines quoted by Athenaeus capture an atmosphere of softness, tenderness, and quiet contemplation. Athenaeus (13.564c) notes only that "Licymnius says that Sleep loves Endymion," and it is impossible to say whether Licymnius dealt with other aspects of the myth too. But other versions, including Sappho's and Nicander's, made Endymion Selene's lover, with whom he had, Pausanias (5.1.4) tells us, fifty daughters – incidentally, an appropriately dithyrambic number.[75] The same softness is underlined by a fragment from a prose work of *ca.* 200 BC that quotes dithyrambic fragments, and in which the names Melanippides, Philoxenus, and possibly Telestes occur:[76]

> μέλος μαλα[κὸν ἡ]γεῖτο πολ[λ]αχοῦ μὲν ἀποφαίνε[σ]θαι, μάλιστα δ' ἐν τῷ
> τίς ἄρα λύσσα νῷ τιν' ὑφαι[
> *PMG* 929a

> He believed that a <u>soft song</u> was produced in many places, but particularly in:

> What madness, pray, (robs?) us both of a . . . ?

[75] Sappho: fr. 199 Voigt; Nicander: *Etym. Magnum* 153. Agapiou 2005 presents two Endymion traditions: the Helladic/Western tradition of King Endymion, and the Asia Minor/oriental tradition of Endymion and Selene, stating "[Licymnius] nous donne une version singulière du mythe" (33). The fact that some versions make Endymion the son of Calyce might be important, as another late classical composer (Stesichorus II) had a (bucolic) song entitled *Calyce*.

[76] Oellacher 1932.

Although many of the passages that appear later in the papyrus seem to relate to Dionysus (b–f), there is one fragment that evokes not only the same theme (Sleep), but also the same images (that of soft eyes and tenderness), creating a charming little tableau:

>]ε μαλακόμματος ὕπ-
> νος [γ]υῖα περὶ πάντα βαλών,
> ὡσεὶ μάτηρ παῖδ᾽ ἀγαπα-
> τ]ὸν χρόνιον ἰδοῦσα φίλῳ
> κ]όλπῳ πτέρυγας ἀμφέβαλεν.
>   *PMG* 929g

> Soft-eyed Sleep (came), enveloping all his/her limbs, as a mother on seeing her beloved child after a long absence folds her wings around him to her loving breast.

The scene is intimate and delicate and evokes characteristics that are typical of what has been described as the "Hellenistic aesthetics."[77] The compound adjective μαλακόμματος, which actualizes the qualities of Sleep (sleep makes the eyes soft), is reminiscent of the adjective used by Aristotle in his hymn to virtue: μαλακαυγήτοιό θ᾽ ὕπνου ("sleep with languid eyes/which makes the eyes soft," *PMG* 842.8). If the fragment that follows is part of the same narrative, some tragic reversal would have happened:

> ὄμματα κλήσας ἐν δι[
> ταις ἄρκυσιν ἤδη βιο[
> δεσμοῖς ἐνέχῃ.
>   *PMG* 929h

> Closing his/her eyes in ... with hunting nets now ... he holds (him/her?) in fetters.

If this were the case, the two elements, romance and adventure, would be once again combined, but this possibility can be little more than speculation.

"Romance" and "drama"

The second meaning of romance is more specifically developed in narratives that have a distinctly bucolic nature. In addition to a fragment of Polyidus that staged Atlas as a shepherd (*PMG* 837), other late classical "bucolic" love titles figure among the *spuria* for Stesichorus I (*PMG* 277–9). The *Marmor Parium* dates the victory of a "second Stesichorus of Himera" (maybe a

---

[77] Fowler 1989.

lucky nickname that a late classical choral composer adopted?) to the early fourth century BC, and a testimony of the historian Marsyas attributes to a Stesichorus a *Cyclops* that was performed for Philip of Macedon in 353 BC (*PMG* 840). Aelian knew of a Stesichorean *Daphnis*, to which he attributes the beginnings of bucolic songs (τὰ βουκολικὰ μέλη).[78] Aristoxenus (fr. 89 Wehrli *ap.* Ath. 14.619e) also records a fragment attributed to a Stesichorus, a composition entitled *Calyce* (*PMG* 277). This work was sung by women of the past (αἱ ἀρχαῖαι γυναῖκες Καλύκην τινὰ ᾠδήν) and told the tale of Calyce, a maiden with a modest character (ωφρονικὸν τὸ τῆς παρθένου ἦθος) who flung herself from the Leucadian cliff out of despair at not being loved back by the young Euathlus.[79] The passage of Aristoxenus that reports this testimony is quoted by Athenaeus in Book 14 of the *Deipnosophistae*, in a context that describes several kinds of bucolic song involving female deaths and musical aetiologies: the preceding quote from Clearchus' *Erotica* (fr. 32 Wehrli) told the story of Eriphanis (the lyric poetess in love with Menalcas and inventor of the *nomion*) and the next stories, from Aristoxenus' *Brief Notes* (fr. 129 Wehrli) and Nymphis in his *On Heracleia* (*FGrH* 432 F 5b), tell, respectively, the story of Harpalyce (responsible for the invention of a song contest among maidens called, in her honor, the *harpalyce*) and of the Bormus dirge (sung among the Mariandynians during a certain harvest festival). All these songs are aetiological tales for musical practice that tie particularly closely the interest in musical heroes (Linus and Hymenaeus) that I have highlighted above to bucolic and romantic interests.

Finally, a fragment of a *Rhadine* (*PMG* 278) can be added to the list of romantic and bucolic plots. The fragment that has been preserved is a traditional invocation of the Muse and invitation to sing (accompanied by the lyre), but the plot that Strabo outlines, with doubts about the Stesichorean authorship (Στησίχορος ποιῆσαι δοκεῖ), combines romance and adventure,

for it tells how when Rhadine had been given in marriage to a tyrant of Corinth, she sailed there from Samus when the west wind was blowing ... The same wind

---

[78] Aelian (*VH* 10.18) attributes to Stesichorus of Himera the origins of this type of melic composition (μελοποιίας) and recounts the plot of the *Daphnis*: the seduction of Daphnis by the nymph Thaleia, their love pact, Daphnis' breaking of the pact and seduction of another girl, and his subsequent blinding. West (1970: 206) suggests that "a poem on Daphnis might suit the fourth-century writer" and proposes that the *Scylla* ascribed to Stesichorus I could also be the work of Stesichorus II. Rose (1932) had already argued for the attribution of the three *spuria* fragments to Stesichorus II and described the *Rhadine* as "smack[ing] strongly of the typical Greek novel" (90). Contra: Lehnus (1975), who attributes the fragments to the sixth-century poetess Mirtis.

[79] Aristoxenus' reference to ἀρχαῖαι γυναῖκες ("women of the past") would seem to point to the period of Stesichorus I, but Aristotle, Plato, and others refer to poets of the previous generation as ἀρχαῖοι.

carried her brother to Delphi in charge of a mission; and her cousin, who was in love with her set out by chariot to find her in Corinth; the tyrant killed both of them and sent off the bodies in a chariot, but later repented, called it back, and gave them burial.

Strabo 8.3.20

The plot focuses on minor heroes (unknown from other sources), romance, reversal of feelings, and adventure. Strabo preserves the opening lines of the song:

> ... καὶ ἡ Ῥαδίνη δὲ ἦν Στησίχορος ποιῆσαι δοκεῖ, ἧς ἀρχή
> ἄγε Μοῦσα λίγει, ἄρξον ἀοιδᾶς †ἐρατῶν ὕμνους†,
> Σαμίων περὶ παίδων ἐρατᾶι φθεγγομένα λύραι
> ἐντεῦθεν λέγει τοὺς παῖδας.

Stesichorus, *PMG* 278 *ap.* Strabo 8.3.20

> ... and the *Rhadine* that seems to have been composed by Stesichorus and starts: "Come clear-voiced Muse, start †the lovely-named† song and tell the story of the Samian children, accompanied by your lovely lyre." And then it talks about the children.

The greater asclepiadeans in which the song is composed are reminiscent of the stichic meters of Alcaeus and Sappho and would be more appropriate for a solo song than for a dithyrambic performance but, more importantly, the characters, intrigues, and atmosphere are reminiscent of the theatrical plots I have highlighted above.[80] Finally, several fragments of Lycophronides draw from a similar type of romantic material in a pastoral setting. One, in particular, is specifically set in a bucolic setting and takes the form of a dedication:[81]

> ὅθεν Λυκοφρονίδης τὸν ἐρῶντα ἐκεῖνον αἰπόλον ἐποίησε λέγοντα·
>
> τόδ᾽ ἀνατίθημί σοι ῥόδον,
> καλὸν ἄνθημα καὶ πέδιλα καὶ κυνέαν
> καὶ τὰν θηροφόνον λογχίδ᾽, ἐπεί μοι νόος ἄλλᾳ κέχυται
> ἐπὶ τὰν Χάρισι φίλαν παῖδα καὶ καλάν.

Lycophronides, *PMG* 844 *ap.* Ath. 15.670e–f

> This is why Lycophronides makes his goatherd in love say: "This rose I dedicate to you, beautiful dedication, and these sandals and cap, and beast-slaying javelin, since my thoughts are poured out everywhere, toward the girl who is dear to the Graces and beautiful."

---

[80] Rose 1932: 91–2 described the song's composer as a "drawing-room singer, as we might say."

[81] On the fragment, Fantuzzi and Hunter 2004: 177; see Sens 2006: 164 for a comparison between Lycophronides and other Hellenistic epigrams.

This kind of dedication is close to Hellenistic literary epigrams such as the following Theocritean example:

> Δάφνις ὁ λευκόχρως, ὁ καλᾷ σύριγγι μελίσδων
>   βουκολικοὺς ὕμνους, ἄνθετο Πανὶ τάδε,
> τοὺς τρητοὺς δόνακας, τὸ λαγωβόλον, ὀξὺν ἄκοντα,
>   νεβρίδα, τὰν πήραν, ᾇ ποκ' ἐμαλοφόρει.
>
> <div align="right">Theoc. <i>Ep.</i> 2 Gallavotti</div>

> White-skinned Daphnis, who sings bucolic songs on his beautiful syrinx, dedicated these things to Pan: his pierced reeds, his shepherd staff and sharp javelin, his fawn-skin and the leather pouch in which he once carried apples.

Narratively, the passages function in the same way: they rely heavily on *deixis* to create a little drama, where the locutor dedicates objects linked with the bucolic and pastoral world. Lycophronides' fragment, however, is mimetic, in that it is spoken in the first person (by a goatherd in love, according to Athenaeus), while Theocritus', which is in the third person, pretends to be an inscription. While Theocritus' epigram does not say why Daphnis dedicated his things to Pan, Lycophronides explains that the shepherd is in love, and pastoral duties are impossible to reconcile with erotic feelings. We know nothing about the genre of the poem, or even the type of poetry that Lycophronides composed, but the fragment could fit well in a dithyramb on a pastoral theme, where the character has to abandon the semi-fantastic bucolic world as a result of suffering real-world passions. The nature of the internal audience of this little drama – the "you" (σοι) of the first line – remains tantalizingly mysterious. While the deictic pronoun (τόδ') gives the audience access to a world present before its (mind's) eyes, there is no need to presume that the σοι was subsumed under the presence of an actual audience *viewing* this drama: once again, the important element is the *enargeia* of the narrative calling the audience in.

Stepping back from our observation of the surviving fragments to facilitate larger considerations, we can recognize that several of the recurrent themes we have found in late classical melic compositions – pastoral settings, travel, adventure, devoted romantic love – have been discussed by Mark Griffith as staples of satyr-drama.[82] Griffith's analysis enriches and nuances our understanding of the mimetic panorama. As Griffith explains, satyr-drama is close to tragedy in its language and its "mimetic" mode but

---

[82] Griffith 2008: 81.

not in its aesthetics and interest in romantic and bucolic themes. More fundamentally, the case of the satyr-drama reveals that

> if . . . we remove from our eyes the critical blinkers (or Aristotelian bifocals) that have conditioned us to think that (i) tragedy and comedy exist naturally and essentially as the two basic, proper, and best forms of drama (even of "world view"), while other dramatic subforms function only as parodies, offshoots, degeneration, etc. of the two "original" masterforms, and (ii) that "drama" as such was really invented in Athens during the fifth century BCE, *then we may come to appreciate better what a wide range of dramatic enactments and choral impersonations could be found all over Greece.*[83]

I emphasize the main clause because it speaks to the idea that I have sought to bring home in this section: careful examination of the surviving fragments of late classical dithyrambs and nomes allows us to map out distinct ways in which the narrative could engage an audience through its mimetic work.[84] On a continuum of narrative *mimēsis*, the dithyramb is thus closer to satyr-drama than to tragedy in terms of its aesthetics and its interest in romantic and bucolic themes. But its mimetic mode remains fundamentally dissimilar to that of both satyr-drama and tragedy, as the performance is non-matrixed. This type of analysis invites us to downplay the idea that dithyrambs and nomes moved toward drama and dramatization mainly, or primarily, by including greater somatic *mimēsis*, including choral impersonation, introduction of soloists, and grand spectacle. Instead, one should think of "drama" and "dramatization" as having a greater range of meaning in themselves, in that lyric narrative was used to create a specific type of relationship between audience and world represented, a relationship that privileged the audience's work of displacement and projection into a narrative world through wish-fulfillment fantasy, rather than a relationship based on a narrative voice that speaks as religious and civic authority, or as its mirror, for the community. The audience's subjectivity that this engagement of audience and narrated world assumes is fundamental and will be studied more closely in one last example, Philoxenus' *Cyclops*, one of the most famous late classical songs.

---

[83] Griffith 2008: 61 (my emphasis).

[84] Fearn (2007: 305–15) offers a compelling reading of the *enargeia* of Bacchylidean dithyrambs, but distinguishes them from the *mimēsis* of the New Music. The parallel with rhapsodes is very suggestive, but I would be more cautious than Fearn, who states: "Plato makes no mention [in *Resp.* 394], and he also ignores the fact that the New Musical *dithyrambopoioi* of his day were likely to have produced extraordinarily mimetic works, far more so than in Bacchylides' day: these are crucial omissions" (307–8). Rather than seeing his silence as a crucial omission on the part of Plato, I interpret it as coming from his familiarity with the nature – still overwhelmingly narrative, and not "acted out" – of the dithyrambs and nomes performed in his day.

Music from the cave: Philoxenus' *Cyclops*

Some of the narrative issues brought up by Philoxenus' *Cyclops* are similar to those raised by Timotheus' *Persians*, including our understanding of *mimēsis*, dramatization, and "dramatization" in theatrical lyric. But while a significant part of the text of Timotheus' nome is extant, barely more than a few complete lines of Philoxenus' *Cyclops* or *Galatea* have survived. Several testimonies (*PMG* 815–24) however inform us about its likely date of composition: sometime after 406 BC (the beginning of the rule of Dionysius I of Sicily, at whose court Philoxenus stayed and with whom the composition of the *Galatea* is commonly associated) and before 388 BC (the date of Aristophanes' *Plutus*, in which the chorus parodies Philoxenus' – recently produced? – dithyramb).[85] A testimony of the historian Marsyas preserved by Didymus in his commentary on Demosthenes' *Answer to Philip's Letter* (11.22, col. 12.43ss) attests to the reperformance in Philip's time (353 BC) of several *Cyclopes* composed by New Musicians:

The story about the pipers is told in the same terms by Marsyas: when Philip was holding musical competitions shortly before his accident [where he lost an eye] it happened by a strange coincidence that all the pipers performed the *Cyclops*, Antigenidas that of Philoxenus, Chrysogonus that of Stesichorus, Timotheus that of Oeniades.

PMG 840

Given the context and performance scenario described (a musical competition and pipe accompaniment), there is little doubt that Philoxenus' *Cyclops* was a dithyramb. It was, however, in dialogue with many dramatic forms: Cratinus had a comedy entitled *Odysseuses* (frr. 143–57 KA), Callias a *Cyclopes* (frr. 5–13 KA); several New Comedy plays (parodying Philoxenus?) were entitled *Galatea* (Nicochares, frr. 3–6 KA) or *Cyclops* (Antiphanes, frr. 129–31 KA, and Alexis, frr. 37–40 KA). The Cyclops was also the theme of satyr-dramas by Aristias (*TGrF* I F 4) and Euripides, of dithyrambs by Stesichorus II and Oeniades (as seen in the quotation above), and of a composition, probably a nome, by Timotheus (*PMG* 780–3), and other references to Cyclopes can be found in late classical fragments.[86]

The two specific features of Philoxenus' *Cyclops* on which critics have focused are its performance scenario, especially the significance of the scholiast's remark that the Cyclops played the cithara, and the thematic

---

[85] Hordern 1999: 445.
[86] *PMG* 925e (mentioning a *Cyclops*); *PMG* 966 (expression from a *Cyclops*) and *PMG* 997, "unconvincingly ascribed to Pindar by Schneidewin" (Campbell 1993: 401). On the *Cyclops* theme and its relationship with the *Odyssey*, see also Brenner 1949.

innovation it introduced in the Homeric narrative, that of the love-interest of the Cyclops. This latter element resonates with the "romantic" features I highlighted above and was recuperated by the Hellenistic poets, not only Theocritus, in two *Idylls* (6 and 11), but also Callimachus, Hermesianax, and Bion.[87] Duris (*FGrH* 76 F 58) finds the origins of this theme in Philoxenus' lack of understanding of the Sicilian landscape and folklore:

According to Duris, in return for the rich pasture for his flocks and for the abundance of milk (τοῦ γάλακτος πολυπλήθειαν), Polyphemus built a temple to Galatea near Mount Etna; but when Philoxenus of Cythera visited and could not figure out the reason for the temple, he invented (ἀναπλάσαι) the story that it was because of Polyphemus' love for Galatea.

PMG 817 = Σ Theoc. 6(f)

The anecdote contradicts the other biographical story about the origins of *Cyclops* or *Galatea,* which I discussed in Chapter 3 (that tells of Philoxenus at the court of Dionysius), and the competition between different stories about the origins of the Galatea element highlights that the need was felt to explain the new character of the Philoxenian Cyclops. Duris' note underlines two important features: the transformation of the way the poet imagined the Cyclops' relationship with nature and the character of the Cyclops himself. In the *Odyssey,* the rusticity of the Cyclops is midway between utopia and uncivilized monstrosity. The Homeric text depicts the Cyclops' relationship with nature as both magical and primitive (there is never a bad crop on the Cyclopes' island yet Cyclopes are ignorant of laws, gods, or boats) and realistic and sentimental (Polyphemus is very organized in his sheep management and cheese production, yet he is tenderly attached to his ram). By contrast, Philoxenus' Cyclops lives a romantic life, erecting a temple to the object of his amorous desire rather than in glorification of nature. One of the two lines that Aristophanes quotes or parodies in his *Plutus* further shows the Cyclops as a bucolic figure, carrying items typically associated with rustic life:

πήραν ἔχοντα λάχανά τ' ἄγρια δροσερά.
Philoxenus, *PMG* 820 = Σ Ar. *Plut.* 296

with a leather-bag and dewy <u>wild</u> herbs.

---

[87]   Callim. *HE* 1047–52, Hermesianax, fr. 7.69–74, *CA*, p. 100 (= *PMG* 815), and Bion (fr. 16 Reed). Anello 1984 argues that Philoxenus' plot might have been inspired by the Sicilian tradition. On the Hellenistic compositions, Hordern 2004. On the changed nature of the Cyclops in the Hellenistic period, Payne 2007, 70–82.

The line is particularly interesting for its reconfiguring of an Odyssean motive, that of the wildness of the Cyclops, called ἄγριος (Hom. *Od.* 9.494): here, however, it is the Cyclops who is domesticated, and the only wildness is that of the aromatic herbs, in a curious mix of lowly objects and tragic diction (δροσερά, "dewy"). With this transfer, the narrative pulls away from the world of folktales and fantasy and into a more realistic universe where the vegan Cyclops in love goes around carrying his vegetables in a bag.[88]

The question of the type of character (ἦθος) Timotheus and Philoxenus represented in their respective *Cyclops* is brought up by a difficult passage of Aristotle's *Poetics*:

Homer represents men as better than they are, Cleophon as they are, and Hegemon the Thasian, the first author of parodies, and Nikochares, the author of the *Deiliad*, worse than they are. The same is true of the composers of dithyrambs and nomes, as is the case [corrupt] of the Cyclopes that a Timotheus and Philoxenus would represent (ὁμοίως δὲ καὶ περὶ τοὺς διθυράμβους καὶ περὶ τοὺς νόμους, ὥσπερ †γᾶς† Κύκλωπας Τιμόθεος καὶ Φιλόξενος μιμήσαιτο ἄν τις).

Arist. Poet. 1448a 11–16 = PMG 782

Are the two *Cyclops* taken as illustrating the same principle (that is, that they *both* represent worse characters), or is the *Cyclops* of Timotheus contrasted with that of Philoxenus, the latter representing men as worse, the former as better than they are?[89] Where the issue of genre classification appears to be leading us into a dead end, the issue of how an audience relates to the new Cyclops and the experience of past story worlds opens up new avenues.

The characterization of the romantic and domestic Cyclops is part of a larger appropriation of the fictional world of the Homeric episode. Sources indicate that Philoxenus was following the Homeric plot and described Odysseus' being trapped in the Cyclops' cave, blinding Polyphemus, and escaping thanks to his resourcefulness.[90] But one of the most important testimonies about the plot is the beginning of a letter by the late

---

[88]   The characteristic lowly πήρα is found in the Theocritus epigram quoted above.

[89]   For an attempt to solve the problem on philological grounds, Hordern 2002: 107–9. A parallel with Pl. *Resp.* 394c intriguingly brings to the fore three aspects of a more base character – sickness, love-sickness, and drunkenness – which all happen to be illustrated by the plot of Philoxenus' *Cyclops*.

[90]   On being trapped: Zenobius quotes a proverb (*PMG* 824), based on what Odysseus said (οἴῳ μ' ὁ δαίμων τέρατι συγκαθεῖρξεν, "what kind of monster has the divinity shut me in with!") when he was shut in the cave of the Cyclops "in a play (δρᾶμα) by the poet Philoxenus." On the blinding, see scholiast (*PMG* 820), quoted below, p. 239. On the tricks: the conclusion of Synesius' parody states ὁ μὲν οὖν Ὀδυσσεύς, ἠδικεῖτο γὰρ ὄντως, ἔμελλεν ἄρα τῆς πανουργίας ὀνήσεσθαι ("so Odysseus, who had really been wronged, was to profit from his resourcefulness").

fourth-century AD Christian writer Synesius, which Bergk identified as a parody of the *Cyclops*:[91]

To Athanasius, diluter of wine. Odysseus was trying to convince Polyphemus to let him out of the cave. "I am a sorcerer (γόης) and I could be of critical help to you who have been unlucky in your aquatic love affair. For I know incantations and binding spells and love charms that Galatea would not be likely to resist even for a second. The only thing you have to do is promise to move the door or, rather, this door stone, which looks to me as enormous as a promontory. For my part, I will win the girl over and return faster than it takes to say it. What I am saying, 'win her over'? I will produce her here for you, rendered submissive by love charms. She will beg you, and entreat you, but you will feign indifference and dissimulate your feelings. But meanwhile I'm worried that the stink of your fleecy blankets might irk a girl who is used to luxury and bathes several times a day: so it would be great if you swept and cleaned your room and burnt incense inside. And it would be even more great if you prepared garlands of ivy and bindweed to adorn yourself and your sweetheart. But why waste time? Why don't you put your hand to the door?" At this, Polyphemus burst out laughing and applauded with all his might. Odysseus thought that Polyphemus could not contain his joy at the prospect of getting his sweetheart, but Polyphemus touched his chin and said "No-Man, you seem to be a sharp one, a consummate businessman. But apply your cunning to something else: you are not getting away from here."

PMG 818 = Synes. *Epist.* 121 (*Patr. Gr.* 66. 1500B–D Migne)

It is obviously impossible to determine to what degree Synesius was faithful to Philoxenus' plot or diction, or even to ascertain definitively that Synesius is parodying Philoxenus at all. But this version of the plot gives an image of a *Cyclops* that is strikingly close to the impression suggested by the collection of titles and fragments discussed above: the basic setting that Synesius describes, including the obstacle of the monstrous door, is reminiscent of the Homeric narrative, but the types of character, their relationship to one another, and the way an audience can relate to them are different from the Homeric model.

First, Synesius' paraphrase suggests that Odysseus was described as trying rhetoric (ἔπειθε) before trickery as a means of escape, playing off the Cyclops' (erotic) appetite, flattering his pride by comparing his strength to that of a puny mortal, and finally giving him love advice, including recommendations on playing hard-to-get (καὶ δεήσεταί σου καὶ ἀντιβολήσει, σὺ δὲ ἀκκιῇ καὶ κατειρωνεύσῃ, "she will beg you, and entreat you, but you will feign indifference and dissimulate your feelings"). In his speech, and the

---

[91] Hordern 1999: 450–1, 2004: 285–7. For a different take: Holland (1884: 192–6), who argued that Synesius knew the story through Middle Comedy.

advice given to the Cyclops, Odysseus allows an audience to imagine both the setting in which the Cyclops currently lives, and, with comic contrast, the locus of the potential romance: his description transforms the smelly room of the pastoral bachelor, with the realistic Homeric dung and goat smell of the cave (τῶν κωδίων ὁ γράσος), into a *locus amoenus* for a loving couple that has been made appropriate to the nature of Polyphemus' darling, a sea creature who, naturally, "is used to luxury and bathes several times a day " (κόρη τρυφώση καὶ λουομένη τῆς ἡμέρας πολλάκις). Moreover, another important element in this characterization of the Cyclops is that, unlike the fantastic Homeric cave dweller, Philoxenus' Polyphemus sees the world in the same terms as Odysseus and is every bit as good and bad as a man: the Cyclops is presented not as a dense brute ignorant of gods and laws, but as a man who has a weakness (his love for his "aquatic darling"), who sees through people, knows how to characterize them (he labels Odysseus δριμύτατον ἀνθρώπιον καὶ ἐγκατατετριμμένον ἐν πράγμασιν, "a sharp one, a consummate businessman") and even knows literary criticism (he uses ποικίλειν, a very apt term to describe Odysseus' *mētis* and persuasion skills). And Odysseus is not the polytropic hero who conquered Troy, but a man part γόης ("sophist") who knows incantations, binding spells, and love charms (ἐπῳδάς, καταδέσμους, ἐρωτικὰς κατανάγκας), and part professional, ready to sell his services. An audience can relate to the world of these characters in a way that would not replicate their engagement with a Homeric heroic character: the narrative holds out the very possibility of putting oneself in the shoes of both Odysseus and Polyphemus, which would be unthinkable for the Homeric epic.

But despite the humor of the situation, these figures in their revised version are not completely base either, as comic figures would be. Some of the fictional weight of the world of the Cyclops comes from his lingering connections with the Homeric narrative. A *Suda* entry notes that Philoxenus was using Homeric vocabulary:

> ἔθυσα, ἀντιθύσῃ.
>
> τοῦτο παρὰ Φιλοξένῳ ὁ Κύκλωψ λέγει πρὸς τὸν Ὀδυσσέα. ἀπεκδέχονται γὰρ τὸ "ἔνθα δὲ πῦρ κείαντες ἐθύσαμεν" παρὰ τῷ ποιητῇ εἰρῆσθαι ἐπὶ τῶν ἀρνῶν, οὐχὶ δὲ τὸ †"ἀπεθύσαμεν"† [ἐθυμιάσαμεν ci. Bernhardy] νοεῖσθαι.
>
> *Suda* E 336 (ii 211–12 Adler) = *PMG* 823

> "You have sacrificed: you will be sacrificed." This is what the Cyclops says to Odysseus in Philoxenus. Homer's 'then we lit a fire and made a sacrifice' [*Od.* 9.231] is misinterpreted as referring to the lambs, as opposed to meaning '†we made offerings†'.

I would suggest that Philoxenus is not misreading the Homeric passage but, rather, is making the Cyclops reinterpret his own poetic ancestry and self-consciously, intertextually, construct his post-Homeric identity. As we have seen in the case of Timotheus, the power of the intertext resides in the transformation of the character from a heroic, mythical, fantastic figure into an individual whose world the audience can approach, and even project into, and whose "texture" is partly familiar (but *only* partly familiar) to them from other fictions, more specifically Homeric fictions.

Besides illustrating the late classical authors' more general interest in erotic themes and adventures in exotic lands, the combination of the love of the Cyclops with the travels of Odysseus opens up the possibility of a more domestic "drama": because the Cyclops is presented as a musical lover, rather than as an anthropophage who cannot hold his liquor, the poet invites an audience to operate the wish-fulfillment fantasy characteristic of the type of subjectivity I have described. The audience of the dithyramb is allowed to overhear the Cyclops' love song meant for his beloved:

> ὦ καλλιπρόσωπε χρυσεοβόστρυχε ⟦Γαλάτεια⟧
> χαριτόφωνε θάλος Ἐρώτων.
> Philoxenus, *PMG* 821

> O beautiful-faced, golden-tressed Galatea, grace-voiced offshoot of the Loves.

Athenaeus, who quotes the passage (13.564e–f), interprets the lack of reference to the nymph's eyes as a premonition of the Cyclops' own blindness and contrasts it with the praise that Ibycus addresses to Euryalus (*PMG* 288). But although Polyphemus' invocation is reminiscent of many archaic addresses, more important is the fact that the metaphorical "offshoot (θάλος) of the Loves" capping his ascending tricolon reflects his pastoral outlook: the Cyclops calls his beloved with the words in which he sees his world. An audience hearing the Cyclops' song reproduces exactly the process Jaś Elsner has described as "the dynamic whereby the Classical viewer observes a world operating on something like the lines of that to which he or she belongs and attempts to relate to that imaginary world, or to draw some conclusions from its lessons that might be valuable to his or her own context."[92]

How does this mimetic creation of the world of the Cyclops in love, and of the new character of the Cyclops, relate to the performance scenario of the dithyramb? One feature that the preserved fragments suggest is that

---

[92] Elsner 2006: 87.

the poetic "I" changes throughout the song (it refers to Odysseus in *PMG* 824, but the Cyclops uses "you" in *PMG* 823). Alternation between *personae loquentes* occurs in other dithyrambs and does not need to be understood as involving a change in speaker, but recent criticism has largely explored Philoxenus' *Cyclops* in this light. On the basis of the scholiast's reference to the Cyclops playing the cithara, it has been suggested that the *Cyclops* was mimetic (dramatic) to the point of including a solo actor, who would have enacted the Cyclops playing the cithara while the chorus played the part of Odysseus and his companions.[93] Part of this interpretation takes at face value the ancient testimonies' vagueness about the performance scenario or genre. The scholiast on Aristophanes' *Plutus* calls Philoxenus a διθυραμβοποιός ("dithyrambic poet"), τραγῳδιδάσκαλος ("leader of the tragic chorus"), or simply τραγικός ("tragic"); he also refers to the *Cyclops* as δρᾶμα ("drama"?)[94] and seems to refer to an actor:

Σ Ar. *Plut.* 296 (RV): "With your leather bag" (πήραν ἔχοντα): this expression too is taken from Philoxenus ... (Junt.) Here the poet playfully reports the words of Philoxenus, who says that (τὰ τοῦ Φιλοξένου εἰπόντος) the Cyclops carries a leather bag and eats vegetables. For this is the way he has made the <u>actor</u> playing the Cyclops who enters the stage (πεποίηκε τὸν τοῦ Κύκλωπος <u>ὑποκριτὴν</u> εἰς τὴν σκηνὴν εἰσαγόμενον). Aristophanes also recalls the blinding, since it was in the poem (ἐν τῷ ποίηματι). All this he says to ridicule Philoxenus as not saying the truth. For the Cyclops, according to Homer, ate flesh, and not vegetables. What Philoxenus said there (ἃ τοίνυν ἔφησεν ἐκεῖ ὁ Φιλόξενος) the Aristophanic chorus repeats.

PMG 820

The entry indicates that the scholiast was thinking of the *Cyclops* as a mimetic (that is, non-diegetic) form, complete with props. The idea is partly derived from Aristophanes' parody itself, which is a dialogue between solo actor (Cario, parodying Polyphemus) and chorus (parodying the dithyrambic chorus).

But while the scholiast refers to props, *skēnē*, and actor, he also describes the *Cyclops* as a ποίημα and refers twice to what Philoxenus "says." The

---

[93] Power (forthcoming) discusses the agonic relationship between cithara music and *aulos* music, as well as between nome and dithyramb. For Power, the "Kyklōps citharōidos" of Philoxenus' dithyramb would be "parodically reenacting 'Timotheus' Polyphemus' in particular – Polyphemus as represented by Timotheus in his *Cyclops*, [a] *nomos* [appropriating the] dramatic and Dionysiac style and content [of a dithyramb]." If I understand Power's point correctly, Aristophanes, in his comedy, would thus be taking it one step further: the comedy would be parodying the (Philoxenian) dithyramb, itself parodying the (Timothean) nome playing off dithyrambic style and content.

[94] Σ Ar. *Plut.* 290 (lines 15 and 19). On the *Cyclops* as drama, Sutton 1983 and Griffith 2008: 67–8. *Suda* T 265 (iv 518 Adler) also calls Telestes κωμικός, his production δράματα.

scholiast's explanation of the other line of Philoxenus parodied by Aristophanes is equally confusing:

Σ Ar. *Plut.* 290: Aristophanes is mocking Philoxenus the tragic poet, who introduced Polyphemus playing the cithara (εἰσήγαγε κιθαρίζοντα). "Threttanelo" is a kind of melody and musical sound... He is mocking the dithyrambic or tragic poet Philoxenus, who had written (ἔγραψε) of the love of the Cyclops for Galatea. Then to imitate the sound of the cithara in the writing (ἐν τῷ συγγράμματι), he uses the word "threttanelo." For there Philoxenus introduces (εἰσήγαγε) the Cyclops playing the cithara and provoking Galatea.

PMG 819

Once again, the scholiast seems to suggest that Polyphemus entered the stage playing the cithara. But εἰσήγαγε τὸν Κύκλωπα can also be interpreted not as the mode of performance of the dithyramb, but as referring to a *thematic* innovation introduced by Philoxenus. Further, indeed, we also have εἰσήνεγκε τὸν Κύκλωπα ἐρῶντα τῆς Γαλατείας, which can only mean "he introduced the theme of the Cyclops in love with Galatea" – not that he brought the Cyclops on the stage as he was loving (kissing?) Galatea.[95] The *Suda* entry to θρεττανελώ seems to confirm this interpretation:

Θρεττανελώ: ἦχος κιθάρας. Φιλόξενον γὰρ τὸν διθυραμβοποιὸν ἢ τραγῳδιοδιδάσκαλόν φασι γράψαι τὸν ἔρωτα τοῦ Κύκλωπος, τὸν ἐπὶ τῇ Γαλατείᾳ. εἶτα κιθάρας ἦχον μιμούμενον ἐν τῷ ἐπιγράμματι τοῦτο εἰπεῖν τὸ ῥῆμα, θρεττανελώ. ἐκεῖ γὰρ εἰσάγει τὸν Κύκλωπα κιθαρίζοντα καὶ ἐρεθίζοντα τὴν Γαλάτειαν. ἐπεὶ οὖν ἔφη ὁ χορός, ὡς ἥδομαι, ἔφη καὶ ὁ οἰκέτης, κἀγὼ βουλήσομαι χορεύειν· καὶ ἅμα ἀναφωνεῖν τὸ μέλος ἐκεῖνο. ἡ γὰρ κιθάρα κρουομένη τοιοῦτον μέλος ποιεῖ, θρεττανελώ, θρεττανελώ.

Suda Θ 475 (ΙΙ 727 Adler)

Threttanelō: the sound of the cithara. The dithyrambic or tragic poet Philoxenus, they say, wrote about the love of the Cyclops for Galatea. Then to imitate the sound of the cithara he uses the term in the epigram/short poem (ἐν τῷ ἐπιγράμματι) *threttanelō*; indeed [Philoxenus] introduces the Cyclops playing the cithara and provoking Galatea. So the chorus says "how happy we are" and the slave also says "and I would like to dance and accompany vocally that melody." For when it is played, the cithara makes the sound *threttanelō, threttanelō*.

---

[95] Similarly, Sommerstein 2001: 156: "some ancient statements imply a performance (contrary to the normal conventions of dithyramb) with individual actors, costumes and properties, but this may be guesswork." Also Torchio 2001: 148–9: "Il fatto che nel *Pluto* θρεττανελώ non sia *extra metrum* indica che *probabilmente nell' originale il ciclope imitava con la voce il suono della cetra*" ("the fact that in the *Plutus* *threttanelō* is not *extra metrum* indicates that probably in the original too the Cyclops was imitating with his voice the sound of the cithara," my emphasis).

The last words spoken by the slave appear neither in Aristophanes nor in the scholia, and it is possible that they were in the original text of Philoxenus. The reference to the epigram/short poem (τῷ ἐπιγράμματι) is equally puzzling. One possible interpretation is that it was the song that Philoxenus was addressing to Galatea. The *Suda* here opens up a different possibility: that the Cyclopic cithara-playing was not *actually* done, but only evoked by the Cyclops in his song or described by the narrator. Aristophanes' parodic θρεττανελώ θρεττανελώ would then be a debunking of the Cyclops' evocation of cithara music in his song rather than of the song's accompaniment, just as τοφλαττοθρατ τοφλαττοθρατ is an Aristophanic shorthand for mocking the archaizing music of Aeschylus, without necessarily implying that Aeschylus' music was actually performed on stage to the cithara, either by Aeschylus or by Euripides.[96] Seen in this light, Aristophanes would be making fun of the love song of the Cyclops, imagined as performed to the cithara and described in the narrative of the dithyramb.

   All in all, the scholiasts' notes with their inconsistencies in the description of Philoxenus (as tragic or dithyrambic poet) and his composition (as drama or dithyramb) are more revealing of the flexibility of the scholiasts' vocabulary than of a change in the mode of performance of the dithyramb, from choral to dramatic or with cithara accompaniment either throughout or episodically.[97] One last detail, of which scholars have made relatively little use in this context, deserves consideration. Plutarch discusses a passage where "Philoxenus says that the Cyclops tries to cure his love 'with the beautiful-voiced Muses'" (Μούσαις εὐφώνοις ἰᾶσθαί φησι τὸν ἔρωτα Φιλόξενος).[98] The scholiast to Theocritus *Idyll* 11 reports the same scenario but adds the pointed detail that the Cyclops "ask[s] the dolphins to report to her [Galatea] that he is healing his love with the Muses" (ταῖς Μούσαις τὸν ἔρωτα ἀκεῖται).[99] The Cyclops' representation of love as something to be cured accords with the "intellectualizing condemnation of the passion of love" that Hellenistic poets will develop further.[100] But more importantly for our purposes here, dolphins, "lovers of the *auloi*" (Σ Theoc. 11.1–3b), were connected with the dithyramb and its mythical inventor, Arion (Hdt. 1.23–4).[101] In telling how the Cyclops uses the dolphins as his messengers – an expedient way for Polyphemus to communicate with his

---

[96] Borthwick 1994: 21–6.

[97] Franklin (forthcoming) argues that there is a tradition of citharodic dithyramb, probably started with Arion. Hordern (2004) minimizes the dramatic element.

[98] Plut. *Mor.* 622c (*Quaest. conv.* 1.5.1) = PMG 822.   [99] Σ Theoc. 11, 1–3b.

[100] Fantuzzi and Hunter 2004: 180–2.

[101] On Dionysus' chorus of dolphins, Csapo 2003. Also Eur. *El.* 435 and the parody at Ar. *Ran.* 1317.

aquatic darling – the dithyrambic narrative performed to the sound of the *aulos* would reinforce a connection with traditional choral performance and showcase the actual *aulos* that was heard on stage. In place of an audience ravished by the spectacle of the Cyclops playing the cithara (and perhaps stealing the *aulos'* show), I propose we picture an audience seduced by the music of the *aulos* leading the dithyramb and *imagining* a cithara-playing Cyclops portrayed in a song itself sung by the fifty-strong chorus (replicating a chorus of Nereids and Dionysus-loving dolphins?).

This interpretation locates the *mimēsis* at a different level, in line with the argument I have made throughout this chapter. Rather than dramatic *mimēsis*, that is, impersonation by a soloist to whom a chorus would be responding, it is the narrative *mimēsis* of the song that interests me. I suggest that through narrative means the *Cyclops* or *Galatea* allowed an audience to get mentally close to a fictional world replete with its space and characters. In part this process took shape by developing the story world of the epic tradition (here *Odyssey* 9). Within this universe, the narrator created a "romantic drama" (in the two senses of exotic fiction and love plot) with which an audience could identify and connect thanks to wish-fulfillment fantasy. Here, then, I have argued, we find the features that most effectively distinguish the narrative of New Music dithyrambs and nomes from earlier, pre-Bacchylidean, lyric: not only the type of character represented but also the way in which the narrator engages his audience, for he does not address them directly, but offers them a world to contemplate in "imaginative absorption"[102] and experience vicariously.

Conclusion: *mimēsis* and the invention of the musical voyeur

This chapter makes a big claim, namely that the principal innovation of late classical lyric is a change in artistic *mimēsis* and the construction of a new type of audience subjectivity. Timotheus' *Persians*, Philoxenus' *Cyclops*, and other surviving fragments of late classical theatrical lyric attest to significant changes in the kind of stories told in theatrical lyrics, in the way these stories were told, and in the response they called for in their audience. More specifically, detailed analysis of Timotheus' *Persians* suggests that the novelty of this nome resided in the type of response it asked for in an audience: mental transport into the partly fictional past of the battle of Salamis, and direct observation of its fantastic characters. Once there, the

---

[102] Elsner 2006: 88.

listener is given multiple speeches to observe and respond to. These speeches are not so much realistic – that is, spoken in the audience's own language – as they are credible, for they are based on other fictions whose language an audience might be familiar with. With the exception of the *sphragis* of Timotheus' *Persians*, which I have analyzed, the narratives of the New Music never address an audience directly: whether in the narration or the direct speeches, the audience is called in to observe a fantastic world full of characters that stimulate the imagination, to which they can respond with a variety of fictional scenarios. In light of this reliance on the audience's subjectivity, the choice of themes cannot be conceived in isolation from the mode of representation: most of the fragments treat themes that are not epic or are previously unexplored myths that left room for emotional responses. These new themes (bucolic, romantic, and escapist intrigues familiar from late-Euripidean tragedy) announce concerns and an aesthetic proper to the Hellenistic age. If one can talk about naturalism, it is to be found less in the conformity of the characters depicted to "real" people or in the representation of their "true" emotions than in the relationship between the audience and these characters, a relationship of voyeurship, rather than a relationship of authority. Language is equally part of this strategy: the language of these fragments is not the language of tradition and authority, with a commanding anchorage in things, but a language that asks a listener to take a position as interpreter and make hermeneutic choices. It is as elusive, and personal, as the relationship the audience establishes with the narrative content. It elicits multiple responses, but it also calls the listener to answer back with an interpretation, both features of the changed role of the audience in the consumption of theatrical lyric.

6 | Sympotic mix: genre, voice, contexts

> I never saw any thing equal to the comfort and style – candles
> everywhere. – I was telling you of your grandmamma, Jane. – There was
> a little disappointment. – The baked apples and biscuits, excellent in
> their way, you know; but there was a delicate fricassee of sweetbread and
> some asparagus brought in at first, and good Mr. Woodhouse, not
> thinking the asparagus quite boiled enough, sent it all out again. Now
> there is nothing grandmamma loves better than sweetbread and
> asparagus – . . . Well, this is brilliant! I am all amazement! Could not
> have supposed any thing! – Such elegance and profusion! – I have seen
> nothing like it since – Well, where shall we sit? Where shall we sit?
>
> Jane Austen, *Emma*

The previous chapter highlighted an important innovation in late classical
theater lyric, namely a change in the nature of the relationship between
audience and world represented that is based on a larger cultural shift
in the construction of audience subjectivity. I now want to extend this
examination of narrative modes and return to the relationship between
fictional world, mode of narrative, and actual performance setting in contexts that extend beyond theater music, by focusing on three late classical texts: Philoxenus' *Dinner Party* (*PMG* 836), Aristotle's *Hymn to Virtue*
(*PMG* 842), and Ariphron's *Hymn to Health* (*PMG* 813). Other than their
dactylo-epitrite meter these three songs have at first sight relatively little in
common. As its title suggests, Philoxenus' *Dinner Party*, a long narrative
attributed to a dithyrambic poet, deals with a gastronomic theme. Aristotle's song, variously called a scolion or a paean, is a short hymn praising
Virtue and celebrating the memory of his friend and father-in-law, Hermias.
Finally, Ariphron's composition, performed by Athenaeus' characters in
the last pages of the *Deipnosophistae* to close the learned symposium, is a
short prayer to Health. Yet, despite these differences in theme and mode
of address, all three songs share, first, that their genre has been a matter
of debate and, second, that they rely in some way on traditional sympotic
themes, motives, and forms known from archaic poetry: Philoxenus' narrative describes a dinner party followed by a symposium and Aristotle's and

Aristonous' compositions rely on motives of songs performed at a symposium. This chapter will first examine how these late classical songs use the memory of older sympotic forms and motives and rework this inherited tradition in new and varied narrative ways, and will then focus on how these songs could, and did, adapt to various performance contexts. My interest is less in defining the genres of these pieces than in arguing, through case studies, against the notion of "generic crossing," a phenomenon often seen as the hallmark of Hellenistic compositions and mobilized to explain the innovative features of some compositions in the early classical period.

Philoxenus' *Dinner Party*: food fiction

Mysterious fare

Philoxenus' *Dinner Party* (*PMG* 836), a description of a sumptuous dinner party followed by sympotic entertainment, is one of the longest surviving sets of late classical fragments, with five fragments amounting to seventy-five lines quoted by Athenaeus. Everything about it is mysterious: its date, its author, its genre, and, most of all, its purpose.[1] I do not claim to solve all of these problems here but, picking up on issues raised in Chapter 5, I focus on a question that has hardly ever been examined, that of the poem's narrative voice and its creation of a fictional world.

The first of the five fragments describes a symposium-like scene:

> κατὰ χειρὸς δ᾽　　　　　　　　　　1
> ἤλιθ᾽ ὕδωρ ἁπαλὸς
> 　παιδίσκος ἐν ἀργυρέᾳ
> 　　πρόχῳ φορέων ἐπέχευεν,　　　　2
> εἶτ᾽ ἔφερε στέφανον
> 　λεπτᾶς ἀπὸ μυρτίδος εὐ-
> 　　γνήτων κλαδέων δισύναπτον.　　3
> Philoxenus, *PMG* 836 fr. a

On our hands, a delicate little slave boy carrying a silver pitcher poured forth much water. Then he brought a wreath made of well-born twigs of delicate myrtle, double-plaited.

---

[1] Because of its narrative content, the song is mentioned in a number of studies about food – Dalby 1987, Olson and Sens 1999: 24–9 and 2000: xxviii–xliii, Wilkins 2000: 341–54 – but it has never been the subject of a detailed literary commentary.

This portrayal is reminiscent of sympotic scenes described by, among others, Xenophanes and Ion of Chios:[2]

νῦν γὰρ δὴ ζάπεδον καθαρὸν καὶ <u>χεῖρες</u> ἁπάντων
καὶ κύλικες· πλεκτοὺς δ᾽ ἀμφιτιθεῖ <u>στεφάνους</u>,
ἄλλος δ᾽ εὐῶδες μύρον ἐν φιάλῃ παρατείνει
κρητὴρ δ᾽ ἔστηκεν μεστὸς ἐυφροσύνης·
ἄλλος δ᾽ οἶνος ἑτοῖμος, ὃς οὔποτέ φησι προδώσειν,   5
μείλιχος ἐν κεράμοις, ἄνθεος ὀζόμενος
ἐν δὲ μέσοις ἁγνὴν ὀδμὴν λιβανωτὸς ἵησιν,
<u>ψυχρὸν δ᾽ ἐστὶν ὕδωρ καὶ γλυκὺ καὶ καθαρόν</u>
παρκέαται δ᾽ ἄρτοι ξανθοὶ γεραρή τε τράπεζα
τυροῦ καὶ μέλιτος πίονος ἀχθομένη·   10
Xenophanes, fr.1.1–10 W²

Now the floor is pure, and everybody's <u>hands</u> and the cups; plaited <u>wreaths</u> are put on, another one puts fragrant myrrh in a bowl; the mixing bowl stands there, full of festive joy; another wine is ready, promising never to abandon us, mild in the jars, giving out its bouquet. And <u>there is water, cool and fresh and pure</u>: yellow bread-loaves are lying at hand, and a majestic table heavy with cheese and rich honey.

and

χαιρέτω ἡμέτερος βασιλεὺς σωτήρ τε πατήρ τε·
ἡμῖν δὲ κρητῆρ᾽ οἰνοχόοι θέραπες
κιρνάντων <u>προχύταισιν ἐν ἀργυρέοις</u>· †ὁ δὲ χρυσός
οἶνον ἔχων <u>χειρῶν</u> νιζέτω εἰς ἔδαφος†.
Ion of Chios, fr. 27.1–4 W²

Let him be welcome, our king, savior, and father: let the wine-pouring servants mix the crater for us <u>in silver pitchers</u>; and let the one who holds [corrupt] wine wash our <u>hands</u> onto the floor.

All three passages describe the same setting and objects, but the performative status, position of the narrator, and speech situation created by each text varies. In Xenophanes, the narrator establishes a sense of immediacy and brings the scene before an audience's eyes by using a deictic (νῦν) and present tenses, creating the illusion of a symposium happening right here

---

[2] On the self-reflexivity of the symposium, Hobden 2013: Chapter 1.

and now. This rhetoric of presence compensates for a lack of visual detail. It is hard to imagine what exactly a "bowl full of joy" *looks* like, but the narrator's main goal may not be to make an audience visualize the crater; the expression works because the narrator assumes an audience familiar with the appearance of a crater and with its connotations (companionship, conversation, education, flirtation). Similarly, the description of wine as "promising never to abandon us" takes the world of the symposium for granted and speaks of a set of values shared by the company for whom the poem would or could be recited. In terms of pragmatics, the opening deictic, νῦν, might speak to the momentary erasure between the time of the poem's performance and the time described in the poem: the adverb works as both intra- and extratextual marker, as it is once the floor of the symposium room has been cleaned and the crowns passed around that the poem about the symposium would be performed. Here, what narratologists call *deixis am Phantasma* (verbal pointing to what one sees in one's mind's eye) joins for a brief moment *demonstratio ad oculos* (verbal pointing to what one sees in front of oneself).[3] In the same way, the passage of Ion creates the situation of a speaker who *is* at a symposium and orders the course of events. The imperative mood of the verbs not only creates the illusion of performance, it also constructs the world in which these words could be pronounced. When this work was performed at a symposium, again the boundary between the world of the poem and the world in which the poem was uttered would momentarily be blurred.

The fragment of Philoxenus creates a different type of presence. Told in the third person and in the imperfect, it puts a scene before its audience's eyes by displacing that audience into the past as in the Timothean narrative discussed in the previous chapter or in Homeric descriptions of preparations for feasting.[4] Each object is described by a select visual characteristic: the boy is delicate, the pitcher is silver, the crowns elaborately woven. But so far, and undoubtedly to some extent because of the fragmentary nature of the passage, the position of the narrator has not been uncovered: we cannot know whether he was part of the scene and for whom the description is

---

[3] The terms come from Bühler 1934. For an explanation of the terms used by Bühler, Bakker 2005: 155–8 and Edmunds 2008: 85–6.

[4] See, for example, the parallel formula χέρνιβα δ' ἀμφίπολος προχόῳ ἐπέχευε φέρουσα | καλῇ χρυσείῃ, ὑπὲρ ἀργυρέοιο λέβητος | νίψασθαι· παρὰ δὲ ξεστὴν ἐτάνυσσε τράπεζαν ("a servant bringing water poured it from a fine golden pitcher, over a silver basin, for them to wash; and alongside she laid out a polished table") in Hom. *Od.* 1.136–8, 4.52–4, 7.172–4, 10.368–70, 15.135–7, 17.91–3.

intended. The same can be said of fragment d, which describes another moment of the party:

> πίνετο νεκτάρεον
>   πῶμ᾽ ἐν χρυσέαις προτομαῖς   1
>   †τε ἄλλων† κεράτων,
> †ἔβρεχον δὲ κατὰ μικρόν†.   2
>   Philoxenus, *PMG* 836 fr. d 1–2

A nectar-like beverage was drunk in golden animal cups †and of others† made from horns, †and they were progressively drenched†.

Here once again the third-person narrative does not reveal the narrator's presence, position, or impressions. Some elements of an answer, however, can be gleaned from another passage in the song.

Enargeia, ekphrasis, phantasia

The second surviving fragment of the *Dinner Party* opens with a description of the preparation of the room, as if a stage is being created in front of the narrator:

> εἰς δ᾽ ἔφερον διπλόοι
>   παῖδες λιπαρῶπα τράπεζαν   1
> ἄμμ᾽, ἑτέραν δ᾽ ἑτέροις,
>   ἄλλοις δ᾽ ἑτέραν, μέχρις οὗ
>   πλήρωσαν οἶκον·   2
> ταὶ δὲ πρὸς ὑψιλύχνους
>   ἔστιλβον αὐγάς   3
> εὐστέφανοι λεκάναις
>   παροψίσι τ᾽ ὀξυβάφων . . .   4
>   Philoxenus, *PMG* 836 fr. b 1–4[5]

A couple of slave boys <u>brought in</u> a gleaming-faced table for us, and another one for others, and another for others, until they filled the room. They <u>shone</u> under the light coming from lamps hung high, graced with plates, and platters and saucers for side-dishes . . .

There is no connection here to a present time nor to the *hic et nunc* of a performance. Instead, and again with the imperfect, which has a "panoramic force," to use Smyth's expression,[6] the passage creates its own sense of time. Long lines and repetition reproduce the extended preparation for the dinner;

---

[5] I quote from Olson's Loeb edition of Athenaeus; my translation is indebted to his.
[6] See Smyth 1956: 425 on the use of the imperfect.

it takes nearly as long to fill the line as to fill the room. The description also delineates space: in describing the placement of the tables, the narrative follows the narrator's gaze, first horizontally as he looks in front of him to the end of the room, then vertically as he looks up from the table to the illumination high above, then from side to side as he surveys the piles of dishes.

Against the background of the displacement created by the imperfect, the anaphora of ἦλθε in the next lines creates the dramatic structure. Dishes start being brought to the table:

> πάρφερον ἐν κανέοις
> 　　μάζας χιονόχροας ἄλλοι·　　　　　　　　　　　　　　　　　6
> <τοῖς> δ' ἐπὶ πρῶτα <u>παρῆλθ'</u>
> 　　οὐ κάκκαβος, ὦ φιλότας,
> 　　　　ἀλλ' †ἀλλοπλατεῖς† τὸ μέγιστον　　　　　　　　　　　　7
> †πάντ' ἔπαθεν λιπαροντες
> 　　εγχελεα τινες ἄριστον　　　　　　　　　　　　　　　　　8
> γόγγροι τοιωνητεμων†
> 　　πλῆρες θεοτερπές· ἐπ' αὐτῷ　　　　　　　　　　　　　　9
> δ' ἄλλο <u>παρῆλθε</u> τόσον,
> 　　βατὶς δ' ἐνέην ἰσόκυκλος·　　　　　　　　　　　　　　10
> μικρὰ δὲ κακκάβι' ἧς
> 　　ἔχοντα τὸ μὲν γαλεοῦ　　　　　　　　　　　　　　　11
> 　　　　τι, ναρκίον ἄλλο <...>
> <...> παρῆς ἕτερον
> 　　πίων ἀπὸ τευθιάδων　　　　　　　　　　　　　　　　12
> 　　　　καὶ σηπιοπουλυποδείων
> <...> ἁπαλοπλοκάμων.　　　　　　　　　　　　　　　　　13
> 　　　　　Philoxenus, *PMG* 836 fr. b 6–13

Others brought snow-skinned barley-cakes in baskets: after these then first came not a cooking pot, my dear, but [corrupt] the biggest †everything he experienced, shining eels and congers, as lunch, cutting in some way†, full and capable of delighting the gods. After this then came another, just as big, which contained a perfectly round skate; and there were small pots, one with a piece of dogfish, another with a ray . . . Another was there, rich, made of squid and cuttlefish-octopus . . . with their delicate locks.

Each verb creates an apparition – baskets of bread (6), a platter full of eels (8), a plate of ray (9) – and the description continues with a small pot of dogfish (11), some squid (12), a bream (14), prawns (16) . . . The list keeps going on and the repetition of παρῆλθ' ("it came") allows the focus to be on the dishes: the slave boys recede into the distant background and the dishes seem to magically appear, as if of their own volition, piling up one after the other over more than thirty lines. The same form can be found in the last fragment, e (*ap.* Ath. 14.642f–643d), which starts with the same verb as fragment b (εἴσφερον, 2) and describes the accumulation of desserts; by the end of the description, even the verbs have disappeared, giving way to an enumeration of sweets.

In some respects the description echoes fantastic accumulations of food found in comedy.[7] Eubulus, for example, enumerates the same type of extravagant dishes in one of his plays, *Laconians* or *Leda*:

> πρὸς τούτοισιν δὲ <u>παρέσται</u> σοι
> θύννου τέμαχος, κρέα δελφακίων,
> χορδαί τ’ ἐρίφων, ἧπάρ τε κάπρου,
> κριοῦ τ’ ὄρχεις, χόλικές τε βοός,
> κρανία τ’ ἀρνῶν, νῆστίς τ’ ἐρίφου,　　　　　　5
> γαστήρ τε λαγώ, φύσκη, χορδή,
> πνεύμων, ἀλλᾶς τε.
>
> 　　　　　　Eubulus, fr. 63.1–7 KA

Beside these dishes <u>you will get</u> a tuna steak, suckling-pig meat, kid sausages, boar liver, ram testicles, beef tripes, lamb heads, kid intestine, hare belly, black pudding, sausage, lungs, and salami.

Yet the Philoxenian narrator is not simply replicating the mode of comedy. For he does more than evoke an enormous quantity of food, fantastic on account of its variety and quantity – which often includes unappetizing extremities, insides, and fatty parts – and because of the random order in which it is recited. Each item mentioned by Philoxenus is made vivid to the audience by being given specific qualities: the bread is snow-skinned (6), the cuttlefish-octopus – with delicate locks (13), the prawns – browned (16), and the list continues for dozens of lines, with abundant adjectives that help create the synaesthetic poetics I described in Chapter 4.[8] This discrepancy between the fantastic quantity of food and the care given to its description creates a tension that might make an audience pause. Because Philoxenus’ long ekphrastic narration puts a world with a real sensual texture in front of us, it is difficult to decide whether the meal described in all its detail is to be understood as a real meal or as fantasy. Two lines at the beginning

---

[7] On a comic list related to a dinner party, in addition to the fourth-century *Attic Dinner Party* of Matro of Pitane, see, for example, Anaxandrides in *Protesilaus* (fr. 42 KA), ridiculing Iphicrates who married the daughter of the Thracian king Cotys, Alexis in *Crateias* or the *Apothecary* (fr. 115 KA), Eubulus in *Amaltheia* (fr. 6 KA). On such lists, Wilkins 2000: 275–311.

[8] See above, pp. 172–6.

of fragment b offer insight into how one might interpret this strange narrative:

$$†πλήρεις† σύν τε χλιδῶσαι$$
$$παντοδαποῖσι τέχνας \qquad\qquad\qquad 4$$
$$εὑρήμασι πρὸς βιοτάν,$$
$$\underline{ψυχᾶς δελεασματίοισι.} \qquad\qquad 5$$

Philoxenus, *PMG* 836 fr. b 4–5

[The tables were] †full† [of saucers for side-dishes] and with every sort of artful invention for enjoying life, <u>lures for the spirit</u>.

The details are much more than part of the scenery and can be read – as modern scholarship on *ekphrasis* likes to point out – as programmatic:[9] through its insistence on invention, artifice, deception, and art of living in its description of the dishes, and not of the food, the text alerts its audience to important issues and provides clues as to its own status.[10] The plates and serving ware are ψυχᾶς δελεασμάτιοι ("lures for the spirit") and more generally embody the text's poetics of enticement, announcing the dinner to come: these inventions for good living are, like the *Dinner Party* itself, the fruit of a τέχνη ("art"), intended to bring pleasure. But whose ψυχαί ("spirit") will the dishes entice? And what τέχνη is referred to? That of the cook, of the potter who made the dishes, or of the poet who ultimately makes these dishes present for an audience? Thinking back to fragment d, which described the drinking, we can see now another aspect of this aesthetics: the animal cups and the cups made of horn are either taken from the natural world or imitations of the natural world unexpectedly transported into a cultural setting in an artful way that is representative of the whole poem. Here the issues raised by the dinner party as a meal overlap with those of the *Dinner Party* as a song.

Mimetic world

On one level and despite its fragmentary nature, the text works as a unit that constructs a consistent fictional universe for the characters who inhabit

---

[9] Elsner and Bartsch 2007. Fowler (1991: 33) had already clearly noted different approaches to *ekphrasis*: "my sympathies [are] still very much with the organicist New Critical approach which would seek links between ekphrasis and the narrative of which it is part, but ... the challenge of post-modern dislike of this as totalitizing and authoritarian need[s] ... to be taken on board."

[10] As Olson and Sens (1999: 24) observe about Matro of Pitane, "literary descriptions of dinner-parties are almost by definition substantial interpretative acts with their own particular interests, tendencies and agenda, and must be read with an eye to both social and historical reality and the way in which they represent (or misrepresent) that reality."

it, the dinner guests. Through its semantic cohesiveness, the song creates a world of luxury eating and develops an aesthetic, to use Austen's words, of "comfort and style," "elegance and profusion." The delicateness of the boy who serves the dishes is recalled by the use of ἁπαλός and compounds based on it that qualify the dishes he serves: the delicate-locked octopus-cuttlefish (σηπιοπουλυποδείων <u>ἁπαλο</u>πλοκάμων, fr. b 13), the delicate cheese (τυρὸν <u>ἁπαλόν</u>, fr. b 37–8), the delicate youth of the chickpeas (ἐρέβιν-θοι <u>ἁπαλαῖς</u> θάλλοντες ὥραις, fr. e 20). The warm water poured in abundance (<u>χλιεροθαλπὲς</u> ὕδωρ ἐπεγχέοντες τόσσον ὅσον <τις> ἔχρῃζ᾽, fr. b 41) and the reference to being soft (<u>χλιδῶσαι</u>, fr. b 4) suggest the comfort of good living. The slenderness of the myrtle wreath (<u>λεπτᾶς</u> ἀπὸ μυρτίδος, fr. a 3) is echoed by the spider's slender web (<u>λεπτᾶς</u> ἀράχνας, fr. e 10). A whole atmosphere of lightness, softness, and elegance is conjured up by the various adjectives: μελικαρίδες <u>κοῦφαι</u> ("light honey cake," fr. b 16), μαλακοπτυχέων ἄρτων ("breads with soft folds," fr. b 37), μαλακοφλοίδων ("soft-leafed," fr. e 21). This gentleness and delicacy in texture is replicated in the passage's attention to gleams, colors, and reflections (in λιπαρῶπα, fr. b 1; ἔστιλβον αὐγάς, fr. b 3; †λιπαροντες εγχελεα †, fr. b 8), white or light colors (μάζας <u>χιονόχροας</u>, fr. b 6; ξανθαὶ μελικαρίδες, fr. b 16; σχελίδας <u>λευκοφορινοχρόους</u>, fr. b 31; <u>ξανθόν</u> μέλι, fr. b 37).

Just as Miss Bates, the narrator of the epigraph to this chapter, insists on candles, light, and luxury, Philoxenus' narrator captures every impressive detail and constructs for an audience a detailed fictional universe to which its senses give access.[11] The text comes back, however, to the question of appearance and illusion at the end of fr. b:

> . . . ὁμοσύζυγα δὲ
> ξανθόν τ᾽ ἐπεισῆλ-
>   θεν μέλι καὶ γάλα σύμπακ-
>   τον, τό κε <u>τυρὸν ἅπας τις</u>   37
> <u>ἦμεν ἔφασχ᾽ ἁπαλόν,</u>
>   κἠγὼν ἐφάμαν.   38
>
> Philoxenus, *PMG* 836 fr. b 37–8

And also, keeping them company, blond honey arrived mixed with curded milk, <u>which anyone would say was soft cheese</u>, as indeed I did.

---

[11] The question is less one of "realism" or "verisimilitude" than one of "credibility," to use Ruth Scodel's words: it is difficult to assess the status of the meal itself in relationship to the audience's beliefs, but at least the facts of the world constructed cohere internally. Scodel 1999: 9: "Verisimilitude is a property of the story itself, and so can be appreciated even when analysis extracts the story from the discourse; credibility belongs to the narrative discourse." For a modern reader, the meal might not be verisimilar, but in the context of Athenaeus' *Deipnosophistae*, for example, it is only one example of many Gargantuan experiences.

The narrator reveals both the nature of the dish and its deceptive appearance, but he does not reveal how the dinner guests discovered what the dish was.[12] And we realize that none of the details of this dinner party ever evoke the pleasure of eating: we are never told if the prawns were spicy or the skate undercooked. This is a feast for the audience's eyes, not for their taste buds. The audience must imagine for themselves what the guests might have experienced, for they are denied the pleasure of an omniscient narrator.

Here, then, is the second level at which the "lures for the spirit" function. The curded milk that looks like cheese (fr. b 37–8) will trick not simply the guests but also the narrator's audience. The credibility of this dinner party is enforced not by descriptions of the food but through the narrator's control of the imagination of his audience and, first of all, of the internal addressee, the friend addressed five times (either as φίλε, φιλότας, or "you") in fragment b.[13] The vividness of the description, the *enargeia* that I have described in the previous chapter in Timotheus' narrative, is the effect of the narrator's *phantasia*, which Longinus defines in the following terms:

καλεῖται μὲν γὰρ κοινῶς φαντασία πᾶν τὸ ὁπωσοῦν ἐννόημα γεννητικὸν λόγου παριστάμενον· ἤδη δ' ἐπὶ τούτων κεκράτηκε τοὔνομα ὅταν ἃ λέγεις ὑπ' ἐνθουσιασμοῦ καὶ πάθους βλέπειν δοκῇς καὶ ὑπ' ὄψιν τιθῇς τοῖς ἀκούουσιν.

[Longinus], *Subl.* 15.1

The term *phantasia* is used generally for anything that in any way suggests a thought productive of speech; but the word has also come into fashion for the situation in which enthusiasm and emotion make the speaker see what he is saying and bring it visually before his listeners.

In this description with no real drama, *enargeia* produces a "feeling of astonishment and consternation which was experienced by those who witnessed the event."[14] Because the speaker sees the scene, he can make it present for the audience. The interruption in the narration (ναὶ μὰ θεούς, fr. b 20) and the direct addresses to the friend suggest that the narrator wants to make the narratee believe in the meal and does so by relaying his own

---

[12] This exception underlines the general aesthetic of the party: in contrast to what happens at Trimalchio's dinner party, where dishes conceal other dishes and are elaborate experiments in culinary deception, in Philoxenus' *Dinner Party* things look like what they are or are what they look like.

[13] *PMG* 836, fr. b 7, 16, 19, 23, 35.

[14] Plutarch's words on Thucydides, on which Chapter 5, p. 197 and n. 21.

emotions and his disbelief at the sight of such a lavish scene, as is evident in fr. b 25–7:

> ἔγωγ᾽ ἔτι, κοὔ κε λέγοι τις   25
> πάνθ᾽ ἃ παρῆν ἐτύμως
>   ἄμμιν, †παρέπεσαι† δὲ θερμόν   26
> σπλάγχνον.   27

And no one could truly tell all that was there for us, but <u>my rash heart</u> †has persuaded me [reading παρέπεισε]†.

But the narrator also conveys much more than what *can* be seen. He delays, for example, the description of the first plate by alluding to an alternate reality, fr. b 7–9 (also quoted above):

> τοῖς> δ᾽ ἐπὶ πρῶτα παρῆλθ᾽
>   <u>οὐ κάκκαβος, ὦ φιλότας,</u>
>   ἀλλ᾽ †ἀλλοπλατεῖς† τὸ μέγιστον   7
> †πάντ᾽ ἔπαθεν λιπαροντες
>   εγχελεα τινες ἄριστον   8
> γόγγροι τοιωνητεμων†.   9

After these then first came <u>not a cooking pot</u>, my dear, <u>but</u> [corrupt] the biggest †everything he experienced, shining eels and congers, as lunch, cutting in some way†.

The suspense not only makes the enumeration more exciting but also creates, and populates, a mental world. The reference to something that did not appear (a cooking pot) brings in an element that the narratee, or audience, might very well *never* have imagined and therefore carries them into the narrator's mental world – or, at any rate, into the mental world he wants to create.

One passage in the last fragment brings this game of viewing, presence, absence, and fantasy to a new level:

> ταῖς δ᾽ ἐν μέσαισιν   4
> ἐγκαθιδρύ-
>   θη μέγα χάρμα βροτοῖς, λευ-
>   κὸς μυελὸς γλυκερός,   5
> λεπτᾶς ἀράχνας ἐναλιγκί-
>   οισι πέπλοις   6
> συγκαλύπτων ὄψιν αἰσχύ-
>   νας ὕπο, μὴ κατίδῃς   7

μαλογενὲς †πῶυ λιπών
      ταῖς ἀνάγκαις†   8
ξηρὸν ἐν ξηραῖς Ἀρισταί-
      ου μελιρρύτοισι παγαῖς·   9
τῷ δ' ὄνομ' ἦς ἄμυλος.   10
            Philoxenus, *PMG* 836 fr. e 4–10

And in the middle, set up as a great delight for mortals, there was a white milky flan, modestly concealing its face under a veil, like a spider's delicate web, lest anyone should see that it had left the sheep-born flock †out of necessity†, dry in the dry springs of Aristaeus flowing with honey. Its name was *amylos*.

The account starts by conveying visual data, but it quickly moves from a description focalized through the narrator's eyes to a picture that cannot be seen with the eyes but is rather a projection of the mental world of the viewer, which here draws on mythical knowledge.[15] The narrator has constructed something more than a scene: he has delivered a gaze that allows the audience to project their own imaginary thoughts into the sight described. The narrator describing his own spectating is a mythically attuned viewer who connects honey and sheep with the hero Aristaeus, and who is sensitive to a modest female gesture of veiling. The process I described when analyzing the audience's relationship with the narrative in the previous chapter can also be observed here: this puzzling depiction in florid diction relays to us an internal viewer's response to a sight that requires interpretation. On hearing that description, the audience is asked, in turn, to lend a reality as familiar as a pudding a richer interpretation.

Indeed, *phantasia* works both ways: not only does it fashion the narrator's skill in communicating his enthusiasm and *seeing* what he wants to say, but it also influences the audience's emotions and imagination and in so doing, reveals the third and final level at which the lure operates. Beyond its power over the internal audience of the poem – the "you" that is addressed throughout – the description, in the end, manipulates the poem's external audience. By means of direct addresses to an absent person that interrupt the description – just as the narrator addresses Jane in the epigraph from *Emma* – the speaker constructs a whole fiction about his own life and that of the addressee. As Mark Payne explains in words that could also apply

---

[15] As Olson (2006–10: VII ad loc.) notes, "the hero Aristaeus was a son of Apollo and the mortal Autonoe and was associated with shepherding and the production of honey and olive oil . . . But exactly what edible substance is being referred to is unclear."

to the anonymous characters speaking in Timotheus' nome, "the dramatic mode [of address] and the speech of characters is crucial in securing our paradoxical assent to the [characters'] manifestly fictional world."[16] In the *Dinner Party*, the characters' fictional world is created, for example, by reference to their idiolect or common tastes:

πυριων τε †στεγαναί
    φυσταὶ μέγαθος κατὰ κάκ-
        καβον γλυκυόξεες < ... >   18
ὀμφαλὸς θοίνας καλεῖται
    παρά γ' ἐμὶν καὶ τίν, σάφ' οἶδα.   19
†εσταδα† ναὶ μὰ θεούς
    ὑπερμέγεθές τι θέμος
        θύννου μόλεν ὀπτὸν ἐκεῖθεν   20
†θερμὸν ὅθεν γλυφις†
    τετμημένον εὐθὺς ἐπ' αὐτάς   21
τὰς ὑπογαστρίδας. <αἷς>
    διανεκέως ἐπαμύνειν   22
εἴπερ ἐμίν τε μέλοι
    καὶ τίν, μάλα κεν κεχαροίμεθ'.   23
    Philoxenus, *PMG* 836 fr. b 18–23

... coated wine-cakes of wheat grains, as big as a three-legged pot, sweet-and-sour ... They <u>are called "the navel of the feast" at your house and at mine</u>, as I know well. [corrupt] it's true, by the gods! An humungous serving of broiled tuna came from there, †hot from there†, carved straight to the belly-cuts: <u>if it were up to you and us to help them along continually, we would greatly enjoy ourselves</u>.

One could even adduce the addressee's culinary preferences:

τουτ< ... >, ὦ φιλότας,
    ἔσθοις κε.   35
    Philoxenus, *PMG* 836 fr. b 35

You would eat that ... dear friend!

Here we encounter again, as in the previous chapter, the voyeuristic pleasures of an audience. That audience overhears a private conversation between friends, a fictional presence in which two anonymous characters share

---

[16] Payne 2007: 83.

experiences in an encounter that parallels the pleasure one might get from reading a novel.[17] The narrator builds for us not simply the world of opulent dining but also the world of his own relationship with the addressee, real or imagined, and this social dimension, as much as the aesthetic display, brings pleasure to his audience. The weight of the meal lies not in the *ekphrasis* of the dinner itself, but in the way the speaker, who remains anonymous for us, appeals to his own feelings and to those of his internal addressee when evoking the scene.

Ultimately, the situation, just as in *Emma*, is simply that of a staged monologue. We know nothing of the addressee and never hear his voice. But in the long description the tone of the narrator's voice keeps changing and real polyphony is created. The language is sometimes riddling, like the language of the symposium with its elements of *ainos* (the wine cakes, for example, are called ὀμφαλὸς θοίνας, "navel of the feast," fr. b 19; the tables are called λιπαραυγεῖς πορθμίδας, "shining freighters," fr. e 1–2).[18] A whole section of the song, with its focus on sausage, tripe, and innards, also recalls iambic poetry, especially in its thematic connection of the consumption of fatty food, excess, and abuse.[19] It shows both the apparently inexhaustible appetite of the guests (χερσὶν δ' ἐπέθεντο < ... > στόμιον μαλεραῖς, "with fierce hands they placed in their mouth," fr. e 10) and their delight in the stuff of comedy – entrails and body ends (ἀκρωκώλια ... ῥύγχη κεφάλαια πόδας τε χναυμάτιόν τε σεσιλφιωμένον, "extremities, snouts, heads, and feet, and a tit-bit cooked in silphium," fr. b 30–1).[20] Some lines are even reminiscent of Homeric formulae: for example, βρωτύος ἠδὲ ποτᾶτος ἐς κόρον ἧμεν ἑταῖροι, "when we had reached our fill of food and drink," fr. b 39, reminds one of the formulaic ἐπεὶ πόσιος καὶ ἐδητύος ἐξ ἔρον ἕντο, "when they had put away the desire for drink and food."[21] The process of referring to things by two names, one used by the gods, the other by men, is also Homeric and is used in the description of a pudding (τὰς ἐφήμεροι καλέοντι νῦν τραπέζας <δευτέρας>, ἀθάνατοι δέ τ᾽ Ἀμαλθείας κέρας, "creatures of one day call [desserts] 'second tables' but the immortals call them 'the horn of

---

[17] Payne 2007: 11.

[18] On moments of collapse between the language of the dithyramb and the language of the symposium, LeVen 2012 and further below, pp. 260–3.

[19] Steiner 2002 and 2009, on the relationship between fatty food and abuse. The comic fragment of Eubulus quoted above was an example of such discourse, focusing on fat and inferior animal parts. The same type of excessively rich food is consumed in Matro of Pitane's *Attic Dinner Party*.

[20] On the same type of ambiguity in Petronius and Roman culture, Gowers 1993: 30–2.

[21] For example, in Hom. *Il.* 1.469, 2.432, 3.67, 4.73, *Od.* 8.72.

Amalthea'," 3–4).[22] Finally, the *recusatio*, "I couldn't tell… my rash heart persuaded me" (if we read, with Campbell 1993, παρέπεισε δὲ θερμὸν σπλάγχνον, 26–7), is a familiar epic trope.[23] Yet, by contrast with Matro of Pitane's *Attic Dinner Party* (a fourth-century parody and cento of Homer), none of the epic echoes in Philoxenus' *Dinner Party* are ever so obscure as to require from the audience great familiarity with Homeric epic if they are to enjoy the poem or even to make sense of any of its details. Besides these epic tropes, the narrator also inserts elements of didactic discourse, especially in the last fragment, which contains four references to naming: the first is the metaphor used for the tables (πορθμίδας, "vessels," 2), then comes the distinction referred to above, between the name for desserts given by mortals and that given by gods (3–4), followed by a reference to the name of the milky flan (τῷ δ' ὄνομ' ἧς ἄμυλος, 10), and finally a reference to "what is called the dessert of Zeus" (ἃ Ζανὸς καλέοντι τρώγματ', 12). All these references to naming are condensed in the first twelve lines of the fragment; there are no more later. The desserts, moreover, seem listed in alphabetical order according to their periphrastic or riddling name – Ἀμαλθείας κέρας, 4; ἄμυλος, 10; Ζανὸς τρώγματ', 11 – in the sort of riddling word game played at symposia.[24] All these voices and associations alternate, as if the narrator is ventriloquizing the cacophony of voices and the types of poetry that might be heard in the symposium, from scolion to iambic abuse, from Homeric recitation to didactic passages and riddling games.[25]

Symposium and performances

Dinner Party *at the symposium?*

Is the symposium, then, the setting that we should imagine for the actual performance of Philoxenus' *Dinner Party*? A direct address to Bromius in fragment c, reminiscent of the situation of elocution I have described for the passages of Ion and Xenophanes, could very well give the illusion that

[22] For example, in Hom. *Il.* 2.813–14 (for the hill that mortals call "Batieia" and gods "burial mound of dancing Murine"), 14.291 (for the bird that mortals call *kymindis* and gods *chalchis*), and 20.74 (for the river that men call Scamandros and gods Xanthos).

[23] For example, before the catalogue of ships in Hom. *Il.* 2.489 (πληθὺν δ' οὐκ ἂν ἐγὼ μυθήσομαι οὐδ' ὀνομήνω, "I could not relate or name the multitude"). One could also read the reference to a "rash heart" (θερμὸν σπλάγχνον) in a more comic light: "but *warm tripes* persuaded me."

[24] Clearchus, fr. 86 Wehrli *ap.* Ath. 10.448c.

[25] On the variety of poetic forms present at the symposium, Ford 2002: 27–58. All these forms are also present in comedy, which often integrated sympotic forms, on which Wilkins 2000: 204–13, and 229–43 on "sympotic elements in comedy."

the *Dinner Party* takes place at a symposium, before the *komos* (drunken revel):

σὺ δὲ τάνδ᾽ †εκβακχια†   1

εὔδροσον πλήρη μετανιπτρίδα δέξαι·

πραῦ τί τοι Βρόμιος

γάνος τόδε δοὺς ἐπὶ τέρ-

ψιν πάντας ἄγει.   3

Philoxenus, *PMG* 836 fr. c 1–3

> But you, accept this †Bacchic?†, after-washing cup, full and with plenteous dew: Bromius, in offering this gentle refreshment, draws all men to enjoy themselves.

The fragment uses deictic markers (τάνδ᾽, 1; τόδε, 3) and verbal forms that could indicate both a speech act of the narrator (δέξαι, "accept," 2), and a *demonstratio ad oculos* in performance. It is unclear whether the deictic and the imperative refer to an object and an interlocutor internal to the narrative, where the after-drinking cup could be the one around which the narrative is sung, or to a situation external to the narrative.[26] All the more puzzling is that, if the latter, then this would be the only moment in the fragments of the *Dinner Party* that have survived where the narrator connects the world described in the poem with that of a performance.

Despite this lone reference, and the general gastronomic and sympotic theme, a sustained exercise in self-referentiality seems to me unlikely, and I do not believe that the symposium was the original performance setting. The surviving examples of archaic and early classical lyric poetry performed at symposia are never concerned with the subject of Gargantuan food, treated at such length. The few references to food in sympotic poetry are much more sober – only honey and bread are cited in Xenophanes, fr. 1, for example. Moreover, the ideology of consumption in Philoxenus' feast is very different from that developed in most surviving archaic sympotic lyric and elegiac poetry: the *Dinner Party*'s endless display of dishes could not be further away from injunctions to moderation (*to metron*) or references to an ideal of orderliness (*kosmotēs*).[27] While some erotic expectation is set up every time a "tender boy" is introduced in the narrative, there is no further reference to *eros* and no mention of religious concerns either, unlike the καθαρόν of Xenophanes or the libations that follow in the next lines of Ion (σπένδοντες δ᾽ ἁγνῶς, fr. 27.5 W²).

---

[26] Campbell (1993, ad loc.) suggests that the imperative is directed at the "friend addressed in (b)."

[27] On the ethics of the archaic and early classical symposium, Ford 2002: 25–45.

More importantly, perhaps, of the elements often mentioned in connection with the symposium (crowns, perfumes, conversation, game of *kottabos*, all of which appear in fr. e 23–4) one is spectacularly absent: there is no music. One could argue that there may have been long passages about music in the parts of the *Dinner Party* that Athenaeus does not quote. But given Athenaeus' interest in musical disquisitions, it would be very surprising if he had omitted them.[28] The music of words themselves might constitute part of the entertainment: some lines – fr. e 17–19, for example – have evocative assonances and alliterations, with sibilant, liquid, and occlusive consonants that alternate with marked rhythmic effects (ἄμυλος πλαθανίτας σασαμοτυροπαγῆ δὲ καὶ ζεσελαιοπαγῆ πλατύνετο σασαμόπλαστα, *amulos plathanitas sasamotyropagē de kai dzeselaiopagē platyneto sasamoplasta*) and work as tongue twisters.

But there is one more way in which to account for this silence about music. That explanation is linked to the mysterious fragment c, with its reference to Bromius and something Bacchic. The passage might mimic the invitation issued by a fictional guest in the *Dinner Party* to take part in the drinking. I have also suggested that it could be a direct invitation spoken by the performer of the song to another guest, calling him to partake of the wine in the real-life sympotic performance context of the *Dinner Party* as song. But the ambiguity of the reference has a double purpose here. Bromius is the divinity not only of the intoxicated symposiasts but also of the theater, and his two worlds often blend, one setting exploiting the other's associations. This exchange is precisely the kind imagined in an Attic scolion in which the speaker of the lines fantasizes about being a lyre moving to the "chorus of Dionysus":

> εἴθε λύρα καλὴ γενοίμην ἐλεφαντίνη
> καὶ με καλοὶ παῖδες φέροιεν Διονύσιον ἐς χορόν.
>
> *PMG* 900

Would that I could become a handsome ivory lyre and that handsome boys carry me to the Dionysiac chorus!

The erotic overtones are obvious enough, but rather than picturing the imaginary *chelys*-lyre (λύρα), symbolic of elite education and sympotic performance, moving to the theater (where she would cut a strange and soundless figure), one should rather interpret this "Dionysiac chorus" as a riddle: playing on the ambiguity of setting, whether inside or outside

---

[28]   On Athenaeus' musical interests, see Chapter 1, pp. 48–50.

the sympotic context, the narrator works with the double network of associations with Dionysus, as both god of the theater and its dramatic and dithyrambic choruses and god of the symposium and its drunken revel.[29] The riddling and periphrastic expression (the "Dionysiac chorus" for the symposium) is further justified by the sociological continuity between the two locations, with the players of the sympotic lyre likely to be also chorus members in Dionysiac drama who performed their elite identity in another kind of musical context.

Pushing this connection between the two types of bacchic chorus (sympotic and theatrical) further, I would suggest that the references to Bacchus and Bromius in Philoxenus' fragment c point not to the sympotic Dionysiac chorus but to the other setting for Dionysiac performance: the theater, and more precisely the dithyramb. The meter (dactylo-epitrites) and the diegetic form are no different from other examples of earlier dithyrambs that include Pindaric and Bacchylidean narrative, and the narrative form of the *Dinner Party* – what I earlier called "a staged monologue" – corresponds to the diegetic mode that Plato makes typical of the dithyramb in *Republic* 394c. One could even venture to suggest that the deictic τόδε in fr. c 3, quoted above, which intradiscursively picks up the "after-washing cup" (τάνδε μετανιπτρίδα, fr. c 2) might point extradiscursively to the other gift of Bromius (Βρόμιος γάνος τόδε δούς), the dithyramb and its entertainment, and that the account in the next lines of the "draw[ing] all to enjoy themselves" (ἐπὶ τέρψιν πάντας ἄγει) is a fitting description of a dithyramb performed at a festival. If the *Dinner Party* is a dithyramb, then it allows an audience to achieve the ultimate democratic experience described in Pericles' Funeral Oration (2.38) by collapsing the distinction between two spheres described as bringing pleasure to Athens: the public competitions at festivals and sacrifices (ἀγῶσι μέν γε καὶ θυσίαις) and the private elegant home (ἰδίαις δὲ κατασκευαῖς εὐπρεπέσιν). The *Deipnon* takes up a theme that is becoming popular in the late fifth and fourth centuries – elegant food and dining – and displays it in the civic context of a public performance to bring its audience, in the words of Thucydides "relaxation from toil to the spirit" (τῶν πόνων πλείστας ἀναπαύλας, Thuc. 2.38).[30]

In addition to the many descriptions and imitations of sympotic moments in comedy, two comic passages support the idea that the theme of the

---

[29] On the ambiguity of setting, whether inside or outside the sympotic context, the classic article is Slater 1976. On sympotic fantasy and songs relying on escape through the imagination, see Bacchylides' encomium fr. 20B, with Fearn 2007: 27–86.

[30] On the topic of food and elegant dining in the classical period, Olson and Sens 1999: 24–33 and 2000: xliv–lv.

symposium itself, sympotic voices, and musical forms could move from symposium to theatrical stage, a transition made even smoother by the presence of *aulos* accompaniment that provides continuity across both forms. The first passage comes from a play by Amphis teasingly called *Dithyrambos* and probably dating from the second half of the fourth century BC. It presents two characters, of which the first must be a musician or composer of dithyrambs:

{Α.} ἐγὼ δὲ τὸν γίγγραν γε τὸν σοφώτατον.
{Β.} τίς δ᾽ ἔσθ᾽ ὁ γίγγρας; {Α.} καινὸν ἐξεύρημά τι
ἡμέτερον, ὃ θεάτρῳ μὲν οὐδεπώποτε
ἔδειξ᾽, Ἀθήνησιν δὲ κατακεχρημένον
ἐν συμποσίοις ἰδίᾳ ᾽στί. {Β.} διὰ τί δ᾽ οὐκ ἄγεις   5
εἰς τὸν ὄχλον αὐτό; {Α.} διότι φυλὴν περιμένω
σφόδρα φιλονικοῦσαν λαχεῖν τιν᾽· οἶδα γὰρ
ὅτι πάντα πράγματ᾽ ἀνατριαινώσει κρότοις.

                                       Amphis, fr. 14 KA

A: As far as I am concerned, it is the *gingras* [which I like/want],
    a very clever thing.
B: What's the gingras?
A: A new discovery of mine, which I haven't displayed in the theater yet.
    But it's already used to great effect in private at symposia in Athens.
B: Why don't you bring it out before the public?
A: Because I'm waiting to get by lot a phyle that's really keen for victory;
    I know it'll heave up everything, like a trident, with the crowd's
    applause.

The movement imagined for the *gingras* (a small *aulos*) is the same that I suggest for the sumptuous dishes of the *Dinner Party*: from the private symposium to the popular stage. The situation in *Dithyrambos* replicates that of the *Dinner Party*: in neither case is a theater audience given anything to see, hear, or taste. There is no *gingras* on stage in the comedy *Dithyramb*, and nothing is said about a dinner party that matches the *Dinner Party*, but the audience's senses are being teased with the anticipation of the imaginary music or the food, just as they would be teased at a symposium with the anticipation of other pleasures. The audience is given only a character's speech about these wonderful symbolic objects, and the speech, just like the song, vicariously brings "tit-bits from the cultural riches of the upper-class private world of pleasure into the world of the mob."[31] Through his use of

---

[31] Wilson 2000: 69–70.

the narrative framework of the symposium, his description of a lavish meal, and even his imitation of its inside voices, the dithyrambist creates for the duration of a performance the world of elite dining, to which the audience can assimilate and in which it can participate through the riddling language common to symposium and dithyramb.[32] In a strategy also noted in the previous chapter, the song does not address an audience directly but instead calls that audience into the world it has constructed with a wealth of sensual details. Furthermore, just as the reader of *Emma* can distance herself from the narrator, be it poor Mr. Woodhouse or silly Miss Bates, an audience can observe the spectacle of the *Dinner Party* and enjoy its imaginary details in their sensual abundance but distance themselves from the spectacle when it verges on disgusting gluttony, thus showing their discrimination and good taste (by contrast with the voracious dinner guests) and replicating the very process of social identification typical of the elite archaic and early classical symposium.[33]

The second passage giving weight to the hypothesis of a dithyrambic performance of Philoxenus' *Dinner Party* is from Cratinus. This text too seems to refer to the phenomenon whereby the private and at times musical pleasures of the symposium were transferred to the public stage. The fragment satirizes the late fifth-century lyricist Gnesippus for his "chorus of plucking girls":

> ἴτω δὲ καὶ τραγῳδίας
> ὁ Κλεομάχου διδάσκαλος
> †μετὰ τῶν† παρατιλτριῶν
> ἔχων χορὸν Λυδιστὶ τιλ-
> λουσῶν <u>μέλη πονηρά</u>.
>   Cratinus, fr. 276 KA

Let even Cleomachus' son, the producer of tragedy, go away †with his† chorus of slave girls plucking <u>vile limbs/songs</u> to a Lydian tune.

---

[32] On the continuity between the language of the symposium and the language of dithyramb, LeVen 2012.

[33] Compare also Matro and the greediness of the guests depicted in lines 70–1, 93–4, 104, 115–20. Olson and Sens (1999: 27) state: "although the narrator's account of the meal contains reports of a number of vivid individual events and a substantial amount of incidental emotional color, therefore, it is structured more as spectacle than as story, and that spectacle has a decidedly ugly side." And, very helpfully for our interpretation of Philoxenus: "[Matro's] *Dinner-Party* can thus be interpreted as simultaneously a greedy fantasy, by means of which the audience is allowed to see what it must be like to dine with the very richest and most powerful men in Athens, and an implicit attack on the behavior of such people" (28–9). Similarly, Wilkins (2000: 208) notes: "the elegant symposia of the rich are represented, perhaps sometimes to astound, but on other occasions to be satirized."

The fragment has been interpreted in various ways, and part of the joke comes from the polysemy of τίλλω, which means both to pluck strings on an instrument in order to make tunes (μέλη) and to pluck hairs from limbs (μέλη). If the chorus that Cratinus describes is a real dramatic chorus, the situation is a perfect parallel to that of the *Deipnon*: that chorus would be replicating, or just evoking, the Lydian tunes played at symposia, thus displacing onto the civic stage and the civic body of the chorus the private pleasures of the symposium and its "plucking" girls, the hetaerae.[34]

But both references to types of musical performance at the symposium, the old (the Lydian tunes) as well as the new (the *gingras*), invite us to move from reflection on the elite symposium as motive to consideration of the late classical symposium as the locus of lyric performance.

Evolving context

Aristophanes and other comic poets provide us with insight into the symposium as performance context and its evolution in the late classical period that, once again, must be evaluated carefully, as I suggested in Chapter 1. Isolated remarks give us the impression that toward the end of the fifth century, the symposium followed the evolution of other musical venues, with changes that brought an end to an era. Singing while accompanying oneself on the lyre, a traditional aristocratic skill practiced in the social and educational setting of the symposium, is presented as giving way to a variety of innovations. In a scene from the *Clouds*, for example, Strepsiades laments the demise of traditional education. When describing the damage that the new (sophistic) education has done to his son, Strepsiades explains that Pheidippides resists his father's request that he pick up the lyre and sing:[35]

> 'πειδὴ γὰρ εἰστιώμεθ᾽, ὥσπερ ἴστε,
> πρῶτον μὲν αὐτὸν τὴν λύραν λαβόντ᾽ ἐγὼ 'κέλευσα   1355
> ᾆσαι Σιμωνίδου μέλος, τὸν Κριόν, ὡς ἐπέχθη.
> ὁ δ᾽ εὐθέως ἀρχαῖον εἶν᾽ ἔφασκε τὸ κιθαρίζειν
> ᾄδειν τε πίνονθ᾽, ὡσπερεὶ κάχρυς γυναῖκ᾽ ἀλοῦσαν.
>
> Ar. *Nub.* 1354–8

For after we had had dinner, as you know, I asked him first to take the lyre and to sing a song by Simonides, the "Shearing of the ram." But he instantly replied that <u>singing and playing the lyre over drinks was old-fashioned</u>, like a woman grinding parched barley.

---

[34] Contra: Hordern 2003. On the passage, see also Prauscello 2006a.

[35] The ἀρχαία παίδευσις that took place at the cithara master's house is contrasted with the new education happening in the agora and the Academy; on this aspect, see Ar. *Nub.* 961–1023.

And to Strepsiades' great distress, Pheidippides despises Aeschylus as "full of sound, incoherent, a ranter speaking crags" (ψόφου πλέων ἀξύστατον στόμφακα κρημνοποιόν, 1367):

> ὅμως δὲ τὸν θυμὸν δακὼν ἔφην· "σὺ δ' ἀλλὰ τούτων
> λέξον τι τῶν νεωτέρων, ἅττ' ἐστὶ τὰ σοφὰ ταῦτα."   1370
> ὁ δ' εὐθὺς ᾖγ' Εὐριπίδου ῥῆσίν τιν', ὡς ἐκίνει
> ἀδελφός, ὦ 'λεξίκακε, τὴν ὁμομητρίαν ἀδελφήν.
> Ar. *Nub.* 1369–72

> However, biting my anger, I said: "At least recite some passage of these new poets, whatever these clever things are." And immediately he recited a rhesis of Euripides, how a brother – O averter of evils! – screwed his uterine sister.

Taking the comic poets at face value, many critics do not hesitate to assume that the portrayal of Pheidippides in the *Clouds* reflects a general change in education practices and the influence that new disciplines – sophistry and, later, philosophy – had on individual musical practice:[36] the singing of wisdom poetry, as a form of education and a means of strengthening elite bonds through the sharing of *sophia*, gives way in Aristophanes' depiction to the recitation of new poetry, of the Euripides type, and to a new form of *sophia* (σοφὰ ταῦτα).[37]

But reflecting on the conflict between fathers and sons in late fifth-century Athens and also starting from evidence gathered from the comic poets, Barry Strauss offers some welcome qualification of this picture: "comedy bites best when it touches raw nerves . . . Aristophanes' use of father–son conflict does not in itself indicate that such conflict was prevalent, although it may demonstrate that it was feared by some (fathers) and wished by others (sons)."[38] Many scenes in Aristophanes do depend on this father–son dynamic and on the failure of the father to educate his son in the old ways, but father and son still have much in common. At the end of the *Wasps*, in the scene in which Philocleon educates Bdelycleon in the ways of the symposium, the father is converted to the ways of the son who aspires to elite status and thus assimilates with its traditional education

---

[36] Pickard-Cambridge (1962: 38–9) describes such an end-of-era scenario: "the younger generation were impatient of the old-fashioned discipline and literature; the lyric poetry of the older writers – Stesichorus, Pindar, and others – a knowledge of which seems to be assumed in his audience by Aristophanes, was no doubt read by cultivated persons, but became gradually more and more unfamiliar and out of date"; see also Wallace 1994 and 1995b.

[37] On Euripides and the sophists, Conacher 1998 and Allan 1999–2000.

[38] On the father–son conflict, Strauss 1993: 4–6, 153–66; 154 for quotation.

model – the symposium. Aristophanes underlines not a conflict of generations characteristic of any time period but the gap between different sub-cultures. And he figures this gap by talking about symposium manners. Although established mores are turned on their head in the *Wasps* with the son teaching his father, the passage plays with ideas of cultural conservatism and reactionary attitudes. The symposium becomes an icon of aristocratic culture and status, one of the cultural battlegrounds of the elite. The practice of the late fifth-century symposium is not Bdelycleon's subject; he tells of an atemporal, ideal, aristocratic gathering. In Angus Bowie's formulation, "the collapse of relationship within the oikos *is figured through* the collapse of the symposium."[39] Aristophanes' use of the symposium is not meant to reflect contemporary reality; rather, the institution itself and its codes are used as norms against which one can evaluate other changes.

Moreover, Pheidippides' recitation of the *neōteroi* at the symposium allows us to observe a dialogue between public and private venues of performance: passages of dramatic *mousikē* make their way into the symposium without necessarily displacing old practices, a process that will continue until the Roman Empire.[40] It might be in this light that we should understand a fragment of Aristophanes, fr. 719 KA, where a character proposes to put on smart words and playful amusement ([ἐνδεικνύναι] ῥήματά τε κομψὰ καὶ παίγνια) at the symposium, perhaps influenced, again, by the sophists.[41] The concluding words of Philoxenus' *Deipnon* also refer to the performance of "some smart new jokelet" (τι καινὸν κομψὸν ἀθυρμάτιον, fr. e 24), which caused the admiration of the audience (θαύμασαν αὖτ᾽ ἐπί τ᾽ ᾔνησαν, fr. e 24). And even though I resist seeing the symposium as the *original* place of performance for Philoxenus' *Dinner Party*, it is tempting to think that having been performed on the dithyrambic stage the song could have been *reperformed* at a symposium. In subsequent recitations in a small

---

[39] A. Bowie 1997: 5 (my emphasis).
[40] The same is true of the anecdote staging Dionysius of Sicily and his company, who go through paeans after dinner (see Chapter 1, p. 16). On sympotic practices during the late classical and Hellenistic periods, Cameron 1995: 71–103, especially 74: "despite the popularity of dramatic recitation at Hellenistic symposia, singing was not entirely a thing of the past. The clearest proof is one of the most interesting of all extant symposium texts, a papyrus published by Wilamowitz and Schubart in 1907." The papyrus in question, known as the Elephantine papyrus, contains the text of several songs, on which see Ferrari 1988.
[41] Hordern 2003: 608–9: "Davidson [2000] suggests that this could refer to putting on mimic pieces, but although the verb (ἐνδεικνύναι) can be used in this way, the juxtaposition of παίγνια with ῥήματα is important; one does not put on 'smart words (or speeches) and *mimes*'. However, the language would be very appropriate as a slighting description of display-oratory in the Gorgianic or Thrasymachean style ('smart words and farcical ideas'?)."

setting after a dinner party (not unlike that of Athenaeus' *Deipnosophistae*), the performer would have the pleasure of excerpting from, and recreating, the *Dinner Party*, in a form of fantastic *mise en abîme*.[42]

Other passages of comedy suggest that the symposium continued being an important place of poetic and musical performances, of increasing variety. A fragment from Eupolis' *Helots* is based on the same dichotomy between old and new types of performances but refers to a different change in musical entertainment:

> τὰ Στησιχόρου τε καὶ Ἀλκμᾶνος Σιμωνίδου τε
> ἀρχαῖον ἀείδειν, ὁ δὲ Γνήσιππος ἔστ᾽ ἀκούειν.
> κεῖνος νυκτερίν᾽ ηὗρε μοιχοῖς ἀείσματ᾽ ἐκκαλεῖσθαι
> γυναῖκας ἔχοντας ἰαμβύκην τε καὶ τρίγωνον.
>
> Eupolis, fr. 148 KA

> It is old-fashioned to sing the songs of Stesichorus and Alcman and Simonides – but Gnesippus, this is the one to hear! For he has invented serenades for adulterers, to attract the ladies with *iambuca* and triangle.

It is hard to establish the tone of the fragment, which, in line with the passage in the *Clouds* that contrasts old and new education, emphasizes the rejection of traditional sympotic poetry, the adoption of "new" authors, and even the creation of a new kind of performance. James Davidson has drawn from this testimony as well as from Xenophon's *Symposium* and a passage from Chionides' *Beggars* (fr. 4 KA) in which Gnesippus is described as a "writer of pleasantries of the merry Muse" (παιγνιογράφου τῆς ἱλαρῆς Μούσης) to argue that the new songs Gnesippus was composing in the 420s were erotic mimes acted by "performers usually drawn from the ranks of the *mousourgoi*, the singing-girls, but it seems possible that the guests themselves might sometimes participate to a greater or lesser extent."[43] There is, however, little, if any, evidence that Gnesippus was introducing innovation

---

[42] A testimony of Aristotle (fr. 83 Rose *ap.* Ath. 1.6d) supports this idea: in a typically spiteful comment about contemporary popular culture, Aristotle says: "they [popular performers] use claptrap in the crowd and spend their whole day doing tricks (ἐν τοῖς θαύμασι) . . . although they have never read (ἀνεγνωκότες) anything but Philoxenus' *Dinner*, and that not entirely." This remark presents Philoxenus' *Dinner* as an iconic song for artists interested in crowd-pleasers (for performance at a festival for instance) but also as a text available for *reading* and thus for recitation. On the relationship between reading and New Music, see Chapter 4, p. 164, on Licymnius.

[43] Davidson (2000: 51) draws on the evidence of Xenophon's *Symposium*, whose dramatic date is supposed to be the 420s, but which was probably composed in the 360s.

into the performance scenario; rather, in Hordern's words, "Gnesippus' poetry was certainly nothing out of the ordinary, and belonged, whatever individual elements he added himself, to a lyric tradition of erotic poetry that went back well into the archaic period."[44] In the fragment of the *Helots*, Eupolis is probably relying on the comic trope of mocking the sympotic tradition of erotic poetry, just as Chionides (fr. 4 KA) mocks the same Gnesippus and Cleomenes, and Epicrates (fr. 4 KA) puts the fourth-century lyricists Cleomenes and Lamynthius in the same category as Sappho and Meletus, called a composer of scolia by Aristophanes in *Frogs* (1302). Rather than introducing radical changes and seeing a disappearance of traditional entertainment practices, the late classical symposium likely continued to accommodate a variety of performances that included love poetry, drinking songs, and hymns of various sorts, while welcoming recitations of compositions originally sung or spoken in much more public settings, such as dramatic speeches and choral odes. This is not, in itself, an innovation of the late classical period, as other types of songs or poems, including elegy and epinicians, also moved from public to private context in the early classical period. The novelty rather resides in the open traffic between private and public fora, with the symposium importing passages from the dramatic stage and exporting some of its traditional motives and forms of expression to more public settings, dramatic and beyond. This last scenario is illustrated by two hymns that I discuss in the next section.

Sympotic fluidity: Aristotle's *Hymn to Virtue* and Ariphron's *Hymn to Health*

Aristotle's *Hymn to Virtue* and Ariphron's *Hymn to Health* are ideal places to explore sympotic fluidity. The songs have much in common, including themes, images, and form of enunciation. Rather than constituting formal or thematic innovations, either experimenting with a mix of genres or addressing abstractions as gods that were not celebrated in hymnic form before, as many scholars have suggested, these lyric compositions continue a tradition in which songs performed a social, ethical, and religious function in the context of the symposium while able to adapt to other contexts of performance (including more public contexts) and other means of performance (including reading).

---

[44] Hordern 2003: 613.

Aristotle's Hymn to Virtue

More or less since its composition, Aristotle's *Hymn to Virtue* has puzzled critics.[45] One of the main questions they have asked is that of the song's generic identity: is it a hymn? a paean? a scolion? an encomium? a mix of all of the above? What was the poet's purpose – and was the author of the *Poetics* breaking generic conventions? Unusually, we know something of the circumstances of the poem's composition.[46] According to Athenaeus, who quotes it, Aristotle composed the *Hymn to Virtue* to celebrate the memory of the philosopher's deceased friend and father-in-law, Hermias, the "philosopher-king" who had been tyrant of Atarneus (*ca.* 355–341 BC) before being treacherously murdered by the Persian King. The form chosen by Aristotle to celebrate the deeds of his friend and relative was felt to be offensive, however, and created, still according to Athenaeus, great controversy:[47]

τούτων λεχθέντων ὁ Δημόκριτος ἔφη· ἀλλὰ μὴν καὶ τὸ ὑπὸ τοῦ πολυμα-
θεστάτου γραφὲν Ἀριστοτέλους εἰς Ἑρμείαν τὸν Ἀταρνέα οὐ παιάν ἐστιν,
ὡς ὁ τὴν τῆς ἀσεβείας κατὰ τοῦ φιλοσόφου γραφὴν ἀπενεγκάμενος Δημό-
φιλος †εἰς αἰδωτε† παρασκευασθεὶς ὑπ᾽ Εὐρυμέδοντος, ὡς ἀσεβοῦντος καὶ
ᾄδοντος ἐν τοῖς συσσιτίοις ὁσημέραι εἰς τὸν Ἑρμείαν <u>παιᾶνα</u>. ὅτι δὲ παιᾶνος
οὐδεμίαν ἔμφασιν παρέχει τὸ ᾆσμα, ἀλλὰ <u>τῶν σκολίων ἕν τι καὶ αὐτὸ εἶδός</u>
ἐστιν ἐξ αὐτῆς τῆς λέξεως φανερὸν ὑμῖν ποιήσω·

Ἀρετὰ πολύμοχθε γένει βροτείῳ,
   θήραμα κάλλιστον βίῳ,
σᾶς πέρι, παρθένε, μορφᾶς
   καὶ θανεῖν ζηλωτὸς ἐν Ἑλλάδι πότμος
καὶ πόνους τλῆναι μαλερούς ἀκάμαντας·   5
τοῖον ἐπὶ φρένα βάλλεις
   καρπόν ἰσαθάνατον χρυσοῦ τε κρείσσω
καὶ γονέων μαλακαυγήτοιό θ᾽ ὕπνου.
σεῦ δ᾽ ἔνεχ᾽ <καὶ> ὁ διὸς
   Ἡρακλέης Λήδας τε κοῦροι   10

---

[45] On the song, Ford 2011a is now fundamental. For general studies, Bowra 1938, Renehan 1982, Furley and Bremer 2001. On the song's relationship with Aristotle's philosophy, Jaeger 1948 and Düring 1957. For the biographical component, Santoni 1993, and on the relationship with inscriptions, Runia 1986 and LeVen 2013c.

[46] On this point, see especially Wormell 1935 and Ford 2011a: 9–26.

[47] Also quoted in Diogenes Laertius (5.7–8) and found in the papyrus of Didymus' commentary on Demosthenes (10.32).

πόλλ' ἀνέτλασαν ἔργοις
   σὰν ἀγρεύοντες δύναμιν·
σοῖς δὲ πόθοις Ἀχιλεὺς Αἴ-
   ας τ' Ἀΐδαο δόμους ἦλθον·
σᾶς δ' ἔνεκεν φιλίου μορφᾶς καὶ Ἀταρνέος   15
   ἔντροφος ἠελίου χήρωσεν αὐγάς.
τοιγὰρ ἀοίδιμος ἔργοις,
   ἀθάνατόν τέ μιν αὐξήσουσι Μοῦσαι,
Μναμοσύνας θύγατρες, Δι-
   ὸς ξενίου σέβας αὔξου-   20
σαι φιλίας τε γέρας βεβαίου.
                Arist. *PMG* 842 *ap.* Ath. 15.696a–d

When these [scolia] had been recited, Democritus said: "What's more, the poem written by the erudite Aristotle in honor of Hermias of Atarneus is not a paean, as opposed to the allegations of Demophilus – who, pushed by Eurymedon, had carried the accusation of impiety against the philosopher [corrupt] – allegations that he makes on the grounds that Aristotle was showing impiety by singing his paean to Hermias every day in the syssities. But that the song does not show any mark of a paean, but is a unique form of scolion, I will make clear to you by the diction of the poem:

Virtue, you who bring many toils to the mortal race, most beautiful thing to be hunted in one's life, it is for the sake of your beauty, maiden, that even death, and the bearing of cruel and indefatigable pains, is an enviable lot in Greece: so great is the fruit that you put in people's heart to make it equal to an immortal's, and better than gold, and parents, and sweet-eyed sleep. For your sake, even the divine Heracles and the sons of Leda suffered many things in their deeds, going after your power; because of their desire for you, Achilles and Ajax went to the dwellings of Hades. For your dear beauty, the nursling of Atarneus bereaved his eyes from the light of the sun. So he is celebrated in song for his deeds, and the Muses, the daughters of Memory, will foster him as an immortal while fostering the majesty of Zeus of Hospitality, and the part of honor of our strong friendship."

The ancient debate that Athenaeus presents as the frame for the discussion of the poem is based on two positions about the notion of genre that I have defined in Chapter 1: some point to formal features (the paeanic cry as marker of a paean, for example), while others think about genre in terms of performance and function (for instance, praise as the function of an encomium). Thus, Democritus argues from the absence of paeanic *epiphthēgma* that Aristotle should not be condemned, as the piece he composed is a scolion, while Demophilus' accusation against Aristotle is founded on the inappropriateness, even the impiousness, of singing a paean to a man (as opposed to a god).[48] Robert Renehan's verdict on Demophilus' indictment is unambiguous: "whatever the specific genre, the charge [of impiety] is an obvious sham."[49] Entering into the genre debate, modern commentators have suggested that rather than belonging to a single genre, Aristotle's poem could constitute an innovation by borrowing from different song types and thus exemplifying the "mixing of genres" that would be typical of the Hellenistic period and was already developing in the late classical period. Thus C. M. Bowra:

> The solution must be that Aristotle modeled his poem on the Paean but added to it some characteristics of the θρῆνος, and addressed in it a power which meant a great deal to him but was not officially in the Greek pantheon. From the θρῆνος he took the lamentation for the dead man . . . But from the Paean he took his structure and his place of singing. *In so combining, or confusing, two types of poem Aristotle followed the tendencies of the fourth century.* A similar confusion may be seen in Philodamus' Paean to Dionysus, in which Dionysus, for whom the right kind of Hymn was the Dithyramb, is addressed in the form proper to Apollo with Apollo's own refrain of ἰὲ Παιάν.[50]

While Bowra thinks about the song as a hybrid, Renehan interprets it as a monster: "Here surely, in this very diversity of opinion, lies the solution. Scholars, in ancient times and modern, have failed to agree on the genre of the poem precisely because it cannot be put into any single category without Procrustean measures. *It is untypical,* even as is its immediate occasion."[51]

Common to both Bowra and Renehan is the idea that Aristotle's composition is some sort of puzzle for which one must seek a "solution," a term used by both critics. Far from moving away from the idea of genre as a fixed category that texts are born into, these two quotations present Aristotle's composition as a form of engineering:[52] hybridity, untypicality, and

---

[48] Whether the accusation is justified or not, paeans sung to dead men were already attested in the late fifth century: paean to Lysander: Plut. *Vit. Lys.* 18.3 (quoting Duris, *FGrH* 76 F 71) = *PMG* 867.

[49] Renehan 1982: 253.   [50] Bowra 1938: 186 (my emphasis).

[51] Renehan 1982: 255 (my emphasis).

[52] The image is borrowed from Barchiesi, see Chapter 1, p. 66.

combination are only positive twists on the notion of confusion. I am not interested as much in assigning a genre label to the song as in understanding how the verbal material of the song, including its enunciation, themes, and images, made it possible for the poem to play its intended function in varied settings, while consistently celebrating the memory of a deceased friend and his deeds of excellence.

The song is composed in dactylo-epitrites, and has a typical tripartite hymnic structure.[53] The first section (1–5) is the *invocatio* to Virtue and a glorification of her power; the second part (6–16) describes the power that Virtue bestows on those who possess her and proceeds to naming mythological *exempla*; the last part (17–22) is a glorification of the addressee of the poem, Hermias, and of the poet himself and his power of immortalization. The hymnic address to Virtue is unparalleled but draws from two traditions: on the one hand, the anthropomorphization or allegorization of Virtue, made a noble and modest-looking lady in Prodicus and presented as dwelling at the top of a steep and long road in Hesiod, for example;[54] on the other, the address to personified abstractions, from Pindaric epinicians that open with an invocation to Tycha (*Ol.* 12) and Hesychia (*Pyth.* 8) to Ion of Chios' *Hymn to Kairos* (*PMG* 742) and an anonymous address to Tyche (*PMG* 1019).[55] Even though it is close to these forms, Aristotle's song also distances itself from them: while invocations of abstractions in the Pindaric opening give way to the celebration of the victor in the rest of the ode, Virtue remains up to the last lines of Aristotle's song the topic in focus and its power is illustrated in the short mythical *exempla*. And while Virtue is described in Prodicus or Simonides, Virtue is made present in Aristotle through a direct address.

The apostrophe in the opening line, to Virtue as most beautiful prey (θήραμα κάλλιστον), points to a specific background against which the poem is to be understood. The particular locus for the articulation of a form of the question "What is the fairest (κάλλιστον)?" is the symposium.[56] This is most clearly expressed, for example, in Sappho 16 Voigt, which opens with a priamel: after a host of horses, foot soldiers, and ships, the narrator abruptly moves from the military field to domestic concerns and declares that what is fairest (κάλλιστον) is the object one loves (ἔμμεναι κάλλιστον,

---

[53] On hymnic tripartite structure, Bremer 1981, Janko 1981, Race 1982, Furley and Bremer 2001: I 50–63, Calame 2004a: 11–19.

[54] Arete personified in Hesiod (*Op.* 289–92), Simonides (*PMG* 579), and Prodicus (quoted in Xen. *Mem.* 2.1.21–34).

[55] On Pindar, Furley and Bremer 2001: I 265. On Ion's hymn, Jennings 2007.

[56] On this aspect, Ford 2011a: 114–21.

ἔγω δὲ κῆν' ὄττω τις ἔραται, 3–4). Theognis relies on the same trope in elegiac form:

> κάλλιστον τὸ δικαιότατον· λῷστον δ' ὑγιαίνειν·
>> πρᾶγμα δὲ τερπνότατον, τοῦ τις ἐρᾷ, τὸ τυχεῖν.
>>> Thgn. 255–6 W²

> Most beautiful is what is most just; and best is to be healthy, but the most enjoyable is to find what one loves.

A similar process appears also in a scolion:

> ὑγιαίνειν μὲν ἄριστον ἀνδρὶ θνητῷ,
> δεύτερον δὲ καλὸν φυὰν γενέσθαι,
> τὸ τρίτον δὲ πλουτεῖν ἀδόλως,
> καὶ τὸ τέταρτον ἡβᾶν μετὰ τῶν φίλων.
>> PMG 890

> Health is the best for a mortal, second comes physical beauty, third, wealth acquired without guile, and fourth, youth in the company of friends.

The song is variously attributed to Simonides (*PMG* 651) and Epicharmus (fr. 250 KA) and is quoted by Athenaeus (15.694e–f), who points out that Plato deemed it "very well phrased" (ἄριστα εἰρημένου, *Grg.* 451e). The speaker Myrtilus also quotes the comic revision of the scolion in a comedy by Anaxandrides (*The Treasure*):

> ὁ τὸ σκόλιον εὑρὼν ἐκεῖνος, ὅστις ἦν,
> τὸ μὲν ὑγιαίνειν πρῶτον ὡς ἄριστον ὂν
> ὠνόμασεν ὀρθῶς· δεύτερον δ' εἶναι καλόν,
> τρίτον δὲ πλουτεῖν, τοῦθ', ὁρᾷς, ἐμαίνετο·
> μετὰ τὴν ὑγίειαν γὰρ τὸ πλουτεῖν διαφέρει·
> καλὸς δὲ πεινῶν ἐστιν αἰσχρὸν θηρίον.
>> Anaxandrides, fr. 18 KA

> Whoever came up with the scolion was right to name health first, as the best thing; but when he made beauty second and wealth third, he was out of his mind. For wealth is next best to health: a handsome man who is poor is an ugly beast.

Different modes of performance are to be imagined for all these passages – sung Aeolic lyrics for Sappho, recited/chanted elegiacs for Theognis, sung Attic scolion for Anaxandrides – but in their diversity they all illustrate that the symposium is a place where, as Ford has noted, values are ranked and discussed, where "one [can] put familiar themes in play within recognizable transformations."[57] But the symposium is also a place where these very values are enacted and reaffirmed in the process of reciting or singing the lines. The social and ideological bonds that link the participants of the symposium are renewed every time the lines are uttered: songs celebrating friendship, excellence, beauty, health, and wealth strengthen the ties between the *kaloikagathoi*, a gathering of wealthy, healthy, excellent, and beautiful friends.[58]

In addition to relying on a central theme celebrated at the symposium – praise of excellence – Aristotle's song uses images clearly associated with that performance setting.[59] The metaphor of the hunt in the description of Virtue as most beautiful prey (κάλλιστον θήραμα, 2), continued in the meaning of the participle "chasing" (ἀγρεύοντες, 12, according to Campbell's supplement), reinforces the network of elite associations, since hunting was "along with the *symposion*, athletics, and battle, a defining activity of the masculine aristocracy," and the metaphor itself could find a visual echo in the hunt motives represented on symposium vessels.[60] The goods celebrated in the priamel are taken from three distinct spheres that define complementary dimensions of the elite symposiast: a physiological good (sleep), which defines him with respect to his body, an ethical good (parents), which defines him with respect to his social group, and a symbolic good (gold), which defines him with respect to the larger society of aristocrats and gods to which he belongs. The last lines of the poem explicitly recall cornerstones of the symposium: the references to the piety of Zeus of hospitality in particular (Διὸς ξενίου σέβας, 19–20) and to the boon of secure friendship (φιλίας γέρας βεβαίου, 21) express and reproduce the social and ethical links between the guests. Even the reference to Hermias, not named explicitly but referred to in riddling form (*ainos*) as the "nursling of Atarneus," continues the modes of expression typical of the symposium and supposes a tight bond between symposiasts, the happy few privy to the meaning of the periphrasis.[61] One could go further and argue that the whole poem can be read as a sort of *ainos*, developing the idea contained in the initial address and the anthropomorphization of Virtue. The quest for an irresistible maiden for the sake of whom all heroes – including the two best Achaeans and the

---

[57] Ford 2011a: 119.

[58] On the ethical meaning of ὑγιής as "sound and healthy," Gentili 1988: 70.

[59] On praise of excellence performed at the symposium, Tyrtaeus, fr. 12.13–44 W², Thgn. 29–30, 315–18, 335–6, 465–6, 933–8, 971–2 W².

[60] Barringer 2001: 7. The importance of the motive of the hunt is confirmed by the parallel with Ariphron, who describes the pleasures of love as Ἀφροδίτας θηρεύομεν ("hunt[ing] Aphrodite," 5).

[61] On *ainos* and symposium, Ford 2002: 72–80.

Dioscuri, mentioned in the priamel – die can be interpreted in the light of Sappho's own mythological example of τὸ κάλλιστον: Virtue is a sort of Helen, the most beautiful exemplum selected by the poet, a "maiden" who embodies desire but brings death in her wake. Taken together these elements suggest that it is more productive to understand the images and modes of expression in the light of a certain socio-cultural performance *setting*, the symposium, rather than as a specific *genre* or performance mode, such as scolion, encomium, or paean. These genres all rely on the same themes but are performed in different ways, metrical, dialectal, and probably instru-mental and musical.

Should we think, then, that Aristotle's song was intended to be per-formed at a symposium, just as Athenaeus' sophists sing (or recite) the scolia collected at the end of the *Deipnosophistae* over desserts and drinks? The only external reference to a performance of the song points to a very different scenario – a choral recitation by diners, at the common meal of the Academy – and some of the song's motives and formal features could be explained by its intended performance setting: the very public and Panhellenic context in which epinicians were performed.[62] Aristotle's choice of mythical exempla is particularly striking. All the heroes, from the first generation of the Argonauts Heracles and the Dioscuri to the Trojan heroes Achilles and Ajax, represent heroic and martial public virtue rather than private domestic virtue.[63] More specifically, the song accomplishes all the functions of an epinician. On the one hand, it praises the dedicatee, his city, the metaphorical contest in which he competed (a contest of excellence, an abstraction of all other contests in which men can show their *aretē*), while aggrandizing the poet.[64] On the other hand, it inserts the object of praise (Hermias) into a social and religious network of communal celebration. The reference to the dedicatee's immortality (ἀθάνατον, 18) through the

---

[62] Renehan 1982, on the song as epinician. I cannot document here the rich debate on the modes and contexts of performance – choral or monodic? public or private? cultic or not cultic? – of epinicians; for recent takes on this large topic see Agócs, Carey, and Rawles 2012, Part 2: 111–245, with relevant bibliography.

[63] On *aretē* understood as a public virtue, Adkins 1960: 31–60 and 153–71, and Whitehead (1993), who underlines changes in the meaning of *aretē* toward a more private virtue in the fourth century. On other uses of *aretē*, in particular in *epitaphioi logoi*, Loraux 1993: 110–12 and 194–7; in encomiastic poetry and public discourse, Dover 1974: 66–73; in the language of public approbation in democratic Athens, Whitehead 1993 and 2009; and in epitaphs, Tsagalis 2008 and LeVen 2013c (on Aristotle's reliance on the language of funerary inscriptions and its use of *aretē*).

[64] With a handful of exceptions, the noun ἀρετή is used in all of Pindar's epinicia. This might be one of the elements that allow epinician reperformance, as the "excellence" of the victor in athletic competition is also a keyword of a symposium where the ode could later be performed.

work of "the Muses, daughters of Memory" (Μοῦσαι, Μναμοσύνας θύγατρες, 18–19), the allusion to the work of the poet who makes the *laudandus*
an object of song (ἀοίδιμος, 17), and the praise of friendship and hospitality
(ξενίου σέβας ... φιλίας τε γέρας, 20–1) are all features of epinicians. One
can even observe all the formal Bundyan elements of an epinician, including name cap, myths, and *gnomai* around which the community hearing
the song can rally. Like an epinician, Aristotle's song oscillates between two
poles: the private, individual, and temporally and locally set (the death of
Hermias of Atarneus and the mourning of a friend) and the public, uni-
versal, generalizing, and Panhellenic (the celebration of Virtue and some
of its Panhellenic heroes, starting with Heracles). These are features that
allow the song, like an epinician, enough flexibility to be relevant both for
a community as a whole and for singers in a private setting. Thanks to the
various motives and images associated with the celebration of Virtue, the
theme is appropriate for varied locations that share the same ethos, be it a
private symposium or a public, civic context. Because of the many different
realms of meaning of *aretē* (ethical, social, physical, and philosophical) and
because of the range of exempla used (from mythological heroes to more
everyday comments on the goodness of sleep), the song can unite around
itself as many audiences as there are contexts. Understanding the poem as
able to adapt to various circumstances and as enabled by the specific choice
of imagery and language to move from one setting to the next is more useful
than thinking of Aristotle's hymn as exploring the boundaries of genres or
trying an "untypical" form that combines generic features or attempts to
evoke a performance context. This is what Andrew Ford has analyzed in his
elegant monograph devoted to Aristotle's composition, where he highlights
the paradoxical critical use of "genre." Refusing to pinpoint one genre, or
several, from which the song would borrow features, Ford asserts:

Whatever we decide is the best way to categorize Aristotle's song, this study of Greek
lyric genres has suggested that they had a paradoxical role. Genre must have acted as
an anchor, a drag on free motion; and yet it was an anchor that could be moved and
set down in new places. In a culture that had at once numerous performance venues
and deeply seated expectations about propriety, genre had to be at once changeable
and authoritative. The genre of Aristotle's song might shift as it moved into new
situations, but in those situations it had to continue to provide some restraint,
limiting and stabilizing meaning before releasing it to move again.[65]

While much of the focus of Ford's argument is on our understanding of
the notion of genre itself (he demonstrates that a song can change genre

---

[65] Ford 2011a: 90.

according to the circumstances of its performance), my analysis has considered the in-built capacity of the song to move, much like an epinician, from one context to the next, between private and public and sacred and secular, and to exploit the specific social associations of these settings while always fulfilling the same function – celebrating the excellence of Hermias while creating, or reaffirming, the social and ethical bonds between a community of excellent men who recognize the beauty of virtue. Rather than seeing Aristotle innovate with his song, I would instead see him as composing according to one of the most traditional rationales of hymnic poetry: he addresses as large an audience as possible to make his object, and his own poetry, as widely known as possible. Aristotle's *Hymn to Virtue* illustrates the very dynamics that I have suggested are at stake in Philoxenus' *Dinner Party*. These compositions attest to the fluidity of the movement between performance settings and between social contexts, and to a rich process of exchange and cross-pollination among symposium, festival, and theater that deserves further examination.

Ariphron's paean

A paean to health by Ariphron of Sicyon (*PMG* 813) reveals further questions about what allows songs to circulate and be performed in varied settings without losing some of their power. Probably composed in the fourth century BC, the hymn is quoted by Athenaeus in the closing pages of the *Deipnosophistae*, referred to by Lucian as "very well known and on everybody's lips" (τὸ γνωριμώτατον ἐκεῖνο καὶ πᾶσι διὰ στόματος, *De lapsu* 6) in the second century AD, and inscribed on stone in different locations, where it is dated to the second or third century AD.[66] The exact composition date of the poem is unknown: an inscription of the early fourth century BC (*IG* II² 3092) celebrates the victory of a chorus trained by a certain Ariphron, but Ariphron was a name popular in the classical period and the poet recorded in that inscription may have no connection with the author of this song. The reasons given by William Furley and Jan Bremer to justify a Hellenistic date are stylistic and thematic but these arguments, as I have noted, are problematic.[67] The composition shares similar features with

---

[66] For epigraphic record, *IG* II² 4533 (from Athens), *IG* IV² 1, 132 (from Epidaurus). The song is quoted in a number of sources: *PMG* 813 = Lucian, *Pro lapsu* 6; Plut. *Mor.* 450b (*De virt. moral.* 10); Max. Tyr. 7.1; Sext. Emp. *Math.* 11.49; Stob. 4.27.9. On the song, Wilamowitz-Moellendorff 1921: 494–5, Maas 1933: 148–50, Keyssner 1933, Bremer 1981: 210–11, Wagman 1995: 159–78, Furley and Bremer 2001: I 224–7, Rutherford 2001a: 37–8, Ford 2011a: 91–7.

[67] See Chapter 1, pp. 43–8.

Aristotle's song, and some unusual expressions that appear in both poems, especially the reference to near divinity, are so close to each other that it is difficult to deny imitation, but there is no certainty about, nor consensus on, the chronological relationship between the two works.[68] Overall, even though the two songs draw on the same tradition, motives, and images, they achieve different purposes.

Ὑγίεια βροτοῖσι πρεσβίστα μακάρων, μετὰ σεῦ
ναίοιμι τὸ λειπόμενον βιοτᾶς, σὺ δέ μοι πρόφρων ξυνείης·
εἰ γάρ τις ἢ πλούτου χάρις ἢ τεκέων
ἢ τᾶς ἰσοδαίμονος ἀνθρώποις βασιληίδος ἀρχᾶς ἢ πόθων
οὓς κρυφίοις Ἀφροδίτας ἕρκεσιν θηρεύομεν,   5
ἢ εἴ τις ἄλλα θεόθεν ἀνθρώποισι τέρψις ἢ πόνων
ἀμπνοὰ πέφανται,
μετὰ σεῖο, μάκαιρ' Ὑγίεια,
τέθαλε καὶ λάμπει Χαρίτων ὀάροις·
σέθεν δὲ χωρὶς οὔτις εὐδαίμων ἔφυ.   10

Ariphron, *PMG* 813

Health, for the human race the most august of the blessed ones, may I dwell with you for what remains of my life, and may you gladly be with me. For if any pleasure found in wealth or children or in the regal power that gives to men a status equal to that of the gods or in the desires that we hunt with the secret nets of Aphrodite, or again if any other delight god-sent to men or any respite from toil exists, it is with you, blessed Health, that it blooms and shines in the converse of the Graces; and without you no man is happy.

The song is a short monostrophic composition in dactylo-epitrites. Athenaeus calls it a paean, but critics attached to the formal definition of genre have observed that the song does not display any of the markers of a paean (including, again, no paeanic *epiphthēgma*) and contains no reference to Apollo. Still, one can argue that Hygieia is traditionally connected with Apollo through her grandfather Asclepius, and that a *iē Paian* could have been added *extra metrum* in performance. Moreover, the song is quoted in the *Deipnosophistae* in a sympotic context, in which, as Ian Rutherford has shown, paeans were sung and toasts for health made.[69] But what makes the short song a striking specimen is that, in addition to being

---

[68] On the chronological relationship between the two, Bowra 1938 and Renehan 1982.

[69] Rutherford 2001a: 50–1, quoting Alcman (*PMG* 98), Dicaearchus (fr. 88 Wehrli), and Plutarch (*Quaest. conv.* 615b) as testimonies for the practice of sympotic paean-singing and health-toasting. See also the parody in comedy, Eubulus, *Semele* (fr. 93 KA), with three bowls for the sound of mind and the celebration of Hygieia, with Wilkins 2000: 225–6.

preserved in quotation in several texts, it was also inscribed on stone in sanctuaries. These unique circumstances raise the question of what made this traditional-looking hymn such a powerful composition that it could be adapted across the centuries to so many different settings – from imagined sung performance at a symposium, to quotation in book-form, and to visual display in a public place.

The first and most obvious background against which one can understand the hymn, just like Aristotle's praise of excellence, is the symposium.[70] I have already quoted the lines in which Theognis (255–6 W²) praises health as a sympotic boon, and the Attic scolion (*PMG* 890) in praise of health that Plato cites in the *Gorgias* (451e) and that he declares "known from everyone." The difference between the way these poems treat health, as a personified abstraction, and Ariphron's deification of Health is barely relevant; as Ford has shown, Greek mythopoetic thought drew no clear line between the two approaches.[71] But even closer to Ariphron's composition is an elegiac fragment of the fifth-century poet Critias that makes Health one of the abstractions present at the ideal symposium:

καλῶς δ' εἰς ἔργ' Ἀφροδίτης
πρός θ' ὕπνον ἥρμοσται, τὸν καμάτων λιμένα,
πρός τὴν τερπνοτάτην τε θεῶν θνητοῖς Ὑγίειαν   20
καὶ τὴν Εὐσεβίης γείτονα Σωφροσύνην.

Critias, fr. 6.18–21 W²

It equips one well toward the deeds of Aphrodite, and for sleep, the harbor of pains, and for Health, the most enjoyable of the gods for mortals, and toward Temperance, neighbor of Piety.

The list of good things present at a symposium is reminiscent of Ariphron's priamel: Critias' "deeds of Aphrodite" recall Ariphron's "secret nets of Aphrodite," and the elegiac description of sleep as "harbor from pains" echoes Ariphron's "delight and respite from toil." These images again recall Aristotle's priamel: like Aristotle, Ariphron alternates description of the enjoyment (χάρις) of social and political goods (πλούτου, "wealth," 3 and ἰσοδαίμονος ἀνθρώποις βασιληίδος ἀρχᾶς, "regal power that gives man a status equal to that of the gods," 4) with more private goods (τεκέων, "children," 3 and πόθων, "desires," 4) and forms of pleasure

---

[70] Also Thgn. 255–6 W², quoted above; Soph. *TGrF* ɪᴠ F 356.2 λῷστον δὲ τὸ ζῆν ἄνοσον ("advantageous is to live disease-free").

[71] Ford 2011a: 93. Health is described as venerable (σεμνή) but is not divinized in Simonides (*PMG* 604 = Sext. Emp. *Math.* 11.49). Only Licymnius (*PMG* 769) comes close to divinizing Health, in a composition that Sextus Empiricus calls a prelude (on which see Chapter 4).

(θεόθεν τέρψις, "god-sent delight," 6 and πόνων ἀμπνοά, "respite from toil," 6–7).

These thematic and poetic features align Ariphron's song with compositions performed at the symposium, yet Ariphron's form of enunciation is different from the gnomic statements made in archaic and classical elegy. Just as in Aristotle's song, here too the poem's form of enunciation enables it to cross between contexts of performance, traveling in this instance from the exclusive world of the symposium to the open air of the sanctuary of Asclepius. And again like Aristotle's song, Ariphron's revolves around the creation of the presence of Health, thanks to an anaphora of the second person that brings unity to the poem (μετὰ σεῦ, "with you," 1; μετὰ σεῖο, "with you," 8; σέθεν δὲ χωρίς, "without you," 10). But by contrast with Aristotle's song, Ariphron also foregrounds a performing "I": after the opening invocation establishing Health as a divine addressee (Ὑγίεια βροτοῖσι πρεσβίστα μακάρων), the song continues with a prayer, in a manner reminiscent of the shorter Homeric hymns, which establishes the presence of the narrator. Just as in the Homeric hymns, a strong reciprocal connection is established from the beginning between god and performer. In Ariphron's song that mutual engagement takes the form of a chiasm, where the speaker's wish "may I live with you for the rest of my life" (μετὰ σεῦ | ναίοιμι τὸ λειπόμενον βιοτᾶς, 1–2) is reinforced by "may you gladly be with me" (σὺ δέ μοι πρόφρων ξυνείης, 2). The prayer is expressed in two different verbal persons and the grammatical reciprocity at the beginning of the poem anticipates the ritual reciprocity at its end. The same rhetoric can be observed after the priamel, in the praise of health's effects, which, similarly, is not expressed as a logical proposition such as "if there is health, then these things (enjoyment, wealth, for example) are possible" but as a performative statement: by noting the pleasures of life first, the speaker establishes the presence of health that makes these pleasures possible, and thus praises its power. Where the sympotic elegies quoted above state a hierarchy of values that reinforces ideological and social ties between members of a group, this song aims at ensuring that the prayer will be answered. That the connection is between performer and song, rather than between song and context, is reinforced by the absence of any markers that tie the song to a specific time or space: indeed, the "what is left of life" (τὸ λειπόμενον βιοτᾶς, 2) has a different span every time the song is sung, and the very meaning of the song is reactivated by each utterance of this line (the healthier I am, the more I will be able to sing this song to health), an idea reinforced by the aspectual feature of the perfect tense (πέφανται, 7; τέθαλε, 9; ἔφυ, 10), which expresses the state resulting from the presence of health.

The last three lines (8–10) respond to the opening section with a direct address. Before stating one last time in gnomic form the boon of living in the company of health (σέθεν δὲ χωρὶς οὔτις εὐδαίμων ἔφυ), Ariphron uses an intriguing expression, "it [health] shines in the company of the Charites" (λάμπει Χαρίτων ὀάροις, 9). On the one hand, this idea is close to that expressed by Aristotle in his reference to the Muses (17–19) and even has Hesiodic overtones: Ariphron's description of the "delights god-sent to men and respite from toil" is reminiscent of what the Muses themselves bring in the *Theogony*, forgetfulness of evils and respite from worries (λησμοσύνην τε κακῶν ἄμπυμά τε μερμηράων, 55), and Ariphron's reference to the delight and the "converse" of the Charites (Χαρίτων ὀάροις), a rare word, echoes the description of what accompanies Aphrodite in the Hesiodic text, maidenly converse and delight (παρθενίους τ' ὀάρους . . . τέρψιν τε, Hes. *Theog.* 205– 6). On the other hand, the reference to the Charites is more specific than the appeal to the Muses one finds in Aristotle's song and characterizes the rhetoric of Ariphron's prayer. *Charis* is mobilized for its polysemy and for the multiplicity of domains it connects: poetic, aesthetic, sensual, and social. Just as there is no grace, charm, or beauty without health, there is no hymn to Health without the Charites, the divinities that give charm to poetry. As Pindar states in his own address to the Charites, in the opening of *Olympian* 14, "even the gods would not arrange choruses or feasts without the august Charites" (οὐδὲ θεοὶ σεμνᾶν Χαρίτων ἄτερ | κοιρανέοντι χοροὺς οὔτε δαῖτας, 8–9).[72] These two settings imagined in the epinician are particularly marked as they correspond to two possible venues and contexts of performance of the epinician itself: the symposium and the chorus. The presence of *charis* and the Charites emphasizes the reciprocity in the relationship between performer, song, and victor and between song and audience.[73] But it also links dedicator and dedicatee of the *agalma*, be it a prayer, a song, or a statue, in a much larger setting.

The parallel that I mentioned earlier between Ariphron's song and the shorter Homeric hymns can be taken further, as the reciprocity between singer and divinity praised can open up to reciprocity in a more materialistic context. The reference to the company of the Charites in Ariphron's song facilitates the inscription of the song, as the divinities are linked to physical qualities: the good of health that makes one metaphorically flourish (τέθαλε) and shine (λάμπει) can also be taken as a reference, literally, to material goods offered in the process of reciprocity (*charis*) as thanks to the goddess, flourishing garlands and shiny *agalmata* (offerings and statues).

---

[72] Ford 2011a: 97–105.   [73] Day 2010: 232–80. On *charis* in epinician, Kurke 1991: 103–7.

Ariphron's song thus relies on language and images that are associated with performance at a symposium, in a context where a group can invoke health as a good that they value in common (along with excellence and beauty) and that ties them together. But the hymn also has features that make it close to other objects used in a relationship of reciprocity with a god: when it is written, couched as an inscription, the song's materiality adds to its symbolic status and power. Prayer, sung performance, and material object (inscription) enter into a series of productive relationships tightly connecting poet, divinity, and audience.

Conclusion: sympotic mix

While scholarship on late classical poetic culture has often emphasized the mixing of genres as a characteristic feature of innovations of that period, this chapter has highlighted instead in three case studies the fluidity of compositions that can move from private to public setting and vice versa and the great receptivity of various contexts to the importation and exportation of songs. The symposium remains an important point of reference, both as a theme in itself that can be narrated and given to see on a stage, and as a context of performance. While it evolves to accommodate an even greater diversity of performances in the early classical period (including recitation of dramatic *rhesis* and new types of songs), traditional sympotic themes, values, and forms are exported in songs that can be performed in other settings, from the theater stage to an open area in a sanctuary. The fluidity that I have observed in the songs is partly a result of their form of enunciation, which involves the audience either as voyeur (as in Philoxenus' *Dinner Party*) or as performer (as in Ariphron's song). The best testimony to the innovative use of tradition and the concern for flexibility is probably the hymn to Hermias that Aristotle wrote: "exploiting the language of tradition and of his time, he made an utterance that was at once intelligible and memorable, well-behaved and distinctive, tightly compact with thought and free to address the future."[74] With its double reference in the final lines to musical aggrandizing (αὐξήσουσι Μοῦσαι, 20–1) and solidity (βεβαίου, 21), the song also opens up the question of its own reproduction and dissemination and enters into a dialogue with other objects of celebration and commemoration, with stones and statues.

[74] Ford 2011a: 165–6.

7 | A canon set in stone? Inscriptions, performance, and ritual in late classical hymns

> Qu'on me touche: toutes ces voix vivent dans ma pierre musicale.
>
> Victor Segalen, *Stèles* (Pierre Musicale, Stèles orientées)

Much of the preceding discussion has focused on performance in the Athenian theater and at the symposium; in this final chapter, I turn to late classical songs inscribed on stone in sanctuaries across the Greek main-land: an anonymous paean to Asclepius, Aristonous' hymns to Hestia and Apollo, and Philodamus of Scarphea's paean to Dionysus, all inscribed in Delphi, as well as Isyllus' paean to Asclepius inscribed in Epidaurus.[1] This corpus presents a new set of problems: we know nothing of the songs' authors except for what the *subscriptio* accompanying the record of the text says; the songs are not usually considered part of the lyric canon, no matter how loosely we understand what constitutes a canon; they are not quoted by our usual sources for lyric fragments, Athenaeus, Plutarch, and Stobaeus; and they are rarely taken into consideration by histories of Greek literature. Their apparent obscurity does not mean, however, that the songs were not popular or knew only a brief moment of glory. The anonymous paean to Asclepius, for example, first inscribed in 380–360 BC, was recorded in four different locations in the Greco-Roman world in the course of 600 years, its transmission attesting to continued ritual and poetic practices. As we have seen in the previous chapter, the hymn to Health by Ariphron of Sicyon was also recorded on stone in different places, including Athens, and according to Lucian was "on everyone's lips" (*Pro lapsu* 6) in the second century AD. These works thus provide us with precious insight into a process of survival very different from that of the literary canon, which included Pindar's paeans. Alexandrian scholars edited the canon of texts for the library of Alexandria; the epigraphic hymns, by contrast, tell of a selection process determined by individual communities and their pri-orities. They also provide another view on the relationship of tradition and innovation. The inscribed religious songs are not simply conservative counterparts to showy theater innovation. They display a very high level

---

[1] Respectively *CA*, pp. 136–8, 162–5, 165–71, and 132–6.

of rhetorical self-consciousness, of engagement with different poetic trad-itions, and of thematic innovation. Some of these inscribed songs even reflect upon issues rarely confronted directly by earlier hymns – their written sta-tus, the process of their material inscription, and their materiality as objects inscribed and dedicated in a religious landscape. In that regard, they occupy the middle ground between, on the one hand, archaic and early classical songs associated with a specific occasion and performance setting and, on the other hand, Hellenistic poems, especially epigrams, which, although not performed, play with the memory of an archaic performance scenario and manipulate the conventions of oral poetry.[2] But this trajectory from occa-sional oral performance to self-conscious metatextuality is itself too simple, for inscribed hymns also enter into a different type of dialogue with the poetic tradition. Melic inscriptions belong to a rich written epigrammatic tradition that started in the eighth century BC, that of the *carmina epigraph-ica Graeca* (collected in Peter Hansen's two-volume edition).[3] As Joseph Day has shown most recently, these epigrams are shaped by the oral culture of their times and constitute a reperformance of ritual.[4] Inscriptions have their own conventions, verbal, ritual, and visual, and inscribed songs engage with other epigrams, as well as with visual culture, through dedicated objects, monuments, and statues with which they share ritual and material space.

   This chapter explores a network of issues: the legitimizing of thematic innovations and authorizing of traditional features, the interaction between oral-ness and written-ness, and the intersection of myth, performance, and religious and political ritual. For the most part, the late classical inscribed melic poems have been examined so far from the point of view of produc-tion, as scholarship has considered how the fourth-century BC inscribed hymns conform, or do not conform, to ideas of genre shaped by earlier specimens of sung hymns and how they fit within a tradition of cultic composition.[5] Three specific areas of inquiry, however, invite us to shift the focus toward the reception of these songs. First, what rhetorical strat-egies does a song use to present new aspects of myth to an audience while continuing a cultic tradition? Second, how does an inscribed text represent performance, either its own or other imagined performances, and what effect does its representation of performance have for further enactments of

---

[2] For an overview of the problems associated with inscriptions and epigrams between the archaic and Hellenistic periods, Livingstone and Nisbet 2010: 22–45. For a series of detailed studies on archaic and classical epigrams, Baumbach, Petrovic, and Petrovic 2010.

[3] Hansen 1983–9.

[4] Day 2010, which develops arguments of Day 1989, 1994, 2000, and 2007. Also Tsagalis 2008: 268–78, on Euripidean diction influencing fourth-century funerary inscriptions.

[5] Käppel 1992, Schröder 1999, Fantuzzi 2010.

the song? Finally, how does the text relate both to its material context and to its own materiality (as physical object rather than evanescent sounds), and what effect does the connection to materiality have for the performance, and reception, of the inscribed song? The surviving corpus allows these questions to be engaged in very different ways: I start with the shorter and simpler cases of the paean from Erythrae and Aristonous' hymns, before turning to the paeans of Philodamus and Isyllus, which combine features of these short poems in more intricate patterns.

Song in stone: script, score, space

As Chapter 1 suggested, the existence of inscribed melic poetry in the fourth century BC is most often explained by reference to an important change in technologies of communication over the course of the classical period. In the archaic and early classical period, the dominant (but not single) mode of transmission for melic poetry was oral; songs were learnt and passed on orally, through school or private instruction, participation in symposia, and cult or competitive choral practice.[6] Songs were usually not inscribed, with the best-known exception recorded by the testimony of Gorgon, author of *On Sacrifices* (Περὶ θυσιῶν), who reports that Pindar's *Olympian* 7 was so admired that it was inscribed in gold letters in the sanctuary of Athena Lindia in Rhodes.[7] This exception in itself raises interesting issues. First, the song was not specifically a cult song composed for the community celebrating a god but an epinician. Its myth glorified Rhodes as a statue or a temple might glorify Athena Lindia, but its original epinician performance was presumably not in an exclusively ritual setting. Second, the location of the inscription – inside the sanctuary, to which access was highly restricted – should remind us that inscriptions were not necessarily intended for public reading.[8] Although reading, and a growing rate of literacy, is generally the reason given to explain the phenomenon of inscribed cult songs that started in the fourth century, a variety of other explanations also throw light on why a song might be written down.[9] Rolls of papyrus were held

---

[6] On the transmission of cultic songs in "literary" authors, see Chapter 1, n. 55.

[7] For Gorgon's testimony, *FGrH* 515 F 18. Also Kowalzig 2007: 224–6. The *Certamen* (line 320) also refers to the Delians' inscription of the Homeric *Hymn to Apollo* on tablets in the temple of Artemis (ἐν τῷ τῆς Ἀρτέμιδος ἱερῷ). Other evidence for inscriptions inside sanctuaries in Herington 1985: 201–3.

[8] Thomas (1989: 35, 49) and Bing (2002 and 2009: 116–46) argue that written inscriptions were not actually read. Contra: Sickinger 1999: 160–87.

[9] See discussion above, Chapter 1, pp. 53–5.

in private archives to preserve a text or as a statement of its importance for a particular family, rather than as a means of transmitting that text or making it available to a larger audience.[10] In that instance, the written status of a text is more closely connected with the issues of prestige, symbolism, and even sacredness than with pragmatic concerns. The recording of poems on stone in public places can thus be understood as the democratization of a longer-standing aristocratic practice that did not necessarily see the transmission and diffusion of the written text as one of its main goals.

Most importantly, the fact that cult songs were literally and metaphorically inscribed in a larger visual and aural landscape of gifts to the gods should make us aware of the various layers of ritual activity with which they engaged. They were part not only of a religious ritual (often referred to in the mythical narrative of the song), but also of the social, and possibly performative, ritual of their inscription itself. To hold that growing literacy and the recording of poems on stone *replaced* live and communal singing would be both insensitive to the diversity of cultural practices and, again, a Platonic way of writing the history of the demise of song culture. Even when songs were inscribed in an accessible place and when people could and would read, there was still a tremendous communal and ritual element to the very practice of making inscriptions. One might not want to go as far as Day in arguing that "vocal readings of epigrams, in the presence of those viewing dedicated objects, might be described as miniature rites of performance,"[11] yet the very fact that inscribed songs belong to a sacred complex of objects, gestures, and other words suggests that they should be read as engaging with their ritual, material, and mythical surroundings.

The Erythraean paeans: the rhetoric of making a god

The Erythraean paean to Asclepius presents a neat case of such interaction of object, gesture, and song. As noted above, copies of the hymn were found in four different places in the Greek world, but the earliest version, which Wilamowitz dated to 380–360 BC, belonged to the Asclepeion of Erythrae and was inscribed on a marble stele, with text on both sides.[12] This copy

---

[10] Herington 1985: 45–7, 201–6.

[11] Day 2010: 15. Although one might take issue with the *vocalization* of the reading, the point remains valid even with a silent reading.

[12] Versions of the song were found in Egypt (in Ptolemais, [P] copy datable to 97 AD), in Athens (in the Asclepeion, [A] copy dating from the first or second century AD), and in Dion, Macedonia (the [D] copy probably dating from the second century AD).

is the most interesting because of its textual layout.[13] The front of the stone contains a *lex sacra* that gives instructions for ritual gestures to be performed by patients seeking the help of the healing god Asclepius: these actions included an animal sacrifice and repeating three times a paean to Apollo while standing (or dancing) around the altar of the god.[14] The stone is broken diagonally and the paean to Apollo itself did not survive in its entirety; only the following words can be read:

> ἰὴ Παιών, ὤ, ἰὴ Παιών
> ἰὴ Παιών, ὤ, ἰὴ Παιών
> ἰὴ Παιών, ὤ, ἰὴ Παιών
> ὤ ἄναξ Ἄπολλον φείδεο κούρων
> φείδ[εο.

> *Iē Paiōn, ō iē Paiōn!* (*ter*) O Lord Apollo, protect the young men, protect.

On the other side of the stone is the paean to Asclepius. It is composed of three strophes in lyric dactyls, marked as strophes on the stone, with a paeanic ritual cry (*epiphthēgma*) marked each time as a refrain (*ephymnion*), ἰὴ Παιάν, Ἀσκληπιόν, | δαίμονα κλεινότατον, | ἰὲ Παιάν, at the end of each strophe. After an invitation to young men to sing Apollo (1–4), it establishes the genealogy and progeny of Asclepius (5–18), and concludes with a prayer to Asclepius (19–27).[15]

> (αʹ) [Παιᾶνα κλυτό]μητιν ἀείσατε
>   [κοῦροι Λατοΐδαν Ἕκ]ατον,
>   ἰὲ Παιάν,
>   ὃς μέγα χάρ[μα βροτοῖσ]ιν ἐγείνατο
>   μιχθεὶς ἐμ φι[λότητι Κορ]ωνίδι   5
>   ἐν γᾶι τᾶι Φλεγυείαι,
>   ἰὴ Παιάν, Ἀσκληπιόν
>   δαίμονα κλεινό[τατ]ον,
>   ἰὲ Παιάν,

---

[13] By "textual layout," I simply mean that the text of the song lies on the reverse side of a stone preserving a *lex sacra*. For a sophisticated interpretation of the disposition of the lyrics on the stone and of the strophic organization of the later versions of the song, see Faraone 2011.

[14] The text of the *lex sacra* is quoted in Wilamowitz' 1909 edition. For details on the *lex sacra*, Wilamowitz-Moellendorff 1909, Käppel 1992: 189–93 (who at p. 191 notes that the ritual itself seems typically Erythraean), Fantuzzi 2010: 188–9, I. Petrovic 2011: 265–9. A similar type of ritual is also mentioned in Eur. *IT* 1467–84, in connection with Artemis.

[15] The text is quoted in Powell's (1925) edition, *CA*, pp. 136–8. For other editions and commentaries, see also Engelmann and Merkelbach 1972, Käppel 1992: Paean no. 37, Schröder 1999: 64–75, Furley and Bremer 2001: I 211–14, II 161–80, Fantuzzi 2010, Faraone 2011.

(β′) [το]ῦ δὲ καὶ ἐξεγένοντο Μαχάων   10
     καὶ Πο[δα]λείριος ἠδ᾽ Ἰασώ,
          ἰὲ Παιάν,
     Αἴγλ[α τ᾽] ἐοῶπις Πανάκειά τε
     Ἠπιόνας παῖδες σὺν ἀγακλυτῶι
     ἐοαγεῖ Ὑγιείαι –   15
     ἰὴ Παιάν, Ἀσκληπιόν
     δαίμονα κλεινότατον,
          ἰὲ Παιάν,

(γ′) χαῖρέ μοι, ἵλαος δ᾽ ἐπινίσεο
     τὰν ἐμὰν πόλιν εὐρύχορον,   20
          ἰὲ Παιάν,
     δὸς δ᾽ ἡμᾶς χαίροντας ὁρᾶν φάος
     ἀελίου δοκίμους σὺν ἀγακλυτῶι
     ἐοαγεῖ Ὑγιείαι –
     ἰὴ Παιάν, Ἀσκληπιόν   25
     δαίμονα κλεινότατον,
          ἰὲ Παιάν.

Sing, young men, Paian famous for his skill, the far-darting son of
Leto – *ie Paian* – he who engendered a great delight for mortals, after
mingling in love with Coronis in the land of Phlegyas – *iē Paian, Asklepios*,
most famous divinity, *ie Paian*.

From him descend also Machaon and Podaleirios and Iasus (Healer) – *ie
Paian* – and fair-eyed Aigla (Radiance) and Panacea (Cure-all), children
of Hepione (Sweetness), along with shining Health, the all-famous – *iē
Paian, Asklepios*, most famous divinity, *ie Paian*.

Hail, in your kindness come to my large-plained city – *ie Paian* – and give
us to delight in seeing the light of the sun, esteemed in the company of
shining Health, the all-famous – *iē Paian, Asklepios*, most famous divinity,
ie Paian.

From the second-person initial address to the hymnic framing and the way
the inscription is laid out, respecting the stanzaic pattern, the text has all
the hallmarks of a composition meant for performance and couched in
stone. What happens to the oral aspect when the song is inscribed? What
is the ritual situation of the text and how does it compare to that of the
song?

So far, critical interest in the Erythraean hymn has focused on its position
in the evolution of the paean genre. The most significant analysis is probably that of Lutz Käppel, who has argued for an automatization of paean

composition in the classical period.[16] According to Käppel, all the formal elements of the songs (the *epiphthēgma*, adjectives, and structure) are dictated by their religious function and imply little poetic creation. Interpreting the use of certain dactylic formulae as *gattungsindifferent* ("indifferent to genre") and as belonging to the stock-in-trade of hymnic poetry, he cites parallels between the paean and the shorter Homeric hymns: the invocation Παιᾶνα κλυτόμητιν ἀείσατε ("sing Paian famous for his skill," 1), for example, is reminiscent of Ἥφαιστον κλυτόμητιν ἀείδεο ("sing Hephaistus famous for his skill," *Hymn. Hom. Heph.* 20.1), the first hymnic relative clause ὃς μέγα χάρμα βροτοῖσιν ἐγείνατο ("who engendered a great delight for mortals," 4) recalls τὸν ἐγείνατο δῖα Κορωνίς . . . χάρμα μέγ᾽ ἀνθρώποισιν ("whom noblest Coronis begat, as a great delight for men," *Hymn. Hom. Ascl.* 2–4); and the closing prayer δὸς δ᾽ ἡμᾶς χαίροντας ὁρᾶν φάος ("give us to delight in seeing the light," 22) echoes δὸς δ᾽ ἡμᾶς χαίροντας ἐς ὥρας αὖτις ἱκέσθαι ("give us to delight in coming again at the due time," *Hymn. Hom. Dion.* 26.12). Both Stefan Schröder and Gianbattista D'Alessio have argued against this automatization theory and see the Erythraean paean as an example of less elaborated cultic poetry. All three scholars, however, converge on one point: they understand the hymn not as an example of great choral production, but as a humble, either very early or belated, example of paeanic celebration, at a time when the genre was not yet, or no longer, at its peak. Yet, in its economical form, the song is remarkably effective and accomplishes an elaborate work of legitimization. The form of enunciation chosen allows the recreation of the god Asclepius as Paian every time the paean is uttered. Rather than seeking to trace the evolution of the "genre," be it by "contamination" or "automatization," we should consider how the features of different hymns bear witness to strategies of adaptation to specific circumstances, both local and temporal. My point is that it is not so much the genre that evolved one way or the other but rather that the features of different hymns bear witness to different strategies of adaptation to specific (local and temporal) circumstances. The mechanics of the enunciative process through which the song gradually justifies extending the Paian epithet to Asclepius have not been examined closely and are ripe for investigation.

The initial word of the poem is Παιᾶνα (Paian), the object of the sung celebration. In place of a direct address to "Paian," the opening line carries an exhortation, in the second person plural, to young men to sing

---

[16] Käppel 1992: 193–6.

the god (ἀείσατε κοῦροι, 1–2).[17] This second-person appeal is typical of
hymnic invocations, which "through the coincidence of discourse and
song... present [themselves] as a speech act – or rather, a song-act":[18]
ascribing to young male performers, an ideal Apollonian chorus, the verbal
action of singing at the very moment this action is being realized in performance not only gives authority to the utterance but projects its authority onto
the rest of the song. The first line develops the main object of the sentence,
Παιᾶνα, with traditional epithets of Apollo (Λατοΐδαν Ἕκατον, "far-darting
son of Leto," 2), but also with an adjective rarely used for Apollo, κλυτόμητιν
("famous for his skill," 1), yet close in sound to the more frequent κλυτόμαν-
τις ("famous for his mantic power") found in other paeans.[19] According to
Philostratus, the adjective κλυτόμητις was used by Sophocles in his paean to
Asclepius.[20] The poem legitimizes the use of the paean form for Asclepius as
it moves from celebrating the father, Apollo, with a term previously applied
to the son (κλυτόμητις in Sophocles) to celebrating the son, Asclepius, with
an adjective fit for his father (κλεινότατον, "most famous"). In line 4, right
after the hymnic relative, the first expression qualifying Asclepius (μέγα
χάρμα βροτοῖσιν, "great boon for mortals") comes before the verb. The
phrase can grammatically agree either with the subject (Apollo Paian, ὅς) or
with the direct object of ἐγείνατο, Ἀσκληπιόν, introduced after three lines
of delay in line 7, as a sort of name-cap to ἐγείνατο. As a result, the religious
syncretism operates again at the grammatical and poetic level: the "great
boon for mortals" is as much Apollo as Asclepius. The last expression of the
refrain (δαίμονα κλεινότατον, ἰὲ Παιάν, "most famous divinity, *ie Paian*," 9)
reinforces the proximity of father and son, since the adjective κλεινότατον
("most famous") picks up the root of κλυτόμητιν ("famous for his skill," 1)
and establishes semantic continuity within the family through the notion
of *kleos*.

   In the second strophe, Asclepius is no longer the grammatical subject of
the sentence and this time the *epiphthēgma iē Paian* is not addressed directly
to him. The god does not figure in the strophe by name, but his power,
and Apollo's, is embodied in the "fair-eyed" Aigla (Αἴγλαια ἐοῶπις, 13)
and "shining" Hygieia (ἐοαγεῖ Ὑγιείαι, 15), the "all-famous" (ἀγακλυτῶι,
14). Although Asclepius is not yet celebrated as Paian, the adjectives used

---

[17] On the exhortation/invocation in Greek hymns, Furley and Bremer 2001: i 52–6.
[18] Calame 2004a: 416.
[19] For example, κλυτόμαντι Πυθοῖ in Paean 6 (fr. 52f.2 SM); κλυτομάντιες in Paean 10(a)
   (fr. 52l.22 SM); κλυτοὶ μάντι[ες] Ἀπόλλωνος in Paean 8 (fr. 52i.1 SM).
[20] Philostr. *VA* 3.17.4, *Imag.* 415.7, *PMG* 737, and Rutherford 2001a: 39. Rutherford even suggests
   that Sophocles may be the author of the Erythraean paean.

to describe his offspring develop the theme of his aretalogy and replace it: Asclepius' offspring embody what the god gives (radiance and health) and what he does (cure and heal). Only in the last strophe is Asclepius addressed directly, in the prayer in the second person. The injunction Χαῖρέ μοι, ἵλαος δ' ἐπινίσεο τὰν ἀμὰν πόλιν εὐρύχορον δὸς δ'ἡμᾶς χαίροντας ὁρᾶν φάος ἀελίου ("Hail, in your kindness come to my large-plained city – *ie Paian* – and give us to delight in seeing the light of the sun," 19–23) is performative. In ordering the god to come, it also states the nature of the transaction: it is an exchange of *charis*. The pleasure that the performers have in making the gift of the hymn (ἡμᾶς χαίροντας, 22) should be replicated by the god's pleasure in receiving it (χαῖρε, 19).[21] By alluding to the nature of the prayer (*da quia dedi*, "give because I have given"), the injunction also asserts that it has done its part and that it is the god's turn to reciprocate (δός, 22). The last time that the *meshymnion* comes, line 21, it is clear that Asclepius *is* Paian, and Asclepius can be addressed directly as Paian in the prayer. The *Paian* cry has been legitimized through the poem: the song that opened with an injunction to sing Paian switches from an address to an imagined chorus of young men to the real addressee, Asclepius. The epithet is not *extended* to Asclepius in a formal innovation or as generic evolution; Asclepius is *made* Paian through a gradual transfer of power from the father to the son and through the combination of ritual performance and performative language.

These poetic dynamics are created by the formal apparatus of enunciation regardless of the geographic or physical characteristics of the inscription. But the fact that the song is inscribed, rooted in a place (a landscape and a setting), changes some of its meaning. First, because it was inscribed, the song could serve as a script that preserved a specific, local Asclepian ritual and through instruction could enable participation in the ritual, even by visitors who had no prior knowledge of the cult. The layout of a later paean to Asclepius by Macedoni(c)us (*CA*, pp. 138–40) that shares many features with the simpler Erythraean paean shows that the stonecutter even made a conscious effort to set the song out in a way that allowed a reader to easily distinguish, visually, the *iē Paian epiphthēgma*, "perhaps to facilitate a choral performance or audience response to a choral performance."[22] Moreover, the continuity across the recto and verso sides of the stone invites us to understand the performative address to young men (κοῦροι) on one side of the stone as activating the *lex sacra* that invites Apollo to "protect young men" (φείδεο κούρων) on the other side. The invocation in the paean can be read as a mark of choral projection, a term that Albert Henrichs has

---

[21] Depew 2000: 70–1, Day 2010: 232–80.   [22] Faraone 2011: 216.

used mainly of tragedy and that describes the poet's use of choral imagery to project the activity of the performers onto another, imagined, chorus located in the past or the future.[23] Any time a chorus sings or even reads the paean, it activates the mechanisms of ritual reciprocity linking the two sides of the stone and connecting god and performer.

The idea of mechanisms of reciprocity can be extended from people to places. In line 19 of the Erythraean paean, the narrative concludes with a reference to a first person, both singular (χαῖρέ μοι, "hail," or, more literally, "be gracious to me," 19, and τὰν ἐμὰν πόλιν, "my city," 20) and plural (δὸς δ' ἡμᾶς χαίροντας, "give us to delight," 22). If the possessive (ἐμάν) is read as part of the apparatus of enunciation and refers to the internal speaker of the poem, "my city" can denote the city of any subsequent visitor to the sanctuary who read the song. But if the song is read as a script for ritual, the deictics connect more specifically the performance with the ritual body of performers (the κοῦροι of Apollo) and the place (the sanctuary of Asclepius at Erythrae) in which the song is inscribed.

This epichoric marker is made explicit in the other inscribed versions of the paean, which have a variant for line 19. The version found in Dion, for example, has Δείων πόλιν ("the city of Dion") instead of τὰν ἐμὰν πόλιν ("my city"), and the version in Ptolemais complements this intra-discursive reference with a very local extra strophe:

> Νείλου δὲ ῥοὰς δώῃς, μάκαρ, ἀϊδίους,
> καὶ τᾷδε πόλει θάλος ἀμβρόσιον,
> πάσῃ τ' ἀγανὸν κλέος Αἰγύπτῳ.   30
> χαῖρέ μοι, ὦ Παιάν, ἐπ' ἐμαῖς εὔφροσι ταῖσδ' ἀοιδαῖς,
> χαῖρ', ὦ Πύθι' Ἄπολλον.

> May you grant, O blessed one, the flowing of the Nile to always last, and to this city may you give divine flourishing, and for the whole of Egypt resplendent glory. Take pleasure, O Paian, in these gracious songs of mine, hail, O Pythian Apollo.

In this context, every time the song is performed, it replicates the original inscription process by not only making explicit the reference to τᾷδε πόλει (specifying κλέος Αἰγύπτῳ, "glory for Egypt"), but also customizing the wishes (asking in this case for the waters of the Nile to be abundant and the city to be fertile). The material gift that the inhabitants of Ptolemais gave to the god by making an inscription on a stone, in the form of a prayer that they be granted "divine flourishing," is doubled by another gift to the god,

---

[23] Henrichs 1996: 49.

the transient performance of the song. One (the stone) commemorates the ritual power of the other (the song).

Besides being an offering to the god, the inscription also makes a claim for the community that inscribes it. Variations in the recounting of the myth of Asclepius' and his progeny's births are also significant, especially two details: the absence of the words ἐν γᾷ in line 6 of the Ptolemais version, instead of ἐν γᾷ τᾷ Φλεγυείᾳ as in the Erythraean version, and the addition of Akeso to Asclepius' progeny in the Dion inscription. Following the line established by Bülow's interpretation of the similarities across later versions as the product of an "Athenian recension," scholars have suggested that the introduction of Akeso to versions of the hymn is indicative of a strong Athenian interest in presenting Asclepius as Epidaurian.[24] These variations suggest that the community was careful to remove any allusion to the Thessalian origins of Asclepius, in an attempt by the Athenians to support the Epidaurians.[25]

The song must have been in dialogue with the aural and visual landscape of the sanctuary, that is with hymns sung in honor of the god and dedications to Asclepius in thanks for healing (ἰάματα).[26] But the song is also in dialogue with performances of a more public kind, as is especially clear from the development of the inscriptions. New text was added to the stone: the Erythraean version, for example, records an adscript, lines 74–6 on the stone, of the beginning of a paean in dactylo-epitrites in honor of Seleucus, which can be dated to 281 BC thanks to a reference to the victory at Kyropedion. In this scenario, the inscribed text of the paean is available to generate endless oral performances; but it is also reactivated in specific socio-political rituals, including an occasion on which the mortal Seleucus was celebrated by a hymn and honored by an inscription. This variation illustrates how forms of celebration, sung/oral and written, religious and political, feed off each other and reinforce each other's power. The same is also true of the prescript to the Ptolemais version of the paean: the song was inscribed by the city on the occasion of a ceremony celebrating the restoration of the temple to Asclepius and Hygieia in Ptolemais, during Pompeius Planta and Calpurnius Sabinus' visit under the rule of Nerva (AD 98–100). Just as in the case of the paean to Seleucus that followed that of Asclepius, this paean

---

[24] See Bülow 1929, Furley and Bremer 2001: I 213–14, Faraone 2011: 210–11.

[25] For Asclepius' birthplace, Edelstein and Edelstein 1945: T. 10–20: testimonies give Tricca (Hom. *Il.* 2.729–31, Strab. 14.1.39), various places in Thessaly (*Hymn. Hom. Ascl.* 3, Pind. *Pyth.* 3, Ap. Rhod. *Argon.* 4.616–17), Messenia (Paus. 2.26.7), Arcadia (Paus. 8.25.11), and Epidaurus. See Furley and Bremer (2001: I 213–14) for the two scholars' evaluation of Bülow's argument in favor of the "Athenian recension," which they deem "not proven."

[26] For Epidaurian inscriptions and dedications as thanksgiving, Girone 1998: 39–74, Osborne and Rhodes 2003: 532–42 (no. 102).

could have been performed at a ceremony; the inscription would have been dedicated during the inauguration of the restored temple and at festivals of Asclepius (and Hygieia), in a continued dialogue between oral and written ritual.[27]

The Erythraean paeans are not a stale example of traditional religious hymns whose composition had been "automatized." Rather, these versions of an anonymous hymn attest to the continued life and ever-renewed uses of a song that facilitated commerce between the divinity and the worshipper and could be accommodated to new religious and civic uses in the mortal community both in and after the late classical period.

Aristonous' Delphic hymns: representing divine exchanges

Songs associated with the name of an author, a given locale, and a specific date present a different scenario. The inscription of a song along with a public decree (of the type Δελφοὶ ἔδωκαν… "The Delphians granted…") gives new status to that song by giving public and official status to its author. The inscription is a public acknowledgment of the importance of the hymn for the community, and its material worth is symbolized by the privileges granted to the poet. The *subscriptio* to the hymns by a certain Aristonous of Corinth, for example, inscribed under the archonship of Damachares, which has been dated to the third quarter of the fourth century BC, informs us of the important privileges Delphi awarded the poet:[28]

> Δελφοὶ ἔδωκαν Ἀριστονό[ωι, ἐπεὶ] τοὺς ὕμνους τοῖς θεοῖς ἐπο[ίησεν], αὐτῶι
> καὶ ἐκγόνοις προξ[ενίαν] εὐεργεσίαν προμαντείαν προ[εδρίαν] προδικίαν
> ἀσυλίαν πολέμου [καὶ εἰ]ρήνης, ἀτέλειαν πάντων καὶ ἐπιτι[μὰ]ν καθάπερ
> Δελφοῖς, ἄρχοντος Δαμαχάρεος, βουλευόντων Ἀντάνδρου, Ἐρασίππου,
> Εὐαρχίδα.

> The Delphians granted Aristonous, because of the hymns to the gods that he composed, to him and to his descendants proxeny, the title of *euergetēs*, right to consult the oracle first, first seats in the theater, priority in trial, inviolability in war and peace, exemption from all public burden, enjoyment of all the public rights of the Delphians, under the archonship of Damachares, while Antander, Erasippus, and Euarchides were council-members.

---

[27] For an evocative description of the cult of Asclepius, Dignas 2007.
[28] For the date, Vamvouri-Ruffy 2004: 211–15.

The accumulation is impressive. Aristonous' compensation was the same as that granted, for example, to a victorious athlete at the Pythian games.[29] Similar generosity can be found in the case of an inscribed poem by Philodamus and his brothers, who upon the inscription of their song were said to have received honors that were extended even to their children:

Δελφοὶ ἔδωκαν Φιλοδάμ[ωι Αἰν]ησιδάμου Σκαρφεῖ καὶ τcῖς ἀδελφοῖς Ἐπι[γ]ένε[ι] | . . νπιδαι αὐτοῖς καὶ ἐκ[γόνοις] προξενίαν προμ[αν]τείαν προεδρίαν προδικ[ίαν | [ἀτέ]λειαν ἐπι[τιμ]ὰν καθ[άπερ Δελ]φοῖς· ἄρχοντος Ἐτυμώνδα, βουλευόντων |...σιστωνος Καλλικρ[άτεος [other indications follow].

The Delphians granted Philodamus son of Aenesidamus of Scarphea and to his brothers Epigenes ... to them and to their descendants proxeny, right to consult the oracle first, first seats at the theater, priority of trial, exemption from public burden and enjoyment of all the public rights of the Delphians. Under the archonship of Etymondas, while ... sistonos, Callicrates were council-members.

Although both poets received great honors, the privileges they were given were not identical, which may be evidence that the value of each hymn was cautiously reckoned, estimated to be worth certain privileges but not others. However, by the same token, such a *subscriptio* also *adds* value to the poem itself and necessarily creates heightened expectation: not only the text but also the judgment on the text and a vetted reception are inscribed in the landscape.

Uniquely, the inscription gives insight into the socio-religious mechanisms of commission and composition. The subscript to the latter inscription, for example, mentions that "Philodamus and his brothers composed the paean to Dionysus according to the oracle given by the god" (Φιλόδαμος καὶ τοὶ ἀδελφοὶ τὸν παιᾶνα τὸν εἰς τὸν Διόνυσον ἐποίησαν ... κατὰ τὰν μαντείαν τοῦ Θεοῦ ἐπαγγείλαντος).[30] It asserts the song's ritual character while throwing light on the social role played by its authors, who channelled the god's voice, as it were. We know nothing of these authors other than what the text and peritext tell us, just as we know nothing of Aristonous and Isyllus, two authors whose poetry the next sections will examine. Philodamus and his brothers could have been itinerant poets, composing for communities

---

[29] Osborne and Rhodes 2003: 466–71, no. 92 (for an athlete) lists (3–5) προξενίαν, προμ[αντεία προεδρ]ίαν, ἀτέλειαν, ἀσυλίαν, προδικί[αν, ἐπιτι[μὰ]ν καὶ τἆλλα ὅσα καὶ τοῖς ἄλλοις προξένοις.

[30] I am giving the text of Furley-Bremer's reconstruction (2001: I 57). Bremer (1981: 82) suggests that the phrase probably means that the brothers were not only commissioned to compose a cult hymn, but also given indications about both topic and focus of the song.

who prescribed a specific format for the song they wanted, who in return for their services were granted privileges, or they could have been members of the local elite, like Isyllus, who devoted some of their wealth in the name of the community – and for the advertisement of their poetic talent.[31]

Beside being associated with a name and a date, the inscribed songs are also grounded in a place: the sanctuary of Delphi, where both stelae were found. The songs all deal with aspects of Delphic myth and ritual and relate to specific features of Delphic sights, sites, and geography, real and imagined. Two issues thus come to the fore: that of the relationship between their original setting at Delphi and future reperformances, either on site or elsewhere; and that of the narrative, ritual, and aesthetic effects of the epichoric character of the song. Each of the three songs engages with these two issues in a different way. I will start with the shortest, a *Hymn to Hestia*, and then see how some of the problems it exemplifies are developed on a larger scale in the other two compositions.

Dancing Hestia

Aristonous' *Hymn to Hestia* is a seventeen-line poem in dactylo-epitrites that displays the tripartite structure characteristic of cletic hymns.[32] The introduction (1–2) invokes the goddess, a main part (2–10), introduced by a hymnic relative, presents her function and power, and a conclusion (11–17) includes a farewell formula and a prayer. The song's principal function is to ask the goddess to grant the performers bliss in exchange for their prayers (*da quia dedi*):

> ἱερὰν ἱερῶν ἄνασσαν
> Ἑστίαν ὑμνήσομεν, ἃ καὶ Ὄλυμπον
> καὶ μυχὸν γαίας μεσόμφαλον ἀεί
> Πυθίαν τε δάφναν κατέχουσα
> ναὸν ἀν᾽ ὑψίπυλον Φοίβου χορεύεις   5
> τερπομένα τριπόδων θεσπίσμασι,
> καὶ χρυσέαν φόρμιγγ᾽ Ἀπόλλων
> ὁπηνίκ᾽ ἂν ἑπτάτονον
> κρέκων μετὰ σοῦ θαλιάζον-
> τας θεοὺς ὕμνοισιν αὔξῃ.   10
> χαῖρε Κρόνου θύγατερ
> καὶ Ῥέας, μούνα πυρὸς ἀμφιέπουσα

---

[31] On the status of these itinerant poets, Hunter and Rutherford 2009.

[32] The hymn is quoted in Powell's (1925) edition, *CA*, pp. 164–5. For other editions, see Furley and Bremer 2001: I 116–18, II 38–45. On the hymn: Wilamowitz-Moellendorff 1921: 496–7, Danielewic 1978, Fantuzzi 2010: 192–5.

βωμοὺς ἀθανάτων ἐριτίμους,
Ἑστία, δίδου δ' ἀμοιβάς
ἐξ ὁσίων πολὺν ἡμᾶς   15
ὄλβον ἔχοντας ἀεὶ λιπαρόθρονον
ἀμφὶ σὰν θυμέλαν χορεύειν.

Let us sing Holy Hestia queen of the holy ones, who holds forever sway over Olympus and the omphalos in the recesses of the earth, and the Pythian laurel, you who dance in the lofty temple of Phoebus, enjoying the oracular voices of tripods, and Apollo's golden seven-string phorminx, whenever he plays it to exalt, with you, the feasting gods in his hymns. Hail, daughter of Cronos and Rhea, who alone brings fire to the honored altars of the immortals; Hestia, give us, in exchange for our prayers, prosperity without impiety and to sing and dance around your bright-throned altar forever.

The main feature that commentators have highlighted in Aristonous' poetry is its "classicism."[33] By this, scholars mean that both hymns rely on images, phrases, and diction familiar from archaic and early classical lyric and only innovate insofar as they combine these expressions in new patterns, including a very skillful *symplokē*.[34] The image of Apollo playing the golden seven-string cithara (χρυσέαν φόρμιγγ' Ἀπόλλων . . . ἑπτάτονον κρέκων, 7–9), for example, is reminiscent of earlier lyric.[35] Some expressions in Aristonous' hymn even seem to echo specifically the diction of Delphic plays, Aeschylus' *Eumenides* and Euripides' *Ion*.[36] The relative clause praising Hestia's power, in particular, and the tight connection between omphalos, mantic power, and choral dancing is reminiscent of Euripides' *Ion* (461–4):

Φοιβήος ἔνθα γᾶς
μεσόμφαλος ἑστία
παρὰ χορευομένῳ τρίποδι
μαντεύματα κραίνει.

. . . where Phoebus' ombilical hearth of the earth offers oracles near the tripod circled by dances.

---

[33] Danielewic 1978: 55, 60.   [34] Furley and Bremer 2001: I 121.

[35] For example, Bacchyl. fr. 20B: ἑπτάτονον λ[ι]γυρὰν κάππαυε γᾶρυν; Eur. *Ion* 881–2 τᾶς ἑπταφθόγγου μέλπων | κιθάρας; Pind. *Pyth.* 1.1–2 χρυσέα φόρμιγξ, Ἀπόλλωνος καὶ ἰοπλοκάμων | σύνδικον Μοισᾶν κτέανον; Timoth. *PMG* 791. 202 χρυσεοκίθαριν.

[36] As Furley and Bremer point out, most of the phrases have many parallels in archaic or early classical lyric, from the reference to the golden throne ('Ἑστία χρυσόθρον' in Bacchyl. 16.1–4) to mentions of πυρὶ φλέγουσα, in lines 12–13 of the inscription, for which there are parallels from Pindar to Euripides.

The same passage also echoes Aeschylus' descriptions of Delphi, called μαντικῶν μυχῶν ("mantic recesses") in the *Eumenides* (180), ἑστία μεσόμ-φαλος ("ombilical hearth") in the *Agamemnon* (1056), and μεσόμφαλόν θ᾽ ἵδρυμα ("ombilical seat") in the *Choephoroi* (1035). But these seman-tic parallels might be more than poetic echoes: the λιπαρόθρονον θυμέλαν ("bright-throned altar," 16–17) in particular recalls not only Aeschylus' λιπαροθρόνοισι ἐπ᾽ ἐσχάραις ("in the bright-throned hearth," *Eumenides* 806) but also one of the two Homeric hymns to Hestia, which describes Hestia as having hair "always anointed by wet oil" (αἰεὶ σῶν πλοκάμων ἀπολείβεται ὑγρὸν ἔλαιον, "moist oil always drips down from your locks," *Hymn. Hom. Hest.* 24.3). More than a generic term of praise, the adjec-tive λιπαρός ("bright, glistening") might be a reference to a specific cult at Delphi, where the omphalos was anointed with oil. So rather than inter-preting Aristonous' poem as recycling the diction of Delphic plays, one should consider in what way all these songs, whether tragic lyric or cult compositions, drew from the same Delphic ritual repertoire, which we no longer have access to. This suggestion invites us to think again about the relationship between these hymns and the notion of "model," as the stone poems constitute a form, and site, of dissemination of Delphic cult diction and images parallel to the Athenian stage that we are more familiar with.

Moreover, the same vocabulary has a very different effect when used in the theater of Dionysus in Athens (in this case, in the *Ion*) and in Delphi: while the *deixis* could only be *am Phantasma* in plays put on in the theater of Dionysus at Athens, it can be *ad oculos* when the stone, set in Delphi, refers to the context in which the ritual took place. The reference to anything μεσόμφαλον ("ombilical"), in particular, can be interpreted as an "intervi-sual" rather than intertextual reference: although there is no deictic in the text referring to the Delphic landscape surrounding the inscription, the song, heard or read, echoes the visual sights – laurel, omphalos, temple, altar, statues of the gods...

A further aspect that distinguishes the song from the Erythraean paeans is that the rhetoric of Aristonous' inscription relies on the dynamic of the represented performance. The goddess is invoked as delighting in the music of Apollo and as participating in choral activity in his sanctuary (ναὸν ἀν᾽ ὑψίπυλον Φοίβου χορεύεις, 5). Even the interweaving of terms to do with singing and dancing links humans and gods in musical practice: ὑμνήσομεν ("let us sing," 2) and ὕμνοισιν ("songs," 10); χορεύεις ("you dance," 5) and χορεύειν ("to dance," 17). These references form a spiral of musical worship: the performers hymn Hestia, who dances in the sanctuary of Apollo (who in turn celebrates other gods by his musical performance), and ask the goddess to give them the fortune to dance around her altar. Musical performance is what gives the hymn its structure and its ritual efficacy. In the midst of all this movement, we might forget that a dancing Hestia is functionally strange:[37] Hestia, as goddess of the hearth, should be the one who stays in place while others dance, as is the case in the passage of Euripides quoted above, where ἑστία (462) is a common noun that designates a place and the performers circle in dance around the tripod.[38] But in Aristonous' song, it is as if the movement of concentric circles (Hestia dancing in Apollo's temple and performers dancing around Hestia) maintains a peaceful yet dynamic harmony. Hestia's dance symbolically signifies her blissful embracing of Apollo's ruling at Delphi and the serene concord between the gods. Even more, it is as if the represented performance itself takes the place of, or reproduces, the mythological narrative; at the end of the song, every time the performers replicate Hestia's choral activity, they justify her power. The short mythical vignette of the goddess dancing to the sound of Apollo's singing and playing simultaneously works as an aitiology for the ritual of choral performance at Delphi in the sanctuary of Apollo, and the choral performance justifies the cult of Hestia at Delphi. Either read or performed, the opening speech act (ὑμνήσομεν, "let us sing") initiates a series of further ritual acts connected with musical performance, all tied to the first one.

Apollo and the traffic in grace

The narrative and performative situation is different in Aristonous' *Hymn to Apollo*, which does not make any reference to divine performance. The song is composed of six strophes of aeolic meters, each repeating twice the pattern of three glyconics followed by a pherecratean.[39] The *meshymnion* is marked by the *epiphthēgma iē ie Paian* and the *ephymnion* concludes with *ō ie Paian*. Despite the presence of these specifically paeanic markers, the inscription describes the song as a hymn to Pythian Apollo (Ἀριστόνοος Νικοσθένους Κορίνθιος Ἀπόλλωνι Πυθίῳ τὸν ὕμνον, "the hymn to Pythian Apollo of Aristonous Nicosthenos of Corinth"). Nothing is known about the

---

[37] There are two references to Hestia's movement: 5 ναὸν ἀν᾽ ὑψίπυλον Φοίβου χορεύεις, "you dance in the lofty sanctuary of Phoibus" and 12–13 μούνα πυρὸς ἀμφιέπουσα | βωμοὺς ἀθανάτων ἐριτίμους, "alone bringing fire to the honored altars of the immortals".

[38] On Hestia's function and relationship with space and movement, Vernant 1963.

[39] The hymn is quoted in Powell's (1925) edition, *CA*, pp. 162–4. For other editions, see Käppel 1992: Paian no. 42 (pp. 384–6); Furley and Bremer 2001: I 119–21, II 45–52. For studies on the hymn, Fairbanks 1900: 112–18, Wilamowitz-Moellendorff 1921: 243, Audiat 1932, Panagl 1969, Vamvouri-Ruffy 2004: 94–6, 206–15, Bommelaer 2005, Fantuzzi 2010: 192.

occasion of the poem's composition, but William Furley and Jan Bremer, in their commentary on the text, arguing from the prominent place occupied by many gods in this hymn to Apollo, have proposed (convincingly in my view) composition for the Theoxenia, a Panhellenic festival for all the gods.

The poem starts with an invocation to Apollo and mention of his genealogy (first strophe) and moves to a quick description of his mantic and musical skills (second strophe). Most of the narrative concentrates on the god's accession to power and his relationship with other gods (third through fifth strophes). It ends with a prayer for the god to come to the city and protect the inhabitants (sixth strophe). In the first strophe, just as in the previous hymn, we find a glorification of Delphi, the place as much as its god:

> Πυθίαν ἱερόκτιτον
> ναίων Δελφίδ᾽ ἀμφὶ πέτραν
> ἀεὶ θεσπιόμαντιν ἕ-
>   δραν, ἰὴ ἰὲ Παιάν,
> Ἄπολλον, Κοίου τε κόρας   5
> Λατοῦς σεμνὸν ἄγαλμα καί
> Ζηνὸς ὑψίστου μακάρων
>   βουλαῖς, ὦ ἰὲ Παιάν.

> Forever occupant of the holy-founded Pythian oracular sanctuary, on the Delphic rock, *iē ie Paian*, [I hail you] Apollo, august delight of Leto, daughter of Coeus, and according to the will of Zeus, highest of the Blessed ones, *ō ie Paian*.

The god's worship is rooted in a definite Delphic geography (Πυθίαν, "Pythian," 1; Δελφίδ᾽ ἀμφὶ πέτραν, "on the Delphic rock," 2) and the diction makes clear that the place is full of the god (ἱερόκτιτον, "holy-founded," 1; θεσπιόμαντιν, "oracular sanctuary," 3; σεμνόν, "august," 6). Moreover, the opening strophe attunes the audience to the vocabulary of cult offering by describing the baby god as an ἄγαλμα ("delight," 6): like the song, and like the inscription or any dedication, the baby is a delightfully beautiful gift, which Zeus and Leto receive with joy. This first reference to a gift announces the gift-giving dynamic of the song, representative of the public offering of the hymn itself.[40]

The next strophe establishes the god's power and the origins of that power, starting from intervisual signs – tripods, laurel, temple – that could

---

40 On the vocabulary of gift and exchange between gods as a paradigm for the reciprocal relationship that men hope to establish with Apollo, Vamvouri-Ruffy 2004: 94–6.

probably be seen around the sanctuary in the vicinity of the inscribed stone:

ἔνθ' ἀπὸ τριπόδων θεο-
κτήτων, χλ[ω]ρότομον δάφναν   10
σείων, μαντοσύναν ἐποι-
    χνεῖς, ἰὴ ἰὲ Παιάν,
φρικώεντος ἐξ ἀδύτου
μελλόντων θέμιν εὐσεβῆ
χρησμοῖς εὐφθόγγου τε λύρας   15
    αὐδαῖς, ὦ ἰὲ Παιάν.

ἁγνισθεὶς ἐνὶ Τέμπεσιν
βουλαῖς Ζηνὸς ὑπειρόχου,
ἐπεὶ Παλλὰς ἔπεμψε Πυ-
    θῶδ', [ἰὴ] ἰὲ Παιάν,   20
πείσας Γαῖαν ἀνθοτρόφον
Θέμιν τ' εὐπλόκαμον θεάν
[αἳ]ἐν εὐλιβάνους ἕδρας
    ἔχεις, ὦ ἰὲ Παιάν.

ὅθεν Τριτογενῆ προναί-   25
αν ἐμ μαντείοις ἁ[γί]οις
σέβων ἀθανάτοις ἀμοι-
    [β]αῖς, ἰὴ ἰὲ Παιάν,
χάριν παλαιὰν χαρίτων
τᾶν τότ' ἀϊδίους ἔχων   30
μνήμας, ὑψίστα<ι>ς ἐφέπεις
    τιμαῖς, ὦ ἰὲ Παιάν.

There, from your holy-founded mantic seat, waving the green-shorn laurel, you pursue prophecy, *iē ie Paian*, from the awe-inspiring inner-most shrine: the sacred law of the future, through prophecies and the voice of the beautiful-sounding lyre, *iō ie Paian*.

Purified in the Tempe River, according to the will of supreme Zeus, when Pallas sent you toward Pytho, *iē ie Paian*, you convinced Gaia, nurse of flowers, and the divine Themis of beautiful locks and you occupy forever the sanctuary rich in frankincense, *ō ie Paian*.

So, honoring Tritogene at the threshold of your temple in the holy sanctu-ary with immortal exchanges, *iē ie Paian*, in eternal recognition of the old kindness she showed then, you proceed to the highest honors, *ō ie Paian*.

The description of Apollo's double power, mantic and musical, creates an intertextual connection with the previous hymn, in the mention of the tripods/oracular seat and the god's *phorminx*. Read together as inscriptions, each hymn would reinforce the effect of the other. But in the Apollo hymn, where the diction is traditional, as in χρησμοῖς εὐφθόγγου τε λύρας αὐδαῖς ("through prophecies and the voice of the beautiful-sounding lyre," 15–16), the word order is elaborate: the chiasm created by the interlacing of genitives and datives gives a false impression of symmetry. The diction in general is more elaborate than in the previous hymn, in a way reminiscent of the late classical poetics that I described in Chapter 4. It is especially clear in the use of hapax and compounds (χλωρότομον, "green-shorn," 10; φρικώεντος, "awe-inspiring," 13; ἀνθοτρόφον, "nurse of flowers," 21) that all contribute to adding layers of imagery to the traditional diction and invite a reading or listening audience to participate in imagining and interpreting a long string of adjectives.[41] The result is a fresher praise of the traditional features of the god: compounds and hapax work as visual, and more generally sensorial, cues for the imagination and are a tool of *enargeia*. One is given, for example, to see the freshly shorn laurel (χλωρότομον δάφναν) more vibrantly because two simultaneous ideas are combined in the compound, that of cutting and that of the color and texture of something still fresh and green. Similarly, in the next strophes, the neologistic compound adjectives are used to evoke an image very different from the traditional narrative of the god's arrival in Delphi. Gaia, who brings forth the monster Typho in the *Theogony* (821–2) and rejoices at Hera's vow of parthenogenesis in the Homeric *Hymn to Apollo* (341–2), is nowhere else called ἀνθοτρόφον ("nurse of flowers").[42] With its nurturing and bucolic echoes, the compound contributes to the rhetoric of sacred concord among the gods, and even among the different generations of gods, at Delphi.

In addition to this poetic work of representation of a sacred epiphany, the narrative performs sophisticated ideological work by telescoping two versions of the myth of Apollo's arrival at Delphi.[43] The first version tells of Apollo's victory over Pytho, which required his ritual purifying in the Tempe and subsequent ousting of the previous Delphic occupants.[44] There is no explicit reference to the event, but Aristonous describes the ritual purification (Ἁγνισθεὶς ἐνὶ Τέμπεσιν, 17) and the "recollection of old *charis* [favor]" (29–31) by Athena, who helped Apollo and hosted him in Athens

---

[41] It is again reminiscent of tragic diction, especially Δελφίδ' ἀμφὶ πέτραν ἀεὶ θεσπιόμαντιν ἕδραν (2–3), which echoes ἁ θεσπιέπεια Δελφὶς πέτρα (Soph. *OT* 463–4); also Eur. *Ion* (94–7 and 145–50) for the beautifying effect of the waters of Castalia.

[42] Compare γαῖα φερέσβιος ("Gaia giver of life"), *Hymn. Hom. Ap.* 341.

[43] On the different versions of the myth, Sourvinou-Inwood 1987.

[44] The narrative differs, for example, from the violent one told by Euripides in *IT* 1234–82, which features the baby god's prowess and Gaia's revenge.

after he fled Delphi upon killing Pytho. The alternate version is much more pacific and describes a smooth transfer of power: Apollo, having persuaded Gaia to cede power, occupies the seat of Themis – a peaceful cession of power that the text had already hinted at in the reference to Apollo's power over θέμιν (line 14), and is further established in the next strophes, where a catalogue of gifts offered by the gods to Apollo replaces a narrative of the god's Pythian aretalogy:

> δωροῦντ[αι] δέ σ᾽ ἀθάνατοι,
> Ποσειδῶν ἁγνοῖς δαπέδοις,
> Νύμφαι Κωρυκίοισιν ἄν-   35
>   τροις, ἰὴ ἰὲ Παιάν,
> τριετέσιν φαναῖς Βρόμιος,
> σεμνὰ δ᾽ Ἄρτεμις εὐπόνοις
> κυνῶν ἐμ φυλακαῖς ἔχει
>   τόπους, ὦ ἰὲ Παιάν.   40
>
> ἀλλ᾽ ὦ Παρνασσοῦ γυάλων
> εὐδρόσοισι Κασταλίας
> να[σ]μοῖς σὸν δέμας ἐξαβρύ-
>   νων, ἰὴ ἰὲ Παιάν . . .

The immortals give you gifts: Poseidon – the holy plain, the nymphs – the Corycian grotto, *iē ie Paian*, Bromius – the torch-lit revels, and holy Artemis keeps the place with the watchful industry of her dogs, *ō ie Paian*.

But you, making your body beautiful in the dewy streams of Castalia from the vales of Parnassus, *iē ie Paian* . . .

The gifts (δωροῦνται, 33) continue the network of χάριτες ("favors"): after the ἄγαλμα ("delight," 6) brought by the baby god and the χάρις ("favor," 19) of Apollo, who gives back to Athena what she had given him, Apollo is now the receiver. All the gifts involve snippets of Delphic landscape, physical and cultic, but they do not point directly to the surroundings. Similarly, the song closes with one last reference to the sacred landscape of the Delphic countryside (Παρνασσοῦ γυάλων εὐδρόσοισι Κασταλίας να[σ]μοῖς, "the dewy streams of Castalia from the vales of Parnassus," 42–3), but there is no explicit deictic connection between song, stone, and landscape.

More surprisingly perhaps in light of the musical description of Apollo in the *Hymn to Hestia*, the poem makes no reference to performance, except at the closing of the last strophe:

> χαρεὶς ὕμνοις ἡμετέροις,   45
> ὄλβον ἐξ ὁσίων διδούς

ἀεὶ καὶ σῴζων ἐφέποις
ἡμᾶς, ὦ ἰὲ Παιάν.

Rejoicing in our hymns, always give us prosperity without impiety and
proceed to protect us, *ō ie Paian*.

The musical relationship (ἀμοιβάς, 14) between the gods and between gods
and men that was so prevalent in Aristonous' *Hymn to Hestia* has been
replaced throughout this poem by references to exchanges (ἀμοιβαῖς, 28–9)
between gods, and parallels between gods and men in his *Hymn to Apollo*.
Activities in the divine realm are verbally replicated in the human world:
ὑψίσταις ἐφέπεις τιμαῖς ("you proceed to the highest honors," 31–2), for
example, is echoed by σῴζων ἐφέποις ἡμᾶς ("may you proceed to protect
us," 47–8), the χάριν (29) that Apollo received, replicated in the favor that
he bestowed on Athena as a token of his appreciation for what she had
done in the past (χαρίτων, 29) is replicated in the pleasure (χαρείς, 45) that
the god is supposed to find in the performers' songs (ὕμνοις ἡμετέροις, 45).
Finally the ἄγαλμα ("delightful gift") brought by the birth of the baby god
is echoed by the ἄγαλμα of the song itself in honor of the god. Whoever
reads the inscription ultimately participates in the economy of praise of
the divine and re-enacts this series of exchanges and continuities. While the
Hymn to Hestia justified its status through the representation of an exchange
of performances, the *Hymn to Apollo* describes its own performance as only
one part of a more complex and abstract network involving an exchange of
material and immaterial gifts, visual and sung, human and divine. Through
this extended network of images, all revolving around the notion of *charis*,
the song justifies its manipulations of the Apollo-at-Delphi myth and its
reshaping of other mythological narratives.

Musical tourism: Dionysus at Delphi

Philodamus' *Paean to Dionysus* presents some of the same challenges
as Aristonous' hymns but develops them on a more spectacular scale.[45]
The song has been analyzed mostly in terms of generic innovation, as it
seems to break down the age-long opposition between paean for Apollo
and dithyramb for Dionysus, by invoking Dionysus with the *iē Paian*

---

[45] The hymn is quoted in Powell's (1925) edition, *CA*, pp. 165–71, with a few modifications, all
marked in the notes. For other editions, see Käppel 1992: Paian no. 39 (pp. 375–80); Furley
and Bremer 2001: I 121–8, II 52–84. For studies on the paean: Fairbanks 1900: 38, Vollgraff
1924, Rainer 1975, Stewart 1982, Käppel 1992: 207–84, Schröder 1999, 77–93, Vamvouri-Ruffy
2004: 187–206, Calame 2009, Fantuzzi 2010: 189–92, I. Petrovic 2011.

refrain.[46] But I hope to show that this is too reductive and misleading a way to interpret the rhetoric and pragmatics of the hymn. The main innovation of the hymn, I will suggest, lies in both its rhetoric of legitimization of the god and its self-consciousness about its own inscription in the sanctuary of Delphi. These two features joined together make for a unique example of cultic song, justifying its status both as performance (and future reperformance) and as written object displayed in Delphi.

The composition was inscribed on a stele in two fifty-line columns organized in twelve stanzas and was found under the pavement of the Sacred Way near the altar of Chios at Delphi. The text and peritext provide data about the circumstances of the composition of the hymn. Strophe 9 refers to the reconstruction of the temple of Apollo in Delphi, the so-called Alcmeonid temple, which had been destroyed in an earthquake and landslide in 373 BC. The god urges the Delphic authorities to finish the process of rebuilding, gives architectural, sculptural, and ritual details, and blesses the human builders. Strophe 9 also contains a reference to the festival of the Theoxenia (ἐν ξενίοις ἐτείοις θεῶν, 110–11), which was likely the performance setting for the premiere of the song. As for the exact date of the inscription, a prose *subscriptio* mentions that the authors of the song, Philodamus and his brothers, were honored for their composition under the archonship of Etymondas, which Brian Rainer has dated to 340/339 BC.[47]

The text offers unique insights into issues raised above. In its physical embeddedness in Delphi and its participation in Delphic honors, the song is close to the hymns of Aristonous and brings to the fore the complex relationship between the ritual dimension of a performance and the ritual dimension of an inscription. Furthermore, it invites us to consider the importance of the relationship between song and stone as objects of transaction between gods and men, and as sites of social and political transaction. But we also need consider the relationship between the original performance of the song and its subsequent performances, and the poetic and rhetorical strategies used in honoring Dionysus with a paean. As Käppel's study has shown, the poet carefully negotiates the use of the paean form, and cry, for Dionysus, and simultaneously uses the rhetoric of the paean to legitimize what Käppel sees as a religious innovation, year-round dithyrambic singing at Delphi rather than the more traditional winter dithyrambs. Less attention has been garnered by the relationships between the physical immobility of the stone and the geographic wanderings of the poem, and between the

---

[46] On which see Chapter 1.   [47] Rainer 1975: 75–141. The subscription is quoted above, p. 295.

materiality of the stone and what I call the "traffic in grace" in the paean. It is these issues that the next pages consider.

The first strophe opens with an invocation of the god (1–4):

> (i) [δεῦρ ἄνα Δ]ιθύραμβε Βάκχ'
> Ε[ὔιε, ταῦρε, κισσο]χαῖ-
> τα, Βρόμι', ἠρινα[ῖς ἵκου]
> [ταῖσδ'] ἱεραῖς ἐν ὥραις.

> Here, lord Dithyrambos, Bacchus, Euoi, Taurus, ivy-crowned Bromius, come in this holy spring season.

The text is conjectural, but three adjectives in the vocative suggest that the hymn opens with a cletic address, with an accumulation of familiar ritual epithets of Dionysus – Bacchus, Euoi, and Taurus.[48] One in particular, διθύραμβε (only recorded in Pratinas, *PMG* 708.15), sounds like the poem's generic signature and makes one expect a dithyrambic performance.[49] But this generic expectation is quickly frustrated: there *is*, of course, a connection between Delphi, Dionysus, and dithyrambs, but as Bacchylides and Plutarch attest, dithyrambs were sung at Delphi in honor of Dionysus only during the three winter months, when Apollo visits the Hyperboreans.[50] The song subverts this traditional association by linking from the outset Dionysus Dithyrambus not with winter but with spring (ἱεραῖς ἐν ὥραις, "in the spring season," 4). Moreover, after the initial invocation of Dionysus, the song abruptly juxtaposes in the *meshymnion* (5) the ritual cries of the two gods: *Evohe ō Bacchus* and *ō ie Paian* (Εὐοῖ ὢ Ἰόβακχ' ὢ ἰὲ Παιάν). Unlike the Erythraean paeans to Asclepius, where the use of the adjective *Paian* for Asclepius is gradually introduced, Philodamus uses *Paian* right from the start, in conjunction with the invocation of Dionysus. When the cry appears for the first time, it seems possible that it introduces Apollo, but as

---

[48] The adjectival form (βάκχειος) is applied to Dionysus in the *Hymn. Hom. Pan* 19.46 and Βάκχος appears throughout Euripides' *Bacchae*. Ταῦρε is also used as a ritual epithet for Dionysus in Eur. *Bacch.* 100 and 618–641, and in a cult song by the women of Elis (*PMG* 871.6–7). On the epithets of the god, Ieranò 1997: T. 2–33, Ford 2011b.

[49] The same would be the case for the paean: an invocation of "Paian" would bring up the generic expectation of a paean. On the similarity between the ritual cry for the god and the song's genre, Käppel 1992: 223, Strauss Clay 1996: 88, Ford 2006 and 2011b.

[50] Bacchyl. 16.8–12: ἵκη παιηόνων | ἄνθεα πεδοιχνεῖν, | Πύθι' Ἄπολλον, | τόσα χοροὶ Δελφῶν | σὸν κελάδησαν παρ' ἀγακλέα ναόν ("you come to seek the flowers of paeans, Pythian Apollo, as many as the choruses of Delphians sing loudly near your glorious temple"). Plut. *Mor.* 389c: "the Delphians perform paeans with their sacrifices during most of the year, but from the beginning of winter they replace the paean by the dithyramb for three months, calling on Dionysus instead of Apollo." On Dionysus at Delphi, see also Ieranò 1997: 283–5, Rutherford 2001a: 88–90, Fearn 2007: 171–4, Calame 2009.

the next lines still focus on Dionysus, the *ephymnion* leaves no doubt that the adjective refers to Dionysus. It is thus *as* Paian that Dionysus is invited to come and protect the city of the speaker uttering the prayer:

> ἰὲ Παιάν, ἴθι σωτήρ,
> [εὔφρων τάνδε] πόλιν φύλασσ᾽
> εὐαίωνι σὺν [ὄλβῳ].

> *Ie Paian*, come saviour, in your benevolence preserve this city with happy prosperity.

With the relative clause that launches the mythic narrative (6), Apollo and Dionysus start to blend:

> [ὅ]ν Θήβαις ποτ᾽ ἐν εὐίαις
> Ζη[νὶ γείνατο] καλλίπαις Θυώνα·
> πάντες δ᾽ [ἀθά]νατοι [χ]όρευ-
> σαν, πάντες δὲ βροτοὶ χ[άρεν]
> [σαῖσι], Βάκχιε, γένναις.   10

> ...whom once upon a time in ecstatic Thebes Thyone bore to Zeus, becoming the mother of a beautiful child. And all the immortals danced and all the mortals rejoiced, Bacchus, at your birth.

The narrative is silent about the modalities of the difficult birth of Dionysus – about the death of Semele and the incubating role of Zeus – and presents the god's birth in terms that recall that of Apollo:[51] Thyone is predicatively called καλλίπαις ("[becoming the mother] of a beautiful child"), an adjective that with its variant εὔπαις ("graced with a beautiful child") usually qualifies Leto.[52] The mortal delight at Dionysus' birth in Thebes (πάντες δὲ βροτοὶ χάρεν σαῖσι, Βάκχιε, γένναις, 9–10) recalls Delos' and Leto's joy at the birth of Apollo in the Homeric *Hymn to Apollo* (σὲ ... Λητὼ τέκε χάρμα βροτοῖσι, "Leto bore you as a joy for mortals," 25; χαῖρε δὲ Δῆλος, "Delos rejoiced," 61; and Δῆλος μὲν μάλα χαῖρε γόνῳ ἑκάτοιο ἄνακτος, "Delos rejoiced much at the birth of the far-shooting lord," 90). Still, despite the parallel with the welcomed birth of Apollo, with the poetic plural (γένναις, 10) the poet might be referring to the problematic double birth of Dionysus Di-thyrambus.[53] But why, one might ask, would the poet allude, even if indirectly, to something that the narrative does its best to conceal? And why would the poet call Semele Thyone (7), which is the name that she received

---

[51] Käppel 1992: 230, Strauss Clay 1996: 84–5, Vamvouri-Ruffy 2004.
[52] For example, Eur. *HF* 689; *TGrF* ii (*Adespota*) F 178.
[53] Ieranò 1997: 18–23, with *T.* 4a, 4b, 15–22 for the explanation of the epithet.

after Dionysus fetched her down from Hades to bring her to Mount Olympus with the other Olympians?[54] These features are part of a process that I term "canonical counterpoint": the poet alludes to more than one version of the myth while diverging from the most common account and justifying his own authority in recounting the myth, just as Aristonous did with the alternative versions of the Delphic aetiology.

This process is at work in the narrative of Dionysus' happy welcome in Greek cities. The narrative introduces a clear deviation from other well-known versions, especially Euripides' *Bacchae*, in which the god, arriving as the Stranger, is initially reviled or hunted. "Those who finally recognize his power and accept his divinity are rewarded, while his opponents are struck with madness and destroyed, usually in a ghastly fashion."[55] Obviously parting from this type of narrative, Philodamus tells of Dionysus' welcomed arrival in Thebes, Delphi, Orchomenus, and other places on the Greek mainland. These peregrinations are reminiscent of Apollo's own travels before his accession to Mount Olympus as recounted in the Homeric *Hymn to Apollo*, and Strauss Clay has highlighted some structural and narrative parallels with the section of the hymn that, in his words, "forms a bridge between the Delian and Pythian narratives":

The new god's initial migration to Delphi (*H. Apoll.*, 182–185, cf. *Paean*, 21–3), his progress to Olympus (*H. Apoll.*, 186–87, cf. *Paean*, 55), his reception by the Muses there (*H. Apoll.*, 189ff., cf. *Paean*, 58–62), and his return to Delphi (*Paean*, 21–3) recalls the epiphany of Apollo (ἀστέρι εἰδόμενος μέσῳ ἤματι *H. Apoll.*, 441) in the company of the wives and daughters of the Krisians. And finally the Hymn ends with Apollo inaugurating his cult by leading to the site of Delphi his Cretan priests, who now for the first time intone the ἰηπαιήον' (517).[56]

A form of oral and musical mimetic continuity between the two gods reinforces those thematic and structural parallels: two ritual cries (Εὐοῖ ὦ Ἰόβακχ' ὦ ἰὲ Παιάν) in the *meshymnion* are interwoven in their adjectival forms, εὔιος in lines 2 and 6, connected with Εὐοῖ, line 5, and remarkably close to the adjective associated with Apollo, εὐαίων, line 13.[57] The song juxtaposes the Dionysiac invocation *iō Bacchus* with the cry *iō Paian*, as if they were variants of each other, a fact that is all the more striking as the cry *ie Paian* is often repeated twice. At the aural level, there seems to be

---

[54] *Hymn. Hom. Dion.* 21; Apollod. *Bibl.* 3.5.
[55] Strauss Clay 1996: 85.   [56] Strauss Clay 1996: 95.
[57] This oral potential of the ritual cry is also exploited in the refrain to Ion's paean in Euripides' *Ion*, 125–7 = 141–3 ὦ Παιὰν ὦ Παιάν, | εὐαίων εὐαίων εἴης | ὦ Λατοῦς παῖ ("O Paian, O Paian, may you be fortunate, fortunate, O child of Leto").

divine *mimēsis* as Dionysus echoes the qualities (εὐαίων) of his brother and replicates features of his identity.

Moreover, the narrative powerfully conflates the identity of the god and that of the geographical areas he covers. Thebes' delight is developed in the second strophe:

> (ii) ἤν, τότε βακχίαζε μὲν
> χθὼ[ν μεγαλώνυμός] τε Κά-   15
> δμου Μινυᾶν τε κόλπ[ος Εὔ-
> βο]ιά τε καλλίκαρπος·
> – Εὐοῖ ὦ Ἰόβ[ακχ᾽ ὦ ἰὲ] Παιάν.

> On that day the famous land of Cadmus rose up to bacchic celebration and the vale of the Minyans and Euboia of beautiful fruits – *Euoi, ō io Bacchus ō iè Paian.*

If the supplement χθὼν μεγαλώνυμος in the first lines is correct, it gives an interesting insight: the land is described as already "famous," and "bearing beautiful fruit" (καλλίκαρπος) is a retrospective construction of the origins and nature of Dionysus. Other places participate in the same dynamic: in a further strophe, for example, the land that Dionysus visits is called "prosperous" (ὀλβίας, 53), as if the god had *already* bestowed happy prosperity upon it in response to the refrain sung by the performers (εὐαίωνι σὺν ὄλβῳ, "with happy prosperity," 52). The same motive is developed in the next strophe, this time in the cultic setting of Eleusis and with added significance:

> (iii)   ]λὲς δὲ χειρὶ πάλ-
> λων δ[έρ]ας ἐνθέοις [σὺν οἴσ-]
> τροις ἔμολες μυχοὺς [Ἐλε]υ-
> σῖνος ἀν᾽ [ἀνθεμώ]δεις·   30
> Εὐοῖ ὦ Ἰόβακχ᾽ ὦ ἰ[ὲ Παι]άν
> [ἔθνος ἔνθ᾽] ἅπαν Ἑλλάδος
> γᾶς ἀ[μφ(ὶ) ἐ]νναέταις [φίλοις] ἐπ[όπ]ταις
> ὀργίων ὁσ[ίων ᵂΙ]ακ-
> χον [κλείει σ]ε· βροτοῖς πόνων   35
> ᾧξ[ας δ ὅρ]μον [

> Brandishing in your hand the . . . hide, with possessed frenzy you came to the recesses of flowery Eleusis – *Euoi, ō io Bacchus ō ie Paian* – and there the whole people of Greece, around the dear[58] locals, initiates of the holy rites, call you "Iacchus." For you have opened a haven . . . for mortals.

---

[58] The supplement is from Furley and Bremer 2001. Powell (1925) prints [φίλιον].

A further strategy that can be detected in the legitimizing work of the song has the god act in the narrative in a way associated with his future devotees. The god is presented as brandishing (πάλλων, 27–8) something, either a torch (σέλας), in Furley and Bremer's (2001) reconstruction, or a hide (δέρας) in Powell's (1925) text. Whatever the object, it is clear that the god is imagined as handling an object that his future worshippers will brandish in bacchic ritual. This strophe also introduces a further important element of poetic and cultic legitimization: gathered at Eleusis, a Panhellenic body of initiates calls Dionysus "Iacchus." By doing so, they, and consequently the narrative, acknowledge Dionysus' healing function specifically in connection with the liberating and saving purpose of the mysteries. By the same token, the narrative retrospectively justifies the *ephymnion*: *because* of his function as healer and provider of peace acknowledged at the Eleusinian mysteries, Dionysus can be hailed as Paian, the healer. The performance of this strophe would thus authorize the extension to Dionysus of the cry *iē Paian*, which the performers had been uttering for the past three strophes.

The next strophe is unfortunately too mutilated to give a good sense of Dionysus' itinerary, but it probably comprised a description of sea travel, as the god puts to shore in Thessaly at the beginning of strophe 5.[59] It is there on Mount Olympus and Pieria that Dionysus' specific powers are recognized:

> (v) [ἔ]ν[θεν ἐ]π' ὀλβίας χθονός
>   Θεσ[σαλίας] ἔκελσας ἄ-
>   στη, τέμενός τ' Ὀλύμπι[ον],   55
>   [Πιερ]ίαν τε κλειτάν·
>   Εὐοῖ ὦ Ἰόβακχ' [ὦ ἰὲ Παι]άν·
>   Μοῦσαι [δ'] αὐτίκα παρθένοι
>   κ[ισσῷ] στε[ψ]άμεναι κύκλῳ σε πᾶσαι
>   μ[έλψαν] ἀθάνα[τον] ἐς ἀεί   60
>   Παιᾶν' εὐκλέα τ' ὁ[πὶ κλέο]υ-
>   σαι· [κα]τᾶρξε δ' Ἀπόλλων.

From that blessed land, you came to shore to the cities of Thessaly, and the Olympian sanctuary, and famous Pieria – *Euoi, ō io Bacchus ō iè Paian* – and immediately the Muses crowned their hair with ivy and they all sang and performed a circular dance and called you with their voice "immortal forever and famous Paian"; Apollo had led them.

---

[59] Again, it might have contained references to another version of the myth, the account of the sailors turned into dolphins, narrated in the *Hymn. Hom. Dion.*

After the local recognition of Dionysus among mortals at Thebes and after the Panhellenic endorsement of Dionysus as savior in Eleusis, the Muses take the god's acknowledgment to the next level by calling Dionysus "Paian." Taking on a Dionysiac identity by crowning their hair with ivy and performing a circular dance, the Muses in exchange officially give the god his epithet Paian. Here again, the mythical narrative legitimizes the cultic work of the song. Narratively, and from an enunciative point of view, there could be no better granter of the authority of Dionysus: the speech act of the Muses analeptically justifies that Dionysus has been hailed as Paian since the opening lines of the hymn. Up to this point in the text, the poem extended the refrain *iē Paian*, "come savior," to Dionysus through his function as "Iacchus," acquired at Eleusis. But after the description of the performative speech of the Muses led by Apollo, the use of the refrain is fully and divinely authorized: it is Apollo himself, through the mouth of the Muses, who made Dionysus Paian. Every time the refrain is uttered, Apollo's authority, and that of the Muses, is also reaffirmed.

These sophisticated enunciative features connect the narrative of Dionysus with the ritual performance of the inscribed song, but they are only one part of a more complex scenario: inscribed in a sanctuary, the song also participates in another network of ritual gestures. It belongs to specific political and religious contexts, not only that of the celebration of the reconstruction of the temple of Apollo in 340 BC but also that of the glorification of the authors of the song, praised for their composition and acknowledged by the Delphic community in the *subscriptio*. After culminating in having the voice of the narrator authorized by Apollo himself, the narrative turns in a new direction. In strophes 9–12 we are abruptly made aware of the connection between mythical narrative and historical situation. The lacuna of three stanzas between strophes 5 and 9 is all the more frustrating because we encounter a distinctly different form of enunciation at the beginning of strophe 9. After the mythological *discours* in which the narrator established proximity to the god by the constant use of second-person markers, we turn to a *récit*, in the present, in strophe 9:

> (ix) ἐκτελέσαι δὲ πρᾶξιν Ἀμ-   105
> φικτύονας θ[εὸς] κελεύ-
> ει τάχος, ὡ[ς Ἑ]κάβολος
> μῆνιν ε[. .] κατάσχῃ,
> – Εὐοῖ ὦ [ἰόβ]ακχ' ὦ ἰὲ Παιάν –
> δε[ῖξαι] δ' ἐγ ξενίοις ἐτεί-   110
> οις θεῶν ἱερῷ γένει συναίμῳ
> τόνδ' ὕμνον, θυσίαν δὲ φαί-

νει[ν] σὺν Ἑλλάδος ὀλβίας
πα[νδ]ήμοις ἱκετείαις.

> The god orders that the amphictyons complete the matter with speed, so that the Far-shooter might prevail upon his wrath[60] – *Euoi, ō io Bacchus ō ie Paian* – and that they show this song for his holy brother to the family of the gods, on the occasion of the yearly Theoxenia, and display sacrifices on the occasion of Panhellenic supplications for the prosperity of Greece.

The Muses' performative naming of the god "forever immortal and Paian" in strophe 5 seems to have given the narrator, in turn, the authority needed to articulate his own message, in the name of the god, and to urge the amphictyons to hasten the reconstruction of the temple of Apollo (the πρᾶξιν, "matter," refered to in 105).[61] Mythical narrative and socio-political agenda mix, and Delphic propaganda is woven into the religious hymn. Maria Vamvouri-Ruffy has summed up how the mythological narrative is modeled after political considerations and how the song not only engages with the present cult but also informs its future, and is therefore part of these future events.[62] Vamvouri-Ruffy's important point can be extended from time to space. The song must have gained particular force in the physical context of the sanctuary and from the intersection of hymnic tradition and other conventions, including sacred laws describing appropriate ritual gestures and official decrees inscribed on stone within the precinct.[63] This is especially striking in the lines where the song refers to itself (τόνδ᾽ ὕμνον, "this song," 112) and to its own original context of cultic performance, the Theoxenia (ἐγ ξενίοις ἐτείοις θεῶν, 110–11), where all gods and mortals are invited to take part in sacrifice and banquet (θυσίαν... σὺν Ἑλλάδος ὀλβίας πανδήμοις ἱκετείαις, 112–14).[64] The song connects its own aetiology with the possibility of future dissemination through the expression τόνδ᾽ ὕμνον δεῖξαι ("display that hymn," 110). The nature of the song as choral performance (the "show" of a chorus, reinforced in the next lines [112–13] with the display, φαίνειν, of sacrifices) is thus conflated in a remarkable way with the nature of the inscription. One of its intended audiences seems to be composed of divine spectators and readers, aware not only of the

---

[60] The text printed in lines 107–8 is that of Furley and Bremer (2001). Powell (1925) prints ὡ[ς ἐπ]άβολος | μὴν ἱκέτα[ς] κατάσχῃ. But ἑκάβολος is such a well established epithet for Apollo that it seems perverse to maintain any other adjective. The motive of the wrath also seems most fitting in the context.

[61] Bremer (1981) describes this process as "imminent poetics."

[62] Vamvouri-Ruffy 2004: 206.   [63] On sacred laws, Petrovic and Petrovic 2006.

[64] It is the festival for which Pindar's Sixth Paean was composed, and for which he uses the same kind of expression: θύεται γὰρ ἀγλαᾶς ὑπὲρ Πανελλάδος (62–3).

text's cultic meaning but also of the double nature of the hymn as both musical and visual *agalma*. A very significant switch takes place, from the consciousness of the song as a form of musical worship to the consciousness of the inscription as object.

In the penultimate set of strophes, the song turns from an address to Dionysus to a *makarismos* directed to the mortals who complete the construction of the temple:

(x) ὦ μάκαρ ὀλβία τε κεί-
νων γεν[εὰ] βροτῶν, ἀγή-
ρων ἀμίαντον ἃ κτίση   120
ναὸ[ν ἄ]νακ[τι] Φοίβῳ.
Εὐοῖ ὦ ᾽Ιόβακχ᾽ ὦ ἰὲ Π[αιάν]
[ν]ε[ο]χρύσεον χρυσέοις τύποις
πα[. . . . .]νθεαιγ κύκλου [. . . . . . .
κῳ[. . . .]δογ, κόμαν δ᾽   125
ἀργαίνοντ᾽ ἐλέφαντι, κ[ρα-
τὸς] δ᾽ αὐτόχθονι κόσμῳ.

(xi) Πυθιάσιν δὲ πενθετή-
ροις [π]ροπό[λοις] ἔταξε Βάκχου θυσίαν χορῶν τε πο[λ-
λῶν] κυκλίαν ἄμιλλαν
Εὐοῖ ὦ [᾽Ιόβ]ακχ᾽ ὦ ἰὲ Παιάν·   135
τεύχειν· ἁλιοφεγγ[έ]σ[ι]ν
δ᾽ ἀ[ντ]ο[λαῖς] ἴσον ἁβρὸν ἄγαλμα Βάκχου
ἐν [ζεύγει] χρυσέων λεόν-
των στῆσαι, ζαθέῳ τε τ[εῦ-]
ξαι θεῷ πρέπον ἄντρον.   140

O blessed and prosperous the generation of these mortals who built a temple, never to age, never to be defiled for Lord Phoebus – *Euoi ō io Bacchus, ō ie Paian* – golden, with golden sculptures . . . goddesses circle around . . . his shiny hair made of ivory, his head adorned with an indigenous crown.

To the ministers of the quadriennal Pythian games,[65] he ordered to organize a sacrifice in honor of Bacchus – *Euoi, ō io Bacchus ō ie Paian* – and a contest for many circular choruses, and to set up a splendid statue of Bacchus, like the sun's bright rays,[66] in a (chariot drawn)[67] by golden lions, and to make a grotto appropriate to the holy god.

---

[65] The text is Furley and Bremer 2001. Powell (1925) prints πενθετήροισ[ι τ]ροπαῖς.
[66] The text is Furley and Bremer 2001. Powell (1925) prints ἀρχο[ύσαις].
[67] The supplement is from Furley and Bremer 2001.

Here, the generation of mortal builders is now defined in terms befitting the gods (μάκαρ, "blessed," and ὀλβία, "prosperous," 118), and the material building is elevated to the status of a divine artifact, "never to age, never to be defiled" – a description also, and even more, appropriate for a song. The next two lines (120–1) further establish the song in a network of commemoration practices in the visual landscape of the sanctuary: in addition to the temple, statues, and sacrifices described in stanza 9, strophes 10 and 11 describe further ways of celebrating the divine brothers, with a splendid statue of Bacchus (ἀβρὸν ἄγαλμα Βάκχου, 137), a grotto (ἄντρον, 140), and contests of circular choruses (χορῶν . . . κυκλίαν ἄμιλλαν, 133–4).[68] All these elements saturate the landscape with brightness, shininess, glitter, and movement – on the background of the sound of choral performances.

The astonishing enunciative journey that opened with the hymn's cletic appeal to Bacchus concludes by asking an audience to call Dionysus (designated by this name for the first time in the surviving stanzas) and to welcome him with ivy-crowned choruses (148):

> (xii) ἀλλὰ δέχεσθε Βακχ[ιά-]
>   [στα]ν Δι[ό]νυσο[ν, ἐν δ' ἀγυι-]   145
>   αῖς ἅμα σὺγ [χοροῖσ]ι κ[ι-]
>   [κλήσκετε] κισσ[οχ]αίταις
>   Ε[ὐοῖ ὦ Ἰ]όβακχ' ὦ ἰὲ [Παιάν]
>   πᾶσαν ['Ελ]λάδ' ἀν' ὀ[λβίαν   150
>   .αν . . . .ιτε πολ..υ..στεα..ϝας..ρεπι
>   λῳ [. . . . . .]ν . . . ιο.ε . . . κυκλι[
>   [ἄ]ϝα[ξ] ὑγιείας.

Come on, receive Dionysus the Bacchic god, and in the streets call him, with ivy-crowned choruses – *Euoi, ō io Bacchus ō ie Paian* – all of fortunate Greece . . . with prosperity . . . lord of health.

While the last line brings to completion the representation, and invocation, of Dionysus as Paian (he has now obtained the qualities of Apollo and Asclepius, ἄναξ ὑγιείας, "lord of health," 153), it also brings to full circle the representation of dancing. The ivy-crowned audience recalls the earlier reference to the Muses who had themselves bound their hair in imitation of Dionysiac identity (58–9). The legitimization of the paeanic form for Dionysus is achieved not just through the rhetoric of the song, its performative language, and its manipulation of the narrative, but also through the *representation* of performance. Choral activity is mentioned eight times

---

[68] On the nature of the statuary representing Dionysus and the syncretism of the features of the representation of Apollo and Dionysus, Stewart 1982.

through the extant stanzas and plays a role at various levels. By following the structure of Apollo's march toward Olympus, it establishes the rightfulness of Dionysus' own position: any place the god visits expresses its joy through choral dancing. The blurring of the two activities of rejoicing and worship is reinforced by the aural proximity of forms of χώρα ("place"), χάρις ("joy"), and χορός ("dance"), which alternate in the text, and by the very polysemy of χάρις ("delight," both felt and produced in performance). The motive of dance allows different forms of danced worship to be connected or to merge: the wild dance that Thebes (14) and Eleusis (28, 34, 40) partake in, as well as the more ordered choral celebrations that we can read from ὑμνοβρύης ("full of hymns," 19) and in the reference to maiden songs (22), the dance of the Muses (60), and the circular dances (134, 146).

This repeated motive of dance, rejoicing, and worship invites us to consider the actual performance, and future performances, of the song itself. We do not know the details of how this paean was performed, but as Ian Rutherford has shown, some paeans could project their own performance scenario and setting onto the narrative, ensuring that future audiences who were not at the original site of performance could imagine the song-and-dance as if it were taking place in front of their eyes.[69] Most of the dances described in Philodamus' paean are "circular choruses," which has led many scholars to conclude that the reference is to dithyrambs. But in his forceful argument against Pickard-Cambridge, David Fearn has convincingly shown that "round chorus" is not strictly synonymous with "dithyramb"; there is no need to imagine a blending of two genres or two performance scenarios.[70] Rather, a circular chorus would be an appropriate way to celebrate both Dionysus and Apollo. One should also note that although the motive of dancing recurs throughout the hymn, there is no imaginary reference to the details of the performances, in ways that could serve as a "script" for future performance. And unlike other Delphic hymns, including those of Aristonous, Philodamus' paean makes no reference to the local geographic context. Neither eyes nor imagination are given clues that would allow listeners to visualize the sanctuary in which the original performance of the paean to Dionysus took place. The only details conveyed are the monument, the statues, and the sculptures, but they are not attributed any visual or sensual

---

[69] On the performance, Rutherford 2001a: 58–68, Vamvouri-Ruffy 2004: 190–6.

[70] *Kyklioi choroi* was probably an umbrella term for a variety of performances, including circular choruses for Apollo at the Thargelia. On the use of both terms and the difference between *kyklios choros* as performance term and dithyramb as cult term, Fearn 2007: 165–225. The contest of circular choruses at Delphi need not therefore be a contest in dithyrambs, contrary to the suggestion of Bremer 1981 and Strauss Clay 1992.

texture. The only deictic in the text refers to the materiality of the inscribed song (τόνδ' ὕμνον, "this song here," 112). The striking self-referentiality of the song actually seems to play on the liminal status of epigrams as both objects that point to their materiality and texts that emphasize their verbal, oral, and musical nature. "This song here" (112) which is to be "displayed" (110) thus highlights the song's self-conscious engagement with a range of practices in which the gods are honored with pleasing gifts (song, temple, sacrifice . . .) and the human community whose cohesion is reinforced by religious and social rituals (chorus and sacrifices) as well as political gestures (inscriptions). Even more, the poetic collaboration of the mortal Philodamus and his brothers is given a divine precedent, since Apollo shows to the rest of the society of the gods "this song" for his brother, who is described with a noun (συναίμῳ, "of common blood," 111) more appropriate for a mortal than for a god.

Finally, the inscription belongs to a civic network of glorification in which Philodamus and his brothers are memorialized and given significant privileges in the sanctuary. The material status of the song, reinforced by its self-description as object of display, inverts the expected relationship between movement and stability: there is no detailed description of the performance of the worshippers. It is the song itself that will travel, although the stone does not move, or rather, because the stone does not move, it allows the song to voyage. One has to note that the stone already embodies geographical mobility: Scarphea, the native place of Philodamus and his brothers, is inscribed in the landscape of Delphi, as are the other communities mentioned in the poem, such as Thebes, Eleusis, and Thessaly, and just as was the case with Aristonous' native town (Corinth) in the poet's song. Finally, visitors to the sanctuary of Delphi, Thebans or Eleusinians for example, can read of the god's travels, which mythologically reproduce the voyage they themselves have made from their city to the sanctuary of Delphi. Having heard a song that celebrates the joy felt by many places at the birth of Dionysus, these visitors can bring back home from the sanctuary some memorable lines about their own polis. Whether the text was performed chorally by visiting *theōroi* who might have learned the song beforehand, or by a chorus attracted by the prospect of winning the competition at the contest of circular choruses set up at Delphi for Dionysus, or by a local chorus performing for visitors assembled for the Panhellenic festival, or was even read by a passer-by/viewer, the Delphic song composed for a specific religious purpose is not entirely Delphi-centered. The traffic in song goes far beyond the precinct of the sanctuary. For international visitors and musical tourists, the inscribed song provides good mental memorabilia in the form of a stanza celebrating their hometown that has been conveniently written out for them to read, perform, memorize, and reperform at home. They might leave behind a statue, offering, inscription, or transient performance, but they can take away a snippet of song that, in turn, glorifies their own place. By being inscribed, the song is not immobilized; on the contrary, that very inscription allows the glorification that the song conveys to flow freely. Dionysus who has been brought to Delphi can be taken back to the rest of the Greek world.

Isyllus' embedded performance: Asclepius at Epidaurus

In this complex relationship of material and immaterial glorification of a god, the inscription containing Isyllus' paean to Asclepius constitutes a particular case, as it *stages* its own written-ness and process of inscription. This work is a good place to conclude our study of late classical songs, since it is chronologically the latest example of a paean in the corpus under consideration here. Only a part of the inscribed text is lyric (a paean to Asclepius), but it is crucial to consider how the paean's physical embedded-ness in the inscription influences our interpretation of the song's rhetoric and performance. The poet has inscribed not only his song but also his voice in the cultic landscape of Epidaurus; he creates his poetic author-ity through an elaborate narrative of cultic legitimization and recourse to earlier poetic models. Rather than thinking about the ways in which the paean breaks generic conventions or invents them, it is more productive to examine how the song reflects on questions of representation, performance, and materiality.

Asclepius at Epidaurus

The 84-line inscription by Isyllus was discovered in 1885 in the sanctuary of Epidaurus.[71] The date of the inscription has been an object of scholarly debate since the end of the nineteenth century:[72] an internal reference to the invasion of "Philip" makes it possible to date the inscription either to the late fourth century (if the text alludes to Philip II's invasion of Laconia in 338 BC or to Philip III and his expedition to Mount Ithome in 317 BC) or to the late

---

[71] The Isyllus inscription is quoted in Powell's (1925) edition (132–6); for other editions, see also Wilamowitz-Moellendorff 1886, Käppel 1992: Paian no. 40 (pp. 380–3), and Kolde 2003. For studies on the inscription, see Fairbanks 1900: 36, Käppel 1992: 200–6; Sineux 1999, Furley and Bremer 2001: I 227–40, II 180–92, Fantuzzi 2010: 183–9, I. Petrovic 2011.

[72] Kolde (2003: 257–301) provides full documentation about the dating of the inscription.

third century BC (if the Philip in question is Philip V, who invaded Sparta in 219 BC). The shape of the letters is typical of late fourth-century inscriptions and works in favor of the former dating. The inscription is remarkable for its structural elaborateness: it falls into seven narrative segments, each composed in a different meter.[73] The narrative structure of the text is far from linear. On the one hand, two different temporal sequences are mixed: the story, in the past tense, of the creation of the cult of Asclepius at Epidaurus (its mythical past, the aretalogy of Asclepius, the aetiology of the cult, and the aetiology of the *lex sacra* that Isyllus invented/found), and the story, in the present tense, of the making of the inscription (a vow to inscribe something, a decision to implement this vow, the actual inscription, and two formulae of dedication, in the first and final lines of the text). On the other hand, each of these temporal sequences mixes different modes of address: first-person narrative (singular and plural, sometimes in the same sequence), address in the second person (either to the god or to a potential reader), and narrative in the third person. But as I have already suggested in the case of Philodamus' paean, Isyllus' strategy of legitimization extends beyond the manipulation of forms of enunciation, of mythic material, and of the representation of performance and encompasses the rhetoric of inscriptions and ritual dedications.

This is already clear in the first section (1–2):

> Ἴσυλλος Σωκράτευς Ἐπιδαύριος ἀνέθηκε
> Ἀπόλλωνι Μαλεάται καὶ Ἀσκλαπιῶι.

> Isyllus of Epidaurus son of Socrates made a dedication to Apollo Maleatas and Asclepius.

The opening is striking. The text clearly adopts the form of a dedication, but the object of the dedication remains unspecified. A reader is left to wonder whether it is the stele that is dedicated, or the text following the dedication, or an object that would have accompanied the text, or even the paean that constitutes the inscription's centerpiece. With its use of the Doric dialect (Ἀσκλαπιῶι) and the mention of Apollo "Maleatas" (a local cult name of Apollo?) and Asclepius, this introduction builds expectation for epichoric elements (Doric being the dialect spoken in Epidaurus), and for paeanic features (through the evocation of paeanic personnel, Apollo and his offspring Asclepius).

---

[73] For metrical analysis of the poem, Kolde 2003: 18–41.

The next lines (A, 3–9), however, do not entirely fulfill this expectation: the spoken, not sung, trochaic tetrameters introduce general political considerations on the best form of government and the benefits of aristocracy, with no reference to either a specific Peloponnesian place or a specific god:

> {A} δᾶμος εἰς ἀριστοκρατίαν ἄνδρας αἰ προάγοι καλῶς,
> αὐτὸς ἰσχυρότερος· ὀρθοῦται γὰρ ἐξ ἀνδραγαθίας.
> αἰ δέ τις καλῶς προαχθεὶς θιγγάνοι πονηρίας   5
> πάλιν ἐπαγκρούων, κολάζων δᾶμος ἀσφαλέστερος.
> τάνδε τὰν γνώμαν τόκ’ ἦχον καὶ ἔλεγον καὶ νῦν λέγω.
> εὐξάμαν ἀνγράψεν, αἴ κ’ εἰς τάνδε τὰν γνώμαν πέτη
> ὁ νόμος ἀμὶν ὃν ἐπέδειξα· ἔγεντο δ’, οὐκ ἄνευ θεῶν.

> If the people leads its men well toward aristocracy, it is itself stronger; for it sets itself straight thanks to manly goodness. If someone raised well, however, touches baseness and goes backward, it is by chastising him that the people will be more secure. That was my opinion then, and I expressed it and I express it now. I promised to inscribe (it), if the law that I published for us came to ratify that opinion. It did, not without the gods.

Presented in the first person, Isyllus' political convictions are expressed with several deictic markers (τάνδε τὰν γνώμαν τόκ’ ἦχον καὶ ἔλεγον καὶ νῦν λέγω, "that was my opinion then, and I expressed it and I express it now," 7) which can operate at different levels: they can be understood as referring both intra-discursively to the text of the preceding lines (the belief in the strength of aristocracy as a political regime) and also extra-discursively to the "now" of the performance of the ritual of dedication, or the now of the reading. Εὐξάμαν ἀνγράψεν ("I promised to inscribe," 8) forces the reader to engage directly with the question of the materiality of the inscription, as the inscription itself is the result of the gods' assistance (οὐκ ἄνευ θεῶν, 9).[74] These lines are the first step in the elaborate process of divine authorization of the mortal author. Further elements can also be identified: not only does Isyllus in this section rely on trochaic tetrameters, the meter used by Solon in his capacity as nomothete, but the text of the law also recalls Solon's conclusive statement after the completion of his political project: ἃ μὲν γὰρ εἶπα, σὺν θεοῖσιν ἤνυσα ("what I have said, I have accomplished with the help of the gods," fr. 34.6 W²). The topic, vocabulary, and diction, as well as the assertive tone (each couplet seems like a *gnōmē*) are even specifically reminiscent of Solon's fragment 6 W², from which the text borrows three

---

[74] The expected paean only comes at line 37 of the inscription.

key words (δῆμος, "the people," ἄριστον, "best," and ἄγειν, "to lead") and an optative statement:[75]

> δῆμος δ' ὧδ' ἂν ἄριστα σὺν ἡγεμόνεσσιν ἔποιτο,
> μήτε λίην ἀνεθεὶς μήτε βιαζόμενος.
>
> Solon, fr. 6.1–2 W²

So best shall be for the people to follow its leaders, neither let too loose nor being oppressed.

The idea of right measure expressed by Solon in the passage quoted above is also the idea set forth by Isyllus in the opening lines of the first section of the Epidaurus inscription (3–4).[76] These resemblances all point to Isyllus' attempt to portray himself as a Solon figure. By presenting himself, in line 7, as both poet and nomothete in lines that echo Solon's poetry, Isyllus claims for himself the authority of Solon and thus justifies his own literary and politico-religious project.

The next part (B, 10–26) states, in dactylic hexameters, how under the inspiration and guidance of the gods Isyllus established a sacred law with, again, both political and religious aspects:[77]

> {B} τόνδ' ἱαρὸν θείαι μοίραι νόμον ηὗρεν "Ισυλλος   10
> ἄφθιτον ἀέναον γέρας ἀθανάτοισι θεοῖσιν,
> καί νιν ἅπας δᾶμος θεθμὸν θέτο πατρίδος ἁμᾶς,
> χεῖρας ἀνασχόντες μακάρεσσιν ἐς οὐρανὸν εὐρύ[ν·
> οἵ κεν ἀριστεύωσι πόληος τᾶσδ' 'Επιδαύρου
> λέξασθαί τ' ἄνδρας καὶ ἐπαγγεῖλαι κατὰ φυλάς   15
> οἷς πολιοῦχος ὑπὸ στέρνοις ἀρετά τε καὶ αἰδώς,
> τοῖσιν ἐπαγγέλλεν καὶ πομπεύεν σφε κομῶντας
> Φοίβωι ἄνακτι υἱῶι τ' 'Ασκλαπιῶι ἰατῆρι
> εἵμασιν ἐν λευκοῖσι δάφνας στεφάνοις ποτ' 'Απόλλω,
> ποὶ δ' 'Ασκλαπιὸν ἔρνεσι ἐλαίας ἡμεροφύλλου   20
> ἁγνῶς πομπεύειν, καὶ ἐπεύχεσθαι πολιάταις
> πᾶσιν ἀεὶ διδόμεν τέκνοις τ' ἐρατὰν ὑγίειαν,
> εὐνομίαν τε καὶ εἰράναν καὶ πλοῦτον ἀμεμφῆ,
> τὰν καλοκαγαθίαν τ' 'Επιδαυροῖ ἀεὶ ῥέπεν ἀνδρῶν,
> ὥραις ἐξ ὡρᾶν νόμον ἀεὶ τόνδε σέβοντας·   25
> οὕτω τοί κ' ἁμῶν περιφείδοιτ' εὐρύοπα Ζεύς.

---

[75] Even more than the idea of leadership of the *demos* (δῆμον ἄγειν, found three times in Solon), it is the structure of the line that reminds of Solon's diction: of the ten times Solon uses the substantive δῆμος, seven are instances where δῆμος is the first word of the line.

[76] The idea of straightening is itself found in another Solonian fragment, 4.36–7 W²: εὐθύνει δὲ δίκας σκολιάς, ὑπερήφανά τ' ἔργα | πραΰνει ("he straightens crooked judgments, and calms overbearing deeds").

[77] For a comparison with other *leges sacrae*, Kolde 2003: 107–13, Petrovic and Petrovic 2006.

Isyllus found this law, made sacred by the divine providence, a not-to-decay, everlasting privilege for the immortal gods, and the whole people has fixed it as a decree of my fatherland, raising their hands to the broad sky to the blessed ones: that the men with the highest distinctions in that city of Epidaurus be gathered and that there be an announcement in the tribes to those who hold statesmanlike excellence and self-respect in their breast: that it be announced that these men walk in a procession, with flowing hair in honor of Lord Phoebus and his son Asclepius the healer, and in white garments; and that they walk in holy procession with wreaths of laurel to the temple of Apollo, and then with sprigs of cultivated olive tree to the temple of Asclepius; and that they pray on behalf of all the citizens and their children that the gods give forever lovely health, and that good order prevail, and peace and blameless riches, and that the Epidaurians choose always nobleness among men, and honor that law forever from season to season: thus far-sounding Zeus may protect us.

In this section, the first person has given way to the third. In addition to acknowledging divine authorization, the author stages the inscription of his own name (Ἴσυλλος, 10) and associates his "invention" with divine help. The verb (ηὖρεν, "he found," 10) is not innocent: it makes Isyllus himself a sort of mythological figure, a *prōtos heuretēs* in the manner of Orpheus, Olympus, and Terpander, all imagined as musical innovators. But Isyllus' contribution is not so much an invention *ex nihilo* as a decision to create a law, according to which the whole people of Epidaurus is to say a prayer accompanied by ritual gestures, while a procession of chosen best men celebrates Apollo and his son Asclepius and asks the gods to bring public and private goods to all the citizens. All these wishes – for health, prosperity, and good order – are very close to the petitions in the prayer of Ariphron and Aristotle's songs, and they are also reminiscent of sympotic motives. But because the law is written, the paean, whose performance was prescribed as restricted to aristocrats, is available for all to see. Paradoxically, while the text argues for aristocracy as the best regime, in practice the inscription works as a democratic tool, or at least continues the civic function of the song by making it visually available to all.

Finally, hexameters and epic diction also work as a form of legitimization to reinforce the authority of the text. By describing the law as ἄφθιτον ἀέναον γέρας ("not-to-decay, everlasting privilege," 11) for the gods, with an adjective (ἄφθιτον, "not-to-decay") that occurs in dactylic hexameter formulae qualifying heroic *kleos*, Isyllus bestows the weight of epic and official pronouncements on his own law. At the same time, by signing his own name at the end of the line, Isyllus guarantees himself by proxy a part of this honor and takes on the authority of the epic bard. The Homeric tone of the passage is reinforced by the reference to "loud-sounding Zeus" (εὐρύοπα Ζεύς, 26), who may take care of the citizens if the Epidaurians respect this law from season to season.[78] But the ambiguity of the Homeric adjective, εὐρύοπα, takes on a new meaning depending on whether one connects the -οπα part to ὄψομαι ("see," thus "far-seeing") or to ὄπ- ("voice," thus "far-sounding"). The whole problem of the pragmatics of the inscription is encapsulated in this adjective signifying the power of Zeus, the one whose authority is manifested both in seeing and in sounding, and in the expression ἄφθιτον ἀέναον γέρας (11, a parallel for which is found in Philodamus' description of Apollo's temple, ἀγήρων ἀμίαντον, "never to age never to decay," 119–20), which can apply both to a song and to a material object.

A third section (C, 27–31, in dactylic hexameters and a pentameter, line 28) describes, without any obvious connection to the previous part other than the mention of the cult of Asclepius, the aetiology of the cult of Apollo Maleatas and the establishment of the sanctuary by a certain Malos, and the connection between this sanctuary and the sanctuary of Asclepius:[79]

> {C} πρῶτος Μᾶλος ἔτευξεν Ἀπόλλωνος Μαλεάτα
> βωμὸν καὶ θυσίαις ἠγλάισεν τέμενος.
> οὐδέ κε Θεσσαλίας ἐν Τρίκκηι πειραθείης
> εἰς ἄδυτον καταβὰς Ἀσκληπιοῦ, εἰ μὴ ἀφ' ἁγνοῦ   30
> πρῶτον Ἀπόλλωνος βωμοῦ θύσαις Μαλεάτα.

> Malos was the first to build the altar of Apollo Maleatas and to make radiant the precinct with sacrifices. And in Thessalian Trikka you would not go down in Asclepius' sanctuary if you had not first sacrificed at the holy altar of Apollo Maleatas.

In the second part of the section, a general statement involves a potential reader of the inscription (in the second person singular: οὐδέ κε . . . <u>πειραθείης</u>, εἰ μὴ . . . θύσαις Μαλεάτα, "<u>you would not go down</u> . . . if you had not sacrificed . . . ," 29–31) in finding out the aetiology of the cult

---

[78] Other Homeric-sounding words in this section give it a heroic character: ἐς οὐρανὸν εὐρύν (13), οἵ κεν ἀριστεύωσι πόληος τᾶσδ' Ἐπιδαύρου (14).

[79] The cult is attested in Epidaurus (Kolde 2003: 50 for a list of inscriptions attesting to the cult there) and Sparta (Paus. 3.12.8). Most scholars make Apollo Maleatas a healing god older than Apollo and later assimilated to him. Various etymologies have been proposed, from the derivation from μᾶλον ("apple," an important fruit in the cult of chthonian gods) to μῆλον ("sheep"). Scholars also underline the parallel with the toponyme Μαλέα, or the name Malos, found later in the poem: "Aux yeux de U. von Wilamowitz, Malos ne doit son existence qu'au besoin du poète de trouver une origine au nom du dieu, tout comme le roi Ἄσκλης a été créé pour les besoins de l'étymologie d'Asclépios; du point de vue linguistique, cette étymologie serait de plus fautive," Kolde 2003: 51.

(underlined by the use of πρῶτος, twice). The hexameter/pentameter combination of the opening is once again particularly appropriate, as it is the type of meter used in monumental epigrams. This time the author has removed himself from the text, and the inscription presents itself as a "speaking stone," addressing the passer-by in direct style.[80] The inscription thus embeds a "real" epigram, which could be another sacred law inscribed on a monument, within the inscription. This strategy empowers the reader and confirms the self-consciousness of the stone, fully aware of its materiality and reliance on the power of other inscribed texts to achieve its purpose – to glorify Asclepius, Apollo, Epidaurus, and Isyllus.

A fourth section (D, 32–5, in prose) relates how the Delphic oracle was consulted to determine whether it would be profitable (λώιον) to inscribe the paean referred to in Isyllus' sacred law (of section B):

> {D} Ἴσυλλος Ἀστυλαΐδαι ἐπέθηκε μαντεύσασθα[ι] οἱ περὶ
> τοῦ παιᾶνος ἐν Δελφοῖς, ὃν ἐπόησε εἰς τὸν Ἀπόλλωνα
> καὶ τὸν Ἀσκληπιόν, ἦ λώιόν οἵ κα εἴη ἀγγράφοντι
> τὸν παιᾶνα. ἐμάντευσε λώιόν οἵ κα εἶμεν ἀγγράφοντι   35
> καὶ αὐτίκα καὶ εἰς τὸν ὕστερον χρόνον.

> Isyllus commissioned Astylaidas to consult the oracle in Delphi about the paean that he had composed for Apollo and Asclepius, and to ask whether it would be profitable to inscribe the paean. The oracle responded that it would be profitable for him to inscribe [the paean], both immediately and for future times.

This section performs the same work as the opening dedication, which is also in prose. The text switches back to the third person singular and names Isyllus, while again making a statement about the authority of the inscribed word. It is reminiscent of the form of sacred regulations in which communities record the god's consultation and response; the very record of the divine response testifies to the importance of the cult. As Ivana Petrovic sums up nicely, "by encouraging Isyllus to inscribe the text . . . the oracle acted not only as religious institution, but also as literary critic."[81] But there is added performative value in the deictic "immediately and for future times" (καὶ αὐτίκα καὶ εἰς τὸν ὕστερον χρόνον, 36). The past "now" of the oracle is activated in the "future times" of the present reading, and the "now" of each present reading looks forward to future instances of reading.

---

[80] On this aspect, Svenbro 1988, Sourvinou-Inwood 1995, Bruss 2005.
[81] I. Petrovic 2011: 279.

In place of the customary oracular response in hexameters that one would expect after the (prose) question to the god, the next section (E, 36–61, in ionics) introduces the paean itself:

{E} ἰὲ Παιᾶνα θεὸν ἀείσατε λαοί,
ζαθέας ἐνναέτα[ι] τᾶσδ᾽ Ἐπιδαύρου.
ὧδε γὰρ φάτις ἐνέπουσ᾽ ἤλυθ᾽ ἐς ἀκοὰς
προγόνων ἀμετέρων, ὦ Φοῖβ᾽ Ἄπόλλων.   40
Ἐρατὼ Μοῦσαν πατὴρ Ζεὺς λέγεται Μά-
λ[ωι] δόμεν παράκοιτιν ὁσίοισι γάμοις.
Φλεγύας δ᾽, [ὃς] πατρίδ᾽ Ἐπίδαυρον ἔναιεν,
θυγατέρα Μάλου γαμεῖ, τὰν Ἐρατὼ γεί-   45
νατο μάτηρ, Κλεοφήμα δ᾽ ὀνομάσθη.
ἐγ δὲ Φλεγύα γένετο, Αἴγλα δ᾽ ὀνομάσθη·
τόδ᾽ ἐπώνυμον· τὸ κάλλος δὲ Κορωνὶς ἐπεκλήθη.
κατιδὼν δ᾽ ὁ χρυσότοξος Φοῖβος ἐμ Μάλου δόμοις παρθενίαν ὥραν ἔλυσε,   50
λεχέων δ᾽ ἱμεροέντων ἐπέβας, Λα-
τῶιε κόρε χρυσοκόμα.
σέβομαί σε· ἐν δὲ θυώδει τεμένει τέκε-
το ἶνιν Αἴγλα, γονίμαν δ᾽ ἔλυσεν ὠδῖ-
να Διὸς παῖς μετὰ Μοιρᾶν Λάχεσίς τε μαῖ᾽ ἀγαυά·
ἐπίκλησιν δέ νιν Αἴγλας ματρὸς Ἀσκλα-   55
πιὸν ὠνόμαξε Ἀπόλλων, τὸν νόσων παύ-
[σ]τορα, δωτῆρ᾽ ὑγιείας, μέγα δώρημα βροτοῖς.
ἰὲ Παιάν, ἰὲ Παιάν, χαῖρεν Ἀσκλα-
πιέ, τὰν σὰν Ἐπίδαυρον ματρόπολιν αὔ-
ξων, ἐναργῆ δ᾽ ὑγίειαν ἐπιπέμποις   60
φρεσὶ καὶ σώμασιν ἀμοῖς, ἰὲ Παιάν, ἰὲ Παιάν.

Ie, sing the god Paian, men who live in this very sacred city of Epidaurus. For it was thus reported to my ancestors, O Phoebus Apollo, that Zeus gave the muse Erato to Malos to be his wife in holy wedlock. Phlegyas, who lived in his native city of Epidaurus, married the daughter of Malos, whom Erato (her mother) bore, and she was called Cleophema. She bore a daughter to Phlegyas, Aigla by name. This was her real name, but because of her beauty she was called Coronis. Upon seeing her in the dwellings of Malos, Phoebus of the golden bow loosened the season of her virginity when he entered her desirable bed, O golden-haired son of Leto. I revere you. In the sweet-smelling sanctuary Aigla gave birth to a son, and the son of Zeus loosened the pains of delivery with the help of the Fates including reverent Lachesis. Apollo named him Asclepius, deriving his name from his mother's, Aigla, the one who puts an end to diseases, granter of health, great gift to mortals. *Ie Paian, ie Paian,* hail Asclepius, who exalts Epidaurus the city of your mother, may you bring radiant health in our minds and bodies, *ie Paian, ie Paian.*

As was the case in the Erythraean paeans, the injunction to people to sing (ἀείσατε λαοί, 37) is a speech act that creates the persona of the performer and realizes the utterance in the moment of its performance. But unlike most paeans, which are composed in non-stichic meters, Isyllus' song uses ionics. Not attested in any other song of the classical period, the meter has been understood as part of the development of so-called literary lyric in the Hellenistic period.[82] Interpreted in context, however, it might be seen as connected with traditional processional use rather than with exploitation of ritual contexts for poetic effects.[83] Given that Isyllus has described the context of performance as a procession, it is only natural that the ionics be used, and the meter might also look forward to a future ritual performance.

The song is embedded in the whole structure of the inscription but also has a structure of its own: it starts with a four-line introduction (injunction to sing the god, ἰὲ Παιᾶνα θεόν, and introduction of the myth, 37–40) and closes with a four-line conclusion (with the *epiphthēgma* ἰὲ Παιάν, ἰὲ Παιάν, celebration of Asclepius, and injunction for him to bless the city with health, 56–61). Thematic unity within the poem is ensured by its emphasis on the local: the paean starts with an initial address to the people of Epidaurus (λαοί, ζαθέας ἐνναέται τᾶσδ᾽ Ἐπιδαύρου, "people inhabitant of this land of Epidaurus," 38), introduces Phlegyas ([ὃς] πατρίδ᾽ Ἐπίδαυρον ἔναιεν, "who lived in Epidaurus, his fatherland," 43), and concludes with an address to the god and Epidaurus, the city of his mother (τὰν σὰν Ἐπίδαυρον ματρόπολιν, 59). Once again a whole song is concerned with sanctioning the use of the paean form for Asclepius. But unlike other hymns, this hymn has no cletic address to the god. There is no enumeration of adjectives qualifying the deity;[84] after the initial ἰὲ Παιᾶνα θεόν there is only one address to Apollo (ὦ Φοῖβ᾽ Ἀπόλλων, 40), and the definition of Asclepius comes over fifteen lines after the beginning of the song: "who puts an end to diseases, granter of health, great gift to mortals" (τὸν νόσων παύστορα,

---

[82] Wilamowitz-Moellendorff 1886: 125–61. See Fantuzzi and Hunter 2004: 26–37, Fantuzzi 2010: 181–3, I. Petrovic 2011, on the relationship with Callimachus.

[83] Ionics were used in processional lyric: Furley and Bremer 2001: ii 183, citing a parallel with Aesch. *Supp.* 1018–73, "a long processional hymn composed almost entirely of *ionici a minore*; *Cho.* 827–30, an ephymnion accompanying Orestes' attack on his mother." See also the parodos of Euripides' *Bacchae*, with Seaford 1996: ad loc. and the Iacchus song of Aristophanes' *Frogs*.

[84] In contrast with the Erythraean paeans, which open with Παιᾶνα κλυτόμητιν Λατοΐδαν Ἕκατον . . . (1–2) and the *Hymn. Hom. Ascl.*: ἰητῆρα νόσων (1), κακῶν θελκτῆρ᾽ ὀδυνάων (4).

δωτῆρ ὑγιείας, μέγα δώρημα βροτοῖς, 56–7).[85] This characterization leads
to the only direct address to Asclepius, called Paian (58). The scarcity of
direct addresses to Asclepius can be linked to the confusion of the identities
of Apollo and Asclepius. From the opening line, the dedicatee of the song
remains undefined. The paean starts with Παιᾶνα θεὸν (37) but the direct
address shifts from Apollo (40) to an indefinite second person singular
(σέβομαί σε, 52) (still referring to Apollo?), then back again to a reference
to Asclepius in the third person singular (νιν . . . Ἀσκλαπιόν, 55–6), and
finally to an address in the second person singular (τὰν σὰν Ἐπίδαυρον
ματρόπολιν, 59). The assimilation of the two gods is thus very gradual and
never taken for granted. This process illustrates a point already tackled with
regard to the Erythraean paeans: by delaying the prayer to the god and the
string of adjectives defining the god, Isyllus exploits cultic and performative
mechanisms that justify the use of the song for Asclepius. The poet does not
deliver a formalized prayer but rather reproduces with narrative progression
the creation of Asclepius, the local god, not only in the myth that he relates
(or invents) but also in the song that he composes. It is only when Asclepius
is born (in the chronological progression of the poem) and firmly rooted in
a place (Epidaurus) that the god gets his adjectives ("the one who puts an
end to diseases," "great boon for mortals," etc.).

Emphasizing Asclepius' Epidaurian origins, Isyllus also includes thematic
innovation. While the myth part is introduced in most hymns after a direct
address to the god with a hymnic relative, Isyllus deviates from that model
by presenting the myth as already an oral tradition (φάτις ἐνέπουσ᾿ ἤλυθ᾿
ἐς ἀκοὰς προγόνων, "it was reported to my ancestors," 39–40). "If this [the
oral tradition] were true," Furley and Bremer comment, "it would be an
interesting reference to oral transmission of a sacred legend."[86] But even if
the oral tradition did *not* exist, the reference to an oral model of knowledge
transmission is a foil to the authority of the stone itself: Isyllus does not need
to cite the precise origin of the story, the nod to oral tradition is authority
enough to ensure the legitimacy of Isyllus' own words.[87] The φάτις is part
of the local aetiology and of the fiction of the origins and inscription of
the paean. This local mythology of Asclepius is closely tied into the prose
inscription (which describes the institution of the sanctuary of Malos) and
the next section (which tells of his aretalogy and his having revealed himself
already to the inhabitants of Epidaurus). The narrative portion of the paean
itself picks up Asclepius' genealogy further upstream than any other paean.

---

[85] An expression comparable to the Erythraean paeans: μέγα χάρμα βροτοῖσιν (4) and to the
   Hymn. Hom. Ascl.: χάρμα μέγ᾿ ἀνθρώποισι (4).
[86] Furley and Bremer 2001: ii 188.   [87] On this, see also Sineux 1999: 166.

Although no other version of the myth confirms this, Zeus is said here to have betrothed the Muse Erato to Malos, a native of Epidaurus. Isyllus thus denies the Arcadian origin that Pindar, for example, gives Coronis' lover (ξένου ἀπ' Ἀρκαδίας, "a stranger from Arcadia," Pind. *Pyth.* 3.25–6) or the Thessalian origins that Pausanias attributes to him (Paus. 2.26.3–6). Finally, with the list of meaningful names of female figures, Isyllus insists on the legitimacy of Asclepius.[88] The whole inscription shows constant concern over naming and inscribing, and it is significant that the heroic Kleo-Pheme and the radiant Aigla, elsewhere unattested in Asclepius' genealogy, are announced or picked up in other parts of the inscription and of the myth of Asclepius. The etymology that Isyllus gives for Asclepius is his mother's name Aigla, announced in ἠγλάισεν (28) and picked up in the reference to bright health (ἐναργῆ ὑγίειαν, 60) and the bright words of the god (ἔλεξας ἐναργῆ, 72) in the last section. Similarly, the connection between father and son complements the semantic links: adjectives connect "Phoebus" Apollo (described as χρυσότοξος, "of the golden bow," 48 and χρυσοκόμα, "golden-haired," 51) and his son Asclepius (σὺνόπλοισιν λαμπόμενος χρυσέοις, "shining in his golden weapons," 68–9) in the last section. The lexical connection even goes further, as the name of Asclepius' grandmother (Κλεοφήμα, 45) is introduced by φάτις (39) and picked up by σώτειραν φήμαν (80) in the next part. The significance of this process of naming is emphasized no fewer than five times – ὀνομάσθη (45 and 46), ἐπεκλήθη (47), ἐπίκλησιν (55), and ὠνόμαξ' (56). All these words attest to the care taken in making the birth of the god appear a necessity, the culmination of a process. But they also point to the meticulous effort invested in the religious legitimization of the god and the social legitimization of his poet, through authoritative speech and performative naming.

The last section (F, 62–84, in dactylic hexameters) consolidates the work achieved by the rest of the inscription. It describes the epiphany of Asclepius to a boy, either the poet himself or his son, in a scene that is close to a *Dichterweihe* and reaffirms the special relationship between poet and god.[89]

---

[88] There is a marked contrast between the myth as told in the Erythraean paeans, concerned with the descendants of Asclepius and their manifestation of the power of Asclepius, and that of Isyllus, concerned with the legitimacy of Asclepius' origins and its local importance.

[89] Depending on how one interprets the reference to ὁ παῖς (67) in that section, either Isyllus as a boy or Isyllus accompanying his son received a sign from the god that he was under his protection. When the god speaks to Isyllus, he does so in a way that recalls the preceding parts of the inscription itself, especially in the μαντευσάμενος Λυκοῦργος (71), which echoes the Ἴσυλλος ἐπέθηκε μαντεύσασθαι (32), and in the address to the god (ὦ μέγ' ἄριστε θεῶν, 74), which uses the political vocabulary of the first lines (ἀριστοκρατίαν, 3; ἀριστεύωσι, 14). Moreover, ἄριστος is rarely used of a god, and the record of the virtue of the god is done in

Once again, the model of the visit of the god to the poet-to-be works in two ways. On the one hand, it allows Isyllus to model himself on Hesiod or Callimachus and to boost his own authority as a poet by aligning himself with an earlier poetic figure. On the other hand, the lines also work as an aretalogy of Asclepius, who manifests the salvatory power that the paean was celebrating in an epiphany recorded by the poet. The inscription, which was already functioning as a record of a *lex sacra*, epigram, and script of a cultic song, here works also as the equivalent of an "act of healing" that preserves the deeds of Asclepius. The last lines (83–4) form a ring-composition with the beginning of the inscription:

> ταῦτα τοί, ὦ μέγ᾽ ἄριστε θεῶν, ἀνέθηκεν Ἴσυλλος
> τι[μ]ῶν σὴν ἀρετήν, ὦναξ, ὥσπερ τὸ δίκαιον.

> These are the events, O great and best of the gods, that Isyllus inscribed in honor of your virtue, O Lord, as is just.

These lines, which foreground the poet as author of the inscription, conclude the extraordinary complex that surrounds the paean to Asclepius. As noted at different points, Isyllus' strategy consists of his validating his authority in order to throw into relief the paean's originality, which includes its thematic and epichoric features. By using distinctively different metric patterns in its various sections, the whole inscription relies on the memory of diverse modes, and contexts, of performance – from inscription in prose to hexametric poetry (the meter used for stone or literary epigrams, sacred regulations, and gnomic poetry), and from spoken meters (trochaic tetrameters) to sung rhythms (ionics) – and thus manipulates its audience's horizon of expectation. The existence of the paean as a song cannot be separated from its existence as a written record, as the parts of the inscription all reinforce each other in the creation of the unique figure who praises himself, his homeland Epidaurus, and his special god Asclepius.

Conclusion

Inscribed cultic songs have until recently been ignored in the study of late classical lyric poetry and remained the province of epigraphists and

---

words that remind of the virtue of the good citizen. This retrospective form of *Dichterweihe*, on the model of Hesiod's, Archilochus', or Callimachus' accounts of their meetings with the god when they were young, is more an aretalogy of Isyllus than an aretalogy of Asclepius and retrospectively provides the audience with a framework of reception for Isyllus' law and the whole politico-religious and poetic project.

historians of religion, or they have been analyzed in the light of their relationship with the Homeric or Callimachean hymns. Scholars interested in ancient genre theory have also regarded the songs as specimens illustrating the evolution and decadence of the paean genre and have argued for important changes in the late classical period. The first goal of this chapter has been to highlight various subtle mechanisms involved in the individual songs: each creates its own enunciative journey and displays an elaborate narrative strategy to justify calling the god it celebrates "Paian." Each song enacts the ritual utterance of the *Paian* cry, either by connecting it to the chronological unfolding of the narrative sequence (as is the case with the Erythraean paeans) or by retrospectively legitimizing the use of the cultic adjective (as is the case in Philodamus' paean). Second, the chapter recognized that very rarely does the interpretation of the song's rhetoric and poetic features take into consideration the material reality of these remarkable texts. Inscribed paeans are not just paeans that happened to be inscribed. Song and performance form only one element in a complex nexus of ritual and commemorative practices that also included gestures and monuments. Even acknowledging the physical dimension of the stone as significant object rather than as material of preservation is not enough, for the system of human and divine relationships in which it is involved also calls for our attention. Inscriptions are the material place where cultic and poetic work achieved by the song meets with political and civic work achieved by the text surrounding the song. At this locus two value systems come into contact: the aesthetic and cultic model of the poet, who aims for maximum poetic efficiency in celebrating the god, and the civic model of the community, or individual, who inscribes the song and celebrates the author of the song. In some cases, the paratext carefully stages the song as dedicated by an individual (as was the case with Isyllus) or legitimized by a community (as was the case with the *subscriptio* of Aristonous' hymns and that of Philodamus' paean, and in the added texts on several versions of the Erythraean paeans, which suggest the reuse of the songs in other ceremonies). Finally, in Aristonous' *Hymn to Hestia* and Philodamus' paean, the song is explicitly in dialogue with its material setting. Overall, to read these songs out of context is to miss one half of a dialogue between site and sound.

Epilogue

The aim of this book has been to re-evaluate a corpus of texts that had been, until very recently, ignored, dismissed, or judged extremely negatively by modern scholars. Starting from the observation that our modern approach to the melic poetry of the late fifth and fourth centuries BC has been hindered by a series of ancient and modern aesthetic and ideological filters, I have sought to present the diversity and vibrancy of the late classical Muse – in other words, its many-headedness.

Taken at face value, a many-headed Muse is an image both disturbing and grotesque, a freakish sight that catches the eye, fascinating and repulsing us at the same time. Reifying one of the leitmotivs of the critical discourse on the New Music examined in Chapter 2, many-ness speaks for the excess that critics have seen as representative of late classical theater *mousikē* and for its socio-political perversion of the classical past. The adjective also encapsulates the technical complexity of the musical features of the New Music, and the expression is an all too apt description of the reception of this phenomenon.

Yet the many heads are not so much an image for the topic of the book as for its method: the book is a challenge to the monolithic approach to late classical lyric, often exclusively equated with the New Music. This study has sought precisely to deconstruct the specter of the New Music, so often depicted in ancient sources as representative of the ethical decadence of democracy, by locating this musical phenomenon within a larger histori-cal, intellectual, cultural, and artistic context. The book takes its lead from studies in the archaeology of the theater and the material history of *mousikē* that have greatly contributed to a re-evaluation of late classical lyric activi-ties, but it has also examined other venues, and types, of lyric performance. By focusing both on the showy pieces of the New Musicians and poetry on stones, by setting in parallel dithyrambic and sophistic language, and by juxtaposing obscure fragments with well-known pieces, it has also sought to shift the focus away from the theater music of Athens and to replace a com-fortable unified critical discourse with a series of more fragmentary insights. The New Music was only one of the musical idioms of its time. Other voices could be heard, in different places and settings (such as the symposia and sanctuaries studied in Chapters 6 and 7), and exchanges took place between performance venues, public and private, dramatic and non-dramatic, oral and written. As Chapter 4 has suggested, this interaction concerned not just performance style but also stylistic features: the spectacularly infamous dithyrambic diction cannot be understood without taking into consideration its dialogue with cultic language, Homeric diction, and other forms of linguistic experiments driven by specific intellectual projects, especially those of the sophists, whom Plato evocatively described as "many-headed creatures."[1]

This study thus widens the scope of inquiry by understanding the New Music within its cultural and social contexts, but it also contributes to the study of late classical poetry by bringing into the analysis of texts (and not just the most-read texts like the *sphragis* of Timotheus' *Persians* but also fragments and narrative parts often left out of critical accounts) the literary critical and interpretive tools that have been employed in the analysis of other poetic corpora. Questions of intertextuality, voice, *deixis*, and narratology (studied in Chapters 5 and 6) have provided productive new ways of interrogating texts that had previously been studied largely for their contribution to the evolution of poetic genres. Close readings have made evident that the stylistic features of the language of New Music (the florid diction and use of periphrases and bold images, for example) should not be understood in isolation or as a shopping list of features, but as interlaced and mutually dependent. The diction, in particular, of late classical dithyrambs and nomes is a way of destabilizing the straight relationship between words, things, and audience. Just as viewers of late classical statues are no longer "participant observer[s], whose viewing fulfilled the work of art by creating a temporary bridge across worlds in archaic art,"[2] audiences of late classical theater lyric are not called upon directly, but are to listen to the narrative of a world described as *like* that which they inhabit and to participate in the construction of meaning. This type of narrative brought by the New Music creates a properly democratic experience, for its meaning depends on the audience's involvement, and listening in, rather than on inherited stable images and ideas. That audience, a musical voyeur, is an interpreter of a world constructed for its sake, a world it connects to by projection and identification. Where early twentieth-century scholars found psychological or aesthetic explanations for the innovative features of dramatic *mousikē* in the late classical period, telling of the "tendencies of the time" or "new feeling for life," this study has suggested that the poets created a different

[1] Pl. *Soph.* 240c.   [2] Elsner 2006: 85.

type of relationship with their audience: along with a new narrative style, the New Music created, and relied on, a new listener.[3]

These new avenues of thought through late classical lyric are well worthy of further exploration. One of those pathways considers reception. Chapter 3, devoted to biographical anecdotes about the poets, has examined how ideas about the relationship between poetry and society circulated in the image of the New Musicians and stories about their lives. These narratives survived by means of their adoption into new traditions. The *chreia* in which Philoxenus is described as spitting in the food so as to prevent others from eating it is repeated, for example, in Rabelais' *Prologue du Quint Livre*: there, just as in Philoxenus' *Dinner Party* and Plutarch's *Moralia* (from which the anecdote is extracted), Rabelais' focus is as much on the relationship between food and words as on food itself. The anecdote has traversed cultures and time to find its way in the French literary terroir. Rabelais, again, in *Gargantua and Pantagruel*, describes in the chapter on the education of young Gargantua the Bible being read in a distinct voice while the giant is being washed: "By this means too Ponocrates was making him forget everything that he had learned from his old preceptors, just as Timotheus used to do with his disciples who had been taught by other musicians."[4] The anecdote has not survived in any Greek text but is certainly in keeping with the image of internal rivalries and competitions and the constant tug-of-war between conservatism and innovation that we find in many other ancient stories. These two examples from Rabelais suggest that the late classical poets, or at least their anecdotal personae, were far less forgotten and far more canonical than twenty-first century readers might think, probably in part because of the pre-eminent position the New Musicians occupied in Athenaeus and in Plutarch, cornerstones of Renaissance education. The afterlife of these poets, their personae and their poetry, and the archaeology of forgetting them form only one area that could be explored further, to continue the rewarding and inspiring activity of reading the late classical lyric corpus.

---

[3] For example, Kranz 1933: 232: "[Die neue Tragik] ist die Frucht *eines neuen Lebensgefühls*" ("the New Tragic is the fruit of *a new awareness of life*") or Webster 1939: 197: "Both [*mannerism and realism*] *are used to express the tendencies of the time,* the desire for escape and novelty on the one hand, and on the other the desire to portray emotion and to represent ordinary life ... The lyrics of the later plays of Euripides are often further removed from the action than the lyrics of his earlier period; they are display-pieces, soft, rich, and exotic ... " (my emphasis).

[4] Rabelais, *Gargantua*, Chapter 21.

Bibliography

Editions and commentaries

Bergk, Th. (1878–82) *Poetae lyrici Graeci* (3 vols.), 4th edn. Leipzig.

Boeckh, A. (1811–21) Πινδάρου τὰ σωζόμενα. *Pindari opera quae supersunt* (2 vols.). Leipzig.

Campbell, D. (1982) *Greek Lyric: Sappho and Alcaeus,* vol. i. Cambridge, MA and London.

(1988) *Greek Lyric: Anacreon, Anacreontea, Choral Lyric from Olympus to Alcman,* vol. ii. Cambridge, MA and London.

(1991) *Greek Lyric: Stesichorus, Ibycus, Simonides, and Others,* vol. iii. Cambridge, MA and London.

(1992) *Greek Lyric: Bacchylides, Corinna, and Others,* vol. iv. Cambridge, MA and London.

(1993) *Greek Lyric: The New School of Poetry and Anonymous Songs and Hymns,* vol. v. Cambridge, MA and London.

Canfora, L. (2001) *I Deipnosofisti: i dotti a banchetto, Ateneo. Prima trad. italiana commentata su progetto di Luciano Canfora; introd. di Christian Jacob.* Rome and Salerno.

Cassio, A. (1977) *Aristofane: Banchettanti.* Pisa.

Cipolla, P. (2003) *Poeti minori del dramma satiresco.* Amsterdam.

Colin, A., and D. Olson (2004) *Aristophanes: Thesmophoriazusae,* edited with introduction and commentary. Oxford and New York.

De Lacy, P., and B. Einarson (1967) *Plutarch: Moralia. That Epicurus Actually Makes a Pleasant Life Impossible. Reply to Colotes in Defence of the Other Philosophers. Is "Live Unknown" a Wise Precept? On Music,* vol. xiv, edited with translation. Cambridge, MA.

Diehl, E. (1942) *Anthologia lyrica Graeca,* vol. ii. Leipzig.

Dover, K. (1968) *Aristophanes: Clouds,* edited with introduction and commentary. Oxford.

(1993) *Aristophanes: Frogs,* edited with introduction and commentary. Oxford.

Drachmann, R. (1903–27) *Scholia vetera in Pindari carmina* (3 vols.). Leipzig.

Dunbar, N. (1995) *Aristophanes: Birds,* edited with introduction and commentary Oxford and New York.

Edmonds, J. (1922–7) *Lyra Graeca: Being the Remains of All the Greek Lyric Poets from Eumelus to Timotheus Excepting Pindar* (3 vols.). London.

333

Fortenbaugh, W., *et al.* (1992–) *Theophrastus of Eresus: Sources for his Life, Writings, Thought and Influence* (2 vols.). Leiden, New York, and Cologne.

Furley, W., and J. M. Bremer (2001) *Greek Hymns: Selected Cult Songs from the Archaic to the Hellenistic Period* (2 vols.). Tübingen.

Gallavotti, C. (1993) *Theocritus quique feruntur Bucolici Graeci*, 3rd edn. Rome.

Gamberini, L. (1979) *Plutarco: Della musica*. Florence.

Gentili, B., and C. Prato (1979–85) *Poetarum elegiacorum testimonia et fragmenta*. Leipzig.

Gomperz, T. (1865) *Philodem Über Induktionsschlüsse. Nach der Oxforder und Neapolitaner Abschrift, hrsg. von Theodor Gomperz*. Leipzig.

Gow, A. S. F. (1965) *Machon: The Fragments*, edited with a commentary. Cambridge.

Grande, C. del (1946) *Ditirambografi: testimonianze e frammenti*. Naples.

Gulick, C. B. (1927–41) *Athenaeus: The Deipnosophists*, with an English translation (7 vols.). London.

Hall, E. (1996) *Aeschylus: Persians*, edited with an introduction, translation and commentary. Warminster.

Hansen, P. (1983–9) *Carmina epigraphica Graeca* (2 vols.). Berlin and New York.

Harding, P. (2006) *Didymos on Demosthenes: introduction, text, translation, and commentary*. Oxford and New York.

Hett, W. (1936) *Aristotle: Problems, Books 1–21*, edited with translation. Cambridge, MA.

Hett, W., and H. Rackham (1937) *Aristotle: Problems: Books 22–38. Rhetorica ad Alexandrum*, edited with translation. Cambridge, MA.

Hock, R., and E. O'Neil (1986) *The Chreia in Ancient Rhetoric*, vol. i. *The Progymnasmata*. Atlanta.

Hordern, J. (2002) *The Fragments of Timotheus of Miletus*. Oxford.

Hunter, R. (1983) *Eubulus: The Fragments*, edited with a commentary. Cambridge.
  (1999) *Theocritus: A Selection*, edited with a commentary. Cambridge and New York.

Ieranò, G. (1997) *Il ditirambo di Dioniso: le testimonianze antiche*. Pisa.

Jacoby, F. (1904) *Das Marmor Parium*. Berlin.

Janssen, T. H. (1984) *Timotheus: Persae*. Amsterdam.

Kemke, J. (1884) *Philodemi de musica librorum quae exstant edidit Ioannes Kemke*. Leipzig.

Lasserre, F. (1954) *Plutarque: De la musique*. Lausanne.

Lightfoot, J. L. (1999) *Parthenius of Nicaea*. Oxford.

Maas, P. (1933) *Epidaurische Hymnen*. Halle.

MacDowell, D. (1971) *Aristophanes: Wasps*, edited with introduction and commentary. Oxford.

Maehler, H. (1968) *Die Lieder des Bakchylides*, vol. i. *Die Siegeslieder: Edition des Textes mit Einleitung und Übersetzung*. Leiden.
  (1997) *Die Lieder des Bakchylides*, vol. ii. *Die Dithyramben und Fragmente: Text, Übersetzung und Kommentar*. Leiden.
  (2004) *Bacchylides: A Selection*. Cambridge and New York.

Matthews, V. J. (1996) *Antimachus of Colophon: Text and Commentary.* Leiden.

Meineke, A. (1855–7) *Ioannis Stobaei florilegium* (4 vols.). Leipzig.

Olson, D. (2006–10) *Athenaeus: The Learned Banqueters* (8 vols.). Cambridge, MA.

Page, D. L. (1942) *Greek Literary Papyri in Two Volumes,* vol. I. *Texts, Translations, and Notes.* Cambridge, MA.

Pearson, L. (1990) *Aristoxenus, Elementa Rhythmica: The Fragments of Book II and the Additional Evidence from Aristoxenean Rhythmic Theory.* Oxford.

Powell, J. U. (1925) *Collectanea Alexandrina: reliquiae minores poetarum Graecorum aetatis ptolemaicae 323–146 AC, epicorum, elegiacorum, lyricorum, ethicorum.* Oxford.

Race, W. H. (1997) *Pindar* (2 vols.). Cambridge, MA and London.

Reed, J. (1997) *Bion of Smyrna: The fragments and the Adonis,* edited with an introduction and commentary. New York.

Rose, V. (1886) *Aristotelis qui ferebantur librorum fragmenta.* Leipzig.

Seaford, R. (1984) *Euripides: Cyclops.* Oxford.

  (1996) *Euripides: Bacchae.* Warminster.

Sevieri, R. (2011) *I Persiani.* Milan.

Smyth, H. (1963) *Greek Melic Poets.* New York.

Sommerstein, A. (1980) *Aristophanes: Acharnians,* edited with translation and notes. Warminster.

  (1982) *Aristophanes: Clouds,* edited with translation and notes. Warminster.

  (1987) *Aristophanes: Birds,* edited with translation and notes. Warminster.

  (2001) *Aristophanes: Wealth,* edited with translation and notes. Warminster.

  (2005) *Aristophanes: Peace,* edited with translation and notes, 2nd edn. Warminster.

Sutton, D. F. (1989) *Dithyrambographi Graeci.* Hildesheim.

Torchio, M. C. (2001) *Il Pluto di Aristofane.* Alexandria.

van der Eijk, P. (2000–1). *Diocles of Carystus: A collection of the fragments with translation and commentary.* Leiden and Boston.

Wagman, R. (1995) *Inni di Epidauro.* Pisa.

Weil, H., and T. Reinach. (1900) *Plutarch: De la Musique.* Paris.

West, M. L. (2003) *Homeric Hymns, Homeric Apocrypha, Lives of Homer,* edited with translation. Cambridge, MA.

West, M. L., and R. Merkelbach (1967) *Fragmenta Hesiodea.* Oxford.

Wilamowitz-Moellendorff, U. von (1886) *Isyllos von Epidauros.* Berlin.

  (1903) *Timotheos: Die Perser. Aus einem Papyrus von Abusir im Auftrage der deutschen Orientgesellschaft.* Leipzig.

  (1909) *Nordionische Steine mit Beiträgen von Dr. Paul Jacobsthal.* Berlin.

Other works

Acosta-Hughes, B. (2010a) *Arion's Lyre: Archaic Lyric into Hellenistic Poetry.* Princeton.

(2010b) "The prefigured muse: rethinking a few assumptions on Hellenistic poetics," in Clauss and Cuypers (2010), 81–91.

Adkins, A. (1960) *Merit and Responsibility: A Study in Greek Values.* Oxford.

Agapiou, N. (2005) *Endymion au carrefour: la fortune littéraire et artistique du mythe d'Endymion à l'aube de l'ère moderne.* Berlin.

Agócs, P., C. Carey, and R. Rawles (eds.) (2012) *Reading the Victory Ode.* Cambridge and New York.

Akrigg, B. (2007) "The nature and implications of Athens' changed social structure and economy," in Osborne (2007), 27–43.

Allan, W. (1999–2000) "Euripides and the Sophists: society and the theatre of war," in Cropp, Lee, and Sansone (1999–2000), 145–56.

Alonge, M. (2005) "The Palaikastro Hymn and the modern myth of the Cretan Zeus," Princeton/Stanford Working Papers in Classics, available at: www.princeton.edu/~pswpc/pdfs/alonge/120512.pdf.

Aloni, A. (2001) "The Proem of Simonides' Plataea elegy and the circumstances of its performance," in Boedeker and Sider (2001), 86–195.

Anderson, W. D. (1994) *Music and Musicians in Ancient Greece.* Ithaca.

Anello, P. (1984) "Polifemo e Galatea," *Seia* 1: 11–51.

Aspiotes, N. (2006) *Prosopographia musica Graeca: Personenlexikon mit Daten zu 2350 (heidnischen) Musikern.* Berlin.

Audiat, J. (1932) "L'hymne d'Aristonoos à Hestia," *BCH* 56: 299–312.

Auerbach, E. (1953) *Mimesis: The Representation of Reality in Western Literature,* trans. W. R. Trask. Princeton.

Bacon, H. (1961) *Barbarians in Greek Tragedy.* New Haven.

Bakhtin, M. (1984). *Rabelais and his World,* trans. H. Iswolsky. Bloomington, IN.

Bakker, E. (1997a) *Poetry in Speech: Orality and Homeric Discourse.* Ithaca.

(1997b) "Verbal aspect and mimetic description in Thucydides," in *Grammar as Interpretation: Greek Literature in its Linguistic Contexts,* ed. E. Bakker. Leiden, 7–54.

(2005) *Pointing at the Past: from Formula to Performance in Homeric Poetics.* Washington, DC.

Bakola, E. (2009) *Cratinus and the Art of Comedy.* Oxford.

Barchiesi, A. (2001) "The crossing," in *Texts, Ideas, and the Classics: Scholarship, Theory, and Classical Literature,* ed. S. J. Harrison. Oxford, 142–63.

Barker, A. (1982) "The innovations of Lysander the kitharist," *CQ* 32: 266–9.

(1984) *Greek Musical Writings,* vol. i: *The Musician and his Art.* Cambridge.

(1988) "Che cos' era la mágadis," in Gentili and Pretagostini (1988), 96–107.

(1995) "*Heterophonia* and *Poikilia*: accompaniments to Greek melody," in Gentili and Perusino (1995), 41–60.

(1998) "Telestes and the 'five-rodded joining of strings'," *CQ* 48: 75–81.

(2000) "Athenaeus on Music," in Braund and Wilkins (2000), 434–4.

(2002) *Euterpe: ricerche Sulla Musica Greca e Romana,* trans. E. Rocconi. Pisa.

(2004) "Transforming the nightingale: aspects of Athenian musical discourse in the late fifth century," in Murray and Wilson (2004), 185–204.

(2009) "Shifting conceptions of schools of harmonic theory, 400 BC–200 AD," in Martinelli (2009), 165–90.

(2011) "Music, politics, and diplomacy in Hellenistic Teos," in Yatromanolakis (2011), 159–79.

Barringer, J. (2001) *The Hunt in Ancient Greece.* Baltimore.

Bartol, K. (2004) "What did he do? Clearchus on Philoxenus (ap. Ath. 1.5f–6a = Clearch. Fr. 57 Wehrli)," *CQ* 54: 292–6.

Bassett, S. E. (1931) "The place and date of the first performance of the *Persians* of Timotheus," *CP* 26: 153–65.

Battezzato, L. (2005) "The New Music of the *Trojan Women*," *Lexis* 23: 73–104.

Baumbach, M., A. Petrovic, and I. Petrovic (eds.) (2010) *Archaic and Classical Greek Epigram.* Cambridge and New York.

Bélis, A. (1988) "La trasmissione della musica nell' antichità," in *Lo specchio della musica: iconografia musicale nella ceramica attica di Spina*, ed. F. Berti and D. Restani. Bologna, 29–39.

(1998) "Un 'Ajax' et deux Timothée: (P. Berol. N° 6870)," *REG* 111: 74–100.

(1999) *Les Musiciens dans l'Antiquité.* Paris.

Bell, J. M. (1978) "Κίμβιξ καὶ σοφός: Simonides in the anecdotal tradition," *QUCC* 28: 29–86.

Benvéniste, E. (1967) "Fondements syntaxiques de la composition nominale," *Bulletin de la Société de Linguistique de Paris* 67.1: 15–31.

Bers, V. (1974) *Enallage and Greek Style.* Leiden.

(1984) *Greek Poetic Syntax in the Classical Age.* New Haven.

Bing, P. (2002) "The un-read Muse? Inscribed epigram and its readers in Antiquity," in *Hellenistic Epigrams*, ed. M. Harder, R. Regtuit, and G. Wakker. Hellenistica Groningana 5. Leuven, 39–66.

(2008) *The Well-Read Muse: Present and Past in Callimachus and the Hellenistic Poets*, revised edn. Ann Arbor.

(2009) *The Scroll and the Marble: Studies in Reading and Reception in Hellenistic Poetry.* Ann Arbor.

Boardman, J. (1956) "Some Attic fragments: pot, plaque, and dithyramb," *JHS* 78: 18–25.

Boedeker, D., and D. Sider (eds.) (2001) *The New Simonides: Contexts of Praise and Desire.* Oxford and New York.

Bommelaer, J.-F. (2005) "Un peu d'air des îles à Delphes?," *Ktêma* 25: 65–74.

Borthwick, E. K. (1959) "Κατάληψις: a neglected technical term in Greek music," *CQ* 9: 23–9.

(1968) "Notes on the Plutarch *De musica* and the *Cheiron* of Pherecrates," *Hermes* 96: 60–73.

(1994) "New interpretations of Aristophanes *Frogs* 1249–1328," *Phoenix* 48.1: 21–41.

Bosher, K. (ed.) (2012) *Theater outside Athens: Drama in Greek Sicily and South Italy.* Cambridge

Bourdieu, P. (1991) *Language and Symbolic Power.* Cambridge, MA.

Bowie, A. (1997) "Thinking with drinking: wine and the symposium in Aristophanes," *JHS* 117: 1–21.

Bowie, E. (1970) "Greeks and their past in the Second Sophistic," *P&P* 46: 3–41.

  (1986) "Early Greek elegy, symposium and public festival," *JHS* 106: 13–35.

  (2000) "Athenaeus' knowledge of early Greek elegiac and iambic poetry," in Braund and Wilkins (2000), 124–35.

Bowra, C. M. (1933) "Ancient lyrical and elegiac poetry," in Powell (1933), 1–67.

  (1938) "Aristotle's Hymn to Virtue," *CQ* 32: 182–9.

  (1961) *Greek Lyric Poetry from Alcman to Simonides,* 2nd edn. Oxford.

  (1963) "Arion and the dolphin," *MH* 20: 121–34.

  (1967) *Ancient Greek literature,* revised edn. Oxford.

Boys-Stones, G. R. (ed.) (2003) *Metaphor, Allegory, and the Classical Tradition: Ancient Thought and Modern Revisions.* Oxford and New York.

Braund, D., and J. Wilkins (eds.) (2000) *Athenaeus and his World: Reading Greek Culture in the Roman Empire.* Exeter.

Bräuning, T. (1881) *De adiectivis compositis apud Pindarum.* Berlin.

Breitenbach, W. (1934) *Untersuchungen zur Sprache der euripideischen Lyrik.* Stuttgart.

Bremer, J. (1981) "Greek hymns," in *Faith, Hope, and Worship: Aspects of Religious Mentality in the Ancient World,* ed. H. Versnel. Leiden, 193–215.

  (1991) "Poets and their patrons," in *Fragmenta dramatica: Beiträge zur Interpretation der griechischen Tragikerfragmente und ihrer Wirkungsgeschichte,* ed. A. Harder. Göttingen: 39–60.

Brenner, G. (1949) *Die Polyphemdichtungen des Euripides, Kratinos und Philoxenos und ihr Verhältnis zur Odyssee.* Vienna.

Brown, N. O. (1947) *Hermes the Thief: The Evolution of a Myth.* Madison.

Bruit Zeidman, L., and P. Schmitt Pantel (1992) *Religion in the Ancient Greek City,* trans. P. Cartledge. Cambridge and New York.

Bruss, J. (2005) *Hidden Presences: Monuments, Gravesites, and Corpses in Greek Funerary Epigram.* Leuven, Paris, and Dudley, MA.

Brussich, G. F. (1970) "La lingua di Timoteo," *Quaderni Triestini per il Lessico della Lirica Corale Greca* 1: 51–80.

  (1990) "L'Inno ad Artemide di Timoteo," *QUCC* 34: 25–38.

Budelmann, F. (ed.) (2009a) *The Cambridge Companion to Greek Lyric.* Cambridge.

  (2009b) "Introducing Greek Lyric," in Budelmann (2009a), 1–18.

Bühler, K. (1934) *Sprachtheorie: Die Darstellungsfunktion der Sprache.* Jena.

Bülow, P. (1929) "Ein vielgesungener Asklepios Paean (von Ptolemais)," in *Xenia Bonnensia.* Bonn, 35–49.

Bundrick, S. (2005) *Music and Image in Classical Athens.* Cambridge and New York.

Burnett, A. (1985) *The Art of Bacchylides.* Cambridge, MA.

Butler, J. (1990) *Gender Trouble: Feminism and the Subversion of Identity*. New York.

Calame, C. (1974) "Réflexions sur les genres littéraires en Grèce archaïque," *QUCC* 17: 113–28.

(1995) *The Craft of Poetic Speech in Greece*, 2nd edn. Ithaca and London.

(1998) "La Poésie lyrique grecque, un genre inexistant?," *Littérature* 111: 87–110.

(2004a) "Deictic ambiguity and auto-referentiality: some examples from Greek poetics," *Arethusa* 37.3: 415–43.

(2004b) "Identités d'auteur à l'exemple de la Grèce classique: signatures, énonciations, citations," in *Identités d'auteur dans l'antiquité et la tradition européenne*, ed. C. Calame and R. Chartier. Grenoble, 11–39.

(2009) "Apollo in Delphi and in Delos: poetic performances between paean and dithyramb," in *Apolline Politics and Poetics*, ed. L. Athanassaki, R. Martin, and J. Miller. Athens, 169–97.

Calvié, L. (2010) *Timothée de Milet: Les Perses. Textes choisis et présentés par Laurent Calvié*. Toulouse.

Cameron, A. (1991) "How thin was Philitas?," *CQ* 41: 534–8.

(1995) *Callimachus and his Critics*. Princeton.

Campbell, D. (1964) "Flutes and elegiac couplets," *JHS* 85: 63–8.

(1983) *Golden Lyre: The Themes of the Greek Lyric Poets*. London.

Carson, A. (1999) *Economy of the Unlost: Reading Simonides of Keos with Paul Celan*. Princeton.

Cassio, A. (1971) "Laso e Damone 'sofisti' e 'novatori'," *PP* 26: 275–80.

Cassio, A., D. Musti, and L. E. Rossi (eds.) (2000) *Synaulia: cultura musicale in Grecia e contatti Mediterranei (AION filol.-lett. 5)*. Naples.

Chafe, W. (1994) *Discourse, Consciousness, and Time: The Flow and Displacement of Conscious Experience in Speaking and Writing*. Chicago.

Chiron, P. (2001) *Un Rhéteur méconnu: Démétrios (Ps.-Démétrios de Phalère). Essai sur les mutations de la théorie du style à l'époque hellénistique*, with a preface by M. Patillon. Paris.

Cingano, E. (2003) "Entre skolion et enkomion: réflexions sur le 'genre' et la performance de la lyrique chorale grecque," in *Colloque la poésie grecque antique: actes*, ed. J. Jouanna and J. Leclant. Paris, 17–45.

Citti, V. (1994) *Eschilo e la lexis tragica*. Amsterdam.

Clackson, J. (2002) "Composition in Indo-European Languages," *TPS* 100.2: 163–7.

Clauss, J., and M. Cuypers (eds.) (2010) *A Companion to Hellenistic Literature*. Chichester and Malden.

Colvin, S. (1999) *Dialect in Aristophanes*. Oxford.

Comotti, G. (1972) "L'endecacordo di Ione di Chio," *QUCC* 13: 54–61.

(ed.) (1979) *La musica nella cultura greca e romana*. Turin.

(1980) "Atena e gli auloi in un ditirambo di Teleste (fr. 805 P.)," *QUCC* 34: 47–54.

(1983) "Un antica arpa, la mágadis, in un frammento di Teleste (fr. 808 P.)," *QUCC* 44: 57–71.

(1989) "L'anabolè e il ditirambo," *QUCC* 31: 107–17.

(1993) "Il 'canto Lidio' in due frammenti di Teleste (frr. 806; 810 P.)," in Pretagostini (1993), vol. ii. Rome, 513–20.

Comrie, B. (1976) *Aspect*. Cambridge.

Conacher, D. J. (1998) *Euripides and the Sophists: Some Dramatic Treatments of Philosophical Ideas*. London.

Connor, W. R. (1971) *The New Politicians of Fifth-Century Athens*. Princeton.

Conti Bizzarro, F. (1993–4) "Una testimonianza su Filosseno nella commedia di messo: Antifane Fr. 207 Kassel-Austin," *Rend. Acc. Archeol. Lett. Belle Arti Napoli* 64: 143–57.

Cousland, J. R. C., and J. R. Hume (eds.) (2009) *The Play of Texts and Fragments: Essays in Honour of Martin Cropp*. Leiden and Boston.

Croiset, M. (1903) "Observations sur les Perses de Timothée de Milet," *REG* 16: 323–48.

Croiset, M., and A. Croiset (1904) *An Abridged History of Greek Literature*, trans. by G. F. Heffelbower. New York and London.

Cropp, M., K. Lee, and D. Sansone (eds.) (1999–2000) *Euripides and Tragic Theatre in the Late Fifth Century (ICS 24–25)*. Champaign.

Csapo, E. (1999–2000) "Later Euripidean music," in Cropp, Lee, and Sansone (1999–2000), 399–426.

(2003) "The dolphins of Dionysus," in *Poetry, Theory, Praxis: The Social Life of Myth, Word and Image in Ancient Greece. Essays in Honour of William J. Slater*, ed. E. Csapo and M. Miller. Oxford, 69–98.

(2004) "The politics of the New Music," in Murray and Wilson (2004), 207–48.

(2008) "Star choruses: Eleusis, Orphism, and new musical imagery and dance," in Revermann and Wilson (2008), 262–90.

(2009) "New Music's gallery of images: the 'dithyrambic' first stasimon of Euripides' *Electra*," in Cousland and Hume (2009), 95–109.

(2010) *Actors and Icons of the Ancient Theater*. Chichester and Malden.

(2011) "The economics, poetics, politics, metaphysics, and ethics of the 'New Music'," in Yatromanolakis (2011), 65–131.

Csapo, E., and P. Wilson (2009a) "Timotheus the New Musician," in Budelmann (2009b), 277–93.

(2009b) "The end of the khorēgia in Athens: a forgotten document," in Martinelli (2009), 47–74.

(2010) "Le Passage de la chorégie à l'agonothésie à Athènes à la fin du ive siècle," in *L'Argent dans les concours du monde grec: actes du colloque international Saint-Denis et Paris, 5–6 décembre 2008*, ed. B. Le Guen. Saint Denis, 83–105.

Culler, J. (1981) *The Pursuit of Signs: Semiotics, Literature, Deconstruction*. Ithaca.

Currie, B. (2005) *Pindar and the Cult of Heroes*. Oxford and New York.

Dalby, A. (1987) "The Banquet of Philoxenus: a new translation with culinary notes," *Petits Propos Culinaires* 26: 28–36.

(1996) *Siren Feasts: A History of Food and Gastronomy in Greece*. London.

D'Alessio, G. (2007) "ἦν ἰδού: ecce satyri (Pratina, 708 *PMG* = 4 fr. 3 *TrGF*). Alcune considerazioni sull'uso della deissi nei testi lirici e teatrali," in *Dalla lirica corale alla poesia drammatica: forme e funzioni del canto corale nella tragedia e nella commedia greca*, ed. F. Perusino and M. Colantonio. Pisa, 95–128.

    (2009) "Defining local communities in Greek lyric poetry," in Hunter and Rutherford (2009), 137–67.

D'Angour, A. (1997) "How the dithyramb got its shape," *CQ* 47: 331–51.

    (2006a) "The New Music – so what's new?," in Goldhill and Osborne (2006), 264–83.

    (2006b) "Intimations of the classical in early Greek mousike," in J. R. Porter (2006), 89–105.

    (2007) "The sound of μουσική: reflections on aural change in ancient Greece," in Osborne (2007), 288–300.

    (2011) *The Greeks and the New: Novelty in Ancient Greek Imagination and Experience.* Cambridge.

Danielewic, G. (1978) "De Aristonoi hymno in Vestam," *Eos* 66: 55–60.

Danielsson, O. A. (1903–4) "Zu den Persern des Timotheos," *Eranos* 5: 1–39 and 98–128.

Davidson, J. (1997) *Courtesans and Fishcakes: The Consuming Passions of Classical Athens.* London.

    (2000) "Gnesippus Paigniagraphos: the comic poets and the erotic mime," in Harvey and Wilkins (2000), 41–64.

Davies, M. (1988) "Monody, choral lyric and the tyranny of the handbook," *CQ* 38: 52–64.

Day, J. (1989) "Rituals in stone: early Greek grave epigrams and monuments," *JHS* 109: 16–28.

    (1994) "Interactive offerings: early Greek dedicatory epigrams and ritual," *HSCP* 96: 37–74.

    (2000) "Epigram and reader: generic force as (re-)activation of ritual," in Depew and Obbink (2000), 37–57.

    (2007) "Poems on stone: the inscribed antecedents of Hellenistic epigram," in *Brill's Companion to Hellenistic Epigram*, ed. P. Bing and J. Bruss. Leiden and Boston, 29–47.

    (2010) *Archaic Greek Epigram and Dedication: Representation and Reperformance.* Cambridge and New York.

Dee, J. H. (2001) *Epitheta deorum apud Homerum: The Epithetic Phrases for the Homeric Gods. A Repertory of the Descriptive Expressions for the Divinities of the Iliad and the Odyssey.* Hildesheim.

    (2002) *Epitheta rerum et locorum apud Homerum: A Repertory of Descriptive Expressions for Things and Places in the Iliad and the Odyssey. With an Extensive Supplement for the Epitheta Deorum and Epitheta Hominum.* Hildesheim.

de Jonge, C. (2008) *Between Grammar and Rhetoric: Dionysius of Halicarnassus on Language, Linguistics, and Literature.* Leiden and Boston.

de Romilly, J. (1975) *Magic and Rhetoric in Ancient Greece*. Cambridge.

(1985) *A Short History of Greek Literature*, trans. L. Doherty. Chicago and London.

Depew, M. (1993) "Mimetic hymn in Callimachus," in *Callimachus*, ed. M. A. Harder, R. F. Regtuit, and G. C. Wakker. Hellenistica Groningana I. Groningen, 57–77.

(2000) "Enacted and represented dedications: genre and Greek hymn," in Depew and Obbink (2000), 81–96.

Depew, M., and D. Obbink (eds.) (2000) *Matrices of Genres: Authors, Canon, Society*. Cambridge, MA.

Détienne, M., and J.-P. Vernant (1974) *Les Ruses de l'intelligence, la mètis des Grecs*. Paris.

(eds.) (1979) *La Cuisine du sacrifice en pays grec*. Paris.

Dignas, B. (2007) "A day in the life of a Greek sanctuary," in *A Companion to Greek Religion*, ed. D. Ogden. Malden, 163–77.

Dinse, H. L. M. (1856) *De Antigenida thebano musico*. Berlin.

Dobrov, G. W. (ed.) (1995) *Beyond Aristophanes: Transition and Diversity in Greek Comedy*. Atlanta.

(2002) "Μάγειρος ποιητής: language and character in Antiphanes," in *The Languages of Greek Comedy*, ed. A. Willi. Oxford, 169–90.

Dobrov, G. W., and E. Urios-Aparisi (1995) "The maculate music: gender, genre and the Chiron of Pherecrates," in Dobrov (1995), 139–74.

Dougherty, C., and L. Kurke (eds.) (2003) *The Cultures within Ancient Greek Culture: Contact, Conflict, Collaboration*. Cambridge and New York.

Dover, K. (1974) *Greek Popular Morality in the Age of Plato and Aristotle*. Oxford.

(1997) *Ancient Greek Literature*, 2nd edn. Oxford.

Duncan, A. (2012) "A Theseus outside Athens: Dionysus I of Syracuse and Tragic Self-Representation," in Bosher (2012), 137–55.

Düring, I. (1945) "Studies in musical terminology in 5th-century literature," *Eranos* 43: 176–97.

(1957) *Aristotle in the Ancient Biographical Tradition*. Göteborg.

Earp, F. R. (1944) *The Style of Sophocles*. Cambridge.

Easterling, P. (1993) "The end of an era? Tragedy in the early fourth century," in *Tragedy, Comedy and the Polis: Papers from the Greek Drama Conference. Nottingham, 18–20 July 1990*, ed. S. Halliwell, J. Henderson, A. Sommerstein, and B. Zimmermann. Bari, 559–69.

(1997) "From repertoire to canon," in *The Cambridge Companion to Greek Tragedy*, ed. P. Easterling. Cambridge, 211–27.

Easterling, P., and E. Hall (eds.) (2002) *Greek and Roman Actors: Aspects of an Ancient Profession*. Cambridge.

Ebeling, H. L. (1925) "The *Persians* of Timotheus," *AJP* 46: 317–31.

Edelstein, E., and L. Edelstein (1945) *Asclepius: A Collection and Interpretation of the Testimonies* (2 vols.). Baltimore.

Eder, W. (ed.) (1995a) *Die Athenische Demokratie im 4. Jahrhundert v. Chr.: Vollendung oder Verfall einer Verfassungsform? Akten eines Symposims 3.–7. August 1992.* Bellagio.

  (1995b) "Die Athenische Demokratie im 4. Jahrhundert v. Chr.: Krise oder Vollendung?," in Eder (1995a), 11–28.

Edmunds, L. (2008) "Deixis in ancient Greek and Latin literature: historical introduction and state of the question," *Philologia Antiqua* 1: 67–98.

Engelmann, H., and R. Merkelbach (eds.) (1972) *Die Inschriften von Erythrai und Klazomenai* (2 vols.). Bonn.

Ellingham, C. (1921) "Timotheus' *Persae*," in Powell and Barber (1921), 59–65.

Elsner, J. (2006) "Reflections on the 'Greek Revolution' in art: from changes in viewing to the transformation of subjectivity," in Goldhill and Osborne (2006), 68–95.

Elsner, J., and S. Bartsch (2007) "Introduction: eight ways of looking at an ekphrasis," in *Essays on Ekphrasis*, ed. S. Bartsch and J. Elsner. Special issue of *CP* 102: i–vi.

Ercoles, M. (2010) "Note a Tim. *PMG* 791, 221–228," *Eikasmos* 21: 111–32.

Fairbanks, A. (1900) *A Study of the Greek Paean.* Ithaca.

Fairweather, J. (1974) "Fiction in the biographies of ancient writers," *Ancient Society* 5: 231–75.

Fantuzzi, M. (1980) "La contaminazione dei generi letterari nella letteratura greca ellenistica: rifiuto del sistema o evoluzione di un sistema?," *Lingua e Stile* 15: 433–50.

  (2010) "Sung poetry: the case of inscribed paeans," in Clauss and Cuyspers (2010), 181–96.

Fantuzzi, M., and R. Hunter (2002) *Muse e modelli: la poesia ellenistica da Alessandro Magno ad Augusto.* Rome-Bari.

  (2004) *Tradition and Innovation in Hellenistic Poetry.* Cambridge and New York.

Fantuzzi, M., and T. D. Papanghelis (eds.) (2006) *Brill's Companion to Greek and Latin Pastoral.* Leiden and Boston.

Faraone, C. (2011) "An Athenian tradition of dactylic paeans to Apollo and Asclepius: choral degeneration or a flexible system of non-strophic dactyls?," *Mnemosyne* 64: 206–31.

Färber, H. (1936) *Die Lyrik in der Kunsttheorie der Antike.* Munich.

Farell, J. (2001) *Latin Language and Latin Culture: From Ancient to Modern Times.* Cambridge and New York.

Fauconnier, G., and M. Turner (2002) *The Way We Think: Conceptual Blending and the Mind's Hidden Complexities.* New York.

Fearn, D. (2007) *Bacchylides: Politics, Performance, Poetic Tradition.* Oxford and New York.

Feeney, D. (1993) "Towards an account of the ancient world's concepts of fictive belief," in *Lies and Fiction in the Ancient World*, ed. C. Gill and T. P. Wiseman. Austin and Exeter, 230–44.

(2007) *Caesar's Calendar: Ancient Time and the Beginnings of History*. Berkeley.

Fehr, B. (1990) "Entertainers at the symposion: the *Akletoi* in the archaic period," in Murray (1990), 185–95.

Ferrari, F. (1988) "P. Berol. inv. 13270: i canti di Elefantina," *SCO* 38: 181–227.

Finkelberg, M. (1998) *The Birth of Literary Fiction in Ancient Greece*. Oxford and New York.

Finley, M. (1954) *The World of Odysseus*. New York.

Firinu, E. (2009) "Il primo stasimo dell'*Ifigenia Taurica* euripidea e i *Persiani* di Timoteo di Mileto: un terminus post quem per il nomos?," *Eikasmos* 20: 109–31.

Fischer-Bossert, W. (2005) "Die Koronis im Berliner Timotheospapyrus," *Archiv für Papyrusforschung* 51: 191–5.

Fleming, T., and E. Kopff (1992) "Colometry of Greek lyric verses in tragic texts," in *Atti del convegno internazionale di Antichità Classica della F.I.E.C, Pisa 24–30 agosto 1989, SIFC* 3rd series, 10: 758–70.

Folch, M. (forthcoming) *The Polis and the Stage: Citizenship, Genre, and the Politics of Performance in Plato's Laws*.

Fongoni, A. (2005) "Antifane e Filosseno," *QUCC* 81: 91–8.

(2011) "Alternanza delle armonie nei *Misi* di Filosseno (Ps. Plut. *De mus.* 33, 1142ef)," *QUCC* 99: 153–64.

Ford, A. (1999) "Reading Homer from the rostrum: poems and laws in Aeschines' *Against Timarchus*," in Goldhill and Osborne (1999), 231–56.

(2002) *The Origins of Criticism: Literary Culture and Poetic Theory in Classical Greece*. Princeton.

(2003) "From letters to literature: reading the 'song culture' of classical Greece," in H. Yunis (2003), 15–37.

(2006) "The genre of genres: paeans and paian in early Greek poetry," *Poetica* 38: 277–96.

(2011a) *Aristotle as Poet*. Oxford.

(2011b) "Dionysus' many names in Aristophanes' *Frogs*," in *A Different God? Dionysos and Ancient Polytheism*, ed. R. Schlesier. Berlin and Boston, 343–55.

(forthcoming) "Language of dithyramb," in Wilson and Kowalzig (forthcoming).

Foucault, M. (1969) "Qu'est-ce qu'un auteur?," in *Dits et Écrits*. Paris, 789–821.

(1985) *The History of Sexuality*, vol. ii. *The Use of Pleasure*, trans. R. Hurley. New York.

Fowler, B. H. (1967) "Aeschylus' imagery," *C&M* 28: 1–74.

(1989) *The Hellenistic Aesthetic*. Madison.

Fowler, D. (1991) "Narrate and describe: the problem of ekphrasis," *JRS* 81: 25–35.

Franklin, J. C. (2012) "The Lesbian singers: towards a reconstruction of Hellanicus' *Karneian Victors*," in *Poesia, musica e agoni nella Grecia antica*, ed. D. Castaldo and A. Manieri. Proceedings of the 2010 MOISA conference. Galatina, 719–64.

(forthcoming) "'Song-benders of circular choruses': dithyramb and the 'demise of music,'" in Wilson and Kowalzig (forthcoming).

Froning, H. (1971) *Dithyrambos und Vasenmalerei in Athen*. Würzburg.

Frontisi-Ducroux, F. (1994) "Athéna et l'invention de la flûte," *Musica e Storia* 2: 239–67.

Gargiulo, T. (1996) "Mare e vino nei *Persiani*: una congettura a Timoteo, fr. 791, 61–62 Page," *QUCC* 54: 73–81.

Garland, R. (1992) *Introducing New Gods: The Politics of Athenian Religion*. London.

Garrod, H. W. (1920) "The Hyporcheme of Pratinas," *CR* 34: 129–36.

Gemoll, W. (1924) *Das Apophthegma*. Vienna.

Gentili, B. (1988) *Poetry and its Public in Ancient Greece: From Homer to the Fifth Century*, trans. A. Cole. Baltimore and London.

Gentili, B., and F. Luisi (1995) "La Pitica 12 di Pindaro e l'aulo di Mida," *QUCC* 49: 7–31.

Gentili, B., and F. Perusino (eds.) (1995) *Mousike: metrica ritmica e musica greca. In memoria di Giovanni Comotti*. Pisa and Rome.

Gentili, B., and R. Pretagostini (eds.) (1988) *La musica in Grecia*. Bari.

Gerber, D. (1986) "The Gorgon's lament in Pindar's Pythian 12," *Museum Helveticum* 43: 247–9.

Gerhard, G. A. (1938) *Griechische Papyri: Urkunden und literarische Texte aus der Papyrussammlung der Universitätsbibliothek Heidelberg*. Heidelberg.

Giangrande, G. (1973) "On the stylistic employment of compound epithets in late Greek epic poetry," *Philologus* 117: 109–12.

Giannisi, P. (1997) "Chant et cheminement en Grèce archaïque," *QS* 23.46: 133–41.

(2006) *Récits des voies: chant et cheminement en Grèce archaïque. Préf. de Jesper Svenbro*. Grenoble.

Gildersleeve, B. (1903) "Brief mention," *AJP* 24.2: 222–38.

Gilula, D. (2000) "Stratonicus, the witty harpist," in Braund and Wilkins (2000), 423–33.

Girone, M. (1998) *Iamata: guarigioni miracolose di Asclepio in testi epigrafici*. Bari.

Goldhill, S. (2002) *The Invention of Prose*. Oxford and New York.

Goldhill, S., and R. Osborne (eds.) (1999) *Performance Culture and Athenian Democracy*. Cambridge and New York.

(eds.) (2006) *Rethinking Revolutions through Ancient Greece*. Cambridge and New York.

Goodwin, W. (1889) *Syntax of the Moods and Tenses of the Greek Verb*. New York.

Gowers, E. (1993) *The Loaded Table: Representations of Food in Roman Literature*. Oxford.

Gray, D. (1947) "Homeric epithets for things," *CQ* 41: 109–21.

Gray, V. (1986) "Xenophon's *Hiero* and the meeting of the wise man and tyrant in Greek literature," *CQ* 36: 115–23.

Graziosi, B. (2002) *Inventing Homer: The Early Reception of the Epic*. Cambridge and New York.

Griffith, M. (1977) *The Authenticity of Prometheus Bound*. Cambridge and New York.

(2005) "Sophocles' satyr-plays and the language of romance," in *Sophocles and the Greek Language*, ed. I. de Jong and A. Rijksbaron. Leiden, 51–72.

(2008) "Greek middlebrow drama (something to do with Aphrodite?)," in Revermann and Wilson (2008), 59–87.

Guilleux, N. (2009) "La Fabrique des hapax et des proton legomena dans l'*Alexandra*," in *Lycophron: éclats d'obscurité. Actes du colloque international de Lyon et Saint-Etienne, 18–20 janvier 2007*, ed. C. Cusset and E. Prioux. Saint-Etienne, 221–36.

Guthrie, W. K. C. (1930) "Epithets in the Orphic Hymns," *CR* 1930: 216–21.

Gützwiller, K. (1998) *Poetic Garlands: Hellenistic Epigrams in Context*. Berkeley.

(2006) "The herdsman in Greek thought," in Fantuzzi and Papanghelis (2006), 1–23.

Hadas, M. (1950) *History of Greek Literature*. New York.

Hadjimichael, Th. (2010) "Bacchylides and the emergence of the lyric canon," thesis, University College London.

Hagel, S. (2000) *Modulation in altgriechischer Musik*. Frankfurt am Main.

(2010) *Ancient Greek Music: A New Technical History*. Cambridge.

Hall, E. (1989) *Inventing the Barbarian: Greek Self-Definition through Tragedy*. Oxford.

(1994) "Drowning by nomes: the Greeks, swimming, and Timotheus' Persians," in *The Birth of the European Identity: The Europe–Asia Contrast in Greek Thought, 490–322 BC*, ed. H. Akbar Khan. Nottingham, 44–89.

(2000) "Female figures and metapoetry in Old Comedy," in Harvey and Wilkins (2000), 407–18.

(2006) *The Theatrical Cast of Athens: Interactions between Ancient Greek Drama and Society*. Oxford.

(2007) "Greek Tragedy 430–280 BC," in Osborne (2007), 264–87.

Halliwell, S. (1990) "The sound of the voice in old comedy," in *Owls to Athens: Essays on Classical Subjects for Sir Kenneth Dover*, ed. E. Craik. Oxford, 69–79.

(2002) *The Aesthetics of Mimesis: Ancient Texts and Modern Problems*. Princeton.

Hamilton, R. (1990) "The Pindaric Dithyramb," *HSCP* 93: 211–22.

Hansen, O. (1984) "On the date and place of the first performance of Timotheus' *Persae*," *Philologus* 128: 135–8.

Harris, W. (1989) *Ancient Literacy*. Cambridge, MA.

Hartwig, A. (2009) "A reconsideration of the musician Chaeris," *CQ* 59: 383–97.

Harvey, A. E. (1955) "The classification of Greek lyric poetry," *CQ* N.S. 5: 157–75.

(1957) "Homeric epithets in Greek lyric poetry," *CQ* N.S. 7: 206–22.

Harvey, D., and J. Wilkins (eds.) (2000) *The Rivals of Aristophanes: Studies in Athenian Old Comedy*. Swansea.

Havelock, E. (1982) *The Literate Revolution in Greece and its Cultural Consequences*. Princeton.

(1986) *The Muse Learns to Write: Reflections on Orality and Literacy from Antiquity to the Present*. New Haven and London.

Henderson, J. (1991) *The Maculate Muse: Obscene Language in Attic Comedy*, 2nd edn. New York.

  (2000) "Pherekrates and the women of Old Comedy," in Harvey and Wilkins (2000), 135–50.

Henrichs, A. (1984) "Ein neues Likymniosfragment bei Philodem," *ZPE* 57: 53–7.

  (1996) "Dancing in Athens, dancing on Delos: some patterns of choral projection in Euripides," *Philologus* 140: 48–62.

Herington, J. (1985) *Poetry into Drama: Early Tragedy and the Greek Poetic Tradition*. Berkeley, Los Angeles, and London.

Hobden, F. (2013) *The Symposion in Ancient Greek Society and Thought*. Cambridge.

Holland, G. R. (1884) "De Poliphemo et Galatea," *Leipziger Studien* 7: 139–312.

Hopman, M. (2009) "Layered stories in Aeschylus' *Persians*," in *Narratology and Interpretation: The Content of Narrative Form in Ancient Literature*, ed. J. Grethlein and A. Rengakos. Berlin, 357–76.

Hordern, J. (1998) "Two notes on Greek dithyrambic poetry," *CQ* 48: 289–91.

  (1999) "The Cyclops of Philoxenus," *CQ* 49: 445–55.

  (2000) "Telestes, *PMG* 808," *CQ* 50: 298–300.

  (2003) "Gnesippus and the rivals of Aristophanes," *CQ* 53: 608–13.

  (2004) "Cyclopea: Philoxenus, Theocritus, Callimachus, Bion," *CQ* 54: 285–92.

Hornblower, S. (1983) *The Greek World 479–323 BC*. London.

  (2012) "What happened later to the families of Pindar patrons – and to epinician poetry," in Agócs, Carey, and Rawles (2012), 93–107.

Hubbard, T. (2004) "The dissemination of Epinician lyric: pan-Hellenism, re-performance, written texts," in Mackie (2004), 71–93.

Hunter, R. (2001) "The poet unleaved: Simonides and Callimachus," in Boedeker and Sider (2001), 242–54.

  (2008) *On Coming After: Studies in Post-Classical Greek Literature and its Reception*. Berlin.

  (2009) *Critical Moments in Classical Literature: Studies in the Ancient View of Literature and its Uses*. Cambridge and New York.

Hunter, R., and I. Rutherford (eds.) (2009) *Wandering Poets: Travel, Locality and Pan-Hellenism*. Cambridge.

Irigoin, J. (2006) "Euripide poète et musicien selon Denys d'Halicarnasse," *Pallas* 72: 219–27.

Irwin, E. (2005) *Solon and Early Greek Poetry: The Politics of Exhortation*. Cambridge and New York.

  (2006) "The biographies of poets: the case of Solon," in *The Limits of Ancient Biography*, ed. M. McGing and J. Mosmann. Swansea, 13–30.

Jacob, C. (2000) "Athenaeus the Librarian," in Braund and Wilkins (2000), 85–110.

  (2001) "Ateneo, o il Dedalo delle parole," in *I deipnosofisti: i dotti a banchetto, Ateneo; prima traduzione italiana commentata, introduzione di Christian Jacob*, ed. L. Canfora. Rome and Salerno.

(2004) "La citation comme performance dans les Deipnosophistes d'Athénée," in *La Citation dans l'Antiquité: actes du colloque du PARSA Lyon, ENS LSH, 6-8 novembre 2002*, ed. C. Darbo-Peschanski. Grenoble, 147–74.

Jaeger, W. (1948) *Aristotle: Fundamentals of the History of his Development*, 2nd edn., trans., with the author's corrections and additions, by R. Robinson. Oxford.

Janko, R. (1981) "The structure of the Homeric Hymns: a study in genre," *Hermes* 109: 9–24.

Jennings, V. (2007) "Ion's Hymn to Kairos," in Jennings and Katsaros (2007), 331–46.

Jennings, V., and A. Katsaros (eds.) (2007) *The World of Ion of Chios*. Leiden and Boston.

Junker, K. (2010) "The transformation of Athenian theatre culture around 400 BC," in Taplin and Wyles (2010), 131–48.

Käppel, L. (1992) *Paian: Studien zur Geschichte Einer Gattung*. Berlin and New York.

Kenyon, F. (1903) Review of *Timotheos, Die Perser* by Ulrich von Wilamowitz-Moellendorff, in *The English Historical Review* 18.72: 762–4.

(1919) "Greek papyri and their contribution to classical literature," *JHS* 39: 1–13.

(1951) *Books and Readers in Ancient Greece and Rome*. Oxford.

Keyssner, K. (1933) "Die Hygieiahymnen des Ariphron und des Likymnius," *Philosophische Wochenschrift* 53: 1289–96.

Kirby, M. (1972) "On acting and not-acting," *The Drama Review* 16.1: 3–15.

Kolde, A. (2003) *Politique et religion chez Isyllos d'Epidaure*. Basel.

König, J. (2009) *Greek Literature in the Roman Empire*. London.

König, J., and T. Whitmarsh (eds.) (2007) *Ordering Knowledge in the Roman Empire*. Oxford.

Kowalzig, B. (2007) *Singing for the Gods: Performances of Myth and Ritual in Archaic and Classical Greece*. Oxford and New York.

Kowerski, L. (2005) *Simonides on the Persian Wars: A Study of the Elegiac Verses of the "New Simonides."* New York.

Kranz, W. (1933) *Stasimon: Untersuchungen zu Form und Gehalt der griechischen Tragödie*. Berlin.

(1962) "Sphragis: Ichform und Name-siegel als Eingangs- und Schlussmotiv antiker Dichtung," *RhMus.* 104: 3–46 and 97–124.

Kris, E., and O. Kurz (1979) *Legend, Myth, and Magic in the Image of the Artist: A Historical Experiment*, with a preface by E. H. Gombrich. New Haven.

Kroll, W. (1924) *Studien zum Verständnis der römischen Literatur*. Stuttgart.

Kurke, L. (1990) "Pindar's Sixth Pythian and the tradition of advice poetry," *TAPA* 120: 85–107.

(1991) *The Traffic in Praise: Pindar and the Poetics of Social Economy*. Ithaca.

(1999) *Coins, Bodies, Games, and Gold: The Politics of Meaning in Archaic Greece*. Princeton.

(2002) "Gender, politics, and subversion in the *Chreiai* of Machon," *PCPS* 40: 20–65.

Laird, A. (1993) "Fiction, bewitchment and story worlds: the implications of claims to truth in Apuleius," in *Lies and Fiction in the Ancient World*, ed. C. Gill and T. P. Wiseman. Austin and Exeter, 147–74.

Lakoff, G., and M. Johnson (1980) *Metaphors We Live By*. Chicago and London.

Lambin, G. (1982) "Le Surnom Βάταλος et les mots de cette famille," *RPh* 56: 249–63.

Leclercq-Neveu, B. (1989) "Marsyas, le martyr de l'aulos," *Mètis* 4: 251–68.

Lefkowitz, M. R. (1981) *The Lives of the Greek Poets*. London.

Lehnus, L. (1975) "Note stesicoree: i poemetti minori (fr. 277–9 *PMG*)", *SCO* 24: 191–6.

Lenfant, D. (ed.) (2007) *Athénée et les fragments d'historiens: actes du colloque de Strasbourg (16–18 juin 2005)*. Paris.

Lesky, A. (1947) *Thalatta: Der Weg der Griechen zum Meer*. Vienna.

(1966) *A History of Greek Literature*, trans. J. Willis and C. de Heer. New York.

LeVen, P. (2010) "New Music and its myths: Athenaeus' reading of the *aulos* revolution," *JHS* 140: 35–47.

(2011) "Timotheus' eleven strings: a new approach (*PMG* 791, 229–236)," *CP* 106, 245–54.

(2012) "'You make less sense than a (new) dithyramb': sociology of a riddling style," in *The Muse at Play: Riddles and Wordplay in Greek and Latin Poetry*, ed. J. Kwapisz, D. Petrain, and M. Szymanski. Berlin, 44–64.

(2013a) "Reading the octopus: authorship, intertexts and a Hellenistic anecdote (Machon, fr. 9 Gow)," in *Intertextuality and its Discontents*, ed. Y. Baraz and C. van den Berg, special issue of *AJP* 126.1: 23–35.

(2013b) "The colors of sound: Poikilia and its aesthetic contexts," *Greek and Roman Music Studies* 1: 229–42.

(2013c) "Aristotle's Hymn to Virtue and funerary epigraphy," in Low and Liddell (2013), 271–87.

Lévêque, P. (1955) *Agathon*. Paris.

Levi, P. (1985) *History of Greek Literature*. Harmondsworth.

Levin, F. R. (1961) "The hendecachord of Ion of Chios," *TAPA* 92: 295–307.

Lissarague, F. (1990) "Why satyrs are good to represent," in *Nothing to Do with Dionysos*, ed. J. Winkler and F. Zeitlin. Princeton, 228–36.

Livingstone, N., and G. Nisbet (2010) *Epigram*. Cambridge.

Livrea, E. (1975) "Telestes fr. 805 (= 1). C. 2 Page," *RhM* 117: 189–90.

Lloyd, G. E. R. (1987) *The Revolutions of Wisdom: Studies in the Claims and Practice of Ancient Greek Science*. Berkeley.

Lloyd-Jones, H. (1966) "Problems of early Greek tragedy," *Cuadernos de la Fundación Pastor* 13: 11–33, reprinted in H. Lloyd-Jones (1990), *Greek Epic, Lyric, and Tragedy: The Academic Papers of Sir Hugh Lloyd-Jones*. Oxford, 225–37.

(1968) "Melanippides Fr. 1, 1–2 (Page *PMG* 757)," *Philologus* 112: 119.

Loicq-Berger, M.-P. (1966) "Le 'Bruxellensis' 11282 et l'activité littéraire de Denys l'Ancien," *Revue Belge de Philologie et d'Histoire: Belgisch tijdschrift voor Philologie en Geschiedenis* 44: 12–20.

Long, T. (1984) *Barbarians in Greek Comedy.* Carbondale and Edwardsville, IL.

Loraux, N. (1993) *L'Invention d'Athènes: histoire de l'oraison funèbre dans la cité classique,* 2nd edn. Paris.

Lorenz, K. (2007) "The anatomy of metalepsis: visuality turns around on late fifth-century pots," in Osborne (2007), 116–43.

Louyest, B. (2009) *Mots de poissons: le banquet des sophistes, livres 6 et 7 d'Athénée de Naucratis.* Villeneuve-d'Ascq.

Low, P., and P. Liddell (eds.) (2013) *Inscriptions and their Uses in Greek and Latin Literature.* Oxford.

Lulli, L. (2011) *Narrare in distici: l'elegia greca arcaica e classica di argomento storico-mitico.* Rome.

Ma, J. (2007) "A Horse from Teos: epigraphical notes on the Ionian-Hellespontine association of Dionysiac artists," in Wilson (2007a), 215–45.

Maas, M. (1992) "Polychordia and the fourth-century Greek lyre," *Journal of Musicology* 10: 74–88.

Maas, M., and M. Snyder (eds.) (1989) *Stringed Instruments of Ancient Greece.* New Haven.

Mackie, C. J. (ed.) (2004) *Oral Performance and its Context.* Leiden and Boston.

Mahaffy, J. (1891) *A History of Classical Greek Literature* (2 vols.). London and New York.

Mantziou, M. (1989) "A Hymn to the Dolphins: fr. adesp. 939 PMG," *Hellenica* 40: 229–37.

Martin, R. (2003) "The pipes are brawling: conceptualizing musical performance in Athens," in Dougherty and Kurke (2003), 153–80.

  (2006) "Outer limits, choral space," in *Visualizing the Tragic: Drama, Myth, and Ritual in Greek Art and Literature. Essays in Honour of Froma Zeitlin,* ed. C. Kraus, S. Goldhill, H. P. Foley, and J. Elsner. Oxford and New York, 35–62.

Martinelli, M. C. (ed.) (2009) *La musa dimenticata: aspetti dell'esperienza musicale greca in età ellenistica.* Pisa.

Mazon, P. (1903) "Timothée de Milet, *Les Perses*: traduction," *Revue de Philologie* 27: 209–14.

McFarlane, K. (2002) "'To lay the shining foundation': the theme of the Persian Wars in classical Greek poetry," PhD dissertation, University of Alberta.

  (2009) "Choerilus of Samos' Lament (*SH* 317) and the revitalization of epic," *AJP* 130.2: 219–34.

McKinnon, J. (1984) "The rejection of the aulos," in *Music and Civilization: Essays in Honor of Paul Henry Lang,* ed. E. Strainchamps. New York, 203–14.

Meyer, G. (1923) *Die stilistische Verwendung der Nominalkomposition im Griechischen: Ein Beitrag zur Geschichte der DIPLA ONOMATA.* Leipzig.

Mikalson, J. (2005) *Ancient Greek Religion.* Chichester and Malden.

Momigliano, A. (1993) *The Development of Greek Biography*, expanded edn. Cambridge, MA and London.

Moreaux, A. (1994–5) "Les Danaïdes de Mélanippidès: la femme virile," *CGITA* 8: 119–51.

Morgan, K. (2012) "Prolegomena to performance in the West," in Bosher (2012), 35–55.

Morris, I. (1986) "Gift and commodity in archaic Greece," *Man* 21: 1–17.

Morrison, A. (2007a) *The Narrator in Archaic Greek and Hellenistic Poetry.* Cambridge.

(2007b) *Performances and Audiences in Pindar's Sicilian Victory Odes.* London.

Most, G. W. (1995) "Reflecting Sappho," *BICS* 40: 15–38.

Muecke, F. (1982) "A portrait of the artist as a young woman," *CQ* 32: 41–55.

Murray, G. (1935) *A History of Ancient Greek Literature.* New York and London.

Murray, O. (ed.) (1990) *Sympotica: A Symposium on the Symposium.* Oxford and New York.

Murray, P., and P. Wilson (eds.) (2004) *Music and the Muses: The Culture of "mousike" in the Classical Athenian City.* Oxford and New York.

Musti, D. (2000) "Musica greca tra aristocrazia e democrazia," in Cassio, Musti, and Rossi (2000), 7–55.

Nagy, G. (1979) *Best of the Achaeans: Concepts of the Hero in Archaic Greek Poetry.* Baltimore.

(1989) "The 'professional muse' and models of prestige in ancient Greece," *Cultural Critique* 12: 133–43.

(1990) *Pindar's Homer: The Lyric Possession of an Epic Past.* Baltimore.

Napolitano, M. (2000) "Note all'iporchema di Pratina: (*PMG* 708 = *TrGF* i 4 F 3)," in Cassio, Musti, and Rossi (2000), 111–55.

Neer, R. (2012) *Greek Art and Archaeology: A New History, c. 2500–c. 150 BCE.* New York.

Nesselrath, H.-G. (1990) *Attische mittlere Komödie: Ihre Stellung in der antiken Literaturkritik und Literaturgeschichte.* Berlin and New York.

Nieddù, G. (1993) "Parole e metro nella sphragis dei Persiani di Timoteo (*PMG* fr.7 91.202–236)," in Pretagostini (1993), 521–9.

Nobili, C. (2011) "Threnodic elegy in Sparta," *GRBS* 51: 26–48.

North, H. (1952) "The use of poetry in the training of the ancient orator," *Traditio* 8: 1–33.

Norwood, G. (1925) *The Writers of Greece.* London.

Nowottny, W. (1962) *The Language Poets Use.* Oxford and New York.

Ober, J. (1989) *Mass and Elite in Democratic Athens: Rhetoric, Ideology, and the Power of the People.* Princeton.

Ober, J., and B. Strauss (1989) "Drama, political rhetoric and the discourse of Athenian democracy," in *Nothing to Do with Dionysus: Athenian Drama in its Social Context*, ed. J. Winkler and F. Zeitlin. Princeton, 237–70.

Oellacher, H. (1932) "Eine exegetische Schrift zum späteren Dithyrambos," in *Mitteilungen aus der Papyrussammlung der Nationalbibliothek in Wien (1)*. Vienna, 136–42.

Olson, S. D., and A. Sens (1999) *Matro of Pitane and the Tradition of Epic Parody in the Fourth Century BCE*. Atlanta.

(2000) *Archestratos of Gela: Greek Culture and Cuisine in the Fourth Century BCE: Text, Translation, and Commentary*. Oxford.

Osborne, R. (ed.) (2007) *Debating the Athenian Cultural Revolution: Art, Literature, Philosophy, and Politics 430–380 BC*. Cambridge.

Osborne, R., and P. J. Rhodes (eds.) (2003) *Greek Historical Inscriptions: 404–323 BC*, edited with introduction, translations, and commentaries. Oxford and New York.

O'Sullivan, N. (1992) *Alcidamas, Aristophanes and the Beginnings of Greek Stylistic Theory*. Stuttgart.

Panagl, O. (1969) "Stationen hellenischer Religiosität am Beispiel des delphischen Sukzessionsmythos," *Kairos* 11: 161–71.

(1971) *Die "dithyrambischen Stasima" des Euripides: Untersuchungen zur Komposition und Erzähltechnik*. Vienna.

Papadopoulou, Z., and V. Pirenne Delforge (2001) "Inventer et réinventer l'aulos: autour de la xiie Pythique de Pindare," in *Chanter les dieux: musique et religion dans l'antiquité grecque et romaine*, ed. P. Brulé and C. Vendries. Rennes, 37–58.

Parker, R. (1996) *Athenian Religion: A History*. Oxford and New York.

Patterson, L. (2010) *Kinship Myth in Ancient Greece*. Austin.

Payne, M. (2007) *Theocritus and the Invention of Fiction*. Cambridge.

Peponi, N. (ed.) (2013) *Performance and Culture in Plato's Laws*. Cambridge.

Peradotto, J. (1990) *Man in the Middle Voice: Name and Narration in the Odyssey*. Princeton.

Perlman, S. (1964) "Quotations from poetry in attic orators," *AJP* 85: 155–72.

Petrovic, A. (2009) "Epigrammatic contests, Poeti Vaganti, and local history," in Hunter and Rutherford (2009), 195–218.

(2013) "Inscribed epigrams in orators, epigrammatic schools, epigrammatic collections," in Low and Liddell (eds.), 197–213.

Petrovic, A., and I. Petrovic (2006) "'Look who is talking now!' Speaker and communication in Greek metrical sacred regulations," *Kernos* suppl. 16: 151–79.

Petrovic, I. (2011) "Callimachus and contemporary religion: the Hymn to Apollo," in *Brill's Companion to Callimachus*, ed. B. Acosta-Hughes, L. Lehnus, and S. Stephens. Leiden and Boston, 264–85.

Pfeiffer, R. (1968) *History of Classical Scholarship from the Beginnings to the End of the Hellenistic Age*. Oxford.

Phillips, D. (2003) "Athenian political history: a Panathenaic perspective," in *Sport and Festival in the Ancient Greek World*, ed. D. Phillips and D. Pritchard. Swansea, 197–232.

Pickard-Cambridge, A. W. (1927) *Dithyramb, Tragedy and Comedy*. Oxford.
   (1962) *Dithyramb, Tragedy and Comedy*, 2nd edn., revised by T. B. L. Webster. Oxford.
Pintacuda, M. (1978) *La musica nella tragedia greca*. Cefalù.
Podlecki, A. (1968) "Simonides, 480 BC," *Historia* 17: 257–75.
   (1969) "The Peripatetics as literary critics," *Phoenix* 23: 114–37.
   (1984) *The Early Greek Poets and their Times*. Vancouver.
Pöhlmann, E. (1960) *Griechische Musikfragmente: Ein Weg zur altgriechischen Musik*. Nuremberg.
   (2011a) "Aristophanes and the 'New Music' (*Acharnians, Knights, Clouds, Birds, Thesmophoriazousai, Frogs*)," in Yatromanolakis (2011), 29–64.
   (2011b) "Twelve chordai and the strobilos of Phrynis in the Chiron of Pherecrates (*PCG* fr. 155)," *QUCC* 99: 117–33.
Pöhlmann, E., and M. L. West (2001) *Documents of Ancient Greek Music: The Extant Melodies and Fragments*. Oxford and New York.
Porter, J. I. (2006) *Classical Pasts: The Classical Traditions of Greece and Rome*. Princeton.
   (2010) *Origins of Aesthetic Thought in Ancient Greece: Matter, Sensation, and Experience*. Cambridge.
Porter, J. R. (1994) *Studies in Euripides' Orestes*. Leiden and New York.
Powell, J. U. (ed.) (1933) *New Chapters in the History of Greek Literature, Third Series: Some Recent Discoveries in Greek Poetry and Prose of the Classical and Later Periods*. Oxford.
Powell, J. U., and E. A. Barber (eds.) (1921) *New Chapters in the History of Greek Literature: Recent Discoveries in Greek Poetry and Prose of the Fourth and Following Centuries BC*. Oxford.
Power, T. C. (2001) "Legitimating the Nomos: Timotheus' *Persae* in Athens," PhD dissertation, Harvard University.
   (2007) "Ion of Chios and the politics of polychordia," in Jennings and Katsaros (2007), 179–205.
   (2010) *The Culture of Kitharoidia*. Washington, DC.
   (forthcoming) "Kyklops kitharoidos: dithyramb and nomos in play," in Wilson and Kowalzig (forthcoming). Oxford.
Prauscello, L. (2006a) "Looking for the 'other' Gnesippus: some notes on Eupolis Fragment 148 K–A," *CP* 101: 52–66.
   (2006b) *Singing Alexandria: Music between Practice and Textual Transmission*. Leiden and Boston.
   (2009) "Wandering poetry, 'travelling' music: Timotheus' muse and some case-studies of shifting cultural identities," in Hunter and Rutherford (2009), 168–94.
   (2011a) "Patterns of chorality in Plato's *Laws*," in Yatromanolakis (2011), 133–58.
   (2011b) "Callimachus and the New Music," in *The Brill Companion to Callimachus*, ed. S. A. Stephens, B. Acosta-Hughes, and L. Lehnus. Leiden and Boston, 289–308.

(2012) "Epinician sounds: Pindar and musical innovation," in Agócs, Carey, and Rawles (2012), 58–82.

Pretagostini, R. (ed.) (1988) "Parola, metro e musica nella monodia dell'Upupa (Aristofane, Uccelli 227–262)," in Gentili and Pretagostini (1988), 189–98.

(ed.) (1993) *Tradizione e innovazione nella cultura greca da Omero all'età ellenistica: scritti in onore di Bruno Gentili.* Rome.

Prioux, E. (2007) *Regards alexandrins: histoire et théorie des arts dans l'épigramme Hellénistique.* Leuven.

(2009) "Machon et Sotadès, figures de l'irrévérrence alexandrine," in *Le Poète irrévérencieux: modèles hellénistiques et réalités romaines. Actes de la table ronde et du colloque organisés les 17 octobre 2006 et 19 et 20 octobre 2007 par l'ENS LSH, l'Université Lyon 2 et l' Université Lyon 3,* ed. B. Delignon, Y. Roman, and S. Laborie. Paris, 115–32.

Pucci, P. (1987) *Odysseus Polutropos: Intertextual Readings in the Odyssey and the Iliad.* Ithaca.

Race, W. (1982) "Aspects of rhetoric and form in Greek hymns," *GRBS* 23: 5–14.

Rainer, B. L. (1975) "Philodamus' Paean to Dionysus: a literary expression of Delphic propaganda," PhD dissertation, University of Illinois at Urbana-Champaign.

Reinach, T. (1903) "Les *Perses* de Timothée," *REG* 16, 62–83.

Renehan, R. (1982) "Aristotle as lyric poet: the Hermias poem," *GRBS* 23: 251–74.

Restani, D. (1983) "Il *Chirone* di Ferecrate e la 'nuova' musica greca," *Rivista Italiana di Musicologia* 18: 139–92.

(1988) "Problemi musicali nel xiv libro dei Deipnosophistai di Ateneo: una proposta di lettura," in Gentili and Pretagostini (1988), 26–31.

Revermann, M. (2006) "The competence of theatre audiences in fifth- and fourth-century Athens," *JHS* 126: 99–124.

Revermann, M., and P. Wilson (eds.) (2008) *Performance, Reception, Iconography.* Oxford.

Rijksbaron, A. (1988) "The discourse function of the imperfect," in *In the Footsteps of Raphael Kühner: Proceedings of the International Colloquium in Commemoration of the 150th Anniversary of the Publication of Raphael Kühner's Ausführliche Grammatik der griechischen Sprache, ii. Theil: Syntaxe, Amsterdam 1986,* ed. A. Rijksbaron. Amsterdam, 237–54.

Robb, K. (1994) *Literacy and Paideia in Classical Greece.* Oxford and New York.

Rocconi, E. (2003) *Le parole delle muse: la formazione del lessico tecnico musicale nella Grecia antica.* Rome.

Romeri, L. (1997) "La Parole est servie," *REA* 15.1: 65–93.

Rose, H. J. (1932) "The Rhadine Fragment," *CQ* 26: 89–92.

Rosenbloom, D. (2006) *Aeschylus: Persians.* London.

Rosenmeyer, T. (1982) *The Art of Aeschylus.* Berkeley.

Roskam, G. (2006) "Philoxenus once again," *CQ* 56: 652–6.

Rösler, W. (1983) "Die Entdeckung der Fictionalität in der Antike," *Poetica* 12: 283–319.

Rossi, L. E. (1971) "I generi letterari e le lora leggi scritte e non scritte nelle letterature classiche," *BICS* 18: 69–94.

Rothwell, J. K. S. (1992) "Identity of the fourth-century chorus," *GRBS* 33: 209–25.

Runia, D. T. (1986) "Theocritus of Chios' epigram against Aristotle," *CQ* 36: 531–4.

Rutherford, I. (1995) "Apollo's other genre: Proclus on nomos and his source," *CP* 90: 354–61.

(2001a) *Pindar's Paeans: A Reading of the Fragments with a Survey of the Genre.* Oxford and New York.

(2001b) "The new Simonides: towards a commentary," in Boedeker and Sider (2001), 33–54.

(2004) "Χορὸς εἷς ἐκ τῆσδε τῆς πόλεως... (Xen. *Mem.* 3.3.12): song-dance and state-pilgrimage at Athens," in Murray and Wilson (2004), 67–90.

(2007) "*Theoria* and theatre at Samothrace: the *Dardanos* by Dymas of Iasos," in Wilson (2007a), 279–93.

Saïd, S. (1984) "Grecs et barbares dans les tragédies d'Euripide: la fin des différences," *Ktêma* 9: 27–53.

Sansone, D. (2009) "Euripides' new song: the first stasimon of *Trojan Women*," in Cousland and Hume (2009), 193–204.

Santoni, A. (1993) "L'inno di Aristotele per Ermia di Atarneo," in *La Componente autobiografica nella poesia greca e latina fra realità e artificio letterario: atti del convegno, Pisa, 16–17 maggio 1991*, ed. G. Arrighetti and F. Montanari. Pisa, 179–95.

Saxonhouse, A. W. (2006) *Free Speech and Democracy in Ancient Athens.* Cambridge.

Schacter, A. (1998) "Simonides' elegy on Plataia: the occasion of its performance," *ZPE* 129: 1–11.

Schmitt-Pantel, P. (1992) *Cité au banquet: histoire des repas publics dans les cités grecques.* Rome and Paris.

Schönewolf, H. (1938) *Der jungattische Dithyrambos, Wesen, Wirkung und Gegenwirkung.* Giessen.

Schröder, S. (1999) *Geschichte und Theorie der Gattung Paian: Eine kritische Untersuchung mit einem Ausblick auf Behandlung und Auffassung der lyrischen Gattungen bei den alexandrinischen Philologen.* Stuttgart.

Schubart, W. B. (ed.) (1911) *Papyri Graecae Berolinenses.* Bonn.

Schultz, P. (2007) "Style and agency in an age of transition," in Osborne (2007), 144–87.

Scodel, R. (1999) *Credible Impossibilities: Conventions and Strategies of Verisimilitude in Homer and Greek Tragedy.* Stuttgart.

Scullion, J. S. (2002) "'Nothing to do with Dionysus': tragedy misconceived as ritual," *CQ* 52: 102–37.

Seaford, R. (1977–8) "The 'Hyporchema' of Pratinas," *Maia* 29–30: 81–99.

Segal, C. (1985) "Choral lyric in the fifth century," in *The Cambridge History of Classical Literature*, ed. P. Easterling and B. Knox. Cambridge, 222–44.

(1994) "The gorgon and the nightingale: the voice of female lament and Pindar's twelfth Pythian ode," in *Embodied Voices: Representing Female Vocality in Western Culture*, ed. L. Dunn and N. Jones. Cambridge and New York, 17–34.

Seidensticker, B. (1995) "Dichtung und Gesellschaft im 4. Jahrhundert: Versuch eines Überblicks," in Eder (1995a), 175–98.

Sens, A. (2006) "Epigrams at the margin of pastoral," in Fantuzzi and Papanghelis (2006), 147–65.

Sickinger, J. P. (1999) *Public Records and Archives in Classical Athens*. Chapel Hill.

Silk, M. (1980) "Aristophanes as a lyric poet," *YCIS* 26: 99–151.

(2000) *Aristophanes and the Definition of Comedy*. New York.

(2010) "The language of Greek lyric poetry," in *A Companion to the Ancient Greek Language*, ed. E. Bakker. Malden, 424–40.

Simpson, M. (1969) "The Chariot and the bow as metaphors for poetry in Pindar's Odes," *TAPA* 100: 235–53.

Sineux, P. (1999) "Le Péan d'Isyllos: forme et finalité d'un chant religieux dans le culte d'Asklépios à Epidaure," *Kernos* 12: 153–66.

Slater, W. (1976) "Symposium at sea," *HSPh* 80: 161–70.

(2007) "Deconstructing festivals," in Wilson (2007a), 21–47.

Slonimsky, N. (1953) *Lexicon of Musical Invective: Critical Assaults on Composers since Beethoven's Time*. New York.

Sluiter, I., and R. Rosen (eds.) (2004) *Free Speech in Classical Antiquity*. Leiden and Boston.

Smyth, H. W. (1956) *A Greek Grammar for Colleges*, revised by G. M. Messing. Cambridge, MA.

Sourvinou-Inwood, C. (1987) "Myth as history: the previous owners of the Delphic oracle," in *Interpretations of Greek Mythology*, ed. J. Bremmer. London, 215–41.

(1995) *"Reading" Greek Death: To the End of the Classical Period*. Oxford.

Stanford, W. (1942) *Aeschylus in his Style: A Study in Language and Personality*. Dublin.

(1973) "Onomatopoetic mimesis in Plato, Republic 396b–397c," *JHS* 93: 185–91.

Stehle, E. (1997) *Performance and Gender in Ancient Greece: Nondramatic Poetry in its Setting*. Princeton.

Steiner, D. (1986) *The Crown of Song: Metaphor in Pindar*. New York.

(2002) "Indecorous dining, indecorous speech: Pindar's first 'Olympian' and the poetics of consumption," *Arethusa* 35: 297–314.

(2009) "Diverting demons: ritual, poetic mockery and the Odysseus–Iros encounter," *CA* 28: 71–100.

(2011) "Dancing with the stars: choreia in the third stasimon of Euripides' *Helen*," *CP* 106.4: 299–323.

Stephanis, I. (1988) *Dionysiakoi Technitai: symboles sten prosopographia tou theatrou kai tes mousikes ton archaion Hellenon*. Herakleion.

Stewart, A. (1982) "Dionysos at Delphi: the pediments of the sixth temple of Apollo and religious reform in the age of Alexander," *Studies in the History of Art* 10: 205–27.

Strauss, B. S. (1993) *Fathers and Sons in Athens: Ideology and Society in the Era of the Peloponnesian War*. Princeton.

Strauss Clay, J. (1992) "Pindar's twelfth Pythian: reed and bronze," *AJP* 113: 519–25.

(1996) "Fusing the boundaries: Apollo and Dionysus at Delphi," *Mètis* 11: 83–100.

Sutton, D. F. (1983) "Dithyramb as DRAMA: Philoxenus of Cythera's *Cyclops or Galatea*," *QUCC* 42: 37–43.

Svenbro, J. (1976) *La Parole et le marbre: aux origines de la poétique grecque*. Lund.

(1988) *Phrasikleia: anthropologie de la lecture en Grèce ancienne*. Paris.

Swift, L. (2010) *The Hidden Chorus: Echoes of Genre in Tragic Lyric*. Oxford.

Taplin, O. (2007) *Pots and Plays: Interactions between Tragedy and Greek Vase-Painting of the Fourth Century BC*. Los Angeles.

Taplin, O., and R. Wyles (2010) *The Pronomos Vase and its Context*. Oxford and New York.

Taylor, C. (2007) "A new political world," in Osborne (2007), 72–90.

Thomas, R. (1989) *Oral Tradition and Written Record in Classical Athens*. Cambridge and New York.

(1992) *Literacy and Orality in Ancient Greece*. Cambridge and New York.

Too, Y. L. (1995) *The Rhetoric of Identity in Isocrates: Text, Power, Pedagogy*. Cambridge and New York.

Trapp, M. (2000) "Plato in the *Deipnosophistae*," in Braund and Wilkins (2000), 353–63.

Trédé, M. (2000) "Aristophane critique littéraire," in *Le Théâtre grec antique: la comédie. Actes du 10ème colloque de la villa Kérylos à Beaulieu-sur-Mer, les 1er et 2 octobre 1999*, ed. J. Leclant and J. Jouanna. Paris, 129–39.

Trédé, M., and S. Saïd (1997) *Littérature grecque d'Homère à Aristote*. Paris.

Tsagalis, C. (2008) *Inscribing Sorrow: Fourth-Century Attic Funerary Epigrams*. Berlin and New York.

Tsitsibakou-Vasalos, E. (2007) *Ancient Poetic Etymology: The Pelopids. Fathers and Sons*. Stuttgart.

Turner, E. (1952) *Athenian Books in the Fifth and Fourth Centuries BC*. London.

(1968) *Greek Papyri: An Introduction*. Princeton.

Vamvouri-Ruffy, M. (2004) *La Fabrique du divin: les hymnes de Callimaque à la lumière des Hymnes Homériques et des hymnes épigraphiques*. Liège.

Van Minnen, P. (1997) "The performance and readership of the *Persai* of Timotheus," *Archiv für Papyrusforschung und Verwandte Gebiete* 43: 246–60.

Vernant, J.-P. (1963) "Hestia-Hermès: sur l'expression religieuse de l'espace et du mouvement chez les Grecs," *L'Homme* 3: 12–50.

Vollgraff, W. (1924) "Le péan delphique à Dionysos," *BCH* 48: 97–208.

Waern, I. (1951) *Gês ostea: The Kenning in Pre-Christian Greek Poetry*. Uppsala.

Walker, A. (1993) "Enargeia and the spectator in Greek historiography," *TAPA* 123: 353–77.

Wallace, R. W. (1994) "Frammentarietà e trasformazione: evoluzioni nei modi della comunicazione nella cultura ateniese tra v e iv sec.," *QUCC* 46: 7–20.

(1995a) "Speech, song and text, public and private: evolutions in communications media and fora in fourth-century Athens," in Eder (1995a), 199–217.

(1995b) "Music theorists in fourth-century Athens," in Gentili and Perusino (1995), 17–40.

(2003) "An early fifth-century Athenian revolution in *aulos* music," *HSCP* 101: 73–92.

(2009) "Plato, *poikilia*, and New Music in Athens," in *Poikilia: variazioni sul tema*, ed. E. Berardi, F. Lisi, and D. Micalella. Rome, 201–13.

Webster, T. B. L. (1939) *Greek Art and Literature, 530–400 BC.* Oxford.

(1956) *Art and Literature in Fourth Century Athens.* London.

(1967) *The Tragedy of Euripides.* London.

(1970) *The Greek Chorus.* London.

West, M. L. (1965) "The Dictaean Hymn to the Kouros," *JHS* 85: 149–59.

(1970) "Melica," *CQ* 20: 205–15.

(1975) "Some lyric fragments reconsidered," *CQ* 25: 307–9.

(1982) "Metrical analyses: Timotheus and Others," *ZPE* 45: 1–13.

(1992) *Ancient Greek Music.* Oxford.

(1993) *Greek Lyric Poetry.* Oxford.

Whitehead, D. (1993) "Cardinal virtues: the language of public approbation in democratic Athens," *CM* 44: 37–75.

(2009) "Andragathia and Arete," in *Greek History and Epigraphy: Essays in Honour of P. J. Rhodes*, ed. L. Mitchell and L. Rubinstein. Swansea, 47–58.

Whitmarsh, T. (2004) *Ancient Greek Literature.* Cambridge.

Wilamowitz-Moellendorff, U. von (1872) *Zukunftsphilologie! Eine Erwidrung auf Friedrich Nietzsches . . . "Geburt Der Tragödie."* Berlin.

(1900) *Die Textgeschichte der griechischen Lyriker.* Berlin.

(1921) *Griechische Verskunst.* Berlin.

Wilkins, J. (2000) *The Boastful Chef: The Discourse of Food in Ancient Greek Comedy.* Oxford.

Willi, A. (2002) "Languages on stage: Aristophanic language, cultural history, and Athenian identity," in *The Language of Greek Comedy*, ed. A. Willi. Oxford, 111–49.

(2003) *The Languages of Aristophanes: Aspects of Linguistic Variation in Classical Attic Greek.* Oxford.

Wilson, P. (1999) "The aulos in Athens," in Goldhill and Osborne (1999), 58–95.

(2000) *The Athenian Institution of Khoregia: the Chorus, the City and the Stage.* Cambridge and New York.

(2003a) "The politics of dance: dithyrambic contest and social order in ancient Greece," in *Sport and Festival in the Ancient Greek World*, ed. D. Phillips and D. Pritchard. Swansea, 163–96.

(2003b) "The sound of cultural conflict: Kritias and the culture of mousike in Athens," in Dougherty and Kurke (2003), 181–206.

(2004) "Athenian strings," in Murray and Wilson (2004), 269–306.

(ed.) (2007a) *The Greek Theatre and Festivals: Documentary Studies*. Oxford and New York.

(2007b) "Performance in the Pythion: the Athenian Thargelia," in Wilson (2007a), 150–84.

(2007c) "Pronomos and Potamon: two pipers and two epigrams," *JHS* 127: 141–9.

(2010) "The man and the music (and the choregos)," in Taplin and Wyles (2010), 181–212.

Wilson, P. , and B. Kowalzig (eds.) (forthcoming) *Dithyramb in Context*. Oxford.

Winnington-Ingram, R. P. (1956) "The pentatonic tuning of the Greek lyre: a theory examined," *CQ* 50: 169–86.

(1988) "Kónnos, Konnâs, Cheride e la professione di musico," in Gentili and Pretagostini (1988), 246–63.

Worman, N. (2002) *Abusive Mouths in Classical Greece*. Cambridge.

Wormell, D. E. W. (1935) "The literary tradition concerning Hermias of Atarneus," *YCS* 5: 57–92.

Xanthakis-Karamanos, G. (1980) *Studies in Fourth-Century Tragedy*. Athens.

Yatromanolakis, D. (ed.) (2011) *Music and Cultural Poetics in Greek and Chinese Societies*, vol. i. *Greek Antiquity*. Cambridge, MA and London.

Yunis, H. (ed.) (2003) *Written Text and the Rise of Literate Culture in Ancient Greece*. Cambridge.

Zimmermann, B. (1986) "Überlegungen zum sogenannten Pratinasfragment," *Museum Helveticum* 43: 145–54.

(1988) "Critica ed imitazione: la nuova musica nelle commedie di Aristofane," in Gentili and Pretagostini (1988), 199–204.

(1989) "Gattungsmischung, Manierismus, Archaismus: Tendenzen des griechischen Dramas und Dithyrambos am Ende des 5. Jahrhunderts v. Chr.," *Lexis* 13: 25–36.

(1992) *Dithyrambos: Geschichte einer Gattung*. Göttingen.

(1993) "Comedy's criticism of music," in *Intertextualität in der griechischrömischen Komödie*, ed. N. Slater and B. Zimmermann. Stuttgart, 39–50.

Index locorum

Subject index

For names of individual musicians and poets, see also Table 1 (pp. 22–32), Table 2 (pp. 34–8), Table 3 (pp. 41–2) and Table 4 (pp. 44–7).

Lightning Source UK Ltd.
Milton Keynes UK
UKHW031940220522
403373UK00005B/151